Lecture Notes in Artificial Intelligence

Subseries of Lecture Notes in Compu

Edited by J. G. Carbonell and J. Siekm

Lecture Notes in Computer Sci

Edited by G. Goos, J. Hartmanis and J. van Leeuwen

Luc Steels   Guus Schreiber
Walter Van de Velde (Eds.)

A Future for Knowledge Acquisition

8th European Knowledge Acquisition Workshop,
EKAW '94
Hoegaarden, Belgium, September 26-29, 1994
Proceedings

Springer-Verlag

Berlin Heidelberg New York
London Paris Tokyo
Hong Kong Barcelona
Budapest

Series Editors

Jaime G. Carbonell
School of Computer Science, Carnegie Mellon University
Schenley Park, Pittsburgh, PA 15213-3890, USA

Jörg Siekmann
University of Saarland
German Research Center for Artificial Intelligence (DFKI)
Stuhlsatzenhausweg 3, D-66123 Saarbrücken, Germany

Volume Editors

Luc Steels
Walter Van de Velde
Artificial Intelligence Laboratory, Vrije Universiteit Brussel
Pleinlaan 2, B-1050 Brussels, Belgium

Guus Schreiber
Department of Social Science Informatics, University of Amsterdam
Roetersstraat 15, 1018 WB Amsterdam, The Netherlands

CR Subject Classification (1991): I.2.4-6, I.2.8

ISBN 3-540-58487-0 Springer-Verlag Berlin Heidelberg New York

CIP data applied for

Typesetting: Camera ready by author
SPIN: 10479023   45/3140-543210 - Printed on acid-free paper

Preface

Knowledge acquisition is a scientific field focused on understanding how knowledge may be elicited from humans for the purpose of understanding, supporting or automating complex problem solving behavior. The problem of knowledge acquisition only came to the foreground when the technology was sufficiently mature to allow the construction of large knowledge systems. Before that, knowledge acquisition took place in an ad hoc way. It is now understood that knowledge acquisition is the most important part of building a complex knowledge system, and that solid methodologies need to be in place.

The European Knowledge Acquisition Workshop (EKAW) is the prime forum for tracking the advances in this area in Europe. It is complementary to the Japanese Knowledge Acquisition Workshop (JKAW) and the yearly Banff Knowledge Acquisition Workshop (KAW). This eight edition of EKAW was held in Hoegaarden near Brussels and confirms the important trends of the last years. It also confirms the depth and progress obtained in the area of methodology, formalisation of knowledge acquisition models, and practical application. In spite of such impressive results, it is often heard that up to now the knowledge-based direction has failed to deliver on its promises. According to some it is even doubtful whether it ever had the potential of doing so. In view of this apparent impasse, EKAW'94 has set itself two main objectives.

The first objective is to demonstrate that work in the mainstream of knowledge acquisition *is* leading to useful results. There are presently several systems available and in use that demonstrate the potential of knowledge technology. The state of the art in knowledge systems is far beyond the rule-based model. The old knowledge extraction view has been replaced with a prominent modelling view. Knowledge level modelling, method configuration approaches, automated knowledge acquisition, knowledge standards, exchange, and reuse are now becoming reality. All of these help to overcome the complexity problems associated with building intelligent systems that up to now hampered widespread deployment of the technology. The various papers in this volume are representative data-points of these trends.

As for its second objective, EKAW'94 puts the knowledge acquisition enterprise in a broader context. This new context derives from the new perspectives on knowledge that are being developed within Knowledge Acquisition and in other areas of Artificial Intelligence or other sciences. For example from linguistics, philosophy of science, learning science, psychology, and sociology one learns how knowledge can be viewed as a social phenomenon, ever evolving and situation specific. This is often seen as an argument against the feasibility of knowledge-based approaches. However, at the same time technological developments in hypermedia and networking are providing us with new tools to explore exactly these issues. These developments offer new opportunities for different and unexplored uses of knowledge technology that are beginning to shape a new future for knowledge engineering.

New uses: in the last few years knowledge acquisition has focussed on consolidation of research results, in part by developing more applications. However, developments in business management and sociology indicate new opportunities for the techniques that we now master. In particular business process re-engineering, knowledge management, and social learning are hot topics and crucial features of successful organisations in the future. This is the case for European organisations in particular, since the larger European market requires ever greater flexibility and adaptability. The knowledge engineering community contributes to this its particular view on the business process, namely the knowledge perspective. For this community, 'knowledge as a crucial asset for success' is more than a cliché but is backed up by solid techniques and methodologies.

New technologies: knowledge engineering has focussed on building intelligent problem solvers or decision support systems, mostly single user and running on a single computer. New technological developments in hyper- and multimedia, and in networking, are creating new ways to put ideas into practice. These developments are a perfect complement to the new uses that were mentioned above. For example the developments in networking allow for realising the infrastructure that is necessary for effective knowledge management in small and medium sized organisations. Similar technology on a larger scale (i.e., the information highways that are being planned for Europe and the US) will allow for easier exchange and reuse of knowledge descriptions.

EKAW'94 featured special contributions to foster debate on the above mentioned topics. Dr. J. Stewart (Institut Pasteur) reports on the consequences of approaching the problems of mind and knowledge from a constructivist perspective. Ken Ford (University of West Florida), on the other hand, argued that positions like these easily go too far in rejecting useful ideas on mental representations. Dr. Attardi (University of Pisa) described evolutions in computing technology and how they are changing the way in which we work, as well as the tools we may find useful.

While preparing for EKAW'94 extensive use was made of the World-Wide Web (WWW). An EKAW WWW server[1] was set up both as an experiment and as a way to support the practical organisation of the workshop. For example, an interactive review form reduced the time and effort to produce and process reviews. The server offers most papers on line, integrated communication between authors, EKAW organisation, and contributers to the discussions, public commentary and annotations, local organisation and registration information. At any time one could find the most recent organisational information (detailed program, deadlines for registration, accommodation). Participants could also use it for confirming registration or accommodation reservation. The use of WWW was an experiment in itself that is fully in line with the trends that

---

[1] The server can be reached at http://arti.vub.ac.be/www/ekaw/welcome.html

were identified above. In the future, easier access to knowledge technology will enhance the effectiveness of businesses, and in particular the smaller ones. The new uses and new technologies will create a market on which specialised services can develop (remote knowledge systems, active documents, intelligent software agents, goal-oriented data use, sharing and reuse of knowledge, ...). For all of these the experience and know-how of knowledge engineering is central.

Overview

This volume contains a selection of the key papers presented at EKAW'94. Other papers were presented in poster form. The following gives the main themes underlying the papers.

Knowledge Modelling Frameworks

Several frameworks are now in place for performing the knowledge modelling task. Modelling at the knowledge level is generally seen as a way to give depth to knowledge acquisition. Ongoing work that is reported in this volume focuses on formalisation, comparison, and extensions to cooperative and multi-agent task settings. Schreiber, Wielinga, Akkermans, Van de Velde, and Anjewierden (*CML: The CommonKADS Conceptual Modelling Language*) summarize the major features of CML, which is a language at the core of the latest KADS developments. Ruiz, van Harmelen, Aben, and van de Plassche (*Evaluating a Formal Modelling Language*) give criteria for evaluating formal languages for knowledge level modelling and they apply these criteria to the language $(ML)^2$. The paper of Fensel and Poeck (*A Comparison of Two Approaches to Model-based Knowledge Acquisition*) gives a thorough comparison of two different approaches to model-based knowledge acquisition: the MIKE approach influenced strongly by KADS and the CRLM approach based on role-limiting methods. Dieng (*Agent-Based Knowledge Acquisition*) proposes a modelling framework that emphasizes the description of multiple agents, their roles, cooperation, and reasoning capabilities. This complements single agent modelling techniques with the aim of building cooperative and distributed knowledge systems.

On the other hand knowledge modelling frameworks are not unchallenged, as witnessed by two other papers. Schmalhofer, Aitken, and Bourne (*Beyond the Knowledge Level: Descriptions of Rational Behavior for Sharing and Reuse*) put forward arguments against present trends in knowledge level modelling as a predictive framework. Instead they argue for behavior descriptions of systems in a given context rather than performance prediction from knowledge and goals. Compton, Preston, Kang, and Yip (*Local Patching Produces Compact Knowledge Bases*) describe a series of experiments with real and artificial experts on the effectiveness of incremental local changes to a collection of ripple-down rules. To the extent that this works, it implies that knowledge-level models and functional architectures are not necessary.

Generic Components

Knowledge acquisition frameworks also serve as frameworks for reuse. When they are used by a substantial group of people, research can focus on an identification of generic components. Such efforts are now taking place: looking to identify generic task structures, problem solving methods, and also ontologies which can be reused across applications.

For a long time now problem solving methods have been regarded as key reusable elements. Breuker (*Components of Problem Solving and Types of Problems*) gives a typology of tasks with the goal of identifying suitable problem solving methods. This work fits within the KADS framework and is one of the cornerstones of the KADS expertise modelling library. A thorough analysis of diagnostic problem solving resulting in the identification of generic problem solving methods is reported by Benjamins (*On a Role of Problem Solving Methods in Knowledge Acquisition – Experiments with Diagnostic Strategies.*), while Cañamero (*Modelling Plan Recognition for Decision Support*) provides a detailed investigation of another class of problem solving methods, geared towards decision support.

More recently, ontologies are receiving attention as a means to facilitate reuse of complex components. The contribution of van Heijst and Schreiber (*CUE: Ontology Based Knowledge Acquisition*) shows how a better formalisation and structuring of ontologies can play a major role in streamlining further knowledge acquisition in the domain of medical systems. Pirlein and Studer (*KARO: An Integrated Environment for Reusing Ontologies*) also propose an extension of a methodological framework and its supporting environment in order to better support the identification of ontologies and their use in a knowledge acquisition project.

At yet another level one is starting to investigate reuse of the knowledge acquisition process. Geldof and Slodzian (*From Verification to Modelling Guidelines*) describe a set of reusable components for meta-projects, i.e., projects about knowledge engineering projects. They illustrate, using verification as a case-study, how a reflective implementation of a knowledge acquisition tool is used to capture and reuse knowledge engineering know-how.

Methodology

There are still gaps in current methodology, particularly in the areas of user modelling, verification, and validation. Several papers address these gaps. An-drienko and Andrienko (*AFORIZM Approach: Creating Situations to Facili-*

tate Expertise Transfer) propose and demonstrate knowledge elicitation techniques based on the presentation of situations to induce the recollection and verbalisation of expertise. These situations are generated by the use of spatial metaphors and graphic images. Improvements of the MACAO methodology are described by Aussenac (*How to Combine Data Abstraction and Model Refinement: a Methodological Contribution in MACAO*). Concrete experiments on combining MACAO with elements of KADS lead to methodological guidelines on how to combine the detailed analysis of expert knowledge with the selection and adaptation of generic models. Brazier and Treur (*User Centered Knowledge Based System Design: a Formal Modelling Approach*) focus on an area in knowledge level modelling that has, up till now, received less attention, namely the modelling of how the user perceives a system and therefore can interact with it. Tourtier and Boyera (*Validating at Early Stages with a Causal Simulation Tool*) present an approach and a tool to capture and validate knowledge about the dynamics of a system. Their approach has the advantage of being applicable before the conceptual model has been operationalised. Yost, Klinker, Linster, Marques, and McDermott (*The SBF Framework, 1989-1994: From Applications to Workplaces*) show that knowledge acquisition must be part of the larger context of analysing business processes.

Architectures and Applications

Knowledge acquisition frameworks and methodologies can be used for a variety of purposes, some of which are less obvious than others. Major, Cupit, and Shadbolt (*Applying the REKAP Methodology to Situation Assessment*) describe the application of their methodology to a problem of situation assessment, covering knowledge acquisition, design, and implementation aspects of system development. Arcos and Plaza (*Integration of Learning into a Knowledge Modelling Framework*) describe NOOS, a reflective architecture allowing for the description and implementation of inference as well as learning components and, most importantly, their integration and combination. Along similar lines, although with greater focus on resolving issues in machine learning, Rouveirol and Albert (*Knowledge Level Model of a Configurable Learning System*) describe the use of knowledge level models to configure learning algorithms and systems. Their approach makes explicit the alternatives in algorithms and biases. Automated (re-)configuration of applications is also the topic of Stroulia and Goel (*Reflective, Self-Adaptive Problem Solvers*). They describe a reflective system capable of identifying gaps in its knowledge and redesigning its own task structure.

The editors are indebted to the members of the EKAW'94 international program committee who contributed to a timely and high-quality review and selection process.

Thomas R. Addis, University of Reading (Great Britain)
Klaus-Dieter Althoff, University Kaiserslautern (Germany)
Nathalie Aussenac, IRIT – CNRS, Toulouse (France)
John Boose, Fred Hutchinson Cancer Research Center, Seattle (USA)
Guy Boy, EURISCO, Toulouse (France)
Jeffrey Bradshaw, Boeing Computer Services, Seattle (USA)
Ivan Bratko, University of Ljubljana, Ljubljana (Slovenia)
Bernard Chandrasekaran, Ohio University, Columbus (USA)
William Clancey, Institute for Research on Learning (USA)
John Debenham, University of Technology, Sydney (Australia)
Michael Freiling, Tektronix Inc. (USA)
Brian Gaines, University of Calgary (Canada)
Jean-Gabriel Ganascia, LAFORIA – Université Paris VI (France)
Thomas Gruber, Stanford University, Stanford (USA)
Yves Kodratoff, LRI – Université Paris Sud, Orsay (France)
Marc Linster, Digital Equipment Corp. (USA)
John Mc Dermott, Digital Equipement Corp. (USA)
Ryszard Michalski, George Mason University (USA)
Riichiro Mizogushi, Osaka University, Osaka (Japan)
Katharina Morik, University of Dortmund (Germany)
Hiroshi Motoda, Hitachi Advanced Research Lab. (Japan)
Mark Musen, Stanford University (USA)
Bruce Porter, University of Texas, Austin (USA)
Ross Quinlan, Sydney University, Sydney (Australia)
Alain Rappaport, Neuron Data (USA)
Franz Schmalhofer, DFKI, Kaiserslautern (Germany)
Nigel Shadbolt, University of Nottingham (Great Britain)
Mildred Shaw, University of Calgary, Calgary (Canada)
Ingeborg Solvberg, Trondheim (Norway)
Hirokazu Taki, Mitsubishi Electric Corporation (Japan)
Axel Van Lamsweerde, Université Catholique de Louvain-La-Neuve (Belgium)
Hans Voss, GMD, Sankt Augustin (Germany)
Masanobu Watanabe, NEC Corporation (Japan)
Bob Wielinga, University of Amsterdam, Amsterdam (The Netherlands)

EKAW'94 was organised with the financial support of MLNet, the European Network of Excellence in Machine Learning, and the Artificial Intelligence Laboratory of the Vrije Universiteit Brussel. Karina Bergen, Sabine Geldof, Siegrid d'Haeseleer, and Brigitte Hönig, all from the Vrije Universiteit Brussel, did an excellent job for the workshop organisation.

The editors, Brussels, July 1994

Table of Contents

Knowledge Modelling Frameworks

Generic Components

Methodology

Architectures and Applications

CML: The CommonKADS Conceptual Modelling Language

Guus Schreiber[1], Bob Wielinga[1], Hans Akkermans[34], Walter Van de Velde[2] and Anjo Anjewierden[1]

[1] University of Amsterdam, Social Science Informatics
Roetersstraat 15, NL-1018 WB Amsterdam, The Netherlands
[2] Free University of Brussels, AI Lab
Pleinlaan 2, B-1050 Brussels, Belgium
[3] Netherlands Energy Research Foundation ECN
P.O. Box 1, 1755 ZG Petten, The Netherlands
[4] University of Twente. Information Systems Department
P.O. Box 217, 7500 AE Enschede, The Netherlands

Abstract. We present a structured language for the specification of knowledge models according to the CommonKADS methodology. This language is called CML (Conceptual Modelling Language) and provides both a structured textual notation and a diagrammatic notation for expertise models. The use of our CML is illustrated by a variety of examples taken from the VT elevator design system.

1 Introduction

In this paper we describe a highly structured, semi-formal notation for the specification of CommonKADS expertise models [16]. This notation is called CML, short for Conceptual Modelling Language. The CML described here covers domain knowledge (including the specification of ontologies), inference knowledge, task knowledge as well as problem solving methods. Below, we discuss the various constructs of the CML for each of these categories in subsequent sections. The practical use of the CML is illustrated by various examples taken from the VT elevator design domain [8, 17], as reanalyzed with the help of the CommonKADS methodology [11].

In an appendix we give the full set of BNF grammar rules defining the syntax of the *textual* CML constructs. In addition to textual CML definitions, we provide a *graphical* notation allowing the knowledge engineer to concisely present the main features of an expertise model in a set of diagrams. We note that the graphical notation is not intended to replace the textual description, as it often abstracts from details that are present in this textual description. On the other hand, a diagrammatic notation is very useful in representing, explaining and communicating knowledge structures in a way accessible to both knowledge engineers and users. Thus, textual and diagrammatic notations have complementary functions. Our graphical notation follows as much as possible the notations used in software engineering, especially with respect to the domain knowledge where we closely follow the object-oriented OMT (Object Modelling Technique) notation proposed by Rumbaugh et al. [9]. In the final discussion section we comment on the relationships and differences of the CommonKADS CML with the OMT and Ontolingua [5] specification languages.

2 Domain Knowledge

The domain knowledge in an expertise model consists of three parts:

1. *Ontology definitions*: sets of type definitions of domain constructs, such as concepts and relations.
2. *Ontology mappings*: a description of how types of one ontological theory can be mapped onto types in another ontology.
3. *Domain models*, denoting knowledge base partitions containing domain expressions that use a set of ontology definitions.

We use the term ontology to denote a "specification of a conceptualisation" [6]. In earlier publications [15, 16] we distinguished two types of ontologies: (i) the *model ontology*, and (ii) the *domain ontology*, defining respectively the PSM-specific and the domain-specific conceptualisations. Since then, it has become clear that it may be useful to make additional distinctions, e.g. within the model ontology. See for a discussion on types of ontologies and their role in knowledge engineering [14, 11]. For the purpose of defining the CML we assume that there is a need to describe various types of ontologies, without committing ourselves to what these ontologies precisely are.

2.1 Ontology definitions

An ontology is defined through the specification of a number of types or "constructs". The CML provides a number of representational primitives each of which is briefly discussed in this section: *concept, attribute, expression, structure* and *relation*. The example definitions are taken from the VT model ontology [11]. The existence of this ontology can be defined in CML as follows (see also the appendix):

> ontology *VT model ontology;*
>   description:
>   This ontology contains domain-independent type definitions for describing
>   structural properties of the VT knowledge base [17].;
>   definitions:
>   < see the sample concept, attribute, expression, structure
>   and relation definitions>
> end ontology

Concept The notion of *concept* is used to represent a class of real or mental objects in the domain being studied. The term "concept" corresponds roughly to the term "entity" in ER-modelling and "class" in object-oriented approaches.

Every concept has a *name*, a unique string which can serve as an identifier of the concept, possible super concepts (multiple inheritance is allowed), and a number of *properties*. a property is a (possibly multi-valued) function into a value set. A number of value-sets are assumed to be pre-defined, such as strings, integers, natural numbers, real numbers and booleans. A newly defined value-set can be a range of integers or reals or an enumeration of strings. For the definition of value sets, see the appendix. Relations of a concept with other concepts, attributes or expressions should be modeled separately with CML relation definitions (see further).

Below two example concepts definitions found in the VT domain are given.

concept *component;*
  description:
      components are part types of an artefact. Instances in the VT domain are: "elevator", "car buffer", "car guiderail", etc.;
end concept

concept *component-model;*
  description:
      represents a particular model of a component, e.g. "car buffer OH1", "car buffer OM14", etc. Component models often have fixed attribute values, such as weight, physical dimensions, etc.;
end concept

Fig. 1 shows the graphical notation for concepts and sub-type relations between concepts. Concepts are indicated with rectangles. Three notations are provided for the sub-type relation between concepts. In principle, the OMT notation with the triangle should be preferred. The other two are included because many knowledge engineers use them as a convenient shorthand. Fig. 5 (see further) shows the graphical representation of concepts in another ontology (the VT domain-ontology).

Attribute An attribute is a reification of a function. One can see it as a shorthand for a concept with no internal structure and with a single "value" property. Attributes are graphically represented as rectangles, just as concepts, but with the name of the value set written as a subscript (see Fig. 4 for an example).

attribute *attribute-slot;*
  description:
      An attribute-slot is used to represent component attributes, such as weight, width, length, etc.;
  value-set: number ∨ string;
end attribute

Expression The notion of expressions as a domain modelling construct is introduced because these occur often in "domain rules" or "domain axioms". An important aspect of the domain modelling enterprise is to describe the structure of these domain rules. This type of domain description is currently lacking in many KBS development projects. The *expression* construct provides a suitable way of modelling the structure of domain knowledge in which simple expressions such as $age(patient) > 65$ and $temperature(patient) = high$ appear.

The general form of expressions is $< operand >< operator >< value >$ where:

- *operand* is a either an attribute or some property of a concept,
- *operator* is one of $=, \neq, <, \leq, >, \geq, \in, \subset, \subseteq, \supset, \supseteq$,
- *value* is a sub-set of the value-set of the function (i.e. attribute. concept property).

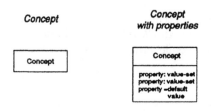

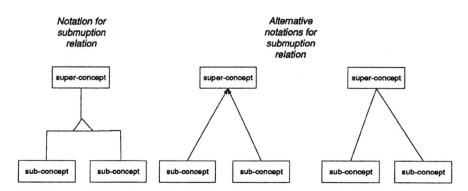

Fig. 1. Graphical notation for concepts (optionally with or without property definitions) and three alternative notations for sub-type relations between concepts. The left-most is the OMT notation and should be preferred

Expressions can be restricted to a particular property of a concept, and to a particular subset of operators. An example of an expression in the VT domain is an equality expression about an `attribute-slot`:

> **expression** *attribute-slot-expression;*
>   **description**:
>   Represents a simple expression about an attribute slot: e.g. "height = 28.75";
>   **operand**: attribute-slot
>   **operators**: = ;
> **end expression**

In the CML description of an expression the specification of operators may be omitted. In that case it is assumed that all legal operators on the values denoted by the properties can be used. For example, if an expression is defined on a property with a numeric value set, the set of possible operators is $=, \neq, <, \leq, >, \geq$, The set operators $(\in, \subset, \subseteq, \supset, \supseteq)$ are typically used with value sets that consist of a set of symbols. Expressions are represented graphically through an oval with the name of the expression and an arrow indicating the operand. Fig. 2 shows the notation for the two types of expression operand definitions.

Structure The notion of structure is used in the CML to describe objects with an internal structure that the knowledge engineer does not want to describe (at this

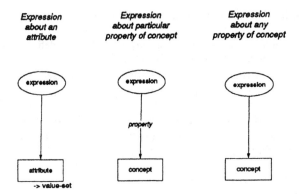

Fig. 2. Expressions are represented graphically through an oval and an arrow indicating the operand. These operands can be of three types: an attribute, some particular property of a concept, or any property of a concept.

moment) in detail. An example in the VT domain for which one could decide to model it as a structure is a *constraint expression*. Constraint expressions represent mathematical and logical dependencies between system variables. The knowledge engineer might want to introduce this as an explicit type in the ontology, without being forced to write down a full syntactical description of the form of constraint expressions. The CML description of structures is similar to that of concepts, but with an additional `form` slot in which the knowledge engineer can give a textual description of this class of objects:

```
structure constraint-expression;
    form:
        any (mathematical, logical) dependency between attribute-slot values.;
end structure
```

```
structure calculation;
    subtype-of: constraint-expression;
    form:
        a constraint expression of the form:
        <attribute-slot> = <mathematical-formula>;
end structure
```

The two examples define the notion of (ii) a constraint expression, without detailing the precise structure of the underlying formula, and (ii) a calculation as a sub-type of constraint expression implying a particular type of formula, again without going into syntactical details. The graphical representation of a structure is a rectangle (see Fig. 4).

Relation The notion of *relation* is a central construct in modelling a domain. In the CML we allow various forms of relations to cater for the specific requirements imposed by knowledge-based systems. The relation construct is used to link any type of objects to each other, including concepts, attributes, expressions, structures and relations.

The grammar rules in the appendix specify the CML for defining relations. The CML supports two types of relation arguments: (i) a single object (e.g concept, attribute, expression, structure, another relation), and (ii) a set of such objects. An example of the second type of argument would be modelling causal relations as a binary relation with a "causes" argument that refers to a set of expressions about some state variable. Relations can themselves also have properties. The classical example of such a property is the wedding date of two married people. Below three example relation definitions of the VT domain are shown.

> **binary-relation** *has-constraint;*
>   description:
>   binary relation linking a component to a constraint expression specifying some
>   dependency between attribute-slot values of this components or its sub-parts.;
>   inverse: constraint-on;
>   argument-1: component;
>   argument-2: constraint-expression;
> **end binary-relation**

> **binary-relation** *has-attribute;*
>   description:
>   binary relation linking components and component models to attribute slots.;
>   argument-1: component ∨ component-model;
>   argument-2: attribute-slot;
>   axioms:
>   ∀ c:component m:component-model a:attribute-slot
>   has-attribute(c, a) ∧ has-model(c, m)
>   → has-attribute(m, a);
> **end binary-relation**

> **relation** *fixed-model-value;*
>   description:
>   binary relation defining fixed values for attribute slots of a component-model;
>   argument-1: component-model;
>   argument-2: attribute-slot-expression;
>   axioms:
>   ∀ m:component-model a:attribute-slot
>   fixed-model-value(m, a = v) → has-attribute(m, a);
> **end relation**

The first relation, has-constraint, links a component to a constraint expression specifying some dependency between attribute-slot values of this components or its sub-parts. The second relation defines the link between components and their models on the one hand and attribute slots on the other hand. The (optional) axioms field states that attribute slots defined for components also apply to their models. The third relation shows the use of an expression construct in a relation definition. This relation (fixed-model-value) links a component model to an equality expression about an attribute slot. This relation can be used to model fixed values for attributes of a component model, e.g. `fixed-model-value(carbuffer OH1, height = 28.75)`.

Graphically relations are represented as diamonds, just as in ER modelling. For binary relations there is an alternative, directional, representation (see Fig. 3). Properties of relations are represented as arrows from relations to value sets. Set arguments of relations are indicated with the join symbol ⋈. Multiple types for an argument are represented through a split line.

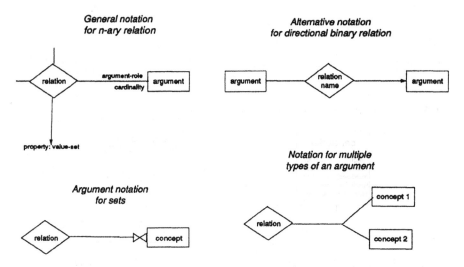

Fig. 3. Graphical notation for relations. For binary relations there is an alternative representation. Properties of relations are represented as arrows from relations to value sets. Arguments of relations can be either single constructs (concepts, attributes, expressions, relations) or sets of these constructs. Sets are indicated with the join symbol ⋈. Multiple types for an argument are shown through a split line

Fig. 4 shows the graphical representation of the CML VT definitions given in this section, plus an additional `has-model` relation. .

2.2 Ontology mappings

In the situation where a KBS is built from scratch it is possible to define one ontology (a model ontology in CommonKADS terms), and view the actual knowledge base as a pure *instantiation* of that ontology. In the light of efforts to share and/or reuse knowledge bases and ontologies, this approach turns out to be insufficient. For example, in the VT example there was an existing domain knowledge base with its own ontology. Some typical fragments of this knowledge base are shown in Fig. 5. We call this knowledge base the VT domain ontology. To use this knowledge base given the VT model ontology, of which parts were defined in this paper, one has to specify a mapping procedure that shows how constructs defined in the domain ontology should be mapped onto the model ontology.

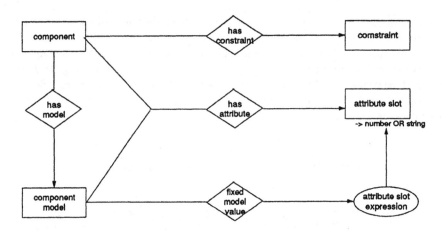

Fig. 4. Graphical representation of the sample VT definitions

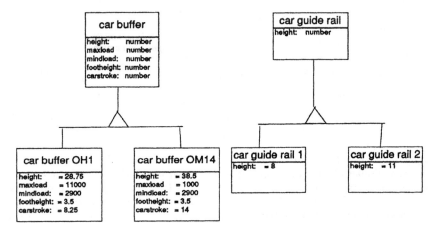

Fig. 5. Domain-specific concepts in VT domain ontology. The notation "property = value" is used to show default values

The purpose of the CML construct **ontology-mapping** is to allow for the (informal) definition of such mappings. An example of the mapping between the VT domain ontology in Fig. 5 and the part of the model ontology shown in Fig. 4 is given below. The mappings are defined here in natural language. In the context of the work on ML^2, [13] a rewrite formalism was developed to specify such mappings in a formal way. Work on the nature of ontology mappings is underway (see, for example, [4]). We expect the CML specification of ontology mappings to be refined in the near future.

```
ontology-mapping
    from: VT domain ontology;
    to: VT model ontology;
```

mappings:
 Concept with no superconcept in the domain ontology
 ↦ component in the model ontology

 Concept with superconcept in the domain ontology
 ↦ component-model in the model ontology

 Sub-type relation between concepts
 ↦ tuple of has-model relation

 Property of concept
 ↦ an instance of attribute-slot plus a tuple of has-attribute

 Default value of concept
 ↦ tuple of fixed-model-value relation, if the concept is a
  component-model;
end ontology-mapping

More details on the mapping shown above is given elsewhere [11, Appendix A].

2.3 Domain models

A domain model is a coherent collection of expressions about a domain that represents a particular viewpoint defined in an ontology. The domain model may therefore embody certain assumptions that are specific for the ontology that it uses.

In the CML a domain model is defined as a composite object. It is defined through a number of parts which contain one or more sets of objects (instances, tuples). The graphical notation for domain models (see Fig. 6) is inspired by the way data stores are represented in data-flow diagrams, because these are intuitively quite similar. Domain models can be viewed as a sort of "knowledge stores". Domain models have an internal structure, represented through aggregate-part links.

3 Inference Knowledge

In this section we define the CML for the specification of inferences and provide a new graphical notation for showing the data dependencies between inferences (the inference structure).

3.1 Inference specification

Names of inferences represent the role these inferences play in solving the problem. Inference names are thus goal-oriented. In addition, we specify the *operation type*: the abstract operation that is performed on some ontology, similar to the inference ontology in KADS-I. For the moment we use the formalised set of inferences defined by Aben [1993] as the basis for describing operation types.

For each role, a mapping is specified to the domain knowledge. For static roles, we may also indicate which domain model should be accessed to find this body of

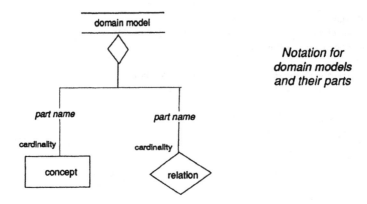

*Notation for
domain models
and their parts*

Fig. 6. A domain model is represented as a "knowledge store" with an internal part-of structure. The "diamond" symbol is overloaded and indicates in this context an aggregate-part relationship

knowledge. Dynamic roles are supposed to be part of the overall working memory of the problem solver and are thus not directly linked to a domain model.

We show two example inferences from the VT application. The *select-parameter* inference selects a parameter to which a value can be assigned. The static roles refer to constraint formulae in two domain models which for reasons of space were not defined in the previous section (see [11]).

inference *select-parameter;*
    operation-type: select;
    input-roles:
        parameter-set → set of attribute-slots;
        parameter-assignments → set of tuples <attribute-slot, value, dependencies>;
    output-roles:
        parameter → single attribute-slot;
    static-roles:
        formulae ∈ domain models *initial-values* and *calculations;*
    spec:
        Select a parameter from the skeletal model that has not been assigned a value
        and for which the preconditions that the domain knowledge (i.e. the *formulae*)
        poses for computing the value are fulfilled. A precondition is the fact that a
        value of some other parameter should be known.
        Formulae in the domain model *initial values* are evaluated as soon as possible.
        A heuristic ordering of components is used to rank the set of parameters. (see
        [17, Start of Sec. 5]);
end inference

The second example inference is *specify value.* This inference uses the constraints in two domain models to compute a value for a selected parameter.

inference *specify-value;*
    operation-type: compute;
    input-roles

parameter → attribute-slot;
parameter-assignments → set of tuples <attribute-slot, value, dependencies>;
output-roles:
parameter-assignment → single tuple <attribute-slot, value, dependencies>;
static-roles:
formulae ∈ domain models *initial-values* and *calculations*;
spec:
Specify the value of a parameter by interpreting the formulae and identify the
parameters that were used in this specification (the dependencies);
end inference

3.2 Inference structure

Inference structures are among the most frequently-used ingredients of KADS. In almost any presentation of an application of KADS, the description of the inference structure plays a dominant role. In this section we define some additional graphical notations to remove a number of ambiguities in inference structures.

Transfer tasks Transfer tasks are treated in the expertise model as black-box functions. Inferences and transfer tasks together form the lowest level of functional decomposition in the expertise model. One could say that transfer tasks are basic functions that do not make any inferences in the domain knowledge. Thus, it seems appropriate to include transfer tasks in an inference structure. A rounded-box notation is used to distinguish transfer tasks from inferences.

Role element vs. set Another issue that has arisen with respect to inference structures concerns the nature of roles. A role constitutes a functional name for a set of domain objects that can play this role. Some inferences operate on or produce *one particular* object, others work on a *set* of these objects. This can lead to ambiguities in inference structures, for example if one inference produces one object and another inference works on a set of these objects, possibly generated by some repeated invocation of the first inference. The graphical CML notation allows for making this distinction explicit: a ⋈ symbol indicates that the input or output should be interpreted as a set of objects playing this role.

Role names Another problem arises from the names given to roles. Some role names constitute a general name for objects involved in carrying out a task. For example, *observable, finding*, and *hypothesis* are such general role names. In addition, more specialised role names are also used. Often, such names are a specialisation of the general categories, e.g. *test observable, discriminating observable*. If one looks upon a role as a container of objects applying that role, a specialised name represents a label for a subset of objects in a container.

Specialized names such as *test observable* are useful and make the inference structure easier to interpret. On the other hand, some inferences may operate on the general category (e.g. observable). One would like to be able to specify both general and specialized role names and still be able to show clearly the dependencies between inferences. We support this in the graphical notation by making the subset structure of containers explicit through a "subset/superset" link between roles. An example of this notation is shown in Fig. 7.

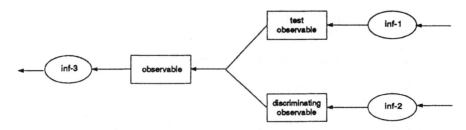

Fig. 7. Introducing general and specialized role names in an inference structure. An object taking the general role *observable* can be generated by two inferences, each using a specialized name for this role (*test observable* and *discriminating observable*). The link between the three roles indicates that *test observable* and *discriminating observable* are in fact subsets of the objects playing the role of *observable*

Static roles Inference structures only used to show the dynamic roles that are being manipulated by an inference. Sometimes, it is also useful to show what type of domain knowledge the inference uses to derive the output from the input (cf. [7]). This domain knowledge is specified through the static roles.

One could argue that this is an unwanted extension of the inference structure, as inferences are in fact domain-independent generalizations of the application of domain knowledge. However, it can be useful at some points during knowledge engineering to make the nature of the domain knowledge explicit, although this destroys the domain-independence of an inference structure. We use a double arrow to indicate the domain knowledge used by an inference, if felt necessary.

Inference and role annotations Optionally, the inferences can be annotated with the operation type of the inference, e.g. the inference "specify-value" can be annotated with the operation type "compute" (see Fig. 9).

Also, dynamic role names may be annotated with the name that is used for this role in the task knowledge. These task role names (see the next section) can be more informative for a user. An example of this type of annotation can be found in Fig. 9 where the role *parameter-assignments* has as a subscript *extended-model* which is the name for this role from the task (goal-directed) point of view.

Fig. 8 summarises the graphical notation for inference structures. Fig. 9 shows the inference structure for the two VT inferences specified previously.

4   Task Knowledge

4.1   Task specification

The knowledge category *task knowledge* describes how a goal can be achieved through a task. A task specification consists of two parts: the *task definition* and the *task body*.

The task definition describes *what* needs to be achieved. It is a declarative specification of the goal of the task. The *task definition* consists of:

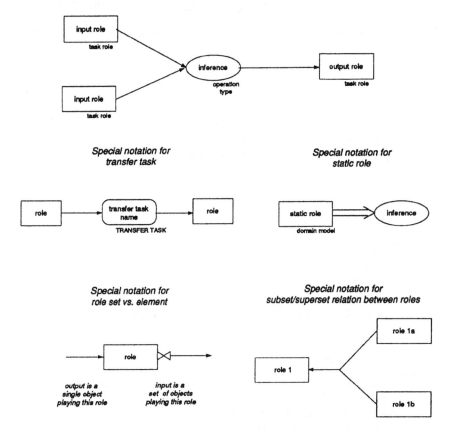

Fig. 8. Summary of the conventional used in the graphical representation of inference structures

Goal A textual description of the goal that can be achieved through application of the task.

Input/Output A definition of the roles that the task manipulates. This definition consists of a name and a textual description. The role is not directly bound to a domain type, as we do not want to have a direct coupling between task and domain knowledge. Instead, the task body (see below) specifies how a role is bound to other task roles and ultimately to dynamic roles of inferences. Only for inferences roles the mapping to domain knowledge is defined.

Task specification A description of the logical dependencies between the roles of the task (e.g. what is true after execution of a task, invariants). This description is optional.

The task definition of the VT design task describes the overall goal of the task and its I/O:

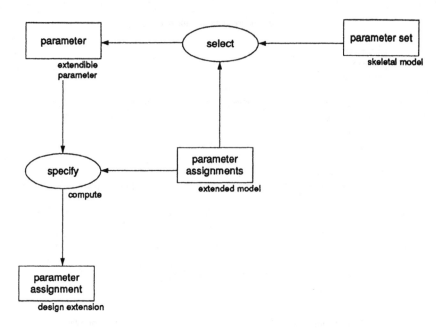

Fig. 9. Inference structure of the *propose* task. The names in the boxes denote inference roles. The annotated names represent the corresponding task role

```
task parametric-design;
  task-definition
    goal: find a design that satisfies a set of constraints;
    input:
      skeletal design: the set of system parameters;
      user-specs: set of parameter/value pairs;
    output:
      design: set of assigned parameters;
  end task
```

The task body describes *how* this goal can be achieved. It is a procedural program, prescribing the activities to accomplish the task. We distinguish three different types of tasks, based on the nature of their task body:

Composite tasks are further decomposed in sub-tasks, e.g. diagnosis is decomposed into generate and test.

Primitive tasks are directly related to inferences. E.g. a primitive abstraction task could be the computation of all solutions of an *abstract* inference, given a particular data-set and a body of domain knowledge

Transfer tasks interact with the world, i.e., the user. The task body of a transfer task is not specified in the expertise model. It is contained in the communication model.

The CML description of the *task body* has the following subparts:

Task type One of *composite* or *primitive*. Task body descriptions of transfer tasks are not part of the expertise model.

Decomposition The sub-tasks that the task decomposes into. These can be other tasks or inferences.

Problem-solving method The PSM that was applied to achieve this decomposition.

Additional roles Additional data stores that are introduced by the decomposition.

Task control Structure The description of control over the sub-tasks to achieve the task.

Assumptions Additional assumptions implied by a decomposition, e.g. concerning certain knowledge structures, concerning the solution, etc. Assumptions are usually introduced by the underlying problem-solving method.

The sample task body of the VT design task is shown below:

```
task parametric-design;
  task-body
    type: composite;
    sub-tasks: init, propose, verify, revise;
    additional-roles:
      extended-design: current set of assigned parameters
        represented as a set of tuples < parameter, value, dependencies>
        where the dependencies constitute a set of parameters that were
        used in specifying the value of this parameter;
      design-extension: proposed new element of the extended model;
      violation: violated constraint;
    control-structure:
      configure(skeletal-design + user-specs → design) =
      init(user-specs → extended-design)
      REPEAT
        propose(skeletal-design + extended-design → design-extension)
        extended-design := design-extension ∪ extended-design
        verify(design-extension + extended-design → violation)
        IF some violation
        THEN revise(extended-design + violation → extended-design)
      UNTIL a value has been assigned to all parameters in the skeletal-design
      design := { <p, v> | <p. v, deps> ∈ extended-design };
  end task
```

The control structure in the example above is written in procedural pseudo code. In principle however, the knowledge engineer is free to use any formalism that s/he finds best suitable for expressing control among sub-tasks. In real-time applications, for example, one could opt for a state transition formalism.

4.2 Task structure

In the process of engineering an expertise model, it is often useful to visualise the current set of tasks as a provisional "inference structure". This is a provisional structure in the sense that the "inferences" in such a diagram can in fact turn out to be (complex) tasks. An example of the use of such provisional inference structures can be found elsewhere [10]. We allow the knowledge engineer to use the same graphical conventions to represent these "task structures"[5] as for inference structures (see Fig. 8), with the exception that the "inferences" are not depicted as ovals but as boxes with rounded corners (similar to the convention used for transfer tasks). An example of a provisional inference structure for the VT example is shown in Fig. 10.

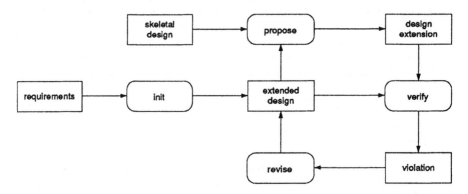

Fig. 10. Top-level data flow in the VT design task

In addition, it is often useful to show graphically the decomposition structure of tasks. An example of such a hierarchical decomposition can be found in Fig. 11. The problem solving methods that generated the decomposition can optionally be written on the lines connecting a task with its subtasks.

5 Problem Solving Methods

For many applications it suffices to specify the domain, inference and task knowledge to build a system. In that case the resulting KBS will have a fixed control structure, i.e. its behaviour is fixed. However, in some circumstances a more flexible form of control can be needed. In CommonKADS such flexibility can be achieved through the introduction of *problem solving knowledge* in the expertise model. Problem solving knowledge comes in two flavours: strategic knowledge and knowledge about problem solving methods [3]. The methods describe how a task definition can be given a task body that describes how to achieve the task goal. The strategic knowledge describes how methods are selected and applied in order to dynamically construct the task model. Below we give a CML definition of the top-level method for Propose-and-Revise.

PSM *propose-and-revise*
  input:

---

[5] The term "task structure" stands here just for a ' "inference structure" representation of a set of tasks and should not be confused with the meaning of the word in KADS-I

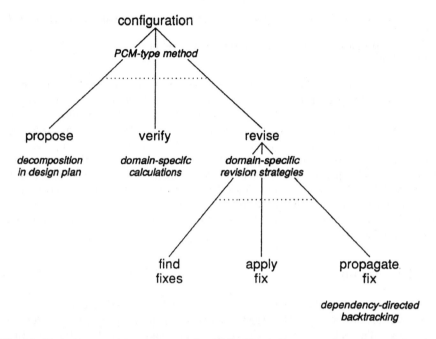

Fig. 11. Task decomposition generated by P&R. The italic annotations characterise the methods that on which the various decompositions are based

```
    skeletal-design: set of parameters;
    requirements: set of operationalised user requirements;
output:
    extended-design: set of parameter assignments;
competence:
    ∀ req ∈ requirements:
      meets(extended-design, req) ∧
      consistent(extended-design, constraints);
sub-tasks:
    propose, verify, revise;
additional-roles
    par: element of the skeletal-design;
    design-extension: newly proposed parameter assignment ;
    violation: violated constraint ;
control-structure-template:
    init(requirements → extended-design)
    FOREACH par ∈ skeletal-design DO
      propose(par + extended-design → design-extension)
      extended-design := design-extension + extended-design
      verify(design-extension + extended-design → violation)
      IF some violation
      THEN revise(extended-design + violation → extended-design) ;
acceptance criteria:
```

1. The requirements are operationalised in terms of initial values for some parameters

2. Design knowledge can be represented as a set of constraints;
end PSM

This problem solving method can be selected when a task definition has to be satisfied that has a goal that matches the *competence* of the method and when the acceptance criteria are met. When applied, the method will decompose the task into three subtasks (propose, verify and revise), introduce several intermediate roles that serve as place holders for intermediate results, and provides a template for a control regime over the sub tasks. This information is essentially sufficient to create a task body. The specification of the problem solving method given above, is largely informal. The CML does not provide explicit mechanisms to apply a method to a task definition, the method specification should be viewed as a structured way to write down knowledge about problem solving. A more formal account of problem solving methods is given in [2].

6 Discussion

In this paper we have described a language for specifying knowledge models: CML. The main advance of the CML is the facility to explicate the *ontology* of the domain knowledge. The ontology can be viewed as a *meta model* describing the structure of the domain knowledge. The mapping mechanism in CML allows the construction of a layered ontology in which higher layers represent abstract knowledge types. This facility is important since ontologies have structure: certain parts are based on generally accepted theory, other parts are based on common practice, useful interpretations or on task oriented notions. As a matter of principle we advocate to distinguish different partial ontologies that are based on different types of ontological commitments. Shareability and reusability of knowledge depend critically on the distinctions between the views that underly the different ontologies.

In many respects, the possibility to specify an explicit and structured ontology is similar to that of Ontolingua [5]. However, Ontolingua does not provide explicit mappings. On the other hand, Ontolingua is a fully formal language, while the CML is semi-formal. The semi-formal nature of CML is an advantage in early stages of the knowledge acquisition process: concepts and relations can be described in natural language. In later stages of KBS development a formal representation is needed. CML allows a formal representation, but does not prescribe a particular representation formalism. In [11] we have shown how CML can be used to specify and transform a formalised knowledge base. Also, tools exists to support structure-preserving operationalisation of CML descriptions in a dedicated executable environment [12].

CML has similarities with OMT [9] and other object-oriented specification frameworks, but offers -apart from the ontology- additional constructs such as *expressions*. Most object-oriented approaches do not separate the meta data model and the actual objects. In CML such a separation is possible through the use of the mapping mechanism. The inference and task layers of the CML have similarities with the control and functional views in conventional software engineering [18]. The graphical notations of CML are similar, but not identical, to the classical counterparts such as data flow diagrams. In CML the links between the different views are made explicit, while most classical approaches leave this link unspecified. In conclusion we claim that CML offers a number of new constructs and mechanisms that could also be of use in the field of classical software engineering.

Acknowledgements The CML notation is the result of a series of discussions in which many participants in KADS-II participated. Helpful comments were received from Christian Bauer, Frank van Harmelen, Andre van Naarden, Olle Olsson, Klas Orsvarn, Guy Saward, Peter Terpstra and André Valente, Manfred Aben built a parser for this CML and corrected in this way many small errors in the CML grammar.

The research reported here was carried out in the course of the KADS-II and KACTUS projects. These projects are partially funded by the ESPRIT Programme of the Commission of the European Communities as project number 5248 and 8145. The partners in the KADS-II project are Cap Gemini Innovation (F), Cap Programator (S), Netherlands Energy Research Foundation ECN (NL), Eritel SA (ESP), IBM France (F), Lloyd's Register (UK), Swedish Institute of Computer Science SICS (S), Siemens AG (D), Touche Ross MC (UK), University of Amsterdam (NL) and Free University of Brussels (B). The partners in the KACTUS project are Cap Gemini Innovation (F), LABEIN (ESP), Lloyd's Register (UK), STATOIL (N), Cap Programmator (S), University of Amsterdam (NL), University of Karlsruhe (D), IBERDROLA (ESP), DELOS (I), FINCANTIERI (I) and SINTEF (N). This paper reflects the opinions of the authors and not necessarily those of the the consortia.

References

1. M. Aben. CommonKADS inferences. ESPRIT Project P5248 KADS-II/M2/TR/UvA/041/1.0, University of Amsterdam, June 1993.

2. J. M. Akkermans, B. J. Wielinga, and A. Th. Schreiber. Steps in constructing problem-solving methods. In B. R. Gaines and M. A. Musen, editors, *Proceedings of the 8th Banff Knowledge Acquisition for Knowledge-Based Systems Workshop. Volume 2: Shareable and Reusable Problem-Solving Methods*, pages 29–1 – 29–21, Alberta, Canada, January 30 – February 4 1994. SRDG Publications, University of Calgary.

3. V. R. Benjamins. *Problem Solving Methods for Diagnosis*. PhD thesis, University of Amsterdam, Amsterdam, The Netherlands, June 1993.

4. J.H Gennari, S.W Tu, T.E Rotenfluh, and M.A. Musen. Mapping domains to methods in support of reuse. In *Proceedings of the Knowledge Acquisition Workshop KAW-94*, Banff, Canada, 1994. SRDG Publications, University of Calgary.

5. T. Gruber. Ontolingua: A mechanism to support portable ontologies. version 3.0. Technical report, Knowledge Systems Laboratory, Stanford University, California, 1992.

6. T.R. Gruber. A translation approach to portable ontology specifications. *Knowledge Acquisition*, 5:199–220, 1993.

7. Marc Linster. *Knowledge acquisition based on explicit methods of problem–solving*. PhD thesis, University of Kaiserslautern, 1992.

8. S. Marcus and J. McDermott. SALT: A knowledge acquisition language for propose-and-revise systems. *Artificial Intelligence*, 39(1):1–38, 1989.

9. J. Rumbaugh, M. Blaha, W. Premerlani, F. Eddy, and W. Lorensen. *Object-Oriented Modelling and Design*. Prentice Hall, Englewood Cliffs, New Jersey, 1991.

10. A. Th. Schreiber. Applying KADS to the office assignment domain. *International Journal of Man-Machine Studies*, 40(2), 1994. Special issue on Sisyphus 91/92 "Models of Problem Solving". In press.

11. A. Th. Schreiber, P. Terpstra, P. Magni, and M. van Velzen. Analysing and implementing VT using COMMON-KADS. In A. Th. Schreiber and W. P. Birmingham, editors, *Proceedings of the 8th Banff Knowledge Acquisition for Knowledge-Based Systems Workshop. Volume 3: Sisyphus II – VT Elevator Design Problem*, pages 44-1 – 44-29, Alberta, Canada, January 30 – February 4 1994. SRDG Publications, University of Calgary.

12. Peter Terpstra. An environment for application design. Deliverable DM7.5a, ESPRIT Project P5248 KADS-II/M7/DD/UvA/072/1.0, University of Amsterdam, 1994.

13. F. van Harmelen and J. R. Balder. (ML)[2]: a formal language for KADS models of expertise. *Knowledge Acquisition*, 4(1), 1992. Special issue: 'The KADS approach to knowledge engineering', reprinted in *KADS: A Principled Approach to Knowledge-Based System Development*, 1993, Schreiber, A.Th. *et al.* (eds.).

14. B. J. Wielinga and A. Th. Schreiber. Reusable and shareable knowledge bases: A european perspective. In *Proceedings International Conference on Building and Sharing of Very Large-Scaled Knowledge Bases '93*, pages 103–115, Tokyo, Japan, December 1-4 1993. Japan Informtation Processing Development Center.

15. B. J. Wielinga, W. Van de Velde, A. Th. Schreiber, and J. M. Akkermans. The KADS knowledge modelling approach. In R. Mizoguchi, H. Motoda, J. Boose, B. Gaines, and R. Quinlan, editors, *Proceedings of the 2nd Japanese Knowledge Acquisition for Knowledge-Based Systems Workshop*, pages 23–42. Hitachi, Advanced Research Laboratory, Hatoyama, Saitama, Japan, 1992.

16. B. J. Wielinga, W. Van de Velde, A. Th. Schreiber, and J. M. Akkermans. Towards a unification of knowledge modelling approaches. In Jean-Marc David, Jean-Paul Krivine, and Reid Simmons, editors, *Second Generation Expert Systems*, pages 299–335. Springer-Verlag, Berlin Heidelberg, Germany, 1993.

17. G. Yost. Configuring elevator systems. Technical report, Digital Equipment Corporation, 111 Locke Drive (LMO2/K11), Marlboro MA 02172, 1992.

18. E. Yourdon. *Modern Structured Analysis*. Prentice Hall, Englewood Cliffs, New Jersey, 1989.

A BNF specification of CML

The constructs of the CML are defined using BNF grammar rules. The conventions used in these grammar rules are summarised in Table A.

```
expertise-model          ::=      EXPERTISE-MODEL Application-name;
                                      domain-knowledge
                                      inference-knowledge
                                      task-knowledge
                                      psm-knowledge
                                  END EXPERTISE-MODEL [Application-name;] .


domain-knowledge         ::=      DOMAIN-KNOWLEDGE
                                      < ontology-def |
                                        ontology-mapping-def |
                                        domain-model >*
                                  END DOMAIN-KNOWLEDGE .


ontology-def             ::=      ONTOLOGY Ontological-theory-name;
                                      terminology
```

Construct	Interpretation
::= * + [ ] ⟨ ⟩ | .	Symbols that are part of the BNF formalism
X ::= Y.	The syntax of X is defined by Y
[X]	Zero or one occurrence of X
X*	Zero or more occurrences of X
X+	One or more occurrences of X
X | Y	One of X or Y (exclusive-or)
⟨ X ⟩	Grouping construct for specifying scope of operators e.g. ⟨ X | Y ⟩ or ⟨ X ⟩*.
SYMBOL	Uppercase: predefined terminal symbol of the language
Symbol	Capitalised: user-defined terminal symbol of the language
symbol	Lowercase: non-terminal symbols

Table 1. Synopsis of the notation used in BNF grammar rules

```
                                  [IMPORT: Ontological-theory-name
                                       <, Ontological-Theory-Name>*;]
                                  DEFINITIONS: domain-construct-def*
                                  END ONTOLOGY [Ontological-theory-name;] .

terminology              ::=      [ < DESCRIPTION: text; > ]
                                  [ < SYNONYMS: text; > ]
                                  [ < SOURCES: text; > ]
                                  [ < TRANSLATION: text; > ] .

domain-construct-def     ::=      object-def | relation-def | value-set-def .
object-def               ::=      atomic-object-def | constructed-object-def .
atomic-object-def        ::=      concept-def | attribute-def structure-def .
constructed-object-def   ::=      expression-def .

concept-def              ::=      CONCEPT Concept-name;
                                       terminology
                                       [SUB-TYPE-OF: Concept-name <, Concept-name >*;]
                                       [properties]
                                       [axioms]
                                    , END CONCEPT [Concept-name;] .

properties               ::=      PROPERTIES: property-def <; property-def>* .
property-def             ::=      Property-name: value-set;
                                       [cardinality-def]
                                       [differentiation-def]
                                       [default-value-def] .
cardinality-def          ::=      CARDINALITY: [MIN natural] [MAX <natural | INFINITE>]; .
differentiation-def      ::=      DIFFERENTIATION-OF Property-name(Concept-name) .
default-value-def        ::=      DEFAULT-VALUE: Value; .
axioms                   ::=      AXIOMS: text; .

attribute-def            ::=      ATTRIBUTE Attribute-name;
```

```
                              terminology
                              [SUB-TYPE-OF: Attribute-name <, Attribute-name >*;]
                              [properties]
                              VALUE-SET: value-set;
                              [axioms]
                          END ATTRIBUTE [Attribute-name;] .

expression-def        ::=   EXPRESSION Expression-name;
                              terminology
                              [SUB-TYPE-OF: Expression-name <, Expression-name >*;]
                              [properties]
                              OPERAND: expression-operand
                                        <, expression-operand>*;
                              [OPERATORS: Operator-symbol <, Operator-symbol >*;]
                              [axioms]
                          END EXPRESSION [Expression-name;] .
expression-operand    ::=   Attribute-name |
                          SOME-PROPERTY-OF Concept-name |
                          Property-name OF Concept-name .

structure-def         ::=   STRUCTURE Structure-name;
                              terminology
                              [SUB-TYPE-OF: Structure-name <, Structure-name >*;]
                              FORM: text;
                              [properties]
                              [axioms]
                          END STRUCTURE [Structure-name;] .

relation-def          ::=   general-relation-def | binary-relation-def .

general-relation-def  ::=   RELATION Relation-name;
                              terminology
                              [SUB-TYPE-OF: Relation-name < Relation-Name >*;]
                              [properties]
                              ARGUMENTS: argument-def+
                              [axioms]
                          END RELATION [Relation-name;] .

binary-relation-def   ::=   BINARY-RELATION Relation-name;
           '                  terminology
                              [SUB-TYPE-OF: Relation-name;]
                              [properties]
                              [INVERSE: Relation-name;]
                              ARGUMENT-1: argument-def
                              ARGUMENT-2: argument-def
                              [axioms]
                          END BINARY-RELATION [Relation-name;] .

argument-def          ::=   argument-type <OR argument-type>* ;
                              [ARGUMENT-ROLE: Role-name;]
                              [cardinality-def] .
```

```
argument-type            ::=    domain-construct-type |
                                SET(domain-construct-type) |
                                LIST(domain-construct-type) .
domain-construct-type    ::=    built-in-type | user-defined-type .
built-in-type            ::=    OBJECT | CONCEPT | ATTRIBUTE |
                                EXPRESSION | RELATION .
user-defined-type        ::=    Concept-name | Attribute-name | Structure-name |
                                Expression-name | Relation-name .

primitive-type           ::=    NUMBER | INTEGER | NATURAL |
                                STRING | BOOLEAN | UNIVERSAL .

primitive-range          ::=    NUMBER-RANGE(Number, Number) |
                                INTEGER-RANGE(Integer, Integer) .

value-set                ::=    primitive-type | primitive-range |
                                Value-set-name | { String-value <, String-value>* } .

value-set-def            ::=    VALUE-SET Value-set-name;
                                   [TYPE: <NOMINAL | ORDINAL>;]
                                   [properties]
                                   < VALUE-LIST: String-value <, String-value>*; > |
                                   < VALUE-SPEC: < primitive-type | text > > ;
                                END VALUE-SET [Value-set-name;] .

ontology-mapping-def     ::=    ONTOLOGY-MAPPING
                                   FROM: Ontological-theory-name;
                                   TO:   Ontological-theory-name;
                                   MAPPINGS: text;
                                END ONTOLOGY-MAPPING .

domain-model             ::=    DOMAIN-MODEL Domain-model-name;
                                   USES: Ontological-Theory-Name;
                                   PARTS: part-def+
                                   [properties]
                                   [EXPRESSIONS: text;]
                                   [ANNOTATIONS: text;]
                                END DOMAIN-MODEL [Domain-model-name;] .

part-def                 ::=  ' Part-name: part-element-def+ .
part-element-def         ::=    part-type ; [cardinality-def] .
part-type                ::=    SET(domain-construct-type) |
                                LIST(domain-construct-type) .

inference-knowledge      ::=    INFERENCE-KNOWLEDGE inference-def*
                                END INFERENCE-KNOWLEDGE .

inference-def            ::=    INFERENCE Inference-name;
                                   operation-type
                                   input-roles
                                   output-role
```

```
                                    static-roles
                                    inf-specification
                                    END INFERENCE [Inference-name;] .
operation-type          ::=     OPERATION-TYPE: text; .
input-roles             ::=     INPUT-ROLES: dynamic-role-mapping+ .
output-role             ::=     OUTPUT-ROLE: dynamic-role-mapping+ .
static-roles            ::=     STATIC-ROLES: static-role-mapping* .
dynamic-role-mapping    ::=     Inference-role-name -> domain-references; .
static-role-mapping     ::=     domain-references IN Domain-model-name; .
domain-references       ::=     <domain-ref <, domain-ref >*> | text .
domain-ref              ::=     domain-construct-type |
                                SET(domain-construct-type) |
                                LIST(domain-construct-type) .
inf-specification       ::=     SPEC: text; .

task-knowledge          ::=     TASK-KNOWLEDGE task-description*
                                END TASK-KNOWLEDGE .

task-description        ::=     TASK Task-name;
                                    task-definition
                                    task-body
                                END TASK [Task-name;] .

task-definition         ::=     TASK-DEFINITION
                                    task-goal
                                    io-def
                                    [task-specification] .
task-goal               ::=     GOAL: text; .
io-def                  ::=     INPUT: role-description+
                                OUTPUT: role-description+ .
role-description        ::=     Task-role-name: text; .
task-specification      ::=     SPEC: text; .
task-body               ::=     TASK-BODY
                                    task-type
                                    decomposition
                                    [psm-ref]
                                    [additional-roles]
                                    [data-flow]
                                    control-structure
                                    [assumptions] .
task-type               ::=     TYPE: < COMPOSITE | PRIMITIVE > ; .
decomposition           ::=     SUB-TASKS: function-name <, function-name >*; .
psm-ref                 ::=     PSM: Psm-name; .
function-name           ::=     Task-name | Inference-name .
additional-roles        ::=     ADDITIONAL-ROLES: role-description* .
control-structure       ::=     CONTROL-STRUCTURE: text; .
assumptions             ::=     ASSUMPTIONS: text; .

psm-knowledge           ::=     PROBLEM-SOLVING-METHODS psm-description*
                                END PROBLEM-SOLVING-METHODS .
```

```
psm-description         ::=     PSM Psm-name;
                                io-def
                                competence-spec
                                decomposition
                                [additional-roles]
                                [data-flow]
                                control-structure
                                acceptance-criteria
                                END PSM [Psm-name] .
competence-spec         ::=     COMPETENCE: text; .
acceptance-criteria     ::=     ACCEPTANCE-CRITERIA: text; .
```

Evaluating a formal modelling language *

Fidel Ruiz[1], Frank van Harmelen[2], Manfred Aben[2], Joke van de Plassche[1],

[1] NICI, University of Nijmegen, The Netherlands
[2] SWI, University of Amsterdam, Roetersstraat 15
1018 WB Amsterdam, The Netherlands
email: frankh@swi.psy.uva.nl.

Abstract. Formal knowledge modelling languages have a number of advantages over informal languages, such as their precise meaning and the possibility to derive properties through formal proofs. However, these formal languages also suffer from problems which limit their practical usefulness: they are often not expressive enough to deal with real world applications, formal models are complex and hard to read, and constructing a formal model is a difficult, error prone and expensive process. The goal of the study presented in this paper is to investigate the usability of one such formal KBS modelling language, called $(ML)^2$. In order to analyse the properties of $(ML)^2$ that influence its usability, we designed a set of evaluation criteria. We then applied $(ML)^2$ in two case-studies and scored the language on our evaluation criteria. A separate case-study was devoted to analysing the possibilities for reusing formal model fragment. $(ML)^2$ scored well on most of our criteria. This leads us to conjecture that the close correspondence between the informal KADS models and the formal $(ML)^2$ models avoids some of the problems that traditionally plague formal specification languages. The case-studies revealed problems with the reuse of formal model fragments. These problems were caused by the (inevitable) ambiguous interpretations of the informal model fragments. Finally, extensive software-support is required when constructing formal specifications. Our case-studies showed that the close correspondence between formal and informal models makes it possible to provide more support (and particularly: different kinds of support) than have traditionally been considered.

1 Introduction

Formal modelling languages have begun to play an increasing role in the knowledge acquisition community in the last few years, as witnessed by a steady stream of proposals for such formal languages for KBS modelling [7, 10, 22, 19, 21]. (e.g. KARL, K_{bs}SF, FORKADS, $(ML)^2$, MoMo, DESIRE). These modelling languages differ from both the high level informal modelling languages, e.g. as used in KADS [23], and from the directly executable languages [12, 14].

* The research reported here was carried out in the course of the KADS-II project. This project is partially funded by the ESPRIT Programme of the Commission of the European Communities as project number 5248. The partners in this project are Cap Gemini Innovation (F), Cap Gemini Logic (S), Netherlands Energy Research Foundation ECN (NL), ENTEL SA (ESP), Lloyd's Register (UK), Swedish Institute of Computer Science (S), Siemens AG (D), Touche Ross MC (UK), University of Amsterdam (NL) and Free University of Brussels (B).

Various authors have argued the advantages of such formal modelling languages: they reduce the vagueness and ambiguity of informal descriptions, they allow for validation of completeness and consistency through formal proofs, and they bridge the gap between the informal model and the design of a system.

However, these advantages come at a price: as is well known from software engineering, these formal languages suffer from problems which severely limit their practical usefulness: they are often not expressive enough to deal with real world applications, formal models are complex and hard to read, and constructing a formal model is a difficult, error prone and expensive process.

1.1 Goal of this Study

The goal of the study presented in this paper was to investigate the usability of one such formal KBS modelling language, called $(ML)^2$. This language has been developed since 1990, and specifically aims at formalising the KADS model of expertise. We conducted this study at a point when the language definition had become stable, and when the language plus a set of tools to support its use had been applied in a number of cases both inside and outside SWI. [4, 24, 18, 8].

1.2 Approach to this Study and Structure of this Paper

In order to analyse the properties of $(ML)^2$ that influence its usability, we proceeded as follows. First of all, we designed a set of criteria to evaluate $(ML)^2$. These are described in section 2. Subsequently, we performed a small case-study, constructing an expertise model in $(ML)^2$, in order to try out and refine our evaluation criteria. Subsequently, $(ML)^2$ was used to construct a second model which formed the basis for our language evaluation. These case-studies (described in section 3) were used to score $(ML)^2$ on our evaluation criteria. The results of this evaluation are reported in sections 4 and 5.. Since reusability is an important topic in knowledge acquisition, we also wanted to study the extent to which a library of model fragments could have been used to construct formal expertise models. The result of this third study is reported in section 6. Section 7 discusses the lessons on tool support for $(ML)^2$ that we learned from these studies and section 8 concludes.

1.3 Brief Description of KADS and $(ML)^2$

We assume that the reader of this paper has a basic knowledge of the structure of KADS expertise models. Knowledge of the $(ML)^2$ language is helpful but not required for reading this paper. In order to remind the reader of the central notions of KADS and $(ML)^2$, we give a very brief description of both. More detailed descriptions can be found in [23] for KADS and [19] for $(ML)^2$.

A KADS expertise model consists of three layers: domain, inference and task layer (for the purposes of this paper we ignore the strategic layer). The *domain layer* contains a description of the domain knowledge of a KBS application. This description should be as much as possible independent from the role this knowledge plays in the reasoning process. In $(ML)^2$, such use-independent descriptions of domain knowledge are formalised as a set of theories in order-sorted first-order predicate logic.

The *inference layer* of a KADS expertise model describes the reasoning steps (or: inference actions) that can be performed using the domain knowledge, as well as the way the domain knowledge is used in these inference steps. In $(ML)^2$, the inference layer is formalised as a meta-theory of the domain layer, and each inference action is represented by a predicate which is axiomatised in an order-sorted first-order theory. The inputs and outputs of an inference action (called knowledge roles) correspond to arguments of these predicates. These roles (terms in the meta-theory) are described in domain-independent terminology, which is connected to domain specific predicates in the domain layer by a naming relation which is specified as a rewrite system (so called lift-operators). The relations between the inference steps through their shared input/output-roles are represented in KADS by a dependency graph among inference steps and knowledge roles. Such a graph is called an inference structure, and specifies only data-dependencies among the inferences, and not the order in which they should be executed.

This execution order among the inference steps is specified at the *task layer*. For this purpose, KADS uses a simple procedural language with primitive procedures to execute inference steps and predicates to test the contents of knowledge roles. These procedures can be combined using sequences, conditionals and iterations. This procedural language is formalised in $(ML)^2$ through quantified dynamic logic [9].

2 Evaluation Criteria

In this section we describe the criteria that we used to evaluate the usability of $(ML)^2$. Although the main aim of this study was to evaluate a specific formal language, we believe that this list of criteria can be of general use in similar evaluation studies.

Expressiveness. A first concern is whether our language was expressive enough. Were certain things impossible to express? Were some things difficult to express?

Frequency of Errors. One of the problems with formal specifications is that their construction is an error prone activity. What were the most common errors made when using $(ML)^2$? What was the frequency of these errors? Can we identify why these errors occurred so frequently? Can we find a way to avoid these common errors?

Redundancy. For reasons of compactness and maintenance, redundancy should be avoided in formal specifications. Was redundancy present in our formal models? Can we identify different types of redundancy? Where does the redundancy occur? Can we think of ways to avoid it? What were the most frequently used constructions in our language? Can we remove or simplify these frequently occurring constructions?

Locality of Change. Since formal specifications will have to be refined and maintained, it is important that changes to a formal model remain local. Do changes propagate through the formal models? If so, what were the causes for global changes, and can they be avoided?

Reusability. Reusability of model fragments and of entire models is an important goal in knowledge acquisition. Do our formal models enable reusability?

Guidelines and Tool-Support. In earlier research, we have developed a set of guidelines on how to construct $(ML)^2$ models [2, chapter 3], as well as a set of software-tools to support the construction process [2]. Were these guidelines useful? Were there any guidelines missing? Was the toolsupport useful? Were any tools missing?

3   Case Studies

In this section we describe the three case-studies that were used to evaluate $(ML)^2$ on the criteria from the previous section.

Adaptation Study. In this study we took an already existing $(ML)^2$ model of a simple scheduling task, plus an alternative model of the same task described in a different language. The task was the incremental propose-test-revise model described in [20], and its $(ML)^2$ formalisation was taken from [4]. The alternative model was formalised in the language KARL and taken from [13]. This alternative model contained a much more elaborate version of the revision subtask. The goal of this study was to adapt the given $(ML)^2$ specification to have the same elaborate subtask as specified in the KARL model, and to observe the effects of these changes on the model as a whole.

Construction Study. In this second study, we performed the process for which $(ML)^2$ is intended: we took an informal conceptual model and constructed the formal version of this model in $(ML)^2$. The particular conceptual model was a simple allocation task, taken from [11]. It allocates employees to offices on the basis of a given set of constraints by choosing a complete allocation and subsequently fixing the constraint-violations that occur.

Reusability Study. Whereas the first two studies were aimed at evaluating $(ML)^2$ by adapting an existing model or constructing a new $(ML)^2$ model, this third study was aimed at evaluating a library of $(ML)^2$ model-fragments by reusing existing model-fragments for the construction process. The basis of this study was the library of formalised inference schemes described in [1]. This library contains formal descriptions of 41 inference schemes, organised in 16 classes of a refinement hierarchy. This study was divided into three separate substudies:

- In the first substudy, we took a number of formal inferences from the models constructed in the adaptation and construction studies, and we analysed whether these inferences could have been obtained by selecting and adapting inference schemes from the library. The result of this study was a a set of adaptation steps that would yield the desired inferences when applied to schemata selected from the formal library.

- In the second substudy we took a number of simple informal inferences from the conceptual model of the allocation study, and investigated whether a formal version of these inferences could be obtained by first selecting formal schemata from the library and subsequently applying the repertoire of adaptation steps from the first substudy to these inference schemes from the library.
- The third substudy was as the second, but this time for more complex inferences.

We carefully chose all inputs to these case-studies to be of a high quality. The inputs for the adaptation study were reviewed publications, and constructed by experts. The input for the construction study was highly rated by KADS experts. This ensured that any problems found by or during formalisation would not be due to flaws in the conceptual model that could reasonably have been avoided.

4 Evaluation of $(ML)^2$

Since we deliberately choose our input models to be of high quality, it is remarkable that the formalisation of the office assignment model revealed many errors in it. We must therefore conclude that formalisation reveals certain aspects that can not be seen in the conceptual model. A logical question is then how formalisation reveals these errors.

We found four ways that formalisation helps in finding errors. The first is that because of the error, a part of the model can not be described in $(ML)^2$. The second is that the detailed examination of the model that is necessary for the formalisation reveals the error. In this case, the erroneous part of the conceptual model can be formalised, but this gives a different interpretation to the model than the intended one. The third is that the formal specification reveals the grainsize of inference steps, which may then turn out to be too complex to be primitive, or too simple for inclusion in the formal model. The final and fourth way of finding an error is that formalisation may reveal redundant parts in the specification, which are repetitions of other parts of the model.

We will take a look at the errors that were found by the formalisation of the office assignment model which was built for the Sisyphus task [15]. This task attempts to assign a given set of employees to a given set of offices under a given set of constraints. We will use one part of this model to illustrate the errors that can occur. We will give a short description of this part of the model.

The office assignment model consists of a propose-test-revise cycle. The propose task generates a complete assignment without considering the constraints. This assignment is tested on the constraints in the test task. If a constraint is violated, a fix is proposed in the revise task. The inference structure of the revise task as it appeared in the conceptual model is shown in figure 1.

The only fix that the revise task proposes for a solution that violates a constraint is an exchange of two employees. Such an exchange is called a transformation. Such a transformation is constructed using the set of conflicts (= the assignments that violate constraints) and the current, incorrect solution. This transformation is used to compute the old local situation, i.e. the two assignments that are going to be switched, and the new local situation, i.e. the two assignments after the exchange. These two situations are compared with respect to the number of requests and requirements that they violate. The

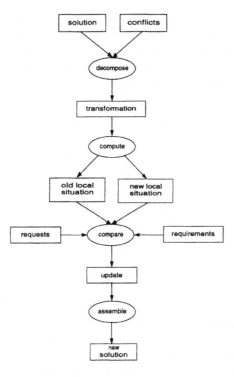

Fig. 1. *the revise task of the office assignment model*

local situation with the least requirement and request violations is passed to `update`. Eventually, this update is used to construct a new solution.

4.1 Incorrect Models can not be Formalised

As the expressivity of any formal language is less than that of natural language, there are certainly models that are expressible in natural or informal language, but that are not expressible in a formal language. Ideally, the formal language would allow a way to write down all methodologically correct models, and disallow all methodologically incorrect models. In our case studies we found that in all cases where $(ML)^2$ precluded us to straightforwardly formalise the models, it turned out that these models where methodologically unsound.

Missing dependencies are the best example of errors that were revealed because it was impossible to formalise the conceptual model. Missing dependencies occur when an output knowledge role of a primitive inference action can not be computed from its input knowledge roles. Sometimes it is difficult to see from the conceptual descriptions what the contents of the knowledge roles is. Therefore, it is easy to make these kinds of errors. Such an error can only be solved by finding the right knowledge roles that contain this knowledge and making this an input to the inference action.

One example of such a missing dependency is concerned with the inference action `compare`. This inference action compares the two local situations with respect to the constraints. However, there are also assignments that are not restricted to these local situations, but involve also other assignments of the solution. As a consequence, we need the knowledge role `solution` as an input to the inference action `compare`. The improved inference structure is shown in figure 2.

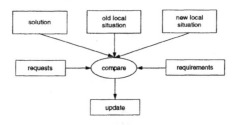

Fig. 2. *the corrected inference structure of compare*

4.2   Detailed Examination reveals Errors

The detailed examination that is necessary for the formalisation of a model often reveals errors. In this case, the erroneous part of the conceptual model can be formalised, but this gives a different interpretation to the model than the intended one.

An obvious objection to the use of formal methods to find imperfections in the informal model would be that taking a closer look at the informal model would have revealed the errors anyway. Our response to this is twofold. First, we took high quality informal models as a starting point: experts in the methodology did not find flaws in the model. Second, formal methods are a tool for having a closer look at the model, providing rigorous support where informal methods apparently fail. Another objection would be to say that implementation of the informal model would have revealed the imperfections anyway. In fact, a detailed look at the implementation of the office allocation task (also given in [11]) shows that the implementation is unfaithful to the informal model at exactly those places where we found the imperfections in the informal model. Indeed, the authors discovered the errors, but since they encoded a correction in the implementation, the implementation does not correspond to the specification anymore, a situation that is highly undesirable from a methodological viewpoint as it hampers maintenance and documentation.

The errors that were revealed in this way are confusing names of inferences and control knowledge that was modelled on the inference layer instead of on the task layer.

Names of Inferences are Confusing. This is one of the most frequent errors. The involved inferences had names that were inconsistent with the conceptual descriptions of these inferences in [5]. The names of the inference action's did not match with the description of the inference actions that took place. This can be very confusing, because it is not clear what inference should be formalised: the inference which is described in the conceptual model or the inference with the same name in [5].

The causes of these errors are the vagueness of the model of expertise and the ambiguous description of the library inferences in [5], which are susceptible to various interpretations[3].

An example of a confusing name of an inference is decompose. The description of this inference action in the conceptual model says that a transformation is proposed which could solve the conflict. This proposition is done by selecting a conflict (= an assignment that violates a constraint) from the set of conflicts, and an assignment from solution that is different from the selected conflict. These two are used to construct a transformation. However, the definition of decompose according to [5] is to choose a set of components from some composite structure. This definition does not match with the conceptual description of the inference action. It seems that the decompose in the conceptual model is a combination of two selects, for selecting a conflict and an assignment, and an assemble, for constructing a transformation.

The Inference Layer contains Control Knowledge. This kind of error occur because control dependencies between modules are represented on the inference layer instead of on the task layer. Often these dependencies are described as conditional actions in the inference action: the decision *when* an inference has to be applied is also part of the inference. Such an error can be solved very easily by modeling this dependency on the task layer.

4.3 Formal Specification reveals the Grainsize of Inferences

In the informal model, specification stops where the knowledge engineer is not interested in further detail. Formalising the informal model by definition adds more detail to the informal model, and reveals differences in complexity of the various inferences in the informal model. Some inferences become very complex, others turn out to be trivial.

Inferences may be Trivial. As formalisation gives us the means to compare inferences and their relative complexity, it can help identifying inferences which "do not do anything", i.e., are formally redundant. In these inferences, the output is equal to the input (mostly there is only one input knowledge role). The cause of these trivial inferences are the vague conceptual descriptions of the input and output knowledge roles, which make it difficult to see the similarities between the two. When such a trivial inference is found it is a modelling decision to remove it or not. There may be conceptual reasons to maintain such inferences. As the inference is trivial the removal of the inference will have no effect on the rest of the model. These errors are revealed clearly in the formal specification of an inference action as it has no body.

The compute inference is such a trivial inference. This inference computes two local situations, the old one and the new one. The old local situation consists of the two

---

[3] In KADS-II this is solved by making a distinction between the type and the name of the inference. The name can be given freely by the domain expert, and the type of the inference maps on an inference from the library.

assignments that are going to be switched, the new local situation of the two assignments after the switch. The computation of the old local situation is, however, redundant as this situation consists of the same assignments as those of the transformation. Removing this output of the inference results in the inference structure that is shown in figure 3.

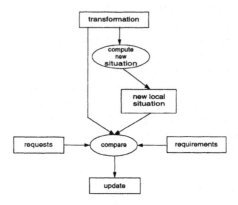

Fig. 3. *the inference structure after removing the computation of the old local situation*

Inferences may be too Complex. When by formalisation an inference turns out to be too complex, it is usually an indication that the conceptual model is not understood well enough. Although it is a modeling decision when to stop decomposing a model, formalisation may show that not all "leaves" of the model are equally primitive. This is usually an indication of complexities in the model that are overlooked in the informal expertise model. If we would have chosen to formalise these inferences, then the formal specification would have been at least two to three times larger than specifications of other inferences. Often it is possible to identify separate parts in the inference. It is better to split up the complex inference in these different parts. This makes the inference structure more clear.

An example of such a complex inference is shown in figure 4, where the inference action `compare` compares the number of constraint violations of an old and a new situation. This inference action can be split up in counting the number of constraint violations for the new situation, counting the constraint violations of the old situation, and comparing these two. This is shown in figure 4.

4.4 Formal Specification reveals Redundancies

Formal specifications also reveal redundancy by establishing that two model fragments are identical, and the inference structure could be improved by removing one of them and restructuring the model.

This can be seen in the revise task of the office assignment model, as it does not completely correspond with the overall interpretation of a propose-test-revise cycle.

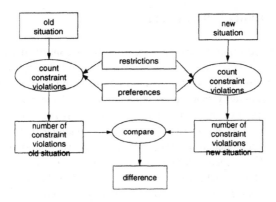

Fig. 4. *the refinement of the inference action* `compare`

Normally, in such a cycle, the test part would examine if the application of a transformation that is proposed in the revise task yields a better solution. However, we can see in figure 1 that the revise part of the office assignment model incorporates another test phase. This makes the test part of the office assignment model redundant. The removal of this extra test from the revise task results in the inference structure that is shown in figure 5.

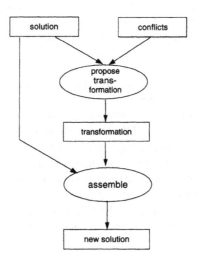

Fig. 5. *the inference structure of revise without the extra test*

5 The Evaluation of the Criteria

Expressivity This criterion, as we have seen before, is concerned with the ability of $(ML)^2$ to describe KADS models of expertise. We encountered no problems that indicate that parts of KADS models of expertise are impossible to express in $(ML)^2$. The problems concerning the expressivity that we encountered were all the result of errors in the models. The limitations of the formal language reveals errors: something that can not be expressed, is often an error. Therefore, we can conclude that $(ML)^2$ is suitable for describing KADS models of expertise. This is not a very surprising conclusion as the structure of $(ML)^2$ depends strongly on the structure of the conceptual modeling language that is used to describe the models of expertise. It is therefore in principle clear how objects in the conceptual description must be mapped onto $(ML)^2$ constructs.

Errors in the Formalisation Process Not many errors were made during the formalisation process: in the beginning approximately three errors per page specification text were made, in the last formalisation only approximately one and a half error per page specification text was made. The most frequent errors are typing errors. Most of these can be located easily with the available tools (a parser and a checker for the syntax of $(ML)^2$). It seems therefore that the formalisation process in $(ML)^2$ is not an error prone activity. We suspect that this is mostly due to the fact that the formalisation process is strongly guided by the conceptual model.

Redundancy and Repetition We can distinguish redundance within models and repetition between models. Redundancy within models occurs if some piece of knowledge has to be represented more than once in the same model. The major disadvantage of this kind of redundancy is that it is difficult to modify the knowledge in a model such that it remains consistent. Fortunately, this kind of redundancy was not present in the conceptual models that we studied, and was therefore also not present in the corresponding $(ML)^2$ models.

Repetition between models occurs when the same piece of knowledge has to be represented for all the models. This kind of repetition is especially present in the task layer of $(ML)^2$ models. Although this kind of repetition is not harmful, it is very time-consuming to generate these parts of the model. However, it is not possible to remove these parts as it is necessary for checking the correctness of the model.

A possible solution would be to generate these parts automatically by a tool. We have found templates for modules that could be used for this purpose (initial and intermediate knowledge role and task programs). Especially the template for task programs is suitable for this. This does not remove the redundancy from the model, but it saves much time in the formalisation process and is not hard to realise.

Locality of Changes With locality of changes we mean the amount of actual changes that are necessary to fix an error in an $(ML)^2$ model or to modify an $(ML)^2$ model. In other words how far do the changes propagate through the model. Therefore, this criterion is important for determining the applicability of $(ML)^2$ in practice. Reusability makes it necessary to (partly) modify an existing model for the formalisation of another model. Also it is inevitable that errors will be made while building formal models. However, we do not want that changes in our model affect significant parts of the rest of the model.

The modifications that we applied in the models all had a local character. The reason for this is the restricted interaction between the various layers, and the modularisation within the layers. Changes in the form of the domain knowledge affect only the lift-rules in the inference layer and changes in the task layer are confined to the modules in the inference and task layer which are part of the modified task. Altogether, we can conclude that modifications in the formal model tend to be local.

Reusability Can we reuse (parts of) the specifications of models for the formalisation of other models? Because modifications in the formal model tend to be local, this reusability depends for a great deal on the similarities between models.

There are two ways that we can syntactically reuse parts of formal models. The first is with the templates that we have found for inference and task layer modules. These templates consist mostly of complete modules and not of smaller portions of a module. This is caused by the grainsize of the reusable elements within KADS conceptual models. The templates we found during the formalisation of the office-assignment model were templates for initial and intermediate dynamic knowledge roles, task programs and the task-definitions module. The modules that belonged to one of these classes of modules all had the same structure.

The second way are general domain theories for various kinds of knowledge like arithmetic and set theory, and property axioms for relations like transitivity, reflexivity and symmetry. A library can be constructed from these general theories, which can then be used in other models by selecting the necessary modules from the library and inserting them in the domain layer.

Here we described reusability with respect to syntactical constructs. In section 6 we will take a look at reusability in a broader context.

Guidelines Generally, the guidelines for constructing a formal model from a conceptual model [2, chapter 3] were clear and easy to follow. The guidelines are quite extensive; there are over 60 of them. These guidelines are organised in different groups, which affect different parts of the model. The first group prescribes how to transform the structure of the informal conceptual model into a skeletal formal model. The second group of guidelines gives suggestions how to add additional structure to the formal model and how to specify the signatures, the axioms and the lift-rules.

The main problem with the guidelines was the fact that their application by hand is very time-consuming. We suggest two ways of improving this process. First we can use *templates*, i.e., reusable syntactic constructs that are essentially compilations of the guidelines. A typical example is the combination of a number of guidelines which each suggest a part of a module in the formal specification into a single template that gives the default structure of the entire module. The advantage of such templates, is that larger parts of the specification are generated quickly, the disadvantage is that these larger templates are less generally applicable.

An alternative way to improve the formal model construction process is automated support by a software tool that takes an informal model and creates an initial formal model. In section 7 we will examine this in more detail.

There are only two issues that are not handled by the guidelines. The formalisation of the primitive inference actions is one of them. The guidelines generate the overall structure of the formal model (for instance the connections in the inference structure), but within this structure, the inference actions are left as "gaps" that must still be filled in. In the next section we will examine if a formalised library of inferences can support this part of the formalisation process. Another lack in the support of the guidelines is the modularisation of the domain layer.

6 Supporting the Formalisation of the Inferences

Whereas the first two studies were aimed at constructing a new $(ML)^2$ model and adapting an existing model, the third study was aimed at reusing existing model-fragments for the construction process and also to examine if these model-fragments can fill the gap in the support of the formalisation process that we identified in the previous section. This gap concerned the formalisation of the inference actions.

In this section we will evaluate the support for the formalisation of the inferences that is given by the formalised library of inferences. This formalised library consists of adaptable components and not 'ready-to-use' components. These components are called inference schemata [1].

There are two goals for a library of formalised inferences. The first is to remove ambiguity from the conceptual descriptions of the library inferences. The second goal is to support the formal specification of inference actions in a model through the selection and adaptation of inference schemata. The inference schemata can be compared much easier than the informal descriptions, because of their formal character. Therefore, the consequences of selecting one schema instead of another is made more clear.

An inference schema is represented as three constituents: a *precondition*, a *body* and a *postcondition* [1]. The *precondition* describes the conditions under which the inference is applicable. The *body* of the inference schema declaritively describes the operation that is performed by the inference on the input knowledge roles to compute the output knowledge role. The *postcondition* describes the properties that hold after the application of the inference.

The selection of the appropriate inference schema or combination of inference schemata can be done on the basis of the postcondition. We compare the postconditions of the inference action with the postconditions of the inference schemata. The inference schema that matches the postconditions of the inference best is selected.

After the inference schema or combination of inference schemata is selected, it has to be differentiated further. The modifications that we apply are strengthening (making a formula more specific), weakening (the inverse of strengthening thus making the formula more general) and reformulation (a syntactical operation that does not affect the strength of an inference). These modifications can be applied to the whole inference schema or to the separate constituents. It is also possible to strengthen some constituents and weaken others. These different modifications result in variations of one inference type.

6.1 Finding the Adaptation Steps

In the first substudy, we used the formal versions of some `select` inferences from the two models of the previous case studies to select an inference schema. These `select` inferences select an element from a given set according to a selection criterion. We adapted these general schemata to fit the specific inferences and examined which adaptation steps they had in common. We used the formal version of these inferences so that we could guide the adaptation process by making the adapted inference schema the same as the inference in the formal model.

The six generic adaptation steps that we found were:

1. Instantiation of the selection criterion or principle (strengthening).
2. Unfolding the definition of an object (reformulation).
3. Folding the definition of an object (reformulation).
4. Removal of a parameter from the head of the body (weakening).
5. Addition of a parameter to the head of the body (strengthening).
6. Joining two (or more) inference schemata into one inference (reformulation).

There were some other adaptation steps, but these were not generic.

In the second substudy, we examined if these adaptation steps could be used to formalise a `select` inference starting from the conceptual description. This resulted in a formal specification of this inference that was better than the original formalisation. The new formalisation corresponded better to the conceptual description of the inference. So it seems that using the library of inference schemata and the adaptation steps we found is a good way to formalise simple select inferences.

6.2 Applying the Adaptation Steps on Complex Inferences

The goal of the third substudy was the same as for the second one, but now we tried to formalise more complex inferences. Using the formalised library by selecting inference schemata and applying the adaptation steps that we found in the previous stage did not succeed for the formalisation of these complex inferences. The problems that we encountered had two causes. The first was that the interpretation of the *names* of the inferences in the models did not match with the standard interpretation. Therefore, it was not possible to rely on the name of an inference for the selection of an inference schema. This is not a severe problem, as selection can also take place on the basis of the contents of the inference action that has to be formalised.

The second cause is more severe, and was that the *contents* of inferences did not match with any inference schema or combination of inference schemata in the library. This made it impossible to formalise these inferences with the help of the formalised library. As these inferences were not primitive inferences, we had to change our inference structure to make it possible to formalise it using the formalised library. This modification of the inference structure is a creative process and is difficult to support. As a consequence, the formalisation of these inferences cost more effort than expected.

Conclusions regarding Reusability. We can conclude from the previous section that the first goal of the formalised library of inferences, namely to remove ambiguity from the descriptions of the library inferences, has been realised successfully, as it was not difficult to find the corresponding inference schema of an inference if there was one.

The second goal of the formalised library has not been realised yet. The formalised library could not give enough support for the formalisation of inferences by *selecting* and *adapting* inference schemata. The cause for this is that the informal model is constructed using the informal library of inferences. The elements from this informal library have various different interpretations. This makes the mapping on the formal library elements difficult, as the formal library incorporates one specific interpretation of the informal library elements.

In other words: not all interpretations of inferences in the conceptual model could be found in the library (the second goal), but those elements that could be found in the library were sufficiently disambiguated (the first goal).

The differing interpretations of the standard inferences in the conceptual model endanger reusability of individual inferences, as it is not clear what a certain inference does. They also endanger reusability of entire interpretation models, as it is probably not known which interpretations of the inferences are used in a model and it is therefore questionable if it is reusable.

As reusability is a crucial aspect of the KADS methodology, this problem will have to be solved. As a solution to this problem, we propose that conceptualisation and formalisation must be viewed as an iterative and not a sequential process. The conceptualisation phase sets up only the global structure of the model, which is then further refined during conceptualisation/formalisation cycles. If formalisation of a model is not possible with the formalised library, then the inference structure must be modified in another conceptualisation phase (and maybe consulting the domain expert). This modified structure is then formalised.

There are some aspects to this solution that need further research. It is obvious that formalisation should follow up the conceptualisation phase sooner, but it is not clear how much sooner this is and how this affects the separate phases. Also research is needed for determining the best support for the formalisation using the inference schemata.

7 Requirements and Evaluation for Software Support

The amount of detail required to ensure the completeness and correctness of a formal model results in two difficulties with formal specification. First, the specifications tend to be big and second, adding the required detail is not always trivial.

Tools and methodology should help in overcoming these difficulties as much as possible. In the following we will analyse the required functionality of software tools, and discuss a number of tools that we used during the experiments. We give some suggestions for more tool support, where we found it lacking during the experiments.

7.1 Current Software Support Tools

Formal specification consists of three phases:

1. Building an *initial* formal specification on the basis of the informal model,
2. *Refining* the formal model until it is sufficiently detailed (e.g. enough to serve as a design document, or such that a certain amount of trust is endowed in the specification),
3. *Analysing* the model for its correctness and completeness.

These phases are often cyclic. Typically, phase 2 depends strongly on the results of phase 3. For each of these phases software support is required. The sheer size and complexity of an average formal specification make it impracticable to write it down and evaluate it with pen and paper. We will describe the required functionality of the tools that support these phases, and we will indicate where such support is already available and evaluated in the course of our evaluation of $(ML)^2$.

The $Si(ML)^2$ toolset [2, chapter 2] has been developed in the course of the KADS-II project. $Si(ML)^2$ consists of a number of tools written in Prolog that support the required functionality sketched above. The toolset uses the facilities of GNU Emacs-19 for interfacing and editing. This toolset has been used during all the experiments and will therefore be discussed in more detail. We will discus the required tool support for the three phases in formal model construction, and indicate which functionality is realised in $Si(ML)^2$.

Initital Formal Model Construction. The result in KADS of the conceptual modelling phase is a structured expertise model. This model is the basis for subsequent formalisation. As we have seen, a large number of guidelines have been developed to help generating an initial formal model on the basis of the expertise model. These guidelines can to a large degree be automated. Many of the guidelines suggest a number of default formalisations, and decisions that are taken in some guidelines determine the decisions that are to be taken in other guidelines. An automated tool can keep track of implications of applying guidelines in a certain way, can avoid errors introduced by manually applying the guidelines and and can help to preview the results. The *transformation tool* included in $Si(ML)^2$ realises this functionality, thereby reducing the number of errors introduced by applying the guidelines manually. The informal constructs that cannot be formalised automatically are inserted as comments at the appropriate places in the formal model, making the specification self-contained and well-documented. For all of the guidelines the tool presents defaults. In combination with an adjustable level of user-interaction, the tool can generate a skeletal model automatically or semi-automatically. The tool became available during the experiments, and is therefore not included in the evaluation. The activities during the case-studies, however, clearly showed the need for such a tool, and in part inspired its construction.

Formal model refinement. The transformation tool generates the initial formal specification. This initial specification contains "holes" where the informal model consists of informal, unstructured text. Formalising these parts is a creative enterprise, and can not be fully automated. However support is still required and feasible. First of all, we need good editing support that can be used to manage the complexity of the formal model. Second, we need support for reusing formal specification fragments, such as the inference schemes.

To manage the inherent complexity of the formal model we need to selectively display parts of the formal model. For instance, when we are sufficiently satisfied that the signatures of the formal modules are complete, we may want to hide them in the editor, such that we can focus on those parts that are still incomplete. Normalisation of the layout and pretty printers make it possible to keep the specification readable.

The $(ML)^2$ *editor* in Si$(ML)^2$ is a customization of GNU Emacs. The editor supports *selective display* which turned out to be very useful for keeping an overview of the specification. Besides the standard navigation facilities offered by Emacs, the editor makes it possible to go through an $(ML)^2$ specification in sensible jumps, e.g., to go to the next module or layer. The editor also supports hypertext navigation through the specification, e.g., to follow import links, or to jump to the place where some term is defined. As the editor constitutes the main interface to all functionality of Si$(ML)^2$, the editor provides functionality to select parts (modules, layers, axioms, etc.) of the specification and subsequently perform an action upon them (e.g., to parse it, to pretty-print it). The pretty printer can be used to normalise layout of the specification in the editor, and to generate LaTeX text.

Apart from managing the complexity of the specification, tool support is required for reusing formal specification fragments stored in a library. Currently the library of inference schemes is not supported by any software tool.

Analysing the specification. We can analyse the (intermediate) results of the fomal specification in various ways. We want to verify the syntactical correctness and to perform static analysis, such as type checking, connections between modules in the specification etc. A third way to analyse the specification is dynamic assessment of the problem solving competence of the formal model.

The Si$(ML)^2$ *parser* is a context-free definite clause grammar parser. The EMACS interface can visualise the parsing process, by using the cursor to display the parsing point. This facilitates finding the cause of a parsing-error. Si$(ML)^2$ includes a *parser generator*, that takes as input a BNF language definition in LaTeX and produces a Prolog parser for that language. This ensures that the definition of the language and the parser for the language are always consistent with each other.

After a text has been parsed, and syntactically accepted, the static semantics of the specification are checked, such as correct typing, valid import relations, defined terms etc. The *checker* generates error messages, which can be interpreted by the editor, allowing to jump to the cause of the error. The tool also heuristically suggests modifications to the specification that would remedy the errors found.

Si$(ML)^2$ contains a *theorem prover* (based on PTTP [16]), which can be used to simulate the execution of a task, and to prove properties of the specification. This part of the toolset was not evaluated in the course of this research.

7.2 Suggestions for Further Support

In the above we described the required functionality for software support tools, and how the Si$(ML)^2$ toolset realises this functionality. There is still some functionality lacking which should be incorporated in a toolset to support the construction of formal specifications.

The main lack in the Si(ML)^2 toolset was *graphical visualisation* and editing of the formal model. We found ourselves sketching the structure of the formal model by pencil and paper, to maintain an overview over the specification. Experiences with tools that do offer graphical support (such as TheME [3]) show the benefits of graphical support is for the construction process of formal specifications.

Another improvement of the toolset would be the ability to show the *evaluation status* of parts of the model. The toolset supports incremental parsing of the specification, but does not show which modules are syntactically accepted, or found to be (in)correct by the type checker.

The selective display that Si(ML)^2 supports is based on the syntactic structure of the specification. One could envisage the support of various *views* on the formal specification. For instance, there may be a view that is more understandable to the domain expert, or a view that is tuned towards the programmer of the target KBS. Such views would not only require hiding detail, but would also require different representations of parts of the formal model. Examples are graphical representations or informal textual *summaries* of specification fragments, or specific syntactic sugar. The editor and parser already support inclusion of *comments* in the specification, and the transformation tool includes CML text as comments, so that could be a starting point.

As remarked above, software support for the selection and adaptation of inference schemes is also neccessary. A library tool requires functionality for selecting and adapting the inference schemes. Given the formal structure of the inference schemes, we envisage theorem proving support for selection and for suggesting adaptations. A library tool should also support the extension of the library with fragments and with adaptation steps.

8 Conclusions

In this paper we investigated the usability of the formal modelling language (ML)^2. We did this by designing a set of evaluation criteria and applying these criteria to (ML)^2 in a number of case-studies. The evaluation criteria were: expressivity, frequency of errors, redundancy, locality of changes, reusability and guidelines/support. In section 5 and 6 we have seen that (ML)^2 scored well on most of these criteria. We contribute these relatively positive results to the close connection that exists between the structure of the informal KADS models and the formal (ML)^2 models. The case-studies revealed problems with the reuse of formal model fragments. These problems were caused by the (inevitable) ambiguous interpretations of the informal model fragments.

Concluding, we can say that formal specification for KBS modelling is both desirable and possible. Formalisation is *desirable* because it reveals errors in conceptual models, even when these were thought to be of high quality. Formalisation is also *possible*, but only when extensive support is given in the form of guidelines and software-tools. The close structural relation between informal and formal model makes it possible to give such extensive support for a number of aspects of the formalisation process.

Besides these positive conclusions concerning desirability and feasibility of using formal languages, there is also a negative conclusion from our work. Our case studies have revealed difficulties with the reuse of model fragments. The ambiguous interpretations of the informal model fragments endangers the reuse of both formal and informal model fragments. In section 6 we have sketched how the problems with reusability of model-fragments might be solved, but further study is certainly needed in this area.

Related Work A recent study of the use of formal methods in industry [6] The recommendations of this study can be summarized as follows. First, the acceptance of formal methods must be improved by integrating the formal methods in a broader methodology and by developing notations that can be used by non-logicians. Second, tools must be robust, and tool support in validation is especially weak. $(ML)^2$ attemps to address both these problems. First, $(ML)^2$ is embedded in the KADS methodology, and especially designed for that methodology. The notations in $(ML)^2$ are tuned towards knowledge engineers that are familiar with the KADS methodology, and avoid the in depth knowledge required for understanding the underlying formal logics. Second, the embedding of $(ML)^2$ in the KADS methodology allows more informed toolsupport.

Limitations and Future Work The first limitation of the research outlined in this paper is that we concentrated mainly on the transformation of the informal model to the formal model. As another goal of the formal model is to bridge the gap between informal model and design model, future research should focus on the question whether the transformation of the informal model to the design model through the formal model is easier and/or gives better results than the direct transformation of the informal model to the design model. The second limitation is that the two models that we used had a restricted domain layer because of the precise knowledge that is necessary for the task. Therefore, our evaluation focussed mainly on the inference layer. Formalisation of a model that has a more elaborate domain layer could focus more on the evaluation of the formal specification of the domain layer. The last topic that needs to be further researched concerns the reusability. The solution that we proposed in this paper is that the relation between conceptualisation and formalisation should not be sequential but iterative. Further research is necessary to examine the effect of this lifecycle to the separate processes.

Acknowledgements. We are grateful to Anjo Anjewierden and Gertjan van Heijst for their critical comments on an earlier version of this paper.

References

1. M. Aben. CommonKADS inferences. Report KADS-II/M2/TR/UvA/041/1.0, June 1993.
2. M. Aben, J. Balder, and F. van Harmelen. Support for the formalisation and validation of KADS expertise models. Report KADS-II/M2/TR/UvA/63/1.0, January 1994.
3. J. R. Balder and J. M. Akkermans. TheME: an environment for building formal KADS-II models of expertise. In *Proceedings of the 12th Int. Conf. on Expert Systems and their Applications*, Avignon, 1992. Also in: AI Communications, 5(3), 1992.
4. J. Balder, F. van Harmelen, and M. Aben. A KADS/ML^2 model of a scheduling task. In Treur and Wetter [17], pages 15–44.

5. J. A. Breuker, B. J. Wielinga, M. van Someren, R. de Hoog, A. Th. Schreiber, P. de Greef, B. Bredeweg, J. Wielemaker, J. P. Billault, M. Davoodi, and S. A. Hayward. Model Driven Knowledge Acquisition: Interpretation Models. ESPRIT Project P1098 Deliverable D1 (task A1), University of Amsterdam and STL Ltd, 1987.

6. D. Craigen, S. Gerhart, and T. Ralston. An international survey of industrial applications of formal methods. Technical report, U.S. Department of Commerce, Technology administration, National Institute of Standards and Technology, Computer Systems Laboratory, Gaithersburg, MD 20899, USA, March 1993.

7. D. Fensel, J. Angele, and D. Landes. Knowledge representation and acquisition language (KARL). In *Proceedings 11th International workshop on expert systems and their applications*, pages 821–833, Avignon, France, May 1991.

8. J. Fox. On the soundness and safety of expert systems. *AI in Medicine*, 5:159–179, 1993.

9. D. Harel. Dynamic logic. In D. Gabbay and F. Guenthner, editors, *Handbook of Philosophical Logic, Vol. II*, pages 497–604. Reidel, Dordrecht, The Netherlands, 1984.

10. L. in 't Veld, W. Jonker, and J.W. Spee. The specification of complex reasoning tasks in $K_{BS}SF$. In Treur and Wetter [17], pages 233–256.

11. J. Kamps and N.J.E. Wijngaards. $(RP)^2$: A KADS–solution for the office assignment problem. student report, July 1992.

12. W. Karbach, A. Voß, R. Schukey, and U. Drouwen. Model-K: Prototyping at the knowledge level. In *Proceedings Expert Systems–91*, pages 501–512, Avignon, France, 1991.

13. D. Landes, D. Fensel, and J. Angele. Formalizing and operationalizing a design task with KARL. In Treur and Wetter [17], pages 105–142.

14. Marc Linster. Linking modeling to make sense and modeling to implement systems in an operational environment. In Thomas Wetter et al., editors, *Current developments in knowledge acquisition: EKAW92, Lecture Notes in AI*, vol. 509, Springer-Verlag, 1992.

15. A. Th. Schreiber. Sisyphus'91: Modelling the office assignment domain. In M. Linster, editor, *Sisyphus'91: Models of Problem Solving*, Arbeitspapiere der GMD 663, chapter 11. GMD, Sankt Augustin, Germany, 1992.

16. M. E. Stickel. A prolog technology theorem prover: implementation by an extended prolog compiler. *Journal of Automated Reasoning*, 4(4):353–380, 1988.

17. J. Treur and Th. Wetter, editors. *Formal Specification of Complex Reasoning Systems*, Workshop Series. Ellis Horwood, 1993.

18. M. van 't Holt. Modelling of visual perception for a recognition task in noise analysis. Master's thesis, Dept. of Information Theory, Fac. of Electrical Engineering, Technical Univ. of Delft, August 1993. (in Dutch).

19. F. van Harmelen and J. R. Balder. $(ML)^2$: a formal language for KADS models of expertise. *Knowledge Acquisition*, 4(1), 1992.

20. I. van Langevelde, A. Philipsen, and J. Treur. An example reasoning task description. In Treur and Wetter [17], pages 7–14.

21. J. Walther, A. Voß, M. Linster, T. Hemman, H. Voß, and W. Karbach. MoMo. Technical Report Arbeitspapiere No. 658, GMD, Juni 1992.

22. T. Wetter. First-order logic foundation of the KADS conceptual model. In B. J. Wielinga, J. Boose, B. Gaines, G. Schreiber, and M. van Someren, editors, *Current trends in knowledge acquisition*, pages 356–375, Amsterdam, The Netherlands, May 1990. IOS Press.

23. B. J. Wielinga, A. Th. Schreiber, and J. A. Breuker. KADS: A modelling approach to knowledge engineering. *Knowledge Acquisition*, 4(1):5–53, 1992.

24. R. Wols. Knowledge acquisition, modelling and formalisation for METEODES. Master's thesis, Dept. of Information Theory, Fac. of Electrical Engineering, Technical Univ. of Delft, July 1993. (in Dutch).

A Comparison of Two Approaches to Model-based Knowledge Acquisition

Dieter Fensel (+) and Karsten Poeck (*)

(+) Institut für Angewandte Informatik und Formale Beschreibungsverfahren
University of KARLsruhe, 76128 Karlsruhe, Germany
phone: 49-721-6084754, fax: 49-721-693717
e-mail: fensel@aifb.uni-karlsruhe.de

(*) Lehrstuhl für Informatik VI
University of Würzburg, Allesgrundweg 12, 97218 Gerbrunn, Germany
phone: 49-931-70561 18, fax: 49-931-7056120
e-mail: poeck@informatik.uni-wuerzburg.de

Abstract. This paper discusses and compares two different approaches to model-based knowledge acquisition. That is, we regard the Model-based and Incremental Knowledge Engineering (MIKE) approach and the Configurable Role-limiting Method approach (CRLM). MIKE is based on the distinction of different phases in the software development process. It uses the formal and operational knowledge specification language KARL allowing a precise and unique description of a model of expertise which is the outcome of the analysis phase. CRLM is based on the role-limiting method approach. Role limiting shells are implementations of strong problem-solving methods and substantially simplify knowledge acquisition through guidance by predefined models of problem-solving and by sophisticated graphical user interfaces. The main disadvantages, namely inflexibility and brittleness, are to some degree overcome by the CRLM where the shell's problem-solving methods are split into smaller parts, which can then be reconfigured allowing the integration of new methods or other method combinations. Although these two approaches are often discussed as contradictory, we, however, experienced that both approaches complete each other very well. As an outcome of our comparison, we outline topics of future research for both approaches.

Introduction

In the paper, we discuss and compare two different approaches to *model-based* knowledge acquisition. Both approaches are *model-based* in the sense that they *explicitly distinguish different types of knowledge* and use *generic problem-solving methods as the behaviour model* of an expert system. Apart from their similarities, the two approaches differ significantly in their underlying principles and points of interest.

Model-based and Incremental Knowledge Engineering (MIKE) [AFL+93] is strongly influenced by the results of the KADS and CommonKADS projects [SWB93] and works in the domain of software engineering and information system design (cf. [AFS90]). It is based on the distinction of different phases like analysis, design, and implementation, in the software development process. An important means of MIKE is the *formal and operational knowledge specification language KARL* (cf. [FAL91], [Fen93a], [AFS94]), which allows a precise and unequivocal description of a model of expertise as the result of the analysis phase.

Configurable Role-limiting Method (CRLM) [PoG93] is based on the role-limiting method approach (see [Mar88], [McD88]). Role-limiting shells are implementations of strong problem-solving methods and substantially simplify knowledge acquisition through guidance by the given model of problem-solving. These shells pre-define the roles that knowledge can play during the problem-solving process and completely fix the knowledge representation scheme for the method such that the expert only has to instantiate given generic concepts. In most of these shells the expert is supported by a sophisticated graphical user interface for knowledge acquisition. Their main disadvantages, that is, their inflexibility and brittleness, are to some degree overcome by the CRLM. In this approach, the problem-solving methods of the shell are split into smaller parts, which can then be reconfigured allowing the integration of new methods or new method combinations. The corresponding knowledge acquisition components can be generated from a declarative description [Flo84]. CLRM tries to preserve the advantages of RLMs such as strong knowledge acquisition support and rapid prototyping, while extending their scope by being more adaptable and therefore less brittle.

The two examined approaches also reflect the two current main streams of research in knowledge acquisition. On the on hand, there are approaches like *KADS* and *CommonKADS* which view the knowledge engineering process of a process of building multiple models. On the other hand, approaches like *PROTÉGÉ-II* [PET+92] or *KREST* [Ste93] aim much stronger at an immediate implementation of a knowledge-based system. Although these different approaches are often discussed as contradictory, we experienced that both approaches complement each other very well. As both approaches emphasize different aspects in the development process of a knowledge-based system, their combination adds to the power of the achieved results. It was already shown in [FEM+93] how an implementation of the board-game method, that is, a role-limiting method, can be combined with a semiformal and formal description by using KARL. [PFL+94] shows a successful solution of the elevator-design problem (i.e., the Sisyphus´93 problem) based on the fruitful combination of the two approaches. In fact, the successful combination of both approaches by solving the elevator-design problem encouraged us to compare both approaches in more detail and depth. The purpose of our study is to get a better insight into the different assumptions implicitly underlying the different approaches by contrasting the two approaches. Additionally, we try to overcome some conceptual miss-matches because a term like knowledge base is associated with different meanings by the two approaches. Finally, we will show how both approaches fit together, that is, how both approaches can be improved by overtaking results of the competitor.

We identified four dimensions for the comparison of both approaches. In each item we *make the different assumptions explicit which underlie the two approaches to model-based knowledge acquisition.* First, we ask how both approaches bridge the gap between informal requirements and implemented systems which meets these requirements. CRLM tries more or less to bridge this gap in one go whereas MIKE makes a walk of several steps. Second, we discuss how both approaches view the difference of problem-solving methods and domain knowledge. The Role-limiting method views problem methods as fixed and implemented whereas MIKE views the problem-solving method as part of the knowledge and aims at its declarative description. The CRLM approach converges into the direction of MIKE but does still regard the problem-solving method not as part of the knowledge base. Third, we ask to what degree both approaches try to mechanize the knowledge engineering process. Whereas MIKE view the knowledge engineer as a necessity CRLM aims on excluding him from the process by offering powerful tool support. The final dimension of our comparison regards the different concepts of reuse which underlie both approaches. In the conclusion, we answer the question whether both approaches are contradictory or rather complementary. It is shown how both approaches converge together starting from very contrary points. Libraries of reusable mechanisms or problem-solving methods seem to unify both approaches. In fact, they require the combination of both approaches.

Our comparison of different approaches in knowledge engineering is not the first one. An early attempt to survey and classify most approaches in knowledge acquisition was given by [Boo88]. Methodologically close in spirit to this work are [KLV90], [NPB+91], [Lin93], and [FeH94]. [KLV90] survey four approaches to model-based knowledge acquisition and extract three common hypotheses which are now common places in knowledge acquisition. [NPB+91] tries to give a complete classification on knowledge acquisition and [Lin93] focuses on solutions of the Sisyphus-I problem. [FeH94] discuss and compare eight formal knowledge specification languages. In this paper we have chosen a different methodological point of view:

- First, we neither aim to give a representative survey on all existing knowledge acquisition approaches nor to classify them. Instead, we chose two different paradigms in knowledge engineering and prototypical approaches for each of them. Therefore, we did not try to abstract and aggregate general features but instead we tried to elicit differences and mutualities of both approach in detail.

- Second, we use a common case study to understand mutualities and differences of both approaches in detail (like [Nwa93] does it for KADS and Generic Tasks). In fact in [PFL+94] we modelled a Sisyphus-II solution by combining both approaches. This case study, even not very often mentioned in the paper, was a rich and powerful source for understanding, comparing and analysing both approaches. In addition, it can be read as a very detailed and broad illustration of our more generic conclusions in this paper.

Therefore, we did not try to get a representative classification by regarding several approaches and aggregating them but we try to take a close view on two different paradigm by choosing two prototypical instances as input for a detailed case study.[1] Our study continues [GaP92] who implicitly compared KADS and their role-limiting method approach by describing how the later can be described using the further one. This is the one of the few approaches which investigates how role-limiting methods can be re-expressed in terms of the general methodological framework of KADS and therefore bridging the dichotomy between methodological and tool-oriented approaches. Compared to our study [GaP92] is much more focused as it asks how to represent a role-limiting method in terms of the KADS model of expertise.

1   How to Bridge the Representation Gap

The development of an (software) artifact contains two main activities. First, the problem to be solved by the artifact must be *analysed and specified*.[2] Second, the artifact

---

1. In social science, this distinction corresponds to the distinction of normative and interpretative oriented techniques and methods (see [Fen92]).

which is to solve the given problem must be *designed and implemented*. Therefore most, if not all, process models in software and knowledge engineering distinguish these two activities in a project even though, in detail, their distinctions are treated in a different way.[3]

MIKE clearly separates the analysis and the design/implementation of an expert system during the project. The outcome of the analysis phase is a (formal) specification of the task which is to be solved by the system and of the knowledge which is required to solve the task effectively and efficiently (without symbol-level control, cf. [Sch92]). The outcome of the implementation phase is a computational agent that solves the problem. This is achieved by a kind of refinement step. The declarative description of a model of expertise in KARL is refined by additional data structures and efficient algorithms which compute the semantics of the model more efficiently [LaS94].

In CRLM, the analysis phase consists of two steps. First, the appropriate problem-solving method and its knowledge representation formalism is selected. Second, the predefined knowledge representation formalism of this problem-solving method guides the acquisition of domain knowledge. Ideally, there is no further design/implementation step in the project because the previous implementation of the problem-solving method (which has been carried out independently of the current project) is reused. The result of the analysis phase is a running system. Yet, it may be necessary to reconfigure a selected method to a specific problem or to implement a new sub-method for a task only partially covered by the selected method combination. While new sub-methods must be explicitly coded, the corresponding knowledge acquisition components can be automatically generated from a declarative description of the knowledge representations and editors. This knowledgeacquisition tools allow domain experts after a training phase to develop the knowledge base by themselves without further guidance by a knowledge engineer [GPS93]. The experts may directly evaluate the knowledge base with test cases without the need for a further precompilation step. While this model of direct knowledge acquisition by domain experts is seen by some as the most important advantage of CRLM, it is for others the cause of important drawbacks. On one hand:

- The quality of the knowledge base is greatly improved since no translation errors occur between the knowledge engineer and the domain experts.
- The maintenance of the knowledge base can be done by the domain experts.

On the other hand:

- The expert has to enter the knowledge without further guidance by intermediate models. He has to analyse and represent his knowledge at the same time.
- Due to the lack of intermediate models the executable knowledge base is the only documentation of the expertise.
- The view of knowledge is obviously determined by the knowledge representation formalism of the chosen shell although the expert only has to deal with the corresponding graphical representations.

Whether the advantages of this process model outweigh the disadvantages cannot be answered in general but depends on the circumstances of the actual project. But we found. that least for classification the experts are comfortable with it and develop

---

2. In the case of a knowledge-based system an integrated part of the analysis phase is the modelling of the knowledge which is required to solve the task.
3. A survey of discussion in software engineering can be found in [ThD90].

knowledge bases with high competence, c.f. [ScS93].

The process model of MIKE is influenced by work in conventional software engineering. In fact it is based on the *spiral model* of [Boe88] and different approaches to *prototyping* of [Flo84]. Its main principles are:

- The entire development process is subdivided into several different phases. Each phase is concerned with a specific aspect of the development process. This defines a clear focus of interest for every activity and reduces its complexity. The four main phases of the process model of MIKE are analysis, design, implementation, and evaluation. Each phase is again split into several subphases.

- As the original life cycle-oriented process models in software engineering rely on unrealistic assumptions (e.g., the waterfall model), the process model of MIKE regards these phases as incremental and cyclic. [Boe88] views this process as a spiral where the entire functionality of the system is achieved by several iterations of these different phases.

- An important aspect of each phase is the evaluation of the achieved results. The main means of evaluation is *prototyping*. The outcome of every phase is an operational description which can be evaluated by prototyping.

The process model of MIKE tries to integrate the advantages of well-structured process models into incremental system development and prototyping. Looking in greater detail at its process model, the large *modelling gap* between informal descriptions of the expertise that are gained from the expert by using knowledge-acquisition methods, and the final realization of the expert system *is bridged* by several intermediate models. Decomposing this gap into smaller ones reduces the complexity of the whole modelling process since in every step particular aspects may be considered independently of other aspects. Five different descriptions of a task and the required knowledge exist in MIKE (see figure 1).

First, knowledge and task are described in *natural-language documents*. These documents may result from interviews or observations, or can already exist as manuals or books, etc. These documents can be structured and represented in a protocol model which uses a hyper media representation. Second, these informal descriptions are transformed into a *semiformal representation* called structure model. For building the protocol model as well as the structure model the hypermedia tool MeMo-Kit (Mediating Model Construction Kit) can be used [Neu93]. As a result, the knowledge and the task are described along the lines of a model of expertise as defined in KADS [SWB93]. The description of knowledge is structured in different layers by using appropriate primitives, which are also associated with a suitable graphical representation. The semantics of elementary knowledge pieces is still defined in natural-language. Such a mediating representation has the following advantages: The structuring process creating the mediating representation provides early feedback for the knowledge engineer and the expert; the semiformal representation of the expertise provides a useful basis for communicating with the expert; the contents of the model may be exploited for the explanation facility of the final system; and the model documents modelling decisions and thus may be used for the maintenance of the final system.

The third type of description is accomplished by using KARL. Knowledge which is represented informally or semiformally is formalized during the *knowledge-formalization step*. The main benefits of formal descriptions of expertise, compared to informal or semiformal representations, are the following: The vagueness and ambiguity

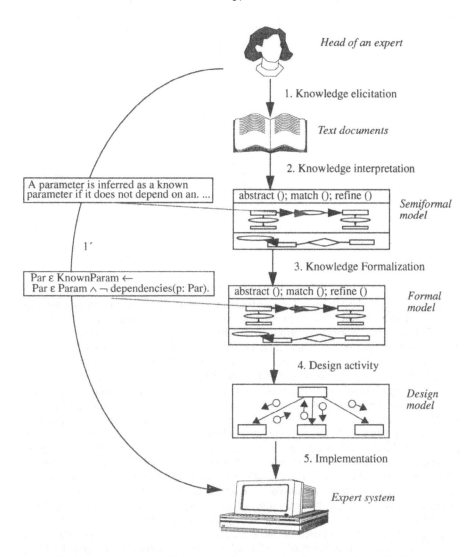

Head of an expert

1. Knowledge elicitation

Text documents

2. Knowledge interpretation

A parameter is inferred as a known parameter if it does not depend on an. ...

abstract (); match (); refine ()

Semiformal model

1´

3. Knowledge Formalization

Par ε KnownParam ←
Par ε Param ∧ ¬ dependencies(p: Par).

abstract (); match (); refine ()

Formal model

4. Design activity

Design model

5. Implementation

Expert system

Fig. 1. The five steps of MIKE (1-5) and the one-step transition (1´) of CRLM.

of natural-language descriptions can be avoided; the formalized problem-solving method can be used to guide the collection of domain knowledge; the formal description can help to get a clearer understanding of single problem-solving steps as well as of complete problem-solving methods, it thus supports their reuse; and a formalized specification can be mapped to an operational one. This allows prototyping or a symbolic execution in order to evaluate the knowledge, thus supporting incremental modelling.

Formalization results in a formal and operational description of the model of expertise. Since a KARL specification is based on the structure of the KADS model of expertise there is a smooth transition from an semiformal to a formal description. The KARL

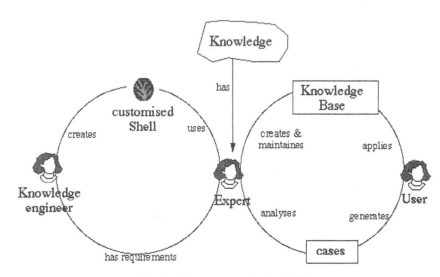

Fig. 2. The process model in CRLM

model is constructed by refining the semiformal model of expertise, e.g., by augmenting an informal description of an elementary inference step in the semiformal model by a formal description. Formal descriptions should not replace informal ones but rather define their meaning precisely and uniquely. Natural language is very useful to outline the general idea of an inference since in a formal description one often cannot see the wood for trees. One the other hand, it is very difficult if not impossible to define the exact meaning of an inference in a precise and unique manner by natural language only. KARL is a customization of first-order logic consisting of the two sublanguages L-KARL that represents static knowledge and P-KARL that represents dynamic knowledge. It has a declarative semantics [Fen93a] as well as an operational semantics [Ang93]. L-KARL is based on Frame-logic [KLW93], which integrates object-orientation into a declarative framework. P-KARL is based on dynamic logic [Koz90], which integrates the representation of procedural knowledge into a declarative framework. The modelling primitives of KARL reflect the structure of the model of expertise of KADS (i.e., the separation of different layers and different modelling primitives at each layer, e.g. inference actions and roles at the inference layer). As a specification in KARL is based on the structure of the model of expertise, there is a smooth transition from an informal to a formal description. Natural-language definitions of the meaning of graphically specified elements of a model are supplemented by formal definitions using KARL.

The fourth description level is defined by the *design model*. The model of expertise finally includes all functional requirements posed on the desired system. For the realization of the final system additional requirements have to be considered which are still independent of the final implementation of the system. They are non-functional requirements such as efficiency of the realization of the problem-solving method, maintainability of the system, persistency of data etc. The design model enriches and refines the model of expertise by taking these issues into account, e.g., by introducing appropriate algorithms and data structures, it takes care for a suitable modularization of the system, etc. Capturing such design decisions in the design model narrows the gap between the model of expertise and the implementation of the final system. For instance, the informal and formal but declarative description of an inference action is supplemented by appropriate data structures and algorithms which support an efficient computation (cf. [LaS94] for more details). The final description is achieved by *implementing the system* in the given hardware and software environment.

When we compare these transitions with respect to the way in CRLM it becomes clear that the expert has to do the first three transitions in one go by directly specifying the domain knowledge in the graphical representation of the language of the chosen shell. He has not to deal with design decisions and the details the language is implemented in, since this is viewed as an fixed and given entity for him as described in the next section. Given feedback by cases from end uses he may have to maintain the knowledge base either by changing existing knowledge pieces or adding new ones. This process becomes more complicated in the case that an appropriate shell is not available. Then the knowledge engineer and the expert have to customize the best fitting shell for the specific needs of the expert. It may even happen during knowledge maintenance that the shell must be adapted to allow the formulation of other knowledge types. This double spiral is shown in the figure 2.

2 Relationship of Domain Knowledge and Problem-Solving Methods

An important common feature of both approaches is *the separation of domain knowledge from generic (i.e., domain-independent) problem-solving knowledge*. The problem-solving knowledge controls the use of the domain knowledge for problem-solving. Yet, the two approaches differ significantly in their way of separating and combining both parts of an expert system.

CRLM clearly separates the problem-solving method from domain knowledge. The problem-solving method, its terminology (i.e., the object and relation types it uses) and the knowledge acquisition environment are an implemented and *fixed* building block which is called an *expert-system shell*. The domain knowledge, which consists of instantiations of the generic object and relation types of the selected problem-solving method, is acquired during the knowledge-acquisition step. The domain knowledge is called the *knowledge base* of the expert system. *The terminology is problem-solving-method-specific, but not domain-specific.* The predefined terminology allows the development of reusable graphical knowledge-acquisition tools for the domain knowledge ([GPS93], [PoG93]). This enables domain experts to enter their knowledge without assistance, that is, without a translation step by a knowledge engineer, and to maintain the knowledge base. The reuse of domain knowledge for different problem-solving methods requires additional effort. Even a method specific knowledge base consists of problem specification and problem-solving knowledge. The problem specification can be reused for other methods, for example in classification the same set of observables and diagnoses may be used for heuristic, case-based and set-covering classification, but the terminology must eventually be mapped. The problem-solving knowledge, e.g. set-covering relations, can only be reused when explicit knowledge transformation procedures are applied as for example in [BGG+93]. These mappings or transformations are significantly eased by the explicit knowledge representation of the role limiting methods, where each knowledge entry is used in exactly in way that is at least informally specified. MYCIN rules in contrast are nearly impossible to reuse since they contain both diagnosis rating and dialogue guidance knowledge in the same place.

The model of expertise as the result of the analysis phase in MIKE clearly separates

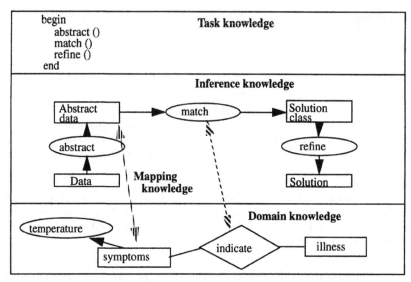

Fig. 3. The model of expertise of heuristic classification in KARL.

three types of knowledge and represents them at three different layers (see figure 2). At the *domain layer*, the domain knowledge is represented independently of its application for the problem-solving process. It consists of the terminology of a domain, a set of rules and constraints which model regularities in this domain, and a set of facts which represent factual knowledge. The *inference layer* is used to represent the inference steps of a problem-solving method and their data dependencies, but also defines a problem-solving-method-specific or task-specific terminology. Domain knowledge and domain terminology are mapped onto the inference layer and its task-specific terminology via view definitions. The *task layer* represents the control flow between the inference steps, that is, it can be used to define sequences, choices, and iterations of inferences. *None of these layers is fixed.* Due to the flexible mapping, a domain layer can in principle be reused for different problem-solving methods [PiS94].[4]

Comparing both approaches with respect to the relationship of domain knowledge and problem-solving method, three main distinctions can be identified (see figure 3):

- CRLM views the problem-solving method as a fixed entity which is not a part of the knowledge base. MIKE views domain knowledge and the generic control knowledge of the inference layer and task layer as part of the knowledge base.
- CRLM only offers a terminology that is specific to a problem-solving method. A model of expertise in MIKE contains two terminologies, that is a domain-specific terminology at the domain layer and a problem-solving-method-specific terminology at the inference layer.
- The relationship of the domain knowledge and the problem-solving method is expressed by the instantiation of a generic terminology in CRLM and by defining

---

4. The different knowledge types can be used to refine the process model of MIKE as their elicitation and modelling define different activities of the development process. The inference and task knowledge can be used as a guidance for modelling domain knowledge, for example (see for more details [NeS92]).

MIKE   **CRLM**

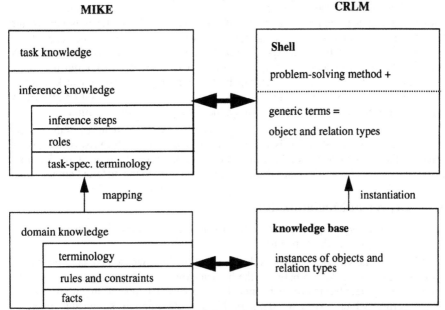

Fig. 4. Relationship of domain knowledge and problem-solving methods in MIKE and CRLM.

a mapping via Horn clauses extended by stratified negation (cf. [Llo87], [Prz88]) in MIKE.

CRLM and MIKE are both methods of developing *expert systems*.[5] Therefore, it is not without interest to ask how both methods view the difference between expert systems and ordinary software programs. The question of how an approach characterizes an expert system is not only of philosophical interest but it also brings up the problem of the scope of its applicability. Both methods aim at supporting the development process of *expert* systems, and not of *arbitrary* systems. Therefore, if one wants to apply one of these methods it must be made sure that one wants to build an expert system in the sense of the selected method.

From the CRLM point of view, the following features are essential for an expert system (despite the fact that the performed task is meant for an expert): transparency, flexibility, user friendliness, and competence (cf. [Pup93]). To that end, the separation of an inference component and domain knowledge is inevitable. The inference component is not viewed as a part of the knowledge base. Domain knowledge (i.e., the knowledge base) can be changed without affecting the inference component. The inference component, that is, the dynamic or control knowledge, is viewed as fixed.

In MIKE, the problem-solving method is regarded as a part of the knowledge which consists of the three parts already mentioned: domain knowledge, inference knowledge,

---

5. To some extent, this is not true for MIKE. In [FAL+93] it is shown how KARL can be used to formalize and operationalize techniques of structured analysis, which is a commonly used approach in software engineering. Therefore, the specification of knowledge-based components can naturally be embedded into the specification of an entire system containing also conventional parts.

and task knowledge. None of these parts is regarded as fixed, and the dynamic or control knowledge which is represented at the inference layer and task layer is part of the knowledge base. Yet, every knowledge type is clearly separated and can be manipulated independently of the others. An expert system is mainly characterized by the kind of task it solves. An expert system is a computer program which solves a task requiring a high amount of knowledge and intellectual capability when a human solves the task, *and* this knowledge is necessary for solving the task, that is, the problem cannot be efficiently solved by a simple complete search through the variety of possible solutions.

While in CRLM an expert system is mainly characterized by the features of the system and its realization, in MIKE it is mainly characterized by the features of the task it solves. This is also reflected in the different degrees of emphasis on the individual life-cycle phases (specification versus design/implementation) in the different approaches.

3   Degree of Mechanization

The view of the *knowledge engineer's* the probably defines one of the most significant differences between both approaches.

In MIKE, the knowledge engineer is the essential medium whose task is to bridge the assumed deep and wide gap between the human expertise and the expert system. The knowledge engineer has to create the model of expertise in cooperation with the expert. The expertise which exists as skills or hidden and implicit knowledge must be transformed into an explicit and formal model. As neither this model exists before the knowledge-acquisition process, nor are the experts very apt at retrospectively developing a model of their own expertise, the development of the model of expertise is mainly the task of the knowledge engineer.

Role-limiting methods provide shells which should enable experts to write expert systems on their own. Therefore, it is assumed that a knowledge engineer is only required during the initial problem analysis when he or she must decide whether there is an appropriate shell for the given task and, if so, which one should be chosen. In CRLM, the role of the knowledge engineer is enlarged to some extent. As an application may not perfectly fit a given shell, or a complex task may require the combination of several shells, the knowledge engineer must configure the appropriate shell. Therefore, he or she must elicit knowledge about the task and the appropriate problem-solving method. The appropriate method is therefore no longer regarded as a fixed precondition for the knowledge acquisition process, but, to some extent it also constitutes a part of its result.

A benefit of the CRLM approach is the *tool support* it offers for knowledge acquisition and knowledge evaluation. As the problem-solving method and its terminology are fixed, the expert only has to instantiate given generic structures. Tools with graphical interfaces can be defined and implemented in order to support this powerful means of knowledge acquisition. Evaluation is supported by the running prototype of the system and by additional tools that use the fixed structure and semantics of the knowledge base imposed by the problem-solving method.

The main means of MIKE are the hypermedia tool MeMo-Kit [Neu93] and the formal and operational language KARL. MeMo-Kit supports the process of building a semiformal model by different customized editors and a library of informally described reusable problem-solving methods. KARL allows a precise and unique description of the knowledge and its evaluation by prototyping. For this purpose, an interpreter and debugger for KARL was developed which is integrated into the MeMo-Kit environment.

4   Reuse By Use of Specification Languages

Both approaches aim at the *reuse* of knowledge and software. [Kru92] compares eight different types of software reuse. One of them is based on *very-high level languages (VHLL)* like KARL which is used by MIKE. VHLL define a higher conceptual level than high-level programming languages like C or Modula by abstracting from efficiency and other implementation details, while having the same or even more expressive power. In comparison to assembler even in a high-level language a considerable reuse rate can be achieved by grouping a set of low-level statements into a single high-level statement. This kind of reuse is extended by VHLLs where it is possible to quickly write powerful (though inefficient) programs. Due to their generality, they can be applied to a broad range of tasks. KARL is neither task-specific nor domain-specific, that is, in principle it should be possible to specify arbitrary tasks and domains in KARL. A significant restriction is the fact that KARL cannot be used to specify real-time problems.

MIKE and CRLM both use *specification languages* which abstract from the implementation, but differ significantly in the level of abstraction of these languages and by the way their semantics is defined. CRLM uses *problem-solving-method-specific representation languages*. Every problem-solving method is combined with a specific representation language that allows the expert to specify knowledge in terms of his or her task without referring to a general-purpose representation formalism. As already mentioned, given a complete graphical interface, this allows non-programmers to program (i.e., to enable them to develop and maintain the knowledge base without assistance). In contrast to KARL, these languages do not have a declarative semantics. Their semantics is only defined by their interpreter, that is, by the shell using the language. An implementation of a problem-solving method together with its specific representation formalism and knowledge acquisition tools can be applied for problems in different domains. [Kru92] classifies this approach as *application generators*, where an application-specific (task-specific or better problem-solving-method-specific in our terms) languages is provided that allow users to think in terms of their application (i.e., task). Comparing both concepts of software reuse, two comments can be made:

- On the one hand, task-specific languages are easier to learn because of their limited range of applicability and there higher conceptual level than that of general-purpose languages. Users can think in terms of their task instead of learning a very general language.
- On the other hand, the limited range of task-specific languages restricts the expressiveness of the language constructs. Different tasks or the combination of several problem solvers require the effort of developing and learning different languages.

Conclusion: Contradiction or Complement?

Finally, we discuss some experiences concerning the combination of MIKE with CRLM. To some extent, both approaches are complementary and supplement each other very well. [FEM+93] already report on a fruitful combination of a role-limiting method approach and MIKE. In its current stage, MIKE offers significant tool support for the early phases in knowledge engineering. The hyper model can be used to semiformally describe a model of expertise and this description can be further refined and operationalized by the specification language KARL. Language and tool support for the design phase is under way. Currently, there is no support for the implementation of a final system. The inverse holds for the CRLM approach which only supplies powerful shells which eliminate or drastically reduce the implementation effort, but provides less support for the early knowledge acquisition phases. By combining both approaches, a description of a system and of the used knowledge at different complementary levels can be achieved: First, the knowledge is described at the *conceptual level* in a semiformal manner by the different layers and primitives of a model of expertise. Second, the knowledge is described at the *formal level* to define a precise and unique meaning. This formal description makes it possible to exactly define the knowledge-based systems without referring to implementational aspects. Third, the knowledge is described at the *implementational level* by a running system. The domain knowledge can comfortably be acquired and efficiently be executed by the shell. Since the implemented problem solver operates directly on a representation corresponding to the problem solving method explanation and maintainability capabilities are significantly improved.

Speaking as a cynic, both approaches fit together and supplement each other because of the incompleteness of their current development state. On the other hand, both approaches seem to converge regarding the kind of *reuse* they aim to support in the near future. The original RLM reused monolithic task-specific shells. An implementation of a problem-solving method together with its task specific representation formalism and knowledge acquisition tools could be applied for problems in different domains. CRLM extend this as also smaller parts of problem solving methods (mechanisms) can be reused, and new methods can be configured from the mechanisms. The knowledge acquisition tools can be generated from a declarative description of the knowledge representation and the views acquired in the knowledge editors. The library of CRLM currently contain mechanisms for heuristic ([PuG92], [GPS93]) case-based [PuG91] and set-covering classification [Pup93], methods for assignment (propose-and-exchange [PoP92]) and for simple configuration (propose-and-revise [PFL+94]).

In MIKE, reuse is enabled by the very-high level language KARL which makes it possible to quickly write powerful (though inefficient) specifications of problem-solving methods and domain knowledge. A further kind of reuse in MIKE is subject of ongoing work. Different problem-solving methods like the *board-game method* [FEM+93], *cover-and-differentiate* [Ang93], *propose-and-exchange* [LFA93] together with their generic terminology have been specified in KARL. These collection of problem-solving methods will be continually extended, and the formal semantics of these models will be investigated in order to support the selection, modification, and combination of these methods based on formal goal descriptions of a given task (cf. [Fen93b]). A library of semiformally specified problem-solving methods which supplements these formal descriptions is described in [Neu94].

The library of semiformal, formal and operational problem-solving methods indicates that MIKE and CRLM are convergent. The main difference concerns the representation of the reusable blocks, e.g. the problem-solving methods, and their descriptions. CRLM provides an informal textual description and an efficient implementation of such a block in a programming language. MIKE provides a semiformal description and a formal (and operational) description, but no implemented building blocks. The formal semantics of it can be used to derive properties of it (e.g., pre and post conditions which can be used to guide the selection process). There is a clear need in the CRLM approach to use some kind of precise and unique description formalisms for its implemented mechanisms in order to support their selection and combination.

A clear distinction between the both approaches arises by the different ways to view domain knowledge: KARL (MIKE) uses a domain-specific and a problem-solving-method-specific terminology. The user can work in terms of his domain or of the applied problem-solving method. In CRLM, only a problem-solving-method-specific terminology is provided and the implemented system does not use the domain-specific terminology. Domain knowledge is assumed to be only factual knowledge. This restriction is necessary to define powerful generic knowledge acquisition tools. A first step to enrich the role-limiting method approach was done by *PROTÉGÉ* [Mus89] which allows the derivation of domain-specific acquisition tools, but requires structural equivalence of domain and task knowledge. Work on the *PROTÉGÉ-II framework* [PET+92] tries to define more flexible mappings between problem-solving methods and domain ontologies which again narrows the gap between both approaches.

Acknowledgement

We thank Jürgen Angele and Dieter Landes who participated on our Sisyphus-II case study, Gabi Rudnick for partial correction of our manuscript, and two anonymous referees for helpful comments.

References

[AFL+93]   J. Angele, D. Fensel, D. Landes, S. Neubert, and R. Studer: Model-Based and Incremental Knowledge Engineering: The MIKE Approach. In J. Cuena (ed.), *Knowledge Oriented Software Design*, IFIP Transactions A-27, Elsevier, Amsterdam, 1993.

[AFS90]   J. Angele, D. Fensel, and R. Studer: Applying Software Engineering Methods and Techniques to Knowledge Engineering. In D. Ehrenberg et al. (eds.), *Wissensbasierte Systeme in der Betriebswirtschaft, Reihe betriebliche Informations- und Kommunikationssysteme, no 15*, Erich Schmidt Verlag, Berlin, 1990.

[AFS94]   J. Angele, D. Fensel, and R. Studer: The Model of Expertise in KARL. In *Proceedings of the 2nd World Congress on Expert Systems*, Lisbon/Estoril, Portugal, January 10-14, 1994.

[Ang93]   J. Angele: *Operationalisierung des Modells der Expertise mit KARL (Operationalization of a Model of Expertise with KARL)*, Ph. D. thesis, University of Karlsruhe, 1993 (in German).

[BGG+93]   S. Bamberger, U. Gappa, K. Goos, and K. Poeck: Teilautomatische Wissenstransformation zur Unterstützung der Wissensakquisition (Semiautomatic Knowledge Transformation Supporting Knowledge Acquisition). In *Proceedings of the 2. Deutsche Tagung Expertensysteme (XPS-93)*, Hamburg, February 17-19, 1993 (in German).

[Boe88]   B.W. Boehm: A Spiral Model of Software Development and Enhancement, *IEEE Computer*, May 1988.

[Boo88]   J. H. Boose: A Research Framework For Knowledge Acquisition Techniques and Tools. In *Proceedings of the 2nd European Knowledge Acquisition for Knowledge-Based Systems Workshop (EKAW-88)*, St. Augustin/Bonn, 1988.

[FAL91]   D. Fensel, J. Angele, and D. Landes: KARL: A Knowledge Acquisition and Representation Language. In *Proceedings of the 11th International Conference on Expert Systems and their Applications, vol.1, General Conference Tools, Techniques and Methods*, 27-31 May, Avignon, 1991.

[FAL+93]   D. Fensel, J. Angele, D. Landes, and R. Studer: Giving Structured Analysis Techniques a Formal and Operational Semantics with KARL. In *Proceedings of Requirements Engineering '93 - Prototyping -*, Bonn, April 25 - 27, 1993, H. Züllighoven (ed.), Teubner Verlag, Stuttgart, 1993.

[FeH94]   D. Fensel and F. van Harmelen: A Comparison of Languages which Operationalize and Formalize KADS Models of Expertise. In *The Knowledge Engineering Review*, vol 9, no 2, June 1994.

[FEM+93] D. Fensel, H. Eriksson, M. A. Musen, and R. Studer: Description and Formalization of Problem-Solving Methods for Reusability: A Case Study. In *Complement Proceedings of the 7th European Knowledge Acquisition Workshop (EKAW'93)*, Toulouse, France, September 6-10, 1993.

[Fen92]   D. Fensel: Knowledge Acquisition and the Interpretative Paradigm. In F. Schmalhofer et al. (eds.), *Contemporary Knowledge Egineering and Cognition, First Joint Workshop*, Kaiserslautern, Germany, February 21-22, 1991, Lecture Notes in Artificial Intelligence, no 622, Springer-Verlag, Berlin, Juli 1992.

[Fen93a] D. Fensel: *The Knowledge Acquisition and Representation Language KARL*, Ph D. thesis, University of Karlsruhe, 1993.

[Fen93b] D. Fensel: Reuse of Problem-Solving methods in Knowledge Engineering. In *Proceedings of the 6th Annual Workshop on Software Reuse (WISR'6)*, Owego, New York, November 1-4, 1993.

[FGS93]   D. Fensel, U. Gappa, and S. Schewe: Applying a Machine Learning Algorithm in a Knowledge Acquisition Scenario. In *Proceedings of the IJCAI'93 Workshop Knowledge Acquisition and Machine Learning*, Chambery, France, August 28th - September 3rd, 1993.

[Flo84]   C. Floyd: A Systematic Look at Prototyping. In R. Budde et al. (eds.), *Approaches to Prototyping*, Springer-Verlag, Berlin, 1984.

[GaP92]   U. Gappa and K. Poeck: Common Ground and Differences of the KADS and Strong-Problem-Solving-Shell Approach. In *Proceedings of the 6th European Knowledge Acquisition for Knowledge-Based Systems Workshop (EKAW-92)*, May 18-22, Heidelberg/Kaiserslautern, 1992, Lecture Notes in Artificial Intelligence, no 599, Springer-Verlag, Berlin, 1992.

[GaP94]   U. Gappa and K. Poeck: An Architecture for Reusing Role-limiting Mechanisms and Knowledge Acquisition Modules, submitted, 1994.

[GPS93]   U. Gappa, F. Puppe, F., and S. Schewe: Graphical Knowledge Acquisition for Medical Diagnostic Expert Systems. In *Artificial Intelligence in Medicine, Special Issue Knowledge Acquisition*, vol 5, 1993.

[KLV90]   W. Karbach, M. Linster, and A. Voss: Models, Methods, Roles, and Tasks: Many Labels—One Idea. In *Knowledge Acquisition*, vol 2, no 4, 1990.

[KLW93]   M. Kifer, G. Lausen, and J. Wu: Logical Foundations of Object-Oriented and Frame-Based Languages. In Technical Report 93/06, Department of Computer Science, SUNY at Stony Brook, NY, April 1993. To appear in *Journal of ACM*.

[Koz90]   D. Kozen: Logics of Programs. In J. v. Leeuwen (ed.), *Handbook of Theoretical Computer Science*, Elsevier, Amsterdam, 1990.

[Kru92]   C. W. Krueger: Software Reuse, *ACM Computing Surveys*, vol 24, no 2, June 1992.

[LaS94]   D. Landes and R. Studer: The Design Process in MIKE. In *Proceedings of the 8th Banff Knowledge Acquisition for Knowledge-Based System Workshop (KAW'94)*, Banff, Canada, Januar 30th - February 4th, 1994.

[LFA93]   D. Landes, D. Fensel, and J. Angele: Formalizing and Operationalizing a Design Task with KARL. In J. Treur and T. Wetter (eds.), *Formal Specification of Complex Reasoning Systems*, Ellis Horwood, Chichester, 1993.

[Lin93]   M. Linster: A review of Sisyphis 91 & 92: Models of Problem-Solving Knowledge. In *Proceedings of the 7th European Knowledge Acquisition Workshop (EKAW'93)*, Toulouse, France, September 6-10, Lecture Notes in Artificial Intelligenc, no 723, Springer-Verlag, Berlin, 1993.

[Llo87]   J.W. Lloyd: *Foundations of Logic Programming, 2nd Editon*, Springer-Verlag, Berlin, 1987.

[Mar88]   S. Marcus (ed.): *Automating Knowledge Acquisition for Experts Systems*, Kluwer, Boston, 1988.

[McD88]   J. McDermott: Premilary Steps Towards a Taxonomy of Problem Solving Methods. In [Mar88].

[Mus89]   M. A. Musen: *Automated Generation of Model-Based Knowledge-Acquisition Tools*, Morgan Kaufmann Publisher, San Mateo, CA, 1989.

[NeS92]   S. Neubert and R. Studer: The KEEP Model. In *Proceedings of the 6th European Knowledge Acquisition for Knowledge-Based Systems Workshop (EKAW-92)*, May 18-22, Heidelberg/Kaiserslautern, 1992, T. Wetter et al. (eds.), *Current Developments in Knowledge Acquisition*, Lecture Notes in Artificial Intelligence, no 599, Springer-Verlag, Berlin, 1992, pp. 230-249.

[Neu93]   S. Neubert: Model Construction in MIKE (Model-Based and Incremental Knowledge Engineering). In *Knowledge Acquisition for Knowledge Based Systems, Proceedings of the 7th European Knowledge Acquisition Workshop (EKAW '93)*, Toulouse, France, September 6-10, Lecture Notes in Artificial Intelligenc, no 723, Springer-Verlag, Berlin, 1993.

[Neu94]   S, Neubert: Modellkonstruktion in MIKE - Methoden und Werkzeuge (Model Construction in MIKE - Methods and Tools), Ph.D thesis, University of Karlsruhe, 1994 (in German).

[NPB+91] H. S. Nwana, R. C. Paton, T. J. M. Bench-Capon, and M. J. R. Shave: Facilitating the Development of Knowledge Based Systems. In *AI Communication (AICOM)*, vol 4, no 2/3, 1991.

[Nwa93]   H. S. Nwana: Using KADS and Generic Tasks to Model a Timetabling Problem. In *Complement Proceedings of the 7th European Knowledge Acquisition Workshop (EKAW '93)*, Toulouse, France, September 6-10, 1993.

[PFL+94] Karsten Poeck, Dieter Fensel, Dieter Landes, and Jürgen Angele: Combining KARL and Configurable Role Limiting Methods for Configuring Elevator Systems. In *Proceedings of the 8th Banff Knowledge Acquisition for Knowledge-Based System Workshop (KAW '94)*, vol 3, Banff, Canada, Januar 30th - February 4th, 1994.

[PET+92] A. R. Puerta, J. W. Egar, S. W. Tu, and M. A. Musen: A Multiple-Method Knowledge-Acquisition Shell For The Automatic Generation Of Knowledge-Acquisition Tools, *Knowledge Acquisition*, vol 4, no 2, 1992.

[PiS94]   T. Pirlein and R. Studer: An Environment for Reusing Ontologies within a Knowledge Engineering Approach. In N. Guarino et al. (eds.), *Formal Ontology in Conceptual Analysis and Knowledge Representation*, Kluwer, Boston, to appear 1994.

[PoG93]   K. Poeck and U. Gappa: Making Role-limiting Shells More Flexible. In *Knowledge Acquisition for Knowledge Based Systems, Proceedings of the 7th European Knowledge Acquisition Workshop (EKAW '93)*, Toulouse, France, September 6-10, Lecture Notes in Artificial Intelligence, Springer, 1993.

[PoP92]   K. Poeck and F. Puppe: COKE: Efficient solving of complex assignment problems with the propose-and-exchange method. In *Proceedings of the 5th International Conference on Tools with Artificial Intelligence*, Arlington, Virginia, USA, November 10-13, 1992.

[Prz88]   T. C. Przymusinski: On the Declarative Semantics of Deductive Databases and Logic Programs. In J. Minker (ed.), *Foundations of Deductive Databases and Logic Programming*, Morgan Kaufmann Publisher, Los Altos, CA, 1988.

[PuG91]   F. Puppe and K. Goos: Improving Case-based Classification with Expert Knowledge. In *Proceedings of the 15th German Workshop on Artificial Intelligence (GWAI-91)*, Bonn. September 16-20, 1991.

[PuG92]   F. Puppe and U. Gappa: Towards Knowledge Acquisition by Experts. In *Industrial and Engineering Applications of Artificial Intelligence and Expert Systems, Proceedings of the 5th International Conference IEA/AIE-92*, Paderborn, June 9-12, 1992.

[Pup93]   F. Puppe: *Systematic Introduction to Expert Systems: Knowledge Representation and Problem-Solving Methods*, Springer-Verlag, Berlin, 1993.

[Sch92]   G. Schreiber: *Pragmatics of the Knowledge Level*, Ph D. Thesis, University of Amsterdam, 1992.

[ScS93]   S. Schewe and M. A. Schreiber: Stepwise development of a clinical expert system in rheumatology, In *The Clinical Investigator*, 1993.

[Ste93]   L. Steels: The Componential Framework and its Role in Reusability. In J.-M. David et als (eds.), *Second generation expert systems*, Springer, Berlin, 1993

[SWB93]   G. Schreiber, B. Wielinga, and J. Breuker (eds.): *KADS. A Principled Approach to Knowledge-Based System Development*, Knowledge-Based Systems, vol 11, Academic Press, London, 1993.

[ThD90]   R. H. Thayer and M. Dorfman (eds.): *System and Software Requierements Engineering*, IEEE Computer Society Press, Los Alamitos, California, 1990.

Agent-Based Knowledge Acquisition

Rose DIENG, Olivier CORBY, Sofiane LABIDI

ACACIA Project, INRIA
2004 Route des Lucioles, BP 93
06902 SOPHIA-ANTIPOLIS CEDEX, FRANCE
E-mail: {dieng, corby, labidi}@sophia.inria.fr
Tel: (33) 93 65 78 10, Fax: (33) 93 65 77 83

Abstract. This paper presents our approach for knowledge acquisition from multiple experts. In order to build a cooperative KBS, representing the knowledge of several experts and intended to multiple users inside an organization, we propose a model of cognitive agent for guiding the process of knowledge acquisition. This model of agent can serve as a basis for specifying the future KBS to be integrated in the organization. An agent-based knowledge acquisition is then seen as the process of identifying the adequate agents and of filling them (both their individual characteristics such as their expertise model or their knowledge graphs, and their social features such as their integration in an organization or their cooperation capabilities).

1 Introduction

The involvement of multiple experts in the development of a knowledge-based system (KBS) can influence problem definition, knowledge elicitation, knowledge modeling, operationalization of the expertise models and validation of the final KBS [28, 21, 27].

A cooperative, explanatory KBS must be able to cooperate with its ends-users for problem solving and to provide them with explanations about its knowledge and its reasoning. The building of such a system involves collaborative knowledge acquisition and collaborative design, as well as the construction of a KBS based on multiple experts.

In both cases (i.e multiple experts and cooperative KBS), models or techniques stemming the field of distributed artificial intelligence (DAI) seem useful: (a) for modelling the organization where the experts and the intended users of the future KBS work, (b) for modelling the experts, their cooperation and their conflicts, (c) for modelling the knowledge acquisition process and specially the cooperation during knowledge acquisition from a group of experts, (d) for modelling the cooperation and explanation processes between the humans (experts or non-experts) in the effective organization and between the future KBS and the future end-users.

We think that a model of cognitive agent can guide the design of such a KBS, specially when this KBS is aimed at relying on some human, social behaviour and at offering a collaboration between an artificial agent and human agents.

Therefore, our knowledge acquisition method relies on a model of cognitive agent aimed at modelling the experts and the intended users in their organization.

In this paper, after studying the link with composite systems, we present our model of cognitive agent. Then, we describe the method of agent-based knowledge acquisition, relying on this model, and we present an application of our method to traffic accident analysis.

2 Composite systems

The notion of composite systems [17], made of heterogeneous (human, software and hardware) agents seems quite relevant for our work. In a previous research [15], we viewed the development of a multi-expert system as a combination of several human and software components, interacting with one another, depending on the phase of development:

- The analysis of the actual organization made of experts (whose tasks will be partially simulated by the future KBS) and of potential users that need assistance from this future KBS helps to identify the human agents that may then take part in the knowledge acquisition phase.
- The knowledge acquisition phase consists of knowledge elicitation and modelling and involves human agents such as experts, knowledge engineers, potential users. The knowledge acquisition tool - that plays the role of an assistant of the knowledge engineer - is an artificial agent, that may itself rely on a multi-agent architecture.
- During the design phase, progressively, the knowledge engineer designs the artificial agents of the final multi-expert system, with the help of human agents such as the experts, the potential users and perhaps specialists in ergonomics or in user interfaces.
- After effective achievement of the KBS, during validation phase, the knowledge engineer and the validating experts are human agents, while the KBS is an artificial agent.
- In the final phase of effective use of the KBS, the introduction of the KBS into the organization transforms this organization. The artificial agent is the KBS that may be composed of a multi-agent system, comprise an explainer and cooperate with the human agents constituted by the end-users.

This vision allows to model the development of a multi-expert application, (in particular the knowledge acquisition phase) as the behavior of a specific society of (human or artificial) agents: it helps to characterize the roles and tasks of each agent and to emphasize the main relations between such agents (knowledge transfer, explanation, validation, assistance to problem solving...) and to analyse the cooperation underlying the process of knowledge acquisition. We also stressed that the notion of agent should allow to model the end-user as an agent and ease the description of a knowledge acquisition methodology involving several human agents. In [14], we had proposed elements of a model of cognitive agent in order to take into account knowledge acquisition from multiple experts.

This analysis confirms the remark made in [32] where the author notices that the process of design of an object multi-agent system relies on several multi-agent systems obtained by composition of the object multi-agent system and of some of the various human agents that may take part in the design (user, application programmer, system programmer, designer...)

Notice that, in our case, two object multi-agent systems can be considered: the knowledge acquisition tool and the KBS can both be based on a multi-agent architecture. For the knowledge acquisition tool, we need a model of the human agents inside the human organization and of the knowledge acquisition process. For the KBS, the model of agent must allow to specify the intended behaviour of the group constituted by the KBS and the users, and how several such agents will cooperate for problem solving and for explanation. In our past research [12], we had proposed a language for describing different relations concerning one agent or linking several agents (e.g. specialists inside one KBS, or several different cooperating KBS). Inspiration can be taken from this idea in order to propose a language for specifying not only the final multi-agent system but the relations of the human / artificial agents in the organization.

The couple "final KBS - user" can be considered as a couple of two agents that must cooperate in order to perform for example cooperative problem solving. It is then interesting to model the group constituted by the KBS and by the user as a multi-agent system compound of two agents: decomposition of the global task between both agents, distribution of subtasks, planning of job among them, possible interactions among them, their interaction points, possible communication language they use, possible conflicts and way such conflicts will be solved [5]. This vision can be extended to several users: in this case, a multi-agent system is obtained, with an artificial agent (the cooperative system) and several human agents (the users), such human agents can interact among themselves or with the KBS. The interaction among the users or with the KBS will be influenced by the organization to which the users belong.

3   A model of Cognitive Agent

A model of agent, intended to model both experts and users involved in the KBS design, must include *individual aspects* (concerning the agent himself independently of the organization in which he is inserted and independently of the other agents) and *social aspects* related to the agent's insertion in an organization and to his interactions with the other agents. The individual aspects include *general features* not linked to the particular problem to be solved (competence domain, high-level goals, tasks, expertise knowledge consisting of domain knowledge, of general problem solving methods used, of possible strategies) and *problem-specific features* that may depend on the phase of the considered problem solving (intentions, plans, actions, commitments and state).

The social aspects include the organizational structure (that can concern either the way a compound agent is organized or the way an agent is included in a given compound agent), the cooperation modes, the communication languages.

We distinguish *simple agents* that are not made of other agents and *compound agents* (also called *organizations*) that are constituted by subagents gathered through an organizational structure, such subagents being themselves simple or compound. This notion of compound agent allows to model for example a group of cooperating experts or a group of collaborating users. The individual (resp. social) aspects of an agent exist, whether this agent is simple or compound.

The next sections describe more thoroughly such features.

3.1 Individual Characteristics

Long-term, Problem-independent Characteristics. Some individual characteristics of an agent are generally long-term and problem-independent. Among such characteristics, let us cite:

- *identity*: an agent is identified by a name characterizing this agent without any ambiguity and known by the other agents that can call him explicitly by his name. Each time a new agent is created, he must at least own a name, different from the already existing agent names. An agent may have several names, but he must not share any name with any other agent. The problems raised by the notion of identity of an aggregate agent (specially when this identity cannot be considered as permanent and can evolve through time) were studied in [22].
- *role, competence domain, high-level goals* and *tasks* : such characteristics summarize what the agent can do. The role of an agent in an organization he belong to must be indicated. If an agent belongs to several organizations, he can have a different role in each of them. The competence domain indicates the special field of expertise of the agent. When he solves a problem in his discipline, the expert aims at one or a few high-level goals, associated to his main task. This main task can then be decomposed into subtasks: this decomposition can be represented through a task structure [6, 8, 33, 30]. Such a task structure may be static or dynamic: in this last case, the task structure should rather be considered as a problem-dependent characteristics instead of a problem-independent feature. Several levels of abstraction can be adopted for this task structure: either it may be close to the expertise domain [16] or generic [6, 8, 33].
  For example, psychology, vehicle engineering and road infrastructure engineering are examples of competence domains of the experts involved in the task of road accident analysis. When analysing an accident, in addition to the comprehension of the accident scenario, cognitive modelling of the drivers and diagnosis of the drivers' errors are the high level goals of the psychologist, while diagnosis of a possible vehicle malfunctioning and proposal of advices for vehicle design and manufacturing are the high-level goals of the car engineer. Extraction of data from the drivers involved in the accident, as well

as analysis of all extracted data (on the drivers, on the vehicles and on the road infrastructure) from a psychology viewpoint are examples of (sub)tasks of the psychologist. The task of data analysis can itself be decomposed into other subtasks.

— *resources*: such characteristics summarize the various resources used by the agent. In the framework of artificial agents, in [7], the authors distinguish sensing resources, sending-receiving resources, acting resources and cognitive resources. For human agents such as experts or users, the relevant resources are rather instruments, software, tools, etc. For example, in traffic accident analysis, the infrastructure engineer and the vehicle engineer may make use of a camera in order to take photographs of the road infrastructure and of the vehicles involved in the accident, while the psychologist uses a cassette recorder in order to record the interviews of the involved drivers, and the vehicle engineer uses a program of kinematics reconstitution, in order to reconstitute the trajectories and speeds of the vehicles.
In addition to classic interviews, analysis of observations or of thinking-aloud protocols can give complementary information on such resources (and specially on the context where the expert makes use of a given resource).

Remark: Knowledge can be considered as a cognitive resource, so significant that we prefer to distinguish a specific characteristics, called *expertise model*, in the model of agent.

— *expertise model*: it helps to model the agent's static knowledge on the domain, his problem solving methods, and his strategies. We adopt the decomposition of expertise knowledge in four layers (domain, inference, task and strategy) proposed in KADS-I [6, 33] [1]. An agent's vision of the domain comprises the concepts or entities he knows, his vision of their structure and of the relations linking them, the parts of them he can access or act upon. If a KADS-I expertise model is associated to the agent, his vision of the domain can be described in the domain layer of this expertise model. Moreover, his strategy can be based on an *evaluation function* allowing him to assess the situations, in order to guide his choices according to the context. The *general preferences* of the agent may also be part of this strategy. For example, the order in which an expert prefer to examine some data, the kinds of models / methods / tools he prefers when several ones are available, are parts of his general preferences.

Remark: We consider that competence domain, high-level goals, resources, knowledge are generally independent of the problem to be solved. It seems to be a reasonable hypothesis. But, in some cases, such features may evolve : for example, a particular problem solving may help an agent (for example, the user of the final KBS) to increase his knowledge and to improve his capabilities. Likewise, the resources used for a given problem solving may depend on the considered problem.

---

[1] We tried to respect the philosophy of KADS-I and have not yet adapted our work to COMMONKADS framework.

When a feature is contextual and not permanent, it is important to acquire all the adequate contextual information indicating the conditions of modification of this feature.

Problem-dependent Characteristics. Other characteristics depend on the problem to be solved and can evolve throughout the problem solving.

- *intentions* or *low-level goals*: during a problem solving, the agent has several simultaneous or successive intentions, that can be explicitly expressed to other agents or remain implicit. A hierarchy may link the different intentions of an agent, as he can handle simultaneously several low-level goals of various levels of abstraction. Of course, such low-level goals can generally be linked (and associated) to the subtasks appearing in the decomposition of the main task of the expert. In [7], the authors distinguish strategic intentions (that are long-term) and tactical intentions (that are short or mid-term).

  So, the knowledge engineer must elicit the possible intentions of the different experts during a problem solving, how such intentions are linked to one another, etc. For example, the analysis of individual thinking-aloud protocols or of case studies can be useful to reveal such intentions, and help the expert to make them explicit and to explain them.

- *plans*: in order to achieve his goals, the agent may make individual plans, perhaps taking into account the common goal(s) of the organization(s) he is included in. A plan is a succession of actions. Of course, a plan should be naturally associated to a task: it can be seen as a detailed description of a possible realization of this task.

  So, the knowledge engineer must elicit the different possible plans each expert has available for a given problem solving, the elementary actions such plans are composed of, the criteria of choice between such plans, the conditions of execution of a plan, its conditions of success, how to repair it in case of need. The way the individual plans of the experts can be integrated in collective plans of the organizations to which the experts belong can also be elicited, through interviews or analysis of observations, case studies or collective thinking-aloud protocols.

- *actions*: we distinguish observable actions, actions having observable consequences, and internal actions without any observable consequence (such as the cognitive actions that are distinct from the effectoric actions, as stressed in [7]). The actions can have different levels of abstraction and different natures (e.g. physical actions versus steps of problem-solving).

  For example, the observable actions of the vehicle engineer are to record the tracks of the vehicles involved in the accident, to examine the photographs of the vehicles and of the road infrastructure, to execute the program of kinematics reconstitution, while his cognitive actions correspond to his internal reasoning and can be simultaneous with the previously described observable actions.

- *state*: several features of the agent can evolve through time, due to the evolution of the problem solving or to the interactions of the agent with the other agents: such features can be considered as parts of the agent's state. The agent has an *information state* (what he knows about data, about the state of the problem solving), an *intentional state* (at a given instant, both his long-term and short-term intentions), a *strategic state* (the chosen strategy among several possible alternatives), an *evaluative state* (at a given instant, the values assigned to the possible choices) [31].

If we consider that the agent's knowledge (i.e. his model of expertise) can evolve, it may also be considered as a part of the agent's state. The model the agent has about the world and in particular, about the other agents and their intentions, may also be considered as a part of the agent's information state.

The state of a compound agent depends on the individual states of his sub-agents, but not exclusively.

— *individual history*: at a given moment of the problem solving, it is constituted by the successive past actions and past states of the agent. Such information on the individual history of an agent during a problem solving could be useful, for example for enabling explanatory capabilities in the final KBS. It can be elicited by analysing case studies, observations or thinking-aloud protocols.

3.2 Social Aspects

When an agent belongs to a multi-agent world, his social characteristics may be described through the features described below.

— *interaction points* [32]: they can be used as an external interface of the agent with the outside world. The requests sent by the other agents to this agent rely on what they know about the official competences of this agent, and the kind of requests he can accept. We distinguish *entry interaction points* (cf the demands the agent can receive) and *exit interaction points* (cf the requests he can send). Requests are linked to particular subtasks the agent is known to be able to perform. For example, an entry interaction point of the vehicle engineer agent is *"extract data on the state of the vehicles involved in the road accident"* since other agents such as the psychologist can need some data on the vehicle, for their own tasks. An agent must be able to link a request received in one of his interaction points, to a task he is able to perform.

In the case of a compound agent, there may be several kinds of relations between his interaction points and the interaction points of his subagents: his interaction points may correspond exactly to the set of all the interaction points of the subagents, or to only a subset or even comprise new interaction points not appearing in any of the subagents.

So, during knowledge acquisition phase, the knowledge engineer must elicit information on what can constitute the interaction points of each expert.

— *model of the world*: the external world of an agent consists of other intelligent agents, and of entities such as facts or data. His interactions with the outside world, and in particular with the other agents help the agent to adapt and modify his model of the world. A *model of the other agents* is part of this model of the world: we can consider that some features of an agent such as domain competence, high-level goals, interaction points can be visible from the other agents. But must they be visible from all agents or not ? Some flexibility on this notion of visibility is needed. For example, the agent psychologist may know the competence domain of the vehicle engineer agent without knowing his intentions or the individual plans he uses for a particular problem solving. An agent may know only the external aspects of another compound agent (competence domain, high-level goals, interaction points) but without knowing his internal structure and the subagents composing this compound agent.

So, the knowledge engineer must elicit what vision each expert has upon the external world and upon the other experts.

— *organizational structure*: a *compound agent* (i.e. an *organization*) is made of several subagents (that may be simple or compound themselves), gathered into an adequate organizational structure and, so, linked by different relations such as cooperative problem solving... This notion of compound agent is close to the notions of *social agent* proposed in [26] or of *aggregate agent* studied in [22]. Some agents can aggregate in order to form a compound agent (seen as a unique agent by the outside world), for a common goal. Such an aggregation is not a simple "concatenation". It must respect an organizational structure. There may be several models of organizational structures, according to which the different agents may aggregate. For example, such agents can be gathered in a horizontal, non hierarchical structure or in a vertical, hierarchical structure. The organizational structure may then influence their types of cooperation: for example, sharing of tasks and of results in a non hierarchical organization, commands, bids and competition in a hierarchical organization... Studies on the roles and responsibilities assigned to distinct agents inside a human organization, on the norms which govern interactions between such agents, on the delegation of tasks to agents can be exploited.

Two different compound agents can be made of exactly the same subagents but gathered through two different organizational structures. For example, there may be a compound agent made of a psychologist, a vehicle engineer and an infrastructure engineer working with a non hierarchical structure, and another compound agent, made of the three same subagents organized hierarchically with the infrastructure engineer coordinating the group work. Both compound agents will exist at different moments of the problem solving; they may also exist simultaneously, with different high-level goals.

The interaction points of a compound agent are not necessarily obtained by the union of the interaction points of the internal agents. When an external agent asks a request to the whole organization, he uses the interaction points of the compound agent. The way this request is then forwarded to all or some subagents of the organization depends on the organizational structure of the compound agent.

The recognized competence of the whole organization may be wider (or even smaller) than the simple union of the individual competences of the agents. The list of the tasks the compound agent can perform can also be wider than the union of the subagent task lists.

An organization can be fixed or evolve through time as new agents can be inserted into it or old agents removed. A given agent may belong simultaneously or successively to several different organizations. Even if he belongs to an organization, an agent can receive individual requests (concerning the agent himself and not the whole organization), on his own individual interaction points.

We will suppose that the high-level goals of the compound agent are common to all his subagents. They may have been common before the aggregation of the agents into the compound agent, or, on the contrary, have become common only because of this aggregation. Likewise, they may disappear after the dissociation of the compound agent or, on the contrary, still exist for the separate agents even after their separation. The distribution of tasks among the different agents can be independent of the problem, or fixed for a given problem or dynamically evolving throughout problem solving. Some aspects of the organization can be global and visible to all internal and external agents, while others can be local to the agent or partially known by only some particular agents. Several studies on organizational models and on science of organizations can be exploited [4, 25, 34]. In [4], the author describes a model for human organizations represented by a set of interacting projects. The agents performing such activities correspond to specialist departments. The model helps to represent goals and tasks. In [25], the authors study the integration of men and computers in firms dispersed geographically. They introduce the notion of computational assistants (or intelligent agents), helping for a task and resorting to the services of other agents in case of need. In [34], a framework is proposed in order to model complex organizations, with three levels of modelling: social, logical and physical. All such research gives indications on the possible organizational models that could be useful.

So, the knowledge engineer must elicit the information on the possible organizational structures of the compound agents that may appear during the problem solving, on the way such organizational structures can evolve, on the contexts where a given compound agent will change his organizational structure. Organizational models proposed in the current state of the art could be gathered in a library of predefined organizational models, that could guide the knowledge engineer: he would have to recognize the adequate model corresponding to his application and exploit this model for eliciting the needed information. In case of need, an adaptation of a predefined model or a combination of existing models would be necessary.

− *cooperation modes*: the agent's mode of cooperation may depend or not on the problem to be solved. For example, the class of problems studied can influence the kind of cooperation: in [3], the study of cooperation among designers influenced the multi-agent architecture implementing such a collaboration. In [10], cooperation relies on the notion of goal adoption, which implies a goal common to the different agents. Different types of cooperation are presented: accidental cooperation, unilaterally intended cooperation, mutual cooperation. Cooperation is considered as a function of mutual dependency among the agents. In [31], the author distinguishes negative cooperation (where the agents avoid to do the same task simultaneously) and positive cooperation (where the agents need one another to perform a task). We can adopt all these types of cooperation as possible modes of cooperation of the agents. They can be permanent (independent of the considered problem) or temporary (dependent on the problem to be solved). They may be independent of the other agents playing the role of partners or, on the contrary, depend on the considered partners.

In [24], different coordination modes inside an organization are described: by mutual adjusting, by direct supervision by standardization of procedures, of results or of qualifications. In some coordination modes such as standardization of procedures, the allocation of roles and tasks is rigid. Studies on the cooperation modes in norm-governed human organizations can be also exploited.

More generally, all this previous work on cooperation (either in the science of organizations or in the field of multi-agent systems) can be useful to propose some predefined models of cooperation [2]. Then, during the knowledge acquisition phase, the knowledge engineer can be guided by such models and try to recognize which predefined models can help describe the actual modes of cooperation used effectively by the experts. For example, collective study cases can be useful to elicit such information. As an agent can change his cooperation modes according to the context of problem solving or according to the other agents, the information on such evolution of cooperation modes and on the conditions where a given cooperation mode is preferable to another, must be elicited.

If the proposed predefined models of cooperation are not convenient, the knowledge engineer can adapt one of them or combine them or propose a new one, more adapted to the way the experts cooperate. This use of a library of cooperation models is very similar to the use of KADS library of interpretation models.

— *communication languages and protocols*: the agent may use various languages and protocols in order to communicate with the other agents, and, in particular, to send them requests, results, explanations... The communication languages may vary according to the considered agent. For example, a vehicle engineer may use a specific language, based on very technical terms, equations and graphics, when he works with another vehicle engineer and a simpler, non technical language when he works with experts of the other disciplines.

---

[2] The meaning we give here to the expression "model of cooperation" is different from KADS [11].

So, the knowledge engineer must elicit the communication languages and protocols of the experts and the contexts in which one expert uses a given language / protocol rather than another.

— *visibility from the other agents*: an agent has visible aspects (for example, observable actions, actions having observable consequences, messages sent to other agents) and internal aspects (for example, knowledge or cognitive actions that have no observable consequences). Some of the internal aspects (such as intentions) can be either explicitly expressed or when they are implicit, can be deduced by the other agents thanks to interpretations of the observable actions of the agent. A compound agent can be sometimes seen as a "blackbox" for the external world that can neither see his subagents nor deal with them directly. But it may be interesting to let the other agents know the structure of the compound agent, even if they cannot directly address requests to such subagents without using the organization interaction points.

— *joint plans, joint actions* and *commitments*: in order to achieve collectively a common goal of a compound agent, his subagents may make joint plans, that may comprise joint actions to be performed collectively by such subagents. The subagents can make commitments on the future.

Analysis of collective studies of cases, or of thinking-aloud protocols during a collective problem-solving by several experts can help to reveal such joint plans and, in particular, indicate the explicit commitments that can be made within a group of experts and the links between the individual plans of the agents and the collective decisions / plans.

— *collective history*: the history of an agent's past interactions with the other agents may be useful, specially for cooperative problem solving or for explanation. His successive integrations in several compound agents, as well as his participation to joint actions inside such compound agents, are part of this collective history. As the agents' individual histories, this collective history can be exploited for explanations.

3.3 Operators on the Agents

Various operators among the agents can be thought out, such as:

— *creation of a new agent* at least identified by his name,
— *sending a message to one or several agents*: request, result, explanation... The addressees of the message must be identified either explicitly by their names or implicitly by the properties they must satisfy.
— *aggregation of several agents*, according to an organizational structure, for a common goal and for a given time duration. This aggregation of agents is a particular case of creation of an agent.
— *decomposition of a task among several agents*: it may be reserved to agents linked through an organizational structure in a compound agent or it may be possible even for separate, independent agents.

- *modification of a compound agent*: he may integrate new subagents, remove some subagents, reorganize himself (i.e. modify his organizational structure).
- *death of an agent*: the dead agent (and in particular, his identity) no longer exists. He is no longer known by any other agent. So, all the compound agents to which the dead agent previously belonged to, must reorganize themselves in order to take this death into account.
- *dissociation of a compound agent*: his subagents become separate, independent agents, and, in particular, the organizational structure of the compound agent disappears, as well as his identity. This dissociation of agents is a particular case of death of an agent.

The knowledge engineer can acquire information on the contexts where such information can be used and exploit them for the design of the final KBS if it is based on a multi-agent architecture.

4 Agent-based Knowledge Acquisition

Knowledge acquisition consists of knowledge elicitation and knowledge modelling. Once the previous model of agent is available, knowledge acquisition can be seen as the process of *identifying the adequate involved agents* and then *building the corresponding artificial agents* in the knowledge acquisition tool and *filling them progressively*.

The identification phase consists of identifying the different kinds of humans involved in knowledge acquisition phase and specially the experts and potential end-users in a given organization. Then the artificial agents that will represent them in the knowledge acquisition tool are progressively identified and built: according to the case, such artificial agents may correspond to one expert (resp. user), to a group of experts (resp. users) or to a combination of subparts of experts (resp. users). So, an agent may represent an expert totally or partially. More precisely, an expert may be represented by a compound agent, made of: a) an agent common to all experts, b) agents common to this expert and to some other experts, c) and an agent representing the specificities of this expert.

The filling of the agents consists of eliciting and modelling knowledge from the adequate human agents (knowledge on the human organization, on the varied expertises, on the cooperation modes, etc.) in order to be able to fill the different individual and social features that must characterize the associated artificial agents. The long-term, problem-independent characteristics such as competence domain, tasks, high-level goals can generally be elicited through individual elicitation techniques. Individual observations or thinking-aloud protocols on case studies by a single expert can reveal also information on problem-dependent, individual features. The expertise model of an individual agent can be built using KADS method and its domain layer structured using our formalism of knowledge graphs. Collective elicitation techniques involving several experts are particularly helpful for refining the previous individual features, but mainly for eliciting the social features of the agents: interaction points, cooperation modes, adaptation of such cooperation modes and of communication language to the context and to the partners, conditions of creation of temporary compound agents for solving a subproblem, etc.

The knowledge engineer can adopt a bottom-up approach (construction of the simple agents and then of the compound agents) or a top-down approach (construction of the compound agents and then of their subagents). The comparison of expertise models can lead to the "decomposition of a given expert" in several subagents ot to the "gathering of several experts" into a single artificial, compound agent.

Identification and filling of the agents are in fact interleaved as, throughout the knowledge acquisition process, the need to split an agent into several ones or to gather several agents into a compound one may appear.

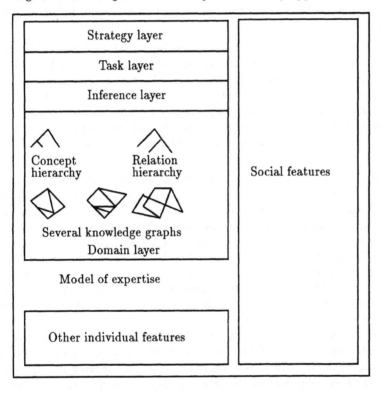

Figure 1: An agent in KATEMES.

The help offered by a knowledge acquisition method / tool can consist of offering a list of predefined possible values, for each characteristics of the model of agent. Such possible values can stem from the state of the art in DAI (in particular, multi-agent systems) or in science of organizations or from experimental results. In the section 3, we studied some of the possible values for the features of our model of agent, by relying on the current state of the art in DAI. Clearly, this work needs to be studied more thoroughly, for example, in order to make choices between several approaches of DAI. We do not intend to offer new DAI concepts or a new DAI tool, but rather to rely on what is currently known and accepted in DAI in order to offer a help during knowledge acquisition phase.

A knowledge acquisition method / tool can offer a library of organizational structures, of cooperation modes, of communication languages based on the current state of the art in DAI, with information on the contexts where each element of the library should be preferably chosen instead of another, and the adequate techniques for eliciting the information needed by this element. Such libraries can then guide the knowledge engineer in a top-down way, in order to elicit knowledge, once he has recognized the model convenient for his application. As for the exploitation of KADS library of interpretation models, he can adapt a model that seems interesting but not perfect, or combine several models, or build a completely new model if none of the predefined models could be adapted or combined.

At present, the proposed agent-based knowledge acquisition method is supported by KATEMES, a knowledge acquisition tool aimed at tackling knowledge acquisition from multiple experts [14]. Notice that KATEMES is not aimed at being a workbench for simulating agents: as it is intended to be used only during knowledge acquisition phase, it only helps to acquire knowledge on the way the human agents behave for problem-solving and for their interaction but it does not simulate such behaviour, and it does not offer any operationalization of the agent model.

For the detection of conflicts among several expertises, KATEMES focuses on the expertise knowledge of the agents. This expertise knowledge is modeled through a KADS-like model of expertise: the reasoning is described through the inference, task and strategy layers. In addition, in KATEMES, the concepts and relations of the domain layer are represented through knowledge graphs. An agent has a hierarchy of concepts, a hierarchy of relations and different knowledge graphs, as shown in Figure 1. Therefore, for the comparison of expertise models, KATEMES focuses on the comparison of such knowledge graphs. The description of our method of comparison of knowledge graphs is out of the scope of this paper and is detailed in [13].

If successful, the algorithm of comparison of the different knowledge graphs of the same nature must lead to unified knowledge graphs, according to the strategy of fusion adopted. Then a new agent must be built, having as expertise knowledge the knowledge common to both experts, i.e. described in the domain layer by the unified knowledge graphs. The remaining parts of each expert (for example, when he owned a knowledge graph for a viewpoint that did not exist for the other expert) constitute his specific knowledge and can be gathered in a new agent corresponding to this expert's specificities (and called agent specific to this expert). For example, for the house building, after comparison of the experts in electricity and in mechanics, the "electrical viewpoint knowledge graph" of the expert in electricity will not be part of the expertise of the common agent and will remain in the electrician's specific agent. Each of the two experts that were compared becomes then a compound agent, made of the common agent and the specific agent.

5 Application

We are applying this agent-based knowledge acquisition method to the design of an expert system in road safety. This application is described thoroughly in [2]. Psychology, vehicle engineering and road infrastructure engineering are the competence domains of the experts involved in traffic accident analysis. We elicited knowledge from two psychologists, three engineers in road infrastructure and two vehicle engineers. Each of the experts, being himself a driver, had at least a common-sense model of the driver, of the vehicle and of the road. But the psychologists had a deeper, finer model of the driver, the vehicle engineers had a finer model of the vehicle and the infrastructure engineers had a finer model of the road infrastructure. Moreover, within a given discipline, there were differences between the specialists: such differences were detailed in [13] and are summed up in figure 2.

For the knowledge elicitation techniques, we used both individual techniques (interview of one expert; thinking aloud protocols of one expert solving a case) and collective techniques (collective solving of a case by several experts either from the same discipline of from different ones; individual solving of a given case by several experts separately, followed by a meeting where they compared their respective solutions and discussed about them, etc.). The individual sessions were helpful to determine the individual characteristics of each expert (competence domain, tasks, high-level goals, resources, expertise model) as well as some social aspects such as the way each expert explicitly described his model of the other experts or his cooperation modes. The collective sessions helped us to refine the individual characteristics and to elicit the social aspects (the experts' interaction points, the way some experts could gather and reorganize temporarily during a given problem solving, their cooperation modes, the way they adapted their communication language to the interlocutor, etc.). The analysis of the case studies gave information on the problem-dependent characteristics of the experts (in particular, their low-level goals, their plans and their successive actions).

The various examples that illustrated the previous section on our model of agent were based on the characteristics obtained for the agents associated to the experts in traffic accident analysis. We will not recapitulate each of such features.

Lastly, the comparison between the experts allowed to progressively determine which artificial agents would represent them. The following comparison procedure seemed interesting: (1) compare both psychologists, (2) compare both vehicle engineers, (3) compare the three infrastructure engineers, either directly, or progressively by first comparing the two infrastructure engineers that know well the region, and had been in the field, and then comparing the obtained common agent with the third infrastructure engineer that has a theoretical background and is not living in the region, (4) compare the three possible common agents obtained.

When the common agent represents only what is really common to the different agents to be compared, the agents obtained are described in figure 2.

Remark: This work is still in progress, as our representation of all the agents and knowledge graphs associated to the different experts is not yet complete.

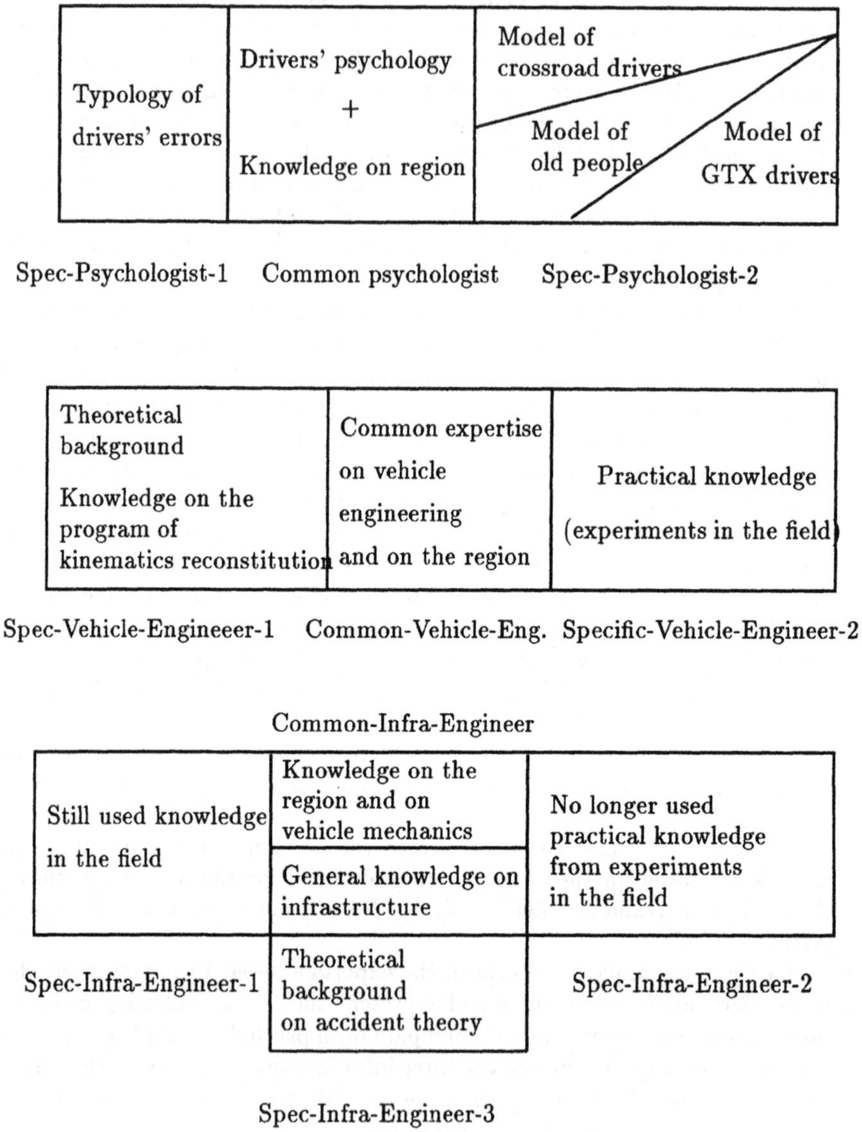

Typology of drivers' errors	Drivers' psychology + Knowledge on region	Model of crossroad drivers
		Model of old people / Model of GTX drivers

Spec-Psychologist-1   Common psychologist   Spec-Psychologist-2

Theoretical background Knowledge on the program of kinematics reconstitution	Common expertise on vehicle engineering and on the region	Practical knowledge (experiments in the field)

Spec-Vehicle-Engineeer-1   Common-Vehicle-Eng.   Specific-Vehicle-Engineer-2

Common-Infra-Engineer

Still used knowledge in the field	Knowledge on the region and on vehicle mechanics	No longer used practical knowledge from experiments in the field
	General knowledge on infrastructure	

Spec-Infra-Engineer-1	Theoretical background on accident theory	Spec-Infra-Engineer-2

Spec-Infra-Engineer-3

Figure 2: The agents involved in traffic accident analysis.

6 Conclusions

This paper proposed elements of an informal model of agent, allowing to represent the different kinds of humans involved in knowledge acquisition phase and specially the experts and potential end-users in a given organization. This model of agent can then serve as a guide for the design of the object multi-agent system. We applied our agent-based knowledge acquisition method to traffic accident analysis.

Related Work

In [19] the link between distributed knowledge acquisition and multi-agent systems is emphasized. The author adopts a blackboard architecture in order to elicit software requirements from multiple clients (approach similar to knowlege acquisition from multiple experts), and in order to solve conflicts thanks to the splitting of agents. Techniques for comparing several viewpoints and solving conflicts among them are described in [18]. We took inspiration of some aspects of such research for the splitting of agents for solving conflicts, but our model of agent and our agent-based knowledge acquisition method offers new features, different from this approach.

The choice of a multi-agent architecture serves as a methodological guide for knowledge acquisition in [20] and the *EMA* knowledge acquisition method handles a notion of agent [29], but, in both cases, the authors do not evoke the possible exploitation of this notion for knowledge acquisition from multiple experts.

CommonKads [1] offers a model of agent that, as the authors indicate, "serves as a link between the task model, the communication model and the expertise model, by modelling the capabilities and constraints that the experts have, which are involved in solving a task". Clearly, our model of agent aims at the same purpose as the one of CommonKads but, in addition, it is actually the central model in our knowledge acquisition method, which is entirely guided by it: moreover, it contains aspects concerning task, expertise, communication and organization, it aims at modelling cooperative problem solving by several agents and it is strongly inspired of work from DAI field.

Our research is also linked to research analysing software design as an agent-based activity, since a KBS is a particular case of software. In [23], the conflicts among design agents (that may be human or artificial agents) can be detected and solved, in a tool aimed at supporting cooperative design. It would be interesting to study whether such techniques, aimed at classic software, can be extended or adapted for cooperative design of a KBS.

6.1 Discussion and Further Work

As indicated earlier, we studied the current state of the art in DAI in order to indicate some of the possible values for the characteristics of our model of agent. In our study of DAI research, we naturally focused on the aspects that could be applied to human agents such as experts and users, since some characteristics of artificial agents in multi-agent systems cannot, of course, be adequate for modelling the capabilities and behaviour of human agents. But our work must not be seen as a workbench for simulating agents: it only aims at helping to acquire knowledge on the way the human agents in the organization behave for problem-solving and for their interaction, but without simulating such behaviour. In particular, it offers nothing for the operationalization of the agent model. It can be considered as a specification of the capabilities and behaviour of the agents that will appear in the final KBS if it based on a multi-agent architecture.

As an extension of this work, we will study more thoroughly how to be able to offer a guide for the construction of the final KBS: how to exploit our model of agent, in particular, if a DAI tool can be used for the generation of the operational KBS ? How to guide this operationalization while respecting the specifications obtained after knowledge acquisition phase on the behaviour of the agents ?

As a further work, we will try to formalize our model of agent: the present description of the agent's characteristics is informal and based on a synthesis of the properties most often evoked in the field of science of organizations or of multi-agent systems; but we intend to offer a more formal basis for such a description. We will try to take benefit of research on formal models of agents, that is carried out in various areas such as software design, requirements engineering, organizational models or composite systems, within the BRA Working Group MODELAGE.

We will also study methods of comparison of the different KADS layers, so that the splitting of an agent into several agents no longer relies only on the comparison of knowledge graphs performed in the domain layer. Last, we will adapt our work to COMMONKADS instead of relying on KADS-I only.

For the validation of our method through a concrete application, we will complete the representation of the different agents for traffic accident analysis.

Acknowledgements

We deeply thank the French "Ministère de la Recherche et de l'Espace" (contract n. 92 C 0757), "Ministère de l'Equipement, des Transports et du Tourisme" (contract n. 2 93 E 403) and the European Community (contract EP:8319) that funded this research. We also thank very much our colleagues of the French Working Groups MULTI-EXP and COOP, the members of the European KARMA Group and our partners of the Esprit Working Group MODELAGE for our fruitful discussions on knowledge acquisition from multiple experts, on models of agents or on cooperative systems. We thank very much our colleagues from the ACACIA project, from INRETS and from Paris V University that took part in the knowledge elicitation phase upon the traffic accident analysis.

References

1. *The Common KADS Agent Model, KADS-II/M4/TR/SICS/002/V1.1.* May 1993.
2. Ch. Amergé, O. Corby, R. Dieng, D. Fleury, A. Giboin, S. Labidi, and S. Lapalut. Acquisition et modélisation des connaissances dans le cadre d'une coopération entre plusieurs experts : Application à un système d'aide à l'analyse de l'accident de la route. Rapport intermédiaire du contrat MRE n° 92 C 0757, décembre 1993.
3. A. H. Bond. *The Cooperation of Experts in Engineering Design*, chapter 18, pages 463–483. Pitman / Morgan Kaufmann Publ. Inc., November 1989.
4. A. H. Bond. A normative model of collaboration in organizations. In *Proc. of 1990 Workshop on DAI*, Bandera, Texas, October 1990.
5. A. H. Bond and L. Gasser. An analysis of problems and research in distributed artificial intelligence. In *Readings in DAI*. Morgan Kaufman Publ., 1988.
6. J. Breuker, B. Wielinga, M. van Someren, R. de Hoog, G. Schreiber, P. de Greef, B. Bredeweg, J. Wielemaker, and J.-P. Billault. *Model Driven Knowledge Acquisition: Interpretation Models*, 1987. Deliverable A1, Esprit Proj. 1098, Memo 87.
7. B. Burmeister and K. Sundermeyer. Cooperative problem-solving guided by intentions and perception. In Werner and Demazeau, editors, *Decentralized AI, 3*, pages 77–92. Els. Sc. Publ., June 1992.
8. B. Chandrasekaran, T. R. Johnson, and J. W. Smith. Task-Structure Analysis for Knowledge Modeling. *Comm. of the ACM*, 35(9):124–137, September 1992.
9. W. J. Clancey. Heuristic classification. *Art. Int.*, 27(3):289–350, Dec. 1985.
10. R. Conte, M. Miceli, and C. Castelfranchi. Limits and levels of cooperation : disentangling various types of prosocial interaction. In Demazeau and Muller, editors, *Decentralized AI, 2*, pages 147–157. Els. Sc. Publ. B.V., 1991.
11. P. de Greef and J. Breuker. Analysing system-user cooperation. *Knowledge Acquisition*, 4:89–108, 1992.
12. R. Dieng. Relations linking Cooperating Agents. In Demazeau and Muller, editors, *Decentralized AI, 2*, pages 51–69. Els. Sc. Publ. B.V., 1991.
13. R. Dieng, O. Corby, and S. Labidi. Expertise conflicts in knowledge acquisition. In *Proc. of the 8th KAW*, vol. 2, pages 23.1–23.19, Banff, Canada, 1994.
14. R. Dieng, A. Giboin, P.-A. Tourtier, and O. Corby. Knowledge Acquisition for Explainable, Multi-Expert Knowledge-Based Design Systems. In Wetter & al editors, *Current Developments in Knowledge Acquisition : EKAW-92*, pages 298–317, Berlin/Heidelberg, May 1992. Springer-Verlag.
15. R. Dieng and P.A. Tourtier. A Composite System for Knowledge Acquisition and User Assistance. In *Proc. of AAAI Spring Symposium on Design of Composite Systems*, pages 1–5, Stanford, CA, March 1991.
16. R. Dieng and B. Trousse. 3DKAT, a Dependency-Driven Dynamic-Knowledge Acquisition Tool. In *Proc. of the 3rd Int. Symp. on Knowledge Engineering*, pages 85–93, Madrid, Spain, October 1988.
17. E. Doerry, S. Fickas, R. Helm, and M.S. Feather. A Model for Composite System Design. In *Proc. of AAAI Spring Symposium on Design of Composite Systems*, pages 6–10, Stanford, CA, March 1991.
18. S. Easterbrook. Handling conflict between domain descriptions with computer-supported negotiation. *Knowledge Acquisition*, 3(3):255–289, September 1991.
19. S. M. Easterbrook. Distributed Knowledge Acquisition as a Model for Requirements Elicitation. In *Proc. of the 3rd EKAW*, pages 530–543, Paris, July 1989.
20. C. Ferraris. *Acquisition des connaissances et raisonnement dans un univers multi-agents : application à la prise de décision en génie civil urbain*, Février 1992. Thèse de Doctorat en Informatique, Université de Nancy I.
21. B. R. Gaines and M. L. G. Shaw. Comparing the Conceptual Systems of Experts. In *Proc. of the 9th IJCAI (IJCAI-89)*, pages 633–638, Detroit, 1989.

22. L. Gasser. Boundaries, Identity and Aggregation: Plurality Issues in Multi-Agent Systems. In Werner and Demazeau, editors, *Decentralized AI, 3*, pages 199–213. Els. Sc. Publ., June 1992.

23. M. Klein. Detecting and resolving conflicts among cooperating human and machine-based design agents. *The Int. Journ. for AI in Engin.*, 7:93–104, 1992.

24. H. Mintzberg, editor. *The Structuring of Organizations*. Prentice Hall Inc., 1979.

25. J. Y. C. Pan and J. M. Tenebaum. An Intelligent Agent Framework for Enterprise Integration. In *Proc. of AAAI Spring Symposium on Design of Composite Systems*, pages 69–96, Stanford University, CA, March 1991.

26. A. S. Rao, M. P. Georgeff, and E. A. Sonenberg. Social Plans: a Preliminary Report. In Werner and Demazeau, editors, *Decentralized AI, 3*, pages 57–76. Els. Sc. Publ., June 1992.

27. M. L. G. Shaw and B. R. Gaines. A methodology for recognizing conflict, correspondence, consensus and contrast in a knowledge acquisition system. *Knowledge Acquisition*, 1(4):341–363, December 1989.

28. M. L. G. Shaw and J. B. Woodward. Validation in a knowledge support system: construing consistency with multiple experts. *International Journal of Man-machine Studies*, 29:329–350, 1988.

29. S. Spirgi and D. Wenger. Generic techniques in EMA: A model-based approach for Knowledge Acquisition. In *Proc. of the 5th EKAW*, Crieff, UK, May 1991.

30. L. Steels. *COMMET: a componential methodology for knowledge engineering.* 1991. Esprit Project CONSTRUCT DWP/2/3/4.

31. E. Werner. Social Intentions. In *ECAI-88*, pages 719–723, Munich, 1988.

32. E. Werner. The design of multi-agent systems. In Werner and Demazeau, editors, *Decentralized AI, 3*. Els. Sc. Publ., June 1992.

33. B. J. Wielinga, A. T. Schreiber, and J. A. Breuker. KADS: a modelling approach to knowledge engineering. *Knowledge Acquisition*, 4:5–53, 1992.

34. E. Yu. Organization Modelling and Composite Systems. In *Proc. of AAAI Spring Symposium on Design of Composite Systems*, pages 122–126, Stanford University, CA, March 1991.

Beyond the Knowledge Level: Descriptions of Rational Behavior for Sharing and Reuse

Franz Schmalhofer[1], J. Stuart Aitken[1] and Lyle E. Bourne Jr.[2]

[1] German Research Center for Artificial Intelligence, P.O. Box 2080, D 67608
Kaiserslautern, Germany email: schmalho,aitken@dfki.uni-kl.de
[2] Department of Psychology, University of Colorado, Campus Box 430, Boulder,
Colo. 80309 email: lbourne@clipr.colorado.edu

Abstract. The currently dominant approach to the sharing and reuse
of knowledge strives to develop ontologies, with clearly constrained interpretations. The idea of ontological commitments is based on the knowledge level perspective. Several shortcomings of the knowledge level have
been identified (Clancey, 1991). Pursuing Clancey's argument, if KBS
are to be situated in ever changing environments, their purposes and
significance will change over time and they have to be redescribed accordingly. The behavior descriptions proposed in this paper emphasize
coherent and consistent descriptions in some given context, rather than
predicting performance from knowledge and goals. When systems are
embedded into larger contexts, their behavior is redescribed so that the
additional significance is shown. Behavior level descriptions thus provide the flexibility for conceptual changes in a knowledge-based system.
We demonstrate how behavior descriptions can be used for documenting
KBS and present an example of the documentation of a KBS for elevator
configuration.

1 Introduction

It has recently been recognized that the development of large knowledge-based
systems which can be successfully used for real world applications requires the
sharing and reuse of knowledge. In the so called knowledge sharing effort (Neches
et. al., 1991)(Swartout, Neches and Patil, 1993) a vision and corresponding technologies are being developed so that a new system need (and must) not be
constructed from scratch but can instead be developed by assembling reusable
components of established knowledge such as ontologies that are already em-
bodied in existing knowledge-based systems (Guha and Lenat, 1990; Breuker
and Wielinga, 1989). On the basis of shared ontologies, even specific system
implementations could be reused when building a new system.

One major working group within the knowledge sharing effort (i.e. the Shared,
Reusable Knowledge Bases group) is concerned with developing a language by
which a consensus on vocabulary and semantic interpretations of domain models
can be established. Gruber (1993) has termed the specification of a vocabulary
for a shared domain consisting of definitions of objects, concepts, classes and
relations an ontology. Ideally, such shared definitions should be specified at the

knowledge level (Newell, 1982), independent of specific representation languages. On the basis of these assumptions an Ontolingua has been developed. Ontolingua is an implemented system (Gruber, 1993, p. 12-2) for translating ontologies from a declarative, predicate-calculus language into a variety of representation systems like a KL-ONE type system

Sharing and reusing knowledge which is specified in some common logic that is independent of any specific representation language is certainly of pivotal importance for developing successful knowledge-based systems. However, Clancey has recently pointed out a number of deficiencies of current knowledge level specifications and proposed respective re-interpretations (1989). Prior to this criticism, Bourne has already argued that the postulate of pure symbol manipulation processes does not set the right stage for a better understanding of complex systems. He furthermore proposed behavior descriptions which would yield a better understanding of the human conceptual behavior (Bourne, 1969; Bourne, Ekstrand and Dominoski, 1971; chapter 1) and which are better suited for building large knowledge-based systems.

Although, proponents of the information or symbol processing hypothesis promptly refuted the notion of behavior descriptions (Newell, 1969), recent research clearly indicates the value and the promises of behavior descriptions and the underlying scientific idiom. Maes (1993) has recently compared knowledge-based to behavior-based artificial intelligence. Behavior-based systems excelled in that such systems can be understood as a part of the environment. Their performance is consequently emerging from the interaction of the system and its environment. They are autonomous open systems and their symbols are grounded in the environment.

The goal of this paper is to provide a formalization of behavior descriptions and to show how the sharing and reuse of knowledge can be accomplished in a ever changing environment. We will first summarize Newell's knowledge level conceptualizations and point out a number of shortcomings. Whereas knowledge level descriptions, which are often viewed as function-structure blueprints, describe an abstract mechanism, behavior descriptions specify the significant relations among various parameters of behavior. After a general exposition of behavior descriptions, it is exemplified how behavior descriptions can be used for the documentation of artificial systems (expert systems and computer programs in general). The sharing and reuse of knowledge is then discussed when the functionality of a knowledge base is to be extended and when a knowledge base is used for purposes, which were not considered at design time.

2 Newell's knowledge level

In his influential paper, Newell (1982) has introduced a level of computer system description called the "knowledge level". Since this time, describing artificial and human systems as a knowledge system has become an important goal in expert system research (Clancey, 1985; Breuker and Wielinga, 1989) as well as in cognitive psychology (Pylyshyn, 1984; Anderson, 1990). When establishing a knowledge level description, a natural or artificial system "is viewed as having a body of knowledge and a set of goals, so that it takes actions in the environment that its knowledge indicates will attain its goals"(Newell, 1992, p. 426). Knowledge systems are one level in the hierarchy of systems that make up an intelligent agent. Lower level descriptions such as the symbol level specify how a knowledge level system is realized in mechanisms (i.e. information processing and representation). The symbol level is described by a memory, symbols, operations, interpretation processes and perceptual and motor interfaces (Newell, 1982). Through knowledge level descriptions, Newell has thus provided us with a possibility for uniformly characterizing natural and artificial systems.

The key assumption underlying the knowledge level is the notion of an idealized rational agent. A rational agent is assumed to have the following attributes: 1) The agent has the ability to perform a set of actions in some environment. 2) The agent has goals about how its environment should be. 3) The agent has a body of knowledge. Its body of knowledge is about the environment, its goals, its actions and the relations between them. The agent also knows all those facts that are a deductive consequence of its body of knowledge 4) The principle of rationality is its single law of behavior. It describes which actions the agent will perform: "If an agent has knowledge that one of its actions will lead to one of its goals, then the agent will select that action" (Newell, 1982, p.102).

The behavior of an agent is a sequence of actions taken in the environment over time. By applying the principle of rationality, one can presumably predict the future behavior of an agent from its knowledge and its goals. Consider for example a chess player as such an ideal rational agent. It has the ability to perform a set of moves on the chess board. It has the goal of winning the game. Its body of knowledge consists of the rules of the chess game, i.e. the starting positions and the legal moves and everything that is deductively derivable from this body of knowledge. Therefore, for every chess board constellation, it knows which move will make it win the game. With the principle of rationality, it is thus predicted that it will play the perfect game of chess.

The assumption of such idealized rational agents has been shown to produce (at least) two substantial problems: 1) Important knowledge differences cannot be expressed in a knowledge level descriptions. The symbol level must consequently be used to denote these important distinctions. This is the problem of confounded knowledge differences. 2) A faithful implementation of a knowledge level description at the symbol level would often require unlimited computational resources. The assumptions made about rational agents may thus be too unrealistic for being particularly useful. This applies for describing human cognition (Anderson, 1990) as well as for specifying and implementing knowledge-based systems (Sticklen, 1989). This is the problem of a too unrealistic idealisation. Sticklen has pointed out the problems of the inability to represent control, the potential computational inadequacy and the non-operational characterisation[3].

---

[3] Schreiber, Akkermans and Wielinga (1990) have rejected these criticisms but we believe the case is not yet closed. We propose skills to avoid introducing control into knowledge descriptions

Confounded knowledge differences: Chess grand masters have spent years of learning for improving their chess game. Unlike beginners, who merely know the rules of the game, chess grand masters are known to have a large vocabulary of different chess board configurations (Chase and Simon, 1973). The chess grand masters thus certainly have more chess knowledge than the beginners. However, in a knowledge level description a la Newell there would be no difference between the beginner and the chess grand master. Because the beginner s body of knowledge would also include everything that is deductively derivable from the rules of the game, he would be said to know everything a grand master can possibly know about chess. In a knowledge level description, a beginner and a grand master would thus be said to have the same chess knowledge.

According to Newell (1982, 1992), the symbol level is described with the following attributes: 1) a memory, with independently modifiable structures that contain symbols; 2) symbols (patterns in the structures), providing the distal access to other structures; 3) operations, taking symbol structures as input and producing symbol structures as output; 4) interpretations processes, taking symbol structures as input and executing operations (the structures thereby representing these operations) and 5) Perceptual and motor interface to interact with an external environment. A symbol level description of a chess player includes its memory for the different types of chess constellations. At the symbol level the chess grand master would thus have dramatically more chess patterns in the symbol structures (chunks) than the beginner.

Unrealistic idealisation: In order to substantiate the body of knowledge of a chess player at the symbol level, one must compute everything that is deductively derivable from the rules of the game. This problem is computationally intractable. In other words, a computational device would be needed that has infinite memory and infinite processing resources. Neither humans nor computer systems can be realistically viewed as such computational devices. Knowledge level descriptions are therefore unrealistic idealisations and not very useful. A knowledge engineer, who wants to implement an expert system from a knowledge level description of the ideal chess player, may not even achieve a rude approximation of the program specification given at the knowledge level (Sticklen, 1989). Since resource limitations are a fundamental characteristic of human cognition (Miller, 1956; Norman and Bobrow, 1975; Simon, 1974), a psychologist, who describes human behavior at the knowledge level would most frequently derive predictions, for which no supporting empirical evidence can be found.

The problems with knowledge level descriptions have been known for some time and various solutions have been proposed (Dietterich, 1986; Schreiber, Akkermans and Wielinga, 1990). These solutions refine Newell's knowledge level notion by imposing more detailed structures on an agent's body of knowledge. They do however not address the root of the problem. Although Newell's proposal of describing natural and artificial systems at a uniform abstract level is extremely important for cognitive psychology and artificial intelligence, his formulation of the knowledge level hypothesis is incomplete and/or misdirected. There are four major misconceptions: 1) Knowledge and goals are in themselves inadequate to fully characterize intelligent systems. 2) Knowledge level descriptions are developed as if intelligent systems were causal systems. 3) For this level of abstract description, the distinction between an agent and its environment is artificial. 4) The knowledge level does not lie directly above the symbol level and there is no tight connection between them. Therefore knowledge level descriptions cannot be reduced to the symbol level (Clancey, 1991).

3 Behavior descriptions

If existing knowledge level descriptions of systems are inadequate, what then does it take to give an adequate and complete description of intelligent behavior? Knowledge is important of course; an intelligent system knows the important facts of its operative domain. But knowledge alone is inert; it does not act on its own. There are other equally important parameters of intelligent behavior, which include, at a minimum, skill, intention , (goals or purpose) and performance. To talk about the behavior of any agent, natural or artificial, one is obliged to make, either explicitly or implicitly, some commitment to the knowledge, skill, intention (or goals) and performance of that agent. It is not enough to say that the agent has the pertinent knowledge and acts rationally. Such a description is at best incomplete, and at worst wrong.

3.1 Extending knowledge level descriptions

What do knowledge, intention (or goals), skill and performance entail and what does it mean to call these parameters of behavior? Basically we agree with Newell about the nature of knowledge. The knowledge is the complete set of discriminations, facts, or concepts available to an agent which have been acquired from past experiences. Knowledge implies that the agent can make distinctions between and among objects, processes, events and states of affairs. It has a basis for treating some things in one way, others in a different way.

But, as the foregoing discussion might suggest, knowledge does not exist independently of, or in isolation from the way it is used. Thus, with respect to any discrimination, fact or concept there is a corresponding skill, which represents its use. It might be helpful to think of knowledge then, in Ryle's sense, as "knowing that x is the case". Skill, then, is "knowing how to act on that knowledge" (Ryle, 1949). The difference captured in this distinction is the difference between "knowing that" and "knowing how". As Ryle (1949, p32) has clearly stated knowing how cannot be defined in terms of knowing that.

Similarly, intentions or goals do not exist independently of knowledge and skill. An intention is the want, desire or need to act upon some existing knowledge in a particular way.

The combinations of knowledge, skill and intention do not cause any particular behavior to be what it is. Neither do they in any intelligible way cause an action. Rather these are merely parameters of a behavior description. But to use the term "merely" is not to minimize their importance. There might be no defensible way to give a valid causal description of behavior.

But we are not yet finished. There is a missing ingredient. To provide a complete behavior description, it is required that some commitment be made to the knowledge, the skill, and the intention of the agent. Knowledge, skill and intentions alone provide only a description of behavior potential. What is required to complete the description of an actual behavior is some performance or action by the agent. Please note, classical behaviorism to the contrary notwithstanding, performance is not equivalent to behavior in this descriptive system. It is merely a component or parameter of behavior, meeting the criteria of consistency and coherence. Rather than causing performance to be what it is, knowledge, skill and intention enable a certain performance in the sense that they make it feasible and intelligible when it occurs. The way we use these concepts entails that each one of them is involved in providing a behavior description.

$$B=R(G,K,S,P)$$

where B is behavior, G are the goals or the intention, K is knowledge, S is skill, P is performance and R specifies the various relationships among G,K,S and P.

These components do not exist independently, in separate systems or in isolation. The knowledge, the skill, and the intention to engage in any action, x, are tightly interconnected. For every quantum of knowledge that allows for discrimination between x and not-x, there is some way of acting on that discrimination and some possibility that the actor will want to take that action. Thus, it does not make sense to look for independent traces of knowledge, skill and intention in separate brain locations of storage mechanisms.

Consider that most adults are able to recognize a case of piano playing when they experience it, even if they have no musical training. I have sufficient knowledge to distinguish piano from non-piano playing in most circumstances (although there might be cases in which it would be difficult for anyone to tell). Furthermore, I have ways of acting on that knowledge, such as calling it a case of piano playing, or a case of bad piano playing, or simply leaving the room where it is being done. I might have the goal of either approaching, because it is good and I want to hear better, or avoiding, because it offends my sensibilities. If that goal is stronger than all other immediate goals, I will take the indicated action. Having done this, I have completed a behavior episode and anyone (including myself) who observed my action and had reason to know or to think about my personal knowledge, skills and intentions, would be correct in describing what happened as an act of behavior.

Because I know what qualifies as piano playing, I can consider hypothetical cases of piano playing. The fact that I know that I know distinguishes me, as a human being capable of intelligent, intentional action, from an automaton. One might realistically say that the thermostat "knows" how to control room temperature, by turning a switch off and on at appropriate times. But it make no sense whatsoever to say that the thermostat "knows that it knows."

The concepts of knowledge, skill, intention and performance are necessary but possibly not sufficient to give a complete description of behavior. There are other constraints of the system that might have to be taken into account in the general case. For almost all purposes of the present discussion, the basic parameters will suffice.

It is tempting to liken the distinction between knowledge and skill in this descriptive system to the concepts of declarative and procedural memory in the contemporary literature of artificial intelligence (Winograd, 1976) and cognitive psychology (Anderson, 1983; Squire and Slater, 1975; Tulving, 1975). It is common to invoke Ryle to argue that memories can be either procedural or declarative.) Declarative memories are memories for facts, either at a general, conceptual or semantic level or as episodes, embedded in some time/space co-ordinates. Most adult human beings know, for example, the concept of a newspaper, or a meal or justice. Further they can be expected to know (at least some of) what they read in the newspaper about the U. S. presidential election at home last night. In the first case, the knowledge is general, semantic and de-contextualized; in the second case, it is embedded in an episode. In either case, the memory is fact-based, and its recollection is always conscious and deliberately achieved (note that a skill is required for this). Procedural memories are memories about doing something. These are the kinds of memories that support acquired skilful performance, as in piano playing, or repetition priming effects, of the sort that make it somehow easier to process a stimulus the second time around, or some classical conditioning phenomena. The basis for these memory effects is nonconscious. It does not appear to be necessary for one to know or to be able to say much about the skill of piano playing in order to play the piano (of course, one would surely know that he is playing the piano, because that's a fact). Moreover, one need not know about or be momentarily aware of a prior episode with a stimulus in order to exhibit (but possibly not experience) a priming effect. To make the distinction between declarative and procedural memories completely clear, some theorists argue that they belong to separate memory systems and never mix. In some cases, the argument is made that procedural memories derive from or are some compiled version of fact-based memories.

We believe that the declarative/procedural distinction is important, but probably muddled in current theorizing. First of all, while it is correct to cite Ryle in support of this distinction, it should be noted that he had a somewhat different meaning in mind. As in the present system, facts and skills were not independent entities for Ryle. Facts and skills go together. For everything you know, there corresponds a way to act upon it. One does not know a newspaper without some related actions (which can, but need not include reading it). There is no evidence of declarative memory without associated action; further there is no case of intelligent action without a basis in knowledge. Which is not to say that skills and repetition effects do not exist. It is indeed possible to exhibit skill without a lot of useful information you can communicate about it verbally or consciously. Repetition priming effects are quite reliable. But the fact that you appear to be unable to report an earlier occurrence of the pertinent stimulus rules out only one possible thing you might know and uses only one possible way to assess what you know about that stimulus. There simply is no compelling evidence at the present time that different memory systems contain declarative and procedural memories. Thus, the distinction will require further sharpening of both a theoretical and an empirical sort.

Clancey (1991, p. 386) has already pointed out that knowledge level descriptions should not be identified with causal mechanisms because they are observer-relative. The regularities in the performance of humans or artificial systems should be viewed as characterizations that are descriptive. In agreement with Clancey's arguments, the relationship among the parameters of behavior is not causal. That is, the conjunction of knowledge and intention (or goals) does not cause an action. Rather the relationships that governs this descriptive system are consistency and coherence. As we will see, the component parameters must make sense together for the behavior described to be accepted as rational. Component inconsistency or incoherence produces descriptions that are irrational or incorrect or unrecognizable as intelligent behavior. In a more technical notion, a description of rational behavior thus consists of the unification of the parameters of behavior.

The environment is as the agent perceives it. That is, within this system, there is no point to the assertion that the environment is one thing and the organism is another. There is no point in separating internal from external. Organisms do not just function within environments, they are part and parcel of the environment. Among other things, it is for that reason that the environment is not the same for all organisms. Now of course the environment is not entirely different for different organisms. There are regularities, and these regularities are what gives us some scientific purchase on behavior.

The environment is an interpreted framework within which behavior takes place. The environment exists for an agent only because the agent has some knowledge about what it perceives, some skills and goals to act on that knowledge, and an ability to carry forward with action or movement. Environments differ among people, because people differ in which way they know about what they perceive. But because to some degree knowledge is shared, environments are shared. To the extent that two people have the same knowledge, skills, goals and performance abilities they will perceive the environment in the same way and they will behave in the same way. The implication for knowledge-based systems is that we must build environments into them. The knowledge-based system must contain not only knowledge in some internal sense (and skills, goals and performance abilities), but also knowledge of the environment (something like cognition-environment relationships in standard terminology) in which the system operates.

The notion of knowledge has traditionally been used to mediate between the internal states of an agent and the states of the world. But there need not be any tight coupling between the symbol processing of an artificial system and its behavior description. Depending upon the scope and context of a behavior description an identical symbol processing and performance may result in different behavior descriptions. And conversely, different symbol processing procedures may be given an identical behavior description.

It is often said that science seeks explanations for natural phenomena. The study of intelligent systems (of the empirical and engineering sciences) is, as it should be, fully as scientific as any of its kindred enterprises. Yet, the system we have presented is called a descriptive system; its goal is to supply complete behavior descriptions. We do not intend, by the use of this term, to diminish its value as a scientific tool. Rather, we are merely following the requirements of good logic. Logically, it is impossible to explain something you cannot in the first place describe to some degree of accuracy and completeness. Because existing systems of description in psychology and artificial intelligence are defective, we need to establish a descriptive idiom that will work. Description must come before explanation. But there is also the possibility that, once an adequate, detailed an complete description of behavior has been achieved, there might be nothing left to explain.

It should be noted that behavior descriptions are not identical to performance. Behavior descriptions encompass the goal, knowledge, skill and performance parameters. Thus, performance is only one of the parameters of behavior descriptions.

3.2 Formal behavior descriptions

In this section we describe the formalization of behavior descriptions. We then show how these descriptions can be used to document computational systems. Documentation is essential for understanding the operation of programs and for their maintenance. Good documentation can aid the reuse of program designs. It can also aid the growth or expansion of the system, and the reuse of program design when the purpose, or use-in-practice, of the system changes. The problem of reusing programs and their designs cannot be solved from symbol level considerations alone. We must relate symbol level computations to abstract level descriptions.

While we are concerned with KBS in complex domains we shall begin by discussing examples in the field of set theory. This choice was made in order to illustrate our ideas clearly, in a concrete and widely understood domain. In section 4 we address the more complex problem of documenting a KBS.

A behavior description is defined by the 4-tuple $< G, K, S, P >$. One or more behavior descriptions may be associated with an agent. The components of the behavior description conform to the following specification, where each description is specified with respect to a particular conceptual theory.

$< G, K, S, P >$ is a behavior description, in a conceptual theory C, where:

G :defines the goal which the behavior description can satisfy,
  the formal language is predicate calculus (extended as defined below).
K :defines knowledge related to the solution of the goal
  the formal language is predicate calculus.

S :describes skills which perform the computation defined in K,
the notation is that of functional programming.

P :describes the performance of the skills, i.e. one or more
concrete examples of the input-output relation, the formal
description is specified by the programming language.

The predicate calculus is extended by the addition of predicates which represent concepts in set theory, for example, set union is formalized by: $\cup(A, B, C)$. However, for clarity, we shall use the standard infix notation of set theory and write $C = A \cup B$ to represent union. In other domains, predicate calculus may not be the most appropriate formal language. In such cases K and G may be described in any suitable formal language which provides appropriate semantics and rules of inference.

It is required that a function, h', must actually exist at the concrete level, in some programming language, before we can confirm the existence of the skill, h. This guarantees that we can obtain examples of actual performances P of the skills. Performances are indexed by the skill they are produced by, the concrete level function name, and the programming language the concrete function is specified in. This method of documentation includes information which can be seen as validating the concrete level code.

The relationships between the various components of the behavior description are illustrated by example in the following documentations of programs.

3.3 Example 1: Set union.

In the framework of simple set theory the union of two sets, A, B, is a set which contains all members of A and all members of B. Elements which occur in both A and B occur only once in the union set. The computation of the union of two sets can be considered to be composed of two operations: the construction of a set C, obtained from B by removing all elements which also occur in A, and then the combination of A and C to yield the output set D. The former computation we call diff and the latter concatenate. The computation is illustrated diagrammatically in figure 1[4], which shows the relationship between data classes and skills. The documentation of this computation in terms of behavior descriptions is given in table 1.

The goal is a summary of the computation, namely that for any sets A and B the union, D, can be calculated. The knowledge component specifies the distinctions which decompose the goal into an equivalent set of formulae, from which the skills can be derived. Formula i. defines the union operator in terms of set membership ϵ and ii. defines an equivalent breakdown of the rhs. of i. which introduces the set C i.e. the set whose members are in B but not in A. The skill $C = \text{diff}(B,A)$ is associated with the distinctions defined by the expression $(f\epsilon C \leftrightarrow f\epsilon B \wedge f \not\epsilon A)$. The skill $D = \text{concatenate}(A,C)$ is associated with $(f\epsilon D \leftrightarrow f\epsilon A \vee f\epsilon C))$, however in this case the context is important as A and C are guaranteed to be disjoint. This association is behavioral, i.e. the skill effects

---

[4] This diagram illustrates the method but not the details of the computation.

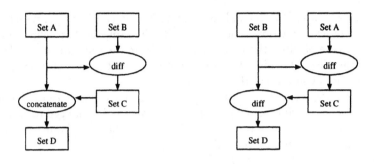

Fig. 1. The Union computation (left) and the Intersection computation (right)

the calculation specified by the knowledge component, as is witnessed by the performance. Where it is possible to prove equivalence between the knowledge component and the concrete function, this is desirable. However, we acknowledge that this may not always be possible in all domains.

LISP, PROLOG and C definitions of the **diff** and **concatenate** skills were defined according the decomposition defined above. It is notable that the structure of the conceptual model of the computation was maintained, for imperative, functional and logic-based programming languages.

Union (simple set theory)

Goal: Construct $D : (\forall A)(\forall B)(D = A \cup B)$

Knowledge: i. $(\forall A)(\forall B)(\forall D)(A \cup B = D) \leftrightarrow (\forall e)(e \epsilon A \vee e \epsilon B \leftrightarrow e \epsilon D)$
            ii. $(\forall A)(\forall B)(\forall C)(\forall D)$
               $((\forall e)(e \epsilon A \vee e \epsilon B \leftrightarrow e \epsilon D)) \leftrightarrow$
               $((\forall f)(f \epsilon C \leftrightarrow f \epsilon B \wedge f \notin A) \wedge$
               $(f \epsilon D \leftrightarrow f \epsilon A \vee f \epsilon C))$

Skill: a.   C = diff(B,A), D = concatenate(A,C)

Performance: 1.   A = '(1 2 3 4) B = '(4 3 5 6)
                D = '(1 2 3 4 5 6) [skill = a, set-union, LISP]
            2.   A = '(a b c) B = '(d e)
                D = '(a b c d e) [skill = a, set-union, LISP]
      ...

Table 1. The behavior description for Union.

It is also possible to define set union as one skill C = union-1(A,B), that is, the skill corresponds to the rhs. of i. In this case the function, at the concrete level, is a synthesis of the diff and concatenate functions. The performance of this new concrete level function is not necessarily the same as that defined in 1. In fact, in the case of LISP, the performance differs in the ordering of the elements of the output list, D. This difference is not significant at the abstract level, in the framework of simple set theory.

The behavior description can therefore document several alternative solutions of the goal. The description of union, defined above, can be changed to encompass the new skill union-1 and the new performances obtained from the concrete implementations by adding the following items:

Skill: b. D = union-1(A,B)

Performance: 1. A = '(a b c) B = '(d e)
             D = '(c b a d e) [skill = b, union-1, LISP]

3.4   Example 2: Set intersection.

The intersection of two sets A and B is the set of all elements of both A and B. The computation of this set can be viewed as the combination of two steps: the calculation of $C = B - A$ and then of $D = B - C$. The set C is composed of those elements of B which are not in A. The goal is to calculate those elements of B which are in A, and this can be obtained by removing all elements of C from B. The computation is illustrated graphically in figure 1. The behavior description of intersection is defined in table 2.

Intersection (simple set theory)

Goal: Construct $D : (\forall A)(\forall B)(D = A \cap B)$

Knowledge: i. $(\forall A)(\forall B)(\forall D)(A \cap B = D) \leftrightarrow (\forall e)(e\epsilon A \wedge e\epsilon B \leftrightarrow e\epsilon D)$
            ii. $(\forall A)(\forall B)(\forall C)(\forall D)$
                 $((\forall e)(e\epsilon A \wedge e\epsilon B \leftrightarrow e\epsilon D)) \leftrightarrow$
                 $((\forall f)(f\epsilon C \leftrightarrow f\epsilon B \wedge f\ \cancel{\epsilon} A) \wedge$
                 $(f\epsilon D \leftrightarrow f\epsilon B \vee f\ \cancel{\epsilon} C))$

Skill: a. C = diff(B,A), D = diff(B,C)

Performance: 1. A = '(1 2 3 4) B = '(4 3 5 6)
             D = '(4 3) [skill = a, set-intersection, LISP]

Table 2. The behavior description for intersection

As in the previous case, the knowledge defines an expansion of the goal into a form where skills can be defined. The skills, or, more precisely, their concrete level counterparts, actually carry out the computation and the performance is recorded. Again, LISP, PROLOG and C versions of this computation were defined using the same abstract model.

4   The documentation of a configuration system

For the simple programs considered so far, it was possible to give a precise definition of the knowledge of set theory represented in the programs. In this section we show how our approach can be scaled up to describe a conventional KBS. We describe a KBS which solves the Sisyphus task of configuring elevator systems (Yost, 1992). Due to space considerations we present only a part of the entire solution.

The Sisyphus task involves the configuration of elevators according to a given design. The aim is to find a configuration which satisfies a number of constraints. We shall not describe the derivation of our solution, in fact we used an approach similar to the KADS methodology[5] (Breuker and Wielinga, 1989), instead we shall focus on the documentation of the solution.

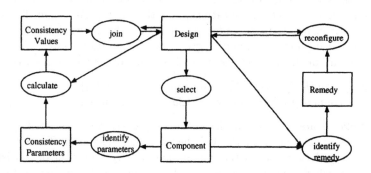

Fig. 2. An inference structure for configuration

A KBS will typically be comprised of function definitions which define the problem solving steps and a knowledge base (KB) which defines domain specific information. The function definitions will normally be task specific but domain independent, as will the schema of the KB. Our solution of the Sisyphus task has exactly this design. It was derived after a knowledge level analysis of the task was performed. The resulting inference structure is shown in figure 2. The method should be understood as beginning with the selection of a *Component* from the *Design*, determining a number of *Parameters* which determine the consistency of this choice, and their values. The checking of the consistency of the choice of component is done by the *id-remedy* knowledge source which finds a replacement component, *Remedy*, if any constraints are violated.

---

[5] We adopt the KADS I terminology

The documentation of the KBS must characterise two distinct types of knowledge: the domain knowledge of the KBS, and the method of the configuration algorithm. The knowledge about the attributes of a particular motor is represented in table 3. The Knowledge component is a formalization of the domain knowledge as arguments of the predicates *instance-of* and *has-attribute*. These predicates have the usual interpretation. The Skill component is the construction of a list where slots in the design are assigned the appropriate value. There is only one possible performance, the slots get the correct values.

The configuration algorithm consists of the recursive function configure, which is defined in terms of two further functions, increment-design and identify-remedy, one list processing function and functions defined in the KB. In order to document the configure function we must specify the goal which it satisfies:

Construct Design = configure(Specification)

We consider the knowledge of configure to be a formalized representation of the inference structure which resulted from the knowledge level analysis. The meta-classes of the inference structure are captured by predicates whose logical domains are sets of domain terms. The dependency of meta-classes upon one another is represented by implications, and the appropriate quantification of variables. For example, in our inference structure the knowledge source *select* selects a *Component* to be configured, given the configuration *Design*. *Component* and *Design* are predicates and the dependency is represented by the formulae:

i. $(\forall d : set)(Design(d) \rightarrow (\exists c : element)Component(c))$
ii. $(\forall c : element)(Component(c) \rightarrow (\exists d : set)Design(d))$

Formula i. states that for all designs a component can be selected, ii. states that if a component has been selected then a design must exist. These formulae define the key data classes of the domain and specify a number of consistency relationships which must hold. Each knowledge source of the inference structure is described in a similar way and the resulting set of formulae describe a set of relations which hold in the inference structure as a whole[6]. This method of describing the inference structure does not define how components are selected, or when, in control terms, the selection inference is made, these aspects are specified in the Skill component.

The Skill component is simply the ordered listing of the definition of *configure*. Details such as terminating conditions are omitted to leave the essential structure of the algorithm.

---

[6] This formalization of the knowledge level does not predict the results of the problem solving, it specifies necessary relationships between KL classes. The role of this formalization is descriptive and not predictive or computational. No stronger formalization of the KL is possible without introducing domain terms and/or control terms.

Instantiate attributes (elevator configuration)

Goal: Construct $Y : Y = instantiate - attributes(motor, 10HP)$

Knowledge: i. $instance - of(10HP, motor)$
               ii. $has - attribute(10HP, model, 10HP)$
              iii. $has - attribute(10HP, maxHP, 10)$
              iv. $has - attribute(10HP, maxCurrent, 150)$
              v. $has - attribute(10HP, weight, 374)$

Skill: a.   **Y** = ((motor.model 10HP) (motor.maxHP 10)
                (motor.maxCurrent 150) ...)

Performance: **Y** = ((motor.model 10HP), (motor.maxHP 10)
              (motor.maxCurrent 150) ...)

Table 3. Domain knowledge about the motor model 10HP

a. <Component,NewDesign> = increment-design(Design,Remedy),
   NewValues = calculate-values(Component,NewDesign),
   NextDesign = join(NewValues,NewDesign),
   NewRemedy = identify-remedy(Component,NextDesign)
   return <O-Design, O-Remedy> = configure(NextDesign,NewRemedy)
   where Design, Remedy are input values,
   and O-Design, O-Remedy are output values

The function increment-design returns a *Component* and an updated version of the design as the outputs. More details of this function are documented in a separate behavior description which shows that increment-design calls the instantiate-attributes function defined above. The relationship between the Skill and Knowledge components is indicated by the variable names, i.e. those which end in Design to be interpreted as instances of the *Design* meta-class.

The Performance component is an example of an execution of the *configure* function.

1. Design = (... (motor.model nil) ...)
   Remedy = nil
   NextDesign = (...(motor.model 10HP) (motor.maxHP 10) ...)
   NewRemedy = 15HP
   O-Design = (... (motor.model 15HP) (motor.maxHP 15) ...)
   O-Remedy = nil
2. Design = (... (motor.model 20HP) ...)
   Remedy = 28
   NextDesign = (...(motor.model 20HP) (machine.model 28) ...)
   NewRemedy = nil
   O-Design = (... (motor.model 20HP) (machine.model 38) ...)
   O-Remedy = nil

The documentation of the KBS differs from the documentation of the set theory programs in that domain knowledge must be described. This is unproblematic. The knowledge of the algorithm, that is, the knowledge of the solution method implemented by the algorithm, cannot be expressed in such a way that the KL definition predicts the symbol level performance. This is a known feature of the knowledge level, the KL cannot be reduced to the symbol level. The set theory programs are exceptional in that the symbol level behavior is precisely that predicted by the Knowledge component, within the physical limitations of the computer which performs the calculation.

In contrast with the KADS approach, we have not specified an implementation where the inference structure is represented as a distinct layer of the design. Instead, we have produced a design which can be easily related to the inference structure and this simplified the implementation. The documentation of our solution includes examples of runs of the program, hence our approach is more empirical than the purely rationalistic KADS method.

5 Sharing and reuse

The idea of significance as related to context is important in our approach to the reuse of behavior descriptions. Consider, for example, that you observe an application of the concatenate function:

concatenate((()(1)(2)(2 1))((3)(3 1)(3 2)(3 2 1))) =
(()(1)(2)(2 1)(3)(3 1)(3 2)(3 2 1))

This function would just be described as concatenating two sets. However, if the following piece of information is added:

powerset((2 1)) = (()(1)(2)(2 1))

then we can see that the first argument of concatenate is the powerset of the set (2 1). If we now add two more pieces of information:

repeated-union((3),(()(1)(2)(2 1))) = ((3)(3 1)(3 2)(3 2 1)) and

split((3 2 1)) = <(3), (2 1) >

we can see that the second argument of concatenate is the list formed by adding (3) to the powerset of (2 1) and that these elements were once composed into a single list (3 2 1). Taken together these functions define an algorithm which computes the powerset of a set. The significance of the particular application of the concatenate function increases as more information about the context in which the evaluation occurs becomes known. We have, of course, only described the process of understanding the significance of the concatenate function in one particular instance, the problem of designing algorithms such as powerset is not addressed here.

In general, we view the significance of a computation as increasing as it becomes embedded in greater and greater contexts, i.e. as the system grows. The problem is to describe and redescribe the computation as this growth happens in order that reuse can occur. Behavior descriptions capture the information required for this purpose.

The complete behavior description of the powerset function is shown in table 4. The computation of this function can be defined recursively as is shown in

Powerset (simple set theory)

Goal: Construct $Y : (\forall A)Y = P(A)$

Knowledge: i. $(\forall A)(\forall Y)(Y = P(A) \leftrightarrow (\forall x)(x \epsilon Y \leftrightarrow x \subseteq A))$
             ii. $(\forall A)(\forall Y)(Y = P(A) \leftrightarrow$
             $(\forall B)(\forall C)(\forall D)(\forall E)(\forall F)(C = A - \{B\}) \wedge (D = P(C)) \wedge$
             $(\forall z)(\forall y)(z \epsilon D \wedge y = \{B\} \cup z \rightarrow y \epsilon E) \wedge (Y = E \cup D)$

Skill: a. $<B,C> =$ split(A), $D =$ powerset(C),
             $E =$ repeated-union(B,D), $Y =$ concatenate(D,E)

Performance: 1. $A =$ '(2 1), $Y =$ '(()(1)(2)(2 1)) [skill = a, powerset, LISP]
             2. $A =$ '(3 2 1)
             $Y =$'(()(1)(2)(2 1)(3)(3 1)(3 2)(3 2 1))
             [skill = a, powerset, LISP]

Table 4. The behavior description of powerset.

figure 3. The powerset Y, of set A, is the set of all subsets of A. The basic insight required to derive the computational method from the requirements is to note that the powerset of a set A can be calculated from the powerset of A minus element B and the set formed by adding B to every subset of D.

The method is to split one element, B, of the input set A, to obtain set C. The powerset, D, of C is calculated and then the set E is created by adding B to each member of D. The union of D and E yields the powerset of A. In fact, as D and E are disjoint (there are no members of B in D), the powerset can be obtained by the concatenation of D and E. This is documented in table 4.

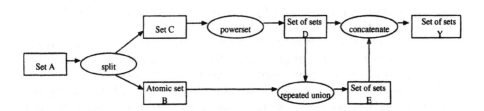

Fig. 3. The powerset computation.

6 Conclusions

We have defined behavior descriptions in order to overcome a number of problems with fixed ontologies. We have shown how behavior descriptions can be formalized and illustrated our proposals by a number of simple examples from set theory. The documentation of a knowledge-based system for the Sisyphus task demonstrates how our approach can be scaled up.

The knowledge level is a rational approach for describing the behavior of a computational system. In addition to this descriptive function, the knowledge level is also used in the development of KBS. Typically, declaratively represented knowledge plays a specific role in a problem solving model, however, the documentation of such a system relies on a fixed interpretation. In contrast, our approach is more evolutionary (Kühn, 1993) (Hinkelmann, Meyer and Schmalhofer, 1994). Behavior descriptions may change over time.

We do not separate the description of the requirements from the description of the implementation (Swartout and Balzer, 1982) and the system is not viewed as being divorced from the environment in which it is used. In comparison with the discussion of the knowledge level/symbol level relationship in Smith and Johnson (1993) we emphasise the notion of *method* in the knowledge level description.

From Clancey's discussion of the frame of reference problem we can conclude that there may be different descriptions for the same system depending upon context. Pursuing this argument, we consider it inevitable that systems will be redescribed for different contexts and purposes. This contrasts with the view of a fixed ontology based upon a uniform KL descriptions. For allowing such conceptual changes on KBS and programs, we proposed the behavior descriptions and provided a formalization which can be used for documentation. Such documentation consists of, 1) the goal or purpose the KBS is used for, 2) the distinctions and categorizations which are made by the system, i.e. representation of declarative knowledge, 3) the computational procedures which are implemented by the system and correspond to the categorization made by the encoded declarative knowledge and 4) the actually observed input-output relations (i.e. the performance of the system on selected test cases).

If the use of a system is not to be limited by the designer's preconceptions, then the abstract descriptions of a system have to be changed according to the new purposes which users may invent. We have shown how behavior descriptions are adjusted to new purposes by assessing the already existing behavior description in the light of the newly emerging conceptualization. It is often assumed that knowledge sharing and reuse is to be accomplished by specifying a (rather) fixed ontology, which is agreed upon by all designers and users. The proposed behavior descriptions provide the flexibility of describing and redescribing systems according to the current purposes. Behavior descriptions thus allow for the sharing and reuse of knowledge as well as for conceptual changes over time (Keil, 1993; Ram, 1993). Specific representation languages may be required for forming such descriptions. A declarative language which allows for knowledge evolution is currently being developed in the VEGA project (Boley, 1993).

We view reuse as a problem of the redescription of computational systems in larger contexts. Components of a system gain significance by being embedded. An example of such an embedding is the reuse of the concatenate function within the powerset function. Another example is the reuse of calculations in a spreadsheet environment by embedding them in a larger workflow e.g. for paying travel expenses (see for example, Dallemagne *et. al.*, 1992). We have not yet presented a technology for reuse, but we have laid some of the theoretical groundwork for such a technology.

Acknowledgements: We would like to thank Otto Kühn, Peter Ossario, Jörg Thoben and Rainer Deventer for their critical and constructive discussions of the issues presented in this paper. This research was supported by grants ITW 8902 C4 and 413-5839-ITW9304/3 from the BMFT and by grant SCHM 648/1 from the DFG.

References

Anderson, J.R. (1983) The architecture of cognition. *Harvard University Press, Cambridge, Massachusetts, 1983*

Anderson, J.R. (1990) The adaptive character of thought. *Hillsdale, New Jersey, Lawrence Erlbaum, 1990*

Boley, H. (1993) Towards evolvable knowledge representation for industrial applications. *in Hinkelmann, K. and Laux, A. (eds) DFKI Workshop on Knowledge Representation Techniques, D-93-11, DFKI, July 1993*

Bourne, L.E. Jr.(1969) Concept learning and thought: Behavior not process. *in ed. Voss, J. Approaches to thought. Columbus OH: Merrill, :167-195.*

Bourne, L.E.,Jr., Ekstrand, B.R. and Dominowski, R. L. (1971) The psychology of thinking. *Englewood Cliffs, N.J.: Prentice-Hall, 1971.*

Breuker, J. and Wielinga, B. (1989) Models of expertise in knowledge acquisition. *In Guida, G. Tasso, C. (Eds.), Topics in expert system design, methodologies and tools Amsterdam, Netherlands: North Holland :265 - 295*

Chase, W.G. and Simon, H.A. (1973) Perception in chess. *Cognitive Psychology, 4, :55-81.*

Clancey, W.J. (1985) Heuristic classification. *Artificial Intelligence 27 (1985) :289-350*

Clancey, W.J. (1989) The frame-of-reference problem in cognitive modelling. *In Proceedings of the 11th Annual Conference of the Cognitive Science Society Hillsdale, NJ: Lawrence Erlbaum :107-114*

Clancey, W. J. (1991) The frame of reference problem. *in ed. VanLehn, K. Architectures for intelligence. Lawrence Erlbaum, New Jersey, 1991. :357-423*

Dallemagne, G. Klinker, G. Marques, D. McDermott, J. and Tung, D. (1992) Making application programming more worthwhile. *in Schmalhofer, F. Strube, G, and Wetter, T. (eds) Contemporary knowledge engineering. Springer Verlag, Berlin, 1992 :6-22*

Dietterich, T.G. (1986) Learning at the knowledge level. *Machine Learning 1:287-316 1986*

Fischer, G. and Girgensohn, A. (1990) End-User Modifiability in Design Environments, *Human Factors in Computing Systems, CHI'90, Conference Proceedings (Seattle, WA) ACM, New York (April 1990), :183-191.*

Gruber, T. (1993) Towards principles for the design of ontologies used for knowledge sharing. *ftp server Stanford*

Guha, R. V. and Lenat, D.B. (1990) CYC: A mid-term report. *AI Magazine 11(3) :32-59*

Hinkelmann, K. Meyer, M. and Schmalhofer, F. (1994) Knowledge-base evolution for product and production planning. *AICOM Vol. 7 Nr. 2 :98-113*

Keil, F.C. (1993) Conceptual change and other varieties of cognitive development: Some distinctions in the emergence of biological thought. *Proceedings of the Conference of the Cognitive Science Society, Boulder, Co. 1993, Lawrence Erlbaum, NJ:4*

Kühn, O. (1993) Knowledge sharing and knowledge evolution. *Proceedings IJCAI 1993 Workshop on knowledge sharing and information exchange.*

Maes, P. (1993) Behavior-Based Artificial Intelligence. *in Proceedings of the Fifteenth Annual Conference of the Cognitive Science Society, June 18-21, 1993, :74-83. Hillsdale, NJ: Lawrence Erlbaum.*

Miller, G.A. (1956) The magical number seven, plus or minus two: some limits on our capacity for processing information. *Psychological Review, 63 :81-97.*

Musen, M. A. (1992) Dimensions of knowledge sharing and reuse. *Computers and biomedical research 25, 435467 (1992)*

Neches, R. Fikes, R. Finin, T. Gruber, T. Patil, R. Senator, T. and Swartout, W.R. (1991) Enabling technology for knowledge sharing *AI Magazine Fall 1991 :36-56*

Newell, A. (1969) Discussion of Professor Bourne s Paper: Thoughts on the concept of process. *in ed. Voss, J. Approaches to thought. Columbus OH: Merrill, :196-210.*

Newell, A. (1982) The knowledge level. *AI 18 (1982) :87-127*

Newell, A. (1990) Unified theories of cognition. *Cambridge, MA: Harvard University Press.*

Newell, A. (1992) Precis of Unified Theories of Cognition. *Behavioral and Brain Sciences, 15, :425-437.*

Norman, D.A. and Bobrow, D.G. (1975) On data limited and resource limited processes. *Cognitive Psychology, 7, :44-64*

Pylyshyn, Z. (1984) Computation and cognition. *Cambridge, MA: MIT Press.*

Ram, A. (1993) Creative conceptual change. *Proceedings of the Conference of the Cognitive Science Society, Boulder, Co. 1993, Lawrence Erlbaum, New Jersey :17-26*

Ryle, G. (1949) The concept of mind. *Harmondsworth: Penguin*

Schmalhofer, F. and Thoben, J. (1992) The model-based construction of a case-oriented expert system. *AICOM Vol.5 Nr.1 :3-18*

Schreiber, G., Akkermans, H. and Wielinga, B. (1990) On problems with the knowledge level perspective. *in. Boose, J. Gainers, B.R. (eds) Proceedings of the 5th Banff Knowledge-bases systems workshop, :30-1 -30-14.*

Simon, H.A. (1974) How big is a chunk? *Science, 1974, 183, :482-488*

Smith, J.W. and Johnson, T.R. (1993) A stratified approach to specifying, designing, and building knowledge systems. *IEEE Expert, 8(3) :15-25*

Squire, L.R. and Slater, P.C. (1975) Forgetting in very long-term memory as assessed by an improved questionnaire technique. *Journal of Experimental Psychology: Human Learning and Memory, 1975, 1, :21-34*

Sticklen, J. (1989) Problem solving architecture at the knowledge level. *Journal of Experimental and Theoretical Artificial Intelligence.*

Swartout, W. and Balzer, R. (1982) On the inevitable intertwining of specification and implementation. *Communications of the ACM, 25, 7 :438-440.*

Swartout, W.R. Neches, R. and Patil, R. (1993) Knowledge sharing: Prospects and challenges. Proceedings of the International conference on building and sharing of very large-scale knowledge bases 1993 :95-102

Tulving, E. (1975) Ecphoric processes in recall and cognition. *in Brown, J. (ed) Recall and recognition. Wiley, 1975*

Winograd, T. (1976) Frame representations and the declarative-procedural controversy. in Bobrow, D.G. Collins, A. (eds) Representation and Understanding. *New York: Academic Press, :185-210.*

Yost, G. (1992) Configuring elevator systems. *AI Research Group, DEC, Marlboro, MA.*

Local Patching Produces Compact Knowledge Bases

P. Compton, P.Preston, B.Kang, T.Yip

School of Computer Science and Engineering,
University of New South Wales,
PO Box 1, Kensington 2033 Australia,
email compton@cse.unsw.edu.au

Abstract. Knowledge acquisition (KA) encompasses working with the expert to model the domain and a suitable problem solving method as preconditions for building a knowledge based system (KBS) and secondly working with the expert to populate the knowledge base. Ripple Down Rules (RDR) focuses on the second of these activities and allows an expert to populate a knowledge base (KB) without any knowledge engineering assistance. It is based on the idea that since the knowledge an expert provides is a justification of his or her judgment given in a specific context, this knowledge should only be used in the same context. Although the approach has been used for large single classification systems, it has the potential problem that the local nature of the knowledge may result in much repeated knowledge in the KB and much repeated knowledge acquisition. The study here attempts to quantitate and compare KB size and performance for systems built by experts with various levels of expertise and also inductively. The study also proposes a novel way of conducting such studies in that the different levels of expertise were achieved by using simulated experts. The conclusion from this study is that experts are likely to produce reasonably compact and efficient knowledge bases using the Ripple-Down Rule approach.

1 Introduction

Current approaches to knowledge acquisition, for example the KADS methodology [32], seem mainly concerned with understanding the type of problem that has to be solved, what methods should be used to solve this problem and what are the elements in the domain that should be taken into consideration and how they should be represented. These are important software engineering issues, but answering these questions does not necessarily eliminate the knowledge engineering bottleneck. A major issue in the knowledge engineering bottleneck [14] is that after the questions above are answered one still has to decide how to incorporate any particular chunk of knowledge into the knowledge base (KB). This is not an easy task. As Grossner et al., point out "the behaviour of large rule-based systems is almost always hard to predict because although individual rules can be easy to understand on their own, interactions that can occur between rules are not obvious" [19].

RDR will be discussed further below, but the essential idea is that any knowledge provided by an expert is used only in the context in which it is provided. Rules are refinements or corrections to other rules, to be used only in the same context as when the other rule fired [10][12]. Conceptually RDR are related to non-monotonic logics, but are aimed at knowledge acquisition with the goal of allowing large systems to be built by experts without assistance from knowledge engineers, apart from setting up the initial data model. RDR have also been proposed as a mediating representation in machine learning [2], as they tend to produce a more compact representation than other approaches [18]. RDR can be PAC learnable [22] and are a useful representation in Inductive Logic Programming [31] and have been included in a CLASSIC like knowledge representation system [16].

The relation to machine learning noted above is not coincidental. RDR are a machine learning like way of knowledge acquisition. Broadly speaking, in machine learning an algorithm is used to decide how to modify or extend a knowledge base to deal with a case the KBS does not yet handle correctly. The algorithm decides where in the knowledge base a change will be made and what that change will be. The RDR structure determines where a new rule will be added, but an expert is used instead of an algorithm to decide what knowledge will be added. The expert is also constrained to provide a rule which is valid. Unlike most machine learning methods, RDR are incremental and are used to add to the knowledge base when a case is misclassified.

There is a clear difference in emphasis between task analysis knowledge acquisition strategies and machine learning like strategies such as RDR. The task analysis strategies seem to believe that if the initial analysis (and tool building) is done well enough it will be very easy for the expert to actually populate the knowledge base. Machine learning like methods on the other hand seem to believe that populating the knowledge base is the more important problem and implicitly, if the method of doing this is strong enough, the initial analysis can be quite weak. It seems that both strategies would like to claim that all KA issues can be addressed with their approach, but despite successful applications there is still insufficient data to draw strong conclusions from comparisons [25]. (Of course a likely conclusion is that both aspects of knowledge acquisition need to be explicitly addressed.)

The major success with RDR is PIERS, an expert system used to add clinical interpretations to chemical pathology laboratory reports [8][13]. PEIRS now has about 2000 rules, covers 25% of chemical pathology (i.e., 100 out of 500 reports per day issued by the laboratory) and is 95% accurate. Rules can deal with temporal data, allow mathematical expressions to be included and new attributes can be added at any time. PEIRS went into routine use with about 200 rules with the rest of the rules added while in routine use. Rule addition is a trivial task taking about 3 minutes per rule, so that knowledge addition for the whole system has taken about 100 hours. Most importantly, all rules have been added by an expert without any knowledge engineering or programming assistance or skill. Rule addition takes about 15 minutes per day and is a trivial extension to an expert pathologist's normal duties. A knowledge engineer/programmer was required only for the initial data modelling.

RDR also shift the development emphasis to maintenance by blurring the distinction between initial development and maintenance. The difficulty of adding a rule to an RDR system is the same regardless of how long a KB has been under development and how large it is. This feature allows a KB to evolve along with the gradual development of domain expertise.

2 Problem, Motivation and Aim

The problem with RDR is that despite the success above of a very large medical expert system in routine use built without a knowledge engineer, by and large, other researchers do not believe that RDR can really work; they believe the results above are a lucky exception. The reason for this belief is the expectation is that since knowledge is used only locally, in context, the same knowledge will be repeated in many places throughout the KB. If inappropriate knowledge is added at the start there will be gross repetition, the knowledge acquisition task will be enormous and the system will never converge towards completion. The aim of this paper is to demonstrate that these problems do not in fact occur.

It seems likely that Platonic assumptions about the desirability of optimal, elegantly organised knowledge are also involved in such a judgment [6]. KBS research has moved away from the assumption of being able to extract expert knowledge to the more reasonable view that the role of an expert is to collaborate in creating a qualitative model [5]. However, the Platonic perspective of searching for archetypal knowledge is deeply ingrained and even the modelling approach can be criticised for its expectations of finding out something about expert knowledge [26].

RDR takes the modelling approach to its logical conclusion. There is no intrinsic reason to prefer one modelling approach over another. So, there is no reason to embark on a costly and demanding exercise to construct a model if a primitive modelling strategy which only allows errors to be corrected is adequate for the task. The knowledge engineer or expert do not have to collaborate on making structural decisions about the KB. The structure is fixed, and the only task is for the expert to fix errors as they occur. This does not require any knowledge of the internals of the system, only domain knowledge as to why the system should make a different conclusion.

The aim of this paper is to show that this approach works, and that the costs of possible repetition are small. The method used in the study is to build and compare a series of RDR KBs using simulated experts. The advantage of simulated experts (provided by another KB) are that different levels of expertise can be compared without the costs of human experts and with better experimental control.

3   Ripple Down Rules

Context in RDR is defined as the sequence of rules that were evaluated leading to a wrong conclusion (or no conclusion). When the rule producing a new conclusion is added, this rule is evaluated only after the same sequence of rules is evaluated. The resulting structure is a set of ordered rules (if .. elseif rules) with exceptions which can themselves be ordered rules and so on [2]. If a rule is satisfied by the data then its conclusion will be asserted unless any of its exception rules are satisfied and so on with the exceptions to the exceptions. The expert need have no knowledge about this structure and how the system appends the rule to the KB. As far as the expert is concerned he or she composes a rule of whatever generality is preferred and the system handles this rule. All rule addition is prompted by the system misclassifying or failing to classify a case.

A second advantage of the approach is that the expert can be constrained to add only valid rules. Each rule is added to the system to deal with a specific case. These cases are stored in conjunction with the rules and are called cornerstone cases. When a new rule is added, the cornerstone case associated with the rule that gave the wrong classification may be misclassified by the new rule, as any case satisfying the parent rule is passed along to the new exception rule. Therefore a new rule should be satisfied by the new case but not by the previous cornerstone case. This can be achieved by requiring the expert to select conditions for the new rule from a list of differences between the case for which the rule is added and the previous cornerstone.

For example:

old case	new case
TSH high	TSH high
T3 low	T3 low
FTI normal	
	TT4 high

The expert must choose either or both the conditions

FTI NOT normal
TT4 high

as conditions in the rule and can optionally chose any of the common conditions to make the rule intelligible. Such a rule is guaranteed to work on the new case but not the old case, so no further checking is required or relevant. Note that for a case that has not satisfied any rule, the difference list includes all the conditions that are true for the case and the rule can use any of these conditions, however, the rule is not evaluated until all previous rules have been evaluated.

In systems like PIERS, the difference list can be very large because of the large number of possible attributes that can be handled. Further, new functions can be defined and quite complex expressions used so that interface issues become important [28]. However the basic feature remains that the expert can make up any rule for the case they choose, but the system only allows the expert to make up a valid rule.

Note that rules are never deleted from the system nor edited, only added. All errors can be dealt with by rule addition and the difference list above except for the rare case of the classification being wrong but the difference list being empty, in other words an expert blunder. This can be corrected by allowing the difference list requirement to be overridden for such a case.

A major limitation of RDR is that an RDR system can only handle single classification problems [7]. Techniques are under development to deal with multiple classification problems [21], and it has been proposed that it may be possible for the knowledge in context validated acquisition strategy to apply to all KBS tasks. In this proposal the data model for the system evolves as the system develops and task analysis [4][32] is a post hoc explanation of what the system is doing rather than a prerequisite to building the system [11].

An apparent restriction with RDR is that all knowledge is added to deal with cases. We believe this is not a restriction in reality. When rules are added in the maintenance phase, this is inevitably to deal with cases not properly handled by the system. Secondly, for any significant system for real world use, there will be extensive evaluation against test cases before deployment. If these are suitable test cases, they would have been suitable cases from which to build a system. Alternatively a system will be closely monitored when put into use, again providing cases for which to add knowledge.

The most obvious limitation of RDR is that a structure may develop with a lot of repeated very specific knowledge. It is the contention of this paper that repetition is not in fact a major problem. If, however, it eventually becomes a problem with a KB, Gaines has proposed a strategy of developing an RDR system manually, running cases through this KB to provide well classified cases and then using the Induct machine learning system to produce a smaller RDR system which can again be used for manual maintenance [16].

4   Experimental Design

We assume that a useful measure of a compact knowledge base is the size of a knowledge base built by induction. A major feature of machine learning research has been algorithms to produce compact knowledge bases. We assume further that the most critical comparison for the size of an RDR KB would be with a KB produced by the Induct machine learning algorithm. Induct performs similarly to C4.5 [15] but in its RDR version generally produces smaller KBs on standard data sets than other methods [18]. Its knowledge bases seem to be roughly one third the size of those produced by alternate methods. The compact representation produced is one of the advantages of RDR as a mediating representation in machine learning [2].

The design is that Induct/RDR is applied to a dataset and a KB produced. The dataset is also used by simulated experts to produce other RDR KBs The expert works through the cases sequentially, running each case through the developing expert system and adding a rule for each case that is misclassified. A stupid simulated expert selects conditions from the difference list. More expert simulated experts are produced by running the case through the Induct/RDR KB and then selecting some conditions from the rule trace to go into the rule. The difference between the Induct/RDR system and the manual RDR system is that the Induct system considers all the cases at once to produce an optimal organisation of the rules according to its algorithm, whereas the manual system is built by adding rules to deal with cases in whatever order the cases occur. However the expertise to deal with the cases is obtained from the Induct/RDR KB. The Induct/RDR KB used as the expert is trained on all possible training cases.

The simulated experts select conditions from the difference list (described above) that also occur in the Induct/RDR KB rule trace. One simulated expert selects four conditions from the top of the rule trace that are in the difference list or all such conditions if there are less than four. Another simulated expert selects a single condition from the top of the rule trace that is also in the difference list. A number of other simulated experts have been studied which, as far as the paper here is concerned, perform similarly to the two simulated experts described.

4.1 Dataset

The dataset was taken from Garvan Institute thyroid data. A subset of this data has been used previously in machine learning experiments [29][30] and is available from the UC Irvine ftp site. The dataset used here is larger and comprises 21,822 cases. The cases here are from the years 1985 to 1990 and were used in historical order as training cases. Up to 15,000 cases were used for training and the last 5,000 cases kept as a test set. The cases were classified by passing them through the original Garvan ES1 expert system [9][20]. A correct classification was defined as that provided by Garvan ES1. This meant that there was no noise which may have obscured the results. Garvan ES1 provides 60 different classifications. The numerical data was also preprocessed to simpler ordinal data (high, low etc) by the preprocessor for the original Garvan ES1 system before being used in these experiments. After preprocessing each case had 32 attributes (1 x 5 values, 5 x 4 values, 7 x 3 values and 19 x 2 values). After preprocessing there were 3,151 different data patterns in the 21,288 cases.

An even larger dataset of some 45,000 cases. is available. However as has been shown, in such real world data, there are significant changes in the data profiles over time [17]. The cases selected for the present study come after the major shift in the data profiles in 1984 to 1985.

4.2 Induct

The Induct algorithm [15] is based on an extension of the Prism algorithm [3]. The algorithm deals with the classes in a dataset one at a time. It evaluates each possible attribute value pair as a class selector. It does this by counting the true and false positives and true and false negatives that result using the selector and then calculating the probability that this result could be achieved by chance with the dataset. An important feature of the method is that these calculations use standard statistical techniques in the normal way [15]. The attribute value class selector that is least likely to have its effect by chance is then chosen as a rule condition. Extra conditions are added to the rule in the same way, however, a condition is not added to a rule if its effect could occur by chance (e.g. > 5%). The probabilities are corrected for the number of possible rules considered so that very specific rules have to perform much better than simpler rules to be selected. The RDR extension to Induct was a simple matter of recursively applying the Induct algorithm to false positives that fell under a rule and the false and true negatives excluded by a rule [16].

5 Results

Fig 1 shows the error rates achieved as the various KBs develop. The test data are the last 5000 cases. The results for Induct show the effect of increasing the training set size. As shown by Catlett , error rates continue to fall as more training cases are added [1], however, note the log scale; the final error rate is 2.2%. There are in fact some 693 data patterns between cases 10,000 and 15,000 that did not occur previously. Note that because there is a default classification the error rate is 22.7% with no KB.

For the various manual RDR KBs the X axis indicates the total number of cases seen by the developing expert system. The number of cases actually used to form rules is seen in Fig 2. The stupid expert chooses the first four conditions from the top of the difference list. The seeming improvement in the error rate of the stupid expert after the first 1000 cases is simply a function of less, and therefore more meaningful, differences between the cases as the KB develops. The two simulated experts perform comparably to Induct, with the 4 condition expert having a slight advantage. Note that the simulated 4 condition expert performs marginally better than Induct. The explanation is that the expert, having been trained on 21822 cases knows more than Induct trained on a smaller data set.

Fig 1 indicated that a manually built RDR KB performed comparably to an inductively built KB. However, the critical question is the KB size to achieve this performance. These results are shown in Fig 2. These results are for the same KBs as shown in Fig 1 except that the data using the entire dataset for training is also shown. The final sizes are: Induct alone 332 rules, clever expert 822 rules, moderate expert 1221 rules and stupid expert 1636 rules. It should be noted that the maximum possible number of rules is 3151, the number of different data patterns amongst the 21822 cases.

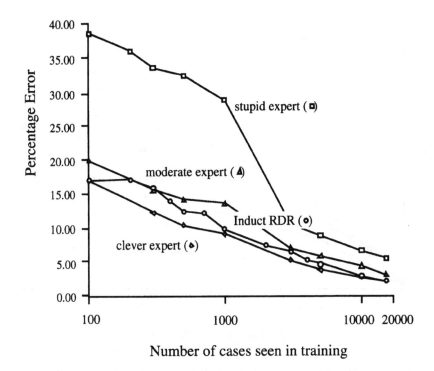

Fig. 1. Error rates on a test set with different simulated experts and Induct alone, provided with different numbers of training cases. The stupid expert selects 4 conditions from the top of the difference list for a rule, the clever expert selects 4 conditions from the top of the Induct rule trace which are in the difference list and the moderate expert selects one such condition.

6 Discussion

These results demonstrate that a manual RDR expert system performs similarly to an inductively built expert system. The error rate versus number of training cases for induction or number of cases evaluated by the manual RDR system is the same. The manual RDR error rate is slightly better than the inductive error rate. These results are not unexpected, in fact we would expect a human expert to do better than the synthetic expert or induction for small training sets. The first 4 conditions in the rule trace are not necessarily the conditions a human expert would use in a rule. In a previous study a human expert built an RDR system with a 12% error rate from 291 training cases versus 74% for C4.5 for the same training cases [23]. (As noted above, Induct performs similarly to C4.5). The test set was 9514 Garvan thyroid cases but importantly the training set was 291 unusual cases which the original Garvan ES1 expert system had used as test cases or which the system had misinterpreted at some stage [20]. Because the cases were diverse this raining set was a challenge for an inductive approach but not for an expert.

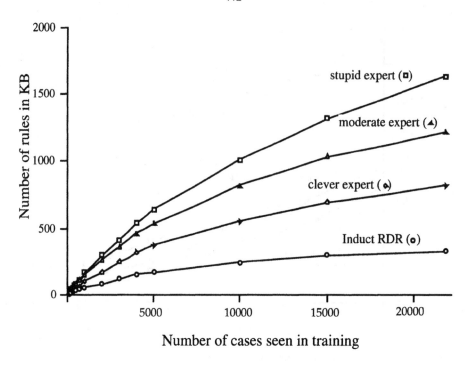

Fig. 2. Size of the resultant KB versus number of training cases seen. The experts are defined as in Fig 1.

Perhaps more surprising initially, is that the best simulated expert produced a KB that was only 2.5 times as large as the inductive KB. Even a stupid expert built a KB only 5 times as large as the inductive KB.

This performance more than meets any real world requirements. If we take the time to add PIERS rules of 3 minutes per rule, the time taken for a human expert to build an 822 rule system similar to the clever expert would be only 41.1 hours over the 5 year period covered by the data. On average the simulated expert here is adding a rule for every 27 cases seen and at the end of the period is adding a rule for every 50 cases seen. It should be noted that the error rate for the inductive KB at this stage is 2.2%. Now either an error rate of 2.2% is acceptable and errors can be ignored or more rules need to be added. If errors need to be picked up and more rules need to be added, then adding one rule every 50 cases for the manual RDR has the same cost as detecting errors from the inductive KB with an error rate of 2.2%.

A separate issue is whether such performance is suitable for all domains. However, before rejecting RDR for alternative methodologies (or none), it reasonable to ask whether similar data is available for the other methods giving information about the relative compactness and performance of the KBS produced by these methods.

We propose to use the same experimental design on other datasets used in the machine learning literature, to confirm that these results are domain independent. The advantage of the current dataset is that it is taken from a real domain. Building a system by taking sequential cases and testing it on cases that occur after the system is assumed complete (here at 15,000 cases) is exactly the scenario that occurs in the real world where one expects the system to apply to future cases. Although the test approach we have used is entirely consistent with a real world system, we propose to use some of the techniques in machine learning for separating test and training sets to provide further comparative data.

The critical issue is why this simple approach of constantly patching errors works as well as it does. Ideally a classification rule will cover all the members of the class but none of the members of other classes. Repetition in the KB will occur where this goal is not achieved and there are false positives and negatives to be handled by further rules. False positives (in this context) are where a rule is too general and some of the cases that fall under it have to be corrected by further rules (which also occur elsewhere in the KB). False negatives (in this context), will occur if the expert makes rules that are too specific so that more rules have to be added (which themselves subsume earlier rules).

RDR should not be confused with general decision tree strategies where if an attribute with poor discrimination goes at the top of the tree, much repetition will result. Normally with a decision tree, the top nodes do not immediately reach a classification and it is assumed that the classification will be produced after further splitting at lower nodes. In this framework the choice of which decisions go at the top is critical. In contrast, with RDR, each rule attempts to deal with a particular class, so if we assume that each rule is perfect and there are no false positives or negatives, it does not matter whether the initial rules deal with classes with many members or few. If a rule (using attribute value pair conditions) is specific to the class, then cases for other classes will fail to satisfy the rule and will result in new rules being created. The order doesn't matter as long as the rules have no false positives or negatives. The critical issue then is the number of false positives. The fewer, the less repetition there will be.

With RDR the expert is asked simply to justify their conclusion in the context in the same way as normal human discourse. An expert is someone who knows the right conclusion and is likely to provide a justification that is both as general and as error free as possible in the context; i.e. it implicitly minimises the false positives and false negatives in the context; i.e. it is a good practical explanation, The RDR approach thus provides a framework where the natural performance of an expert will tend to produce a compact KB.

Fig 3 shows that for PIERS human experts do tend to produce rules that are very general, and so would produce few false negatives while at the same time producing few false positives needing further correction (see also [27]). The rules tend to have only one or two conditions in them and on average only two to three rules have to be satisfied to reach the correct conclusion. Fig 3 also shows that the total number of conditions that have to be satisfied in reaching a conclusion. The corresponding graph for the simulated clever expert is very similar. Induct produces similar results, except that it tends to produce rules with more conditions than a human expert [18]. With all RDR KBs it is much more likely that a new rule will be added to cover a case not yet covered than to add a correction rule, so that the resultant structure is closer to a the flat shape of a list of ordered rules rather than the triangular shape expected with a decision tree.

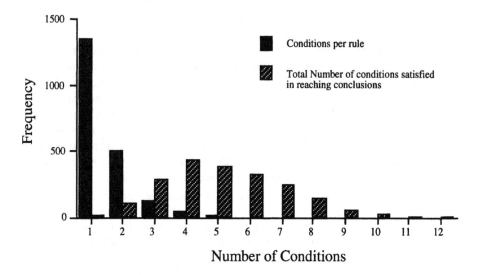

Number of Conditions

Fig. 3. The complexity of rules in terms of number of conditions in individual rules, and the total number of conditions in rules satisfied in reaching a conclusion for the PIERS expert systems R28.

Of course repetition does occur, the clever expert KB in Fig 2 is 2.5 times the optimal size. This repetition can be dealt with by Gaines strategy [16] as discussed. The point of the paper here is that reorganisation of the KB is likely to be a secondary or rare requirement, with the results in Fig 1 and 2 not indicating any pressing need to reorganise the KB.

Since RDR have been compared here to induction, the question arises of why not simply use induction. For induction all the training cases need to be well classified by an expert prior to use and in many domains such cases are not available. For RDR the cases only need to be well classified by the expert when they are used to add a rule to a system. Hence, a good way of preparing cases for induction would be to build an RDR system which produces a version of the required KB in the process. As the PIERS experience shows this can occur while the developing KB is in routine use.

The conclusion from this work is that the effort that is put into trying to organise knowledge into an optimal model is often unnecessary. It is perfectly adequate merely to keep patching errors with local corrections. Not only is this practical, but the task does not require a knowledge engineer or knowledge engineering skills, thus transforming the practical possibilities of KBSs.

Finally this is seen as a counter intuitive result, probably because of the underlying Platonic motivation in much AI of finding the right model, the right representation, the right knowledge. Something that works and is simple, but is not elegant and demanding, is perhaps not seen as attractive. The situated cognition perspective on the other hand suggests that since the knowledge experts construct is always gong to be justification constructed on the fly in context, a local patch approach is an appropriate solution. Testing and fixing is perhaps a more naturally human approach than trying to do sufficient analysis to get the system right [25].

The critical question for the RDR approach is whether a local patch approach can be found for tasks other than single classification. It appears that a solution can be found for multiple classification problems [21] and preliminary results using the simulated expert technique suggest that the size of the knowledge acquisition task is similar to ordinary RDR. It remains a (hopeful) conjecture as to whether this can be used as a basis for other tasks, removing the need for task analysis [11] and perhaps even being able to use an evolving domain model [24].

Acknowledgments

This work has been funded by the Australian Research Council. The authors are grateful to Brian Gaines for making available the Induct software and his encouragement in these studies.

References

1. Catlett, J.: Megainduction: machine learning on very large databases. Machine Learning: Proceedings of the Eigth International Workshop.
2. Catlett, J.: Ripple-down-rules as a mediating representation in interactive induction. R. Mizoguchi, H. Motoda, J. Boose, B. Gaines and R. Quinlan (eds.):Proceedings of the Second Japanese Knowlege Acquisition for Knowledge-Based Systems Workshop. Kobe, Japan, (1992) 155–170
3. Cendrowska, J.: An algorithm for inducing modular rules. International Journal of Man-Machine Studies 27 (4) (1987) 349–370
4. Chandrasekaran, B.: Generic tasks in knowledge-based reasoning: high level building blocks for expert system design. IEEE Expert 1 (3) (1986) 23–30
5. Clancey, W.: Viewing knowledge bases as qualitative models. IEEE Expert Summer (1989) 9–23
6. Compton, P.: Insight and knowledge. J. Boose, W. Clancey, B. Gaines and A. Rappaport (eds.):AAAI Spring Symposium: Cognitive aspects of knowledge acquisition. Stanford University, (1992) 57–63
7. Compton, P., Edwards, G., Kang, B., Lazarus, L., Malor, R., Menzies, T., Preston,P., Srinivasan,A., Sammut, A.: Ripple down rules: possibilities and limitations.

J. Boose and B. Gaines (eds.):6th Bannf AAAI Knowledge Acquisition for Knowledge Based Systems Workshop. Banff, (1991) 6.1–6.18

8. Compton, P., Edwards, G., Srinivasan,A., Malor, R., Preston,P., Kang, B., Lazarus, L.,: Ripple down rules: turning knowledge acquisition into knowledge maintenance. Artificial Intelligence in Medicine 4 (1992) 47–59

9. Compton, P., Horn, R., Quinlan, R., Lazarus, L.,: Maintaining an expert system. J. R. Quinlan (eds.): Applications of Expert Systems. London: Addison Wesley (1989) 366–385

10. Compton, P., Jansen, R.: Knowledge in context: a strategy for expert system maintenance. C. Barter and M. Brooks (eds.): Proc AI 88. Berlin: Springer-Verlag (1990) 292–306

11. Compton, P., Kang, B., Preston, P., Mulholland, M.: Knowledge acquisition without analysis. N. Aussenac, G. Boy, B. Gaines, M. Linster, J.-G. Ganascia and Y. Kodratoff (eds.): Knowledge Acquisition for Knowledge Based Systems. Lecture Notes in AI (723). Berlin: Springer Verlag (1993) 278–299

12. Compton, P., Jansen, R.: A philosophical basis for knowledge acquisition. Knowledge Acquisition 2 (1990) 241–257

13. Edwards, G., Compton, P., Malor, R., Srinivasan, A., Lazarus, L.: PEIRS:a pathologist maintained expert system for the interpretation of chemical pathology reports. Pathology 25 (1993) 27–34

14. Feigenbaum, E.: The art of artificial intelligence: themes and case studies of knowledge engineering. Proceedings of the Joint International Conference on Artificial Intelligence. (1977) 1014–1029

15. Gaines, B.: An ounce of knowledge is worth a ton of data: quantitative studies of the trade-off between expertise and data based on statistically well-founded empirical induction. Proceedings of the Sixth International Workshop on Machine Learning. San Mateo, California, Morgan Kaufmann (1989) 156–159

16. Gaines, B.: Induction and visualisation of rules with exceptions. J. Boose and B. Gaines (eds.):6th AAAI Knowledge Acquisition for Knowledge Based Systems Workshop. Bannf, (1991) 7.1–7.17

17. Gaines, B., Compton, P.: Induction of meta-knowledge about knowledge discovery. IEEE Transactions on Knowledge and Data Engineering 5 (6) (1994) 990–992

18. Gaines, B., Compton, P.: Induction of ripple down rules. A. Adams and L. Sterling (eds.):AI '92. Proceedings of the 5th Australian Joint Conference on Artificial Intelligence. Hobart, Tasmania, World Scientific, Singapore (1992) 349–354

19. Grossner, C., Preece, A., Chander, G., Radhakrishnan, T., Suen, C.: Exploring the structure of rule based systems. Proceedings of the American Association of Artificial Intelligence. Washington, MIT Press, Cambridge (1993) 704–709

20. Horn, K., Compton, P., Lazarus, L., Quinlan, J.: An expert system for the interpretation of thyroid assays in a clinical laboratory. Aust Comput J 17 (1) (1985) 7–11

21. Kang, B., Compton, P. : Knowledge acquisition in context: the multiple classification problem. Proceedings of the Pacific Rim International Conference on Artificial Intelligence. Seoul, (1992) 847–854

22. Kivinen, J., Mannila, H., Ukkonen, E.: Learning rules with local exceptions. Proceedings Euro-COLT. (1993)

23. Mansuri, Y., Compton, P., Sammut, C.: A comparison of a manual knowledge acquisition method and an inductive learning method. J. Boose, J. Debenham, B. Gaines and J. Quinlan (eds.):Australian workshop on knowledge acquisition for knowledge based systems. Pokolbin, (1991) 114–132

24. Menzies, T.: Maintaining procedural knowledge: ripple down functions. A. Adams and L. Stirling (eds.):AI'92, Proceedings of the 5th Australian joint conference on artificial intelligence. Hobart, World Scientific, Singapore (1992) 335–342

25. Menzies, T., Compton, P.: Knowledge acquisition for performance systems; or: when can "tests" replace "tasks"? J. Boose, B. Gaines and M. Musen (eds.):Proceedings of the 8th AAAI-Sponsored Banff Knowledge Acquisition for Knowledge-Based Systems Workshop. Banff, Canada, (1994) 34.1–34.20

26. O'Hara, K., Shadbolt, N.: AI models as a variety of psychological explanation. International Joint Conference on Artificial Intelligence. Chambery, (1993) 188-193

27. Preston, P., Edwards, G., Compton, P.: A 1600 rule expert system without knowledge engineers. J. Leibowitz (eds.):Proceedings of the Second World Congress on Expert Systems. Lisbon, Pergamon (1993) in press

28. Preston, P., Edwards, G., Compton, P.: A 2000 rule expert system without a knowledge engineer. B. Gaines and M. Musen (eds.):Proceedings of the 8th AAAI-Sponsored Banff Knowledge Acquisition for Knowledge-Based Systems Workshop. Banff, Canada, (1994) 17.1–17.10

29. Quinlan, J.: Simplifying decision trees. Int. J. Man-Machine Studies **27** (1987) 221–234

30. Quinlan, J., Compton, P., Horn, K., Lazarus, L.: Inductive knowledge acquisition: A case study. Applications of Expert Systems. London: Addison Wesley (1987) 159–173

31. Siromoney, A., Siromoney, R.: Local exceptions in inductive logic programming. Proceedings of the 14th Machine Intelligence Workshop (1993) to appear

32. Wielinga, B., Schreiber, A., Breuker, J.: KADS: a modelling approach to knowledge engineering. Knowledge Acqusition **4** (**1**) (1992) 5–54

Components of Problem Solving and Types of Problems

Joost Breuker *

University of Amsterdam
Department of Social Science Informatics
Roeterstraat 15
NL–1018 WB Amsterdam, the Netherlands
email breuker@swi.psy.uva.nl

Abstract. A typology of problems is presented that is used for indexing and accessing reusable problem solving components in a library that supports the *Common*KADS methodology for building knowledge based systems. Eight types of problems, such as planning, assessment etc., are distinguished, and their dependencies are explained. These dependencies suggest that the typology is to be viewed as a "suite" rather than the usual taxonomy of "generic tasks". Developing the suite has lead to some new insights and elaborations of [Newell and Simon, 1972]'s theory for modeling problem solving.

- *Tasks* are distinguished from problem definitions. A tasks is constructed by finding and configuring problem solving methods (PSMs), which are suitable for solving the (well-) defined problem. Tasks and PSMs therefore have a one to one correspondence ([O'Hara and Shadbolt, 1993]), while there is a one to many corresponce between a problem definition (type) and PSMs.
- Three phases are proposed that turn spontaneous, ill-defined problems into well-defined ones, respectively. into problem solving tasks.
- A complete *solution* consists of three components: a case model, an argument structure and a conclusion. The conclusion is a sub-part of both other components.
- Tasks (PSMs) package recurring chains of dependent types of problems in variable ways.
- The availability of behavioural models, or of structural/behavioural models in a domain determines to a large extent which types of problems can be posed and solved.

1 Introduction

In the *Common*KADS methodology for constructing knowledge based systems, a Library of reusable problem solving components takes a central role in top-down support of knowledge acquisition [Valente et al., 1993, Breuker and de Velde, 1994]. It performs the same role as the KADS-1 library of "interpretation models", but

---

* The research reported is partially funded by the Esprit programme of the European Commission, P-5248, KADS-II. I would like to thank André Valente for commenting on this paper. A different, and far more elaborate version of the framework presented this paper can be found in [Breuker, 1994b]

differs in content and structure [Breuker et al., 1987]. The new Library's content no longer consists of only highly abstract inference structures — one for each type of task — but of linked components of different grain-size levels, allowing for refinement by selection and combination to fit the application domain.

The components come in a large variety. They may range from a full generic model that needs only to be instantiated by domain terms, to a simple inference function. The components are expressed in CML, the Conceptual Modeling Language [Wielinga et al., 1993], and can be semi-automatically translated into ML^2, the formal language of *CommonKADS* [van Harmelen and Balder, 1993]. The most abstract description of a component is a *function*. A function has input- and output roles.

This Library has two divisions: the Task division, where problem solving methods (PSMs) are stored, and the Domain division, containing reusable ontologies. The Domain and Task divisions are linked by features (assumptions), representing interactions between PSMs and domain knowledge. In this paper, we are concerned with the Task division, and more precisely with one of its major accesses: a *typology of problems*. This typology differs in two major respects from current approaches, such as Generic Task [Chandrasekaran, 1983, Chandrasekaran and Johnson, 1993], "role limiting methods" [McDermott, 1988], [Clancey, 1985]'s taxonomy, or the KADS-1 one [Breuker et al., 1987, Schreiber et al., 1993]. First, the typology is about "well defined" problems, and not about tasks. As will be explained below, a task consists of a problem definition and a configuration of PSMs. The problem definition is used to find an appropriate PSM in the Library. Second, the typology is not a taxonomy (see Fig. 1), but a "suite", consisting of rational dependencies in the breakdown of any problem. See Fig. 7 for what is meant by a suite.

It is based on dependencies between problems instead of a classification of their properties. What started as a revising the taxonomy of KADS-1 (Fig. 1), ended in redefining many taken for granted concepts such as task, solution, problem space, etc. To a large extent, this paper can be taken as revisiting Newell & Simon's classical problem solving paradigm that is still prevailing in AI [Newell and Simon, 1972]. The results of this exploration are rather elaborations of this paradigm, than complete revisions or an alternative view. Some of these results are new. For instance, it appears that the solutions are not simple answers to questions, but complex objects, consisting of two strongly related parts or sides: a case model *and* an argument structure. This double side of a solution is also reflected in problem solving methods (PSMs) and the their "generate & test" structure.

2 Problems and Tasks

The classical definition is that problems are some conflict between a current state and a goal state [Newell and Simon, 1972]. However, many (everyday life) problems are not so obviously goal related:

> *An old lady wants to visit her friend in a neighbouring village. She takes her car, but halfway the engine stops after some hesitations. On the side of the road she tries to restart the engine, but to no avail.*

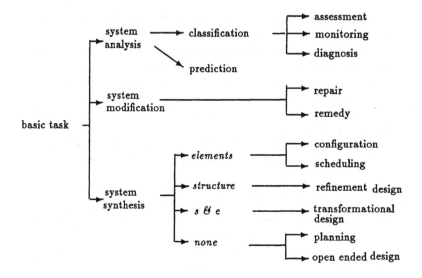

Fig. 1. Taxonomy of "basic tasks": the revised KADS-1 taxonomy of generic tasks [Aamodt et al., 1992, App.C.]

In this story, the goal is to visit a friend, and one may assume that the old lady's plan to do so may take a multitude of intermediary subgoals, but none of these is in conflict with the current state of the malfunctioning engine. The term "goal" would become highly inflated if it should cover any expected state, including those assumed states as subsumed under the 'frame problem'. The old lady's assumption about a correctly functioning car is violated, when she perceives that there is no longer a correspondence between her foot's pressure on the accelerator and the car's speed. Therefore, it is more appropriate to speak about *norm states* than about goal states. Identifying a discrepancy between a current state and a norm or expected state leaves us with an ill defined problem. The discrepancy itself does not say anything in which direction a solution should be found.

Problems are *well-defined* when there is a simple test to conclude that a solution is a solution. This view stated by [McCarthy, 1956] is at the basis of Newel & Simon's description of these problems by their problem space [Newell and Simon, 1972, p. 72-78]. This notion has been widely accepted, but further discussions on this theme are rare. [de Velde, 1988] elaborates the notion of problem space, as a triple $\Omega = <P, S, solution>$, where P is the set of problems, S is the set of solutions, and *solution* is the relation that should hold between both sets. This definition explains the competence in problem solving, because it focuses on the relation between input (P) and output (S). The meaning of this relation (*solution*) is generally that a solution (s) satisfies some problem (p). A diagnosis solution, consisting of a faulty component that explains the malfunctioning of some device, is an example. Besides 'satisfies', 'is-consistent-with' may be an interpretation of the *solution* relation (see section 3). From a performance perspective, the solution set P may not be known, because the problem space has not been completely explored, or the set may be infinitely large. Moreover, it takes a rather strong interpretation of McCarthy's prescript of testability. Of course the simplest and most complete test to see whether a particular solution s is a solution is by finding it as a member of the set of possible solutions S. However, the test may imply no more and no less than whether some attributes are part of the solution s. From a performance perspective, requirements on solutions are available rather than sets of solutions. Therefore it appears here that a problem is defined by some *abstract description of a solution*, rather than some (enumerable or typical) set of solutions.

When the solution is given *in abstracto*, problem solving is a process of refinement of an abstract solution with the help of more specific, but still generic domain knowledge, and of 'filling' the structure of the solution with the specific data from the current state. [Clancey, 1985] was the first to propose this combination of abstraction and refinement as the major operators in the heuristic classification method. [de Velde, 1988] took this view of Clancey, which is blurred by so many other interesting observations, in a more generic and principled way, and showed that all problem solving can be characterized by abstraction and refinement procedures, which come in two major but mixable flavours: classification and construction. We will return to this issue in the last section of this paper.

A problem may be well-defined but that does not make it a task. For instance, the old lady may define her problem as one that should lead to an outcome that is some repair of her car. Note that many alternative problem definitions may have occurred. She might have, for instance, decided to find alternative means for transportation, or to give up her current plan. The difference between a well-defined problem and a task looks rather subtle. A problem can be solved, and a task is executed. The distinction is hardly noteworthy if we see in solving a problem the controlled execution of problem solving methods. However, with task we also mean something that can be repeated, that can be distributed and that contains a plan, i.e. a configuration of PSMs. A task differs therefore from a problem, because in a task the problem solving methods are known, and for a problem these still have to be found. Of course, in a more dynamic view where problem solving consists of defining new subproblems and solving these, the distinction is less sharp. However, in knowledge engineering the problems to be automated are so routine that they are tasks, rather than problems for human agents. People may complain that they have problems; not that they have tasks at their work. This means that problems are deviations and complications, and tasks are not.

Going from an ill-defined problem to a task can be described as an ontogenesis of three steps (see Fig 3 for a summary).

Problem Identification. The output of the first stage is a *conflict* between a current state and a norm state: these two states are inputs to problem identification. The conflict is a "spontaneous" problem: it has the role of a 'complaint'. The complaint is the inducement or trigger for a (well defined) problem, a p in Van de Velde's formula. The conflict is not the cause of the problem. Finding the cause of a problem is a problem by itself (diagnosis, or reconstruction). The conflict describes the difference between what is the case, and what should have been the case. What should have been the case, i.e. the norm, may have two different meanings. The first one is an expectation, i.e. a state that is predictable on the basis of knowledge about the world. The malfunctioning car of the old lady is an example. The second type of norm is a desire, i.e about states in the world that *ought* to be the case. The distinction between these types of norms is of importance, because different types of inference are involved (e.g. [Sergot and Jones, 1992], [Breuker, 1993], [Valente and Breuker, 1994]).

Problem Definition. This second step takes as its input the conflict, and produces as its output some abstract solution, or, as we will see in the next section, a *generic conclusion*. A problem definition turns a spontaneous problem into a well-defined one. It establishes the problem space, Ω. A problem definition is a necessary step to provide sense to a problem. For instance, the old lady of our story may decide to have first her car diagnosed and repaired, and may then continue her journey. An alternative is, that she may have a taxi pick her up and have a garage take care of her car. Or she may give up the goal — visiting her friend — altogether. Problem definition is a *planning* activity, which is guided by the dependencies between abstract solutions (= problem types: see Fig. 7). The sense of a problem definition is the fact that the chain of the potential solutions in the plan aim at a *goal*.

Task Specification. Well-defined problems change into *tasks* by finding or constructing appropriate PSMs. In organizations, recurring well-defined problems are planned as tasks, and distributed over agents and other resources. These scheduled tasks have often lost their relation with spontaneous problems, which means that tasks have not necessarily some violated norm as their direct origin. [2]. Task specification has as its inputs a defined problem, and one or more PSMs which should solve the problem. The controlled configuration (decomposition) of PSMs forms the 'task-body', while the problem definition is its 'header'. Fig. 2 shows the structure of task knowledge. The "assumptions" slot of the task structure refers both to the required data, and to the required (generic) domain knowledge.

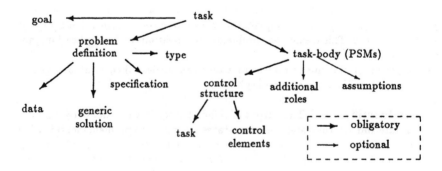

Fig. 2. Structure of task knowledge

---

[2] Indirectly they have, as the goals of a task are the operationalization of some 'desire'

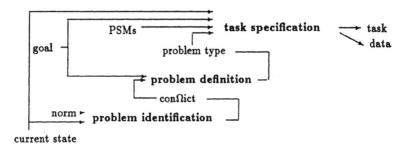

Fig. 3. Three steps in going from problem to task

3   What's in a Solution?

Problems are defined by their generic solutions. This is also the philosophy behind the various taxonomies of problem/task types refered to in Sec. 1. Newell & Simon observe that the term solution may mean different things [Newell and Simon, 1972, p. 76]. They distinguish between solution-objects, solution-paths, and solution-action sequences . The first is what we normally would see as a solution: some outcome or conclusion of the reasoning. For instance, the solution-object in diagnosis is the set of faulty components. Solution paths take the reasoning itself as its objective. In finding a proof in a geometry problem we are not so much interested in the outcome — that was already given or hypothesized — but in the way it can be argued. Solution-action sequences are plans or instructions that lead to the required solutions: they are plans, or rather: problem solving methods (PSMs).

In later literature one will find no explicit elaboration on this observation, but rather varied descriptions of what solutions consist of. A good example can be found in the work of Clancey. In [Clancey, 1985] he shows that in analytic types of problems, the solution is part of the knowledge base, i.e. the solution is to be found by classification rather than by construction. For instance, in medical diagnosis, the solution may be the name of one or more known diseases. The solution is here the *conclusion* of applying a PSM, and coincides with Newell & Simon's "solution object". However, in later publications, notably [Clancey, 1992], he convincingly argues that this is too meager a view, and that a solution is rather constructed as a situation specific, or *case model* (cf. [Steels, 1990]). At the end of the article (sec. 7) the emphasis is no longer on modeling, but on the way evidence supports the case model components. This is a "process model relational structure", which "can be interpreted like a proof". From these three distinctive aspects of solutions of problems, it is possible to synthesize the notion of a *complete solution* to a problem. We propose that a complete solution has three components. (1) The *case model* represents the understanding of the problem. (2) The *conclusion* is the answer to the question posed by the problem definition, while the supportive evidence forms (3) the *argument structure* that states what evidence supports the conclusion (see Fig 4).

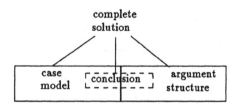

Fig. 4. Components of a solution

The conclusion is a part both of the argument structure, and of the case model. From the perspective of the argument structure, a conclusion is the "sentence" or theorem which is supported by all the evidence. Evidence may be empirical (data, requirements), or based on common knowledge, which may range from simple facts to as-valid-accepted structures or procedures of argument. From the perspective of a case model, the conclusion is that part of the case model which is of interest (input) in solving a next problem (see Sec. 6 for an explanation). The argument structure is not independent of the case model. It refers to facts or entities in the case model. The argument structure is linked to the case model by making references to its behaviours and/or components. Complete solutions are rare, or rarely made explicit, because one may be interested in only one component (e.g. conclusion, argument strcucture), or because it is assumed to be known by the 'user' (e.g. (large parts of the) case model). The roles of these three components of a solution with respect to communication to the user are the following :

Explanation: The CASE MODEL has the role to explain the data.
Justification: The ARGUMENT STRUCTURE justifies the conclusion.
Result: The CONCLUSION is an input for another problem definition, or (sub)task. This (sub)task may be executed by another agent than the one who produced the solution (see also [Breuker and de Greef, 1993])

3.1 Problem Type and Components

The way the conclusion covers the other two components is not fixed, but depends on the *problem type*. For instance, if the problem is to find a proof, the conclusion coincides fully with the argument structure. In design, the conclusion — some structure — covers completely the case model, i.e. there is no distinction between these two components. [3] The argument structure consists of the set of explicitly satisfied requirements. For diagnosis problems, the conclusion consists of the identification of one or more faulty components, while the case model includes also the correct ones and their structural description [de Kleer et al., 1992]. Here the argument structure is built up from the tests performed to show that the faulty components are indeed faulty, and the correct ones correct — or can still be assumed to be working correctly. It should be noted that the argument structure is not simply the trace of

---

[3] In Fig 4 the dashed box 'conclusion' should then cover the box 'case model' completely.

some problem solving process: it is largely its restructuring in terms of argument relations between case model components and evidence. Assessment is concluded by a decision class or metric attributed to a case model [Valente and Löckhoff, 1994]. The argument structure for the complete solution of this type of problems is very thin. It suffices to show that the terms used in the norms of the decision class are applicable to the case [Breuker, 1993].

Usually the case model is described as a situation specific version of generic domain models (e.g. [Steels, 1990]). Similarly, the argument structure can be viewed as a problem specific version of the rationale of a PSM (see [de Velde, 1993] about the "competence" of a PSM). The rationale of a PSM describes how and under what assumptions a method yields valid results.

3.2 Problem Solving Methods and Components

A good example of the different contributions to the solution components is provided by PSMs for solving diagnosis problems of devices. The conclusion of such a diagnosis consists of the set of abnormal component(s). This set is the only relevant one for the dependent problem: the repair of the device. However, some of these PSMs may as well be aimed at the construction of a more complete case model by identifying the normal components as well. Requirements on the completeness of the solution has direct consequences for the cost-effectiveness of a PSM. It is cheaper to identify only faulty components, instead of also the correctly working ones, because a single deviant value is sufficient evidence for a fault, whereas establishing the correct working of a component may involve checking its full behavioural repertory. Minimal solutions may be tractable, where a slightly more complete solution may easily make the problem too complex [de Kleer et al., 1992].

PSMs may also differ whether they reach the conclusion by modeling or by argumentation. This can be illustrated by the two major approaches in model based diagnose. [4]

In consistency based diagnosis (e.g. GDE [deKleer and Williams, 1987]), the abnormal components are identified when their behaviour is inconsistent with the model of their correct behaviour. These conclusions are reached in a deductive way, and primarily by argumentation. The behaviour of the smallest set of remaining components that cannot be explained by models for normal components "must be" abnormal components. The price payed is that we have an incomplete case-model, because we do not know what the faulty behaviour of the abnormal components is. Note also that the other components are *assumed* to be working properly, because no falsifying evidence has been obtained in testing. Therefore, also the argument structure is incomplete, but the conclusion — the set of abnormal components — is completely justified.

In *abductive diagnosis*, the abnormal components are not only identified, but they are modeled as well. Generic models of faulty behaviour are matched against the data

---

[4] We will use the convention to denote tasks or methods by a verb — e.g. (to) diagnose —, while problem types will be indicated by nouns, e.g. diagnosis. Sometimes, this convention is hard to maintain for PSMs, because of the use of adjectives to denote a specific method, e.g. in heuristic classification.

to obtain explanations (covers). The case model, therefore, explains the abnormal components [Console and Torasso, 1991]. Abductive PSMs can only be justified by assuming the domain to be a closed world. It is easy to see how consistency based diagnosis can be extended by the use of fault models. In this way abductive and consistency based approaches are complementary (e.g. [Console and Torasso, 1991], [de Kleer et al., 1992]).

4 Problem Types

Problems can be characterized by their (minimal) solutions, i.e. their generic conclusions. A generic conclusion is an abstract description of an object that covers the set of conclusions. The generic conclusions can be thought of as types, and there exists also a fair consensus on a number of these types. Diagnosis, design, planning are well established ones. We will identify another five types: assessment, monitoring, modeling, assignment (including scheduling and configuration) and prediction. We do so, not only because some of these (assignment, monitoring) are still the largest common denominators in the various typologies proposed for knowledge acquisition (see also [Breuker, 1994]), but also because these additional types fill up holes in the systematic view we will develop in the next section. These definitions are still tentative and will be the object for further study, in particular by formalization. For some problem types formalizations can be found in the literature: [de Kleer et al., 1992] for diagnosis; [Poeck and Gappa, 1993] for assignment.

Modeling is concerned with the identification of what is a system and what is its environment, or more precise: what is its interface with the environment. This interface is consists of behaviour (input/output state dependencies): a behavioural model. The model may be a partial one, as in functional specifications.

Design has as its conclusion a structure of components and their connections. The components may be objects or processes, physical or symbolic.

Planning delivers sequences of causally/teleologically connected states (behaviour) in the world, which may be filled by actions. If the final state(s) are not intended future states (goal states), but states in the past, the planning problem is called *reconstruction*.

Assignment distributes (additional) elements (components, actions) over a structure. If the structure is a plan, the assignment problem is generally called *scheduling*. If the structure is a design the problem is often called *configuration*.

Prediction delivers the resulting states of a system over time, starting with an initial state. When one derives an initial state from some output states one may speak of *postdiction*.

Monitoring yields a discrepancy between a predicted state and an observed state.

Assessment provides a measurement that classifies behaviour according to norms.

Diagnosis finds components or structures which conflict with their behavioural model or design.

Table 1 summarizes the typology.

major type	type of problem	generic conclusion
synthesis	modeling	behavioural model
	design	structure of elements
	planning/reconstruction	sequence of actions
modification	assignment (scheduling, configuration)	distribution/assignments
analysis	prediction	state of system
	monitoring	discrepant states
	diagnosis	faulty element
	assessment	class/grade attribution

Table 1. Type of problem and corresponding generic conclusions

5 A Framework for Analyzing Tasks

By finding relevant distinctive properties, these generic conclusions may be categorized in a taxonomy. The advantage of a taxonomy is that it provides coherence (abstraction; exclusion). However, for a typology of problems, a single taxonomy appears to work as a Procrustian bed. There is a wide consensus on the first major distinction, i.e. between synthesis and analysis problems. [Clancey, 1985] gives a most eloquent view on this difference by arguing that analysis problems deal with operations on known systems — "models of systems in the world" — while in synthesis problems there is not yet a model-of-a-system available. However, beyond this distinction, further refinements become problematic, because distinctive properties represent different views. For instance, synthesis problems can be distinguished by the number and nature of dimensions of the generic conclusion. A plan is one dimensional, over 'time'. A design is multi-dimensional and generally involves 'space'. Moreover, these problem types may also be distinguished by the nature of internal requirements, i.e. whether the elements and/or the structure of the system to be designed or planned are given, or have to be found (see Fig. 1). A third problem with these taxonomies is that when they go deeper than one ply, consistency is easily lost.

Therefore, we have looked for another principle to arrive at a collection of problem types, which has the same properties as taxonomies (exclusion, covering), but not the problems that are the consequence of 'multiple inheritance'. These have been found in looking at the the way problems are related to one another by the fact that the results of one problem are necessary to define a dependent problem. These dependencies, i.e. the generic conclusions, between well-defined problems are a more consistent organizer of problem types than a taxonomy, and have moreover the advantage of a practical analytic tool for identifying configurations of problems and tasks, as they occur in real life.

5.1 Some Typical Tasks and Their Problems

The suggestion to look rather for the dependencies between problems as they are packed in a task, than for a set of distinctive properties of generic conclusions that could serve as the basis for a taxonomy, comes from experiences with the KADS-1 taxonomy of generic tasks (see e.g. [Breuker et al., 1987, Ch. 8, Real Life Tasks]). In real-life applications, a problem type hardly ever comes alone, but rather in chains that reflect the fact that the conclusion of one problem is a required input to solve a next problem. These dependencies between problem types — i.e. their generic conclusions — can be easily overlooked because task decompositions (PSMs) may break up the task in sub-tasks which may cover more than one problem, and one problem may be solved by more than one subtask. In the next sections we will provide evidence for the view that by distinguishing the problems from the tasks, common and rational dependencies between problems become visible.

Problems in Diagnose Tasks The minimal solution of a problem is a conclusion. Conclusions may be needed to resolve a next problem. The conclusion of a diagnosis problem — a set of faulty components — is a necessary input for a repair task. The repair is dependent on the results of a diagnosis problem. In well organized, routine problem solving, the problems and their dependencies are packed into tasks and task decompositions. This packing is provided by a PSM, and each PSM may pack problems in a different way. Here we will discuss some examples from diagnose tasks.

A very simple version of a diagnose task is exemplified by the a common practice in finding faulty computer components by replacing the boards in a systematic way. This replacement is a repair, and can be conceived as a very simple *assignment* problem in which a new component is assigned to the position of a failing or suspect component. In this simple task, the diagnosis and assignment problems are configured in such a way, that repairs are used to test diagnosis hypotheses, and the solutions to the diagnosis problem are used as hypotheses. This alternation between simple hypothesis generation and test-by-repair stops, when a repair yields a correctly functioning device (see Fig 5).

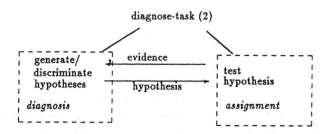

Fig. 5. Decomposition of a simple diagnose task with implied problem types (in italics). The test-task consists of solving a repair problem

However, this configuration will only work under specific conditions (cost of replacement, easily decomposable device etc.) and assumptions (single fault). In most other practical diagnose tasks the solution of repair problems is postponed until this task has been definitely concluded, for instance, when a single fault has been identified.

In the diagnose-by-repair task there is still a one to one correspondence between the problems to be solved and the subtasks. The generate-hypotheses subtask covers the diagnosis problem, and the repair subtask stands for solving the assignment problem. Another, more common structure of a diagnose task with a different set and distribution of problems is the following (see Fig 6). A diagnosis problem can only exist, when some malfunction or complaint has been observed. A malfunction or complaint is a discrepancy between what a system should do according to its design/model and what is observed. Stating how the system should behave — given some input — is the result of some prediction. This prediction problem can be solved by derivation from structural/behavioural models, or by instantiating a behavioural model (e.g. a causal model, or an associational model based on empirical correlates). However, in this diagnose task one is not free to choose from either option. If the diagnose task indeed implies a real diagnosis it should lead to pointing out which components in the structure are the cause of the complaint. It should take a structural model as its road map, and behaviour models of the components as input for prediction, or testing. The requirements of the diagnosis problem dominate the dependent test subtasks. A combination of prediction and monitoring of the actual behaviour of the components of a device provides the primary ingredients for a *test* task. The test task, or rather the conclusion of the monitoring problem in this task, may result in a discrepancy. This discrepancy may play two roles. The first one is the input-role for a diagnosis problem, as a complaint. In this way a diagnose task can be triggered, because a fault has been monitored. The second role is an 'evidence' role, and is also an input to a diagnosis problem. In that case, the test has become a proper subtask in a diagnose task, rather than a 'front-end' task to a diagnose task. This distinction can be expressed in the control over the test (sub)task and diagnose task. In the first role, the test task is followed by a diagnose task; in the second role, the test task is a subtask and is used in an iterative way to refine the hypothesized diagnoses (output of the diagnosis problem). The conclusions of the diagnosis problem take the role of hypotheses. The diagnosis problem does not have a single solution, but all solutions. However, the diagnose *task* uses the hypothesis generation and empirical testing cycle — a PSM — to bring this number down to a minimal set that explains the malfunction. It is the control over these problems that constitutes the task and provides roles to the conclusions of these problems. Note that the generic nature of the problems remains the same, while for each iteration the specific problem to be solved is a different one.

In Fig 6 the relation between this diagnose task decomposition, and the implied problems is presented.

Whatever the packing of problems in these diagnose tasks (and its monitoring "front-end", respectively assignment (repair) "back-end"), a common chain of dependencies between the types of problems can be abstracted:

$$prediction \rightarrow monitor \rightarrow diagnosis \rightarrow assignment$$

Other types of problems may enter the diagnose task as well, in particular in providing evidence (test roles). We have already mentioned the assignment problem, that can be used in two roles: as a test, and as a "back-end" to the diagnose task proper. However, more complicated versions of diagnose may occur. For instance, when observations are difficult or impossible to obtain in a direct way, test may

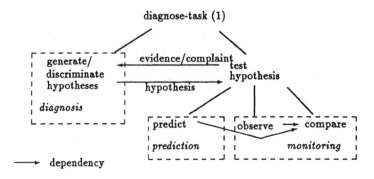

Fig. 6. Decomposition of a typical diagnose task with implied problem types (in italics)

be performed by reconfiguring a system. For instance, a cheap test for stereo-audio equipment is to switch channels, when the complaint is in one of the channels. The configuration problem that is solved is not part of a test, and does not feed in one of the problems of the test, but it changes the diagnosis problem, because the system description of the device has been changed. This dependency with the configuration problem can be simply added to the chain above (we will use here the standard term assignment for configuration):

$$assignment \rightarrow prediction \rightarrow monitor \rightarrow diagnosis \rightarrow assignment$$

Another type of problem that can be observed in real life diagnose tasks is planning. The sequence (or tree) of hypothesis testing can be governed by a plan or schedule e.g. as to maximize the effectiveness and minimize costs of tests (cf. MOL-GEN, [Stefik, 1981]). The chain of problems is as follows:

$$planning/assignment \rightarrow prediction \rightarrow monitor \rightarrow diagnosis \rightarrow assignment$$

Model and Design Tasks; Levels of Understanding Before problems with a system can be identified and diagnosed, the system has to be understood. This means that a (case)*model* has to be constructed. Generic versions of such a model may already be available, thus reducing the model task to an instantiation or adaptation of this generic model of a system. For instance, we may know the global structure and behaviour of amplifiers, which we may use to diagnose a particular type and exemplar. Understanding is not an all or nothing process. For all practical purposes, a system can be understood at three levels:

- By classification: the properties of a system are known, which distinguish a type of system from another type. For instance, a taxonomy of bacterial diseases is a very simple model of malfunctions of the body caused by bacteria.
- By understanding its *behaviour*, i.e. by modeling how changes in the environment, i.e. input to the system, affect the state of the system.

- By understanding its working. This implies not only to have a model of its behaviour, but also a description of what causes this behaviour. There are two major types of *causal models*:

  - The causal model describes the behaviour of a model by intermediary, internal processes or states of a system. For instance, in describing diseases in terms of processes (syndromes), intermediary states such as "immunosuppressed" may provide explanations to account for bacterial diseases which normally would not interfere with the normal processes in the body.

  - The deepest form of understanding consists of relating the causal model to a (physical) structural description that explains by its connections how causes flow through a system. The components of such a system are viewed as subsystems, for each of which a behavioural model may be available, for which again a structural description may be used for more detailed understanding. An example of a structural model is the wiring diagram of an electrical circuit.

When we use the term causal model, we mean in general only the first type of model, while the one that has a mapping between causal chains and physical connections or components is more precisely denoted by the term *structural/behavioural model*.

A structural model of a system is the result of solving a design problem. In the construction of artifacts (devices), the design problem is solved by a *design task*. [5] However, we use the term to *model*, when it concerns the design of causal or structural models of natural systems. Both model and design tasks appear to produce the same kinds of models, and there are more striking similarities. A design or a model is tested. A design is tested against its functional requirements, i.e. against the behaviour that it is intended to exhibit in interacting with its environment (including a user), while an empirical model is tested against its predicted behaviour. These tests look exactly the same as the tests performed in diagnose task; the difference is that this testing is not focussed on explaining a particular discrepancy, but may imply the full behavioural repertoire of the designed or observed system.

There is a growing literature on design and model tasks. A typical example of the PSMs for these tasks can be found in the work of Chandrasekaran. As a first decomposition of these tasks, the following subtasks are identified: "Propose, Verify, Critique, Modify (a design)" [Chandrasekaran, 1990]. Other versions of the same decomposition can be found in the "propose & revise" PSM for configure tasks [Marcus and McDermott, 1988], or the "generate, test & debug" paradigm of [Simmons, 1992] for plan and reconstruct tasks. The Propose subtask is the only task that contains the design problem. The Verify, Critique and Modify subtasks represent process control cycles, which check whether the current state of the design is sufficiently close to (a subset) of the requirements. Therefore, the design task appears to imply the following chain of problems, where Verify implies monitoring, Critique diagnosis and Modify an assignment:

$$design \rightarrow prediction \rightarrow monitor \rightarrow diagnosis \rightarrow assignment$$

---

[5] Here we intend the verb "to design"; not the substantive "design" which we use for problems.

A design problem is solved by the construction of a structural model. The nature of the structure may be explicitly required — internal requirement —, or may be part of a design option. The structure is created to satisfy functional/behavioural (external) requirements. These are the result of solving a *modeling* problem. Within a model/design task one may often find the design problem and the next dependent *assignment* problem quite entangled, because the design problem delivers the structure, while the assignment fills it with elements. Because of interaction problems [Simmons, 1992], it is far more efficient to solve both problems in the same refinement cycles. A similar weaving is found in schedule tasks where the planning and assignment problems are often solved in a combined way [Valente, 1994, Sundin, 1994]. The same can be the case for diagnose and repair (assignment) [Friedrich, 1993]. Therefore, the full chain implied in model or design tasks looks as follows:

modeling → *design* → *assignment* → *prediction* → *monitor* → *diagnosis* → *assignment/design*

Similar analyses as those for diagnose, model and design tasks can be performed for other kinds of tasks. In [Breuker, 1994], other tasks are described. For instance, in process control and device manipulation one finds the follwing chains:

planning/assignment → *prediction* → *monitor* → *diagnosis* → *assignment*

planning/assignment → *prediction* → *assessment* → *assignment*

Similar chains are to be found in test, evaluate and remedy tasks. and diagnose tasks which are aimed at the reconstruction of actions that have lead to a failure.

6 A Suite of Problem Types

These chains of problems which are identified in a large variety of tasks exhibit congruent patterns, which can be integrated into a graph: a suite of problem types (see Fig. 7).

The graph can be divided into two overlapping perspectives: a behavioural and a structural one. A behavioural perspective is taken when its is not possible or feasible to control a system by encapsulating causal effects into physical structures, or to know how causal effects 'propagate' through the physical structure. In that case we have to plan or assess actions. By planning we make a spatio-temporal arrangement that enables causal propagation for a specific situation. For instance, a travel plan (schedule) consists of local and temporal contingencies ("connections") and actions (components). Therefore, the perspectives are relative, and the graph may be collapsed into a single chain. However, we think that the split is highly relevant, because it reflects two ways to control our world: by material technology where we pack causality in (increasingly complex) devices, which leads to mechanization and automation, and by enabling chains of actions: the latter being the default option.

In a very abstract sense we can now explain the ontogenesis of problems and their packing into tasks by PSMs, as a tracing — mainly backtracking — along the suite.

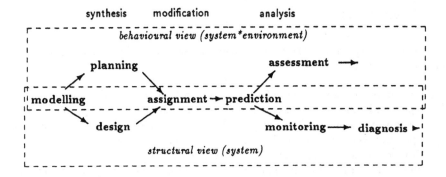

Fig. 7. A suite of problem types, dependencies and views

Spontaneous, ill-defined problems are identified by solving (permanent) monitoring or assessment problems. The spontaneous problem is an indication that somewhere earlier in a dependent problem a solution is no longer valid. This backtracking in problem definition has a minor or a major scope over the suite, dependent on the nature of available domain knowledge and information (data) in the situation. The minor type of problem definition consists of a *refinement* of the conflict (ill defined problem) to allow a minimal, local change — modification — to a system (repair) or a course of action (remedy): both modifications involve an assignment problem. The required refinement may be obtained by solving a diagnosis problem. In diagnosis faulty components instead of the faulty system are identified. Refinement may also be obtained by assessing the conflict, e.g. in terms of classes of malfunctions. If the problem cannot be refined further or cannot be solved by assignment (repair; remedy), more drastic problem solving is required, i.e. one has to start at the modeling entry of the suite.

In this way, a problem definition may consist of more than a single type of problem. As we have seen in Sec 5.1, a task covers in general more than one problem type. This is for two different reasons or *rationales*. The first one is based upon the fact that more than one dependent problem may have to be solved, as in the case of a diagnosis and an assignment (repair). We have seen the packing of combinations of problems by a single method/task in particular for reasons of *efficiency* (see e.g. [Friedrich, 1993]). However, we have also found other chains of problems. In all those cases these problems are packed into tasks because of the different roles that are involved in arriving at a *complete* solution. The rationale for these additional tasks is not that they are intermediary steps towards some goal, but that they constitute a *test or evaluation* cycle that builds the argument structure of a solution. Despite the fact that this control cycle is never a main task, but a rather universal subtask, it also follows the dependencies in the suite. For a further elaboration of the consequences of the reappearance of the 'generate & test' paradigm, the reader is refered to [Breuker, 1994].

7 Conclusions

These new conceptualizations of the elements of solutions, and the problem typology have a number of advances:

- By distinguishing problem definitions from tasks a smaller, less variant set of types can be identified. Tasks and their decompositions hide the problems they are to solve. Moreover, the names and 'real life' appearances of tasks such as 'operation control', '(medical) diagnosis', 'trouble shooting', 'verification' etc. obscure the their commonalities and distinctive features. The typology of problems is at least more parsimonious and appears thus far sufficient to characterize the problems that are solved by (real life) tasks.
- It is assumed that this parsimonious typology also provides a more strict classification of problem solving methods (PSMs). Ideally, for each problem type exclusive PSMs should be identified. There is not yet enough evidence to warrant such a claim, but we have at least shown that by disentangling problem types from (sub)tasks we get a better view of what problem(s) a PSM is supposed to solve, and what task-goals it is aimed to accomplish. For instance, it can be understood why many PSMs for medical diagnose are not diagnostic methods at all, but rather aimed at assessment (normative classification) (e.g. [Clancey, 1985]).
- The view that a *complete solution* to a problem has two major components or 'sides of the same coin' — a case model and an argument structure — clarifies why some PSMs justify conclusions (partial solutions) — e.g. tests which check observations against hypotheses — and other PSMs focus on a coherent interpretation — e.g. causal abduction. More in general, the 'generate and test' paradigm that is observed in all complex tasks reflects the separation of the construction of the case model and of the argument structure.
- Conclusions are that part of a case model and/or argument structure, that answer the question implied by a problem. Conclusions are necessary inputs to solve a 'next', related problem, and for that reason sufficient as a minimal solution to a problem.
- The pattern of dependencies between problem types forms a "suite", i.e. rational sequences of conclusions, which start in principle with modeling, but may be triggered by monitoring or assessing (one's own) activities. The suite avoids the inconsistencies in (single view) taxonomies of problem, or task typologies proposed in the literature. Moreover, it provides guidance for understanding the structure of real life tasks.
- The genesis of problems and tasks may be modeled by three steps:
  - A problem is identified as the discrepancy between some norm(al) state and an actual state.
  - The ill-defined problem is turned into a well-defined one, i.e. one for which a generic conclusion is found. The problem type suite reflects the typical (sequences of) generic conclusions.
  - In task-specification for a well-defined problem appropriate problem solving methods (PSMs) are found or constructed.

Besides these practical consequences of the rather theoretical exercise presented here, the more specific application is of course in the Common KADS library tools, as currently under development. Further research is going on, aimed at a formalization of the problem types to assess the detailed structure of the problem types (generic conclusions) and the consistency of the dependencies.

References

[Aamodt et al., 1992] Aamodt, A., Bredeweg, B., Breuker, J., Duursma, C., Löckenhoff, C., Orsvarn, K., Top, J., Valente, A., and van der Velde, W. (1992). The CommonKADS Library. Deliverable 1.3. KADS-II/T1.3/VUB/TR/005/1.0, KADS Consortium, Free University, Brussels.

[Breuker, 1993] Breuker, J. (1993). Modelling Artificial Legal Reasoning. In Aussenac, N., Boy, G., Gaines, B., Linster, M., Ganascia, J., and Kodratoff, Y., editors, *Knowledge Acquisition for Knowledge Based Systems, Proceedings of the EKAW-93*, pages 66 – 78, Berlin. Springer.

[Breuker, 1994] Breuker, J. (1994). A suite of problem types. In Breuker, J. and de Velde, W. V., editors, *The CommonKADS Library for Expertise Modeling*. IOS-Press, Amsterdam.

[Breuker and de Greef, 1993] Breuker, J. and de Greef, P. (1993). Modelling system-user cooperation. In Schreiber, G., Wielinga, B., and Breuker, J., editors, *KADS: a Principled Approach to Knowledge Engineering*, pages 47 – 70. Academic Press, London.

[Breuker and de Velde, 1994] Breuker, J. and de Velde, W. V., editors (1994). *The CommonKADS Library for Expertise Modeling*. IOS-Press, Amsterdam.

[Breuker et al., 1987] Breuker, J., Wielinga, B., van Someren, M., de Hoog, R., Bredeweg, B., Wielemaker, J., Billault, J.-P., Davoodi, M., and S, H. (1987). Model Driven Knowledge Acquisition: Interpretation Models. Esprit P1098 KADS A1, University of Amsterdam.

[Chandrasekaran, 1983] Chandrasekaran, B. (1983). Towards a Taxonomy of Problem Solving Tasks. *AI Magazine*, 4(1):9 – 17.

[Chandrasekaran, 1990] Chandrasekaran, B. (1990). Design problem solving: a task analysis. *AI Magazine*, pages 59–71.

[Chandrasekaran and Johnson, 1993] Chandrasekaran, B. and Johnson, T. (1993). Generic tasks and task structures. In David, J.-M., Krivine, J.-P., and Simmons, R., editors, *Second Generation Expert Systems*, pages 232 – 272. Springer, Berlin.

[Clancey, 1985] Clancey, W. (1985). Heuristic classification. *Artificial Intelligence*, 27:289–350.

[Clancey, 1992] Clancey, W. (1992). Model construction operators. *Artificial Intelligence*, 53:1–115.

[Console and Torasso, 1991] Console, L. and Torasso, P. (1991). A spectrum of definitions of model based diagnosis. *Computational Intelligence*, 7(3):133 – 141. extension of paper from the ECCAI-90 Proceedings.

[de Kleer et al., 1992] de Kleer, J., Mackworth, A., and Reiter, R. (1992). Characterizing diagnoses and systems. *Artificial Intelligence*, 56(2–3):197 – 222.

[de Velde, 1988] de Velde, W. V. (1988). Inference structure as a basis for problem solving. In Kodratoff, Y., editor, *Proceedings of the 8th European Conference on AI*, pages 202 – 207, London. Pitman.

[de Velde, 1993] de Velde, W. V. (1993). Issues in knowledge level modelling. In David, J.-M., Krivine, J.-M., and Simmons, R., editors, *Second Generation Expert Systems*, pages 211 – 231. Springer, Berlin.

[deKleer and Williams, 1987] deKleer, J. and Williams, B. (1987). Diagnosing multiple faults. *Artificial Intelligence*, 32:97–130.

[Friedrich, 1993] Friedrich, G. (1993). Model-based diagnosis and repair. *AI Communications*, 6(3/4):187 – 206.

[Marcus and McDermott, 1988] Marcus, S. and McDermott, J., editors (1988). *Automating Knowledge Acquisition for Expert Systems*. Kluwer, Reading MA.

[McCarthy, 1956] McCarthy, J. (1956). The inversion of functions defined by Turing machines. *Automata Studies, Annals of Mathematical Studies*, 34:177 – 181.

[McDermott, 1988] McDermott, J. (1988). Preliminary steps towards a taxonomy of problem-solving methods. In Marcus, S., editor, *Automating Knowledge Acquisition for Expert Systems*, pages 225–255. Kluwer Academic Publishers, The Netherlands.

[Newell and Simon, 1972] Newell, A. and Simon, H. (1972). *Human Problem Soving*. Prentice Hall, Englewood Cliffs, NJ.

[O'Hara and Shadbolt, 1993] O'Hara, K. and Shadbolt, N. (1993). Locating generic tasks. *Knowledge Acquisition*, 5(4):449 – 481.

[Poeck and Gappa, 1993] Poeck, K. and Gappa, U. (1993). Making role-limiting shells more flexible. In Aussenac, N., Boy, G., Gaines, B., Linster, M., Ganascia, J., and Kodratoff, Y., editors, *Knowledge Acquisition for Knowledge Based Systems, Proceedings of the EKAW-93*, pages 103 – 122, Berlin. Springer.

[Schreiber et al., 1993] Schreiber, G., Wielinga, B., and Breuker, J. (1993). *KADS: a Principled Approach to Knowledge Engineering*. Academic Press, London.

[Sergot and Jones, 1992] Sergot, M. and Jones, A. (1992). Deontic Logic in the Representation of Law. *Artificial Intelligence and Law*, 1(1):45 — 64.

[Simmons, 1992] Simmons, R. (1992). The role of associational and causal reasoning in problem solving. *Artificial Intelligence*, 53(2–3):159–207.

[Steels, 1990] Steels, L. (1990). Components of expertise. *AI Magazine*, 11(2):28–49.

[Stefik, 1981] Stefik, M. (1981). Planning with constraints (MOLGEN: Part 1). *Artificial Intelligence*, 16:111 – 140.

[Sundin, 1994] Sundin, U. (1994). Assignment and scheduling. In Breuker, J. and de Velde, W. V., editors, *The CommonKADS Library for Expertise Modeling*. IOS-Press, Amsterdam.

[Valente, 1994] Valente, A. (1994). Modeling components for planning problems. In Breuker, J. and de Velde, W. V., editors, *The CommonKADS Library for Expertise Modeling*. IOS-Press, Amsterdam.

[Valente and Breuker, 1994] Valente, A. and Breuker, J. (1994). A commonsense theory about normative systems. In Breuker, J., editor, *Proceedings of the ECAI Workshop on Artificial Normative Systems*. ECAI.

[Valente et al., 1993] Valente, A., Breuker, J., and Bredeweg, B. (1993). Integrating modelling approaches in the Common KADS library. In Sloman, A., Hogg, D., Humphreys, G., Ramsay, A., and Partridge, D., editors, *Prospects for Artificial Intelligence, Proceedings of the AISB-93*, pages 121 – 130. IOS Press, Amsterdam.

[Valente and Löckhoff, 1994] Valente, A. and Löckhoff, C. (1994). Assessment. In Breuker, J. and de Velde, W. V., editors, *The CommonKADS Library for Expertise Modeling*. IOS-Press, Amsterdam.

[van Harmelen and Balder, 1993] van Harmelen, F. and Balder, J. (1993). ML^2: a formal language for KADS models of expertise. In Schreiber, G., Wielinga, B., and Breuker, J., editors, *KADS, a principled approach to knowledge based system development*, pages 169 – 201. Academic Press.

[Wielinga et al., 1993] Wielinga, B., de Velde, W. V., Schreiber, G., and Akkermans, H. (1993). Expertise model definition document. Esprit P5248 KADS-II/M2/UvA/026/1.1, University of Amsterdam. date May 24 1993.

On a Role of Problem Solving Methods in Knowledge Acquisition
– Experiments with Diagnostic Strategies –

Richard Benjamins

Laboratory of Integrated Systems
Escola Politécnica of the University of São Paulo (EPUSP)
Av. Prof. Luciano Gualberto 158 - trav. 3, 05508-900 São Paulo, Brazil
email: richard@lsi.usp.br, richard@swi.psy.uva.nl

Abstract. Libraries with re-usable knowledge components are becoming increasingly important in Knowledge Acquisition. We propose a library of problem solving methods for diagnosis and describe some experiments and results concerning the usefulness of such a library for constructing and analyzing diagnostic strategies. A key notion is that each problem solving method is associated with suitability criteria, which are exploited in the process.

1 Introduction

Modeling approaches for Knowledge Acquisition such as KADS [7], Component of Expertise [22], Generic Tasks [8], Spark, Burn, FireFigther [16], PROTÉGÉ-II [19] and Problem Solving Methods [17] stress the importance of libraries with reusable modeling components. A library is supposed to support the knowledge engineer in constructing the required model. Examples of library ingredients include domain models, generic tasks, inference structures, mechanisms, problem solving methods, task features, etc.

The aim of this paper is to explore the usefulness of a library of problem solving methods, each associated with applicability conditions, to construct and analyze reasoning strategies. Our task of interest is diagnosis. We present a library with 36 problem solving methods, which are originally described in [3]. We have implemented the library to enable experiments that answer questions such as: "given a certain strategy, what conditions should be satisfied to apply it successfully", and "given some characterization of the domain at hand, what are the possible strategies to solve diagnostic problems".

Modeling approaches to Knowledge Acquisition reside at the Knowledge Level [18]. Consequently, the diagnostic strategies we discuss in this paper are knowledge level strategies.

In Section 2 we define the diagnostic task. Section 3 defines relevant terms. In Section 4 the library with problem solving methods for diagnosis is presented, including suitability criteria. In Section 5 we describe four experiments, that use the program TINA, and in Section 6 we discuss their results. Section 7 relates this work to that of others. Section 8 concludes the paper.

2 Diagnosis

We view diagnosis as the task of identifying the cause of a fault that manifests itself through some observed behavior. In the work described here, diagnosis is conceived as consisting of three subtasks, namely 1) *symptom detection*: finding out whether the complaints are indeed symptoms, where a symptom is defined as an observation that deviates from its expectation, 2) *hypothesis generation*: based on the symptoms, generating possible causes that take into account the initial observations, and 3) *hypothesis discrimination*: discriminating between the generated hypotheses based on additional observations. This decomposition of the diagnosis task (which we refer to as the "prime diagnostic method" (PDM)) is motivated by the work of Davis and Hamscher [12], and further elaborated on in [3, 5]. The presented library contains problem solving methods that can realize these subtasks.

3 Terminology

The goal of this paper relates to the construction and analysis of strategies using a library. We define the terminology necessary for this goal including: task, primitive inference, problem solving method, strategy and suitability criterion.

Task. A task has a goal and is characterized by the type of input it gets and the type of output it produces. It is a specification of *what* needs to be achieved. For example, the goal of diagnosis is to find a solution that explains the initial and the additional observations. A task can be decomposed into subtasks.

Problem Solving Method. A problem solving method (method or PSM) defines a way *how* the goal of a task can be achieved. A method is associated with a goal that it is able to achieve, and has input and output roles[1] that define the roles that the domain concepts can play in the reasoning process. A method decomposes a task into subtasks and/or primitive inferences. In addition a method specifies the data flow (in terms of roles) and the control knowledge over its constituents. It is possible to describe a problem solving method *without* control knowledge, but then it refers to a *family* of methods [10, 27, 5]. Finally, a method has suitability criteria (see below).

Primitive Inference. A primitive inference (inference) defines an inference that can be carried out using domain knowledge to achieve a goal. An inference is associated with a goal that specifies the relation between its output and input. It has an inference body that specifies how the goal can be achieved using domain knowledge[2]. Inferences form the actual building blocks of a problem solver and they (partly) compose a strategy.

---

[1] A PSM only includes so-called *dynamic* roles of CommonKADS [27].

[2] The reference to the relevant domain knowledge is the equivalent of a *static* role in CommonKADS.

Relation between the concepts. Figure 1 illustrates the relations between tasks, methods and inferences, and is referred to as a task-method decomposition. It is a kind of tree, where a task may be realized by different methods (OR-relation) and a method consists of several subtasks or inferences. Actually the structure is a tangled hierarchy (referred to as "task-structure" in [10]) because the same inferences, tasks and methods can appear at several places (e.g. inference1 in Figure 1), which means that they are reusable. Note that the data flow and the control knowledge of the methods are not shown in the figure (they are not of central importance to this paper).

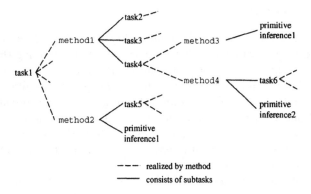

Fig. 1. The relations between tasks, methods and inferences. Dashed lines denote that methods are alternatives for realizing tasks. Solid lines decompose a method in subtasks and/or inferences.

Strategy. A strategy for solving a problem is constituted by 1) a particular configuration of inferences (the building blocks), and 2) control knowledge specifying the overall control over the inference configuration. Note that 1) resembles a KADS inference structure. A strategy can be constructed by recursively applying methods to tasks until all tasks are decomposed into primitive inferences. Because the PSMs have a control regime, so does the final structure of inferences: it is a combination of the control regimes of the methods involved. Consequently there are two ways to refer to a strategy: as a sequence of inferences or as a tree of methods, where the leaves represent the inferences. In this work, we present strategies as a method tree.

Suitability criterion. The relation between a PSM and domain knowledge is formed by so-called "suitability-criteria". They are reminiscent of task features [1], of the set of criteria for choosing alternative methods in [9], of the "sponsors" in TIPS [20], and of the applicability conditions in [26] (see Section 4.1).

4 A library of problem solving methods for diagnosis

The library we experiment with consists of PSMs with their suitability criteria, tasks and inferences. It is discussed in detail in [3, 5]. Because in this paper we are more concerned with the use of the library than with its content, we only explain those library components that are involved in the experiments (see Section 5). Table 1 shows the tasks, methods and inferences currently included in the library. The right column shows the subtasks and/or inferences of the methods (*inferences* appear in italics).

4.1 Suitability criteria

A suitability criterion represents the applicability of a method. It is a requirement reflecting features of a method, that are relevant for determining the method's appropriateness. Such features are local, meaning that they refer only to features of the method itself, and not to other methods. The locality of suitability criteria facilitates modularity and modification of the library. However, global knowledge (global relations, restrictions) between methods is also relevant for composing a strategy. In this paper we only deal with local criteria (but see Section 6).

We distinguish three types of criteria, corresponding to relevant categories of knowledge to consider in knowledge acquisition.

Epistemological criteria specify the type of domain knowledge that has to be available in order to make the PSM work. For example, a simulation method requires that the entities (e.g. components) in the device model have simulation rules (behavioral constraints) that relate inputs to outputs, such that behavioral consequences can be derived.

Environmental criteria refer to environmental requirements that have to be met before a PSM becomes applicable. For instance, a method for testing hypotheses by measuring, requires that the device is accessible for measurements, and that measuring tools are available.

Assumption criteria specify underlying assumptions of the method (e.g. the single fault or non intermittency assumption).

Table 2 gives an overview of the suitability criteria currently included in our library. The criteria are statements that should be true before a method can be applied to a task. For instance, the criterion "causal model" means that it has to be possible to construct a causal model. For explanation of the criteria see [3].

Organization of criteria. Analogue to the task-method decomposition, criteria can be hierarchically organized according to their generality. Lower level criteria are more specific versions of the higher level ones. Figure 2 shows an example of such an organization. The figure illustrates that the criteria "simulation rules", "inference rules" and "fault simulation rules" are more specific than the criterion "dependencies in model", which is more specific than the criterion "device model". Such an organization of criteria enables us to make the

Task, hierarchical level	Method (short names)	Subtasks and *Inferences*
diagnosis 1	prime diagnostic	{symptom detection, hypothesis generation, hypothesis discrimination}
symptom detection 2	compare classify ask user	{generate expectation, compare} {*classify*} {*ask user*}
generate expectation 3	lookup simulate	{*lookup*} {*simulate*}
compare 3	exact order of magnitude threshold teleological statistical historical	{*equal check*} {*determine-oom*, compare} {*determine ratio, check against threshold*} {*teleological abstract*, compare} {*statistical compare*} {*historical compare*}
hypothesis generation 2	model based- hypothesis generation empirical hypothesis- generation	{find contributors, transform to hypothesis set, prediction based filtering} {*associate*, *probability filter*}
find contributors 3	trace back causal covering prediction	{*find upstream*} {*causal covering*} {*simulate*}
transform to hypothesis set 3	set cover intersection subset minimality cardinality minimality	{*set cover*} {*intersect*} {*subset minimality cover*} {*cardinality minimality cover*}
prediction based filtering 3	constraint suspension corroboration fault simulation	{select hypothesis, *suspend constraint*, *simulate*, check consistency, *delete*} {select hypothesis, *simulate*, compare, *delete*} {select hypothesis, *select fault model*, *simulate*, compare, *delete*}
hypothesis discrimination 2	discrimination	{select hypothesis, collect data, interpret data}
hypothesis selection 3	random smart	{*select random*} {estimate cost hypothesis set, order hypothesis set, select first}
estimating the cost of testing the hypothesis set 4	based on local costs on the number of tests based on overall costs	{*estimate local cost*} {*estimate number of tests*} {*estimate overall cost*}
collect data 3	compiled test probing manipulating replacing	{*compiled test*} {*obtain*, generate expectation, compare} {*deduce input vector, simulate, obtain*, compare} {*replace hypothesis*, generate expectation, compare}
interpreting data 3	interpret in isolation split-half interpret model based- hypothesis generation	{*delete*} {*split hypothesis set*}

Table 1. An overview of tasks, problem solving methods and their constituents currently included in the library. The numbers (bold) denote the hierarchical level in the task decomposition. In the right column *primitive inferences* appear in *italics*.

Epistemological criteria	Environmental criteria
causal_model	components_easy_replaceable
component_hypotheses	components_replaceable
correct_device_model	device_accessible
cost_info	device_stable_in_time
dependencies_in_model	failure_rates_equal
device_model	(im)precise_values
empirical_associations	additional_observations
expected_value_database	many_initial_observations
expected_values_obtainable	measuring_points_reachable
fault_behavior_not_constrained	measuring_tools
fault_simulation_rules	net_fanout_structure
historical_info	reachability_equal
hypothesis_set_dependent	user_knowledgeable_symptoms
hypothesis_set_independent	**Assumption criteria**
inference_rules	complete_association_set
knowledge_about_teleology	complete_expected_value_database
knowledge_for_classifying_symptoms	complete_fault_model
local_cost_info	exhaustivity_assumption
probability_information	hypotheses_can_be_generated
simulation_rules	independence_of_hypotheses
statistical_info	no_fault_masking
tests_associated_to_hypotheses	non_intermittency_assumption
threshold_info	single_fault_assumption

Table 2. Overview of (local) suitability criteria of problem solving methods for diagnosis.

following deductions: if C_x is true and *more_specific*(C_x, C_y), then C_y is true, and if C_y is false then C_x is false. For example, if there are simulation rules, then we can derive that there are dependencies in the model. And, if there are no dependencies in the model, we can derive that there are also no simulation rules. The hierarchical organization is used to evaluate criteria concerning their truth value.

4.2 Representation of the library

The library is represented as a quadruple $< D, T, PI, PSM >$. T denotes the set of tasks relevant for diagnosis D. PI stands for the set of primitive inferences. PSM is the set of problem solving methods that decompose tasks into subtasks or inferences. Suitability criteria are defined for each method in PSM. D is the root from which strategies are generated. In terms of a grammar, D would be the start symbol, T the non-terminals, PI the terminals and PSM the rewrite rules.

We use the Definite Clause Grammar (DCG) of Prolog to represent our library.

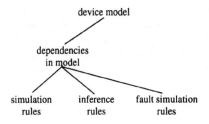

Fig. 2. Example organization of suitability criteria according to their generality.

% The prime diagnostic method for the diagnosis task
    diagnosis ⟶
            {criteria(prime_diagnostic_method)},
                symptom_detection,
                hypothesis_generation,
                hypothesis_discrimination.
% Methods for the symptom detection task
    symptom_detection ⟶
            {criteria(ask_user_method)},
                [user_judgment].
    symptom_detection ⟶
            {criteria(compare_symptom_detection_method)},
                generate_expectation,
                compare.
% Methods for the hypothesis generation task
    hypothesis_generation ⟶
            {criteria(empirical_hypothesis_generation_method)},
                [associate],
                [probability_filter].
    hypothesis_generation ⟶
            {criteria(model_based_hypothesis_generation_method)},
                find_contributors,
                transform_to_hypothesis_set,
                prediction_based_filtering.
% Method for the hypothesis discrimination task
    hypothesis_discrimination ⟶
            {criteria(hypothesis_discrimination_method)},
                select_hypothesis,
                collect_data,
                interpret_data.

Fig. 3. Some grammar rules of the library with diagnostic methods. The term at the left side of the arrow in a grammar rule represents a task. The right part of the arrow represents a method. It consists of a reference to the method's suitability criteria, and a set of subtasks and/or inferences. The [inferences] appear between squared brackets.

```
epistemological(model_based_hypothesis_generation_method, device_model).
epistemological(constraint_suspension_method, simulation_rules).
epistemological(constraint_suspension_method, inference_rules).
assumption(corroboration_method, no_fault_masking).
environmental(probing_method, device_accessible).
```

Fig. 4. Some examples of PSM suitability criteria indexed by their type.

Because DCG allows for normal Prolog code within the grammar, we can easily include the suitability criteria. Figure 3 shows some rewrite rules. In the actual implementation the grammar includes additional variables to build the method tree, but these are left out in the figure for clarity. The suitability criteria of the methods we have implemented separately from the grammar. Figure 4 shows some representations of suitability criteria.

5 Experiments with the library

We present some experiments that illustrate the usefulness of a library with problem solving methods and suitability criteria. In the following when we write requirements of a method, we mean the suitability criteria to be satisfied before the method is applicable.

Suitability criteria form the connection between a problem solving method and the application or problem domain. The former requires characteristics of the application domain while the latter can be described as having certain characteristics. In the real world they may be expressed in different terms depending on the point of view. For the sake of simplicity, in the experiments we will use the same terms for both, in particular the suitability criteria. That is, an application domain is described by characteristics using the terminology of suitability criteria. If some domain characteristic can not be expressed, this indicates the incompleteness of the criteria set. Following we illustrate how some domain characteristics can be expressed using criteria terms. The experiments should be read in a similar way.

A particular domain has certain characteristics. For example a camcorder (a video camera and recorder in one device) can be, among others, described by the following characteristics (we analyzed this device in the Dutch SKBS-A$_2$ project [4]). The device can be modeled in terms of its constituting components. Due the complexity of the behavior of the components it is difficult to construct a simulation model. However, dependencies between components can be specified. These characteristics can be expressed by the criteria "dependencies_in_model" (and thus also by "device_model", see Section 4.1), and "component_hypotheses" (the entities in the device model are components). Because there is no simulation model, expected values of outputs and measuring points are taken from a database, expressed by the statement "expected_value_database". A camcorder can be unfastened when additional observations are required, thus it has the characteristic "device_accessible". Measuring points are known ("measuring_points_reachable" and "local_cost_info") and suspected components can be replaced by correct ones ("components_replaceable"). Most of the observations are done with an oscilloscope ("measuring_tools") which presents a video-signal: a roughly defined pattern on the scope ("imprecise_values") which is correct or incorrect according to some threshold ("threshold_info"). Most of the faults turn out to be single faults ("single_fault_assumption").

We have implemented a small Prolog program called TINA[3], that consults the grammar and performs the experiments. The word "experiment" should be understood as a tentative to discover the possibilities of the library, rather than as a thorough way of testing the library.

Experiment 1 — Given a particular domain generate the applicable strategies. The aim of this experiment is to evaluate whether the library can generate reasonable diagnostic strategies given a particular domain. The domain of the camcorder can be described by the following characteristics (some of them are shortly explained at the right hand side, the others are described in the text):

```
EPISTEMOLOGICAL CHARACTERISTICS
    component_hypotheses
    cost_info                       :cost of testing hypotheses
    dependencies_in_model
    device_model
    hypothesis_set_dependent        :hypotheses are related to each other
    local_cost_info                 :e.g. reachability of measuring points
    threshold_info
ENVIRONMENTAL CHARACTERISTICS
    additional_observations
    components_replaceable
    device_accessible
    imprecise_values
    measuring_points_reachable
    measuring_tools
ASSUMPTIONS
    complete_expected_value_database
    hypotheses_can_be_generated     :all possible causes can be generated
    no_fault_masking
    non_intermittency_assumption
    single_fault_assumption
```

If we provide TINA with these domain characteristics it generates 4 possible strategies, that is, strategies whose criteria match the domain characteristics. The strategy illustrated below is shown as a method tree (containing only methods and inferences). The leaves of the tree represent the inferences that actually do the job, and they are generated by recursively applying methods. Notice that

---

[3] Whether **TinA** is an acronym for **T**ool **in A**cquisition or for **T**his **is** **n**ot **A**cquisition is left to the Knowledge Acquisition community.

substituting a method in a strategy with another method defines a new strategy. Variations of the strategy are shown at the right hand side. The cross product yields the 4 different strategies.

```
prime_diagnostic_method
    compare_symptom_detection_method
        lookup_method
          lookup
        threshold_compare_method
          determine_ratio
          check_against_threshold
    model_based_hypothesis_generation_method
        trace_back_method
          find_upstream
        intersection_method
          intersect
        corroboration_method
          select_random
          simulate_hypothesis
          compare
          delete
    hypothesis_discrimination_method
        smart_select_hypothesis_method
          estimation_based_on_overall_cost_method
            estimate_overall_cost
          order_hypothesis_set
          select_first
        probing_method          | replace_method
          obtain                |   replace_hypothesis
          generate_expectation  |   generate_expectation
          compare               |   compare
        spilt_interpret_method  | model_based_hypothesis_generation_method
          spilt_hypothesis_set  |   model_based_hypothesis_generation
```

The three subtasks of the PDM: symptom detection, hypothesis generation and hypothesis discrimination are respectively realized by the compare symptom detection method (CSDM), the model based hypothesis generation method (MB-HGM) and the hypothesis discrimination method (HDM). The CSDM compares expected values to initial observations. In the strategy above, expected values are obtained from a data base (the lookup method). The comparison is carried out by the threshold compare method, which considers two different values still "equal" as long as a certain threshold is respected (in the example a value is a scope signal). The method consists of the inferences determine ratio and check against threshold. The output of the CSDM is a statement whether the initial observations are normal or abnormal. The MBHGM consists of the subtasks find contributors, transform to hypothesis set and prediction based filtering. The find contributors task is carried out by the trace back method that consults the model representation and traces back the dependencies between the components (performed by the find upstream inference). When there are multiple contributor sets, they can be intersected under the single fault assumption by applying the intersection method. This yields a provisional hypothesis set, which is filtered using the corroboration method. For every component hypothesis the method performs a high level simulation to see whether the component is involved in a correct observation. If so, it is presumed innocent and deleted from the hypothesis set. The method assumes that no fault masking occurs. The HDM consists of three subtasks: select hypothesis, collect data and interpret data. To select a hypothesis the smart select method is applied. For every hypothesis, the cost is estimated of testing the hypothesis set based on overall costs (including reachability of measuring points and the expected number of tests to be performed), starting with that hypothesis. Based on these costs the set is ordered and the first is selected to collect additional data about. The probing method is used to collect data. It obtains an additional observation by asking the user to carry out a measurement. Regarding this observation an expected value is generated using the same lookup method as earlier in the strategy. The lookup method does not appear twice in the strategy, but we assume that if within one strategy a task is performed more than once, it will be realized by the same method. An alternative for the probing method is the replace method (shown at the right side of the probing method). Instead of carrying out a measurement, a suspected component is replaced with a correct one, and the result is observed. The criteria of both these methods are met. The interpret data task is performed by the split interpret method that splits the hypothesis set in two parts based on the test result. But it can also be performed by calling the MBHGM[4] again, but now with the additional observation unified with the initial observations.

Thus simply by providing TinA with the characteristics of the application domain (in terms of the suitability criteria), the library (grammar) generates applicable strategies. It is difficult to "prove" that the generated strategies are the best strategies. But we can demonstrate that some strategies *not* generated are not the best. For example, the generated strategy selects a hypothesis to be tested based on the *overall* cost of testing hypotheses and not on the *number* of expected tests. In diagnosis, hypothesis selection based on the number of expected tests only makes sense if the reachability of the measuring points and the failure rates of components are more or less equal. This is not the case in the camcorder.

TinA includes a so-called "aha erlebnis" feature that recognizes known strategies described in the literature, when generated. For this we have defined several known strategies in terms of the library components (see experiment 3).

Experiment 2 — Allow relaxation of some suitability criteria. In some cases it is possible that the requirements of the domain are too constraint, and no applicable strategy can be generated. To deal with such a situation we added to TinA the possibility to relax some criteria according to the knowledge engineer's

---

[4] In [15] it is correctly pointed out that this ignores the fact that the hypothesis set decreases monotonically.

insight. The relaxation strategy proposed here is rather naive and ad hoc, but experts should to be able to provide a more realistic one.

To continue the example of the camcorder, suppose we take the following domain characteristics away: "complete_expected_value_database" and "threshold_info" (implying that the lookup and the threshold compare method are not applicable anymore). If we now ask TINA to generate the applicable strategies it responds with "no strategies applicable in this situation". TINA can start the following dialogue with the knowledge engineer to relax some constraints.

```
How many methods of each strategy can have unfulfilled criteria?
(type a number or "dontcare".)
|: 3.


What criteria type might be relaxed?
1   epistemological
2   assumption
3   environmental
4   dontcare

Select option : 1.

How many failed epistemological criteria do you allow for each method?
Note that the other criteria types should be without problems!
(type a number or "dontcare".)
|: 3.
```

The first question ("How many methods ...") allows the knowledge engineer to specify that some methods that compose the strategy may have unsatisfied criteria (in this case 3). The next question asks which type of criterion might be relaxed. The reason behind this is that in some domains not all domain characteristics are unchangeable ("hard"). For instance, some assumptions might be relaxed, or domain knowledge that is not directly available could, with additional effort, be supplied. They are soft characteristics. Other characteristics might be inherent to the domain and can not be changed (often environmental characteristics). For example, if a device can not be unfastened, and therefore is not accessible for measurements, there is not much that can be done about it. It is a "hard" characteristic. TINA lets you choose one from three options that reflect the three different types of criteria. The not chosen ones are thus considered as hard characteristics. In the example, we chose to relax some epistemological requirements. The next question asks how many of them can be relaxed within *each* method (3 in the example).

TINA reports that under this relaxation 10 applicable strategies can be constructed. The output consists of two parts: the strategy itself (method tree) and the methods whose criteria are not completely satisfied. Among the 10 strategies suggested are (of course) the four strategies generated in experiment 1. For example, TINA generates the strategy shown in experiment 1 along with the following problem:

```
required(compare_symptom_detection_method,
  [epist([expected_values_obtainable])])
required(probing_method, [epist([expected_values_obtainable])])
required(threshold_compare_method, [epist([threshold_info])])
```

This means that the strategy of experiment 1 is applicable if extra domain knowledge ("expected_values_obtainable" and "threshold_info") can be provided. Expected values are needed to compare observations with their expectations. Note that the problem reported resides in "expected_values_obtainable", while we retracted the domain characteristic "complete_expected_value_database". However the latter is a more specific version of the former (see Section 4.1).

A slightly different strategy (from the one in experiment 1) suggested is that instead of the compare symptom detection method the classify method is applied. But then its epistemological requirements have to be taken care of. In this strategy 2 methods (3 were allowed) have each 1 epistemological criterion not fulfilled (maximum was 3). It is up to the knowledge engineer to decide whether this knowledge can be supplied or not.

```
required(classify_method, [epist([knowledge_for_classifying_symptoms])])
required(probing_method, [epist([expected_values_obtainable])])
```

The first two experiments take as starting point a characterization of a specific domain and suggested applicable strategies. The next two experiments deal with the opposite situation: it starts with a strategy, analyzes it and generates requirements.

Experiment 3 — Provide a strategy and obtain the corresponding requirements. Another knowledge acquisition situation could be that there exists an idea of what strategy to use to solve a diagnostic problem. TINA can then be used to generate the requirements of the supplied strategy. It is up to the knowledge engineer to see whether they can be met. The given strategy has to be a legal one according to the grammar.

Using the methods, tasks and inferences from the library we have modeled several strategies described in the literature (see [3]), such as DART [14], GDE/GDE+ [13, 23], CHECK [11], FAULTY [4]. Note that the same strategies are exploited in the "aha erlebnis" feature. As an example of a well known strategy, we input a combination of GDE/GDE+ and show the requirements generated. The strategy is shown below in a method tree.

```
prime_diagnostic_method
    compare_symptom_detection_method
        simulate_method
          simulate
        exact_compare_method
          equal_check
    model_based_hypothesis_generation_method
        prediction_based_method
```

```
      simulate
    subset_minimality_transform_method
      subset_minimality_cover
    fault_simulation_method
      select_random
      select_fault_model
      simulate_hypothesis
      compare
      delete
hypothesis_discrimination_method
    smart_select_hypothesis_method
      estimation_based_on_overall_cost_method
        estimate_overall_cost
      order_hypothesis_set
      select_first
    probing_method
      obtain
      generate_expectation
      compare
    model_based_hypothesis_generation_method
      model_based_hypothesis_generation
```

For symptom detection the CSDM is used, which consists of the simulation method and the exact compare method. For generating hypotheses, GDE uses the MBHGM consisting of the prediction method for finding contributors, the subset minimality cover method for transforming the contributor sets to a hypothesis set[5], and the fault simulation method for filtering the hypothesis set (GDE+). To realize the hypothesis discrimination task GDE applies the following methods. It selects a hypothesis to test based on an estimation of the overall cost (number of tests and failure rates) using the notion of minimal entropy. The probing method is used to collect additional data about the hypothesis. To interpret the data, the MBHGM is used again, which means that the collected data are processed in the same manner as the initial data.

TINA generates the following requirements for the strategy. The first argument of "required" is the method name, the second a list with its requirements. This list is divided in at most three parts representing epistemological, assumption and environmental requirements.

```
Required criteria:
required(prime_diagnostic_method,
  [assum([hypotheses_can_be_generated]),
   envir([additional_observations])])
required(compare_symptom_detection_method,
  [epist([expected_values_obtainable])])
required(simulate_method, [epist([simulation_rules])])
required(exact_compare_method, [envir([precise_values])])
```

---

[5] This means that a hypothesis should not have an empty intersection with any of the contributor sets, and that there is no other valid hypothesis which is a subset of it.

```
required(model_based_hypothesis_generation_method,
  [epist([device_model]), assum([non_intermittency_assumption])])
required(prediction_based_method, [epist([simulation_rules])])
required(subset_minimality_transform_method,
  [epist([fault_behavior_not_constrained]),
   assum([independence_of_hypotheses])])
required(fault_simulation_method,
  [epist([fault_simulation_rules]), assum([complete_fault_model])])
required(hypothesis_discrimination_method,
  [assum([non_intermittency_assumption])])
required(smart_select_hypothesis_method, [epist([cost_info])])
required(estimation_based_on_overall_cost_method,
  [epist([hypothesis_set_dependent]), envir([cost_info])])
required(probing_method, [epist([expected_values_obtainable]),
                          envir([device_accessible, measuring_tools])])
required(model_based_hypothesis_generation_method,
  [epist([device_model]), assum([non_intermittency_assumption])])
```

We shortly explain some of the requirements. The PDM assumes that hypotheses can be generated, or more precise, there should be no hypothesis that would be considered as a possible cause, while it can not be generated by the hypothesis generator. An environmental requirement is that it has to be possible to obtain additional observations. In order to select a next measurement GDE minimizes the overall cost of the tests to perform. This requires that the hypotheses in the set are dependent on each other and that cost information is available (third "requirement" from the bottom).

Experiment 4 — Provide a partial strategy and obtain its possible completions along with the requirements. This experiment is an extension of the previous one, but here the knowledge engineer has only an idea about parts of the strategy to solve the problem. Instead of providing TinA with a complete strategy, a partial strategy can be given. Partial in the sense that the major part of the strategy is known (in terms of inferences), but some inferences are unspecified. This is a strong version of top-down acquisition, because the completion of the strategy is strongly guided by what already has been specified so far. It has also a bottom-up part because the criteria of the completing method(s) have to be satisfied.

In the partial (simple) strategy shown below there are two unspecified inferences (in the place of the hypothesis generation task). If we feed this partial strategy to TinA, it suggests to complete it with the empirical method for generating hypothesis. The restriction for a method to be applicable (apart from its suitability criteria) is that the number of inferences that constitute the possible completing method(s) must be equal to the number of unspecified inferences (2 in this case).

```
user_judgment
UNSPECIFIED_INFERENCE1
UNSPECIFIED_INFERENCE2
select_random
compiled_test
delete
```

Here is what TINA generates (the completions are marked with *):

```
prime_diagnostic_method
    ask_user_method
        user_judgment
    empirical_hypothesis_generation_method*
        associate*
        probability_filter*
    hypothesis_discrimination_method
        random_select_hypothesis_method
          select_random
        compiled_test_method
          compiled_test
        interpret_in_isolation_method
          delete
```

```
Required criteria:
required(prime_diagnostic_method,
  [assum([hypotheses_can_be_generated]),
   envir([additional_observations])])
required(ask_user_method, [envir([user_knowledgeable_symptoms])])
required(empirical_hypothesis_generation_method,
  [epist([empirical_associations, probability_information]),
   assum([complete_association_set])])
required(hypothesis_discrimination_method,
  [assum([non_intermittency_assumption])])
required(random_select_hypothesis_method,
  [epist([hypothesis_set_independent])])
required(compiled_test_method, [epist([tests_associated_to_hypotheses])])
required(interpret_in_isolation_method,
  [epist([hypothesis_set_independent])])
```

TINA finds thus a legal completion of the partial strategy along with the requirements to be met. This experiment deals with a very simple strategy. The user is asked to decide on the (ab)normality of the initial observations. These are associated to hypotheses (empirical method) yielding a hypothesis set. This set is exhaustively tested by the compiled test method, where a test is explicitly associated to each hypothesis. Test results are interpreted in isolation, that is, not considering the impact of the result on other hypotheses. This makes sense if the hypotheses in the set are unrelated to one another.

Depending on the number of inferences not specified, TINA generates many or few strategies. In this experiment 2 of 6 inferences were unspecified. In another experiment we supplied TINA with a more complex partial strategy consisting of 17 inferences, leaving unspecified 6 of them. 8 possible completions were generated.

6 Discussion

With the 4 experiments we have demonstrated that the library is useful in various ways for constructing and analyzing diagnostic strategies. Of course, the "goodness" of a strategy depends on the quality of the library components, in particular on the methods and the criteria. We do not claim that the library presented here is complete. For instance, Case-based and Bayesian approaches to diagnosis are not considered. However, we do claim that the library covers most strategies used in the mainstream approaches to diagnose faults in technical devices and some strategies in the medical domain [5]. With respect to the completeness of the suitability criteria set we have to be more cautious. This is a rather new area and more research is needed.

Generation versus analysis of strategies. The power of the current library lies in 1) generating strategies in restricted domains, 2) analyzing strategies and generating their domain requirements, and 3) completion of partial strategies. It lies not in the generation of all strategies that one could think of. In principle the grammar could be used to generate an infinite number of strategies because of its recursive nature. In the implemented grammar we took some recursion away. Still, the grammar generates 32928 different strategies, not considering the criteria of the methods. With only the most common methods to compare observations with expected values (2 instead of 6), the amount of possibilities is reduced to 10656. Even if we could generate strategies assuming that all criteria of all methods are satisfied, many strategies (a large part of which uninteresting) would be generated. However, some criteria are contradictory to each other (they can not be true at the same time), therefore a statement about the number of possible strategies, assuming all criteria are satisfied, is not possible: strategies are related to domains (see later).

For experimenting with the generation of strategies, the library would need to include knowledge about global constraints and relations between the methods. Such constraints limit the number of possible combinations of methods and thus the number of strategies. Global constraints should be represented separately from the grammar, in another part of the library. An example of a global relation is: if the simulate method is used to generate expectations as part of the symptom detection task, then the find contributors task should also use the simulate method. Once global relations are included, less strategies will be generated and it would be interesting to analyze them in detail.

Underlying assumption. If in a particular strategy different methods use different domain models, there is an underlying assumption that the different domain models are compatible with each other. For example, to combine a method that uses a causal model with a method that reasons with a component model requires that these models "know" about each other's content. Often this is not an optimal situation because once a certain domain model is constructed (which can be quite a difficult task), preferably this model is used in as much methods as possible. This problem could be dealt with by adding a general global constraint which states that methods should as much as possible use the same domain model. However, in some diagnostic domains the use of multiple domain models might be a necessary feature (e.g. when reasoning in one model leads easily to an impasse [2]).

Top-down versus bottom-up acquisition. Using the library for strategy analysis construction combines top-down and bottom-up acquisition. Top-down acquisition analyzes a strategy and generates its requirements, while bottom-up works from domain characteristics to strategies. As the experiments show there are variations possible moving the emphasis towards bottom-up (experiment 1 and 2) or towards top-down (experiment 3 and 4).

Generalizing from the experimental results. What do the experimental results mean in general for constructing diagnostic strategies with a library? Let L be the library. C_D denotes the set of characteristics (in terms of the suitability criteria) that defines an application domain D. The set S_D represents all strategies that are applicable in D. We could write this as $L(C_D) = S_D$. The applicable strategies are a function of the domain characteristics, where the function is defined by the library. If we could define typical problem domains D in terms of their characteristics C, then we could generate the sets of applicable strategies S_D in D using the library L. This would be a valuable extension to the library for diagnosis, because *clusters* of strategies can be represented for *types* of domains. We have made a first attempt to define some typical domains including empirical, medical, simple technical and complex technical domains (thus: $C_{empirical}$, $C_{technical}$, etc.). L then defines the generative relation between C_D and S_D, thus for example $L(C_{empirical}) = S_{empirical}$. The quality of such relations, however, depends on the completeness and correctness of the library (i.e. the PSMs and the sets of suitability criteria). Since these can not yet be guaranteed, it is too early to make such general conclusions. However it indicates an interesting direction for further work.

Possible extensions of TINA. TINA exploits some possibilities of the library represented in the grammar. Extensions are however possible.

If one is willing to represent some meta-knowledge about primitive inferences or tasks in the library, some interesting features could be realized. For instance, if we include knowledge about which inferences interact with the user (e.g. so-called "transfer tasks" in KADS [21]), then we could generate strategies that minimize on user interaction. In diagnostic applications this is important because getting information (e.g. provide the diagnostic system with more observations) can be a cost determining factor.

In this paper we distinguished between three types of criteria: epistemological, environmental and assumption. Another (orthogonal) dimension for characterizing suitability criteria reflects their strictness: necessary or useful [3]. We have only considered necessary criteria which refer to knowledge, without which a method cannot work. "Useful" criteria on the other hand, refer to knowledge that hints at the *rate* of applicability of the method. If such criteria are considered in the process of generating strategies, the result would not only be a set of possible strategies, but an ordered set based on their rate of applicability.

7   Related work

Considering tasks and subtasks in terms of a grammar is not a new idea. It is among others applied in KEW [25]. There the construction of a strategy is depicted as a gradual refinement process where the knowledge engineer interactively decides which rewrite rule to apply next, thereby considering the conditions of each rewrite rule (and possibly acquiring the domain knowledge). The result of a KEW session is one particular "inference structure" that satisfies the constraints at hand. We have implemented our library in the KEW formalism [3] and it supports the construction of diagnostic strategies. The difference with TinA is, that TinA can work in two directions: generation and analysis. Moreover it generates not one strategy, but all of them. It is then up to the knowledge engineer to select the most suitable.

Our library of problem solving methods could be considered as constituting part of the CommonKADS library[6] [24]. Using CommonKADS terms, our library represents one *basic task* (function), namely diagnosis. It presents so-called *complete* methods that can be applied to the diagnosis task. Complete methods in CommonKADS are a combination of expansion methods (that decompose a task in subtasks) and control methods, that specify control knowledge.

8   Conclusions

In this paper we present a library with reusable diagnostic components. The major part of the library is constituted by problem solving methods. We show some ways of how the library can be used in Knowledge Acquisition by exploiting so-called suitability criteria of methods. In particular we demonstrate the following possibilities. 1) Given a particular domain generate the applicable strategies. 2) In case no applicable strategies can be found, allow relaxation of some suitability criteria and generate the legal strategies along with their not fulfilled criteria. 3) Given a particular strategy, obtain the corresponding requirements. 4) Given a partial strategy, obtain its possible completions along with the requirements. The quality of the strategies and of the requirements generated, depends on the correctness and completeness of the methods and the suitability criteria. These can not yet be guaranteed, but strategies described in the main

---

[6] Some of the reasons why actually it is not, are outlined in [15, 6]. I agree with most objectives in [15], but only with some in [6]. Some modifications of our library are pointed out in [5].

stream approaches to technical diagnosis, are covered [5]. More research has to be conducted to assure reasonable completeness of the suitability criteria.

There is another application of the library, not so much concerned with knowledge acquisition as well with flexible (dynamic) reasoning. Instead of constructing one particular strategy, and implement that one in a diagnostic system, one could let the diagnostic system itself choose the best applicable method *on the fly*. Such diagnostic systems manifest fine tuned and more robust behavior, however at the expense of efficiency (computational overhead to select the best method for realizing tasks). This line of library use is discussed in [3, 10, 20, 26].

Finally, the approach should not only work for diagnosis, but for any tasks for which a library can be constructed. This is exactly the claim of modeling approaches to Knowledge Acquisition.

Acknowledgement

This paper has partly been written as a response to a question of Luc Steels (VUB) while I was defending my Ph.D. thesis. Ameen Abu-Hanna, Wouter Jansweijer and Leliane Nunes de Barros are acknowledged for their contribution. The work has been supported by the Dutch SKBS-A$_2$ project (performed at SWI/UVA) and by a scholarship of the Brazilian government (CNPq - RHAE nr. 610145193).

References

1. A. Aamodt, B. Benus, C. Duursma, C. Tomlinson, R. Schrooten, and W. Van de Velde. Task features and their use in commonkads. Technical Report KADS-II/T1.5/VUB/TR/014/1.0, Free University of Brussels & University of Amsterdam & Lloyd's Register, 1992.

2. A. Abu-Hanna. *Multiple domain models in diagnostic reasoning.* PhD thesis, University of Amsterdam, Amsterdam, 1994.

3. V. R. Benjamins. *Problem Solving Methods for Diagnosis.* PhD thesis, University of Amsterdam, Amsterdam, The Netherlands, June 1993.

4. V. R. Benjamins and A. Abu-Hanna. FAULTY: A shell for diagnosing complex technical systems. Technical Report SKBS/A2/90-1, SWI, University of Amsterdam, Amsterdam, 1990.

5. V. R. Benjamins and W. N. H. Jansweijer. Towards a competence theory of diagnosis. *IEEE-Expert*, 9(4), august 1994.

6. B. Bredeweg. Model-based diagnosis and prediction of behaviour. Technical Report KADS-II/M2/UvA/1.0, SWI, University of Amsterdam, Amsterdam, 1994.

7. J. A. Breuker, B. J. Wielinga, M. van Someren, R. de Hoog, A. Th. Schreiber, P. de Greef, B. Bredeweg, J. Wielemaker, J. P. Billault, M. Davoodi, and S. A. Hayward. Model Driven Knowledge Acquisition: Interpretation Models. ESPRIT Project P1098 Deliverable D1 (task A1), University of Amsterdam and STL Ltd, 1987.

8. B. Chandrasekaran. Generic tasks as building blocks for knowledge-based systems: The diagnosis and routine design examples. *The Knowledge Engineering Review*, 3(3):183–210, 1988.

9. B. Chandrasekaran. Design problem solving: A task analysis. *AI Magazine*, 11:59–71, 1990.

10. B. Chandrasekaran, T. R. Johnson, and J. W. Smith. Task-structure analysis for knowledge modeling. *Communications of the ACM*, 35(9):124–137, 1992.

11. L. Console and P. Torasso. Hypothetical reasoning in causal models. *Int. J. of Intelligent Systems*, 5(1):83–124, 1990.

12. R. Davis and W. C. Hamscher. Model-based reasoning: Troubleshooting. In H. E. Shrobe, editor, *Exploring Artificial Intelligence*, pages 297–346. Morgan Kaufmann, San Mateo, California, 1988.

13. J.H. de Kleer and B.C. Williams. Diagnosing multiple faults. *Artificial Intelligence*, 32:97–130, 1987.

14. M. R. Genesereth. The use of design descriptions in automated diagnosis. *Artificial Intelligence*, 24:411–436, 1984.

15. K. Orsvärn. Towards problem solving methods for sequential diagnosis. Technical Report KADS-II/M2.3/TR/SICS/001/1.0, SICS, 1994.

16. G. Klinker, C. Bhola, G. Dallemagne, D. Marques, and J. McDermott. Usable and reusable programming constructs. *Knowledge Acquisition*, 3:117–136, 1991.

17. J. McDermott. Preliminary steps towards a taxonomy of problem-solving methods. In S. Marcus, editor, *Automating Knowledge Acquisition for Expert Systems*, pages 225–255. Kluwer, Boston, 1988.

18. A. Newell. The knowledge level. *Artificial Intelligence*, 18:87–127, 1982.

19. A. Puerta, J. Egar, S. W. Tu, and M. A. Musen. A multiple-method knowledge-acquisition shell for the automatic generation of knowledge-acquisition tools. In *Proc. 6th Banff Knowledge Acquisition Workshop*, pages 20.1–19, Canada, 1991. SRDG Publications, University of Calgary.

20. W.F. Punch. *A Diagnosis System Using a Task Integrated Problem Solver Architecture (TIPS), Including Causal Reasoning.* PhD thesis, The Ohio State University, Ohio, 1989.

21. A. Th. Schreiber, B. J. Wielinga, and J. A. Breuker, editors. *KADS: A Principled Approach to Knowledge-Based System Development*, volume 11 of *Knowledge-Based Systems Book Series.* Academic Press, London, 1993.

22. L. Steels. Components of expertise. *AI Magazine*, Summer 1990.

23. P. Struss and O. Dressler. Physical negation – integrating fault models into the general diagnostic engine. In *Proc 11th. IJCAI*, pages 1318–1323, Detroit, 1989.

24. A. Valente, B. Bredeweg, J. Breuker, and W. van de Velde. A library of re-usable knowledge models and components. In *Proc. of the Conference of the Brazilian Computing Society*, Florianópolis, august 1993.

25. G. van Heijst, P. Terpstra, B. J. Wielinga, and N. Shadbolt. Using generalised directive models in knowledge acquisition. In Th. Wetter, K. D. Althoff, J. Boose, B. Gaines, M. Linster, and F. Schmalhofer, editors, *Current Developments in Knowledge Acquisition: EKAW-92*, Berlin, Germany, 1992. Springer-Verlag.

26. J. Vanwelkenhuysen and P. Rademakers. Mapping knowledge-level analysis onto a computational framework. In L. Aiello, editor, *Proc. ECAI-90*, pages 681–686, London, 1990. Pitman.

27. B. J. Wielinga, W. Van de Velde, A. Th. Schreiber, and J. M. Akkermans. The Common KADS framework for knowledge modelling. In B. R. Gaines, M. A. Musen, and J. H. Boose, editors, *Proc. 7th Banff Knowledge Acquisition Workshop*, volume 2, pages 31.1–31.29. SRDG Publications, University of Calgary, Alberta, Canada, 1992.

Modeling Plan Recognition for Decision Support

Dolores Cañamero

CNRS-LRI
Université Paris-Sud, Bât. 490
91405 Orsay Cedex, France
lola@lri.lri.fr

Abstract. Plan recognition consists of building an interpretation of an observed behavior in terms of the plans and goals that can be attributed to an agent. It can be thus considered as a form of understanding. Plan recognition is often compared with planning—they are considered as opposite processes according to two criteria: the mechanism employed to reach the solution—selection or construction—and the knowledge involved in both forms of plan reasoning. On these grounds, plan recognition has often been considered as an ill-defined "understanding task", different from problem solving. Also, while knowledge-level models of planning can be found in the literature, the main modeling approaches have made no attempt to rationalize plan recognition. In this paper, plan recognition is analyzed as problem solving behavior, and an interpretation model for this task is proposed. The situation considered is one of keyhole recognition from low-level data in a dynamic environment, with the aim of providing decision support in a critical domain.

1 Introduction

Plan recognition can be broadly defined as the interpretation by an observer of another agent's behavior. This interpretation comes generally in the form of a set of plausible goals and plans that the observer attributes to the agent on the grounds of some observed actions and previous knowledge. Many factors can affect the plan recognition situation, such as the features of the environment (static, dynamic, etc.), the relationship between the observer and the agent (e.g., degree of cooperation to the recognition on the part of this latter, previous knowledge that the observer has about the agent), the type of interaction the observer has with the environment (e.g., easy or difficult, direct or indirect access to data). In the plan recognition situation considered in this paper, the agent behaves in a dynamic environment. It is unaware of being observed, and so the result of the observations do not affect its actions. The observer has a very limited interaction with the environment—she can only observe, and has no possibility to act upon it. Moreover, the observability conditions are also very restricted—she sees the agent as if through a keyhole, and only gets punctual and not completely reliable information, like snapshots of the behavior. To make things worse, the observer knows nothing about the agent, that is to her as a 'black box'. In this situation, the best the observer can do in order to understand what the agent is doing is to think that the agent "knows what it is doing". In other words, the observer assumes that the agent is acting that way because of some reason, because it has thought about the problem situation, and because it knows that, in that specific situation, that course of actions will lead to the accomplishment of the searched goal. It is thus assuming that the agent's behavior is both rational and practical. This way, the observer will be able to make sense out of the sparse information she can get, i.e., she will be able to build an interpretation, a model of the situation. What the observer is doing is to consider the agent "at the knowledge level" [13]. A knowledge-level account (from the observer's point of view) of plan recognition seems thus a quite adequate description of this problem-solving behavior. Analyzing plan recognition from a knowledge-level perspective is the topic of this paper.

In Sect. 2, the nature of the plan recognition problem solving task is investigated from a general perspective. In Sect. 3, the specific circumstances of the plan recognition task—the 'task features'—and the plan recognition system considered in this analysis are detailed. In Sect. 4 a knowledge-level model of the problem solving behavior involved in this task—an interpretation model in the sense of the KADS methodology—is outlined. Section 5 draws some conclusions.

2 The Plan Recognition Problem

2.1 Plan Recognition versus Planning

Plan recognition is often opposed to planning. This opposition can be summarized in two types of arguments: the nature of the solution—whether it is constructed or selected—and the knowledge involved in both reasoning processes.

On the one hand, plan recognition and planning are opposed on the grounds of the type of mechanism employed to reach the solution—construction or selection. Planning is usually considered as a construction problem, while the solution to a plan recognition problem is supposed to be selected out of a set of predefined possibilities (plans). This opposition is a simplification which only holds in some cases, since construction and classification are to be seen as two extremes of a spectrum of problem-solving methods, and most problem solving behavior occurs between those extremes [7, 20]. In fact, planning may involve classification as well as construction. When a predefined set of plans is available that describe how to achieve a predefined set of goals, and the goal being pursued belongs to that set, planning is trivially reduced to selecting the adequate plan. On the contrary, if such predefined sets are not available, the solution to the planning problem must be constructed. The same holds for plan recognition. For example, in Mooney's system GENESIS [12], two types of techniques are used for plan recognition. Schemata already incorporated into the system allow to interpret events in a text—schema-based understanding—whereas plan-based understanding is used to construct a new schema when none of the existing ones can be applied. The choice between construction and classification will rely on the amount of expert knowledge available in the domain. The type of plan recognition considered in this paper proceeds through classification, as a library of prototypical plans—reflecting the standard behavior of an agent in some given circumstances—are used to interpret the actual agent's behavior.

Plan recognition and planning are also considered as inverse processes which involve the opposite in terms of what is known and what must be computed [25, 26]. Planning involves assessing a situation, deciding what goals to pursue, creating plans to obtain these goals, and eventually executing those plans. On the contrary, recognizing the behavior of an agent implies finding an interpretation that makes sense out of some available information. More precisely, it involves inferring the goals, plans, and (in some cases) actions of the agent in a given situation from available evidence, and relating these elements to each other. On the grounds of this opposition, the AI literature has usually given a different status to both plan reasoning activities. While planning is seen as a problem-solving task, plan recognition is often considered as an "understanding task", which may be a relative of problem solving but that is not entailed by, nor dependent upon it [25]. As pointed out by Hoc [11], this opposition is very common in natural language comprehension, where it is stressed that:

- In *problem solving*, the agent knows the goals to be reached and must find the sequence of actions that should be accomplished to attain these goals.
- In *story understanding*, procedural knowledge—what the actors do—is the only information available to the reader, who must infer the declarative knowledge involved in the story— the goals pursued by the actors and justifications of their actions.

In this view, problem solving is limited to the process of taking actions to attain goals. This corresponds to the view of Newell in his theory of the knowledge level [13]. However, broader definitions of problem solving can be found in the literature that allow to include understanding— and more specifically, plan recognition—within problem solving. Van de Velde [21], lists three ways of viewing problem solving besides Newell's: (1) as an input-output process, (e.g., the KADS methodology [4]); (2) as a process of model transformation (e.g., the Componential Methodology [18]); and (3) as the 'creation' of a suitable case model (van de Velde's own approach). Let us consider the input-output approach applied to both planning and plan recognition. A general characterization of both types of problems is given in [23]. A classical **planning problem** typically has the following form:

GIVEN (a) a set of goals, (b) a set of allowable actions, and (c) a planning environment—a description of the world in which the plan is to be executed (initial state),

FIND a sequence of actions that will bring about a state of affairs in which all of the desired goals are satisfied.

A typical **plan recognition problem** consists of the following elements: (a) a set of allowable actions, (b) a set of observed actions, and (c) a plan recognition environment—description of the world in which the observed actions are performed. The goal of plan recognition is to find an interpretation that explains the observed actions. A *solution* to this problem includes some of the following elements: (a) a set of expected goals; (b) a library of typical plans; (c) a preference ordering over the space of plans.

While the reasoning process leading from a planning problem to its solution has been widely analyzed by the main modeling approaches to knowledge engineering (e.g., [4, 18]), these methodologies have paid no attention to the plan recognition reasoning process. In this paper I examine in which sense plan recognition is a problem solving activity (Sect. 2.2) and analyze the reasoning involved in this process in terms of a knowledge-level model (Sect. 4).

2.2 Plan Recognition Problem Solving

The goal of plan recognition is to find an interpretation that explains a observed set of actions. This corresponds to what understanding a situation means—building an interpretation of that situation. Plan recognition is thus a form of understanding. Several ways of building such an interpretation, which correspond to various meanings of the word "understanding", have been distinguished in cognitive psychology [15], namely

- Construction of a interpretation by particularization of a schema;
- Construction of a conceptual structure giving rise to a network of relations;
- Construction of a particular model of the situation from general information, giving rise to a mental picture of the situation; and
- Construction of an interpretation by analogy with a known situation.

The plan recognition task considered in this paper fits within the first sense of understanding—an interpretation of the observed behavior is built by particularizing one or several schemata (*XPlans*; see below, Sect. 3) out of a predefined library. This particularization serves two purposes: (1) it provides an interpretation of the observed evidence by relating it to a general framework, which also allows to infer missing pieces of information and to predict the agent's future behavior; (2) it provides a general meaning that groups together several pieces of information (e.g., if it has been observed that a car has gone to the left lane, has accelerated until driven past a car situated on the right lane, and has gone back to the right lane, I can summarize all this information by saying that the car has overtaken another car). Particularization allows the observer to construct a model of the situation every time a new observation is input to the system—the model is updated as new data arrive and are interpreted. The way this model is built is the object of Sect. 4.

This problem solving behavior corresponds to the view of problem solving as the construction of a suitable (case) model of the situation, which "at every moment during problem solving summarizes the agent's understanding of the problem, and allows it to eventually conclude that the goal has been reached" [21, page 220].

Another main feature of plan recognition—and in general of understanding—is its purposive[1] nature: not only it relies on the construction of an interpretation or model of the situation, but the construction of this model is guided by an external purpose. This purpose imposes constraints on the form and the content of the interpretation. In our case, the purpose for which the interpretation is built is providing decision support in critical domains, as explained in next section.

2.3 Plan Recognition for Explanation-Based Decision Support

The decision making situation the user of the plan recognition system is faced with is an example of what has been called the explanation-based decision making model [14]. In this framework, a typical decision-making problem presents the following features: (1) a massive amount of evidence is found; (2) evidence comes in a scrambled order; (3) the evidence is fragmentary and there are numerous gaps in its depiction of the actual behavior—data are incomplete, some critical events may have not been observed, and information about the agent's motivations is missing; and (4) subparts of the evidence are meaningless by themselves—the meaning of a piece of evidence depends on the meanings of related pieces of evidence. A decision maker reasons about evidence in order to build an intermediate representation of the evidence—a "story"—that makes sense out of it. This intermediate representation is an interpretation of the original evidence, and will constitute the basis of the final decision, rather than the original "raw" evidence. Using this interpretation "facilitates evidence comprehension, directs inferencing, enables the decision maker to reach the decision, and contributes substantially to the confidence assigned to the accuracy or success of the decision" [14, pages 124–125]. The role of our plan recognition system is to assist the decision maker by providing her with advice in the form of this intermediate interpretation that proposes a way of making sense out of the raw evidence, and hence will serve as a basis for her decisions.

The decision process can be further decomposed into three sub-processes: (1) constructing a causal explanation that accounts for the available evidence in the form of a "story"; (2) looking for a set of alternatives that could likewise explain the evidence; (3) reaching a decision through the classification of the "story" into the best-fitting alternative. In providing decision support, the plan recognition system covers subtasks 1 and 2. The advice (interpretation of the evidence) proposed to the user allows her to build a "story" that accounts for what the observed agent is trying to do. If several alternative interpretations are found, they will be ordered according to their degree of plausibility and presented to the decision maker. The decision (subtask 3) is left to the user, who will try to optimize the choice between alternatives.

---

[1] My translation of the French term *"activité finalisée"*, as defined in [11, 15].

3 Plan Recognition Based on XPlans

3.1 Plan Recognition for C^3I

The plan recognition system used in this analysis [3] has been designed in the context of Command, Control, Communication, and Intelligence (C^3I). This system is a module to be integrated in the MATIS[2] model [2]. MATIS is designed to provide support for military decision in critical or difficult situations, within the context of C^3I. However, it can be of use in all civilian contexts in which decision making becomes difficult. It covers a comprehensive range of tasks, from the processing of basic raw data (generally numeric) to the handling of "knowledge objects", i.e., elements which carry some direct relevance for the decision maker. Its architecture (Fig. 1) consists of several interpretation layers, with very little feedback among them[3].

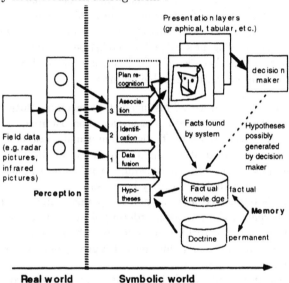

Fig. 1. MATIS architecture and knowledge processing. The plan recognition system can be seen as a fourth layer in this architecture. Feedback occurs only through factual knowledge

Initially, some hypotheses[4] are used to somehow anticipate the situation by taking into account some knowledge stored in the memory of the system. This

---

[2] MATIS: *Modèle d'Aide à la décision par le Traitement de l'Information Symbolique.*

[3] There is deliberately no feedback from the symbolic to the numeric level, nor from a given semantic level to a lower one. Consequently, the acquisition of data cannot be controlled from the higher level (e.g., by reorganizing the sensors or focusing on a particular area of observation), and the relevance of information increases along the process. This imposes more robustness on the higher modules to be able to achieve acceptable recognition in spite of uncertain, missing, and wrong data.

[4] There is no need for these hypotheses to be exact at first, since they are mainly used to initialize the model, and they will be changed according to the situation as perceived by the upper layers.

knowledge consists of facts already known about the situation, which are confirmed by the doctrine. These hypotheses can be seen as a layer previous to MATIS *interpretation layers*. The first layer is a perceptual system made of a number of sensor families which track various physical parameters. It performs data fusion on basic data observed by the sensors—*observations*. The numeric output from the sensor families is converted to symbolic format by a first interpretation treatment—*perception*. The second layer identifies elements relevant to the action, e.g., a car, the order of battle, etc. It attributes a name to each relevant element, or *entity*. The third layer groups entities into significant collections of objects—*association*. These three layers progressively enrich the information flowing through the reasoning system of MATIS, mainly by increasing the semantic content of each knowledge object. The plan recognition system can be seen as a fourth layer, as shown in Fig. 1. It handles the semantically richest information of the third layer. The fourth layer does not bear just on objects, but rather on their behavior, which it interprets in terms of predefined plans and goals. This system is "real-world" as it has to deal with real data. Data have been partially collected by intelligent services[5], and must be understood by them. Hence, we must adapt to their knowledge representation for our input/output. In particular, the data present six undesirable features:

1. Measures are taken in a fixed way. This means that incoming data may not contain the information characterizing a situation. For example, in order to recognize that a car stopped at a traffic light, one usually assumes that the car is recorded while stopped at the light. This may not be true for our data, which may only report of a car slowing down before a light, and the measurement of the car at null speed may be missing.
2. Since measurements performed at some point may take some time to reach the interpretation center, the temporal ordering of input data may not be the same as that in the real world. Consequently, a hypothesis must never be discarded on the grounds of missing data at a given time, as confirming data may arrive later.
3. There are different granularity levels in the data. For example, some information may be relevant for a combat section but not for a company.
4. For every level of granularity, the units perform tasks at which they normally collaborate. Each agent is intelligent in its way, but it is not free to threaten in any way the general plan (on a battle field, "backtracking" usually implies heavy losses). Freedom is strongly limited, but never totally absent.
5. Data are lacunary (some of them may lack indefinitely) and can be noisy.
6. Data contain information about actions which take place at specific locations and at specific points in time.

A seventh requirement of a different nature must also met. Since a C^3I system is intended to help a commander who has heavy responsibilities, it is not

---

[5] Our other sources of information are the three lower levels of MATIS.

possible to make decisions on data fusion in a way which is not directly understandable to the commander. Explanations that serve as a basis for the decision
making process must be provided to the commander in her own language. This
explanatory faculty is also a requirement of real-life—a C^3I system which does
not explain its actions will at best be reluctantly accepted under heavy constraints. Indeed, the overall objectives the system can be defined as: (1) relating
the observed behavior described in terms of low-level data to high-level structures
which describe the tactics or strategy applied by a rational agent in a particular
situation; (2) interpreting this behavior in terms of the agent's motivations; and
(3) providing satisfactory explanations in response to user's questions.

Strong specifications as the seven above cannot be exactly met in the present
state of the art, that only provides partial answers to these problems (see [3]).
Plan recognition is generally considered in an ideal context, where the input is
supposed to be 100% correct (violating requirement 5) and consists of actions,
that is, chunks of activity representing well-defined transitions in the situation
(violating requirement 1). Such ideally clean contexts can be described in strong-
theory domains, and make it possible the application of formal techniques such
as abduction [1, 19] or syntactic parsing [22]. On the contrary, in a realistic
context, plan recognition must be done on an evolving situation described at a
level which is lower than that of self-contained actions, and which consists of
punctual events. Such a context imposes weak-theory modeling and incremental
evidence assignment. This robust approach is adopted in our system. Several
characteristics follow from this approach:

- The input consists of an imposed sequence of *events*, and not of actions.
  Events present the following features: (1) they are snapshots of the observed
  activity—they have no duration—situated at whatever point of the behavior
  of the agent (actions, on the contrary, span some amount of time); (2) they
  are measured at regular intervals; therefore, measurements are not necessarily performed at the time of a qualitative transition[6].
- The system must be able to process massive input, and to smooth out the
  incidence of false data.
- The output must include a list of plausible plans. The confidence rate for
  these plans must be incrementally confirmed.
- The system must interpret low-level data in terms of high-level concepts so
  that the advice provided can be easily understood by the user. This advice
  must also be satisfactorily justified.

Some of this specifications are to be taken as facts upon which we have no
power, such as the general non-recursive nature of the system. In this sense, the
system is also "real-world" as we had to adapt to previous decisions.

---

[6] Qualitative transitions have to be reconstructed from events, e.g, the system must
find out that the car is turning left, based on the position and speed of the car at
various instants.

3.2 The Plan Recognition Situation

The domain chosen for the initial modeling had to present the features listed above. In a car driving domain, the system must face the following type of problems. A car—the *agent*—is moving. Its driver is supposed to be a rational agent with goals or motivations (e.g., saving time, saving gas) that will lead her to drive in a certain way rather than another in order in a specific situation. The *observer*[7] cannot see the car directly. In principle, it knows nothing about the agent. The recognition situation is a case of keyhole recognition [8], i.e., the agent is unaware of being observed, and the observer cannot attribute to the actor any intention to cooperate in the recognition process. The only information the observer has available are sets of low-level data such as speeds, positions, and distances, which arrive periodically. As additional assumption, the observer considers this agent "at the knowledge level". That is, it considers this agent, which is embedded in a task environment, as composed of bodies of knowledge (about the world), some of which constitute its goals, and some of which constitute the knowledge needed to reach these goals—the agent processes its knowledge to determine the actions to take. Its behavioral law is the principle of rationality—"If an agent has knowledge that one of its actions will lead to one of its goals, then the agent will select that action" [13, page 102]—but in its more pragmatic form of the two-step rationality theory [21]. In this form, the practical application of the principle of rationality is constrained by the boundaries of a model of the problem-situation (KL-model), which takes into account the specific circumstances in which the task is to be solved—'task features'. This way, the assumption is made that the behavior of the agent is both rational and practical. Based on this assumption, and from the available low-level data, the observer must interpret the car driver's behavior. In particular, it must explain: (a) what the driver seems to be doing, e.g., overtake a car, approach a red light; (b) how she does it, e.g., faster than it would be safe; and (c) why she acts this way rather than another—what her goals or motivations are (saving time, etc.).

3.3 The XPlans Representation

Structure and Organization of XPlans. XPlans [9] are inspired by Schank's *Explanation Patterns* [16], but they present some substantial differences, since our context is entirely different from Schank's. We have to consider an evolving situation in which massive, uncertain and lacunary input corresponding to events arrives in an uncontrollable flow. Therefore, we need a more elaborated domain knowledge in order to give a logic and understandable interpretation to row data that do not have a meaning by themselves. Additionally, we consider two points of view: (a) that of a standard agent, who is supposed to behave in a rational way, i.e., planning sequences of actions in order to attain some goals—*planning knowledge*; and (b) that of an observer who tries to understand what a real agent

---

[7] The observer is the plan recognition system with cooperation from the user—the decision maker.

is doing by comparing the information she gets to her knowledge about what a standard agent should do in that circumstances—*recognition knowledge*. We need thus two types of semantically different rules: planning rules and recognition rules, which are based on the planning ones. Both types of rules are integrated in complex structures—schemata—including, among other information, the rule application context. Recognition knowledge is highly contextual, since one action can respond to different causes in various contexts, and hence must be given different interpretations. For example, excessive speed would be associated to different interpretations in the context of a plan for overtaking a car or in the context of a plan for approaching a red light. Among other information, XPlans include the following elements:

- *Parameters*: List and description of the variables used, including confidence value.
- *Preconditions*: The basic facts that must hold for the plan to be considered. When they hold, the plan is said to be *active* and its recognition algorithm is applied.
- *Planning algorithm (PA)*: Description of the behavior of a standard (ideal) driver in the situation described by the XPlan. It consists of the sequence of *phases* that the agent should follow to accomplish the plan. Every phase has associated two different types of rules: *activation rules*, which call another plan (and optionally deactivate the plan) when preconditions do not hold anymore, and *behavior rules*, which result in the modification by the agent of the value of one or more parameters.
- *Recognition rules (RR)*: They control the modification of the confidence value of the plan, and assign an interpretation to the observed behavior, according to behavior rules in the PA.
- *Postconditions*: They describe sufficient conditions—elements of the world description after completion of the plan—for deactivating the plan, both in the case the plan has succeeded and in the case it has failed[8]. Alternative plans are also deactivated.
- *Motivations*: They represent the goal pursued by the agent when adopting a specific strategy rather than another to accomplish a task.

XPlans are organized in the form of a hierarchy (Fig. 2) which constitutes a library of prototypical cases. There are two main types of links in this taxonomy. The first type of link (dark arrows) expresses the specialization of the context (preconditions) in which the XPlan takes place. The XPlan that this type of link gives rise to corresponds to a task that the agent must perform. The other type of link (gray arrows) expresses that the child XPlan is a consequence of a choice of the driver—a prototypical strategy chosen to perform a task according to a certain motivation.

---

[8] Failure postconditions are considered because something external to the agent may happen that prevents it from accomplishing the plan (e.g., car_2 suddenly stopped and car_1 collides into car_2). This is because in this domain the situation changes not only as a consequence of the agent's behavior, but also independently of it.

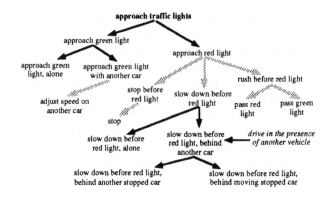

Fig. 2. A subpart of the hierarchy of XPlans relative to driving

The Recognition Process. The plan recognition process consists basically of the retrieval of cases (prototypical plans) from the XPlan hierarchy in order to interpret and explain the behavior of the agent from the low-level data feeding the system. The uncertainty inherent to an uncontrolled flow of input and the presence of lacunary data make difficult the retrieval of cases. This led us to develop an algorithm for partial and progressive matching of the target case onto some of the source cases stored in the library. This matching amounts in practice to a credit assignment mechanism, included in a recognition algorithm associated with each XPlan. In order to recognize the plan that the agent is applying, we try to follow her steps by producing interpretative hypotheses, as specific as data allow, and prudently confirming or disqualifying them as new data arrive. This mechanism is somehow comparable to spreading activation: plans activate one another down the hierarchical structure of the plan library, or across the hierarchy. Several concurrent hypotheses can be plausible interpretations of the agent's behavior—multiple plans can be simultaneously active.

The *general loop* for the processing of an event is as follows. Initially, only the root node is active. The postconditions of active plans are examined first; the plans whose postconditions hold are deactivated, as well as their concurrents. Then a depth-first search on the preconditions of children plans is started; if the preconditions of a plan hold, it is activated and the parent plan is deactivated. At this point, a *recognition algorithm* is applied to every single active plan. If the recognition rules of a plan cannot be applied, its confidence value is slightly decreased. If the confidence value of a plan is smaller than a certain threshold (fixed to 0.1), it is deactivated (its confidence value is forced down to 0).

The *recognition algorithm* applied on each plan is the following. For every new input event, the XPlan activation rules are checked and triggered if applicable; other plans are activated as specified in that rules, and the plan itself can be deactivated. If the plan is still active, for each applicable behavior rule, the ideal value of the parameter used as a reference is calculated and compared to the measured actual value. Based on their difference, the plan's confidence value is adjusted—it is increased if the difference is small or null, decreased else.

When all the plans in a branch have been deactivated, the root node becomes active again. This corresponds to the case when a sequence has come to an end (e.g., a car has driven past the traffic lights) and a new situation is considered.

3.4 Providing Advice for Decision Support

Advice is given as a causal interpretation (see Sect. 2.3), from the observer's point of view, of low-level input data in terms of the agent's plausible plan, strategy, and motivation in a specific situation. This interpretation (and more generally the explanations provided by the system) is the result of a trade-off among three factors: (1) the constraints imposed by the robust approach to plan recognition, (2) the purpose of the recognition task—decision support in critical domains—and (3) the user's needs for information. Three main types of needs—and hence of explanations—are distinguished:

1. A reliable source of information. The interpretation provided is aimed at understanding a situation in the world by relating it to some predefined high-level concept;
2. A means to test the user's own hypotheses. They are considered and, if plausible, added to the list of possible explanations;
3. Justification of different elements of the interpretation, to ensure that the system's reasoning and/or conclusion can be trusted.

Only explanations of types 1 and 2 take part in the plan recognition problem-solving process. Explanations of type 3 are considered only upon user's request (see [5]). They are constructed after plan recognition problem solving has taken place, and its generation constitutes a complex problem-solving process itself; therefore, they are not included in the model of plan recognition (next section).

4   An Interpretation Model for Plan Recognition

In our case, plan recognition is an interpretation problem as defined by Hayes-Roth, i.e., "inferring situation descriptions from sensor data" [10, page 14]. The recognition process presents the overall form of heuristic classification [7], as shown in Fig. 3. Initially, a set of observables in the form of low-level data arrives to the system. This set of observables is transformed into a form that can be matched against the preconditions of XPlans in the hierarchy, i.e., in terms of the parameters defined in the system model. Abstracted data are matched onto a hierarchy of pre-enumerated solution abstractions (XPlans) by non-hierarchical, uncertain inferences based on assumptions of typicality, which may relate the abstracted data to one or more hypotheses anywhere in the hierarchy. This matching operation generates a set of active hypotheses—differential. Each hypothesis in the differential is further refined, in several steps, into a more specific solution which proposes an interpretation of the situation in terms of the plausible agent's goal, what the agent seems to be doing, the strategy applied, and the possible motivations for having chosen that strategy. This solution must be consistent with the observations, although it is not necessary that the observations be fully explained by it. The solution is assumed to be within the differential. The differential is reduced as new evidence arrives that allows to discriminate between competing hypotheses.

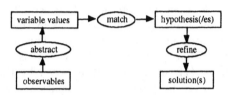

Fig. 3. Plan recognition can be analyzed in terms of heuristic classification

The task decomposition of the plan recognition task is given in the next section, and its corresponding detailed inference structure in Sect. 4.2.

4.1 Task Decomposition

The main task of the system—plan recognition for decision support—is decomposed into two main subtasks[9] (Fig. 4), as suggested by the Componential Methodology [17].

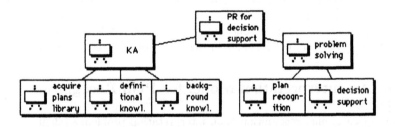

Fig. 4. Top level of the overall task decomposition structure for plan recognition

First, a knowledge acquisition subtask, which consists of acquiring the predefined library of plans (the 'system model'), as well as definitional and background knowledge that will be used for some of the plan recognition subtasks—the abstraction operation and the classification of the difference between standard and observed behavior respectively. For plan recognition purposes, all this knowledge is given—this task gives rise to the domain models that will not be affected by

---

[9] In the following, I will use both terms, subtasks and tasks, to refer to subtasks.

the problem solving process. On the other hand, a problem solving subtask splits into plan recognition and decision support subtasks[10]. In this paper, I will only consider the plan recognition task.The task decomposition structure for plan recognition is depicted in Fig. 5.

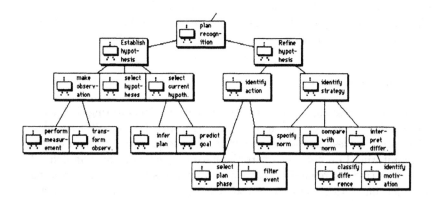

Fig. 5. Task decomposition structure for the plan recognition problem solving task

Plan recognition is divided in two subtasks—establishing a likely hypothesis that might account for the observed data, and refining the proposed hypothesis. *Establishing a hypothesis* implies selecting a list of plausible hypotheses by matching the (transformed) observables against the predefined library of XPlans, and choosing from that list the most plausible hypothesis—that with the highest confidence value. The selected hypothesis provides two elements—a possible goal (corresponding to the postconditions of the XPlan, e.g., car_2 has driven past car_1), and plan can be attributed to the agent (e.g., overtaking another car). This plan is further refined. If several candidates are found, each of them is refined by decreasing order of their confidence values. *Refinement* proceeds as follows. First, the action the agent is trying to perform is identified (actions correspond to phases in the planning algorithm of the XPlan, e.g., accelerating on the right lane). Then, the way in which the agent performs that action or strategy (e.g., the car accelerates more than it is needed) is identified by comparing the standard behavior in that situation, as contained in the XPlan, with the agent's current behavior, and a motivation is attributed to the agent as the reason for having chosen that strategy (e.g., save time). The result is a case model containing, for every active hypothesis: (a) the plausible agent's goal; (b)

---

[10] Even though plan recognition in our case is intended for decision support, and this latter task imposes constraints on the output of plan recognition, they are conceptually two different steps.

the plan it is likely to be applying in order to achieve that goal; (c) the current plan phase (action); (d) the way in which the plan or the action is being carried out (strategy); and (e) the reasons the agent might have to follow the strategy chosen (factor or motivation). The inference structure corresponding to this task decomposition is presented in the next section.

As we will see below (Sect. 4.3), the whole process is repeated at regular intervals (every time a measurement is performed by the system, i.e., every time an event is input to it). This may lead to a modification of the case model—the confidence values of the active hypotheses may change, and hypotheses may be added or removed from the list.

4.2 Inference Structure

The recognition process can be seen as a combination of monitoring or chronicling the behavior of an external agent, and diagnosing. Like monitoring, plan recognition presupposes an existing system model and an actually running system. By monitoring I do not mean here the narrower sense of the term defined in [4], i.e., detecting discrepancies between a running system and a pre-existing system model, but rather the wider sense given in [7]—detecting discrepancies in behavior or simply characterizing the current state of the system. The diagnose task is also interpreted in the sense given in [7]—explaining monitored behavior in terms of discrepancies between the actual (inferred) behavior and the standard behavior.

The detailed inference structure is shown in Fig. 6. Following the usual representation in the KADS methodology [24], ovals represent knowledge sources (inference steps) and boxes stand for meta-classes (roles). Static roles are represented by thick boxes. Knowledge sources are as follows:

obtain The plan recognition process starts by performing a measurement on the running system, which results in a set of numeric low-level data such as positions, speeds, etc.

transform These observables are transformed into a set of variable values that correspond to parameters and concepts used in the system model (in the preconditions of XPlans), so that they can be matched against it.

match The set of variable values ('variable-values-1') is matched against the library of prototypical plans ('system model') through preconditions of XPlans. If a differential already exists, the matching is first performed on it. A confidence value is attributed to each hypothesis according to the degree of match (number of parameters involved).

select–1 One hypothesis is selected for further consideration ('current-hypothesis'). Selection can be based on confidence values—the hypothesis (XPlan) with the highest confidence value is selected—on additional evidence, or on both. Evidence ('evidence-1') consists of the user's expectations based on external information not available to the system, i.e., a goal or a plan that can be attributed to the agent. Two meta-classes are singled out: a plausible agent's

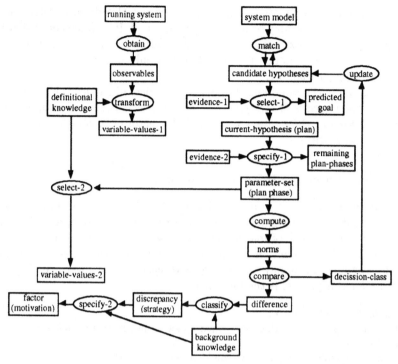

Fig. 6. Inference structure for plan recognition. Ovals represent knowledge sources (inference steps) and boxes stand for meta-classes (roles). Static roles are represented by thick boxes

goal, which corresponds to the success postconditions of the XPlans, and a plan that the agent may be applying.

specify-1 The name and the set of parameters defining the current phase of the plan that the agent seems to be applying are specified. Additional evidence can be considered. This evidence consists of the 'remaining-plan-phases' that were predicted in a previous recognition cycle. The remaining phases of the plan are also specified.

select-2 Variables are selected which are also parameters of the system model ('plan-phase'), so that they can be compared with norms.

compute The expected values of the parameters in the selected set are deduced ('norms') from the system model. The values of dependent parameters are also calculated.

compare The standard (parameter) values and the actual (variable) values are compared. This produces two outputs: the difference for each compared value (a number or a percentage) and a decision class, which attributes a degree of plausibility to the plan (confidence value) according to the results of the comparison.

update From the confidence value attributed to the plan by the decision class, the differential is updated. If the hypothesis was already in the differential, its confidence value may be increased or decreased. If its value goes below 0.1, the hypothesis is extracted from the differential. In the case the hypothesis is a new one, it is added to the differential only in the case its confidence value is higher than 0.1.

classify From background knowledge, the numerical difference is classified into a discrepancy class or strategy (e.g., car_2 is overzealous in slowing down).

specify–2 Finally, the strategy is attributed a factor or motivation (e.g., motivation is security).

4.3 Control over the Inference Structure

Task Structure. In our case, the plan recognition process is data-driven in the sense that (a) it proceeds as new data arrive to the system, and (b) it has no control over the flow of information. Also, selection of parameters from the system model is dependent on the variables coming from the observations of the running system, and it may be changed with each monitoring cycle. The task structure for this process is the following:

task *data-driven-plan-recognition*
goal execute a plan recognition cycle when a new event arrives to the system.
control-terms
differential = candidate-hypotheses (confidence-value > 0.1)
situation = agent's goal, plan, current-plan-phase, remaining-phases, strategy, factor
current-plan-phase = parameter-set
task-body
recognize (situation) =
  obtain (running-system → observables)
  transform (observables + definitional-knowledge → variable-values–1)
  IF differential = empty
    match (variable-values–1 + system-model → candidate-hypotheses)
  ELSE
    match (variable-values–1 + differential ± system-model → candidate-hypotheses)
  DO FOR EACH hypothesis ∈ candidate-hypotheses
    select–1 (candidate-hypotheses ± evidence–1 → predicted-goal, current-hypothesis)
    specify–1 (current-hypothesis ± evidence–2 → parameter-set, remaining-phases)
    select–2 (variable-values–1 + parameter-set → variable-values–2)
    compute (parameter-set → norms)
    compare (variable-values–2 + norms → difference, decision-class)
    IF decision-class-value > 0.1
      update (decision-class → differential)
      classify (difference + background-knowledge → discrepancy)
      specify–2 (discrepancy + background-knowledge → factor)
    ELSE get current-hypothesis out from differential

From another point of view, the strategy applied for recognizing the plans of the agent corresponds to what has been called a hypothesis-driven or hypothesize-and-revise strategy in the plan recognition literature [6], since a hypothesis is formulated concerning the agent's plan, including observed actions (in our case, inferred from low-level data and the system model) and expected ones, and this hypothesis is revised on the grounds of new evidence. This is by opposition to a data-driven or wait-and-see strategy, where hypothesizing the agent's plan is deferred until all the actions that constitute a plan have been observed (in our case, inferred).

Time Cycle. Like monitoring, plan recognition is a continuous task which proceeds in cycles. Due to the fragmentary and lacunary nature of our input, several events are usually necessary before a hypothesis has accumulated evidence enough to be acceptable. As we have seen above (Sect. 3.1), measurements are taken at regular points is time. This may affect the quality of data, since information which is essential to characterize a situation may be lost; however, the system has no possibility of control over the flow of data—it cannot know in advance when a relevant event will happen, nor force the arrival of data. A recognition cycle starts every time a new event is input to the system. The length of the intervals between cycles will depend on the application domain, but in any case it is imposed by the system (or rather by its user). The execution of each recognition cycle has an impact on the degree of confidence attributed to each of the alternative hypotheses that may explain the agent's behavior, thus possibly modifying the list of active hypotheses—differential. A recognition process comes to an end when no hypothesis remains in the differential. This corresponds to the case when the agent has ended a sequence of actions leading to the attainment of the desired goal (e.g., a car has driven past the traffic lights) and a new situation has to be considered. The solution to the plan recognition problem is thus the last hypothesis that remained in the differential before it became empty. The fact of the differential being empty may also correspond to the case when the system failed to recognize the agent's behavior—no solution to the plan recognition problem was found.

Selection of Active Hypotheses. In addition to the differential generated by the system, the user may also propose alternative hypotheses to be considered, possibly on the grounds of additional information not available to the system. The user's hypothesis can be run on past or future data, in isolation or together with the set of active hypotheses. The system monitors the evolution of the hypothesis which, if plausible, is added to the list of active hypotheses. In this case, only part of the task structure in Sect. 4.3 would be executed. We could call this new task structure "hypothesis-driven-plan-recognition":

task *hypothesis-driven-plan-recognition*
goal execute a PR cycle when the user proposes a hypothesis to the system.
control-terms
differential = candidate-hypotheses
current-hypothesis = possible agent's plan proposed by the user
task-body
recognize (current-plan-phase, remaining-phases, strategy, factor) =

obtain (running-system → observables)
transform (observables + definitional-knowledge → variable-values–1)
monitor (current-hypothesis) =
  specify–1 (current-hypothesis ± evidence–2 → parameter-set, remaining-phases)
  select–2 (variable-values–1 + parameter-set → variable-values–2)
  compute (parameter-set → norms)
  compare (variable-values–2 + norms → difference, decision class)
  IF decision-class-value > 0.1
    classify (difference + background-knowledge → discrepancy)
    specify–2 (discrepancy + background-knowledge → factor)
    update (decision-class → differential)

5 Conclusion

In this paper I have analyzed plan recognition—the process of interpreting an observed behavior—in terms of problem solving. This view is contrary to the approaches that define plan recognition as a not very well defined "understanding task" and confront it to problem solving. This opposition results from adopting a too restricted definition of problem solving. Plan recognition is indeed a form of understanding—situation understanding—but it is also a problem-solving behavior, as broader definitions of this latter concept have allowed us to show. The problem-solving reasoning underlying plan recognition has been investigated from a knowledge-level perspective. The plan recognition situation considered for this analysis has been one of keyhole recognition of an agent's behavior in a dynamic environment from low-level data, where purpose of the recognition task is providing support for decision making in a critical domain. A first knowledge-level model—an interpretation model in terms of KADS—for this task has been proposed.

References

1. Allen, J.F., Kautz, H.A., Pelavin, R.N., and Tenenberg, J.D.: Reasoning about Plans. Morgan Kaufmann, 1991.
2. Barès, M.: Aide à la décision dans les systèmes informatisés de commandement: rôle de l'information symbolique. DRET Report, July 1989, Paris.
3. Barès, M., Cañamero, D., Delannoy, J.-F., and Kodratoff, Y.: XPlans: Case-Based Reasoning for Plan Recognition. Applied Artificial Intelligence **8**, Vol. 3, (1994) (forthcoming).
4. Breuker, J. (ed), Wielinga, B., van Someren, M., de Hoog, R., Schreiber, G., de Greef, P., Bredeweg, B., Wielemaker, J., and Billaut, J.-P.: Model Driven Knowledge Acquisition: Interpretation Models. Deliverable A1, ESPRIT Project 1098, Memo 87, SWI, University of Amsterdam, 1987.
5. Cañamero, D., Delannoy, J.-F., and Kodratoff, Y.: Building Explanations in a Plan Recognition System for Decision Support. Proceedings of the ECAI Workshop on Improving the Use of Knowledge-Based Systems with Explanations, Vienna, Austria, August 1992; Rapport LAFORIA 92/21, Université Paris VII, France, 35–45.

6. Carberry, S. and Pope, A.: Plan Recognition Strategies for Natural Language Understanding. Int. J. Man-Machine Studies **39** (1993) 529-577.

7. Clancey, W.J.: Heuristic Classification. Artificial Intelligence **27** (1985) 289-350.

8. Cohen, P.R., Perrault, C.R., and Allen, J.F.: Beyond question answering. In W. Lenhert and M. Ringle (eds.): Strategies for Natural Language Understanding. Lawrence Erlbaum, 1981, 245-274.

9. Delannoy, J.-F., Cañamero, D., and Kodratoff, Y.: Causal Interpretation from Events in a Robust Plan Recognition System for Decision Support. Proceedings of the Fifth International Symposium on Knowledge Engineering, Sevilla, Spain, October 1992, 179-189.

10. Hayes-Roth, F., Waterman, D., and Lenat, D. (eds.): Building Expert Systems. Addison-Wesley, 1983.

11. Hoc, J.-M: Psychologie cognitive de la planification. Presses Universitaires de Grenoble, France, 1987.

12. Mooney R.J.: Learning Plan Schemata From Observation: Explanation-Based Learning for Plan Recognition. Cognitive Science **14** (1990) 483-509.

13. Newell, A: The Knowledge Level. Artificial Intelligence **18** (1982) 87-127.

14. Pennington, N. and Hastie, R.: Reasoning in Explanation-Based Decision Making. Cognition **40** (1993) 123-163.

15. Richard, J.-F.: Les activités mentales : Comprendre, raisonner, trouver des solutions. Armand Colin, Paris, 1990.

16. Schank, R.C.: Explanation Patterns: Understanding Mechanically and Creatively. Lawrence Erlbaum Associates, 1986.

17. Steels, L: Components of Expertise. AI Magazine **11** (1990, Summer) 28-49.

18. Steels, L: Reusability and Knowledge Sharing. In L. Steels and B. Lepape (eds.): Enhancing the Knowledge Engineering Process—Contributions from ESPRIT. Amsterdam, North-Holland, 1992, 240-268.

19. van Beek, P. and Cohen, R: Resolving plan ambiguity for cooperative response generation. Proceedings of the 10th AAAI, 1991, 938-944.

20. van de Velde, W.: Inference Structure as a Basis for Problem Solving. Proceedings of the 8th European Conference on Artificial Intelligence (ECAI-88). London, Pitman, 1988, 196-207.

21. van de Velde, W.: Issues in Knowledge-Level Modeling. In J.-M. David, J.-P. Krivine, and R. Simmons (eds.): Second Generation Expert Systems. Springer-Verlag, 1993, 211-231.

22. Vilain, M.: Getting serious about parsing plans: A grammatical analysis of plan recognition. Proceedings of the 9th AAAI, Boston, MA, 1990, 190-197.

23. von Martial, F.: Coordinating Plans of Autonomous Agents. Springer-Verlag, LNAI **610**, 1992.

24. Wielinga, B.J., Schreiber, A.Th., and Breuker, J.A.: KADS: A Modeling Approach to Knowledge Engineering. Knowledge Acquisition **4** (1992) 5-53.

25. Wilensky, R.: Meta-Planning: Representing and Using Knowledge About Planning in Problem Solving and Natural Language Understanding. Cognitive Science **5** (1981) 197-233.

26. Wilensky, R.: Planning and Understanding: A Computational Approach to Human Reasoning. Addison-Wesley, 1993.

CUE: Ontology Based Knowledge Acquisition *

Gertjan van Heijst and Guus Schreiber

University of Amsterdam
Department of Social Science Informatics
Roetersstraat 15
NL–1018 WB, Amsterdam
{gertjan,schreiber}@swi.psy.uva.nl

Abstract. This paper presents CUE, a knowledge engineering workbench that supports the development of knowledge based systems according to the GAMES methodology, which is also briefly described. CUE contains tools that support the three steps involved in model based knowledge acquisition: model construction, model instantiation and model refinement. Two of the tools that are part of the workbench are described in detail. The first of these, QUOTE, is an editor for the definitions of ontologies. The second, QUAKE, exploits the ontologies defined with QUOTE to elicit domain knowledge in a focused way. In the context of QUAKE an analysis of possible knowledge elicitation strategies is presented. Finally, the strengths and weaknesses of CUE are discussed and the system is compared with other knowledge acquisition environments.

1 Introduction

In this paper we analyse the state of the art with respect to knowledge acquisition (KA) tools based on the model-based KA paradigm. There appears to be an emerging theory of the various steps in this process and of the role of tools in supporting this process. We present CUE as an KA environment that operationalizes this theory. Many of the underlying ideas of CUE are thus not new, but are just an explicit integration of principles underlying existing tools. Our major aim is to use CUE as a testbed for extending this, emerging KA process theory, in particular in the area of (i) exploiting a *library of ontologies*, and (ii) the exploration of the notion of *knowledge elicitation strategies*. A library of ontologies acts as a repository of previous knowledge engineering experiences, and enables the knowledge engineer to reuse descriptions of the *structure* of domain knowledge that have proven useful in the past. Knowledge elicitation strategies are principles for organising the knowledge elicitation dialogue, and present an alternative for the existing techniques that are either completely user- or system-driven.

* The research reported here was carried out in the course of the GAMES-II project. This project is partially funded by the AIM Programme of the Commission of the European Communities as project number A2034. The partners in this project are SAGO (Florence, Italy), Foundation of Research and Technology (Crete, Greece), Geneva University Hospital (Switzerland), the University of Amsterdam (The Netherlands), University College of London (UK), the University of Pavia (Italy) and the University of Ulm (Germany). This paper reflects the opinions of the authors and not necessarily those of the consortium.

The next section describes the paradigm of model based knowledge acquisition, and some tools that have been developed to support it. Sec. 3 presents the GAMES methodology, which forms the immediate context of the CUE system. In Sec. 4 and Sec. 5 two tools that are part of the the CUE workbench are described in detail. The first of these, QUOTE, is an editor for the definitions of ontologies. The second, QUAKE, exploits the ontologies defined with QUOTE to elicit domain knowledge in a focused way. In the context of QUAKE an analysis of possible knowledge elicitation strategies is presented. In Sec. 6 the CUE is compared with PROTÉGÉ-II and KEW, and future extensions are described.

2 Background

2.1 Model Based Knowledge Acquisition

Model based knowledge acquisition, the main paradigm for acquiring knowledge for knowledge bases, has three basic subtasks: (i) skeletal model construction, (ii) model instantiation, and (iii) model refinement. The first of these subtasks, skeletal model construction, involves the creation or selection of an abstract specification of the knowledge that is required to perform a particular task in some domain. Such skeletal models may come in different flavors, and they vary in the amount of detail that they specify. For example, *generic tasks* [Chandrasekaran, 1987] specify both the method that is used to perform a task and the way that domain knowledge must be represented. In contrast, KADS *interpretation models* [Wielinga et al., 1992] specify the method (using control knowledge and inference structures), but they do not specify how the domain knowledge must be represented. In the PROTÉGÉ approach [Musen, 1989a], both the method and the domain specific classes are specified in the skeletal model. Here, only the instances of the classes and their relations are unspecified.

Model instantiation, the second step in KBS development, involves "filling" a skeletal model with domain knowledge, to generate a complete knowledge base. Many well-known knowledge elicitation tools concentrate on this step in the knowledge acquisition process [Boose, 1985, Shaw & Gaines, 1987, Marcus, 1988, Musen *et al.*, 1988]. For example, SALT concentrates on the elicitation of knowledge that is required for the Propose-and-Revise skeletal model. In the model instantiation step the elicited knowledge is often, but not always, represented in a non-executable "knowledge level" language.

The third step in model based knowledge acquisition is refinement of the instantiated skeletal model. In this step, the instantiated skeletal model is validated using a number of selected test cases. When the KBS does not solve the test cases correctly, or produces invalid explanations, this provides feedback about erroneous or missing knowledge in the knowledge base. A prerequisite of the model refinement step is that the knowledge is represented in an executable language. Therefore, an additional translation step is required in cases where the model instantiation step produces knowledge level descriptions of the domain knowledge.

Fig. 1 shows the three basic steps in model based knowledge acquisition. It should be emphasized that this task breakdown does not imply that the three subtasks are necessarily performed sequentially. As argued by [van Heijst *et al.*, 1992], the KA

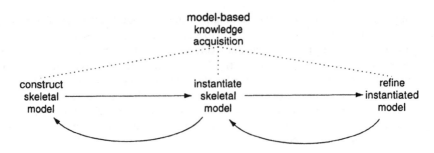

Fig. 1. The three basic steps in model based knowledge acquisition

process is typically a cyclic process where model construction, instantiation and refinement are highly intertwined.

The three steps require different kinds of expertise [Musen, 1989b] and different types of support tools. Whereas the model construction step is inherently difficult and requires the expertise of a knowledge engineer, the knowledge instantiation step can often be performed by domain experts, after some initial explanation of representation and tool usage. The knowledge refinement step can also be performed by domain experts, provided that they understand the control regime of the inference engine [Davis, 1979].

2.2 Brief Overview of Automated Knowledge Acquisition

In this section we give a historic overview of developments in automated knowledge acquisition and illustrate these with references to some well known tools that have been developed. However, we do by no means intend to present a complete overview of all existing KA tools.

Looking at the history of automated knowledge acquisition, a remarkable trend can be observed to concentrate on ever earlier steps in the knowledge acquisition process. KA tools of the first generation, such as KAS [Duda *et al.*, 1979], EMYCIN [van Melle, 1979] and TEIRESIAS [Davis, 1979], barely supported model construction, while the support for model instantiation was limited to symbol level facilities such as rule editors. Tools of this generation assumed that the domain expert or the knowledge engineer was able to build an initial knowledge base without extensive (tool) assistance. Only after this initial knowledge base was available could the tools support the KA process by providing feedback about the origin of erroneous solutions. The power of these tools was purely based on the explanation facilities of their inference engines, which facilitated the job of locating missing or incorrect parts of the knowledge base.

The second generation of knowledge acquisition tools also supported the model instantiation step. These tools were capable of knowledge level communication with domain experts to build an initial knowledge base. The type of support provided by second generation tools varied widely. For example, in MOLE and SALT the knowledge of the underlying skeletal model was used to engage in a structured dialogue with the domain expert. In OPAL, the model instantiation step was supported by the use of a graphical interface, and the tool was able to interact with the domain experts in terminology that is familiar to them. In this tool, model instantiation amounts to a kind of form filling, where the forms resemble the paper forms that the domain experts are used to work with. A third group of tools of this generation based their support on psychological techniques. Typical examples of this category are tools such as ETS [Boose, 1985], which embodies the repertory grid technique and ALTO [Major & Reichgelt, 1990], which is based on the laddering technique.

Only recently have tools been built that support skeletal model construction. In contrast with the tools of the first and the second generation, which are often presented as stand-alone programs, these tools are usually embedded in larger knowledge engineering environments, called KA workbenches. One of the first tools that supported model construction was PROTÉGÉ. This tool uses an abstract model of a problem solving method, and allows the knowledge engineer to associate the knowledge roles of the method with domain specific labels. Based on these associations, PROTÉGÉ can be used to generate model instantiation tools such as OPAL, which interact with experts in domain specific terminology. A limitation of PROTÉGÉ is that it is based on one problem solving method: episodic skeletal plan refinement. The commitment to one problem solving method defines the scope of this approach. Current work on PROTÉGÉ-II attempts to overcome the limitations of PROTÉGÉ. PROTÉGÉ-II is a large environment that embeds a number of tools, most of which are currently under development. We will return to the work on this system in Sec. 6.

Another tool that supports model construction is SPARK, which belongs the SPARK-BURN-FIREFIGHTER (SBF) environment [Klinker et al., 1991]. SPARK allows the user to indicate which of the tasks in a particular industrial environment should be performed by a KBS. To do this, the tool employs a general model of the tasks that are performed in some domain. Based on this task analysis, SPARK generates a specification of the method of the KBS, in the form of a configuration of mechanisms. This mechanism configuration is then used by BURN, the model instantiation tool of the SBF workbench, to elicit the domain knowledge that is required by the method.

KEW [Anjewierden et al., 1992], another third generation KA environment, is a large system that embodies a variety of knowledge elicitation and knowledge refinement tools. The skeletal models that are built with KEW's model construction tool are called generalized directive models (GDMs) [van Heijst et al., 1992], and they are similar to KADS interpretation models. In contrast with the original KADS approach, KEW does not merely provide a library of such skeletal models, but it actively supports the construction of these models, using a collection of model refinement operators specified as a rewrite grammar. The model refinement operators may only be applied if their associated conditions have been satisfied. The applicability conditions can express dependencies on task features (as in SPARK), or dependencies on domain features.

The COMMET workbench [Steels, 1993] is yet another example of a third generation KA environment. In this system, which is based on the componential framework [Steels, 1990], skeletal model construction consists of two parts: (i) the construction of a task structure, which is a task decomposition tree, and (ii) the construction of a model dependency diagram, which is a specification of the domain models that are needed to perform a particular task.

As mentioned above, the different approaches and workbenches use different types of skeletal models, with varying degrees of restriction. Whereas some types of skeletal models, such as interpretation models, only weakly constrain the ways that they can be filled in the model instantiation step, others, such as the ones created with PROTÉGÉ, are very specific about the nature of the domain knowledge that they require. There is a direct relation between the amount of detail of the skeletal model and the amount of guidance that the model can provide for the model instantiation step.

CUE, the system presented in this paper, is another third generation knowledge acquisition environment. In CUE, a descendant of KEW, the skeletal models consist of a task model and an *application ontology*, which is an explicit representation of the structure of the domain knowledge for a particular application. It will be argued in this paper that the availability of an explicit representation of the application ontology enables CUE to provide strong guidance for the model instantiation step.

3   Context: Knowledge Modeling in GAMES

A knowledge acquisition environment should be based on a particular view of how the knowledge acquisition process should be organized, or in other words, a methodology. CUE is being developed as part of the GAMES-II project, which develops a methodology for the construction of medical knowledge based systems [van Heijst *et al.*, 1993]. The GAMES methodology views the KBS development process as consisting of the construction of two models: the *epistemological model*, which is a knowledge level description of the knowledge that is required to perform the expert task, and the *computational model*, which is a symbol level specification of the representations and algorithms required to have a computer perform that task. This distinction is similar to that between the conceptual model and the design model in KADS [Wielinga *et al.*, 1992]. The epistemological model consists of three parts: (i) a task model, (ii) an application ontology, and (iii) the application knowledge. In the terminology of the previous section, the task model and the application ontology together form the skeletal model. They specify what kind of application knowledge is required to solve problems in the domain. Only after the task model and the application ontology have been specified in the model construction step can the application knowledge be elicited (model instantiation). The result is an epistemological model that is specified in a knowledge level language.

As mentioned, the third step in knowledge acquisition, model refinement, requires that the knowledge is represented in an executable environment. In GAMES this executable environment is specified in the computational model. The computational model may be regarded as a specification of a blackboard system where different steps in the task model may be realised by different problem solvers, which may use different internal representations. The diversity of the problem solvers makes it difficult to develop a general knowledge refinement tool. For this reason the current version of CUE provides only problem solver specific knowledge refinement tools.

Nature of the GAMES skeletal model In this paper we concentrate on CUE's model construction and model instantiation tools, which both work on the level of the epistemological model. Fig. 2 shows a simple example of such a model.

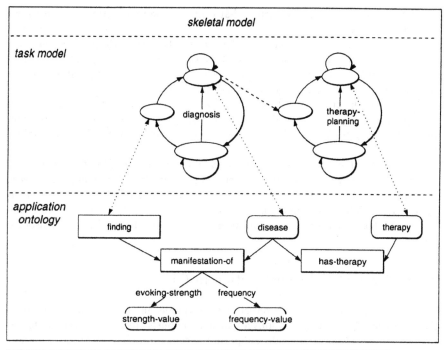

application knowledge

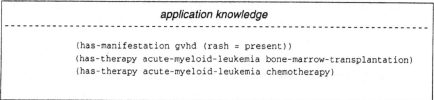

Fig. 2. A simple example of a GAMES epistemological model.

A GAMES task model consists of a configuration of instances of one generic inference model, the *Select and Test Model* (STModel) [Ramoni *et al.*, 1992], and their data dependencies. It is assumed that the three fundamental tasks in medical reasoning, diagnosis, therapy planning and patient monitoring, can be regarded as specializations of the STModel. This model, which is based on the work of the philosopher Peirce, [Peirce, 1932] distinguishes four fundamental reasoning steps: data abstraction, abduction of hypotheses, deduction of predictions, and inductive verification of the predictions. Furthermore, the model distinguishes two additional activities: deciding in which order the hypotheses will be tested (ranking) and requesting new data.

In Fig. 2, the circular objects with bubbles and arrows represent instances of the generic STModel. The arrows represent inferences and the bubbles represent knowledge roles. This task model consists of two STModels, one for diagnosis and one for therapy planning. The arrow that connects the two STModels represents a data dependency.

The second part of the skeletal model is a specification of the application ontology. As mentioned, the application ontology specifies the structure of the domain knowledge. The application ontology shown in Fig. 2 specifies that diseases may have findings as manifestations, and that these relations may be qualified by an evoking-strength attribute and a frequency attribute. To facilitate the development of application ontologies, the GAMES methodology provides a library of reusable medical ontologies that can be connected and fine-tuned for a particular application.

After the task model and the application ontology have been built, the third step in the construction of the skeletal model is the specification of a mapping between the knowledge roles in the task model and the classes and relations specified in the application ontology. The mappings, shown in Fig. 2 by dotted lines, indicate how the knowledge specified in the application ontology will be used in the reasoning process.

4 Skeletal Model Construction in CUE

The skeletal models in GAMES consist of a task model and an application ontology. For both constituents CUE contains a tool that supports their construction. QUITE, the task model editor, graphically supports the configuration of STModel instances into a task model for the application. Because only a first prototype of this tool has been implemented at the moment, we will concentrate here on QUOTE, the tool for application ontology construction.

4.1 Application Ontologies

Application ontologies determine which knowledge is required to solve problems in the domain of the KBS under development. For real applications, they can become very complex and their development is a difficult and error prone activity.

Ontologies need to be specified in a language. In CUE, Ontolingua [Gruber, 1992] is used for this purpose. Ontolingua, which is developed as part of the Knowledge Sharing Effort [Neches et al., 1991], is based on predicate calculus, but supports the explicit representation of additional knowledge differentiations such as the distinction between definitional and assertional knowledge and it provides theory inclusion as a modularity construct. Ontologies written in Ontolingua consist of definitions of classes, relations, functions and in some cases instances. The definitions can be formulated using a collection of representational primitives which are defined in the Frame Ontology.

4.2 QUOTE

QUOTE can be used for three purposes: (i) the development of application ontologies from scratch, (ii) the fine tuning of ontologies that are selected from CUE's ontological theory library for a particular application, and (iii) the development of reusable ontologies that are to be stored in the ontology library. We will illustrate the functionality of QUOTE by showing how the tool supports the development of an application ontology such as the one shown in Fig. 2. QUOTE's theory inclusion graph viewer, which is shown in Fig. 3, visualizes the theories that are part of the application ontology and their inclusion relations. A theory must include another theory when the definitions in the former depend on definitions in the latter. For example, the theory finding which contains the definition of the concept "finding" includes the theory observable which defines the concept "observable", because findings are defined as expressions about observables. All theories that are part of the inclusion graph in Fig. 3 are loaded from the GAMES supplied library of reusable ontological theories.

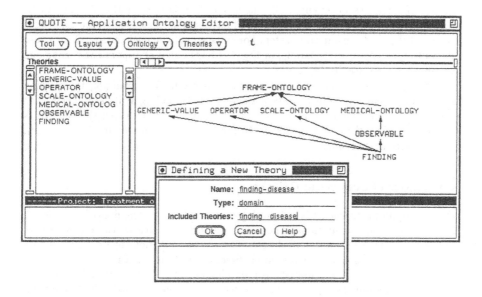

Fig. 3. A visualisation of the theory structure of an application ontology in QUOTE. The arrows indicate direct inclusion relations. When the user presses the OK button, the theory finding-disease is added to the graph.

In Fig. 3, the user is defining a new theory: finding-disease, in which the concepts will be defined that specify how diseases are related to findings in the current domain.[2] Since the definitions of these concepts depend on the definitions of findings and of diseases, the theories that contain these definitions are included in the new theory.

When the new theory is created it is automatically added to the theory inclusion graph. The contents of new theories can be specified by means of theory editors, in which new concepts may be defined and existing definitions may be altered. The

---

[2] In reality, finding-disease is also part of the ontology library. We assume here that it must be defined by the knowledge engineer to illustrate the functionality of QUOTE.

user interface of a theory editor consists of two areas (see Fig. 4). The upper area contains a number of browsers which show the classes, relations and functions that are defined in the theory, and another browser which shows the theories that are directly included by the theory. The lower area shows a graphical representation of the structure of the theory. The rounded boxes in the lower area of the tool represent already defined classes, and the rectangular boxes represent defined relations. The texts finding-importance and evoking-strength represent functions.

QUOTE distinguishes between intensionally and extensionally defined classes. For extensionally defined classes, the instances are also defined as part of the application ontology, while the instances of intensionally defined classes are considered to be part of the application knowledge. The difference between these two types of classes is important because it affects the knowledge acquisition process: the definition of instances of extensionally defined classes is part of the skeletal model construction step, whereas the definition of instances of intensionally defined classes is part of the model instantiation step. For extensionally defined classes, QUOTE also shows the instances. For example, in Fig. 4 the instances of importance-rate and strength-value are displayed.

The arrows in the graph indicate type constraints. For example, the relation manifestation-of is defined to have a disease and a finding as its arguments. The user can edit the definitions by opening a definition editor, in which the definitions can be altered on the Ontolingua level. In Fig. 4 the user is modifying the definition of the function frequency.

4.3   Levels of Support in QUOTE

QUOTE supports the definition of ontologies at three levels. The first of these is the level of Ontolingua definitions. The definitions editors, such as the one shown in Fig. 4, facilitate the definition of classes, relations and functions by syntax checking, automatic indentation, and by providing direct access to relevant parts of the on-line documentation that is distributed with Ontolingua. Therefore, every definition that is created or modified in QUOTE is guaranteed to be consistent with the Ontolingua language definition.

The second level of support of QUOTE is that of theories. QUOTE graphically shows the type constraints that are specified in the definitions. Whenever a parameter of a relation or a function is not typed, a warning is signaled.[3] QUOTE also warns the user when definitions refer to classes, relations or functions that are not defined in the theory or its included theories. Furthermore, warnings are given when concepts are defined more than once.

The third level of support that QUOTE provides, has to do with the selection of theories from a library. The graphical interface of QUOTE enables users to get a quick overview of the contents of an ontological theory, without an analysis of the internal details of the definitions.

---

[3] In principle, nothing is wrong with untyped parameters. Neither Ontolingua nor QUOTE enforce such typing. However, the ontologies defined in QUOTE are intended for driving the knowledge elicitation process, and type constraints on parameters are important for the validation of elicited knowledge.

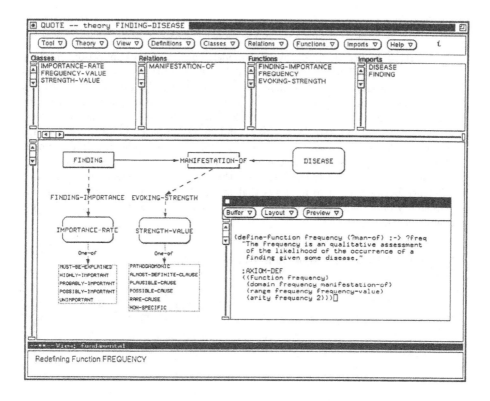

Fig. 4. QUOTE's theory editor

A final aspect of QUOTE that should be mentioned is that the tool works directly on Ontolingua theories. The theories that are created using QUOTE are saved as Ontolingua files, and can therefore directly be used as input for the Ontolingua translators described in [Gruber, 1993]. Furthermore, the tool can also be used to edit or visualize Ontolingua files that were not created using QUOTE. For these reasons the tool might also be used outside the CUE framework and independent of the GAMES methodology.

As can be deduced from the description above, the support provided by QUOTE is to a large extent based on three types of functionality: syntax checking, type checking and graphical visualisation. Although these functionalities significantly facilitate the definition of ontologies, it remains a passive kind of support: the user defines the concept, and the tool warns that something might be wrong or missing. The creative aspect of ontology construction remains a task for the user. However, the GAMES supplied library ensures that in many cases application ontology construction amounts to library selection.

5 Model Instantiation in CUE

As described in Sec. 3, CUE's skeletal models consist of an application ontology and a task model. Thus, the skeletal model specifies which kinds of knowledge are needed for the application, and how this knowledge will be used in the reasoning process. The purpose of QUAKE, CUE's model instantiation tool, is to interact with the domain expert to collect the domain knowledge that is specified in the skeletal model and store it in a knowledge base. It should be emphasized that this knowledge base only acts as a repository, it is not executable. QUAKE can be used in two modes of interaction: (i) passive, where the user determines the structure of the knowledge acquisition dialogue, and (ii) active, where the tool acts as an interviewer. The main difference between the two modes is that in passive mode QUAKE checks only for consistency of the entered knowledge, whereas in active mode the tool also aims for completeness.

5.1 QUAKE as a Passive Consistency Checker

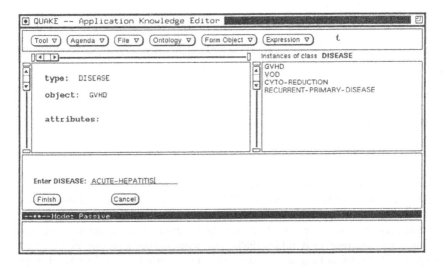

Fig. 5. QUAKE after the domain expert has entered some diseases. The entered diseases are visualised in the browser on the right side of the tool. The user has just entered a fifth disease (ACUTE-HEPATITIS). In the object window the tool shows the available information about one of the diseases: GVHD.

QUAKE is equipped with a limited user interface. Only the parts of the underlying knowledge base that are directly relevant for the current elicitation activity are shown to the user. QUAKE's user interface, which is shown in Fig. 5, consists of three areas. The upper left area, the object window, shows information about the object that is the current focus of the elicitation activity. The right upper area contains a multi-functional browser. Depending on the nature of the current elicitation activity, this browser shows different types of objects. The lower area of the tool is the interaction window. In this window the user is prompted to assert new knowledge in the knowledge repository.

The use of QUAKE in passive mode will be illustrated with a part of a knowledge elicitation scenario for a system that diagnoses graft-versus-host disease (GVHD). For this scenario, we use the application ontology which is described in Sec. 4. The scenario will also be used in Sec. 5.2 to describe some more advanced features of the tool.

A knowledge elicitation scenario In the example scenario, the domain expert starts the knowledge elicitation session by entering diseases. Therefore, the tool is focused on the class **disease**, which turns the browser into a browser for disease instances. The expert enters the names of some diseases that are relevant in the application area. The result is shown in Fig. 5.

Once five diseases have been entered, the user decides to concentrate on one of them: GVHD. The disease is selected and visualised in QUAKE's object window. As can be seen in Fig. 5, there are no attributes defined on instances of class disease in the application ontology. Therefore, the user decides to ask the tool for the relations that are defined on diseases. According to the application ontology, there are three kinds of relations defined on instances of the class disease: **disease-subtype**, **manifestation-of** and **has-treatment**. The relations are shown in the browser, which is now used as a relation browser. In Fig. 6, the relation **disease-subtype** is mentioned twice, because GVHD can play two roles in this relation. In the first relation specifier GVHD plays the role of the subtype, whereas in the second specifier GVHD would be the supertype.

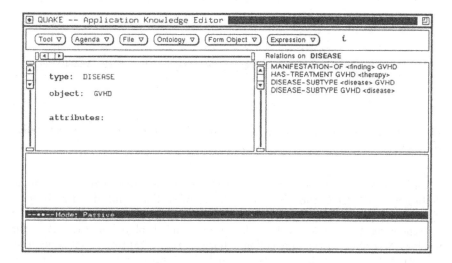

Fig. 6. QUAKE showing the relations defined on the class of GVHD.

The domain expert decides to work first on the manifestations of GVHD, so that relation is selected in the browser. The tool responds by showing all the findings that are defined as manifestations of GVHD. However, in this case there are as yet no findings associated with GVHD. The domain expert decides to enter the presence of a rash as a manifestation of GVHD and selects the corresponding pulldown option, which results in the tool showing a template for the manifestation-of relation in the interaction window. Because the domain expert is working on GVHD, the disease parameter is already instantiated. As illustrated in Fig. 7, the user types the finding in the text field. When the OK button is pressed QUAKE checks the entered expression for syntactic and ontological correctness. If the new expression is correct and does not conflict with previously entered information, it is asserted in the QUAKE knowledge base. An example of a possible conflict would be that the domain expert had already asserted that rash is an instance of disease. Since in the application ontology findings are defined to consist of observables, operators and values and disease is not specified as a subclass of observable or vice versa, QUAKE would in that case refuse to accept the entered finding.

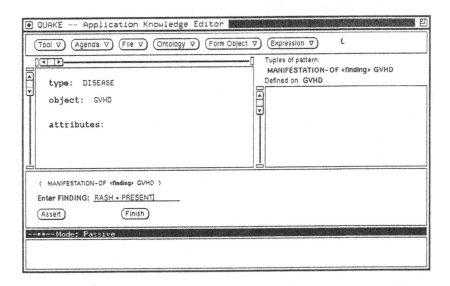

Fig. 7. QUAKE when the domain expert enters that the presence of rash is a manifestation of GVHD.

In the scenario, the domain expert continues by asserting that another manifestation of GVHD is the presence of fever. After that (s)he decides to specify some further qualifications of the first mentioned manifestation. Therefore the corresponding tuple is selected in the browser and displayed in the left upper window. According to the application ontology, manifestation-of relations have two attributes: the evoking-strength and the frequency.[4] The user first se-

---

[4] QUAKE interprets unary functions as attributes.

lects the **evoking-strength** attribute and as a result a template for the function appears in the interaction window (Fig. 8). Because in the application ontology **evoking-strength** is defined to have a **strength-value** as its value, which is an extensionally defined class, QUAKE is able to generate the list of possible values for the attribute. This list is used to support the auto-completion facility which is also displayed in Fig. 8. This example clearly illustrates the importance of the distinction between intensionally and extensionally defined classes mentioned in Sec. 4: in the model instantiation phase it is not possible to define instances of extensionally defined classes.

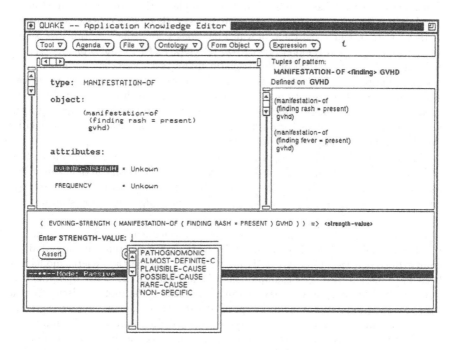

Fig. 8. QUAKE when the domain expert enters the evoking strength of the presence of rash for GVHD.

The scenario shows that QUAKE uses the application ontology to provide strong guidance to the model instantiation process. The tool prevents the user from entering expressions that conflict with the definitions in the ontology, and the tool interacts with the user in domain oriented terminology: it prompts for diseases and findings, and not for method specific knowledge types such as hypotheses and data or for symbol level constructs such as rules or constraints. Furthermore, QUAKE confronts the user with a limited amount of information at a time. For instance, Fig. 8 shows only the manifestations of GVHD, and the evoking-strength and the frequency for one of these manifestations. The rationale behind this approach is that this narrow, focused view on the underlying knowledge base guards the domain expert from not seeing the wood for the trees. It is our experience that domain experts often get confused when large amounts of heterogeneous domain facts are displayed at a time.

5.2   QUAKE as an Active Knowledge Collector

Experience with QUAKE as a passive application knowledge editor has revealed some shortcomings. The problem is that QUAKE's narrow view on the knowledge base causes the user to loose touch of the overall picture. The user very quickly forgets which knowledge still has to be entered. For example, in the scenario described in the previous section, the user first entered five diseases, then (s)he concentrated on one of these, GVHD, and asked the tool which relations were defined on this disease. Of the four relations, manifestation-of was selected, and two tuples of this relation were entered. In the course of this scenario many tasks were left unfinished. For instance, besides the five diseases shown in Fig. 5 other diseases need to be entered which also have findings as manifestations. Further, the disease hierarchies (the disease-subtype relations) must be specified, etc. The problem is that QUAKE, when used in passive mode, leaves the navigation in the knowledge space defined by the skeletal model completely to the user.

To overcome this difficulty, QUAKE is also equipped with a more active interaction style. In active mode, the tool not only waits for the user to take action, but it can also take the initiative. The active component of the tool consists of two parts: (i) an agenda mechanism and (ii) an interpreter for knowledge elicitation strategies.

Agenda mechanism The purpose of the agenda mechanism is to keep a record of which parts of the skeletal model are fully instantiated, partially instantiated, or empty. In some cases, QUAKE can decide whether a part of the skeletal model has been fully instantiated. For example, one of the assumptions made by QUAKE is that an attribute must always have a value.[5] Therefore, the tool can decide that a particular attribute still needs to be specified without bothering the user. Furthermore, sometimes the application ontology explicitly defines that a specific number of relation tuples or class instances must exist. For instance, in the application ontology described in Sec. 4, one of the constraints defined on the class disease says that every disease must have at least one finding as a manifestation. QUAKE's agenda manager can use such information to decide whether parts of the skeletal model are fully instantiated.

Most of the time however, the decision as to whether a part of the skeletal model is fully instantiated must be taken by the domain expert. In the example, it was the domain expert who had to decide that all the relevant diseases were entered, that all the manifestations of all the diseases were specified etc. In active mode, it is up to QUAKE to keep the agenda up to date. Whenever a user decides to start working on another part of the knowledge base and the tool cannot determine by itself that the

---

[5] This does not mean that QUAKE assumes that the values of all attributes of all objects can always be determined during knowledge acquisition. However, when an attribute value may be unknown, the value unknown (or something similar) must be specified explicitly as an admissible value for the attribute in the application ontology.

job that was worked on has been completed, QUOTE asks the user. For example, when the user in the scenario in Sec. 5.1 decided to start working on the manifestations of GVHD, in active mode the tool would first ask whether the entered diseases are all the diseases that are relevant for in the domain of the application. The response of the user would then be used to update the agenda. Fig. 9 shows QUAKE's agenda after the five diseases and the two manifestations have been entered.

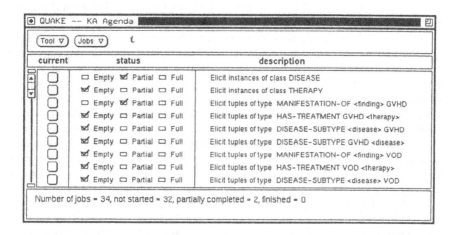

Fig. 9. QUAKE's agenda mechanism

Knowledge elicitation strategies The agenda mechanism maintains a list of knowledge elicitation activities that are completed, partially completed, or not yet initiated. However, the decision in which order the different elicitation activities are performed is still left to the user. For example, in the scenario in Sec. 5.1 it was the user who decided to start working on the diseases, and it was the user who decided to select the **manifestation-of** relation from the relations defined on GVHD. After a while, the decision as to which knowledge elicitation activity should be performed next becomes a complicated task in itself, because the number of activities rapidly increases as new knowledge is entered. For example, in the above scenario, four activities are added to the agenda for every disease which is entered in the knowledge base (elicitation of the manifestations, treatments, subtypes and supertypes of the entered disease).

Many second generation tools that are specialised in the model instantiation step of the knowledge acquisition process, take a more active role. For example, MOLE and SALT instantiate their skeletal models using a dialogue where the initiative is taken completely by the system. Here, the system decides which knowledge should be elicited when. We call the structuring principles for such a dialogue a *knowledge elicitation strategy*. Thus, a knowledge elicitation strategy is a specification of the order in which the domain instances and expressions must be elicited.

In the abovementioned second generation KA tools, it was possible to hardwire the knowledge elicitation strategies in the program, because these tools were based on a fixed skeletal model. MOLE for example, begins a knowledge elicitation session by asking the user to list some of the complaints that would indicate that there is a problem to be diagnosed. After these are entered, the tool asks for states or events that explain these complaints. In turn these states may also need to be explained. In this way MOLE builds, in a breadth-first manner, a network of causally related states and events. MOLE derives its power from the strong assumptions that it makes about the structure of the causal network that is required for the Cover-and-differentiate problem solving method.

Unfortunately, it is not possible to use built-in knowledge elicitation strategies in systems like CUE, where the construction of the skeletal model is also considered part of the knowledge acquisition process. Because the appropriateness of a strategy depends heavily on the nature of the skeletal model, the strategy can only be determined after the skeletal model has been constructed. This problem can be addressed in two ways. Firstly, it is possible to make the specification of the knowledge elicitation strategy part of the construction of the skeletal model, as is also done in DIDS [Runkel & Birmingham, 1994] and COMMET [Steels, 1993]. The second way is to formulate the knowledge elicitation strategies on an ontology-independent level. Currently, the first option is used in QUAKE. However, as a part of our project we are also investigating the possibility of the second, more ambitious option.

To formulate knowledge elicitation strategies as part of the skeletal model, a simple LISP based language has been defined which can be interpreted by QUAKE. This language allows the knowledge engineer to express ordering constraints in terms of the application ontology. A very simple example of a knowledge elicitation strategy defined in this language is the following.[6]

```
(define-ka-strategy
   (elicit-all ?d (disease ?d))                        [1]
   (for-each ?d (disease ?d)                            [2]
      (elicit-all ?f (manifestation-of ?f ?d))))
```

The first expression tells QUAKE to start eliciting all the diseases in the domain. The second specifies that, once the diseases have been elicited, all the manifestations for each disease must be elicited. The language is basically a query language that is extended with constructs for sequencing, iteration and simple conditionals.

A disadvantage of using such a language is that it allows the specification of arbitrary knowledge elicitation strategies. It is left to the knowledge engineer to decide which strategies are sensible. This is an undesirable situation because it makes the job of the knowledge engineer more difficult. What is needed are some general guidelines for the formulation of these strategies. Such guidelines could be used by QUAKE to generate strategies that are appropriate for the instantiation of its current skeletal model. This is the second option that was mentioned above. Unfortunately, such general principles are not available at the moment. However, the possibility of specifying arbitrary strategies for QUAKE makes this tool an excellent instrument for experimentation. In GAMES we are now beginning to formulate hypotheses for candidate principles.

---

[6] The syntax of the language has not yet stabilized.

Because the question of which dialogue structuring principles are sensible is basically an empirical one, a good place to start the investigation are the already existing tools that engage in such a dialogue. For one of these tools, MOLE, we have already described its KA-strategy. SALT constructs its knowledge base in a similar way. The skeletal model of this tool requires three types of knowledge: procedures, constraints and fixes. The knowledge pieces are organized in a dependency network with three types of relations: contributes-to, constrains, and suggests-revision-of. To instantiate this skeletal model, the tool allows the user to start elicitation at any point in the network. SALT then cues the user for appropriate links and keeps track of how the elicited knowledge pieces are fitting together, and it also warns for inconsistencies.

ALTO [Major & Reichgelt, 1990] is a tool for the elicitation of concept hierarchies, based on the laddering technique. The underlying skeletal model distinguishes two types of knowledge: concepts, which are organized in is-a hierarchies, and attributes of those concepts. ALTO starts the elicitation process by asking for a seed item. From this seed item, the user may move up the hierarchy, move down the hierarchy, or move to the siblings of the seed item. After that, the attributes of the new concept are elicited and the process continues with the elicited concept as the new seed item.

Analysis of the three knowledge elicitation strategies described above reveals some striking similarities. All these tools seem to do some kind of "graph traversal". This is one example of a potential general principle for formulating knowledge elicitation strategies.

Whereas the previous principle could be formulated in ontological terms (objects and relations), other principles might be easier to formulate in terms of the dynamic knowledge roles of the task model. For example, one of the heuristics that is used in KEW's advice and guidance module is that it is often sensible to start with the elicitation of potential solutions for the application task. For synthetic tasks, where the number of potential solutions is not enumerable, the heuristic is used to start knowledge acquisition with the elicitation of solution components. Because these heuristics are formulated in terms of the task model, the potential for QUAKE to implement such strategies depends on the mapping between the task model and the application ontology. For example, in the GVHD domain, QUAKE should know that the potential solutions for the diagnostic problem are diseases.

As a final remark about KA-strategies it should be emphasized that we are not aiming for a tool like MOLE that completely dictates the knowledge elicitation dialogue. Our goal is a mixed initiative dialogue that allows users to decide on which parts of the knowledge base they want to work, and that makes sensible decisions when they indicate that they don't know how to continue. This is one of the reasons why the agenda mechanism is implemented independently from the KA-strategy interpreter.

6 Discussion

In this paper we have described two tools that are part of the CUE knowledge engineering workbench. As mentioned in Sec. 2, CUE is a descendant of KEW. CUE deviates from KEW in two ways. Firstly, CUE's skeletal models that are used to drive the KA process are much more restrictive than those of KEW. One of the lessons from KEW was that the KADS-like skeletal models did not sufficiently constrain the knowledge elicitation step. Therefore, the skeletal models in CUE were augmented with application ontologies.

The second way in which CUE differs from KEW is that it is much smaller. Whereas KEW contains about fourteen different tools, the current version of CUE consists only of three tools. Although the system will be extended with some other utilities in the near future, its size will remain relatively small. The decision to reduce the number of tools in CUE was based on the experience that domain experts often get confused when they have to work with different elicitation tools.[7] Therefore, it was decided to equip CUE with one general purpose model instantiation tool, which can be specialised according to the skeletal model defined with QUITE and QUOTE.

The work on CUE advances the state of the art in knowledge acquisition in two ways. Firstly, the use of explicitly represented and editable application ontologies allows tools to provide strong support for the knowledge elicitation process, while they remain generally applicable. Secondly, the introduction of user definable knowledge elicitation strategies allows us to investigate how the knowledge elicitation dialogue must be organized, a topic that has long been ignored by the knowledge acquisition community.

The main advantage of a general purpose model instantiation tool is that domain experts can easily become acquainted with the UI-style and the underlying rationale of the tool. Furthermore, the use of a single tool made it easy to build an agenda mechanism that automatically remains up to date, and it allows us to experiment with knowledge elicitation strategies.

However, the use of a general purpose model instantiation tool has drawbacks as well. One of the advantages of tools that have built-in skeletal models is that they can visualize knowledge in a way that is appropriate for the kind of knowledge that they are intended for. ALTO, for instance, visualizes the elicited concept hierarchies in the form of directed graphs. Such a specialized visualization is possible because the tool makes ontological assumptions about the structure of the knowledge. In contrast, QUAKE cannot make such ontological assumptions because it must be able to instantiate arbitrary ontologies defined with QUOTE.

A challenging future research issue is how to extend QUAKE with the ability of specialized visualization while maintaining its general purpose character. One way to realize this is to make explicit the underlying ontological assumptions upon which specialized visualizations are based. This makes it possible to decide whether a particular class or relation can be displayed with a specialized visualization based on the definition of that class or relation in the application ontology. For example, to depict the tuples of a relation using tree-like visualizations as in ALTO the relation must be binary, transitive, irreflexive and anti-symmetric. For every relation for which these properties hold (e.g. disease-subtype-of, causes) the tuples may be visualized using such directed graphs.

The work that is most closely related to the work presented here is that on the PROTÉGÉ-II system. In particular, the work on DASH [Eriksson et al., 1994] is in a

---

[7] This is not a user interface problem. In KEW a great effort was made to keep the UI-styles of the different tools consistent. However, the tools were often also based on different views on the nature of knowledge.

similar spirit. DASH is a tool that can be used to build knowledge elicitation tools from application ontologies specified in MODEL, the PROTÉGÉ-II ontology language. The relation between QUAKE and DASH is similar to that between an interpreter and a compiler. Whereas QUAKE interprets application ontologies to communicate in domain specific terminology, DASH uses these ontologies to generate other tools that communicate in domain specific terminology. DASH generated tools act as user-friendly front-ends for the underlying knowledge base. They are similar to QUAKE in passive mode in that they do not aim for completeness. That is, they do not actively search for missing information. Therefore it is to be expected that users of DASH generated tools will face the same problems as the users of QUAKE in passive mode.

The DIDS approach [Runkel & Birmingham, 1994] has a facility for specifying knowledge elicitation strategies. They distinguish two elements that drive knowledge elicitation, namely (i) "mechanisms for knowledge acquisition" (MeKA), which define for each knowledge construct in the ontology an elicitation, verification and generalization procedure, and (ii) a "knowledge acquisition method" which defines the sequencing of MeKAs. The main distinction is that the DIDS strategies appear to be more coarse-grained. For example, one could only define that diseases need to be acquired before findings. The strategy shown in Sec. 5.2 requires switching between MeKAs.

As already indicated, the CUE system is still under development. However, the tools described in this paper are implemented and relatively stable. Our long term goal is to develop a knowledge engineering environment that supports the knowledge engineering process from the initial task analysis phase to the delivery of the final application system. Of course, such a workbench should be built on the firm grounds of a sound methodology. However, we believe that the development of such a methodology requires an environment that allows experimentation to verify the ideas that the methodology is based on. The current version of CUE is intended for this purpose.

Acknowledgements We are grateful to Anjo Anjewierden and Jan Wielemaker for their implementation support. Manfred Aben, Anjo Anjewierden, Lynda Hardman, Frank van Harmelen, André Valente and an anonymous reviewer provided valuable comments on earlier drafts of this paper.

References

[Anjewierden *et al.*, 1992] ANJEWIERDEN, A., SHADBOLT, N., & WIELINGA, B. J. (1992). Supporting knowledge acquisition: The ACKnowledge project. In *Enhancing the Knowledge Engineering Process – Contributions from ESPRIT*, pages 143–172. Amsterdam, The Netherlands, Elsevier Science.

[Boose, 1985] BOOSE, J. H. (1985). A knowledge acquisition program for expert systems based on personal construct psychology. *International Journal of Man-Machine Studies*, 23:495–525.

[Chandrasekaran, 1987] CHANDRASEKARAN, B. (1987). Towards a functional architecture for intelligence based on generic information processing tasks. In *Proceedings of the 10th IJCAI*, pages 1183–1192, Milan, Italy.

[Davis, 1979] DAVIS, R. (1979). Interactive transfer of expertise. *Artificial Intelligence*, 12(2):121–157.

[Duda et al., 1979] DUDA, R., GASCHING, J., & HART, P. (1979). Model design in the PROSPECTOR consultant system for mineral exploration. In Michie, D., editor, *Expert Systems in the Micro-Electonic Age*, pages 153-1674. Edinburgh University Press.

[Eriksson et al., 1994] ERIKSSON, H., PUERTA, A., & MUSEN, M. (1994). Generation of knowledge acquisition tools from domain ontologies. In Gaines, B. & Musen, M., editors, *Proceedings of the 8th Banff Knowledge Acquisition for Knowledge-Based Systems Workshop.*, pages 7-1 - 7-20, Alberta, Canada. SRDG Publications, University of Calgary.

[Gruber, 1992] GRUBER, T. (1992). Ontolingua: A mechanism to support portable ontologies. version 3.0. Technical report, Knowledge Systems Laboratory, Stanford University, California.

[Gruber, 1993] GRUBER, T. (1993). A translation approach to portable ontology specifications. *Knowledge Acquisition*, 5:199-220.

[Klinker et al., 1991] KLINKER, G., BHOLA, C., DALLEMAGNE, G., MARQUES, D., & MC-DERMOTT, J. (1991). Usable and reusable programming constructs. *Knowledge Acquisition*, 3:117-136.

[Major & Reichgelt, 1990] MAJOR, N. & REICHGELT, H. (1990). ALTO: an automated laddering tool. In Wielinga, B. J., Boose, J., Gaines, B., Schreiber, G., & van Someren, M., editors, *Current trends in knowledge acquisition*, pages 222-236, Amsterdam, The Netherlands. IOS Press.

[Marcus, 1988] MARCUS, S., editor (1988). *Automatic knowledge acquisition for expert systems*. Boston, Kluwer.

[Musen, 1989a] MUSEN, M. A. (1989a). *Automated Generation of Model-Based Knowledge-Acquisition Tools*. London, Pitman. Research Notes in Artificial Intelligence.

[Musen, 1989b] MUSEN, M. A. (1989b). Automated support for building and extending expert models. *Machine Learning*, 4:347-376.

[Musen et al., 1988] MUSEN, M. A., FAGAN, L. M., COMBS, D. M., & SHORTLIFFE, E. H. (1988). Use of a domain model to drive an interactive knowledge editing tool. In Boose, J. & Gaines, B., editors, *Knowledge-Based Systems, Volume 2: Knowledge Acquisition Tools for Expert Systems*, pages 257-273, London. Academic Press.

[Neches et al., 1991] NECHES, R., FIKES, R., FININ, T., GRUBER, T., PATIL, R., SENATOR, T., & SWARTOUT, W. R. (1991). Enabling technology for knowledge sharing. *AI Magazine*, pages 36-56. Fall.

[Peirce, 1932] PEIRCE, C. (1932). *Collected Papers of Charles Saunders Peirce*, volume 2, Elements of Logic. Cambridge MA, Harvard University Press.

[Ramoni et al., 1992] RAMONI, M., STEFANELLI, M., BAROSI, G., & MAGNANI, L. (1992). An epistemological framework for medical knowledge based systems. *IEEE Transactions on Systems, Man and Cybernetics*, 22:1361-1375.

[Runkel & Birmingham, 1994] RUNKEL, J. & BIRMINGHAM, W. (1994). Separation of knowledge: a key to reusability. In Gaines, B. & Musen, M., editors, *Proceedings of the 8th Banff Knowledge Acquisition for Knowledge-based Systems Workshop*, pages 36-1 — 36-19.

[Shaw & Gaines, 1987] SHAW, M. L. G. & GAINES, B. R. (1987). An interactive knowledge elicitation technique using personal construct technology. In Kidd, A. L., editor, *Knowledge Acquisition for Expert Systems: A Practical Handbook*, New York. Plenum Press.

[Steels, 1990] STEELS, L. (1990). Components of expertise. *AI Magazine*.

[Steels, 1993] STEELS, L. (1993). The componential framework and its role in reusability. In David, J.-M., Krivine, J.-P., & Simmons, R., editors, *Second Generation Expert Systems*, pages 273-298. Berlin Heidelberg, Germany, Springer-Verlag.

[van Heijst et al., 1993] VAN HEIJST, G., LANZOLA, G., SCHREIBER, A. T., & STEFANELLI, M. (1993). Methodological foundations of medical KBS construction. Technical Report

GAMES-II/T1.1/UvA/PP/011/1.0, University of Amsterdam and University of Pavia. Submitted for publication. Available from: University of Amsterdam, Social Science Informatics, Roetersstraat 15, NL-1018 WB, Amsterdam, The Netherlands.

[van Heijst et al., 1992] VAN HEIJST, G., TERPSTRA, P., WIELINGA, B. J., & SHADBOLT, N. (1992). Using generalised directive models in knowledge acquisition. In Wetter, T., Althoff, K. D., Boose, J., Gaines, B., Linster, M., & Schmalhofer, F., editors, *Current Developments in Knowledge Acquisition: EKAW-92*, Berlin, Germany. Springer-Verlag.

[van Melle, 1979] VAN MELLE, W. (1979). A domain independent production rule system for consultation programs. In *IJCAI-79*, pages 923–925.

[Wielinga et al., 1992] WIELINGA, B. J., SCHREIBER, A. T., & BREUKER, J. A. (1992). KADS: A modelling approach to knowledge engineering. *Knowledge Acquisition*, 4(1):5–53. Special issue 'The KADS approach to knowledge engineering'. Reprinted in: Buchanan, B. and Wilkins, D. editors (1992), *Readings in Knowledge Acquisition and Learning*, San Mateo, California, Morgan Kaufmann, pp. 92-116.

KARO: An Integrated Environment for Reusing Ontologies

Thomas Pirlein*[†]   Rudi Studer[†]

*IBM Germany Development   [†]University of Karlsruhe
AE Software Architectures   Institute for Applied
and Technologies   Computer Science and Formal
2300, 7030-91   Description Techniques
D-71003 Böblingen   D-76128 Karlsruhe
tpi@aifb.uni-karlsruhe.de   studer@aifb.uni-karlsruhe.de

Abstract

This paper shows how KARO (*Knowledge Acquisition Environment with Reusable Ontologies*) supports the development of the domain layer in MIKE (*Model-based and Incremental Knowledge Engineering*). KARO supplements the reuse of generic problem-solving methods at the task and inference layers in MIKE with a commonsense ontology at the domain layer. The intention is to make the development process easier and the final domain layer more robust.

In order to reuse ontologies powerful and integrated tools and methods are absolutely necessary. Therefore, we will describe the formal, linguistic and graphical methods, the architecture and other properties of KARO. We will enrich this survey with several examples which clarify the modeling process of the domain layer in a scheduling task using MIKE. We will show the integration of KARO and MIKE in respect of the development of the domain layer of a model of expertise. We finish the paper with a comparison of related approaches.

1   Introduction

Ontologies and their relationship to problem-solving methods (PSM) in order to reuse KBs is of growing interest in the knowledge engineering (KE) community. Unfortunately, there is also a growing confusion about the notion of 'ontology'. To clarify the different understandings, we will briefly discuss the different points of view.

In the knowledge representation and reasoning community (KR&R) the reuse of ontologies was first discussed in an approach to overcoming the brittleness of expert systems (see [16]) and was meanwhile also subject of projects like CYC [22]. Even though there were some back-strokes, the optimism is still existing as can be seen in a paper about 'The future of knowledge representation':

Definition 1: Issues of *ontology* will be among the most important and most talked about topics in the next few years. How to build the 'upper model' – the topmost levels of a large hierarchy of commonsense knowledge, how to integrate parts created by different people, and how to control revisions will be important considerations. [4, p.1089]

Besides the motivation for research in the field of ontologies, Brachman defines ontology as the topmost level of a large hierarchy of commonsense knowledge, i.e., knowledge about time, space, objects, etc. In respect of reuse in KE, efforts in this direction are trying to build KBs which are domain-independent and can therefore be reused in several applications. So domain-independence and reusability is achieved by providing very general knowledge clusters.

In contrast to this definition, Gruber [12] within the KE-community sees ontologies not as a bunch of very general knowledge but as an agreement of several agents in the use and reuse of a shared vocabulary:

> **Definition 2:** A specification of a representation vocabulary for a shared domain of discourse – definitions of classes, relations, functions, and other objects – is called an *ontology*. [12]
>
> An *ontology* is an explicit specification of a conceptualization. The term is borrowed from philosophy, where an ontology is a systematic account of Existence. For knowledge-based systems, what 'exists' is exactly that which can be represented. [13]

Following this point of view, several task-oriented KE methododologies have created their own subtypes of ontologies with different generality, e.g., the KADS group [38]: 'domain ontology, domain-model oriented ontology, task-type oriented ontology, method-specific ontology', and PROTEGE-II [10]: 'editor-interface ontology, input ontology, method ontology, application ontology'. The legitimation for the different ontologies comes from the different sources of ontological commitments, e.g., commitments about general domain theories, the type of the task to be solved or the method chosen to solve the task [38, p.198].

Although defintions 1 and 2 are obviously conflicting, the term 'ontology' has in principle a similar meaning: *a theory of what exists*. The difference between KR&R, KE, cognitive sciences, and philosophy lies in the viewpoint of the scientist, i.e., in the question *for whom does something exist?*:

- in (most parts of) philosophy the things exist *per se* without an agent assuring the existence of these things. Ontology is therefore the study of entities independent of our knowledge of them (simplified).
- the KE community uses the term with respect of what exists *in or for a program* to a given point in time (see definition 2).
- People from the KR&R and cognitive science community (see definition 1) usually speak of ontologies as commonsense ontologies, i.e., things that exist as knowledge about the world that is possessed *by every schoolchild* inclusive the methods for making obvious inferences from this knowledge [25]. Already Hobbs [18] noted that in AI most accounts on ontology have been concerned with the organization of structure of human knowledge of reality rather than with the reality itsself.

According to [12, p.215]) we will call ontologies related to definition 2 *representation ontologies*. They provide a framework, but do not offer guidance about how to represent the world. On the contrary, we will call ontologies in accordance with definition 1 *commonsense ontologies*.

In the following we will only speak from ontologies as commonsense ontologies, i.e., a collection of general top-level categories and associated relations and assumptions. That implies that an ontology is rather domain–independent. However, an ontology is typically not totally task–independent since in all practical cases it can be assumed that the knowledge engineer constructed them with at least a very general task in mind. Domain independence in combination with a variable granularity paves the way for refining an existing ontology in order to build up a domain model for the application domain at hand.

Therefore, KARO (*Knowledge Acquisition Environment with Reusable Ontologies*) deals with two main research directions: firstly, with developing commonsense ontologies and reusing them for modeling other domains. Secondly, with supporting the domain-modeling process with an integrated environment which provides several means for defining, retrieving, and adapting fragments of the ontology in order to incorporate it into the domain-model-KB. Additionally, we support the MIKE approach [1] in building up the domain layer.

Since the first topic is already documented elsewhere[1] we will focus on the second topic, i.e., the methods and tool support in KARO and its usage in the MIKE approach. We will provide only the most important features and the principles of KARO (see section 4). Additionally, we will give an impression of how to use KARO by a few examples (see subsection 5.2). In section 5 we illustrate the profit of using KARO in the development process of MIKE and refer to an already formalized PSM which was published in [21]. We will show how the domain layer can be worked out *easier* and made more *robust* in respect of the usual case of modifications which is of special importance in real world applications (see subsection 5.3). Due to space limitations, the benefit of KARO in earlier phases of MIKE can be discussed just briefly (see subsection 5.5) . To understand how and why KARO was integrated in MIKE we will show the principles of MIKE in the next section.

2   MIKE: Model-based and Incremental Knowledge Engineering

The MIKE approach [1] defines an engineering framework for eliciting, interpreting, formalizing, and implementing knowledge in order to build knowledge based systems. KE is seen as a modeling process which aims at creating a computer model providing results in problem solving which are similar to those generated by an expert. Since such a modeling process is cyclic and reversible and consists of a stepwise refinement KE is considered as an incremental process.

In accordance with the different models which are incremetally created during the modeling process the KE process itself is divided into different phases which are carried out in a cyclic way based on a spiral model. Only some of the phases are relevant in the context of this paper. We will therefore confine ourself to a description of the most important phases, i.e., elicitation phase, interpretation phase, and formalization phase.

---

[1] For the origin, content, and structure of the LILOG ontology see [19]. For practical experiences in reusing ontologies see [32], [33].

2.1 Elicitation

The result of the knowledge *elicitation phase* is the so-called elicitation model (see figure 1), a model on the linguistic level. It contains accordingly interrelated knowledge protocols stemming, e.g. from interviews with the expert.

2.2 Interpretation

Among the models which are built up in the *interpretation phase* are the structure model (see figure 1), and the documentation model (see [29]). The structure model, a model on the conceptual level, is based on hypermedia principles and offers semi-formal descriptions of the problem solving activities on the one hand and of concepts and relationships between concepts on the other hand. The documentation model provides a documentation of the knowledge acquisition process itself by, e.g., capturing modeling decisions about the structure model.

2.3 Formalization

The model of expertise (see figure 1) is the result of the *formalization phase* and offers an expertise description on a logical level using the formal and operational specification language KARL [1]. It is constructed on the one hand from the semi-formal structure model, on the other hand by reusing generic problem solving methods (PSM) from the MIKE library. We will follow the second way of construction in section 5 'Developing the Domain Layer of a Design Task with KARO'.

The model of expertise is separated into three layers (see KADS [37]): The *domain layer* contains the domain model with knowledge about concepts, their features, and their relationships. The *inference layer* contains the inference model with knowledge about the problem-solving methods used; and the *task layer* contains the task model with knowledge about the control flow of these problem-solving methods. The model of expertise also provides means for defining the mapping between the generic concepts and the domain specific concepts at the domain layer.

A KARL specification of a PSM is divided into several parts, namely a collection of processing modules, which decompose the inference and task layer into smaller pieces, and a set of domain modules, which group domain knowledge.

3 An Environment for Knowledge Acquisition with Reusable Ontologies

In the next subsection we will briefly discuss the ontology and inference engine of KARO. The integration of KARO in MIKE and the several means of KARO will be subject of the following sections.

3.1 Architecture of KARO

The ontology we are using in KARO was developed in the LILOG project[17] within approximately four years by the Universities of Stuttgart, Hamburg, Bielefeld, Osnabrueck, and by IBM Germany. The knowledge base consists of

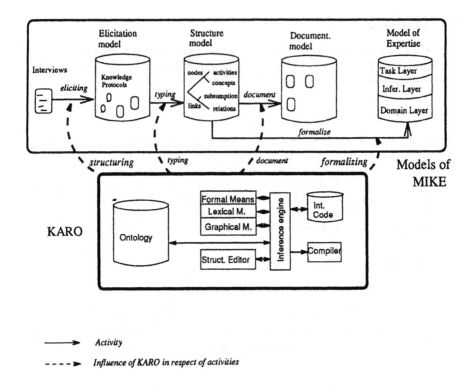

Fig. 1. Relationship between KARO and some models of MIKE

about 700 concept definitions. The number of attributes for each of these concepts averages around 20. The number of axioms is approximately 300. The following knowledge clusters are represented in the LILOG ontology: *Space* (such as shape, orientation, dimensions, etc.), *Objects* (conscious beings, persons, animals, plants, buildings, abstract objects, etc.), *Time and Events* (e.g. relations between time intervals), *Qualities, Quantities, and Measuring Scales* (size, weight, color, etc.), *Energy and Motion* (e.g. movable vs. unmovable objects) *Assemblies and Matter* (e.g. parts of objects).

The ontology is formalised in L_{LILOG} [34] which is a logic-based hybrid representation formalism similar to KL-ONE (cf. e.g. [5]). L_{LILOG} serves for representing the terminology of the domain by means of sort expressions for classes of entities, organized hierarchically as sets and subsets (i.e., the logical subsumption relation), and two-place predicates and functions (i.e., features and roles), attached to specific sorts constituting functional and relational connections between sorts. Therefore, a concept hierarchy is coded as a sort lattice and interconnected by axiomatic definitions. Additionally, axioms of first–order predicate logic which express inferential dependencies between domain terms can be expressed. Due to space limitations, we refer to [19] and [17] for a more detailed discussion on the content and structure of the LILOG ontology.

The inference engine[2] can be considered as a modular theorem–proving shell since it is possible, for example, to exchange inference calculi and search strategies very easily.

The different kinds of models of MIKE were already discussed in the last section. The data flow and control flow in KARO and MIKE will be subject of the next subsection and the different means of KARO will be described in section 4.

3.2 Integration of KARO in MIKE

Figure 1 describes the architecture of KARO and its integration into MIKE. We will briefly discuss the items to be found in the figure.

The broken line between KARO and the models of MIKE can be explained as follows:

Structuring: by showing structural dependencies between entities which often belong together in the ontology, KARO gives guidelines for the KE in respect of 'undiscovered' concepts, attributes, etc. In an interview, for example, the expert mentions a concept 'engineer'. The KE recognizes in KARO additional features relating to the definition of 'engineer' e.g. skills and is motivated to ask the expert about this knowledge (see subsection 5.5)

Typing: KARO tries to support what [38] called 'knowledge typing': knowledge elements are assigned basic types such as concept, attribute and relation. KARO provides several criteria for supporting this decision process (see subsection 4.4). The entity 'schedule', for example, can be represented as event, concept, or predicate (see subsection 5.5).

Documenting: the modeling decisions and the whole development process for conceptual dependencies is stored in KARO. For example, the decision why 'schedule' was represented as 'concept' can be stored in the documentation model (see subsection 4.4 and 2.2).

Formalizing: since already formalized knowledge entities are provided by an ontology, the formalization of semi-formal knowledge is a main topic of KARO, e.g., the KE can search with linguistic expressions and retrieve the corresponding formal expressions from the ontology (see the example for retrieval by lexical means in subsection 5.3).

3.3 Data flow and control flow in KARO

When trying to reuse components in KARO in a systematic way we can lean on experiences made in traditional software reuse. According to [30] the reuse of existing software can be performed in four phases:

- the definition phase describes the component which needs to be constructed.
- the retrieval phase retrieves candidate components from the source KB.
- the adaption phase generates the desired target component out of these candidates.
- the incorporation phase integrates the target component into the rest of the target KB.

---

[2] KARO is based on the inference engine of LILOG-KR (see [17])

In respect of these phases, there are two possible ways of working with KARO. The first one is **phase-driven**, i.e., the availability of operations or means in KARO depends on the reuse phase in which the system is (see the option *Reuse_phases* in figure 3). It is, for example, unnecessary to offer a destructive operation (e.g. del_sort) in the definition phase. The second way is means driven, i.e., the user decides to work for example with the entire collection of graphical means.

Additionaly, all facilities which are independent of the means or reuse status can be selected. These are the documentation of modeling decisions, the guidelines for modeling activities (e.g. criteria if a construct should be represented as a concept or as a relation), and others (see the option *Means* in figure 3). .

4 Means of KARO

The idea of reusing the ontology of LILOG has been of practical interest (see [2]). But experience in reusing general knowledge clusters such as Space, Objects, Qualities, Time, etc. for the modeling of a concrete domain (Business Process Management [32]) showed that the support of powerful and integrated tools is absolutely necessary. Therefore, we have developed our environment in which the different types of means all operate on the same internal code and are therefore integrated (see figure 1). This provides for a free switching between the means.

In figure 2 a screendump of the user interface for the graphical means of KARO is shown. Most of the windows available are hidden for reasons of clearness. The main window ('graph') shows a section of the time cluster where the sort lattice is visualized as a network. The graph window is overlaped by the browsable 'features' window (upper left corner) which shows all features contained in the ontology. In the middle of the 'graph' window we find a menue (focus, superiors,..) which is explained in figure 4. The window in the upper left corner shows the structure editor with the definition of Timeinterval. An important window (command, quit,..) is right under the 'clock-window': the 'menue-window' serves in controling the different services and means of KARO. The current menue-window shows the option mode of the graphical means. Figure 3, figure 4, figure 5, and figure 6 show the different menue windows for the most important operations in KARO.

4.1 Semi-formal Means of KARO

KARO provides graphical means for manipulating the graphical representation of the ontology and also a structure editor for macro-editing the code structure.

Graphical Means of KARO: In contrast to the other operations the graphical operations presuppose a preselection of a sort in the graphic browser by clicking with the right mouse button on it. An explanation of some of the graphical operations can be seen in figure 4.

Structure Editor in KARO: The programmable editor of KARO has an interface to the inference engine. Therefore several operations in KARO can be executed from and to the editor. The exchange of control and data between the

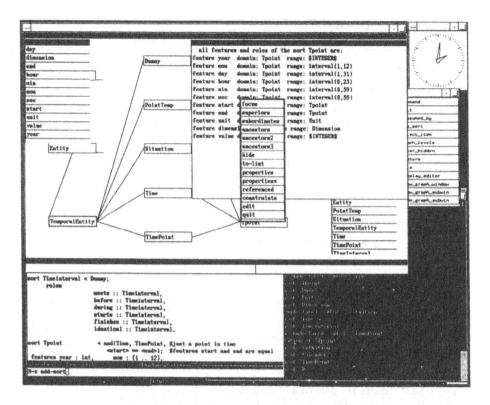

Fig. 2. Screendump of the user interface of KARO

editor and other means is supported. It is possible for example to point from sort definitions in the editor (formal definition) to the graphical representation in the gaphical means and vice versa . The structure editor provides of course some standard commands such as find_sort (feature, role), del_sort, add_sort, etc.

4.2 Lexical Means

The separation between language processing and knowledge processing in KARO gives us the possibility of defining linguistic operations (word class operations, homonymy, synonymy, ..) and knowledge processing operations (classification, subsumption, inheritance, ..) on our ontology in order to retrieve fragments (see [33] for more details). An overview of the most important lexical operations can be seen in figure 5.

4.3 Formal Means of KARO

Code fragments to be retrieved from the ontology can be defined with expressions of the formal representation language L_{LILOG} . Fragments are retrieved either by theorem proving or by classifying concept descriptions with the classification algorithm of KARO. Retrival, adaptation, and incorporation can be performed with a set of predefined operations (about 70) which are provided by an interface module to the taxonomy. One of these operations add_sort is described in more detail below.

Operations	Description
Reuse_phases	(Definition, Retrieval, Adaptation, Incorporation)
Means	(Formal_means, Linguistic_means, Graphical_means)
Documentation	(see section 4.4, 2.2)
Decision_criteria	(see section 4.4: 'Decision_criteria')
Integrity	(see section 4.5: 'Integrity-Checks')
Ontologies	provides operations like: *display_all_ontos* since ontologies in our sense are (more or less) domain-independent but sometimes task-dependent, KARO provides a list of Ontologies from which the most appropriate one is choosable. *documentation_of_onto* provides documentation of the selected ontology and references for further information. As mentioned above it is not trivial to select the right ontology for a given task. Other operations for managing ontologies are provided in addition.
Options	see the *menue*-window in figure 2

Fig. 3. Part of the top level menue of operations in KARO

Operations	Description
focus	sets the selected sort in the lower left corner of the browser window.
superiors	shows all direct subsumers of a sort
subordinates	shows all direct subsumees of a sort
ancestors	shows all ancestors of a sort
hide	hides the sort and its subsumees in the browser
properties	shows all defined properties of a sort
properties*	shows the defined and inherited properties of a sort
referenced	shows where a sort is used in another sort definition
constraints	shows all constraints of a sort
edit	goes to the formal definition of the sort in the editor.

Fig. 4. Part of the menue of graphical operations

Operations	Description
search_word	tries to find a word (or its hyperonyms, synonyms, etc.) in the lexicon and its sortal expression in the ontology.
determine_word_class	tests a word if its word class is noun, verb, adjective, etc. This makes sense for the supervising the modeling criteria (see subsection 4.4)
show_lexicon	shows a pretty print of the lexicon in the editor.
synonym_lexicon	shows a pretty print of the lexicon for synonyms in the editor
define_word_and_sort	interrelates word expression with sort expressions.
load_new_lexicon	loads lexicon
remove_lexicon	removes lexicon from the library
hyperonym	gives all hyperonyms for a word
synonym	gives all synonyms for a word

Fig. 5. Part of the menue of lexical operations

The consistency of the taxonomy after having applied these operations is assured. A direct manipulation of the formal code of the concept-definitions is not allowed.

The explanation for the formal means in KARO which are provided by a mouse sensitive menue-window can be seen in figure 6.

Operations	Description
prove	proves a theorem
classify	classifies a sort expression in the sort lattice
subsumed_by	tells whether a sort is a subsort of another
subsume_all_sorts	performs a subsumption check between any two sorts of an ontology
compile_onto	although KARO supports the investigation of only one ontology at a time, several ontologies can be hold in the workspace of KARO. The membership of each sort is coded in the internal representation of each sort definition. The compilation of knowledge bases into an internal representation provides for an efficient handling of the ontology.
codegen	the compilation and generation process is necessary for checking the semantical and syntactical constraints by the inference machine.
pp_construct	prettyprints the definition of a construct where a construct can be a sort, feature, role, or axiom.
add_construct	typical operations on constructs (sorts, feature, role, axiom), i.e., *del_construct, rename_construct, move_construct*

Fig. 6. Part of the menue of formal operations

Classification as a Retrieval Process: Entering and accessing knowledge of a knowledge base requires knowing how the information is structured in the ontology. Brooks [6] supposed that *invisibility* is one essential difficulty in building large software applications.[3] Information systems such as LaSSIE [9] incorporate a large KB and a semantic retrieval algorithm based on formal inference. The advantage of semantic retrieval is that one just has to know *what* kind of information shoud be retrieved but not *where* to find it. The problem of locating a sort expression S in a sort lattice (caused by invisibility) is automatically solved by, e.g., a classification algorithm[4]. The usefulness of classification as a retrieval instrument opposed to simple syntactical matching in a sort lattice can be shown by the following example:

Given:

```
sort Engineer < Person,
        feature employeed : Corporation.
```

---

[3] Invisibility means that the structure of software (unlike those of buildings or automobiles) is hidden. The only external evidence we have of software is its behaviour when executing or interpreting.

[4] for details on the implementation of a classification algorithm see [24], [31].

```
sort Student < Person,
      feature immatriculated : University.

sort Student-engineer < and(Engineer, Student).

sort Woman < Person
      feature  sex : female.
```

Classify: Dummy = and(employeed : Corporation,
immatriculated : University, sex : female).

Result: subsort(Dummy, and(Woman, Student-engineer)).

When refining the concept Dummy as a, e.g., Female-Student-engineer with appropriate features, etc., we are able to locate it as subconcept of Woman and Student-engineer.

In large ontologies with complex interdependencies, definitions are difficult to *locate* without classifier.[5] Especially when using the lexical means of KARO in order to match synonyms such as Corporation and Enterprise or homonyms such as University and Educational-institution during the classification process, the KARO-classifier has been proven as a powerful tool.

For the use of *documentation* the classification process can be made explicit and stored. Another example for classification as a retrieval instrument is shown in section 5.2.

4.4   Criteria for Modeling Decisions and their Documentation

Besides the extensional definitions of concepts in the ontology[6], KARO provides several criteria how to make modeling decisions. We will provide only a short overview and refer to [33] for more details.

The linguistic test of Woods [39] provides criteria of deciding whether an attribute or predicate is appropriate in a certain modeling case. Attribute names are constrained to nouns, therefore employeed in the example above should not be allowed as a attribute in our case. Instead, employeed should be replaced by employment.

As already mentioned above, the adaption of existing definitions is one phase of reuse. If we want to add a feature designs which is resticted to Machines to the definition of Engineer, we were warned either to model designs as a concept (with attributes, like agent, medium), or as a predicate. During the knowledge acquisition process KARO checks the attribute names in the lexicon and warns the knowledge engineer in case of violated name convention (see next subsection).

Besides the linguistic test, we provide other guidelines such as the modeling criteria mentioned in Guarino [14], which stand in the tradition of the philosophical distinction between substance and essence (see [33]).

---

[5] For reasons of simplicity we have not introduced role-hierarchies, which is quite usual for showing the strenght of classification [31].

[6] Concepts already existing in the ontology and theories behind the concepts determine the conceptual structure of new definitions.

In the end, the KE has to decide if s/he wants to accept the modeling principles or overwrite them. In the latter case, the decisions are at least documented in the documentation model of MIKE.

4.5 Integrity Checks

Every constructive or destructive sort operation has preconditions and postconditions to guarantee the closure principle [27, p.190]: any change operation should lead to a well-defined ontology (avoid multiple introductions of the same atomic term, avoid terminological cycles, take care of unintroduced atomic terms, etc.). In the following the sort operation *add_sort* is described as an example for checking the integrity of the ontology (in pseudocode):

```
add_sort(S,Subsumers,Subsumees,Ontology)
        IF test_precondition(S,Subsumers,Subsumees,Ontology) THEN
                execute_add_sort(S,Subsumers,Subsumees,Ontology),
                test_postcondition(Ontology)
        ENDIF.
```

The operation *add_sort* introduces a new sort expression S with the subsorts *subsumees* and the supersorts *subsumers* in a chosen *ontology*. *test_preconditions* tests if the preconditions are given, i.e. all specified sorts exist, the new sort name is not already introduced and the modeling criteria are fulfilled. Then the sort operation is executed. Finally, the operation *test_postcondition* tests whether the ontology is still consistent.

PRECONDITION
```
test_precondition(S,Subsumers,Subsumees,Ontology)
        test_existence(S,Subsumers,Subsumees,Ontology),
        test_unique_name_assumption(S,Ontology),
        test_modeling_decisions(S,Ontology).
```

First, every sort which was specified as a subsumer or subsumee is checked for existence. The operation *test_unique_name_assumption* tests if the definition of the sort already exists. Then the new sort is checked, e.g., whether the name of the sort is a noun, which is one of the modeling criteria given in KARO. If not, the KE has the opportunity to overwrite the suggestion and document the violation of this criterion.

IMPLEMENTATION
```
execute_add_sort(S,Subsumers,Subsumees,Ontology)
        del_subsumption(Subsumees,Subsumers,Ontology),
        add_subsort(S,Subsumees,Ontology),
        add_supersort(S,Subsumers,Ontology).
```

del_subsumption deletes the subsumption relation between Subsumees and Subsumers. S is then introduced as a supersort of Subsumees and as a subsort of Subsumers.

POSTCONDITION
test_postcondition(Ontology)
    recompile_ontology(Ontology),
    cycle_test_onto(Ontology),
    check_lattice(Ontology),
    all_sorts_consistent(Ontology).

The function *recompile_ontology* tests the unique-name-assumption and the existence of all constructs and computes the subsumption relations of the taxonomy again. In some cases of ontology revision the changes in the sort lattice can be kept local but very often the update of one definition causes changes which concerns the whole taxonomy[7] (see examples in [27]). *cycle_test_onto* tests whether the ontology contains sorts that are defined cyclically. *check_lattice* checks if there are sorts with no connection to top. *all_sorts_consistent* tests for all sorts of the ontology whether they stand for the empty set (e.g., statement $A \wedge \neg A$).

After having described the means and methods of KARO, we will now explain how KARO in interaction with the MIKE approach can be used to build up a domain layer of a model of expertise.

5   Developing the Domain Layer of a Design Task with KARO

Usually the domain layer is not provided with more data than necessary in a specific application domain, i.e., with more knowledge than is needed to solve the task at hand. But we think that there are several reasons for avoiding this kind of domain modeling:

- The construction of a domain model as part of a model of expertise is made much *easier* and more *robust* by offering means for selecting and adapting parts of an ontology.
  Easier means to provide domain-independent structures of knowledge that the designer could use as a starting point for encoding his domain model. The intention is to give the designer a modular system and managing tools to handle these modules in an adequate way so that these modules can be used as an 'upper structure' (or blue-print) in the new KB and the designer can insert his own domain model in the 'lower structure' consistently.
  The development of a *robust* KB tries to achieve a deep reconstruction of the domain which is embedded in a world model. It is intended to represent more of the domain than actually needed in order to 'catch unpredicted cases' and to overcome the wellknown brittleness of conventional expert systems. In the usual case of changing specification requirements, the required domain theories (time, space, etc.) need not be developed from scratch again.
- The modeling process becomes more *standardized* by reusing predefined categories and by checking syntactic, semantic, ontologic, and linguistic constraints when introducing new definitions. These means of standardization

---

[7] There are obviously two ways of reacting to update operations: every constructive or destructive operation releases an automatic reclassification (e.g. like the BACK system [31]) or requires an explicit user demand (e.g. like the SB-ONE system [20]). We support the second alternative.

are preconditions for enabling the distributed development of large knowledge bases.

- The continous use of the same upper models for objects, time, space, etc. in multiple applications supports a better and faster understanding of the modeling principles underlying a model - especially when *making oneself acquainted with* an unknown model or when *maintaining* applications developed by other people. Even when several ontologies are used for one cluster (e.g., time interval logic vs. time point logic for the time cluster) the knowing of a theory behind the model is a good starting point for understanding the modeling principles.

For showing the practical usefulness of KARO in respect of the items mentioned above, we have used [21] as a pattern. There, the problem to be solved is given as a *design problem*. The PSM that fits best has already been identified as propose-evaluate-revise. As in [21] we assume that former phases of the KE process (e.g., elicitation, interpretation) have already been carried out and that we choose the PSM from a library. This PSM has to be connected to the concrete application task, i.e. the domain layer has to be developed from scratch and mapped to the inference layer. In the former solution by [21] the domain layer was developed closest to the application at hand.

In the following we describe the PSM from the library in KARL. Then we explain how the upward and downward mapping from inference layer to domain layer is defined. Finally, the domain layer definitions of KARO proclaiming the advantages mentioned above are given.

5.1 Task- and Inference Layer of the Design Task

Syntactically, problem-solving structures consist of the following constituents:

- the control part specifies the flow of control between the inference actions contained in the PSM (Lines 05 to 22)
- the inference part describes elementary and composed inference actions which are part of the PSM. For each of the inference actions, premises and conclusions are given. Additionally, stores, views, and terminators can be defined which appear for the first time at this level of refinement. For views and terminators, a connection to domain knowledge has to be specified in mapping clauses (see lines 32 and 44).

```
01 PROCESSING_MODULE design
02   INTERFACE
03     REFINEMENTS propose, evaluate, revise;
```

Three basic steps of the PSM for solving the problem are identified (see line 03):

- a **propose** step which is concerned with making new assignments.
- an **evaluation** step which checks the solution found so far against the requirements.
- a **revision** step which tries to make some modifications in case that the evaluation indicates the need to do so.

The composed inference structures will not be refined (see [21] for a complete description) since *all important references to structures of the domain layer are already given at this level of abstraction*. This points to the fact that KARO is already at a very high level of PSM refinement advantageous for developing the domain layer.

```
04
05   CONTROL
06      VAR failure, end;
07      SUBTASK design
08
09         failure := FALSE;
10         end := FALSE;
11         propose(IN: d_states, components, slots, prefer; OUT: d_states);
12         WHILE NOT failure AND NOT end DO
13            evaluate(IN: d_states, components, slots; OUT: p_modifications);
14            WHILE NOT EMPTY(p_modifications) AND NOT failure DO
15               revise(IN:p_modifications, d_states, prefer; OUT:d_states);
16               evaluate(IN:d_states, components, slots; OUT: d_states);
17            ENDWHILE;
18            propose(IN:d_states, components, slots, prefer; OUT: d_states);
19         ENDWHILE;
20         IF NOT failure THEN select(IN:d_states; OUT:design);
21         ENDIF;
22      ENDSUBTASK;
```

The problem solving starts with the assignment of an activity (component) to a timeperiod (slot). Furthermore, a new design state containing this assignment is generated (propose in 11). The new design is then evaluated with respect to the validity of individual assignments and conflicts between assignments. If necessary, potential modifications are made (evaluate in 13) and applied (revise in 15) which resolve that conflict. Since the application of a modification may resolve one conflict but cause another, the evaluate/revise cycle is repeated until a consistent design is reached or no further proposed modifications (p_modifications) are possible.

```
23
24   INFERENCE
25      VIEWS
26         VIEW components
27            DEFINITIONS
28               CLASS components
29                  ELEMENT_ATT
30                     name:{STRING};
31               END;
32            UPWARD_MAPPING
33               USE activity FROM DOMAINMODULE Scheduling Data
34               VAR Obj: ELEMENT; Name: VALUE.
35               Obj[name:Name] is_element_of components
36                     <- Obj[name:Name] is_element_of activity.
```

The mapping clause expresses that the elements of the generic class components at the inference layer, correspond to the elements of the object class activity in line 33 at the domain layer. The same holds for slots and timeperiod in line 45 below.

```
37        END;
38        VIEW slots
39          DEFINTIONS
40            CLASS slots
41              ELEMENT_ATT
42                name:{STRING};
43            END;
44          UPWARD_MAPPING
45            USE timeperiod FROM DOMAINMODULE Scheduling Data
46            VAR Obj: ELEMENT; Name: VALUE.
47            Obj[name:Name] is_element_of slots
48                  <- Obj[name:Name] is_element_of timeperiod
49        END;
```

For our purpose this level of refinement is sufficient. Thus the definition of stores, terminators, and the refinement of inference actions is omitted (see [21] for a complete description of the PSM.).

The definition of the classes activity (in line 33) and timeperiod (in line 45) will be shown next.

5.2 Domain Layer of the Design Task

Even at this abstract specification level of the PSM we have found a connection to the domain layer by the upward mapping of the concept activity (in line 33), which is defined in the domain module SchedulingData as follows:

```
52        CLASS activity
53          ELEMENT_ATT
54            name:{STRING};
55        END;
```

In the original context of [21], activity has only one attribute name (the same holds for timeperiod: there is no starting_point, ending_point, etc.). Other deficiences are the absence of attributes like agent, patiens, location which are important for modeling real world scheduling tasks (see section 5.4).

```
47        CLASS schedule
48          ELEMENT_ATT
49            activity:{activity};
50            schedule_at:{timeperiod}
51        END;
```

A time calculus is only given by the following axiom (transitivity of timeintervals):

```
57        VAR X,Y,Z:ELEMENT;
58        timeorder(before:X,after:Y)
59        <-  timeorder(before:X,after:Z) and timeorder(before:Z,after:Y)
```

Theories of time and action have a longstanding tradition with multiple interdependencies in the fields of philosophy, linguistic, cognitive science, etc. We can't go into deeper theoretical details of our ontology (see [17] and [19] for an overview). Instead we will show in the next subsection how the relevant structures can be defined, retrieved, adapted, and incorporated in our domain layer.

To summarize, we have investigated the solution of a scheduling task by a formal problem solving method *propose-evaluate-revise*. In order to solve the application problem, the PSM was connected to the smallest domain model possible. We have detected several disadvantages of this kind of modeling.

5.3   Modeling the Domain Layer with KARO

To show how KARO provides appropriately structured models as well as a well-defined process model for reusing knowledge base components for building up a domain layer easier and more robust, we will give two examples and discuss advantages of KARO and MIKE in real world applications.

Example for retrieval by classification:
The situation is as follows: The class activity in 52 only exists as a reference without a formal definition, i.e., without appropriate axioms, features, acompanying classes, etc. Therefore, we are looking for a definition of activity in KARO. We choose *definition* in the menue *Reuse_phases* and then *Formal_means* in the menue *Means* of figure 3, and finally *classify* in the menue of formal operations in figure 6. The structure editor appears with a mask for a classification task and appropriate guidelines. We insert

```
sort Dummy = and(before : Dummy, after : Dummy).
```

since we don't know the exact name but expect that the definition of an activity in the context of a scheduling task should have the attributes above. We call the classification process.
The information appears:

```
subsort(Timeinterval,Dummy).
```

Dummy was classified as a supersort of Timeinterval. We choose the menue of graphical operations to visualize the sort lattice (see figure 4). The inspection of the L$_{\text{LILOG}}$ definition can be performed by clicking the *edit* button of timeinterval in the browser (see figure 7). The following definitions appear in the editor window:

```
sort Time              <  TemporalEntity;
  features start       : Tpoint,
           end         : Tpoint,
           unit        : Unit,
           dimension   : Dimension,
           value       : int;
  disjoint Situation.

sort Timeinterval < TemporalEntity;
  features meets : Timeinterval,
           before : Timeinterval,
           during : Timeinterval,
           starts : Timeinterval,
           finishes : Timeinterval,
```

```
       identical : Timeinterval,
       .............
```

```
sort Tpoint < and(Time, TimePoint, %just a point in time
                  <start> == <end>);  %features start and end are equal
features year : int,      mon : [1 .. 12],
         day  : [1 .. 31], hour : [0 .. 23],
         min : [0 .. 59], sec : [0 .. 59].
```

```
sort Situation   < and(TemporalEntity,
       .............
```

Now the user recognizes that there is a difference between timeintervals and activities. The user guesses that there must be a connection so he selects the graphical interface and chooses *references* of timeinterval and finds the class event connected to timeinterval by the attribute duration. Furthermore he can inspect the event cluster and time cluster by navigating through the ontology definitions and using the documentation and explanation facilities of KARO.

Example for retrieval by lexical means:
Instead of using formal means for retrieving activity we will now illustrate the use of KARO by retrieving timeperiod with linguistic means. In order to give an example of the synonym lexicon and the decomposition algorithm we will start with a synonym of timeperiod: lapse.

Definition step: We choose *definition* in the menue *Reuse_phases* and then *Linguistic_means* in the menue *Means* of figure 3. Now we click on *search_word* in the menue of lexical operations in figure 5 and enter lapse.

Retrieval step:

```
Scanning input phrase: lapse
Unknown word: 'lapse'
Select information you will provide or quit.
proper_name hyperonym synonym correction quit
-> synonym
Please enter synonym of 'lapse'
-> timeperiod
Scanning input phrase: timeperiod
Unknown word: 'timeperiod'
Trying to decompose word...
May I use 'interval' instead of 'period'?
-> yes
Synonym found: 'Timeinterval'. The words 'Lapse' and 'Timeperiod'
   correspond to the class  'Timeinterval'
```

KARO automatically retrieves Timeinterval and Lapse, respectively. The user may now switch to *documentation_of_onto* in the top-level menue (in figure 3) and get information to questions like 'what is a timeinterval, theory of time, etc.'.

Finally, he runs into the **adaptation phase** where he may use destructive and constructive operations to adapt the domain layer to the specific application, e.g. inserting missing classes by applying add_sort.

The last phase, the **incorporation phase**, provides means for specifying a set of definitions in L$_{LILOG}$ and translating it into KARL code. Although the formalism L$_{LILOG}$ and KARL are different in several aspects they are quite similar at the domain layer (e.g., multiple inheritance, subsumption, etc.). The semantics of the translation is grounded on work reported in [7].

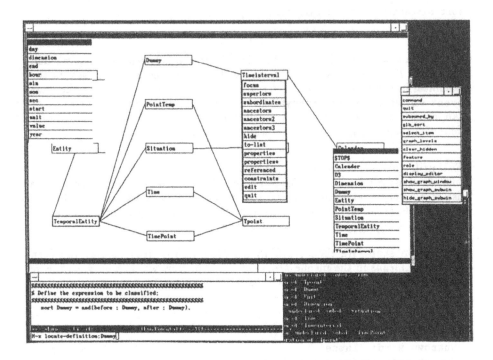

Fig. 7. Screendump of graphical representation of timeinterval

In the last sections we gave an impression of how the models of time and activities in KARO can be reused in order to meet the criteria mentioned in the begining of section 5. In the next subsection we will show that when changing to real world applications the use of KARO is even more important.

5.4 Real World Applications

The solution described in [21] is very abstract and is not concrete in respect of a specific application. One assignment is preferred over another if the time period involved in the first assignment precedes the time period of the second. In typical Production Planning and Scheduling (PPS) applications decision processes are much more complex as described for example in [3]. A realistic PPS problem in the area of pharmaceutical production planning can be described as follows:

- There is a set of orders to be produced. Each order specifies a *product*, an *amount*, and a *due date*. Orders are also assigned *priorities*.
- Each product can be produced in a number of variants. Each variant consists of a number of *production steps*, and each production step can be carried out on a number of different *machines*.
- Machines have different characteristic features; not every step of a variant can be produced on every machine. But since the machines are multi-purpose machines as they can do many different jobs, they should be *scheduled* to achieve highest efficiency.
- There are different *specialists* for every machine. Some are specialists for more than one machine others are only *temporary-workers*.
- *Production constraints* have to be obeyed. For instance, the individual production steps of a given variant must be executed in a predefined sequence, without any time delay between them.

In this problem description the definition of complex concepts, the optimization of distances and other economical and efficiency factors play a crucial role. Especially the entities in italics *product, amount, due date, priorities, production steps, machines, temporary-workers, schedule,* and *production constraints* have to be structured, characterized, and interrelated. The need of general models of space, objects, etc. for doing this in an adequate way is obvious. As can be seen when changing to real-world problems, additional help and support in respect of an environment such as KARO arises.

5.5 Former KE-phases and KARO

Up to now we have only investigated the Model of Expertise and the development of the domain layer with KARO. But as already mentioned in section 2.3, the model of expertise is usually constructed from the semi-formal structure model of MIKE.

How KARO is involved in the elicitation and interpretation phase can be shown as follows: a good example for a knowledge protocol (outcome of the elicitation phase, see figure 1) is the text about pharmaceutical production planning (see above) which could very well stem from an interview with an expert. The transition from the elicitation phase to the interpretation phase requires that entities have to be identified from knowledge protocols. KARO supports what [38] called 'knowledge typing': knowledge elements in the knowledge protocols are assigned basic types such as concept, attribute, and relation. The representation of the entity schedule in line 47 as a class (*schedule* in the text above) has to be motivated since a predicate or attribute would also be acceptable. In the philosphical discussion events or activities mostly had no conceptual status for the reason of ontological economy (Ockham's razor). In knowledge engineering or in general representation tasks this principle is opposed to Russel's razor which demands a most simple logical calculus (see for example [8]). When reifying predicates or events such as schedule or drive then they have concept status in the domain model. This technique enables us to model events in an analogical manner to case frames for verbs in the lexicon.

Besides the event-cluster the ontology of KARO entails also an object-cluster where general concepts and relationships between concepts for modeling objects are provided. This includes, among others, a model of humans which gives guidelines for representing employees, specialists, and temporary-workers (e.g., students). How a concept Student_engineer or more special Female_student_engineer can be retrieved from the ontology was already subject in the discussion of classification processes in subsection 4.3. The modeling decisions are checked for plausibility and documented (see the example about representing 'Temporary-worker' and 'Student' in [33]).

KARO supports the interpretation and structuring of knowledge protocols by providing formal definitions of entities in the protocols. If the definitions reveal several possible new attributes, the KE is motivated to ask the expert about these dependencies. So the formal definitions can initiate a new development cycle of the spiral model starting from the elicitaion phase and resulting again in the formalization phase.

6   Related Work

Before comparing KARO with other approaches, we will first list the special features of our environment. This will serve as a scale for measuring similarities and differencies:

1. **Ontologies**: how many ontologies are selectable, how are they documented, are they philosophicaly, linguisticaly, etc. founded?
2. **Means**:
   - **Formal means**: see subsection 4.3.
   - **Formal semantics**: a formal semantic of a formalism gives us the foundation for inferencing and understanding the formalism.
   - **Semi-formal means**: such as graphical operations and a structure editor (see subsection 4.1)
   - **Lexical/linguistic means** see subsection 4.2
   - **Integrity checks**: see subsection 4.5
3. **Phase oriented reuse**: does the approach provide facilities for phase-oriented reuse which guides the user during the reuse process: definition, retrieval, adaptation, incorporation (see subsection 3.3)?
4. **Process model for KE**: does the approach provide a phase-oriented knowledge engineering methodology?
5. **PSM oriented approaches**: does the environment support a KE methodology based on generic PSMs (see subsection 5)?
6. **Modeling decisions and documentation**: does the environment provide means to support modeling decisions and documentation (see section 4.4)?

As we have said in the introduction, we are able to distinguish between two notions of ontologies: representation ontologies and commonsense ontologies. Obviously, we can also distinguish between environments or tools corresponding to these different notions of ontologies.

6.1   Environments for approaches with commonsense ontologies

Environments which use ontologies for conceptual modeling of the domain layer are, e.g., CODE4 [35], ONTOS [26] , HKE [36]. Since ONTOS was already compared to KARO in [33], we will confine ourself to CODE4 and the knowledge editing interface HKE for the CYC-project.

The CODE-project

CODE [35] is a general purpose management system with a wide variety of functions and is intended to serve as a KE 'rapid prototyper'. In contrast to the MIKE/KARO environment, where expertise is developped in a model- and phase oriented way with clear separations between different development stages, CODE is a mixture of formalisms and functions. The user may freely mix formalisms: a CODE knowledge base can have a free combination of both informal phrases and first-order logic axioms. CODE provides an interactive graphic interface with means for syntatctic and semantic checks. The question of how a mixture of several (in)formal representations can be checked for consistency and integrity remains open. Documentation facilities are given, support for modeling decisions are not. Similar to KARO a commonsense ontology is given. However, means to find and retrieve components from this ontology are only given in form of a graphical browser. Also similar to KARO is a lexical interface for translating and verbalizing knowledge elements. This subcomponent is primarily made for experts and seasonal KEs who want to input their knowledge directly without intensive training for CODE.

The CYC-project

The HITS Knowledge Editor (HKE) has been designed to assist users in the task of knowledge editing for the CYC-project. A graphical interface with browsing facilities is provided to support this issue.

In HKE knowledge editing is seen as a cooperative activity that requires editors to reach consensus as they represent information in a KB. Consensus is achieved by discussing sketches (temporary buffers of parts of the KB), applying simple consistency checks, and design recording.

Design recording shows the vocabulary that previous users have found appropriate for representing a domain. It records particular facts that users asserted about objects in a domain. These facts can be used as a template. HKE does not capture the design rationale behind the representational decisions. In contrast to KARO the editing process is mainly seen from an incorporative view: different means for finding, retrieving, and adapting concepts from CYC are not discussed. In our opinion, the main issue of HKE is to provide a graphical interface to the KB for discussing and for reaching consensus for the modeling process.

A final remark on environments for the CYC-project: [15, p.32 and p.353] describe a knowledge editing environment for CYC with the functionality of a simple class browser and some consistency checks. Even in newer publications Lenat et.al. [23] doubt the usefulness of sophisticated environments: "similarly, having a fancy graphical interface for CYC is a potential distraction, a time-sink we occasionally find ourselves tempted by". In contrast to this we agree with B. Neches [28, p.153] who remarks: "I see the development environment as the key point where sharing and reuse is either enabled or fatally hindered. If a new application is going to tap into Cyc's knowledge, application builders need to be able to uncover what is already out there in the knowledge base related to the application's concerns. Then, they need to determine how their new knowledge relates to that pre-existing knowledge and how to express things to achieve the appropriate interlinking. .....This is why development environments are needed.

I have some trouble understanding how people are going to use it without more investment in tools than appears evident."

The Knowledge Sharing Effort Project (KSE)
Since KSE provides for topic-independent ontologies (time, causality,..) and application-dependent ontologies (closely related to 'representational ontologies'), it lies between the approaches described in this subsection and the next.

KSE tries, among other things, to develop shared ontologies in order to provide a basis for packaging knowledge modules and to integrate different KBs into a unifying framework. The top-level ontologies (such as our ontology) embody representational choices ranging from domain independent (e.g. models of time or causality) to domain specific but still application independent knowledge. The difference to KSE is that KARO does not use ontologies as a communication medium for sharing theories across different domains, but for supporting the development of new conceptual models of a domain.

As far as we know, up until now efforts in KSE have been mainly in the direction of standards for knowledge sharing and not in the development of sophisticated environments specially taylored for commonsense ontologies (in contrast to the remarks of B.Neches above).

Also the **translation approach** to portable ontology specifications [12], which is closely related to KSE, is concerned with describing mechanisms for defining representational ontologies that are portable over representation systems. Ontologies are specified in a standard, system-independent form (Ontolingua) and translated into specific representation languages. Ontolingua was in the first place designed as a language for defining representational ontologies and not as a tool.

When comparing Ontolingua to our approach, we have to determine that in contrast to Ontolingua, KARO provides method and tool support for the reuse of a commonsense ontology. Furthermore, KARO is phase-oriented and embedded in the MIKE approach, and supports the elicitation, structuring, formalizing, and documention of knowledge items.

6.2 Environments for representational ontologies

Since representational ontologies in PSM-oriented approaches do not provide guideance on how to represent the world at the domain layer, e.g., with theories about domain-independent clusters, they do not need mechanisms and tools to define, retrieve, adapt, and incorporate concepts from an already exisiting commonsense ontology. Although these approaches often have tools for reusing PSM from a library, the domain layer itself is mostly built up without support of tools or domain-independent concept libraries. For example in Protege-II an ontology editor MAITRE [11] was developed which maintains frame based definitions in the tradition of more or less sophisticated class browser or knowledge representation environments such as BACK [31], SB-ONE system [20]. Compared to KARO these environments often only have means for classification, inferencing, integrity checking, and GUIs for browsing.

7 Conclusion

In this paper we have shown the basic architecture and the formal, semiformal, and linguistic means of KARO. Moreover, we described the integration of KARO into a knowledge engineering environment MIKE. Our efforts for reusing a commonsense ontology for modeling a domain grew out of practical interest - the motivation, experiences, and results are reported in [2] and [33]).

To summarize, the following features of KARO are of importance:

- KARO attends the development of a model of expertise in respect of the domain layer in MIKE.
- KARO provides a theory of the represented domain, i.e., a deep representation of conceptual dependencies.
- KARO makes the modeling of conceptual dependencies easier, faster, and more robust.
- KARO provides an integrated set of means for defining and retrieving class definitions from an ontology in order to incorporate and adapt it to new domain models. Integrated means that all operations are based on an intermediate formal representation.
- KARO supports the distributed development of KBS since it provides a reference model and a standardization of the terminology in a domain.
- KARO supervises constraints and checks integrity conditions.
- KARO provides means for modeling decisions.
- KARO provides means for documenting decisions.
- KARO supports the elicitation phase, interpretation phase, and formalization phase of the life cycle of a KBS.

Navigating in a more or less unknown ontology requires tool support. Especially in KARO we provide for re/using more than one ontology. To support the user in finding the appropriate ontology for solving his task is an ongoing subject of research not only in the KARO approach but also in several related approaches.

Acknowledgements

For helpful discussions on the KARO topic we would especially like to thank Sven Lorenz, Ralf Becker, and Udo Pletat. The MIKE approach has been developed to a large extent by Susanne Neubert, Jürgen Angele, Dieter Fensel, and Dieter Landes.

References

1. J. Angele, D. Fensel, D. Landes, S. Neubert, and R. Studer. Model-based and Incremental Knowledge Engineering: The MIKE approach. In J. Cuena, editor, *Proceedings of the IFIP TC12 Workshop on Artificial Intelligence from the Information Processing Perspective (AIFIPP'92)*, Madrid, Sept. 1993. Elsevier Science Publisher.
2. R. Becker and T. Pirlein. Executable design specifications through the use of knowledge-based technologies. In *Proceedings of FLAIRS-94*, Pensacola, Florida, May, 4-6 1994 (to appear).
3. C. Beierle. An overview on planning applications in protos-l. In *Proceedings 13th IMACS World Congress on Computation and Applied Mathematics*, Dublin, Ireland, 1991.
4. R. J. Brachman. The future of knowledge representation. In *Proceedings Eighth National Conference on Artificial Intelligence*, pages 1082–1092, Menlo Park, etc., 1990. AAAI Press / The MIT Press.

224

5. R. J. Brachman and J. G. Schmolze. An overview of the KL-ONE knowledge representation system. *Cognitive Science*, (2):171–216, 1985.

6. F. P. Brooks. No silver bullet: Essence and accidents of software engineering. *IEEE Computer*, 4:10–19, 1987.

7. S. Buvak and R. Fikes. *Semantics of Translation*, pages 12–16. Chambery, France, August, 28th. 1993.

8. D. Davidson. The logical form of action sentences. In N. Rescher, editor, *The Logic of Decision and Action*, pages 81–95. University of Pittsburgh Press, Pittsburgh, Pennsylvania, 1967.

9. P. Devanbu, P. Selfridge, B. Ballard, and R. Brachman. Lassie: A knowledge-based software information system. *Communications of the ACM*, 34(5):249–261, 1991.

10. H. Erikson, A. Puerta, and M. A. Musen. *Generation of Knowledge-Acquisition Tools from Domain Ontologies*, volume 93-56 of *Medical Computer Science*. Knowledge Systems Laboratory, Stanford, University, 1993.

11. J. Gennari. *A Brief Guide to MAITRE and MODEL: An Ontology Editor and a Frame-Based Knowledge Representation Language*. Number 94305-5479. 1993.

12. T. Gruber. A translation approach to portable ontology specifications. *Knowledge Acquisition*, 5(2):199–221, 1993.

13. T. Gruber. Toward principles for the design of ontologies used for knowledge sharing. In N. Guarino and R. Poli, editors, *Formal Ontology in Conceptual Analysis and Knowledge Representation*, Dordrecht, Boston, Lancaster, Tokyo, 1994 (to appear). Kluwer Academic Publishers.

14. N. Guarino. Concepts, atrtibutes and arbitrary relations. *Data and Knowledge Engineering*, 8:249–261, 1992.

15. R. V. Guha and D. B. Lenat. Cyc: A midterm report. *AI Magazine*, (11 No. 3):32–59, 1990.

16. P. Hayes. The naive physics manifesto. In D. Michie, editor, *Expert systems in the micro-electronic age*, pages 243–270. Edinburgh University Press, Edinburgh, Scotland, 1978.

17. O. Herzog and C. Rollinger, editors. *Text Understanding in LILOG*, volume 546 of *Lecture Notes in Artificial Intelligence*. Springer-Verlag, Berlin, Heidelberg, New York, 1991.

18. J. R. Hobbs. Ontological promiscuity. In *Proceedings of the 23rd annual meeting of the Association for Computational Linguistics*, pages 61–69, Chicago, Illinois, 1985. Association for Computational Linguistics.

19. G. Klose, E. Lang, and T. Pirlein, editors. *The Ontology and Axioms of the LILOG knowledge base (in German)*, volume 307 of *Informatik-Fachberichte*. Springer-Verlag, Berlin, Heidelberg, New York, 1992.

20. A. Kobsa. The SB-ONE knowledge representation workbench. In *Preprints of the Workshop on Formal Aspects of Semantic Networks*, Two Harbors, Cal., February 1989.

21. D. Landes, D. Fensel, and J. Angele. Formalizing and operationalizing a design task with KARL. In J. Treur and T. Wetter, editors, *Formal Specification of Complex Reasoning Systems*. Ellis Horwood, Chicester, 1993.

22. D. Lenat and R. Guha. *Building Large Knowledge-Based Systems: Representation and Inference in the CYC Project*. Addison-Wesley Publishing Company, Menlo Park, CA, 1990.

23. D. Lenat and R. Guha. Re: Cycling paper reviews. *Artificial Intelligence*, 61:149–174, 1993.

24. T. Lipkis. A KL-ONE classifier. In J. Schmolze and R. Brachman, editors, *Proceedings of the 1981 KL-ONE workshop*, pages 128–145. 1982.

25. J. McCarthy. Programs with common sense. In *Proceedings Symposium on Mechanisation of Thought Processes I*. London, 1959.

26. I. Monarch and S. Nirenburg. The role of ontology in concept acquisition for KBS. *Proceedings of the First European Workshop on Knowledge Acquisition for Knowledge-Based Systems*, 1987.

27. B. Nebel. *Reasoning and Revision in Hybrid Representation Systems*. Lecture Notes in Computer Science 422. Springer-Verlag, Berlin, Heidelberg, New York, 1990.

28. R. Neches. Book review of Lenat, D.B. and Guha, R.V.: Building large knowledge-based systems: Representation and inference in the CYC project, addison-wesley, reading, MA, 1990. *Artificial Intelligence*, 61, 1993.

29. S. Neubert. Model Construction in MIKE. In *7th European Knowledge Acquisition Workshop-93 (Toulouse)*, Lecture Notes in Artificial Intelligence, Berlin, Heidelberg, 1993. Springer Verlag.

30. E. Ostertag, J. Hendler, R. Prieto-Diaz, and C. Braun. Computing similarity in a reuse library system: An AI-based approach. *ACM Transaction on Software Engineering and Methodology*, 1(3):205–228, 1992.

31. C. Peltason, A. Schmiedel, K. Kindermann, and J. Quantz. *The BACK system revisited*, volume 75 of *KIT Report*. Department of Computer Science, Technische Universität Berlin, Berlin, 1989.

32. T. Pirlein. Reusing a large domain-independent knowledge base. In C. Chang, editor, *Proceedings of Fifth International Conference on Software Engineering and Knowledge Engineering*, pages 474–482, San Francisco Bay, CA, June 16-18 1993. Knowledge Systems Institute.

33. T. Pirlein and R. Studer. An environment for reusing ontologies within a knowledge engineering approach. In N. Guarino and R. Poli, editors, *Formal Ontology in Conceptual Analysis and Knowledge Representation*. Kluwer Academic Publishers, Dordrecht, Boston, Lancaster, Tokyo, 1994 (to appear).

34. U. Pletat. The knowledge representation language L-LILOG. In O. Herzog and C. Rollinger, editors, *Text Understanding in LILOG*, volume 546 of *Lecture Notes in Artificial Intelligence*, pages 357–379. Springer-Verlag, Berlin, Heidelberg, New York, 1991.

35. D. Skuce. A multi-functional knowledge management system. *Knowledge Acquisition*, 5(3):305–346, 1993.

36. L. Terveen and D. Wroblewski. A tool for achieving consensus in knowledge representation. In *Proceedings AAAI-91*, pages 74–79, Anaheim, CA, 1991.

37. B. Wielinga, A. T. Schreiber, and J. Breuker. KADS: A modelling approach to knowledge engineering. *Knowledge Acquisition*, 4(1):127–161, March 1992.

38. B. Wielinga and T. Schreiber. Conceptual modelling of large reusable knowledge bases. In K. Luck and H. Marburger, editors, *Management and Processing of Complex Data Structures*, volume 777 of *LNCS*, pages 181–200. Springer, Berlin, Heidelberg, New York, 1994.

39. W. A. Woods. What's in a link: Foundations for semantic networks. In D. Bobrow and A. Collins, editors, *Representation and Understanding: Studies in Cognitive Science*, pages 35–82. Academic Press, New York, N.Y., 1975.

From Verification to Modelling Guidelines

Sabine Geldof, Aurelien Slodzian

VUB AI Lab
Pleinlaan 2, 1050 Brussel Belgium
Tel. (32-2) 641.37.00
Fax. (32-2) 641.37.29
sabine/aurelien@arti.vub.ac.be

Abstract. In this paper, we discuss the verification of knowledge systems by means of knowledge level reflection techniques. Our claim is that knowledge level reflection enables for a principled, customisable and reusable way of performing verification. As a consequence, the knowledge engineer obtains more meaningful results from verification while developing his application and can use them as guidelines for further development. We illustrate how this is done through the MetaKit in the KresT workbench.

Keywords knowledge level reflection, integrated verification, knowledge level verification, modelling, KBS development process,

1 Introduction

In this paper we will focus on verification[1] of knowledge systems. Although it is generally acknowledged that verification (and validation) of knowledge systems is very important for their quality it has not become common practice yet. Developers regard it as an extra burden on their work, not as a help. If they perform verification at all, it is rather at the end of the development process when the project consists of a very tight network of interfering components, where the consequences of one modification are not foreseeable. We argue, like others before ([Bensabat and Dhaliwal, 89], [Sierra et al., 91], [Cañamero et al., 93]), that verification should be intertwined with the development process and that different types of verification should take place in different phases of the development process. Verification needs to be done in such a way that it can contribute positively to the development process, that results of verification are useful for the developer.

In order to improve the possibilities of performing verification in the perspective just described, the verification process should be customisable and produce significant results. Indeed, different types of verification are needed, according

---

[1] according to Hoppe and Meseguer's definition: 'checking a KBS against its formalizable specifications' as opposed to validation: 'assuring that the final KBS complies with user needs and requirements [Hoppe and Messeguer, 91]; cfr. also Boehm's 'building the system right' vs 'building the right system' [Boehm, 84]

to different phases in the development process and to the development style. The ACKnowledge project, for instance, aimed at developing a knowledge engineering workbench where validation is closely tied to knowledge acquisition ([Mengshoel, 91], [Shadbolt, 91]). Our paper treats more generally the integration of validation in the modelling process, we will not consider verification of the contents of knowledge bases. The second requirement relates to the kind of information that is expected as a result of verification: rather than an unstructured list of detailed failures difficult to interpret, the developer should be given an overview about the state of his project and guidelines about how to best continue development. The need for development guidelines has also been put forward in [Vanwelkenhuysen, 93].

We see several major developments in the field of knowledge engineering that contribute to the achievement of the above mentioned goals and requirements. They are all operationalised in the KresT workbench. The first is the idea of knowledge models, mostly used in the practical sense of 'a structure that is imposed on knowledge when it is being put to use in a class of problem situations' [Van de Velde, 93], but derived from the original notion introduced by Newell in [Newell, 82]. It is a generally acknowledged way of providing a meaningful description of a project. Wielinga et al. argued for the need for knowledge level verification and validation [Wielinga et al., 93]. KresT supports knowledge level modelling and systematic linking to symbol level. Applications are developed as white-boxes that can easily be inspected. Another important innovation is the idea of knowledge level reflection, which was latent in the knowledge level theory of Newell. For an overview of its implications see [Wielinga and van Harmelen, 93]. In this paper, we want to demonstrate that this perspective provides an appropriate framework to perform principled, customizable verification and to integrate verification with the other Knowledge System (KS) development activities.

A framework has been developed and operationalised in the MetaKit [Slodzian, 94], an extension of KresT, which makes it possible to perform operations on knowledge level or symbol level descriptions of projects. One of the possible applications is verification. These operations at a meta-level are modelled and implemented in the same way as (object) applications and equally benefit from reusability, configurability and a (knowledge engineering) methodological base. We argue that this allows for more efficient and more meaningful verification in comparison with existing verification procedures. We will show how fragments of meta projects act as verification procedures, providing guidelines for further modelling of the knowledge system.

In section 2 we summarise the main characteristics of the componential methodology (ComMet), the tool KresT and we introduce the principles of knowledge level reflection and the MetaKit that operationalizes them. In the remainder of the paper we will distinguish between two types of verification that both produce information interesting as guidelines for further development of the project.

In section 3 we elaborate on a first type of verification intended to discover incompleteness at the macro level (structure of the project). Formally and conceptually it can be characterised as one-step verification.

In section 4 we discuss a more sophisticated type of verification. There the results of several one-step verification tasks are used as input to another task. This inference task looks for dependencies between symptoms of incompleteness at the micro level (description of components). Formally and conceptually, this is two-step verification.

In section 5 we formulate our conclusions and an outlook on this research field.

2 Background

2.1 ComMet & KREST

The componential methodology [Steels, 90, Steels, 93] belongs to the mainstream of the knowledge engineering field that considers knowledge acquisition as a modelling activity. In ComMet, a coherent model that forms the basis of the application is made up by identifying and integrating a series of components. They belong to three different but complementary perspectives: tasks, methods and models — all of which are necessary to ensure the completeness of the knowledge level description of the application. Models contain data relevant for the application. Identifying the tasks means thinking about what needs to be done to solve the problem that the application addresses. The method perspective specifies how the knowledge can be used to perform the task.

The code level, as opposed to the knowledge level, refers to the machine symbolic representation (in a programming language) of the components identified at the knowledge level. The execution level considers the internal objects created in the machine as the code is installed.

KresT [McIntyre, 92b], [Goossens et al., 93], [Jonckers et al., 92] is an environment that puts into practice the principles of the componential methodology. It improves the process of knowledge engineering in several ways. By conceiving an application as a white-box, it makes possible a principled design and implementation of knowledge systems, offers the possibility of reusing components, and aims at configuration of applications by non-programmers.

In KREST, different types of diagrams visualise the identified components as well as their relationships. Task and subtask relationships are reflected in the Task Structure (TS) (see figure 4). Model-Method and Model-Task relationships are visualised in Model Dependency Diagrams (MDD). As shown in figure 3, the MDD also visualises information concerning the methods. The labels on the arrows indicate the role that the model plays w.r.t. the method associated with the task.

In order to be useful and complete, knowledge level descriptions should not be limited to what can be represented graphically in diagrams. KREST supports extended knowledge level descriptions based on feature structures [Kay, 86]. Feature structures are frame-like representations that can be combined and compared using the unification mechanism. A simple example for a model is presented in figure 1.

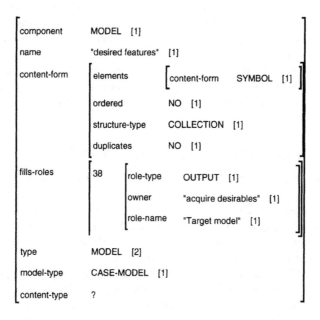

Fig. 1. Feature Structure of a model

Unification[2] serves both as an information-spreading mechanism that can combine partial descriptions drawn from different sources and as an admissibility test based on constraints. These constraints are represented as feature structures, checking consists in comparing the feature structure describing the desired structure (constraint) with the feature structure containing the actual structure (component) [McIntyre, 92a, McIntyre, 92b]. The feature structures of components incorporate the information in the diagrams but also more specific information like the form of the contents a model. Feature structures can be inspected and edited by the user.

In addition to editing of knowledge-level specifications KREST supports the linking of different levels of representation (knowledge-code-execution). The user can link knowledge-level objects to their code-level realisations[3] or encode

---

[2] Unification has mostly been used in natural language processing, but it is also an appealing mechanism for knowledge engineering support. One important characteristic is that unification does not impose an order on the design process. Therefore it fits perfectly our requirement for a mechanism which allows dependencies between components to be captured without thereby imposing a rigid order.

[3] The linking is currently realised via a separate code file for every object. A link for a knowledge level object could also consist in a pointer into a single code file for the complete project.

knowledge-level to code level objects automatically. Code files can also be generated from execution-level objects. The linked code can be inspected and selectively executed.

Finally, KresT may be customised by extending the ontology of the knowledge level description and by enriching the symbol-level library of methods and object classes. It is considered as a good practice to provide both extensions together, in order to preserve the code generation capacities of KresT. Such extensions of KresT are called "application kits" or AppKits. They are most generally specialised either in one domain of application or in one type of operations. The next section presents one of them, which was used to construct the examples of this document.

2.2 Knowledge level reflection and the MetaKit

The MetaKit [Slodzian, 94] is a KresT application kit for knowledge-level reflection.

As an application kit, it consists of a series of specialised knowledge level descriptions of components (models and methods), together with their corresponding symbol level implementations. It also includes a library of ready-made fragments that may be pasted into user projects.

The MetaKit is intended to cover the domain of meta-level operations: it provides tools to design projects working on the properties of other projects.

The main principle of the MetaKit is to separate the object-level and the meta-level. On one hand, we will consider object-projects, which do effective problem solving and result in the deliverable application. On the other hand, we find meta-projects, the task of which being to analyse and manipulate the descriptions of other projects. This distinction between object- and meta-level allows for a clearcut definition of procedures like verification as meta operations. In this scheme, the knowledge engineer can reuse, inspect and modify verification procedures in the same principled way as he can manipulate parts of object-level projects. In its current implementation, the MetaKit is limited to analysing knowledge-level descriptions and does not allow neither modification of these descriptions nor access to the symbol-level descriptions.

Practically, the link between the meta-level and the object-level is made through models in the meta-project representing various parts of the object-project. There are thus no intrinsic causal relations between those projects. This means that the object project is completely independent of the meta-project, and may be modified, encoded and run without any reference to any meta-level concept. The other consequence is that the meta-project may operate on different object projects, just by changing the value of some models.

The MetaKit library provides knowledge-level descriptions for the following types of models, through the 'content-form' attribute:

Projects Models of this type represent KresT projects, either complete ones or simple fragments.

Components Models with 'model', 'task' or 'method' content-forms refer to such components in the object project.

Method-roles Models in the meta-project may also represent relations between methods and models or tasks in the object-project.

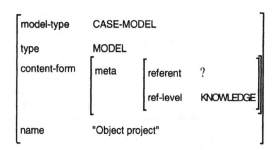

Fig. 2. The feature structure of a "meta" model.

The basic template for these models of the meta-project is presented in figure 2. It introduces the 'referent' attribute which is used to specify the type of the object of the object-project which is referred to. It may be one of the symbols Project or Method-role or one of the structured values [component model], [component task] or [component method].

The contents of such models are accessed by some specialised methods provided by the MetaKit's symbol-level library. Roughly, project-models are filled in by reading files, then component related models may be extracted from the "project" model. There are also methods to inspect components and follow the links between them. In the example presented in figure 3, there is an acquisition task for the model 'object project', which reads from a KresT project file selected by the KresT user, it is followed by an "extraction" task which will build-up the set of the tasks contained in the project. The user intervenes again to select a task from this set and the task 'Look for subtasks' will finally build the set of the subtasks of the selected task.

It is a common practice to consider objects and meta-objects strongly tied together, for example classes and meta-classes, but it is not the case here: one and a same meta-project may be applied to several object-projects. Formally we could say that a meta-project may be instanciated into the meta-level of different object-projects. This instanciation consists in the acquisition of the contents of the meta-project's models. So, during the modelling phase of the meta-project, there is no reference to any particular object-project. Note also that the well known problem of the infinite reflective tower can not occur here for the same reason: a meta-project simply operates on an object project, and there is no upward link from the object to the meta level.

The aim of the MetaKit is to provide a complete and generic tool-set so as to allow the design of any kind of meta-level operation. We are especially inter-

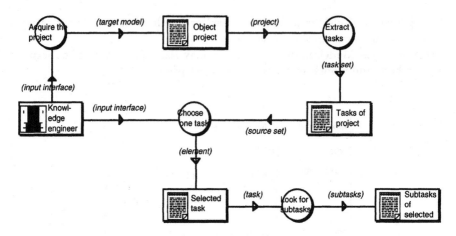

Fig. 3. A mini meta-project

ested in those operations that support the development of knowledge systems: verification, repair of detected errors, guidelines for further development. We want to provide a practical and methodological basis for these activities. The limitations of the current version make it suitable almost only for verification related operations. The next steps are to allow modification of the descriptions of object-projects, and give control over their code and execution level representations.

3 Macro verification: targeted verification

3.1 Principle

The goal of this first type of verification is to get an overview of the project's state of development rather than to verify the project in tiny details. The term "Macro verification" refers to a class of verification procedures, their particularity is to be each targeted to one specific aspect of the project. They can be formulated as concrete questions and the results will point clearly to places where the project needs further development. This type of verification intends to identify gaps in the structure of the project or conceptually important components that might be missing. This is likely to be useful in a rather early phase of the development process, especially for large projects, where it is difficult to keep an overview of the project.

The verification procedure should be flexible and customisable. In ComMet, the three types of components are equivalent, developers can either start from the model, task or method perspective. This may depend on the domain, the development style of the knowledge engineer, his amount of knowledge about the application or the particular application at hand. Unlike more directive tools for KS development, where predefined verification tools are used, we need to provide in KresT the possibility of adapting verification procedures and of creating new ones. This is enabled via the meta level and reflection. The reader will notice in the examples of verification fragments given below that they mainly focus on models and tasks, but also that it is straightforward to build other ones. We will also show how these fragments are built up from reusable fragments and components and how they can be modified. We have elaborated a number of verification procedures that each check one particular specification to be met by a KresT project in order to be sound. The following subsections (3.2 to 3.6) describe some of these procedures.

In practice, verification can be performed as follows: the developer opens an existing meta-level project for verification or configures one with fragments provided in a specialised appkit. After acquiring the knowledge level description of a particular object project (as contents of the models of the meta-level project) he can run the verification procedures on these models.

3.2 Is there a leaf task with a task decomposition method assigned?

Specification : Leafs of the task tree must not be associated with methods of the "task decomposition" family.

Indeed, leaf tasks with a task decomposition method assigned are conceptually contradictory: a task performed by a task decomposition method should be decomposed in subtasks. The detection of such cases can serve as a guideline for the developer: he should develop subtasks for this task.

As shown in figure 4, the task structure of the verification fragment just described consists of two main branches. First the leaf tasks of the object project are identified, then it is tested whether these tasks' methods are of type 'decomposition'. Figure 5 shows model dependencies in this fragment.

In this type of diagram, the rectangles are models (note the difference between case and domain models) and the circles are tasks. The labels on the arrows show the role assigned to the model with respect to the method. For instance, the domain model 'decomposition methods' plays the role *'set'* in the method 'test if member' that will perform the task 'test if decomposition method'.

The three subtasks of the 'detect decomposition tasks' task will be executed for each of the leaf tasks identified in the first part of the fragment. First the method component is retrieved, then its type is compared to the set of known decomposition methods. Depending on the result, the task component will be recorded or discarded.

The model containing the detected leaf tasks can be presented to the user as the guideline: 'since they have a decomposition method assigned, the following leaf tasks of the project need further decomposition'.

This fragment is provided in the MetaKit's verification library, a knowledge engineer can retrieve it, paste it into his particular verification project and modify it if necessary. Suppose, for example, that he wants to examine the leaf tasks whose method is of type 'execution', he could simply replace the domain model

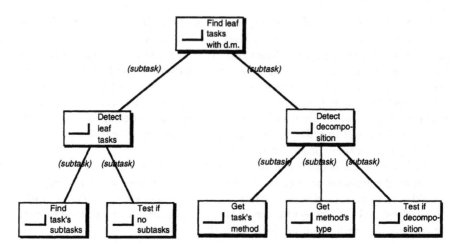

Fig. 4. Task structure of the fragment 'find leaf tasks with a task decomposition method'

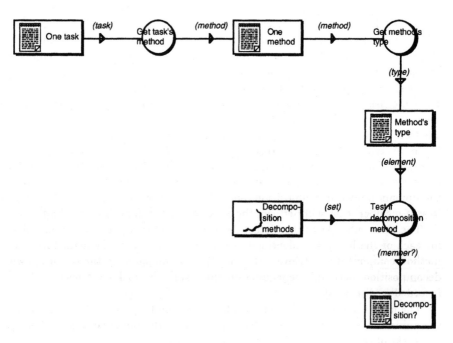

Fig. 5. Subtask model dependency diagram for 'detect decomposition tasks'

'decomposition methods', with a new one containing the list of execution methods. The MetaKit is specially intended to support such operations. Any part of such a fragment can be cut and pasted into another (meta) project, as described for KresT (object) projects in [Steels, 93, Geldof, 94].

3.3 Which leaf tasks have no input or output model yet?

Specification : Leaves of the task tree should have at least one input and one output model.

In a KresT project, the leaf tasks are mainly the ones through which the data flow occurs. Tasks higher in the task tree have decomposition methods and will generally not transform or create data. Thus, in order to have a consistent data flow there must be a chain of corresponding input and output models along subsequent leaf tasks, as the one depicted in figure 5. Therefore it is useful to check whether there are leaf tasks with no input or output model. The developer can then decide whether this really indicates a gap in the data flow: if such a task is not the first (neither the last) in the chain then it should have an output and an input model.

The fragment that enables to check this incorporates a part of the one described in 3.2, namely 'detect leaf tasks'.

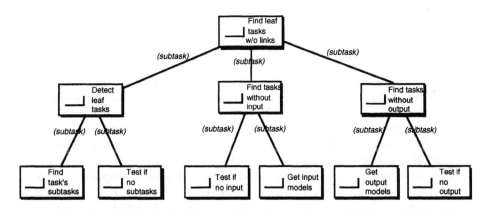

Fig. 6. Task structure for 'find leaf tasks with either no input or no output'

There is also reuse within that fragment: the third subtask ('find tasks without output') is copied from the second, as shown in the task structure, figure 6, and the subtask model dependency diagram, figure 7.

For every leaf task, the input (resp. output) models are identified and this set is tested for emptiness. If the set of input models is empty, the task under consideration is added to the model 'tasks without input (resp. output) model',

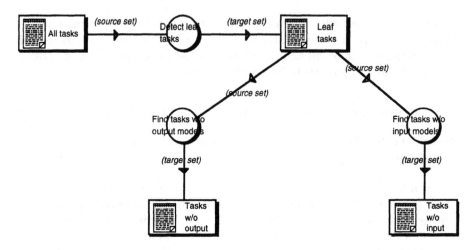

Fig. 7. Model dependency diagram subtasks of 'find leaf tasks with either no input or no output'

which is finally presented to the developer as the guideline: 'the following tasks might need an input or output model to ensure data flow in the application'.

3.4 Is there more than one tasks without parent task?

Specification : All tasks of a project should be gathered in a single task tree. In other words, there should be only one, connected, task tree.

Another indication of incompleteness of a project might be that there is a portion of a task structure that is not integrated in the main task structure.

In line with the Componential Methodology, KresT allows for flexibility in development. Development of a knowledge model consists in identifying components, but there is no rigid sequence: the developer can work on some part of the application for a moment, then switch to another part or to another perspective (for instance focus on the models when getting in an impasse with the task decomposition). As the project becomes very large after a while, the developer might not be aware that he left some part unfinished and need guidance on how to further develop his project. Macro verification is targeted to detect these spots. We have developed a fragment that detects floating pieces of task structure, they could be presented as a guideline: 'check whether these tasks are connected to the global task structure'.

3.5 Which models are not input to any task, output from any task?

Specification : Each model should be used as input (resp. as output) of at least one task.

Similarly, floating models might be interesting to detect. If a model is not read nor written to by any task, it is useless.

This indicates either a model that has been created at some point in the development process, but abandoned for some reason, in which case it should be removed. Either it points to a model that still needs to be connected to a task. Such models might also draw the developer's attention to larger portions of a project that need further development. In the MetaKit library the developer will find a fragment that can check projects on this matter, it produces a guideline for further development: 'these models are worthwhile considering with respect to their connection to tasks'.

3.6 Which domain models still need a knowledge acquisition task?

Specification : Each domain model should be output of at least one acquisition task.

At the end of the development of the project, the knowledge engineer needs to make sure that there should be an acquisition task for each of the domain models used in the application, as such models are usually acquired from the expert and not by computation.

In fact this is a special case of the verification mentioned in 3.5: only domain models and acquisition tasks (i.e. tasks performed by an acquisition method) need to be considered. One could produce the fragment for this verification on the basis of the one for 2.4: detect unwritten models, filter out the domain models and present them to the user. However, this is not exactly the answer to the above question: domain models that are updated in the course of the inference process might still not have an initial acquisition task. The fragment included in the MetaKit makes the difference by examining all the tasks writing to a particular domain model and verifying whether one of these is performed by an acquisition method. The guideline here would be: 'make sure that there is an acquisition task for the following domain models'.

3.7 Conclusion

In this section we have demonstrated that verification can be performed from the meta level, using fragments built with the Meta-kit, meaningful and straightforward to interpret. The fragments presented in this section are so generic that they could be provided as additional functionality in the workbench. The developer would then activate them via a menu and not have access to the way these functionalities are performed. This is what most verification tools provide. The advantage of KresT and the Meta-kit however, is that the developer can inspect the fragments that implement the verification functionalities, reuse and/or modify other fragments to suit his needs.

4 Micro verification: exhaustive verification and analysis of results

4.1 Principle

The verification procedures described so far are very global, analysing the overall structure of the project. Towards the end of the development process, however, the developer will have to focus on aspects of another level of grain-size. The structure of the project is then supposedly reliable and complete, but the detailed descriptions of the different components need to be verified. The developer has to make sure that his model is coherent and complete until the last detail and therefore he will have to focus on other aspects of the description (i.e. method and model types).

The results of such scrutinous analysis however tend to get cluttered: long lists of small fixes to be performed (e.g. method-types that need to be filled in, roles that need to be assigned and model-types that need to be specified). This bunch of information is not easy to interpret by the developer and is far from the desired guidelines for modelling that we are interested in.

To solve this problem in the context of KresT, we will use the modelling constraints included in the knowledge engineering know-how of an AppKit as a structuring mechanism for the verification report. In the Structured BaseKit currently provided with KresT as an example application kit, the choice of a particular method type imposes constraints on the models that fill the roles defined by the method. As a simple example consider the method 'filter' which takes a model for the *source-set* role and a number of tasks as subtasks. The method consists in executing the different subtasks for each of the elements of that source set. The method imposes on that role that it should be of type `ordered-set`. Development of a model of an application supposes that each component satisfies the constraints imposed by its relationship with other components. In the BaseKit, there is a waterfall of constraints that need to be satisfied: method type, method roles, model type of role-fillers. This aspect of the model under development should also appear through the results of the verification, so that the developer gets a good overview of where his description is incomplete and how incompleteness propagates to other parts of the project.

Verification in two steps is needed to provide guidelines for development based on exhaustive verification. So far we could develop verification fragments like the ones in section 3, specialised for the methods: detect all method components without method type specified, detect all method-roles without fillers and detect all under-specified models. However, since all these aspects are interrelated, the developer would be better off with a network of missing parts of descriptions reflecting this waterfall structure. Such an overview will serve as a guideline for development better than a simple list of 'things that need to be repaired'. Also for repairing the detected failures, it is recommended to tackle all related aspects in the same context. Here verification in two steps is required: not only detection of the problems, but also dependencies between these problems should be identified. Figure 8 shows that the two types of verification are complementary.

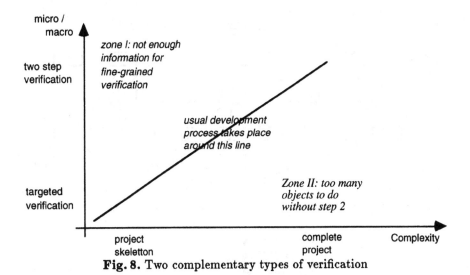

Fig. 8. Two complementary types of verification

This figure represents the need for the second verification step according to the complexity of the project. The oblique line indicates roughly the correlation between these two concepts. Above this line, we find the case of applying complex verification strategies to poorly developed projects. This is almost meaningless as there is not enough information to make inferences. Under the line are already grown up projects to which basic verification procedures are applied. In that case, the problem will be an overflow of uncorrelated error reports, with possibly one cause reported as many times as it has consequences.

Like for macro verification flexibility and adaptability is a crucial aspect of the verification procedures. The example illustrated below shows one way of performing exhaustive verification, adapted to the constraints that hold within the BaseKit and with a particular type of presentation. They could be adapted to another application kit where methods would impose constraints on particular attribute-values of tasks, for example.

4.2 Example

The task structure of the fragment that ensures verification of methods (see figure 9) shows three similar subtasks for the different aspects related to method description. These are correlated as follows: method type (filled in or not?), if the method type is filled in: roles (are all of them assigned to models or tasks?) for assigned roles: fillers (is the model type filled in?).

The structure of each of these subtasks consists of a task for data-collection (e.g. 'collect roles'), one for checking and identifying the components that are incomplete (e.g. 'look for unfilled roles'), finally a task that prepares useful data for the next branch (e.g. 'look for filled in roles'). The collecting and checking

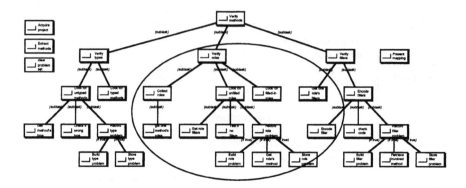

Fig. 9. Task structure of the fragment 'Verify methods'

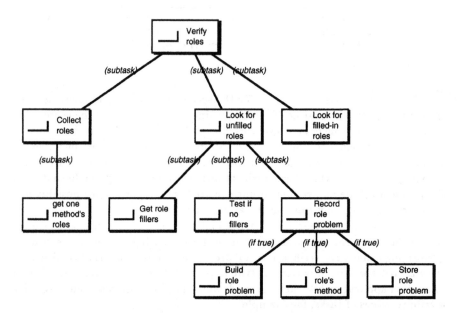

Fig. 10. Detail of the branch 'Verify roles'

tasks are part of the first step in the verification. They are similar to the verification procedures described in section 3. The bookkeeping task however (e.g. 'record role problem') makes explicit the second step in the verification: ordering the results. It creates an object of type 'problem' and writes it to a presentation model (report), making sure that it is listed as a sub-problem of the method that it is connected to. This way, a structured report of the verification results will progressively be built up. In a certain sense, the task 'look for filled-in roles', which passes the data to continue with to the next branch also makes explicit the second step in the verification procedure. It will sort out the models that fill a method role. Only these will be considered, since they are related to the other reported problems. Without the waterfall structure, such a task would not be necessary. It also serves as an optimisation, it ensures that only relevant components are scrutinised. Figure 11 shows an example of presentation for an object project about menu planning. The developer gets a list of methods that he has to inspect, and indications whether their type is filled in or whether there are problems with its roles and/or role fillers.

```
The following methods were found to have problems
---------------------------------------------------
(METHOD::'present dishes' --> (MODEL 'menu' can't be encoded)
METHOD::'find dishes' --> (ROLE 'Subtask' of 'find dishes' has no filler
                          ROLE 'Condition' of 'find dishes' has no
                          filler)
METHOD::'propose first dishes' --> (ROLE 'Input interface' of 'propose
                                              first dishes' has no filler)
METHOD::'copy poss. first dishes' --> (ROLE 'Input interface' of 'copy
                                              poss. first dishes' has
                                              no filler)
METHOD::'update constraints' --> (Method has no type)
METHOD::'find main dish' --> (Method has no type)
METHOD::'knowledge acquisition' --> (Method has no type)
METHOD::'find desert' --> (Method has no type)
METHOD::'test if satisfying menu' --> (Method has no type))
```

Fig. 11. Verification report of running the fragment 'Verify methods' on a project called 'menu advisor'

Like for the other verification fragments described above, all the methods that are used in the meta-project are taken from the MetaKit. In practice, this fragment was built by assembling and partially modifying three similar branches. It was first built as a one-step verification procedure, the book-keeping tasks were plugged in afterwards, as well as the optimisation tasks. The developer can thus adapt his verification project to his own needs, customise it for his domain or for a particular verification strategy.

5 Conclusion

We have illustrated how knowledge level descriptions of applications can be verified trough knowledge level reflection. In particular we described how in KresT the developer can configure meta level projects out of fragments provided in the

MetaKit. The resulting metaprojects inspect the knowledge level descriptions of other projects and produce verification reports, useful for the developer as modelling guidelines along the development process. In its current state, the MetaKit already enables for the straightforward design of meta level operations. Further research and development on this topic will first be aimed at providing also analysis of code level description as to enable verification of contents of knowledge bases. In a second phase, modification of projects via the metalevel will be investigated, leading to full fledged knowledge level reflection.

Acknowledgements

The authors wish to thank Walter Van de Velde for suggesting the topic of the paper. The research reported here is part of the CONSTRUCT project. This project is funded by the Belgian Ministerie van Wetenschapsbeleid (InterUniversitaire Attractie Polen IUAP).

References

[Bensabat and Dhaliwal, 89] Bensabat, I. and Dhaliwal, J. S. (1989). The validation of knowledge acquisition: Methodology and techniques. In *Proceedings of the 3rd EKAW*, 215–233.

[Boehm, 84] Boehm, B. (1984). Verifying and validating software requirements and design specifications. *IEEE Software*.

[Cañamero et al., 93] Cañamero, D., Geldof, S., and McIntyre, A. (1993). Coupling modeling and validation in COMMET. In Meseguer, P. (Ed.). , *Proceedings of EUROVAV '93*.

[Goossens et al., 93] De Vroede, K. and Goossens, L. (1993). The basekit manual (v5.0). Technical report, Knowledge Technologies, Brussels, Belgium.

[Geldof, 94] Geldof, S. (1994). Towards more flexibility in Reuse. In *Proceedings of the International conference on Artificial Intelligence, KBS, Expert systems and Natural Language*, 65–75, Avignon, Paris: EC2.

[Hoppe and Messeguer, 91] Hoppe, T. and Messeguer, P. (1991). On the terminology of VVT. In *EUROVAV 91*, 3–13, Jesus College, Cambridge, England.

[Jonckers et al., 92] Geldof, S., Jonckers, V., and Devroede, K. (1992). The COMMET methodology and workbench in practice. In *Proceedings of the 5th International Symposium on Artificial Intelligence*, 341–348, Cancun, Mexico.

[Kay, 86] Kay, M. (1986). Parsing in functional unification grammar. In Grosz, B., Spark Jones, K., and Lynn Webber, B. (Eds.). , *Readings in NLP*, 125–138. Morgan Kaufmann Publ. Inc., Los Altos, CA.

[McIntyre, 92a] McIntyre, A. (1992a). Commet workbench reference manual. Technical report, VUB AI Lab, Brussels, Belgium.

[McIntyre, 92b] McIntyre, A. (1992b). Feature-based representation in knowledge-level design. Technical Report 92-08, Knowledge Technologies, Brussels, Belgium.

[Mengshoel, 91] Mengshoel, O. (1991). KVAT: a tool for incremental knowledge validation in a knowledge engineering workbench. In *EUROVAV 91*, 239–245.

[Newell, 82] Newell, A. (1982). The knowledge level. *Artificial Intelligence*, 18, 87–127.

[Shadbolt, 91] Shadbolt, N. (1991). Building valid knowledge bases, an ACKnowledge perspective. In *EUROVAV 91*, 195–210, Jesus College, Cambridge, England.

[Sierra et al., 91] Sierra, C., Agustí-Cullell, J., and Plaza, E. (1991). Verification by construction in milord. In *EUROVAV 91*, 211–226, Jesus College, Cambridge, England.

[Slodzian, 94] Slodzian, A. (1994). Knowledge level reflection. Technical Report 94-1, VUB AI Lab.

[Steels, 90] Steels, L. (1990). Components of Expertise. *AI Magazine*, 11(2), 29–49.

[Steels, 93] Steels, L. (1993). The componential framework and its role in reusability. In Jean-Marc David, J.-P. K. and Simmons, R. (Eds.). , *Second Generation Expert Systems*. Springer Verlag, Berlin.

[Van de Velde, 93] Van de Velde, W. (1993). Issues in knowledge level modelling. In David, J.-M., Krivine, J.-M., and Simmons, R. (Eds.). , *Second Generation Expert Systems*, 211 – 231. Springer, Berlin.

[Vanwelkenhuysen, 93] Vanwelkenhuysen, J. (1993). *Participative design of industrial knowledge based systems*. PhD thesis, Vrije Universiteit Brussel, Brussels, Belgium. Also as VUB AI-Lab TR-93-1.

[Wielinga et al., 93] Wielinga, B., Ackermans, H., and G.Schreiber (1993). Validation and verification of knowledge based systems. In Meseguer, P. (Ed.). , *Proceedings of EUROVAV '93*.

[Wielinga and van Harmelen, 93] Wielinga, B. and van Harmelen, F. (1993). Knowledge-level reflection. Technical report, Universisty od Amsterdam.

AFORIZM Approach: Creating Situations to Facilitate Expertise Transfer *

Gennady L.Andrienko and Nathalia V.Andrienko

Pushchino State University
B-35-38, Pushchino, Moscow reg,
142292, Russia
phone 7 (095) 923-80-03
e-mail: and@adm.pgu.serpukhov.su

Abstract. The recognition of the fact that a human expert is often incapable of realizing and reporting his own knowledge induces to search for the situations that might facilitate the processes of recollection and verbalization of the expertise. Such situations were found in cognitive psychology and proved to be of great use for the acquisition of knowledge about properties of objects. Suggested here are some other situations and knowledge elicitation methods based on them. One method is applicable to obtain criteria and preferences for solving the tasks of optimum selection and the other is designed to elicit knowledge about actions to be used in planners. The situations productive for knowledge elicitation can be generated by the use of spatial metaphors and graphic images which provide a vivid, easily perceived and understood form of the tasks given to the expert. The examples of images fruitful for the elicitation of different types of knowledge are given.

1 Motivation

It is widely recognized that a human usually faces significant difficulties when attempting to give an account of his knowledge or to explain the way of solution of some problem. As a human expert still remains a major source of knowledge for knowledge based systems the need arises in special techniques and expedients of inquiring experts that could help them in recollecting and verbalizing the expertise. Such techniques and expedients should be particularly carefully chosen when designing automated means of knowledge elicitation: as compared to knowledge engineers, these means cannot be flexible enough to find the proper way of interviewing the expert in the course of interaction with him but must follow the predefined scenario.

The repertory grid technique is widely and successfully used in various automated knowledge elicitation systems (see KITTEN [1], AQUINAS [2] etc). The advantage of the technique is that it stimulates the recollection of knowledge by

---

* This work was partly supported by Russian Fund for Fundamental Research, grant No 94-01-00950.

an expert suggesting him certain relatively simple auxiliary tasks. These tasks engage the expert into the situations in which he has to compare some objects and reveal their similarities and differences. The situation of comparison turns out to be productive for the expert to recall and verbalize the properties of objects.

Some time ago we put ourselves the question whether there exist similar situations (we call them the reflection stimulating situations, or *RSS*) that allow to obtain other types of knowledge. Now we may give positive answer to this question as we have managed to find such situations. On their basis several knowledge elicitation methods were developed and implemented as the components of the knowledge elicitation system named AFORIZM. When building this research system we have seen our primary objective in creating and testing computer knowledge acquisition methods based on *RSS*. We tried to elaborate such methods for various types of expert knowledge: properties of objects, selection criteria and preferences, knowledge about actions etc.

In this paper two of the *RSS*-based methods implemented in AFORIZM are briefly described. Section 2 deals with the *RSS* productive for eliciting preconditions and postconditions of actions to be used in solving planning tasks. This situation is exploited in the relation analysis method. The other *RSS* given in section 3 is applicable to obtain selection criteria for problems in which optimum choice is needed. The situation is created by means of a business game, or dialog in roles.

As a computer knowledge elicitation tool that strives to direct the expert's mental processes towards revealing this or that kind of knowledge usually does this by posing certain questions or tasks to the expert the form of these questions and tasks may become significant. They must be chosen so that the expert can perceive and understand them easily. The questions asked in text form should not be too long and compound. This restriction can become critical for some methods. The possible way out of this difficulty is the use of computer graphics. The meaning of graphic scene is grasped more easily than the same situation described in text form. Section 4 suggests some examples of the use of graphic images in creating different *RSS*.

Section 5 gives a brief description of the integrated system AFORIZM that unites several knowledge elicitation methods and thus allows to work with knowledge and problems of different types.

2 Revealing knowledge about actions

The computer problem solvers intended to build sequences of actions that lead to certain goals (plans) use the following knowledge about actions: (1) conditions under which fulfillment of an action is possible, usually termed preconditions; (2) conditions which take place in the world as a result of fulfillment of an action, so called postconditions. As such knowledge is needed to automatically solve some problems the issue of its acquisition deserves consideration.

To obtain knowledge of this kind the use of some *RSS* is desirable. It was observed that when an expert thinks about some action he easily recalls the facts relevant to the primary goal this action is usually done for. At the same time some of the prerequisites of doing the action and its side effects are very probable to be forgotten when an expert is directly inquired about the properties of the action. For example, when somebody is asked to describe the results of the action "wash the clothes" the fact "the clothes are clean" is recalled sooner than the fact "the clothes are wet". It is necessary to stimulate in this or that way the recollection of facts not referring to the primary goal of an action.

Evidently, the repertory grid technique helps little in this case as we can *COMPARE* only close entities having much in common. Thus, we can speak about similarities and differences of actions "go by a train" and "go by a car" but it is hardly reasonable to compare in this manner "go by a train" and "buy a ticket for a train". But we can see that last two actions are somehow related and the consideration of this relation can be useful for our purposes: the latter action is needed to make the former possible to fulfil, and this allows to remember the fact that a ticket is needed to travel by a train.

This reasoning has lead us to an idea of the following *RSS*: the expert is proposed to consider pairs of actions and to determine the relation between them giving justification to his answer. In doing this the expert necessarily mentions some facts from the pre- or postconditions of these actions. Based on this idea the relation analysis method was developed and implemented. Five types of relations were chosen by us for this purpose:

1. Doing the action A makes it possible to do the action B, for example, "buy a ticket" and "go by a train";
2. Doing the action B is impossible immediately after the action A is done, like "take the ladder" after "paint the ladder";
3. The fulfillment of the action A is necessarily followed by the action B, for example, having done "wash the clothes" one needs to "dry up the clothes";
4. The actions are alternative, that is, can be used with the same purpose. Such are the actions "go by a train" and "go by a car". It should be noted that this is the case when they can be *COMPARED*;
5. The actions are contrary (implying their results). Example is provided by the pair of actions "ship the goods" and "unload the goods from the ship".

When some of these relations is found to take place for a pair of actions the expert gives a justification to his opinion being prompted by auxiliary questions. The questions are predefined and chosen according to the relation analysed. For example, "What result of A prevents B from being done?" is asked for a relation of the kind (2), and "What is unsatisfactory after A has been done that B becomes necessary?" is chosen when relation (3) is found. In answer the expert is expected to formulate some statements (facts), like "the clothes are wet". These facts are considered to belong to the pre- or postcondition of one of the actions, depending on the relation under analysis. For example, "the clothes are wet" belongs to the postcondition of "wash the clothes" and at the same time to the precondition of "dry up the clothes".

Table 1 shows the questions asked to the expert when each of the relations is found and demonstrates how the expert's answers are interpreted. To denote the relations the abbreviations are used: mp - makes possible, mi - makes impossible, nf - necessarily follows, alt - alternative to, cont - contrary to. In the columns under A and B "post" means that the facts given in answer to the question belong to the postcondition of the corresponding action, "pre" denotes that such facts belong to the precondition.

Table 1. The questions asked in the process of relation analysis and the ways of interpreting the answers.

N	Relation	Questions	A	B
1	A mp B	What is needed by B and created by A?	post	pre
2	A mi B	What takes place after A that makes B impossible?	post	
		What is needed by B that is destroyed by A?		pre
3	B nf A	What takes place after A that makes B necessary?	post	pre
		How this is changed after B is done?		post
4	A alt B	What is common in the results of A and B?	post	post
		What is different in the results of A and B?	post	post
		What is the difference of the situations in which A and B are done?	pre	pre
5	A cont B	What are the contrary results of A and B?	post	post
		What is contrary in the situations in which A and B are done?	pre	pre

As one can see from the table 1, the elicitation of the relations is not the final goal of the method. The role of the relations is to allow us to approach the specific kind of knowledge, namely preconditions and postconditions of actions.

The facts obtained in course of relation analysis are used as source material for generating more formal structures called attributes. For this purpose the expert is asked to pick groups of related facts. For each group he is asked to denote the integral property the chosen facts refer to. The given name is treated as a name of an attribute. Based on the facts chosen the set of possible values of the attribute is defined. For example, we may obtain the attribute "The state of the clothes" with the values "dirty", "clean", "wet", "dry". The analysis of the history of obtaining each fact allows to infer additional information concerning the attribute: which of the values are mutually exclusive, which are desirable and so on. Such information may be of use for planners.

Some description of the procedure of revealing relations for further analysis should be given. This is done in one of the following ways:

1. A pair of action is chosen from the whole set of known actions. The expert is proposed to select one of the five relations which fits best the given pair.
2. An action is chosen and one of the relations is fixed. The expert is asked what other action is associated with the given one by this relation. Note

that this task can help the expert to recall an action which was missed on the stage of listing the actions available.

3. The expert is asked to find a pair of actions associated by the given relation.

These tasks are alternated being chosen depending on the knowledge currently available.

Interesting is the question whether there are other relations to be exploited in the interests of the elicitation of knowledge about actions. By this time we haven't find any that would differ significantly from the given five and offer similar opportunities. On the other hand, this set of relation was sufficient so far for our research purposes.

3 Role dialog for criteria elicitation

Many of the intellectual problems solving of which can be supported by knowledge based systems require choice of the best solution from a set of alternative solutions. To make the choice one should know the criteria that may be treated as attributes with ordered scales of values: for each two values it is defined which of them is preferable. The other kind of knowledge needed is the characteristics of each possible solution in terms of these criteria.

The *RSS* allowing to elicit both kinds of knowledge is created by means of the "Conversation in roles" method having a form of a business game. In this game possible solutions (objects) are treated as goods intended for sale. The expert is proposed to play a role of an agent for a firm producing some of the goods available, the other ones are considered to be the products of imaginary competitors. The knowledge elicitation system (further referred to as system) plays a role of a customer. The game objective of the expert is to persuade the customer into buying one of the goods produced by his firm.

The expert's playing role of advertising agent is very beneficial for our purposes: this induces him to demonstrate the properties of the objects to the customer which is supposed to make a selection. In so doing the expert recalls the properties which he usually takes into account in the course of problem solving. The task of the system is to be captious enough to make the expert search for more advantages of his goods. It should also be clever enough not to allow the expert to praise his goods to the skies and to cast slurs upon those produced by the competitors. The conversation should be designed so as to induce the expert to be less biassed.

To meet these requirements the system constantly analyses the knowledge obtained yet and generates its utterances so to make the expert give a comprehensive characteristic for each object. In fact, all utterances of the system propose the expert to compare objects to reveal the advantages of one over the others. However the specific form of the cues varies depending on such factors as the "quality" of the "goods" being considered and whether they belong to the expert's firm or to its competitors. For this purpose certain quantitative heuristic estimations are made: relative quality of two objects and absolute quality of an object.

The evaluation of relative or absolute quality becomes possible as soon as at least one attribute with its values ordered by preferences is obtained. Therefore the dialog is initiated with the phrase "Please tell me something about your goods" addressed to the expert. When the expert enters some fact concerning one of his goods he is asked to formulate the criterion this fact refers to, to enumerate all possible values of the criterion (in the order of decreasing preference) and to assign each object a certain value of the criterion. The same procedure is applied for each attribute elicited in the course of the dialog.

The relative quality of the object O_1 with respect to the other object O_2, $QR(O_1, O_2)$, is appraised according to the heuristic formula $(P_1 - P_2)/N$, where N is the number of attributes obtained by the given moment, P_1 and P_2 are the numbers of attributes the characteristic values of which for O_1 are respectively more and less preferable than that for O_2. The absolute value of $QR(O_1, O_2)$ thus calculated is compared with two thresholds TR_1 and TR_2. If it exceeds TR_1 one of the objects O_1 and O_2 is regarded as being much better than the other while the sign of QR indicates which of them is better. If the absolute value of $QR(O_1, O_2)$ is less than TR_2 then the objects O_1 and O_2 are considered to be of equal worth.

The absolute quality of the object O_1, $QA(O_1)$, is heuristically evaluated as L/N, where L is the number of attributes the characteristic values of which for O_1 fall into the left half of the range of their values ordered from the best to the worst. The value of QA is compared with the thresholds TA_1 and TA_2. If $QA(O_1)$ is less than TA_1 then the object O_1 is regarded as bad, if $QA(O_2)$ exceeds TA_2 then O_1 is supposed to be good, otherwise O_1 is treated as the object of medium worth. The specific values of TR_1, TR_2, TA_1, TA_2 may vary. In our implementation of the "Conversation in roles" the following values of the thresholds turned out to be reasonable: $TR_1 = 0.5$; $TR_2 = 0.2$; $TA_1 = 0.3$; $TA_2 = 0.5$.

Decision concerning the next step in the dialog is made on the basis of calculations of QA for each object and of QR for every pair of objects. If there is an object with its absolute quality less than TA_1 the expert should be proposed to reveal some advantage of the object. If the QA of some object exceeds TA_2 this means that the expert praises it too much and therefore should be asked about its shortcomings. If there exists a pair of objects with their QR exceeding TR_1 by its absolute value the system must ask about the advantages of the worse of these two goods (or about the shortcomings of the better one).

In case of conflict the system first takes into account the absolute quality. Yet the system tries to avoid the monotony and to alter the form and contents of the tasks given to the expert. Thus, if the previous task was to reveal the shortcomings of some object enormously praised the next step will require the comparison of two objects. When the decision is already made about the form of the task (one or two objects should be considered) then the specific values of QA or QR are taken into account. From the objects with QA less than TA_1 or more than TA_2 the object is chosen with the maximum difference between QA and one of the thresholds. ¿From the pairs of objects with QR exceeding TR_1

the pair is chosen with the greatest value of the QR. If there is no pair with the upset balance of advantages and shortcomings two objects of equal worth are chosen.

Table 2 summarizes the patterns of the utterances given by the system depending on the quality of the object(s) chosen and on their belonging to the expert's firm or to the competitors' (abbreviated as exp. and comp. respectively). It should be noted that the system generates more extended and emotionally colored phrases than given in the table 2 for the sake of brevity. Each statement is illustrated with the characteristics of the objects in terms of the criteria currently available. In answer the expert is expected to enter some fact that is followed by the elicitation of an attribute and evaluation of the objects with respect to its values as was shown above. The expert is allowed to refuse to answer.

Table 2. The forms of the utterances of the system

O_1	O_2	quality	task
exp.	-	$QA(O_1) > TA_2$	You must be unbiased and tell about shortcomings as well
comp.	-	$QA(O_1) > TA_2$	The article of your competitors is good. Maybe it has some disadvantages?
exp.	-	$QA(O_1) < TA_1$	Why does your firm propose such a bad product? Has it any merits?
comp.	-	$QA(O_1) < TA_1$	You are biassed and hide the merits of the articles of your competitors!
exp.	exp.	$QR(O_1,O_2) > TR_1$	Why does your firm produce goods so differing in their quality? Has O_2 some advantages over O_1?
exp.	comp.	$QR(O_1,O_2) > TR_1$	It is unlikely that O_2 is so bad compared to your O_1. Please don't hide its merits.
comp.	exp.	$QR(O_1,O_2) > TR_1$	I see you try to push off the bad thing. How can you persuade me in buying it?
exp.	exp.	$QR(O_1,O_2) < TR_2$	I don't know what to choose. Tell me more about these articles.
exp.	comp.	$QR(O_1,O_2) < TR_2$	The article of your competitors is almost the same! Can you help me to choose?

As may be seen from the table the tasks are chosen so to prevent the expert from being biassed: some tasks suppose him to find the advantages of the goods of his competitors. However, as the expert may refuse to answer the situation when his articles are much better than those suggested by the competitors remains possible. If such situation does take place the system proposes the expert to advertise the goods which were initially ascribed to the competitors.

The dialog is finished when the expert can't recall any more significant criterion. This situation is recognized by repeating refusals to answer the questions.

Now the system stops the game after 3 refusals happening in succession.

The organization of the role dialogue favours the expert giving full and unbiased characteristic for each object. In general, the form of a role game proves to create favorable conditions for the elicitation of knowledge for solving problems of optimum selection.

It should be noted that the role game described above allows to acquire some other types of knowledge: relative significance of criteria, fuzzy estimations of relative preference of values etc. However the review of these issues is beyond the scope of the report.

4 Graphic images and knowledge acquisition

It is well-known that drawings and graphic scenes are easily perceived and understood by humans and therefore widely used to illustrate material presented in text form, to explain complicated conceptions and ideas, to find solutions of knotty problems or even as the means of intercourse between people that strive for the best understanding of their thoughts and statements. This peculiarity of graphics should be given a proper attention in the field of knowledge elicitation.

Our particular interest in graphics concerns first of all the opportunities they may provide for creating RSS. We believe that the use of spatial metaphors and graphic images for this purpose allows, on the one hand, to enhance the expert's perception and understanding of the tasks (which may be too long and complicated when given in text form) and, on the other hand, to facilitate the processes of recollection and verbalization of knowledge as the expert's image thinking is drawn to participate in them.

The key to the use of graphic scenes in knowledge elicitation is given by the observation that all known RSS allowing to approach the knowledge of interest are created by exploiting some **relations** between entities (the term "relation" should be understood here in a wide, non-formal sense). The commonly known example is the similarity-difference relations in the repertory grid technique. For the most of such relations the evident visual representation by spatial relations and images can be found. For example, it is habitual to represent the similarity of some objects by the spatial nearness of graphic images accepted to symbolize these objects.

Each RSS created in some knowledge elicitation method supposes the expert to perform some actions in connection with the relation used: selection of participants for the given relation or relation for the given participants, specification of their places in the relation, giving some characteristics of the participants etc. When a relation is represented visually the expert can do these actions by manipulations with graphic images on the screen. This is more convenient than answering questions in text form.

Given below are some examples of the use of graphic images for the acquisition of different types of knowledge: properties of objects, taxonomies, preferences, pre- and postconditions of actions. Designing these graphics-based RSS we have adhered the principle that graphic symbols should be chosen so to be familiar to the expert. Therefore we have taken our symbols from the area of common notions.

4.1 Using graphics to obtain the properties of objects

As was shown, the similarity-difference relations facilitate the approach to the expert's knowledge about the properties of objects, and these relations can be visually expressed through the distance between the images symbolizing the objects. This fact has lead us to the idea of creating some knowledge elicitation programs with vivid graphic interface. Thus, the program "Regatta" proposes the expert a picture of yacht as a symbol of an object and engages him into the game where yachts must pass under bridges of various construction and go round certain obstacles. The task of the expert is to navigate the yachts in such a way that only similar ones go to the same span of a bridge or to the same side of an obstacle. Each bridge or obstacle corresponds to one of the attributes of the objects. The expert is expected to name the bridge (thus formulating the attribute) and to give captions for the bridge spans (treated as the values of the attribute).

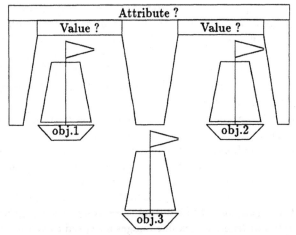

Fig.1. One of the pictures given to the expert as the task to tackle.

The task shown in Fig.1 can be considered as the modification of that proposed by the repertory grid technique: the expert is asked to decide whether the object "obj.3" is similar to the "obj.1" or to the "obj.2" and to find the attribute with different values for the "obj.1" and the "obj.2" such that one of the two values is characteristic also for the "obj.3" (Note that the text suggested to explain the picture is more difficult for understanding than the picture itself). Here we have represented graphically the similarity-difference relation with partly defined participants.

The metaphor accepted allows to create a great variety of comparison RSS that facilitate revealing of the properties of objects. Certain role in generating scenes is played by the construction of the bridges and by the disposition of the obstacles: a scene may be designed so that each receptacle allows the expert to put the predefined number of objects into it. For example, when a bridge span allows exactly one yacht to be put in it the expert is induced in choosing the object that significantly differs from the others. Interesting situations are created by the use of "unknown" yachts: the expert is proposed to detect them taking into account their positions as related to the positions of the known ones.

The experiments with the program "Regatta" have shown that graphic pictures generated on the screen are easily perceived and understood by the expert irrespectively of the number of yachts and spans present. Very often an RSS represented by a picture would require 4-6 sentences to formulate the corresponding task in text form.

It is possible to invent a lot of ways of representing similarity by spatial nearness. The discretization of the space through the use of receptacles (e.g. bridge spans) isn't necessary. For example, let us represent an object by some species of trees and propose the expert to create a botanical garden by arranging the given set of species (corresponding to the set of objects dealt with in the given knowledge based system). The expert is expected to arrange them according to their similarities. In so doing he decides by himself whether to make fences or lanes in the garden thus created. This expedient may be useful for acquiring taxonomies of objects.

4.2 Images to approach the other types of knowledge

As was mentioned in section 3, for problems in which optimum selection is needed the preferences should be acquired. The relation of preference is quite naturally associated with the spatial "higher-lower". Therefore one of the suitable graphic metaphors to elicit this kind of knowledge may be the scene with the image of a bird or a squirrel symbolizing an object and the image of a tree with its branches as the receptacles for the birds.

Such scene may be used in following way: when some fact concerning one of the solutions considered becomes known (for example, obtained in role dialog described earlier) the expert is asked to place the symbols of all known solutions on the branches so to reflect the relative position of these solutions with respect to the criterion the fact refers to. The expert is expected also to formulate a meaningful name of the tree. This name is treated as the name of the new criterion. As to the values of the criterion, the expert can either assign names to the branches of the tree or merely mark somehow the lowest and the highest branch. In the latter case the criterion is considered to have a continuous scale, and the objects are characterized by a (fuzzy) number reflecting their positions between the worst and the best possible values. Thus, the metaphor chosen allows to elicit (1) the name of the criterion; (2) the ordered scale of its possible values; (3) the estimations of the solutions with respect to the criterion.

When some knowledge elicitation method exploits relations that can be in this or that way held to interrelations between sets the useful metaphor is geometries which can overlap, incorporate other ones etc. For example, according to the relation analysis method described above, the recollection of pre- and postconditions by the expert is facilitated through the establishment of one of the five predefined relations between actions. Let us represent an action by a diagram

where S_{pre} is the situation in which the action is fulfilled and S_{post} is the situation to take place after the action is fulfilled. The relation "action A makes possible to fulfil action B" can be represented graphically in a following way:

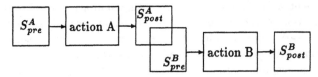

Now we can ask the expert to think about the common part of S_{post}^A and S_{pre}^B and then about the rest of these geometries. This is equivalent to the following task: "What properties are established in the world after the action A that make possible to fulfil the action B? Which of the properties established after the action A are irrelevant to the action B? What properties are needed to fulfil the action B but cannot be established by doing the action A?" As is seen, the graphic formulation of the task is much more compact and easily understood.

In general, graphical and spatial metaphors and images prove to be productive for the elicitation of knowledge of various types from human experts. The advantages of "graphical" knowledge elicitation techniques are following:

— creation of situations that stimulate the expert's reflection over the contents of his mind involving the capabilities of image thinking;
— improvement of the expert's perception and understanding of tasks posed to him due to their vivid visual form;
— attractive and convenient interface with the expert.

Note that "graphical" knowledge elicitation methods can exploit not only various spatial relations but any other means of graphic representation: colour, shape, signs, icons and so on. Interesting opportunities for knowledge elicitation can be created by presenting graphic images in dynamic. It seems to us that a careful study of expressive capabilities of graphic images can significantly contribute to the progress in the domain of knowledge elicitation.

5   A sketch of AFORIZM system

Though the description of AFORIZM system as a whole was not primarily seen as one of the objectives of this paper it seems reasonable to give a brief outline of its architecture and functioning. As is shown above, we have several knowledge elicitation methods designed to obtain different types of knowledge. A system having these methods as its components is expected to make the decision what of the methods to choose in each particular case. It should also combine two or more of them when necessary and determine situations when none of the methods can be used.

With these requirements in mind the following approach was implemented in AFORIZM system. Each knowledge elicitation method is oriented to certain problem type. AFORIZM has an internal knowledge base (KB) where these types are defined in terms of properties the problems belonging to each of them generally have:

- goals pursued by solving problems of each type;
- a nature of possible solutions;
- types of information needed to solve the problems;
- possibility to subdivide the solution process into steps;
- possibility to fix the order of steps.

This allows the system to classify a problem it is applied to by asking the expert about its characteristics and to determine situations when the system cannot be used. For each problem type it is indicated in the internal KB (1) which of the knowledge elicitation methods correspond to them, (2) the sequence of their work (when one of the methods must follow another), (3) how to make choice when several alternative methods exist for the same type (including questions asked to the expert). Based on this knowledge the system triggers knowledge elicitation method or methods according to the type the problem of interest belongs to.

Current version of AFORIZM system includes knowledge elicitation methods oriented to four problem types. Knowledge based architecture of the system allows to extend it easily to new knowledge elicitation methods and new problem types. Here are the types admitted in AFORIZM now:

1. *CLASSIFICATION*: determine the class some object fits into by considering the features of the object;
2. *SELECTION*: select the best solution from the given set of possible solutions with respect to certain criteria;
3. *ROUTINE CONTROL*: fulfil the given set of steps (actions) in an order prescribed by a scheme where conditional branching accounts for possible situations that may happen in course of problem solving and affect the sequence of doing actions;
4. *PLANNING*: build a scheme from the given set of actions that will allow to achieve the desired situation from the given initial situation.

Besides these types, the system is built so to work with compound problems containing components of different types. Such work is based on the assumption that it is possible to consider any problem on such level of abstraction that it is seen as belonging to single problem type. This allows to apply to it one of the type-specific methods. As a result of the work of the method certain notions are acquired according to the type of the problem. Then these notions should go through an analysis that can lead to revealing subproblems. It is meant by analysis of a notion that the expert is asked special questions to determine whether some reasoning or actions are associated with it. For example, when some property is obtained the expert is asked whether it is observed directly or needs some reasoning to determine its current value. Table 3 shows the types of notions acquired for different problem types and how subproblems associated with some of the notions can be revealed.

Table 3. Problem types, corresponding knowledge types and subproblems

Problem types	Knowledge types	Questions to reveal subproblems
Classification	classes, properties and their values	What to do if object belongs to class How to obtain current value of property
Selection	alternatives, criteria, their values and preference order	What to do when alternative is chosen
Routine control	steps (actions), sequences, conditions to choose alternative branches	How to do each action How to determine which condition is true
Planning	actions, pre- and postconditions	How to do each action How to determine which condition is true

If it has been detected during the work of some method that a subproblem is associated with a notion the latter is specially marked in the KB being built and the method continues its work. After this work is finished the system AFORIZM finds marked notions in the KB and applies to them the same procedure "detect problem type - call corresponding method" as for the initial problem.

Suppose, for example, that an expert system is built to support the technology of building expert systems. At the highest level of abstraction "building an expert system" can be seen as a problem of the routine control type: its solution consists of certain stages which follow each other in the predefined order. Therefore AFORIZM should trigger a method designed to acquire the scheme of problem solving. Then each step of this scheme is analysed as separate problem and the notions thus acquired are further analysed. On so doing subproblems of different types will necessarily be revealed: besides routine control, there will be classification and selection subproblems (find proper methods of knowledge representation and inference, select a tool for expert system development etc.).

As a result of knowledge elicitation by AFORIZM system the initial problem is represented in KB as a sophisticated hierarchy of problems which may belong to different types. Therefore a need arises in special tool able to (1) present the structure of the problem and contents of the KB in convenient form; (2) support navigation through the KB; (3) provide calls of knowledge elicitation methods, editors, inference engine according to the type of subproblem currently analysed. For these purposes a hypertext environment is used in AFORIZM. The structure of the hypertext and contents of its nodes are generated automatically so to reflect the current state of the applied KB. Each node presents some subproblem or notion from the KB in the form of text description illustrated when necessary by tables and diagrams. Fig.2 shows how the integrated work of different program components of AFORIZM is achieved.

6 Discussion and related works

The necessity to invent special techniques allowing to access the realm of human's conceptions and ideas was first realized by psychologists. Such techniques as repertory grids, psychological scaling, laddering were intended to bypass cognitive defenses and elicit the key notions, relationships and attitudes that characterize a person's view of the world. As the problems of knowledge engineering have much in common with those of cognitive psychology these techniques has become widely used in knowledge acquisition for knowledge based systems (see, for example, [3], [4], AQUINAS [2], KITTEN [1]). Each of the psychological techniques creates, in our terms, the reflection stimulating situation. It can be observed that each RSS consists in simultaneous consideration of two or more entities and relations between them, the similarity and difference relations being the most frequently revealed and analysed.

However the existing psychological methods are not suited for the acquisition of some types of knowledge. As is shown, for example, in [5], they alone don't allow to build knowledge base for planning or design activities etc. The problem of developing new knowledge elicitation methods for different types of problems remains urgent. The RSS-based methods suggested in the paper apply the principles lying under the psychological techniques to obtain knowledge needed for reasoning about actions (relation analysis method) and for optimum choice (role dialog).

The acquisition of knowledge about actions is given much attention in AI literature. Some authors apply machine learning techniques for this purpose. Thus, in ASK [6] the knowledge elicitation system analyses an example of problem solving suggested by the expert by requiring justification for each step of solution. Justification is the set of parameters and their values given in answer to the question "Why have you chosen this action?" It was shown earlier that such direct interrogation is insufficient for obtaining preconditions and side effects of actions. The other system, DICIPLE [7], attempts to generate the justification by itself based on the relations between objects mentioned in the example. Both systems try to generalize the example received. In so doing they generate their own examples and give them to the expert for evaluation. Both systems require certain knowledge to be available beforehand: structure of the problem or domain objects and relations between them.

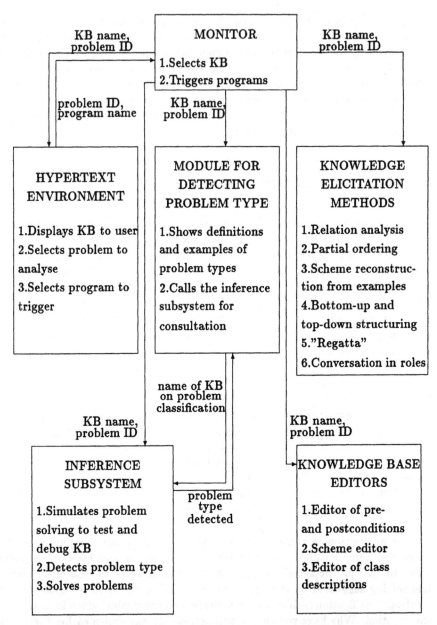

Fig.2. The structure of AFORIZM system and interrelations between its program components. ID - a unique identifier of a (sub)problem in KB.

Our relation analysis method offers the approach other than machine learning techniques. This prevents an expert from the necessity to choose carefully learning examples. Building of initial knowledge base is not required. It may appear that the method requires a set of all possible actions to be known beforehand. In fact, the dialog with the expert can be built in such a way that the list of actions is obtained in parallel with revealing relations. At the very start the expert is asked to remember at least one action relevant to the problem. Having this action the system asks to find another one which becomes possible after the first action, or necessarily follows it and so on. The same procedure may be applied to each of the acquired actions.

In principle, the other approach is possible: to obtain a set of actions by the analysis of protocols or other texts, like in KRITON system [8] where the operator-argument structures are acquired from protocols. However, in KRITON these structures don't undergo any analysis, they are given to the expert as the possible components of rules he is expected to generate.

In [9] the use of predefined relations is found. The paper is devoted to the elicitation and representation of knowledge about stereotyped situations for situation assessment needs. Events comprising a situation are represented by slots with constraints imposed on them. The relations "causes", "enables", "precedes" and "accompanies" are used to establish these constraints. As in relation analysis method, the expert is inquired about the relations taking place between the slots. Unlike our method, the role of the relations is not to simplify the recollection of some knowledge by the expert but to allow to automatically determine the constraints.

Some works touch upon the basic relations to be used in conceptual structures representations [10]. It should be noted that our relation analysis method doesn't represent the relations in the resulted knowledge base: they are used merely as the means to access the pre- and postconditions of actions.

The method of role dialog has much in common with knowledge elicitation on the basis of the repertory grid technique ([1], [2]). However the latter method is not so focussed on the acquisition of criteria and preferences as the former one. The situation created in the business game is close to the situation of real choice which takes place in expert's professional activities. Therefore it is believed that the criteria obtained in the game are the same as used by the expert in solving real selection problems.

The development of the role dialog method was greatly inspired by the works carried on in the Laboratory of AI Systems at the Institute of Mathematics of Academy of Sciences (Kishinev, Moldova). The team of this laboratory suggested to use specially designed computer games for the purposes of knowledge elicitation. This approach was successfully implemented in several interesting and original knowledge elicitation tools. The work of the laboratory is summarized in [11]. Our method differs from the other game methods in type of problems it is applied to (selection vs classification) and type of knowledge it allows to acquire (attributes with ordered values). It also should be noted that role dialog doesn't require any knowledge or examples previously entered into knowledge base to start its work while the other game methods must have partial domain model and a set of examples.

We see some weakness of the role dialog in the procedure used to acquire criteria. It seems somewhat cumbersome and drops out of the game character of the method. The graphic implementation of the procedure, as outlined in 4.2, allows to overcome this drawback.

The fact that graphics can give the expert convenient means for representing his knowledge is widely recognized. This is manifested in creation of a great variety of computer knowledge engineering tools with graphic interface. Some of them allow the expert to enter graphs representing the domain concepts and relations between them (CHECK [12], KEATS [13]). In KNAPS system [14] the expert is proposed to formulate his knowledge in the form of decision tree. In [15] the system LIFT is described in which the expert must build a diagram of problem solving using the given basic types of nodes.

In fact, all such systems propose the expert the language to formulate his knowledge by himself, without rendering him any help or prompt. In other words, they don't use graphics to generate *RSS* as is done in our methods. Our research has shown that graphic images can stimulate expert's mental processes and facilitate revealing and verbalization of knowledge. This opportunity is not exploited in the graphic knowledge acquisition tools listed above while it is of primary concern in AFORIZM approach.

It may be argued that our methods don't allow to obtain deep knowledge [16]. The merit of our approach is that it can be used on the early stages of knowledge acquisition. The knowledge obtained by the methods presented can be further analysed to refine it and to obtain deep knowledge on its basis.

Only sketchy description of the knowledge acquisition system AFORIZM is given to show how it integrates different knowledge elicitation methods and decomposes problems into subproblems of different types. The detailed consideration of these issues as well as of the other knowledge elicitation methods implemented in AFORIZM, the issues of knowledge representation and inference is beyond the scope of the paper.

7 Conclusion

The approach described in the paper consists in the use of reflection stimulating situations to help the expert to recollect and verbalize his knowledge. The idea of *RSS* is psychologically justified and in fact originates from the psychological methods.

The use of each *RSS* is restricted to the specific type of knowledge. The paper describes the *RSS* applicable to obtain knowledge about actions and knowledge of criteria and preferences. So the need in new *RSS*-based methods still exists. It is obvious that a careful analysis of different kinds of knowledge to be used in knowledge based systems will result in inventing such methods that would be of great benefit for knowledge engineering.

Graphic metaphors proved to be very useful in knowledge elicitation. Their advantage as the means of communication between the knowledge elicitation system and the expert is evident. To our regret, we can say little about the role of graphic images in expert's mental activities. Evidently, this issue deserves further investigations.

Acknowledgements

We would like to thank our colleagues from the Laboratory of Artificial Intelligence Systems of the Institute of Mathematics of the Moldavian Academy of Sciences where our work originates from. Seminars and informal discussions held in the Laboratory allowed us to develop and refine our ideas. We wish to express our special appreciation to the Head of the Laboratory Yu.Pechersky for providing favorable atmosphere for creative work of the personnel and S.Solowiev who was our scientific advisor in the period of preparing Ph.D. theses. Useful comments of referees are appreciated.

References

1. Shaw, M.L.G., Gaines, B.R.: KITTEN: knowledge initiation and transfer tools for expert and novices. Int. J. Man-Machine Studies **27** (1987) 251-280
2. Boose, J.H., Shema, D.B., Bradshaw, J.M.: Recent progress in Aquinas: a knowledge acquisition workbench. Proceedings of the European Knowledge Acquisition Workshop (EKAW'88) (1988) 2.1-2.15
3. Cooke, N.M., McDonald, J.E.: The application of psychological scaling techniques to knowledge elicitation for knowledge-based systems. Int. J. Man-Machine Studies **26** (1987) 533-550
4. Chignell, M.H.: The use of ranking and scaling techniques in knowledge acquisition. Expert systems in government, Symposium (1986) 64-72
5. Anjewierden, A.: Knowledge acquisition tools. AI Communications **0** (1987) 29-38
6. Gruber, T.R.: Acquiring strategic knowledge from experts. Int. J. Man-Machine Studies **29** (1988) 579-597
7. Kodratoff, Y., Tecuci, G.: Learning at different levels of knowledge. Proceedings of the European Knowledge Acquisition Workshop (EKAW'88) (1988) 3.1-3.17
8. Linster, M.: A knowledge elicitation tool for expert systems. Proceedings of the European Knowledge Acquisition Workshop (EKAW'88) (1988) 4.1-4.19
9. Noble, D.F.: Schema-based knowledge elicitation for planning and situation assessment aids. IEEE Trans. on System, Man and Cybernetics **19** (1989) 473-482
10. Berg-Cross, G., Price, M.E.: Acquiring and managing knowledge using a conceptual structures approach: introduction and framework. IEEE Trans. on System, Man and Cybernetics **19** (1989) 513-527
11. Andrienko, G., Andrienko, N., Ginkul, G., Solowiev, S.: Automatized Systems for Knowledge Acquisition. Computer Science Journal of Moldova **1** No.3 (1993) Kishinev, 42-50
12. Console, L., Fossa, M., Torasso, P.: Acquisition of causal knowledge in the CHECK system. Computers and Artificial Intelligence **8** (1989) 323-345
13. Eisenstadt, M., Dominique, J., Rajan, T., Motta, E.: Visual knowledge engineering. IEEE Trans. on Software Engineering **10** (1990) 1164-1177
14. Lee, N.S.: Graphical knowledge programming with KNAPS. Int. J. Man-Machine Studies **31** (1989) 611-641
15. Lee, J.K., Lee, I.K., Sung Mahn Ahn: Automate rule generation by the transformation of expert's diagram:LIFT. Int. J. Man-Machine Studies **32** (1990) 275-292
16. Steels, L.: The deepening of expert systems. AI Communications **0** (1987) 9-16

How to combine data abstraction and model refinement: a methodological contribution in MACAO

AUSSENAC-GILLES Nathalie
IRIT-URA 1399 du CNRS - UPS
118, route de Narbonne - F- 31062 TOULOUSE Cedex
aussenac@irit.irit.fr

Abstract: This paper deals with methodological aspects of knowledge acquisition and modelling. We focus on how the problem solving can be modelled. Our analysis relies on two experiments where we combined MACAO and KADS to develop knowledge based systems: a technical diagnosis support application and a system that helps to assess debt recovery files. The paper reports these experiments as well as the conclusions drawn. Their evaluation underlines the advantage of combining a detailed analysis of the expert's reasoning with the selection and adaptation of generic models and problem solving methods. Moreover, from this work, we derive guidelines on how to apply practically this combination. We propose to integrate these results in MACAO and improve the methodology by this means.

Key words: Methodology for Knowledge Acquisition, Knowledge Engineering, Modelling, Problem Solving Method.

1. Introduction

Several knowledge acquisition methodologies consider knowledge modelling as the bottom-up design of a conceptual model (CM): expert's protocols and domain data are analyzed to build up the model [BOO,89]. These methodologies (for instance KOD [VOG,88] or the first definitions of MACAO [AUS,88]) propose the knowledge engineer guide-lines that help him abstract the relevant domain concepts as well as the expert's method for solving problems. Then, the obtained models often result in descriptions of the expert's knowledge without any characterization. Either they list his heuristics or they present the steps he follows when solving a problem. Because they are very close to the domain knowledge, they are considered as ill structured or difficult to be maintained.

On the other hand, approaches such as KADS [BRE,87], Generic Tasks [CHA,86] or Components of Expertise (and the KREST workbench) [STE,92] have developed generic models of problem solving and pre-defined methods for various kinds of tasks. Reusing generic components transforms constructing the model into configuring blocks. The components provide precise guidance for expertise analysis and focus on the knowledge to be acquired. As a consequence, it is often easier to build and adapt the models. The definition of the criteria for selecting and indexing components requires the characterization of the various kinds of tasks and means to perform them [VAL,93].

In short, the bottom-up analysis helps in better characterizing the expertise whereas reusing generic components facilitates the control of the designed model [LIN,92], [KRI,91]. The complementary advantages of these two ways of building a conceptual model led us to investigating their combination both experimentally and through the literature. From these analyses, we derived conclusions on how to integrate these two approaches in the knowledge acquisition methodology we develop: MACAO.

In this paper, we list the dimensions we consider in our analysis. Then, we report two experiments where we applied MACAO and KADS one after the other in order to evaluate the possibility of combining them. The first experiment relates to a diagnosis expertise in space applications. The second one deals with designing a system to help lawyers evaluate loan files. For both of the experiments, we compare the difficulties met when constructing the model as well as the models resulting from to the two approaches. Then, we propose an evolution of the MACAO methodology. We want it to benefit from the combination of bottom-up and top-down phases with the reuse of generic components. We focus on the interest of differentiating specific models for each category of problem before defining the complete conceptual model. We finally confront our conclusions with the state of the art.

2. Combining two ways of building a conceptual model

2.1. Modelling expertise: possible alternatives

We differentiate four main steps in the knowledge acquisition and modelling process [AUS,92]: (1) data driven elicitation, (2) building of a Framework[1] of the conceptual model, (3) instanciation and refinement of this framework in order to obtain the complete conceptual model, and finally (4) model operationalisation and validation (Fig. 1). This decomposition remains valid for most of existing methodologies, although some of them may not support all four steps. The concern of this paper is to experimentally compare step (2) in the KADS and MACAO methodologies, or, in other words, to compare two ways of designing the framework of a conceptual model: by abstraction with MACAO or by reusing an interpretation model with KADS. This diagram enables one to localize the specificity of a given methodology and associated tool (if any).

---

[1] We call Framework of the conceptual model an abstract, rather general and domain knowledge independant representation of the problem solving. It characterizes the content of the conceptual model. The problem solving method is part of this framework [AKK,93].

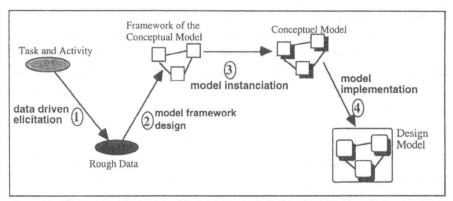

Figure 1: Four tasks can be identified in any knowledge acquisition method promoting a modelling process. The diagram indicates the data used as input and output of these tasks. It does not refer to the exact sequence in which they are performed; many loops and backtracks are implicit.

We bring to light some of the features related to the methodology that we consider as significant dimensions for our analysis:

- *Which of the steps does the methodology or tool actually support?* For instance, for the tools dedicated to Role Limiting Methods (RLMs) such as MOLE, MORE or SALT [MAR,88], steps (1) and (2) have been done as they were developed whereas the knowledge engineer using them performs step (3); these tools automatically carried out step (4), by directly writing rules from knowledge given during step (3). On the contrary, KREST gives no indication about step (1) and more generally about how to acquire the knowledge to be embedded in the model [STE,92]. Moreover, many acquisition methodologies suppose that step (4) is carried out within a different environment from the acquisition one, and assimilate it to the system development.

- *How important is each step?* For example, KADS-I suggested to dedicate very little time to step (1). Difficulties experimented during step (2) proved the importance of acquiring relevant data before, so that KADS-II now pays more attention to step (1). Step (2) becomes major in approaches such as Generic Tasks, where the structure of the conceptual model cannot easily be modified once it is defined. On the contrary, when the framework of the CM can be refined and corrected such as in OMOS or KREST, steps (2) and (3) have a similar scope.

- *Is it possible to backtrack or loop from one step to another?* KREST or OMOS promote a continuity between steps (2), (3) and (4), and prone interactions and refinements even after the model is operational. On the contrary, approaches like Generic Tasks or RLM force the structure of the model to 'freeze' once and for all as it is encoded after step (2). In that case, no back-track is possible and the acquisition must be straightforward, whereas the first kind of approach is based on a cycle including the first three steps.

- Which methods does it suggest to carry out each step? One of the most significant variation for the design of the model framework (step (2)) opposes the model abstraction from the expert's behavior and domain data (like in MACAO) to the reuse and adaptation of generic components (as promoted by KADS-II or KREST). During step (3), the framework of the model guides somewhat powerfully the model instantiation and knowledge acquisition. Some tools like PROTÉGÉ or RLM tools offer specialized editors and apply heuristic knowledge about the model structure to focus on the acquisition of relevant knowledge. A significant dimension to compare methodologies during step (4) is whether the conceptual model continues or not to be refined while it is made operational. OMOS promotes the elicitation of detailed knowledge in parallel with the model operationalisation. KREST suggestion is similar because the model can still be modified after the code is written. On the contrary, with KADS-II, the conceptual model must be complete before it is made operational or encoded in a knowledge base.

It is obvious that other slight differences between existing methodologies may remain implicit through this diagram. Since most of the models set domain apart from problem solving knowledge, it now appears useful to address questions about their interactions like: Is there any other view? Which one is considered first? Does knowledge modelling through one view influence knowledge in another one? etc. For instance, KREST suggests to alternatively consider three views (models, methods and tasks), with strong interactions, which means modifying one view may lead to reorganizing parts of other views. On the contrary, KADS four layers can be assimilated as four views that, until recent evolutions, were presented as weakly connected. Moreover, a full analysis should also bear on the model itself (expert or cognitive model versus system model) and the knowledge representation in it (structures used, etc.).

2.2. MACAO: Presentation

With the aim of experimenting and validating our ideas concerning knowledge acquisition, we use and develop MACAO, a general purpose Knowledge Acquisition methodology [AUS,88]. MACAO provides techniques and guidelines for expert knowledge elicitation, analysis and modelling with a specific knowledge representation. First, we briefly present this language. Second, we report some of the principles of the method. Third, we stress its strengths and weaknesses, which motivated our work.

2.2.1. Knowledge representation in MACAO

The conceptual model is built up using MONA, a formalism defined for MACAO so that knowledge is represented as precisely as possible, easily formulated and structured[2]. Knowledge representation in MACAO has evolved from the one presented in [AUS,94a] towards MONA in order to facilitate the connection between the model and an operational language: LISA[3] [DEL,93]. A connection between structures makes explicit the LISA structures that encode one or several MONA structures. Each structure corresponds to an object defined with slots. It can be first described with comments in natural language, and progressively be made formal before being connected to an operational LISA structure.

The conceptual model built with MACAO is twofold: the domain model is apart from the problem-solving model. So, the knowledge representation separates two inter-dependent networks. One can edit, create and modify parts of the whole network through graphic editors (graph or tree editors). Moreover, views combining problem solving and domain knowledge (such as the concepts playing one role) are under development to make the model instantiation easier. Concepts or instances of concepts as well as links are used to describe domain entities and their relations. Goals and methods represent problem solving knowledge. Modelling how a problem is solved consists of decomposing the main goal into subgoals and of listing and defining the applicable methods for each of the goals.

To facilitate the understanding of domain knowledge and the dialogue with the expert and users, a third part of the model deals with the management of texts and terms. As a consequence, different views exist on the model: an unstructured one in texts and terms, a conceptual one in the models and a design one in the operational model. The management of direct links from raw data (in texts) to structures (in the conceptual and then in the operational models) is under development.

2.2.2. Characterization of the method

Our presentation of MACAO answers the questions posed in section 2.1.:

- *Which of the steps does the methodology or tool actually support?* MACAO supports the four steps of the modelling process. However, no specific tool besides structure editors is available for the model instantiation. The most relevant help is provided during steps (1) and (2), for any elicitation task and for structuring the expert's knowledge.

---

[2] The MONA language is detailed in [AUS94] and [MAT,94].
[3] The LISA language was defined at EDF and LRI (Univ. Paris Sud) by I.Delouis. LISA is written in Le_Lisp (by Ilog) and is used to design operational conceptuel models.

- *How important is each step?* As a mainly bottom-up process, knowledge acquisition with MACAO requires spending more time on the first two steps, where raw data is collected and a model abstracted from it. The model instanciation should be less costly as a lot of knowledge is already available. However, it may take time because the knowledge engineer must decide how to organize the available knowledge inside the model.

- *Is it possible to backtrack or loop from one step to another?* Going from step (3) back to step (2) is rather easy since the framework of the conceptual model can be modified all along the MACAO four steps. In addition to this flexibility, the connection between conceptual and operational structures facilitates the influence of step (4) over the results of step (3). We can say the model is progressively refined.

- *Which methods does it suggest to carry out each step?* Each step of the method defines a cycle including elicitation, conceptualization, structuring and validation.

2.2.3. Main steps of the method

Besides a very classical familiarization stage, step (1) consists in characterizing the expertise (the domain theory and the problem solving), in observing and analyzing the activity at work to gather precise data on how problems are solved. The knowledge engineer selects and classifies cases to identify categories of problems. MACAO offers a repertory grid tool for this classification. With the expert, he defines a set of sample problems from the various categories. The expert is asked to think aloud while he simulates their solving and later to explain his reasoning. From these verbalizations, the knowledge engineer builds up models of problems. These models form a useful and rich data set, a "zoom" on the expertise to be used later on. However, they contain a large amount of very low level knowledge that may be difficult to organize and abstract.

In MACAO, the result of step (2) is a two part framework characterizing the domain and the problem models. Until now, MACAO proposed to abstract this framework directly from the models of the problems solved in step (1). First, a model is associated to each category of problems to describe the way they are solved. Second, from these models and taking into account the system specifications, an expertise model is built up. For the experiments reported in this paper, we also used interpretation models from the KADS library.

Step (3) is dedicated to the acquisition and modelling of domain specific knowledge through the guidelines provided by the framework of the model. The problem and category models embody part of this knowledge. What remains must be asked of the expert or found in documents. The expert and knowledge engineer check together whether all the domain knowledge required by the model has been identified. The syntax of the structures helps in this verification. At the end of step (3), the model is not directly operational. Step (4) consists in interactively translating it into an operational modelling language, LISA [DEL,93], with a double purpose: validating and refining the conceptual model.

2.3. Motivations of our work

With the purpose to compare how KADS and MACAO can be applied, we carried out two experiments and analyzed them through the same grid. In the first parts of sections 3 and 4, we note the effort spent to acquire raw data; we analyze how and when MACAO suggests to abstract a framework of the conceptual model from this data; we evaluate the relevance of the recommendations provided by the methodology; we finally characterize the nature of this framework. In both of the cases, the model built following MACAO is specific to the expertise it represents, whatever the view or the level at which it is considered. This makes it difficult to compare to other models, complex to maintain and impossible to reuse. Most of all, incremental design, based on data abstraction, results as time consuming since the model offers too little guidance.

In order to overcome these limitations of MACAO, we applied KADS and experimented some of the principles of top-down methodologies such as Generic Tasks [CHA,86], KREST [STE,92] or KADS [WIE,92] and related works: MODEL-K [KAR,91], MIKE [NEU,93] or OMOS [LIN,93]. These methods put forward several refinement stages to build an expertise model from a generic one selected in a library. First, the generic model must be adapted to form the framework of the conceptual model. The resulting model stands as a framework to elicit and analyze the knowledge that will instanciate it. Since modelling by reusing components is considered easier that building a model from scratch (or rather from raw expertise data), these methods erase most of the problems occurring during step (2) and bring efficient help to step (3).

For these applications, the knowledge engineer integrated MACAO and KADS and combined a thorough analysis of the expert's knowledge with the adaptation of generic components (Fig. 2). In the following parts of sections 3 and 4, we answer questions such as why we decided to use KADS generic models, how we selected and adapted these models. We compare the resulting framework of the conceptual model to the one obtained with MACAO.

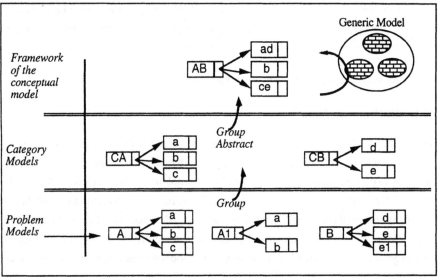

Figure 2: Abstracting the problem solving model with MACAO. Knowledge structures taken from problem models are grouped, reorganized or abstracted to form the category models. The process is similar to build up the expertise model from the category models. It is combined with the reuse of KADS interpretation models: models of categories are compared to select and adapt a generic model.

3. Applying the method to acquire a technical diagnosis expertise

We refer here to an application already mentioned in several papers concerning MACAO [AUS,93] [AUS,94b]. Our first interests were determining the abstraction level of the problem solving model, identifying the kind of knowledge it should contain as well as improving the knowledge representation in MACAO. Since then, the first conceptual model built with MACAO has been improved with the help of additional documents about the expertise and mainly by using generic diagnosis models of the KADS library. We report here how we applied the MACAO and KADS methodologies to build and improve the model; we present the various models obtained and analyze the complementarity of these approaches.

3.1. The problem

Integrating the various components of a spatial sub-system (part of a launcher or space-craft) requires a test stage to demonstrate that the whole system meets design requirements. The test plan organizes the test procedures that start the sending of electrical commands to the systems under test, receive its answer and compare it to the expected one. They warn the test operator of potential incidents. As soon as an incident is mentioned, the operator starts by diagnosing the failure with the aim of localizing the faulty equipment. Then if he can, he identifies the possible reasons for this fault [SOL,93]. A knowledge based system has been developed to diagnose and identify faulty equipments during the integration tests of the vehicle equipment bay of the ARIANE4 launcher[4].

3.2. The modelling process and resulting models

3.2.1. Determining raw data

The expertise context and the task were identified by observing the expert's activity at work and through interviews. A complementary analysis exploited the documents used during the tests. The expert mentioned several examples of problems he had solved [SOL,93]. He classified them into about ten categories, corresponding to the various kinds of faulty equipment. In fact, these categories were so familiar to the expert that he could have listed them quite spontaneously. The expert defined one or sometimes two problems for each of the categories and simulated their solving. He modelled them himself, which is an adaptation of MACAO. These models chronologically describe with domain terms the actions performed to diagnose a fault. For instance, to identify an error on a wire transmitting sequential data, the approach consists in analyzing the test output message, in correlating it with other parameters, in checking the absence of any other kind of fault and, in that case, in testing the various possible hypotheses. These tests consist of four simple checks because the expert knows very this specific kind of problem, so well that he can directly tell the possible causes as well as the way to prove them.

3.2.2. Bottom-up construction of a framework of the conceptual model

Together the expert and the knowledge engineer tried to organize a first framework of the problem solving model that would be valid for all the problems and categories of problems. They wanted this framework to be described with less domain specific terms. This model came from the analysis and comparison of the problem and category models. For this expertise, as most of the selected problems were prototypical of their category, the models of categories were little exploited. Problems and categories were considered as identical, which erases the benefit of a two step abstraction process.

We obtained a framework of the conceptual model (Fig. 3) where the goal decomposition is similar to the one of the example described in section 3.2.1. One significant difference is that hypothesis generation is now dissociated from hypothesis evaluation. In the example, generation was omitted because the expert could directly list his hypotheses and evaluate

---

[4]This work took place at the Matra Marconi Space plant of Toulouse.

them one by one. However, hypothesis generation may be much more complex and require a very precise knowledge of the equipment assembled on the bay.

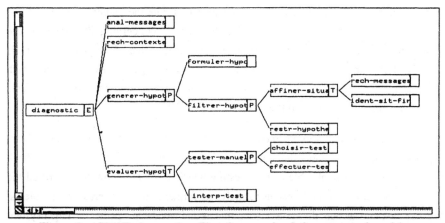

Figure 3: ARIANE 4 expertise: First framework of the conceptual model.
Diagnosing a failure means analyzing the messages issued after the test, scrutinizing the context in which they were produced, generating and later evaluating hypotheses. Capital letters beside the names of the *schemas* refer to the instruction that controls their decomposition: E for AND, O for OR, T for WHILE, C for CASE and P for THEN.

The method followed by the expert to generate hypotheses depends on the complexity of the problem and on the frequency of its occurrence [AUS,93] [MAC,93]. He may either apply heuristics associated to the situation or build hypotheses from an analysis of the situation and his knowledge of the structure of the equipment bay. If we consider the *schema* generate-hypothesis (formuler-hypothèse) in the model, we notice it is not decomposed into other *schemas*. However, its description in natural language reports the various ways of generating hypotheses. In fact, the descriptions in the problem models are too specific to be gathered under more generic labels, and make it harder to explain how the task is performed.

As a consequence, the model presented in Fig. 3 does not precisely report how the expert solves problems. The task decomposition is quite well defined, but most of the problem solving methods remain either approximate (they do not precisely define the control over the solving process) or too specific (the applied procedure is described with domain heuristics without characterizing a method). This remark confirms that MACAO does not really encourage deep progress in the expertise analysis. We built a second model to improve the first one, to make the methods more explicit, also to compare it with what could be obtained with KADS.

3.2.3. Using KADS to refine the framework of the conceptual model

We applied a reduced part of KADS: we were not interested in the full methodology but rather in the inference structures that could help us refine the diagnosis model of our application. Most of the recent and detailed results concerning diagnosis in the CommonKADS library come from [BEN,93a]. To select some of the possible methods proposed for diagnosis, we followed the interactive process suggested by the author, which consists in alternatively considering problem solving and domain knowledge. This approach is similar to the one promoted by KEW [VHE,92].

Each potential problem solving method is associated with a suitability criterion, that expresses expectancies about domain knowledge [BEN,93a]. This criterion helps check whether a method is applicable or not. Testing whether domain knowledge verified the criteria of the various methods lead us to analyzing further how the expert solves problems. We also took into account the system requirements and wondered whether the target system should use the same methods or a different (more efficient) one. The simple fact of being able to select among existing results changed our way of considering the model: we thought more of designing a system and considered all the possible alternatives for each diagnosis task.

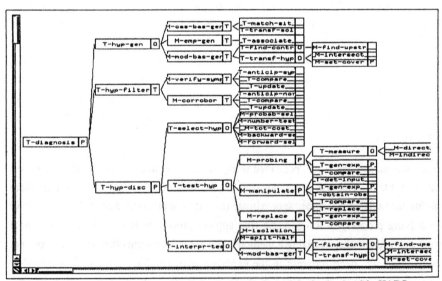

Figure 4: Part of the framework of the conceptual model obtained with KADS.
The names of the methods start with an M, those of goals or tasks with a T. The diagnosis consists in generating hypotheses, filtering a relevant sub-set and discriminating them one by one until the fault is identified.

Our analysis of the expert's methods of solving problems relied on the problem models. However, the answers required to evaluate the suitability criteria of the methods should refer to prototypical reasonings, which normally are described in models of categories. For this application, as previously said, the category models were assimilated to the problem models. The final model resulting from this refinement (fig. 4) is much more precise and structured than the one obtained with MACAO.

To generate hypotheses, the expert first tries to associate the current problem with cases previously solved. If he cannot find a similar situation, he exploits his knowledge of the bay structure (a functional model) and suspects the components preceding the one where the symptom appeared. This alternative corresponds to two possible methods that we associated to the hypothesis generation in our model: empirical-generation (*M-emp-gen* in fig. 4) and model based generation (*M-mod-bas-gen* in fig. 4) [BEN,93b].

Before evaluating his hypotheses by testing each of the suspected components, the expert filters the set of hypotheses he generated by acquiring additional information. An analysis of how this filtering was performed in the problem models reveals two possible ways. They correspond to two of the methods proposed by [BEN,93a]: the expert may filter his hypotheses by anticipating the symptom effects on the set of components (*M-verify-symptoms* in fig. 4); another possibility is that he predicts the normal behavior of the equipment bay and compares the message that should have been obtained with those reported after the test (*M-corroborate*).

Instead of testing all the components implicated in the hypotheses, the expert selects the component according to the hypothesis with highest probability of success. He also classes it according to the fault risk of each component, the cost of its testing and the difficulty of its access. Each of these criteria defines a method to select the next hypothesis to be evaluated (first task of the hypothesis discrimination). This is why we selected and adapted several methods proposed by [BEN,93a]. A similar investigation of the test interpretation showed that several methods are applicable, according to the nature of the test and to the expert's knowledge.

3.2.4. Building and validating the complete conceptual model

It is not our purpose to develop these steps here. We will just mention that the two models were implemented in two different systems. However, for project reasons, the first framework was used to organize the domain knowledge available in the models, and also to acquire additional domain knowledge. The second framework helped improve this first conceptual model. The expert verified it before it was made operational and tested. This last step provoked modifications in the model and the acquisition of extra knowledge.

4. Modelling an assessment law application

4.1. The problem

The granting and control of loans for real estate acquisition by employees of EDF-GDF companies are managed through files corresponding to each loan. Once a request is examined and the partners sign the contract, the files are surveyed during the debt redemption. They are said to be open. Whenever the contract is repudiated, the file is considered as closed. From this situation, the file can turn back to redemption or it can keep on being managed out of the initial contract.

The SADE knowledge based system capitalizes the skill of those who deal with closed files, to help them to better analyze loan redemption files and to perform more adequate procedures for debt recovery [LEP,93]. Evaluating a file not only requires the application of written law rules such as the loan contract clauses and the company regulation. It also relies on the expert's experience. Moreover, the final decision often is influenced by social, political and economical considerations about debt recovery. We report below how this expertise was modelled, mainly by applying the MACAO methodology, but also by reusing some results of the KADS library. A more detailed comparison of the two approaches is developed in [LEP,94].

4.2. The modelling process and resulting models

4.2.1. Determining raw data

Preliminary interviews were made with the people involved in the project. To identify categories of problem, the experts selected a set of twenty files for their representativeness and their diversity. They classified problems into four main classes (divorce, death, breaking of contract and debt overflow). Here again, the result of the repertory grids confirmed the categories formulated by the experts. The experts were asked to simulate the solving of several problems (files) in each category. They worked in their usual environment and were given information concerning the file little by little, as they needed it [LEP,93], [LEP,94]. They were asked explanations afterwards. The knowledge engineer considered it as a long and costly task to build the models of these problems.

4.2.2. Bottom-up construction of a framework of the conceptual model

From the problem models, the knowledge engineer built a problem solving model for each category of problem. This integration was made easy by the similarities between the various problems. The stages in the process were the same for all the problems of one category, only the applied rules differed. Building the category models improved the way the problem solving was decomposed and the labels identifying each step (the names of the *schemas*) [LEP,93]. By comparing and gathering common steps in the various models of categories, a first framework of the conceptual model was obtained (Fig. 5) [LEP,94]. This framework represents how an expert deals with a file. Terms from the domain, a little more abstract than those used in the category models, label the various steps of the process.

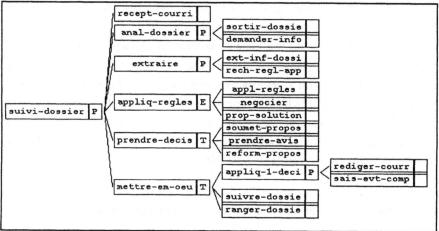

Figure 5: Framework of the conceptual model built with MACAO for SADE.
Assessing a file *(suivi-dossier)* starts with analyzing received mail and selecting the corresponding file. Then relevant information is extracted *(extraire)* from the file *(ext-inf-dossier)* and applicable rules are determined *(rech-regl-app)*. Then, these rules are applied *(appliq-regles)* and decisions taken about the file *(prendre-decis)*, which may include a negotiation *(negocier)*. Finally, the decisions are applied *(mettre-en-oeuvre)*.

4.2.3. Using KADS to refine the framework of the conceptual model

A second framework of the conceptual model was later developed according to KADS, by adapting the assessment interpretation model proposed in [VAL,93]. The KADS-I library describes assessment as a task where a case description is evaluated in reference to some system model (or norm) and mapped onto a decision class [BRE,87]. Valente defines it as *a problem type in which a case description (input) is mapped onto a decision class (output) according to a system model (input).* If the case and the system model are not located at the same abstraction level, then the first one must be abstracted and/or the second one specified in order to be able to apply the model to the case.

From the first interviews of the expert, we identified the expertise as an assessment task: the loan file and associated information can be considered as the case model; the actions to be performed to get the debt recovered correspond to decision classes and the regulations, and legal rules against which the file is evaluated form the system model. As the case description (file) and the system model (regulations and law) are not located at the same abstraction level, the assessment includes abstraction and specification inferences before the norm can match the case description. In the model built with MACAO (Fig. 4), these tasks are gathered in the *Extract* schema: extracting information from the file corresponds to the case abstraction (schema *ext-inf-dossier)* whereas the specification of the system model consists in determining the applicable rules (schema *rech-reg-applicables).* The matching is decomposed into *appliq-règles, prendre-décision* and *mettre-en-oeuvre.*

We then specified these three inference steps by answering the questions proposed by [VAL,93]. Thanks to the preliminary work done when designing the category models, understanding these questions was quite straight-forward. Otherwise, this would have required a significant adaptation in order to understand which domain knowledge was related to each generic term. Questions were formulated using an abstract and domain independent vocabulary, which made them hard to understand in the context of a given expertise. In fact, the category model also contained most of the answers to these questions, which partly avoided new interviews of the expert. The selection of the inference steps and their refinement is detailed in [LEP,94].

The inference structure presented in Fig. 6 describes how the target system will assess a file. This model uses domain independent terms and can be interpreted as follows:

- The abstract description of a file (*abstraction*) takes into account the rules that will be applied. These rules (*system description*) are a sub-set of all the applicable rules in this domain (they are a *specification* of the system model). Building the case structure results in characterizing the kind of file to be evaluated, which is recognizing a category of problems (with MACAO meaning). From then on, the applicable rules are known (*rule filtering*).

- A problem is not solved when one solution is found but rather when several solutions are proposed, classified according to the means they require. This remark is not obvious if one looks at the problem models, where the expert suggested only one solution. However, it appears clearly in the expert's explanations concerning his own solutions. So, the applicable rules must be specified into norms that deduce decision classes (*specify filter*). Moreover, a measurement system must be specified from the focused system model (*specify system*). It serves to define conflict resolution criteria (*specify criteria*).

- After the rules have been applied to the case, conflicts are solved between potential solutions (*solve conflicts*) to classify potential decision classes.

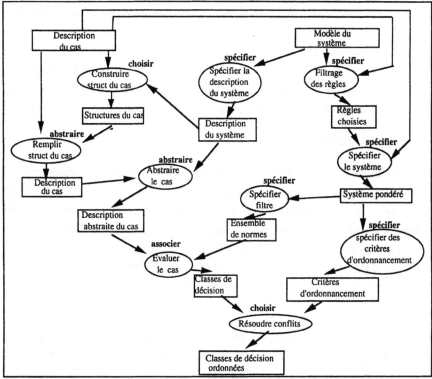

Figure 6: Inference structure of the SADE system obtained with KADS.

4.2.4. Building and validating the complete conceptual model

Only the framework built with MACAO (Fig. 4) was instanciated with domain knowledge. First, parts of the category and problem models were integrated in the framework after their reorganization. Then, additional knowledge was acquired from the experts [LEP,93]. The complete model was validated by the experts and made operational with the LISA language so that its behavior could be tested.

5. Discussion

5.1. Conclusion of the experiments

These experiments confirm the importance of focusing as soon as possible on a framework of the conceptual model to guide knowledge acquisition. In both of the cases, too much time was spent on the elicitation of raw data before knowing how to structure it. They stress the efficiency of reusing generic components in comparison with abstracting data when building such a framework. They also prove the necessity of a thorough analysis of domain knowledge, and particularly the interest of modelling problem simulations, before reusing generic components. The problem models and mainly the models of the categories helped in selecting and adapting these generic models. In other terms, the first steps of MACAO facilitate a model selection and adaptation. These case-studies finally demonstrate the close interdependency between domain and problem solving knowledge for their analysis and modelling: knowing more about one view on the expertise guides in acquiring knowledge about the other view. These results confirm those established in [LER,94].

5.2. Related works

We recall here some results about the reuse of generic components, such as those proposed by KADS [WIE,92], Generic Tasks [CHA,86] or Components of Expertise [STE,92]. These works mainly bear on how to build up libraries of problem solving methods or domain ontologies in order to keep and reuse parts of existing models. Each approach is characterized by the content of the proposed libraries (nature, grain size, formalization and abstraction of the components or the knowledge stored in there), their indexing, the way a component is supposed to be reused as well as the diversity of their content.

KADS proposes Interpretation Models classified according the type of task solved with these models, which are close to problem solving methods [BRE,87]. Current developments aim at indexing these models, providing guidelines such as decision trees that can help in selecting and adapting these models as well as defining models for new types of task [BEN,93a] [VAL,93]. Chandrasekaran's Generic Tasks allow the reuse of pre-defined methods for identified types of tasks. These methods are encoded and each one is located in a different environment. The only possible adaptation consists in combining them or combining several sub-tasks implemented in the various environments. Steels' Components of Expertise promote the idea that any knowledge component defined in the KREST workbench can be reused, whatever its abstraction level, its formalization, its grain size or its genericity. One just has to keep track of the application context in which this knowledge was defined and used.

However, as far as the methodology is concerned, the knowledge engineer is given very few indications to recognize or select a generic component: In the expertise, which are the indications of a type of task, of a method? How to validate the relevance of a modelling decision? How to adapt generic components to an expertise? For instance, it is only by applying KADS to a real problem that one can understand how to analyze an expertise and how to select relevant generic components. KADS proposes to characterize the expert's task from protocols [VAL,93]. In the case of CERISE, a financial diagnosis application developed with KADS, an early expertise analysis lead to the conclusion that the task included diagnosis and assessment [VIC,93]. The application inference structure was derived from the combination of two interpretation models from the KADS library: the diagnosis and the assessment models. In the MIKE method, based on KADS [NEU,93], the task is characterized after an analysis that consists in determining types of problems, which is similar to the categorization of problems in MACAO.

5.2. Future directions for MACAO

Among the results of this analysis, the most important one for MACAO is the necessity to combine bottom-up (abstraction) and top-down (reuse) analysis as well as guidelines to make the best of this combination:

- knowledge acquisition is more efficient when lead by the framework of a conceptual model;
- dedicate the required time to the building of this framework even though it can be later refined;
- to build this framework, we prone a first thorough analysis of the expertise, based on raw data abstraction before trying to reuse generic components;
- the framework of the conceptual model is all the more relevant as the reused components are modified and adapted so that its vocabulary and the selected methods suit the expertise, the domain and the system users.

Even if most of the previous assertions are not new, we recall them to integrate them better in the methodology. To direct the abstraction stage, current recommendations in MACAO form a good basis to which we propose to add the following remarks:

- *Reduce the time dedicated to problem modelling*, because of its high cost, and concentrate more on analyzing problem simulations to *build up category models as soon as possible*.
    - Problem models are just means to build the conceptual model, not goals of the acquisition. So, it does not matter if they are not precise and complete. All the available knowledge after the simulations and the expert's explanations should be exploited. Acquiring additional knowledge is useless at this level and should be done when building the category models. Moreover, the first models should guide the acquisition.
    - We recommend to give up modelling problems of a category as soon as the category model can be organized. The simulation data that were not modelled can be directly used to improve the category model.
- *Fully exploit the problem models* in different ways in order to reduce the number of interviews with the expert:
    - the problem models serve for the category model design;

- they provide examples of how the expertise is applied to solve a problem that help select the convenient problem solving method for the expertise modelling.

- they contain detailed knowledge to be used for the model instanciation.

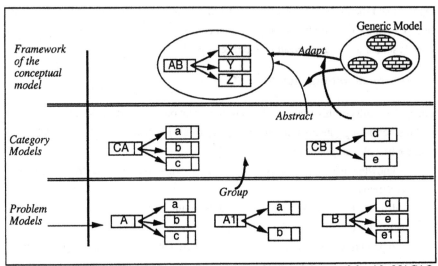

Figure 7: Evolutions of the construction of the problem solving model with MACAO.
Problem models remain in use to build the category models. But the category models are used twice: once to abstract a first expertise model; and mainly to select and adapt generic models or problem solving methods such as those proposed by the Common-KADS library.

- *Analyze the expertise by the means of the categories* as early as possible (Fig. 7):

- an analysis at this level helps characterizing the task because it urges one to consider the problem solving with a significant distance;

- knowledge in a category model provides answers to select a model in a library;

- this knowledge is easily reused to refine and instanciate the conceptual model because it is described at a more convenient abstraction level than problems.

Concerning the reuse of knowledge components, we suggest the knowledge engineer to use available results in CommonKADS or KREST libraries. These are interpretation models or problem solving methods identified by questions or selection criterion such as decision trees (cf. [VAL,93]). We promote the following guidelines:

- refer to a library only after categories have been modelled so that enough detailed knowledge is available in a structured way that could help to select a component;

- try to answer the questions raised in the libraries with the available knowledge in the problem or category models. This avoids new interviews of the expert.

- take into account all existing models, analyze their differences and similarities when refining them or building new models;

- adapt any select component with the domain vocabulary to make it understandable by the expert for validation, by a developer for maintenance and by the end-users;

- do not hesitate in combining generic components to fit better the expert process and/or the system requirements. Keep a reference to the original generic blocks.

6. Conclusion

Our experiments with MACAO as well as the analysis of other methodologies prove that knowledge engineering solutions to build conceptual models tend to become unified. They prone an analysis and abstraction of the expertise followed by the selection and adaptation of generic components and finally the instanciation of these components with domain knowledge. In fact, although approaches promoting the reuse of generic building blocs, such as KADS, GT or KREST, minimises the expertise abstraction step, once these approaches are applied to real applications, the importance of this abstraction is obvious. This is why these methods start proposing guidelines to carry out this first analysis.

On the other hand, the limits of a pure bottom-up design of the conceptual model proved the necessity to rely on a set of reusable generic components that focus on what is being built. A temporary solution for MACAO is to take advantage of existing works in the literature. A direct consequence of this work is an evolution of MACAO methodological guide. We wish to experiment it on new applications.

Acknowledgement

We warmly thank N. Matta and P. Lépine who contributed significantly to earlier versions of this paper. We could not have written it without the works of C. Soler, D.P. Vo and P. Lépine who were patient enough to use MACAO to model their applications. We had fruitful collaborations with them. We also wish to thank R. Benjamins for his major contribution to modelling the diagnosis expertise with KADS.

References

[AKK,93] H. Akkermans, B. Wielinga, G. Schreiber, Steps in Constructing Problem Solving Methods, *Proceedings of EKAW*, Toulouse and Caylus, Sep 1993. N. Aussenac, G. Boy, M. Linster, B. Gaines, J.G. Ganascia and Y. Kodratoff Ed, Lecture Notes in AI 723. Bonn: Springer Verlag.

[AUS,88] N. Aussenac, Soubie J.L., Frontin J., *A knowledge acquisition tool for expertise transfer*, Proceedings of EKAW 88. GMD Studien N 143. pp 8.1 - 8.12.

[AUS,92] N. Aussenac-Gilles, J.P. Krivine, J. Sallantin. Editorial of a special issue of *Revue d'Intelligence Artificielle* about Knowledge Acquisition, Ed: N. Aussenac-Gilles, J.P. Krivine, J. Sallantin, Paris: Hermès, Vol. 12, 1991/2.

[AUS,93] Aussenac-Gilles N., Matta N. Enjeux d'une acquisition des connaissances basée sur l'explicitation d'un modèle plus générique de l'expertise, *Actes des 4ème JAC 93*, St Raphael, Mars 1993.

[AUS,94a] N. Aussenac-Gilles, N. Matta. Making the method of problem solving explicit with MACAO, *International Journal on Human-Computer Studies* (1994) 40, Special issue: the Sisyphus project, M. Linster Ed., London: Academic Press. pp 193-219.

[AUS,94b] Matta N., Aussenac-Gilles N., Problèmes méthodologiques liés à la construction d'un modèle conceptuel avec MACAO, *In Actes des 5ème JAC 94*, Strasbourg (F), 21-23 Mars 1994. pp N.1-N.14.

[BEN,93a] Benjamins R., Problem Solving methods of diagnosis, *Thesis Universiteit van Amsterdam*, With index ref. ISBN 90-9005877-X, Amsterdam, 1993.

[BEN,93b] Benjamins R. *Report of work at Aramiihs*, Toulouse, June 1993.

[BOO,89] Boose J., A survey of knowledge acquisition techniques and tools, *Knowledge Acquisition*, Vol. 1, N 1, London: Academic Press. pp 3-39.

[BRE,87] Breuker J., Wielinga B., Van Someren M., De Hoog R., Schreiber G., De Greef P., Bredeweg B., Wielemaker J., Billault J.P., Model-Driven Knowledge Acquisition: Interpretation Models, *Deliverable task A1, Esprit Project 1098 Memo 87, VF Project Knowledge Acquisition in Formal Domains*, Amsterdam 1987.

[CHA,86] Chandrasekaran B., Generic Tasks in Knowledge based reasoning: High-level building blocks for Expert System Design, *IEEE Expert*, Autumn 86, pp 23-30.

[DEL,93] Delouis I., LISA: Un langage réflexif pour la modélisation du contrôle dans les systèmes à base des connaissances. Application à la plannification dans les réseaux électriques, *Thèse de l'Université de Paris Sud Centre d'Orsay*, Paris, 1993.

[KAR,91] W. Karbach, A. Voss, R. Schukey, U. Drouven, MODEL-K: Prototyping at the knowledge level, *Proceedings of the first international Conference on Knowledge Modelling and Expertise Transfer*, Sophia Antipolis, 1991. IOS Press, Amsterdam.

[KRI,91] Krivine J.P., David J.M., L'acquisition des connaissances vue comme un processus de modélisation; méthodes et outils, *Intellectica, (12)*, Paris dec. 1991.

[LIN,92] M. Linster, *Knowledge Acquisition Based on Explicit Methods of Problem Solving*, Ph.D. Dissertation, D 386, Univ. of Kaiserlautern (G), Feb. 1992. 220 p.

[LEP,93] P. Lépine, Contribution à la validation pratique de la méthodologie et de l'outil d'acquisition de connaissances expertes MACAO, *mémoire d'ingénieur CNAM* - Paris, déc 1993.

[LEP,94] P. Lépine, N. Aussenac-Gilles, Modélisation de la résolution de problèmes: comparaison expérimentale de KADS et MACAO, *Actes des JAC*, Strasbourg, Mars 1994.

[LER,94] B. Leroux, De l'expertise de modélisation, *Actes des 5èmes Journnées Acquisition des Connaissances*, Strasbourg, Mars 1994.

[MAR,88] Marcus S., *Automating Knowledge Acquisition for Expert Systems*. Kluwer Academic Publisher. Sandra Marcus Ed. . 1988.

[MAT,94] Matta N., Modèle Conceptuel: une représentation intermédiaire entre une conduite observée et un code implementé, Paper submitted to "Conférence des Jeunes Chercheurs en Intelligence Artificielle", Marseilles (F), sept. 1994.

[NEU,93] Neubert S., Model Construction in MIKE (Model-Based and Incremental Knowledge Engineering), *Proceedings of EKAW*, Toulouse and Caylus, Sep 1993. N. Aussenac, G. Boy, M. Linster, B. Gaines, J.G. Ganascia and Y. Kodratoff Ed, Lecture Notes in AI 723. Bonn: Springer Verlag.

[SOL,92] C. Soler, Système Expert d'aide à l'intégration Ariane, *Ingénieur CNAM* - Toulouse, déc 1992.

[STE,92] L. Steels, Reutilisability and configuration of applications by non-programmers, *Vrei Universiteit of Brussels-AI Lab, memo 92-4*.

[VHE,92] Van Heijst G., Terpstra P., Wielinga B., Shadbolt N., Using generalised directive models in knowledge acquisition. In Wetter T., Althoff K, Boose J., Gaines B., Linster M., Schmalhofer F., *Current trends in Knowledge Acquisition: EKAW 92*, Berlin (G). Springer-Verlag. 1992.

[VAL,93] Valente A., Lockenhoff C., Organisation as guidance: A library of Assessment Models, *Proceedings (complement) of EKAW'93*, Toulouse and Caylus, Sept 1993.

[VIC,93] Vicat C., Bussac A., Ganascia J.G., CERISE: A cyclic Approach for Knowledge Acquisition, *Proceedings of EKAW'93*, Toulouse and Caylus, Sept 1993. N. Aussenac, G. Boy, M. Linster, B. Gaines, J.G. Ganascia and Y. Kodratoff Ed, Lecture Notes in AI 723. Bonn: Springer Verlag.

[VOG,88] Vogel C., *Génie cognitif*, Masson , Paris. 1988.

[WIE,92] Wielinga B., Schreiber A., Breuker J., KADS: a modelling approach to knowledge acquisition, *Knowledge Acquisition*, Vol. 4, N°1, March 1992. pp 5-54.

User centered knowledge-based system design: a formal modelling approach

F.M.T. Brazier and J. Treur

Vrije Universiteit Amsterdam
Department of Mathematics and Computer Science
Artificial Intelligence Group
De Boelelaan 1081a, 1081 HV Amsterdam, The Netherlands
{frances,treur}@cs.vu.nl

1 Introduction

The problems users encounter when interacting with conventional automated systems are often manifold: varying from very basic key- stroke level problems to problems caused by conceptual mismatch of the users' expectations with what the system effectively does. The likelihood that problems will occur increases when the system with which the user interacts not only directly executes the instructions provided by the user, but also reasons about the current situation using knowledge not directly available to the user. This frequently holds for users' interaction with knowledge-based systems. In such environments the system is an intelligent agent with which the user cooperates.

As in all interactions between a system and a user, the user's expectations depend on the mental model (s)he forms of the system (Norman, 1983). For interaction with an intelligent agent not only the global metacommunication incorporated in the user-interface (and other materials such as manuals) is of importance, but also the way in which the domain dependent interaction between the system and the user is modelled. In cooperative environments in which the user interacts with knowledge-based systems to perform specific tasks, the *user* can often directly influence the systems' performance by providing input to the reasoning process. An accurate mental model of the system's functioning is crucial. In addition, the *system* needs to possess a model of the task and of the interaction process and may also need to have specific knowledge of the user in order to adapt the interaction to previous interaction and to specific user characteristics. This also holds for knowledge concerning interaction with the external material world. Both the system and the user must have an idea of how and when external factors can influence task execution.

Iterative, user centered design mandates that the delegation of tasks to the system and the external world are clearly defined in terms of the user's perception and understanding of the task environment and of the task requirements. A shared task model is the result of the knowledge and task analysis phase in the system's design. This model forms the basis of interaction between the user, the system and the external material world (see also (Ford et al, 1993; Brazier & Ruttkay, 1993)). The mapping between these tasks and the tasks which are most basic to the user (the user's unit task) and to the system (the system's basic tasks) is clearly defined in agreement with the user and thus transparent to the user in interaction with the system (Moran, 1983, Payne, 1987, Tauber, 1990, Brazier & Veer, 1991, Sutcliffe, 1989).

In this paper it is shown that a formal, declarative, multi-level compositional analysis (Langevelde, Philipsen & Treur, 1992) based on task models provides a means not only to construct conceptual models of cooperative agents, but also to structure interaction with the user. All knowledge incorporated in a system is defined in a declarative framework. Using this knowledge the system is capable of reasoning about its own knowledge, about the user's model of the system, the external material world and possibly about other systems' models of the system, but also about interaction with all three types of external agents. This, in turn, holds for each of the participating agents: they may all be capable of reasoning about their own knowledge, about other agent's knowledge and about the communication between agents. A satisfactory model of the task, which captures all relevant functions and operations (Chignell, Hancock and Loewenthal, 1989) is the basis of an intelligent interface providing the required interaction. The approach presented in this paper is based on both fundamental research (e.g., Treur, 1994; Engelfriet & Treur, 1994; Gavrila & Treur, 1994) and applied research. Interactive knowledge-based systems have been designed and implemented in a number of domains varying from intelligent decision support in environmental policy making to dynamic process control and medical diagnosis (e.g., Brumsen, Pannekeet & Treur, 1992; Geelen & Kowalczyk, 1992).

The role of a task model in a cooperative environment in which intelligent agents interact with each other and with the outside world, in which the types of knowledge involved and the roles of the agents are defined and illustrated with an example, is discussed below. In section four a formal approach to the analysis of the required functionality is presented. This approach is discussed in Section 5 and directions for further research are proposed.

2 Task model

The model of the task on which interaction is based is the result of knowledge acquisition and task analysis. The user, a knowledge-based system, and other external agents use this model as the frame of reference for task execution. This model will have different connotations for each of the participating agents: the roles agents play will may differ significantly. The main role fo the external material world is that of information provider. For the sake of clarity the interaction in the model presented below will be limited to interaction between one user, one knowledge based system and the external material world.

The task model on which the agents have agreed, the shared task model defines the roles of each of the agents: the user, the knowledge-based system and of the external world, in relation to the sub-tasks and their interaction. In this example all agents are cooperative participants in the problem solving process. Knowledge to this extent is included in the knowledge-based system's knowledge base. To illustrate the concept of modelling interaction between a user, a knowledge-based system and the external world, a simplified version of a task model for a diagnostic decision-making process (based on a task model designed for medical diagnosis) will be employed. The five modules in this model, as shown in Fig. 1 are:

1. *hypothesis determination*: possible hypotheses are explored, and evaluated as to their applicability to a given situation. Specific hypotheses are selected for further examination.

2. *test determination*: given one or more hypotheses the possible ways to test the hypothesis or hypotheses are determined and compared. The most suitable tests are selected.

3. *test execution*: the requirements of the tests selected in the previous module are fulfilled and the test executed.

4. *result interpretation*: the results of test execution are examined, interpreted and evaluated with respect to the relevant hypotheses.

5. *diagnostic process control*: on the basis of the hypotheses, tests and test results, either a final diagnosis is made or the process of hypothesis selection, test determination, test execution and result interpretation, is continued.

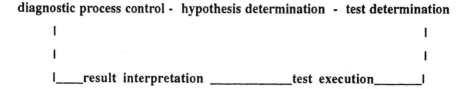

Figure 1: Shared task model for diagnostic decision making

Each of these components represents a sub-task to which both the user and the system can refer: the model as a whole (including the interactions between the modules) can be seen as a shared model of the task. Decisions concerning task delegation within each sub-task require analysis of the desired functionality. Both parties must fully comprehend their role with respect to their own knowledge, the task model, the external world and the other agent. The system and the user may differ significantly with respect to their detailed knowledge of the task at hand: in general one of the two agents will have more knowledge of a particular task within a sub-task for which (s)he is responsible than the other. An example of further task decomposition and task delegation for each of the components in diagnostic decision making is shown below in Fig. 2.

The two agents and the external world each play different roles within each of the sub-tasks in the shared task model. The user and the system are knowledgeable of the roles the other agent plays and of the interaction between the agents. Within hypothesis determination, the system generates possible hypotheses with an ordering of preference on the basis of known factors (for example likeliness, urgency and criticality) in view of the current state of the process, and the user selects one or more hypotheses to explore.

Likewise within test determination the system generates possible tests with an ordering of preference on the basis of known factors (for example expected information value and cost) in view of the current information process and the user selects one or more tests to acquire additional data.

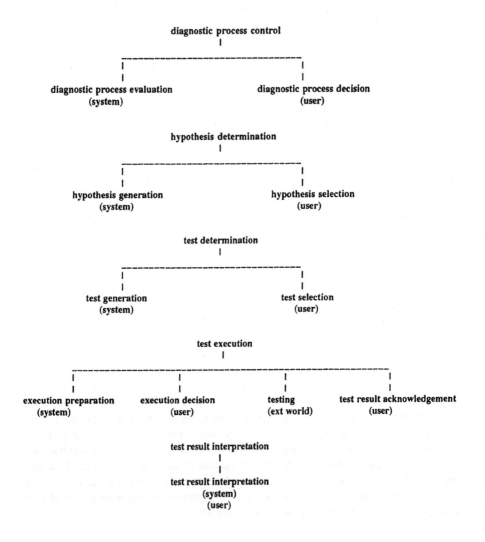

Figure 2: Task decomposition and task delegation

In test execution the data known to the system to be required to perform the test are generated by the system. The user passes the request for additional information to the external world, checks to make sure the results have been obtained and passes the results on to the system for further interpretation.

Both the user and the system examine and interpret the results of the tests in test result interpretation. On the basis of the interpretations of the results the system evaluates the current state of the diagnostic process; e.g. it determines whether a final diagnostic conclusion can be drawn. If so, this decision is proposed to the user, together with the grounds on which the decision is based. The user decides whether (s)he wishes to come to a decision or whether (s)he wishes to explore additional hypotheses.

The control knowledge required to execute the task as a whole has been implicitly defined in the above description of the task. This knowledge, the knowledge of which component activates which other component when, is explicitly specified as a result of the knowledge modelling process. This also holds for knowledge of the mental models, the mental worlds: the user assumes knowledge of the mental world of the system, the system assumes knowledge of the user's mental world. This knowledge is used to define possible interactions during the diagnostic problem solving process.

3 The roles of the three parties

As in our view an agent is an autonomous reasoning and acting entity capable of performing complex tasks, our first concern is to clearly define a transparent structure. Our compositional formal specification framework DESIRE for reasoning systems for complex tasks will be used for this purpose; see (Kowalczyk & Treur, 1990, Langevelde et al, 1992; Treur & Wetter, 1993; Gavrila & Treur, 1994).

3.1 Domains of knowledge of an agent

Intelligent agents are knowledgeable agents: agents with knowledge of themselves and other agents, of the types of interations required between themselves and the other agents, but also of the external world and the necessary interaction (see also (Oberquelle, Kupka, Maas, 1983). Each agent has knowledge within these domains of knowledge, namely (cf. (Dunin Keplicz & Treur, 1994)):

(1) knowledge of the mental world of the agent itself
(2) knowledge of the mental world of other agents,
(3) knowledge of the interaction between the agent and other agents,
(4) knowledge of the exernal material world,
(5) knowledge of interaction between the agent and the external material world.

The agent's knowledge of its own mental world, of its own information state, guides the agent's reasoning process. This includes knowledge of the agent's own goals, of its success and failure in achieving these goals, of assumptions which have been made and when, of information which has been sought and not yet found, of information which has not yet been explored, et cetera. It also includes knowledge of the agent's own reasoning and strategic preferences.

The agent's knowledge of other agents' mental worlds includes knowledge of which information is available in other agents and which tasks they are capable to do. To this purpose knowledge of other agents task models, their goals and success, are required.

Knowledge of the interaction between the agent and other agents is required to know when and how information can be obtained from other agents and when, which tasks can be delegated to other agents and when, et cetera.

For most tasks knowledge of the external material world is required during task execution: knowledge about the specific situation at hand, extending knowledge previously available to the system.

Interaction with the external material world mandates knowledge about which information can be requested from the external material world and how.

3.2 Describing the roles in the example task

The five domains of knowledge distinguished for both the user and the system are described below with respect to the diagnostic task (see also Fig. 3).

3.2.1 The system's role

The domains of knowledge with which the system reasons are:

(1) Mental world of the system itself

To reason about the diagnostic (problem solving) process the system has knowledge of its own state and reasoning behaviour with respect to both the global problem solving process and the hypotheses. This type of knowledge is found in two components:
- diagnostic process evaluation
- hypothesis generation

(2) Mental world of the user

To reason about the diagnostic process the system needs information about the user's contribution to the task, e.g., which (sub)tasks can performed by the user, which subtaks have already been performed and which have succeeded, et cetera. Moreover, the system needs information about certain characteristics (user model) of the user's style of diagnosis, such as: the relative priorities (trade-off) the user employs between aspects like criticality and probability of a hypothesis in the hypothesis determination task; how the relative priorities between information value and costs in the test determination task. This type of knowledge is found in two components:
- user's tasks
- user's characteristics

(3)   Communication with the user

As interaction with the user is required to execute tests, the system requires knowledge of how and what to communicate with the user with respect to these tasks. This knowledge is included in:
- test generation
- test execution preparation

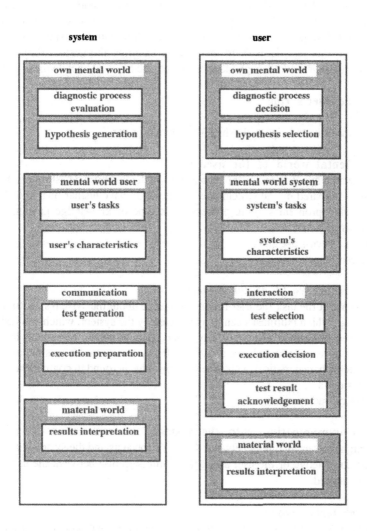

Figure 3: System and user domains and components

(4)   Material world

To reason about the material world the system uses observational (test) information it receives (via the user) about the world and knowledge enabling it to draw conclusions from this information, i.e., based on the outcomes of tests it draws conclusions about the diseases the patient has. This type of knowledge is found in:
- system's result interpretation

(5)   Interaction with the external (material) world

Although it is not difficult to imagine a system that is connected to a test device in the external world, requiring knowledge of the interaction with the external world (e.g., when to use this test device), in this simple example the system only indirectly interacts with the world: through the user. Hence, the required knowledge is trivial.

3.2.2   The user's role

The domains of knowledge with which the user reasons are:

(1)   Mental world of the user itself

To know which hypotheses are applicable and which diagnostic decisions can be made, using input prepared by the system, the user needs to have his/her own knowledge of the diagnostic problem solving process. This type of knowledge is found in two components:
- diagnostic process decision
- hypothesis selection

(2)   Mental world of the system

To reason about the task the user needs knowledge about the system's contribution to the task, e.g., which (sub)tasks can be performed by the system, which sub-tasks have already been performed and which have succeeded, et cetera. Moreover, the user is assumed to have some knowledge about how the system comes to its solutions of sub-tasks (system characteristics). This type of knowledge is found in components:
- system's tasks
- system's characteristics

(3)   Communication with the system

As a straightforward mapping between the user's concepts and the system's concepts is assumed, knowledge of the user about the communication between the user and the system is limited.

(4)   Material world

Just as the system the user uses observational (test) information it will receive about the world and knowledge to reason about the material world enabling it to draw conclusions from this information. The system's and user's knowledge may have an overlap but may also differ; i.e., the user has knowledge the system lacks and vice versa. This type of knowledge is found in only one component:
- user's result interpretation

(5) Interaction with the material world

The user knowledge about which test to perform and related activities are considered part of this domain of knowledge. This type of knowledge is found in three components:
- test selection
- test execution decision
- test result acknowledgement

3.2.3 The external (material) world

The state of the world is modelled in a separate component in which the information on an object or subject (patient) to be diagnosed is specified.

4   Specifications of the example

4.1   A brief introduction to compositional modelling in DESIRE

Within DESIRE, a formal framework for the design and implementation of compositional meta-level knowledge-based systems, task analysis results in a task decomposition in which the components represent sub-tasks. Each component contains static knowledge (knowledge that holds in all states of the domain, the knowledge base) and dynamic knowledge (knowledge that depends on the "current" domain state, the object information state). The object information state of a component represents the explicit information currently available in the component (i.e., input and derived facts). In specifications of actual systems, knowledge bases have, to date, been expressed in rule format. All information states can be represented by sets of closed literals, or, equivalently, by partial models for the signature of the component.

A given component can have a combined information state (for more details, see (Treur, 1991; Langevelde et al, 1992 Gavrila & Treur, 1994; Treur, 1994)) in which two types of information are combined:
- an object-information state: the information the component has about the domain state, (as defined above);
- a meta-information state: information about the state of the reasoning of the component, including explicit information about what is (not) known (at the moment).

The meta-information state specifies all information relevant to the state of the reasoning of the component; it summarizes a number of descriptors characterising these process states, for example:
- the truth value of object statement **a** has not been determined;
- the object statement **h** is considered as a goal for the reasoning process;
- the component can not continue reasoning since information on some object statement **b** has not been determined yet and is needed for the current goal;
- the degree of exhaustiveness of the reasoning.

The distinction between meta- and object level information is crucial to the compositional meta-level approach because it enables a component **C**'s reasoning process to be the subject of the reasoning of another component **D**. If the component **D** reasons at a meta-level, the current meta-information state of **C** provides the domain state for **D**.

During task execution basic steps can be modelled by transitions between information states. One information state can change into another by means of:
- inference process;
- interactions between components.

By making inferences in a component both the object and meta-information states will change. Changes in the object information state are refinements: the object information state becomes more complete. Inferences are assumed to be conservative and monotonic. In practice this means that components have a memory: they store and keep all information obtained earlier. Changes in the meta-information state are, in general, in contrast to changes in the object level information state changes, not refinements, but non-conservative transitions. For example, when an unknown object-level atom **a** becomes known. For more details, see (Gavrila & Treur, 1994; Treur, 1994).

The control structure in DESIRE is formally specified (see (Langevelde et al, 1992)). The formal specifications indicate when and how each component is activated. Activation of a component entails the specification of a number of interactions that should be performed in order to provide input facts for the component, including its exhaustiveness, together with a reference to its target set. This exhaustiveness type can be any, any-new, every or all-possible. Together with a target set it specifies the goal the component has to attain in order to terminate successfully.

The condition that specifies when a component has to be activated is described in terms of the termination status of some other component. If this other component has attained its goal, specified when it was activated, its termination status is defined as succeeded. If it has not reached its goal, and it may reach its goal if additional input is provided (without revisions), its status is failed, otherwise, if it can only reach its goal if some of the inputs are revised, it is c-failed.

The control flow of the system is specified by means of supervisor rules. The start and stop rules are specific supervisor rules that specify which component is to be activated first and when the problem solving process is to terminate. A simple example of a supervisor rule is the following.

> **if termination**(design_object_evaluation, evaluation, **succeeded**)
> **then next-module**(design_process_evaluation, violation, **data-driven, any**)
> **and next-pre-trans**(reflect_up_design_description)

This rule specifies that, if the component design_object_evaluation has succeeded w.r.t. the target set evaluation, the transformation reflect_up_design_description is applied, the component design_process_evaluation is activated, and it should try to derive any element of the target set violation.

4.2 Example specifications

Generic specifications of the components distinguished in Section 2 are presented in this section. Irrelevant details have been omitted.

4.2.1 The system's modules

Hypothesis Generation Module
The module receives epistemic information about what has become known on symptoms and hypotheses sofar, as input. Applying its (domain-specific) strategic knowledge it first determines the current degree of belief and basic priority (e.g., criticality) of hypotheses. Then it generates conclusions of the form hyp_priority(h, pf), where h is a hypothesis and pf is the priority factor assigned to it. It makes use of one of the user's characteristics, namely the characteristic knowledge specified by the predicate h_prior_comb(DOB, B, PF) where DOB denotes the value of the degree of belief, B the basic priority value of a hypothesis and PF the priority value the current user wishes to assign. The generic specification of the module is as follows:

module hypothesis_generation : **reasoning**

input signature symps_and_hypos_presence
      sorts   Hypotheses, Symptoms,
                            DOB_values, B_values, H_prior_values
      relations   h_prior_comb :   DOB_values * B_values * H_prior_values ;
                            present, not_available :   Symptoms ;
                            rejected, confirmed :   Hypotheses ;
endsig

output signature hypos_priorities
      sorts   Hypotheses, H_prior_values
      relations   hyp_priority :   Hypotheses * H_prior_values ;
endsig

internal signature hypos_criteria
      sorts   Hypotheses, DOB_values, B_values
      relations   degree_of_belief :   Hypotheses * DOB_values ;
                            basic_hyp_priority :   Hypotheses * B_values ;
endsig

knowledge base
      if   degree_of_belief(H: Hypotheses, D: DOB_values)
      and   basic_hyp_priority(H: Hypotheses, B: B_values)
      and   h_prior_comb(D: DOB_values, B: B_values, PF: H_prior_values)
      then   hyp_priority(H: Hypotheses, PF: H_prior_values) ;

endmod

Test Generation module

This module receives information of the form "to_be_investigated(h)" as input. This module collects symptoms that are relevant for determining h. Applying its strategic knowledge it generates information on the (estimated) information value and costs of testing a symptom and then combining these factors according to the user characteristic draws conclusions of the form sym_priority(s, pf), where s is a symptom and pf the priority factor assigned to it. The input for this module also contains epistemic information about symptoms.

module test_generation : **reasoning**

input signature symps_presence_and_hypos_in_focus
          sorts   Hypotheses, Symptoms,
                                    IV_values, C_values, T_prior_values
          relations   t_prior_comb :   IV_values * C_values * T_prior_values ;
                                    present :   Symptoms ;
                                    not_available :   Symptoms ;
                                    to_be_investigated :   Hypotheses ;
endsig

output signature symps_priorities
          sorts   Symptoms, T_prior_values
          relations   sym_priority :   Symptoms * T_prior_values ;
endsig

internal signature sym_criteria
          sorts   Symptoms, IV_values, C_values
          relations   information_value :   Symptoms * IV_values ;
                                    basic_sym_priority :   Symptoms * C_values ;
endsig

knowledge base
          if   information_value(S: Symptoms, I: IV_values)
          and   basic_sym_priority(S: Symptoms, C: C_values)
          and   t_prior_comb(I: IV_values, C: C_values, PF: T_prior_values)
          then   sym_priority(S: Symptoms, PF: T_prior_values) ;

endmod

Execution Preparation module

To verify the presence or the absence of a symptom, a measurement is needed. For example, to verify whether the patient has a fever or not, the patient's temperature has to be measured, and according to the result an answer may be given (e.g., if the temperature is higher than 38° then the symptom "fever" is present). The task of the Test Evaluation module is to propose measurements for given tests. This module is specified as follows:

module execution_preparation : **reasoning**

input signature　selected_symptoms
　　　sorts　　　　　Symptoms
　　　relations　　　needed : Symptoms ;
endsig

output signature　measurement_specification
　　　sorts　　　　　Measurements
　　　relations　　　proposed :　　　　Measurements ;
endsig

target-sets
　　dynamic_targets

knowledge base

endmod

System's Results Interpretation module
When a new indication is found to hold, some hypotheses can be confirmed or rejected
on the basis of (domain specific) rules which express logical relations between
indications and hypotheses. The **System's Results Interpretation** module
performs this:

module systems_results_interpretation : **reasoning**

input signature　s_measurements_presence
　　　sorts　　　　　Measurements
　　　relations　　　is_the_case :　　Measurements ;
endsig

output signature　s_hypos_presence
　　　sorts　　　　　Diagnoses
　　　relations　　　diagnosis :　　Diagnoses ;
endsig

knowledge base

endmod

Diagnostic Process Evaluation module
The role of this module is to determine whether the diagnostic process should be continued or not. The "not" decision may be taken in two cases: either a certain hypothesis has been found to be true (i.e., an atom of the form confirmed(h) has been found to be true), or the system was not able to confirm any hypothesis, even though it has explored all possibilities. The specification of this module is as follows:

module diagnostic_process_evaluation : **reasoning**

input signature hypos_presence
      sorts   Hypotheses
      relations   rejected, confirmed :   Hypotheses ;
endsig

output signature diag_decisions
      sorts   Hypotheses
      relations   to_be_continued, unable_to_conclude_anything ;
                      concluded :   Hypotheses ;
endsig

knowledge base

endmod

User's Task module
Left unspecified.

User's Characteristics module
This module stores the user's characteristics about combining the values of different criteria for hypothesis and test priorities as mentioned earlier:

module users_characteristics : **reasoning**

input signature in_characteristics
      sorts   DOB_values, B_values, H_prior_values,
                      IV_values, C_values, T_prior_values
      relations   h_prior_comb :   DOB_values * B_values * H_prior_values ;
                      t_prior_comb :   IV_values * C_values * T_prior_values ;
endsig

output signature out_characteristics
      sorts   DOB_values, B_values, H_prior_values,
                      IV_values, C_values, T_prior_values
      relations   hyp_priority :   DOB_values * B_values * H_prior_values ;
                      test_priority :   IV_values * C_values * T_prior_values ;
endsig

knowledge base

endmod

4.2.2   User modules

Hypothesis   Selection module
Based on the output of the **Hypothesis   Generation** module, the **Hypothesis Selection** module makes a choice of a hypothesis to be investigated. Its output consists of atoms of the form to_be_investigated(h). It can simply be the highest of the list offered by **Hypothesis Generation**, but any other choice is possible.

module hypothesis_selection : **reasoning**

input signature   hypos_priorities
    sorts   Hypotheses, H_prior_values
    relations   hyp_priority :   Hypotheses * H_prior_values ;
endsig

output signature hyp_in_focus
    sorts   Hypotheses
    relations   to_be_investigated :   Hypotheses ;
endsig

knowledge base

endmod

Test Selection module
As in the case of hypothesis selection, based on the output of the **Test Generation** module, the **Test Selection** module makes a choice of the test that should be performed. Its output consists of atoms of the form needed(s).

module test_selection : **reasoning**

input signature   symps_priorities
    sorts   Symptoms, T_prior_values
    relations   sym_priority :   Symptoms * T_prior_values ;
endsig

output signature symps_in_focus
    sorts   Symptoms
    relations   needed : Symptoms ;
endsig

target-sets
    initial_targets

initial   meta-facts
    target(initial_targets, needed(S: Symptoms), **confirm**);

knowledge   base

endmod

Test Execution Decision module

module test_execution_decision : **reasoning**

input signature   measurement_proposals
      sorts   Measurements
      relations   proposed :   Measurements ;
endsig

output signature   selected_measurements
      sorts   Measurements
      relations   selected :   Measurements ;
endsig

target-sets
      initial_targets

initial   meta-facts
      target(initial_targets, selected(M: Measurements), **confirm**);

knowledge base

endmod

Test Results Acknowledgements module
Left unspecified.

User's Results Interpretation module
The **User's Results Interpretation** module is just a copy of the module **System's Results Interpretation**. However, the domain-specific content of the knowledge bases may differ.

module users_results_interpretation : **reasoning**

input signature   t_measurements_presence
      sorts   Measurements
      relations   is_the_case :   Measurements ;
endsig

output signature   t_hypos_presence
      sorts   Diagnoses
      relations   diagnosis :   Diagnoses ;
endsig

knowledge base

endmod

4.2.3 The external world

The External World module
This is not a real knowledge-based module. Its role is to provide specific information concerning various aspects of the object being diagnosed.

module external_world : **conventional**

output signature measurement_results
      sorts   Measurements
      relations   is_the_case :   Measurements ;
endsig

target sets
      dynamic_targets

knowledge base

endmod

4.3 Transformations
To illustrate the way in which specifications are formulated the interaction between the user and the world in which the user asks the external world to perform the selected measurements:

transformation ask_measurement : **object-target**

domain test_execution_decision
      object output signature selected_measurements;

co-domain external_world
      target input signature target_input_external_world

sort links
      (Measurements, OA)

atom links
      (selected(X: Measurements), target(dynamic_targets, X: OA, determine)) :
            <<true, true>, <false, false>, <unknown, unknown>>

endtrans

The other transformations are rather trivial.

4.4   Control

Global control of component activation is defined in the supervisor: task sequence is specified on the basis of sub-task success. In the diagnostic decision task, each execution of a new sub-task entails the activation of a new agent.

5   Conclusions and further research

In knowledge modelling the user is not frequently treated as an essential and central part of the analysis. Often a task model is designed and then, in addition, a so-called cooperation model is devised. In user centered design the user is an integral and central part of the knowledge model right from the start. This implies the requirement that the dynamics of the interaction between user and system must be expressed in the task model. This shared task model provides the basis for interaction and cooperation between system and user. Formal modelling languages make this possible. In this paper this issue has been investigated for one of the existing formal modelling languages (Treur & Wetter, 1993): DESIRE. In an earlier study (Dunin Keplicz & Treur, 1994) it was shown that DESIRE offers interesting possibilities to model the dynamics of cooperation between complex agents in a multi-agent architecture. Combining this with earlier ideas about strategic interaction and revision in compositional knowledge-based systems (Pannekeet, Philipsen & Treur, 1993; Treur, 1993) resulted in the framework presented in this paper for modelling the knowledge involved in a problem solving process with explicit roles for system and user, interacting both at object level and at strategic level.

Specifications in this framework have been shown for an example task in which a user and a knowledge based system need to cooperate. In the current form the problem solving method is explicitly defined at a global level: the sequence of task component activation defines a highly interactive problem solving process. The user, the knowledge-based system and the external world are all assigned tasks which directly influence the problem solving process. In future research a more flexible version of control, in which the involved agents can participate in the problem solving process, for which the sequence is not predefined, will be explored.

Acknowledgements

This research has been partially supported by SKBS.

References

Brazier, F.M.T. and van der Veer, G.C., 1991. Design decisions for a user interface. In Ackerman, D. & Tauber, M. (eds), Mental Models and Human Computer Interaction. North Holland: Amsterdam.

Brazier, F.M.T. and Ruttkay, Zs., 1993. A Compositional, Knowledge-based Architecture for Intelligent Query User Interfaces, Adjunct proceedings of INTERCHI'93 ACM Press, Amsterdam, 1993. 145-146.

Brumsen, H.A., Pannekeet, J.H.M. and Treur, J., 1992. A compositional knowledge-based architecture modelling process aspects of design tasks. In: Proc. of the 12th Int. Conf. on AI, Expert systems and Natural Language, Avignon'92, Vol. 1: pp. 283-294.

Chignell, M.H., Hancock, P.A. and Loewenthal, A. 1989. An introduction to intelligent interfaces. Intelligent interfaces: Theory, Research and Design. North Holland: Amsterdam, 1-27.

Gavrila, I.S. and Treur, J., 1994. A formal model for the dynamics of compositional reasoning systems, in A.G. Cohn (ed.), Proceedings of the 11th European Conference on Artificial Intelligence, ECAI'94 , John Wiley & Sons, Chichester.

Dunin Keplicz, B. and Treur, J., 1994. Compositional formal specification of multi-agent architectures. In: M. Wooldridge & N. Jennings (eds.), Proc. ECAI'94 Workshop on Agent Theories, Architectures and Languages.

Engelfriet, J. and Treur, J., 1994. Temporal theories of reasoning, Proc. Fourth European Workshop on Logics in AI, JELIA'94, Springer Verlag.

Ford, K.M., Bradshaw, J.M., Adams-Webber, J.R. and Agnew, N.M., 1993. Knowledge Acquisition as a Constructive Modeling Activity, IJIS, Vol 8, 9-32, Wiley, N.Y.

Geelen, P.A. and Kowalczyk, W., 1992. A knowledge-based system for the routing of international blank payment orders. In: Proc. of the 12th Int. Conf. on AI, Expert Systems and Natural Language, Avignon'92, Vol. 2, pp. 669-677.

Huhns, M. (ed.), 1987. Distributed Artifical Intelligence, Morgan Kaufman.

Jennings, N.R., 1992. Towards a cooperation knowledge level for collaborative problem solving, in B. Neumann (ed.), Proceedings of the 10th European Conference on Artificial Intelligence, ECAI'92, John Wiley & Sons, Chichester, pp. 224-228.

Kowalczyk, W. and Treur, J., 1990. On the use of a formalized generic task model in knowledge acquisition, In: B.J. Wielinga, J. Boose, B.R. Gaines, A.Th. Schreiber, M.W. van Someren (eds.), Current Trends in Knowledge Acquisition (Proceedings EKAW-90), IOS Press, Amsterdam, pp. 198-221.

Kowalczyk, W. and Treur, J., 1990. Formal specification of task-specific architectures, Report IR-232, Department of Mathematics and Computer Science, Vrije Universiteit Amsterdam.

Langevelde, I.A. van, Philipsen, A.W. and Treur, J., 1992. Formal specification of compositional architectures, in B. Neumann (ed.), Proceedings of the 10th European Conference on Artificial Intelligence, ECAI'92, John Wiley & Sons, Chichester, 1992, pp. 272-276.

Moran, T.P., 1983. Getting into a system. External-Internal task mapping analysis. CHI'83 Proceedings. North Holland: Amsterdam, 51-56.

Norman, D.A., 1982. Some observations on mental models. In: Gentner, D., Stevens, A.L. (eds), Mental Models, Erlbaum Ass, Hillsdale, N.J.

Oberquelle, H., Kupka, I. and Maass, S., 1983. A view of human-machine communication and co-operation, Int. Journal of Man-Machine Studies, 1983, pp. 309-333.

Pannekeet, J.H.M., Philipsen, A.W. and Treur, J., 1992. Designing compositional assumption revision, Report IR-279, Department of Mathematics and Computer Science, Vrije Universiteit Amsterdam, 1991. Shorter version in: H. de Swaan Arons et al., Proc. Dutch AI-Conference, NAIC-92, 1992, pp. 285-296.

Payne, S.J., 1987. Complex problem spaces: modelling the knowledge needed to use interactive devices. In: H-J Bullinger, B. Schakel (eds), Human-Computer Interaction - Interact 87. North Holland: Amsterdam, 203-208.

Sutcliffe, A., 1989. Task analysis, systems analysis and design: symbiosis or synthesis? Interacting with Computers.

Tauber, M.J., 1990. ETAG: Extended task action grammar - a language for the description of the user's task language. In: D. Diaper, D. Gilmore, G. Cockton & B. Schakel (eds), Human-Computer Interaction - INTERACT 90 Elsevier: Amsterdam. 1,1, 6-12.

Treur, J., 1991. Interaction types and chemistry of generic task models, in: M. Linster, B. Gaines, (eds.), Proc. EKAW'91. GMD Studien 211, 1992, pp. 390-414.

Treur, J., 1993. Heuristic reasoning and relative incompleteness, Int. Journal of Approximate Reasoning 8 (1993), pp. 51-87.

Treur, J., 1994. Temporal semantics of meta-level architectures for dynamic control, Proc. META'94.

Treur, J. and Wetter, Th., 1993. Formal Specification of Complex Reasoning Systems, Ellis Horwood, 1993.

Wilson, S., Johnson, P., Kelly, C., Cunningham, J. and Markopoulos, P. 1993. Beyond Hacking: a Model Based Approach to User Interface Design. In Proceedings HCI'93. Cambridge University Press.

Validating at Early Stages with a Causal Simulation Tool

Paul-André Tourtier and Stéphane Boyera

INRIA, ACACIA project
F-06902 Sophia-Antipolis Cedex, France
E-mail: {tourtier, boyera}@sophia.inria.fr

Abstract. Validating the dynamics of a conceptual model of expertise is a crucial task which is too often neglected and sometimes relegated after the implementation's phase. The motivation for this work is to capture and to simulate the dynamics of a modeled system during the early phases of design. In this paper, we present an approach and a tool based on a general and powerful simulation engine. We assume that the dynamics of a system can be viewed as a causal graph, where the nodes represent the parameters of the system and the links represent causal influences between these parameters. In a given state, the belief on the value of a parameter is an uncertain quantity represented by a probabilistic density over its domain of variation. We consider then semi-quantitative parameters and show that, using some results on discrete probabilities, we can exhibit a simulation method based on matrix calculus. We describe MORSE, a prototype based on a simple simulation algorithm, and illustrate its use on an example. Finally, we discuss the current limitations of this method and conclude about future developments of this work.

1. Motivations

1.1. Validating at early stages

The essence of Knowledge Acquisition relies on making explicit the models that underlie an expert's reasoning. It is crucial to validate such models before entering the implementation phase [8]. However, in the current state of the art, as the expert can hardly verify the whole behaviour of the model built by the knowledge engineer, it is often difficult for him to determine potential incoherences.

The motivation for this work is to propose a solution to detect model incoherences during the early phases of the design. The difficulties of this task are well known. As soon as a knowledge engineer (KE) builds some conceptual model underlying an expert's reasoning, the issue of validating this knowledge emerges as a crucial task: are all the relevant parameters considered? does the model give pertinent predictions? is there any problem of coherence? etc. In that matter, the experience seems to prove that there is one major rule: the sooner, the better.

Usually, it is better to see the model working: consider a typical case, test the predictions, understand the reasoning path, correct or complete the model, retry a new case, etc. However, this process is often executed «at hand» by lack of convenient tool; sometimes, the testing phase is even relegated after the implementation of the first prototype because, at an early stage of development, the models include many incomplete, uncertain, and heterogeneous informations.

What we need is a framework for integrating homogeneously these disparate data, and a tool for simulating the behaviour of the system being modeled, preferably at a macroscopic level.

1.2. Capturing the dynamics

We need first to define what we mean by «behaviour» and «dynamics». Generally speaking, a conceptual model of expertise can be viewed as a graph, i.e. as a set of concepts representing objects or processes together with a set of relations between these concepts; an object can have attributes, subparts, etc. We call *static knowledge* those informations that describe a stable state of a system, i.e. facts that do not change or are not considered to change significantly as far as the current point of view is concerned: e.g. «the temperature of the room is 20°C». By contrast, the *dynamic knowledge* captures informations about a variation of state over one or more dimensions, either spontaneously or provoked by some action: e.g. «if the heater is on, then the temperature increases over time».

Actually, a major problem of the validation is to understand and to simulate the dynamic features of a model. Those informations are not always explicitly stated and it is often difficult to predict the state and the evolution of a modeled system in a particular case. Typically, the state of a system will be described by a set of variables (or parameters) associated with a domain of variations and linked by various relations or constraints. Experts, as most human beings, tend to search the causal relations that underlie such a model in order to understand how the variation of some parameters may affect the variation of some others. This is typically the case when the model represents the behaviour of some device.

1.3. Designing a simulation tool

The considerations above lead us to the idea of designing a simulation tool with the following requirements:
- use heterogeneous informations (e.g. qualitative as well as quantitative);
- deal with uncertainty and probabilities;
- capture causal relationships;
- provide a simple and homogeneous knowledge representation scheme; and
- estimate the degree of confidence in the presented results.

In the following, we consider more closely the consequences of these requirements and describe an approach that attempts to integrate within a coherent framework the various pieces of knowledge that capture the dynamics of a conceptual model.

2. An approach based on causal graphs

Let us consider a system S that we want to model. Our approach is based on the following assumptions:
- The state of the system can be described by a finite set of variables (we call here *variables* those properties, subject to significant variations, that are relevant to the current point of view);
- The dynamics of the system can be described as a finite set of causal influences between those variables.

2.1. Qualitative vs. quantitative parameters

First, let us consider the nature of the variables describing our system. Traditionally, different kinds of variable are distinguished given the nature of their domain of variation. One calls
- quantitative, a variable attached to a numeric interval;
- qualitative, a variable whose domain is an unordered set of symbols;
- semi-quantitative, a variable defined by a numeric interval and an ordered set of symbols, where each symbol is associated to a subrange of that interval.

Note that the term «range» can be taken here in a broad sense: a subrange may be defined by a subinterval, a fuzzy set, or any probabilistic distribution.

However, it seems restrictive to consider only one domain of variation for a parameter. An expert may use different scales for the same concept (e.g. two scales with different units). In the same way, a «semi-quantitative» parameter is nothing but a parameter with two scales of different nature (a quantitative one and a qualitative one) linked by a simple relation (a qualitative value is defined by a subrange of the quantitative domain). We may also want to distinguish the point of view of different experts.

More generally, we will consider that a variable can be associated to one or several scales, either qualitative or quantitative, that are linked by transfer relations. Each different scale will then correspond to a specific viewpoint on the variable, defined by different granularities, units, etc.

2.2. Dealing with uncertainty

Most of the data that are collected at this stage are by nature incomplete or uncertain. For instance, an expert's belief on the value of some parameter X can be:
- quantitative («X=3.0», «2.9 < X < 3.1»)
- qualitative («X is high»);
- bounded («X is lower than 4»);
- fuzzy («X is around 3», «X is high with 80% of certainty»; or
- probabilistic («X follows a normal distribution law centered around 3»).

Intuitively, as we want to treat such beliefs in an homogeneous way, the idea is to represent an uncertain quantity by a «density of belief» over its domain of variation.

More formally, the parameters of the system are considered as random variables and we are interested in the probability distribution of those variables. We need also a second-order measure of uncertainty, i.e. an estimation of the difference between the estimated and the real value of the parameter. Instead of trying to bound the maximum error margin, we will consider here the probable error on the value (as in the Monte Carlo approach).

Therefore, we will represent a belief on the *value of a parameter* X as an uncertain quantity noted $v_X = (f_X, d_X)$ where f_X is a function of density (e.g. a centered normal distribution) and d_X is a probable error margin (e.g. 2%).

We define also a the state of a system as a set of values associated to each parameter of the system. Given an initial (incomplete) probabilistic state and a set of variations, we want to be able to compute the estimated probabilistic state of the whole system.

2.3. Representing causal links

Informations that represent influences or constraints between parameters can be expressed through various ways, e.g.:
- mathematical equations («$X = Y + k.Y^2$»),
- rules («if X is low, then Y is high»),
- bayesian associations («$P(X=a / Y = b) = 0.8$»),
- topoi («the higher X, the lower Y»),
- or any combination of the above.

Intuitively, if we have some knowledge about the values of some parameters of the system, the relations above can give us information on how to estimate the values of the remaining (unknown) parameters. The problem is to represent explicitly those informations in a suitable manner.

We will assume here that the network of constraints between the parameters of the considered system can be represented in the form of a causal graph. A causal graph is a body of knowledge that models the causal dependencies between various parameters of a system. It can be represented as a network where the nodes are the considered parameters, and the links are oriented N->1 relations that specify how the value of the target parameter is influenced by the value of the source parameters. If a parameter is influenced by more than a causal link, then we will assume the existence of a combination function that specifies how the value of the parameter can be estimated given the various influences that affect this parameter (for instance, by adding all the influences).

Formally, we will represent a causal relation $(Y_1, \ldots Y_n \rightarrow X)$ by a function noted $F_{X/Yi}$ such as: if $\forall$ i, f_{Yi} is a density on Y_i, then $F_{X/Yi}(f_{Y1}, \ldots, f_{Yn}) = f_X$ is a density on X.

2.4. Design choices

In order to use the previous framework for practical applications, we need to make some design choices.

First, we have to decide how we are going to represent the density of a variable. In order to have an efficient and quick simulation method, we need to choose a family of functions and approximate any density by a function of this kind. Let us call Ω this family of functions. Let A and B be two parameters associated with their densities d_A and d_B (each belonging to Ω) such that A causes B. A basic inference step would be: given d_A, we can determine d'_B (using the fundamental transformation law of probabilities) that is the «real» density of B and then approximate d'_B by d_B that is a function of Ω. Let ψ be the direct transformation $\psi(d_A) = d_B$. ψ belongs to a family of transformations Ψ, and Ψ and Ω are related (the properties of Ψ depend on the nature of Ω).

One important goal is to determine the properties of Ψ, according to the chosen family Ω. Ideally, we want to chose a family such that: there exists an (efficient) algorithm for approximating any «common» density; we can estimate the error of such an approximation; we can store and handle efficiently the approximated functions (e.g. as a finite set of parameters).

Then, we need to define a second-order measure of uncertainty and how to update it given the errors that are done during the approximation.

We need also to determine the kind of relations that we would allow, given that: there exists an algorithm for approximating the functions associated to the relations; we can estimate the error of such an approximation; and we can efficiently store and handle such functions. Probably, we want to propose a predefined set of relations and, ideally, a way to expand this set.

Finally, we have to design a simulation algorithm that would handle such representations.

3. Principles of the simulation

In order to explain the main principles of this approach, we will focus here on qualitative parameters. Actually, we will show in the next section how these results can be reused for semi-quantitative parameters.

3.1. Representing beliefs by density vectors

Let A be a qualitative parameter whose quality space is $\{A_1, ..., A_n\}$. Let us then consider the random variable associated to the space of probability $\{A=A_1, ..., A=A_n\}$, where the event $\{A=A_i\}$ represents the hypothesis that the value of A is A_i.

In the following, we will assume that the events $\{A=A_i\}$ are disjoint, i.e. that we have a mutually exclusive and exhaustive set of hypotheses.

Definition 1. *We call **density vector** of A the tuple $d_A = (\alpha_1, ..., \alpha_n)$ where each coefficient $\alpha_i = P(A=A_i)$ is the probability for A to have the qualitative value A_i.*

Lemna 1. $\quad |d_A| = \sum \alpha_i = 1.$

Note that a density vector d_A represents a belief on the value of the parameter A.

For instance:

belief	density vector
«A= Ai»	$d_A=(0,..., 1, 0,... 0)$
«A=?»	$d_A=(1/n,..., 1/n)$
«A= A1, A2 or A3»	$d_A=(1/3, 1/3, 1/3, 0,... 0)$
«A= A1(20%) or A2(80%)»	$d_A=(1/5, 4/5, 0,..., 0)$

From a practical point of view, the problem is to know how we can compute the density vector of a parameter, given its causal dependencies. In the next section, we present some results drawn from the Theory of Discrete Probability that show that these vectors are linked by relations of matrix calculus (proofs of the theorems are given in [2]).

3.2. Single causal dependencies

Let A and B be two qualitative parameters associated respectively with the density vectors $d_A = (\alpha_1, ..., \alpha_n)$ and $d_B = (\beta_1, ..., \beta_m)$. In the following, we will use the notation «A --> B» for «B is causally depending on A».

Definition 2. *The matrix of conditional probability $M_{B|A}$ is the (n, m) matrix of general term $M_{ij} = P(B=B_j / A=A_i)$.*

Theorem 1. *If A-->B, then : $d_B = M_{B|A} * d_A$*

Let A, B be two parameters, if there exists a causal relation such that «A causes B», the application which determines the density vector of B from A's one is a linear application represented by the matrix of the conditional probabilities of B knowing A.

This result can be extended to the case of multiple causal dependencies. We will present here the results for two variables, which are easily generalizable to the case of n variables.

3.3. Multiple causal dependencies

Let us first define the two operators $\otimes$ and $\circledR$.

Definition 3. *If α is the vector $(\alpha_1, ..., \alpha_n)$ and β is the vector $(\beta_1, ..., \beta_m)$, then $\alpha \otimes \beta$ is the vector $(\alpha_1*\beta_1, \alpha_1*\beta_2, ..., \alpha_n*\beta_m)$ of size $n*m$.*

This operator can be seen as a kind of cross product between two vectors.

Definition 4. *If P is a $(t, n*m)$ matrix and Q is a (n, m) matrix, then $M = P \circledR Q$ is a (n, t) matrix of general term: $M_{ik} = \sum_j P_{k,n*i+j}, Q_{ij}$.*

This operator makes a block to block matrices product. The left matrix is cut in many blocks and each block is multiplied by the right matrix.

Let us consider now three qualitative parameters A, B, and C and let $d_A=(\alpha_1,...,\alpha_n)$, $d_B=(\beta_1, ..., \beta_m)$, and $d_C=(\gamma_1, ..., \gamma_t)$ be their density vectors.

Definition 5. *The matrix of conditional probability $M_{C|A,B}$ is the $(t, n*m)$ matrix of general term $M_{k,m*i+j-m} = P(C=C_k / A=A_i \cap B=B_j)$.*

Theorem 2.1. *If A, B --> C and if A and B independent, then: $d_C = M_{C|A,B} * (d_A \otimes d_B)$*

Let A, B, C be three parameters such that A and B are independent and such that there exists a causal relation «A and B cause C». Then, the application which associates C to the product $A \otimes B$ is a linear application represented by the matrix of conditional probabilities of C knowing A and B.

Theorem 2.2. *If A, B --> C and if A --> B, then: $d_C = (M_{C|A,B} \circledR M_{B|A}) * d_A$*

Let A, B, C be three parameters such that A and B are causally dependant («A causes B») and such that there exists a causal relation between A and B and C («A and B cause C»). Then the density of C depends only on A's one, and the application which associates the density of C to the density of A is a linear application represented by the matrix result of the product by $\circledR$ of the matrix of conditional probabilities of C knowing A and B and of the matrix of conditional probabilities of B knowing A.

If the dependency between A and B is not as simple as a direct relation, the matrix $M_{B|A}$ that we need is not explicitly available. However, if there exists an oriented path from A to B, we have developed methods to compute this matrix in all the cases (e.g. $M_{B/A}$ can be computed from $M_{B/A,X}$). These methods will not be detailed here (see [2] for further information).

4. A prototype: MORSE

4.1. Overview

The MORSE system is a simulation tool based on the previous principles. As any prototype whose goal is to validate theoretical research, the current version of MORSE supports only a limited set of features. In the current version, the functions used to express the causal dependencies are restricted to: linear functions, multiply, divide, functions defined by user's associations, or combination of the above (add, min., max., etc.).
Written in Lisp, this implementation is independent of the knowledge representation formalism used for storing the nodes and the relations, thanks to a clean software interface. This feature allows MORSE to be used with any graph formalism.

As far as the simulation is concerned, the system uses by default a depth-first strategy for navigating through the nodes of the graph. However, this feature can be customized by the user for a particular application.

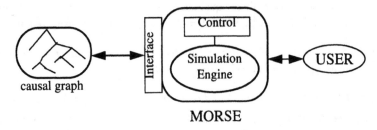

MORSE

After having defined the different scales for each parameter of the graph, the user (usually a knowledge engineer) can for instance initiate a set of simulations, analyse the results, and compare their accuracy with real test cases. If the results were not satisfying, the user could also modify the causal graph and test interactively the new behaviour of the system.

4.2. Design choices

In the design of the prototype, we have decided to represent densities by piecewise constant functions. This choice is motivated by three main reasons:

From a mathematical point of view, this family of functions is particularly convenient because, as such functions of density can be seen as discrete functions, we can fruitfully use the results of the previous section on discrete probabilities. Moreover, it is quite easy to approximate any continuous distribution by a piecewise constant function and to estimate this error:

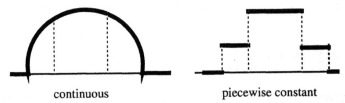

continuous   piecewise constant

From a KA point of view, this kind of information is also easy to elicit. What is needed to define the value of a variable is simply a set of coefficients (one for each scale level). In most cases, even a rough approximation of these coefficients is sufficient for validation's purposes. A more fine-grained specification of the values of the parameters, if possible, would probably not have a major influence on the behaviour of the system at the macroscopic level. Moreover, there is often no need of such complex fuzzy informations in the final expert system.

Finally, from an operational point of view, the results given by the system require little, if any, need of interpretation. Semi-quantitative parameters can be directly associated to a qualitative value. As for quantitative parameters, it is usually enough for the user to know a range of possible values for the parameters, together with some estimation of the probability that the value of the parameter be a given subrange.

4.3. Simulation algorithm

It is easy to see that we can determine the distribution of an output parameter from the distributions of its input parameters, as far as the matrix representing the relation is available. In [2], we describe various methods to compute this matrix according to the nature of the relation, including:
- linear functions;
- monotone functions;
- polynomial functions (in the 1:1 case);
- functions defined by user associations.

The principle of the simulation algorithm presented below is the following:
- before any simulation, the system is initialized by computing the matrix attached to each causal relation;
- then, a set of simulations can be initiated by setting the values of some parameters and propagating the beliefs on the other nodes.

Algorithm.

```
var R:= set-of-relations (system)
var N:= set-of-nodes (system)
function initialization
    for each r ∈ R do
        matrix(r):= compute_causal_matrix (r)
    end initialization
function simulation (list_entries)
    list_nodes:= list_entries
    while list_nodes ≠ empty do
        Let e:= first (list_nodes)
        if value(e) is undefined then
            list_nodes:= list_nodes - {e}
            merge(list_nodes,children(e)) % depth-first
        else if ∀ a ∈ ancestors(e), value(a) is defined then
            value(e):= compute-value(ancestors(e))
        else for each a ∈ ancestors (e) do
                if value(a) is undefined then
                    list_nodes:= {a} U list_nodes
    end while
end simulation
```

4.4. An example: the breakwater construction

The graph presented below is a simplified part of a causal graph used in the EXPORT expert system for breakwater constructions ([14]). The problem is to decide whether one should take the decisions to build a breakwater by considering the various aspects involved: utility, security, budget, loans, etc.

Although very simple, this example illustrates how the system can be used in practice. We suppose that a first (incomplete) model of expertise has already been built. The goal of the user is to examine, validate and complete such a model, e.g.:
  - the user can test the predictions and understand the reasoning steps of the system by changing the context (e.g. increase the estimated price of cement and assume that the budget of the town is probably low) and examine the outputs of the system: the decision of construction (e.g. the town should build the breakwater, with 90% of certainty) and the level of loan (e.g. the town has to borrow between 2 and 3 millions of french francs in order to build the breakwater).
  - it is then possible to complete, refine, or update the model as desired.

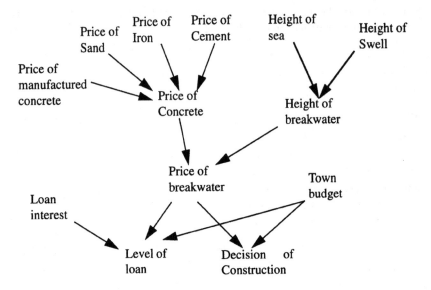

5. Evaluation and extensions

The first experiments that we have conducted with MORSE have stressed out the current limitations of the system and led us to plan a few enhancements for the near future.

5.1. Cyclic graphs

A major limitation of the current system is that it does not allow to work with **cyclic graphs**. This is a problem in some complex domains that involve some kind of feedback process.

This extension requires mainly to modify our simulation algorithm in order to deal with loops. We are currently working on an iterative propagation algorithm similar to those used for neural networks: changes are propagated along the links and each node may be re-computed more than once. The problem is then to decide when the algorithm should stop; the algorithm uses predefined termination criteria in order to check whether an equilibrium state has been reached (success) or whether such an equilibrium cannot be reached with the given conditions (contradiction).

5.2. Implicit dependencies

Finally, our system cannot detect implicit dependencies between variables: if there is no causal path between two variables A and B, then we assume that they are independent. This seems reasonable but it might turn out to be a problem in the case of a shared ancestor (e.g. X-->A; X-->B; and A, B --> Y). Currently, we cannot deal with this kind of situation because it is impossible to determine the matrix $M_{B|A}$ if we do not know, either that A and B are independent, or that they are causally dependent.

We are now studying new methods for detecting this kind of situation and generating equivalent graphs where such implicit dependencies would be eliminated.

5.3. Backward-chaining

Currently, our simulation engine uses a kind of forward-chaining inference scheme (supporting the so-called *what-if reasoning*, i.e. estimating the values of output parameters according to the values of input parameters). However, it is often useful to use some kind of backward-chaining (or *how-to reasoning*, determining the values of input parameters, given the values of output parameters).

We plan to add this feature in the next version of MORSE thanks to the same computational principles, i.e. by determining the *inverse* matrix associated to each causal link. This makes sense if we can make the assumption that the causal model fully captures all the possible causes of change that might occur in the considered system.

5.4. Fuzzy intervals

Due to our choice of piecewise constant functions for representing the probabilistic densities, we have a classical brittleness problem: in the worst case, a small quantitative variation in the inputs may induce a large qualitative step in the results. In the same way, it may seem restrictive to use only scales with disjunctive levels (no overlapping between intervals is allowed) because it is not always easy for an expert to give such accurate limits for a concept. Therefore, an extension of this work would be to use a family of continuous functions (e.g. piecewise linear distributions) and to consider fuzzy intervals.

However, some care should be taken not to loose in simplicity and computational efficiency what we could gain in sensitivity. Moreover, it is always possible, in the current approach, to approximate a continuous function by a piecewise constant function: surprisingly, it seems that this brutal method gives good results in practice, although it does not preserve the continuity property.

5.5. Generic libraries

An interesting way of research would be to emphasize the structural properties of causal graphs. The idea is to define a causal graph as a composition of interconnected components, where a component is a module defined by an interface part (a set of input and output variables) and by a body part (the causal structure describing the influence of the inputs on the outputs). The main advantage of this approach is obviously to encourage a greater modularity and to favour the re-usability of such components. The system could even provide a library of generic components that the user could use, combine, or enrich when needed in order to build a causal graph suitable to his particular application.

Studying the connections that such a library could have with other existing generic libraries, e.g. such as those used in CommonKADS, seems of prime interest to us. In particular, we foresee that it will give us some insight on how this approach could take place within a general K.A. methodological framework.

6. Related Work

This work has required the integration of related works from various fields.

Surprisingly, only a few works in Knowledge Acquisition deal with the problem of qualitative simulation and more generally, the use of qualitative knowledge. We have reused the idea of a Parameter Dependency Oriented Graph in [8] and have extended its expression power. We were also influenced by Clancey's works on qualitative models ([4]). Finally, an interesting approach is developed by H. Akkermans and J. Top in [1].

Following the considerable work relevant to the integration of quantitative with qualitative knowledge ([10, 11]), we used the idea to associate a qualitative value to a quantitative range by defining landmarks that will decompose a quantity space in a finite set of ranges (disjoint intervals or fuzzy sets).

The idea to represent beliefs as probability distributions across competing hypotheses and the use of conditional probabilities for propagating beliefs are similar to Bayes' theory and its use in belief networks. However, our approach differs significantly because it does not require to determine all the conditional probabilities in advance; we compute these data using higher-level knowledge on the causality of the system to be modeled. This is particularly crucial in the K.A. domain where this kind of information is usually very hard to elicit directly from experts.

The principles of our engine are based on the various researches on Qualitative Simulation, namely the idea of predicting the set of qualitatively possible behaviours of a mechanism given a qualitative description of its structure and initial state ([6, 9, 12, 13]). The need for a new tool came from the observation that most QS systems are not adapted to the K.A. domain and suffer from important limitations such as an unnatural knowledge representation, a primitive or implicit notion of uncertainty, counter-intuitive results, or computational inefficiency. For the same reasons, we have decided not to follow a classical Monte Carlo approach: our matrix-based approach is more efficient and more intuitive.

Only a few attempts ([5, 7, 15]) have been made incorporating uncertainty within Qualitative Reasoning (QR) researches. To the best of our knowledge, none approach deals with second-order uncertainty (sensitivity of results).

Finally, our notion of module is closed to the notion of component as defined in DPS ([18]); we tried to extend this idea in the sense of a generic library of reusable components, as used in the KADS approach.

7. Conclusion

We defend here the idea that testing the dynamics of a model of expertise is a crucial task that should be undertaken as soon as possible in the process of knowledge modeling. However, the lack of convenient tool and the top-down strategy of most existing K.A. methodologies tend to postpone validation and testing after the operationalization phase. For instance, it is quite difficult for an expert to validate the «inference level» of KADS because the proposed inference schemes are too abstract and disconnected from his or her real-world problems. By contrast, to consider a real or a simulated case and to test interactively the dynamics of the system's model is a powerful way to have the expert think and react in an appropriate cognitive context; i.e. a real problem-solving situation, not in an artificial situation where the expert must validate his(er) own reasoning process.

We think that the benefits of using a qualitative simulation tool in the early stages of knowledge modeling would be quite substantial. However, existing tools are not dedicated to the K.A. domain and suffer from important limitations. Most of them require informations difficult to elicit or to interpret, and cannot deal with incomplete, uncertain, and heterogeneous informations.

We have proposed in this paper an approach based on causal graphs: the dynamics of a system is viewed as a set of causal influences that links the parameters that describe the system; a belief on the state of a system is then defined as a probabilistic distribution of the values of its parameters over their domain of variation. In the case of qualitative and semi-quantitative parameters, it can be shown that we can represent the state of a system by a set of density vectors linked by relations of matrix calculus. A simple simulation algorithm has been exhibited that determines the probable state of a system in a given situation (i.e. given some beliefs on the value of the exogeneous variables of the system).

We have also presented MORSE, a causal simulation tool dedicated to the validation of the dynamics of conceptual models. The current prototype has restricted features (acyclic graphs, limited set of relations) but is a simple and efficient tool with a clean architecture (independence towards the graph representation, user-controllable search strategy). Major enhancements are planned, and are currently under way: cyclic graphs, fuzzy intervals and relations, etc.

Interestingly enough, we feel that our approach favours an incremental and opportunistic view of Knowledge Acquisition. Instead of following a definite plan, leading to distinguish disjoint stages in the knowledge acquisition process, it seems that experts and knowledge engineers most usually react to specific opportunities of eliciting, modeling, or validating some piece of knowledge. To be able to «work» rapidly on the dynamics and the validation of the emerging models seems to us a good way to provoke such opportunities. Although a real understanding of the complete behaviour of the future KBS cannot be drawn from such a limited and rough simulation, it increases the chance of detecting potential inconsistencies or limitations of the knowledge being modeled. It may also improve the confidence and the interest of the experts in the design of such an -- otherwise abstract -- artefact.

More work is clearly needed to study the impact and the interests of such tools during knowledge modeling. We are about to use our prototype in a complex real-world domain: the analysis of road collisions. We hope to get then some insight on the outcomes and the limitations of this method, and on its integration with current state-of-the-art methodologies. We foresee that, more than a validation tool, MORSE might turn out to be also an important communication tool between the various agents involved: experts, knowledge engineers and application programmers.

References

1. H. Akkermans, J. Top: Tasks and ontologies in engineering modeling. Proceedings of Knowledge Acquisition for Knowledge-Based Systems Workshop, Banff, 1994.

2. S. Boyera: Un générateur de graphes pour KATEMES. rapport de DEA, Université de Nice, 1993.

3. K. Bousson, L. Traves-Massuyes: Fuzzy causal simulation in process engineering. Proceedings of the 13th IJCAI, Chambery, 1993.

4. W. Clancey: Viewing knowledge bases as qualitative models. IEEE expert journal, Volume 4, pp 9-23, 1989.

5. B. D'Ambrosio: Extending mathematics in qualitative process. Proceedings of the 6th national conference on artificial intelligence, pages 595-599, 1987.

6. J. De Kleer and J.S. Brown: A qualitative physics based on confluences. Artificial Intelligence, N°24 (7-83), 1984.

7. D. Dubois and H. Prade: Order-of-magnitude reasoning with fuzzy relations. Proceedings of IFAC symposium on advanced information processing in automatic control, Nancy, 1989.

8. R. Dieng, B. Trousse: 3DKAT, a Dependency-Driven Dynamic-Knowledge Acquisition Tool. 3rd International Symposium on Knowledge Engineering, Madrid 1988.

9. K.D. Forbus: Qualitative process theory. Artificial Intelligence, N°24 (85-168), 1984.

10. K.D. Forbus: Interpreting measurements of physical systems. Proceedings of AAAI 86, 1986.

11. B. Kuipers et D. Berleant: Using incomplete quantitative knowledge in qualitative reasoning. Proceedings of the 7th AAAI, Saint-Paul, 1988.

12. B. Kuipers: Qualitative Simulation. Artificial Intelligence N°29, 1986.

13. B. Kuipers: The use of Qualitative Simulation in support of Model-based Reasoning. SPIE Vol. 1293,
Applications of Artificial Intelligence VIII, 1990.

14. B. Neveu: EXPORT: An expert system in breakwater design. ORIA 87, Artificial Intelligence and Sea, Marseille 1987.

15. Q. Shen and R.R. Leitch: Fuzzy qualitative simulation. IEEE Transactions on Systems, Man and Cybernetics, 23(4), 1993.

16. P. Struss: Problems of interval-based qualitative reasoning. Readings in qualitative reasoning about physical systems, Morgan Kaufman Publishers, 1990.

17. L. Traves-Massuyes, K. Bousson, J. Evrard, F. Guerrin, B. Lucas, A. Missier, D. Rahal, M. Tomasena, L. Zimmer: Modélisation et simulation qualitatives, représentation, algorithmes et applications. 4ème Journées du PRC-IA, Marseille, 1992.

18. M. Vescovi: La représentation des connaissances et le raisonnement sur les systèmes physiques. PhD, Université de savoie, 1991.

The SBF Framework, 1989-1994: From Applications to Workplaces

Gregg R. Yost, Georg Klinker, Marc Linster, David Marques, John McDermott

Workplace Integration Technologies Group, Digital Equipment Corporation
200 Forest St. (MR01-3/J14), Marlboro, MA 01752
yost,klinker,linster,marques,mcdermott@guess.enet.dec.com

Abstract. The SBF (Spark, Burn, Firefighter) project began five years ago. Its goal was to develop a framework for making it easier to evolve effective application programs. Its approach was to provide an integrated set of tools to help developers create applications by configuring and customizing reusable software components, called mechanisms. SBF aimed to be usable by both programmers and non-programmers. SBF has undergone major changes several times, motivated by user feedback and data collected in usability studies. The emphasis has shifted from understanding how applications can be built to understanding what assistance is needed in a workplace and how some automation might best be introduced into an integrated workplace. This paper describes how SBF has evolved over the years, and, more importantly, what motivated the major changes.

1. Introduction

The SBF (Spark, Burn, Firefighter) project began five years ago. Our goal, as initially formulated, was to create a framework that would make it easier to develop application programs. Our approach was to provide an integrated set of tools to help developers (non-programmers as well as programmers) create applications by configuring and customizing reusable software components, called *mechanisms*. SBF has undergone major changes several times as the hypotheses that underlay its design proved to be either untenable or incomplete

Our first attempt at an automatic mechanism configurer in SBF v1 (see Section 3) failed because non-programming domain experts were unable to understand the questions Spark (the configuration system) asked in order to select appropriate mechanisms. At first it seemed to us that Spark failed because its questions were cast in terms that were too close to programming terms. We later realized that that was only a symptom — we were expressing the questions in thinly-veiled mechanistic terms primarily because we had no other context within which to frame them. So began our continuing exploration of *task context*, a topic that will appear throughout the paper. The current version of SBF is radically different from SBF v1 in many ways, and the changes we have made over the years may have seemed rather ad-hoc to the readers of our papers describing the various SBF versions. The primary motivator of the most significant changes, however, is our evolving understanding of what constitutes useful contextual information and the many ways it can be used.

The contextual information we chose to use in SBF is models of the workplaces and work processes involved in a task. While we initially introduced these models to facilitate communication with the task developer, we soon began to use the workplace context for other purposes as well. Among our current uses for the workplace context are indexing into workplace-model and mechanism libraries, and managing the flow of tasks and information in a workplace. More significantly, we believe, our incorporation of the workplace context has caused us to rethink what SBF's product should be. Early on, we took the traditional expert-system view that there was a predetermined task that was to be automated, and that the problem was to acquire and operationally represent the knowledge required to perform that task. The product in this traditional view is an application program that automates the task in isolation. When one considers the workplace context of a task, however, it becomes clear that this is unlikely to be desirable. One task is merely a part of a workplace, and to be effective an application (or a person!) must not only perform its task well, but also work well together with related activities and actors in the workplace. Further, complete automation of a given task may not be the most desirable option; it might be better to automate some activities, assist with others, and leave yet others to be performed by people. So, in our most recent version of SBF, the product is not an application program but a set of coordinated applications that work together with each other and with people in the workplace to provide effective task support. The workplace context has proved to be a very effective framework for considering appropriate ways to provide integrated automated assistance in a workplace.

This paper describes how each SBF version differs from the prior one, and, more importantly, why we made the changes we did. Section 1 describes the main research efforts that led to SBF. Sections 3 through 5 describe successive versions of SBF and show how and why each evolved from its predecessor. We conclude with a discussion of the implications that our most recent version of SBF has for the way effective computer-based workplace support can be developed.

2. SBF's Pre-history

By the mid-to-late 1980's, an approach to knowledge-based system development we'll call *model-based knowledge acquisition* had become a popular research topic. This approach involves building tools that interact with the task developer at the *knowledge level* (Newell, 1982). Ideally, the need for a highly-trained programmer is eliminated, since the domain expert can interact directly with the tool using the concepts of the domain. Model-based tools of the time included CGEN (Birmingham & Siewiorek, 1989), KNACK (Klinker, 1988), MOLE (Eshelman et al., 1988), OPAL (Musen et al., 1988), and SALT (Marcus, McDermott and Wang,

1985; Marcus, 1988). These tools got their power by exploiting knowledge of a particular domain or problem-solving method. By 1988, researchers were gaining a good understanding of the general characteristics of the model-based approach, and at least two frameworks for discussing this work were emerging (generic tasks (Chandrasekaran, 1986) and role-limiting methods (McDermott, 1988)).

Model-based tools proved to have many strengths, but researchers also recognized a number of disadvantages, as partially discussed in (Musen & van der Lei, 1988; Chandrasekaran & Johnson, 1993). Model-based tools obtained their power at the expense of generality: each tool used a problem-solving method and external language that was appropriate for only a very narrow range of tasks. Furthermore, model-based tools spanned only a small fraction of potential tasks, and there were tasks for which no appropriate model-based tool had been constructed, despite serious efforts (for example, the computer configuration task performed by the XCON expert system (Barker et al., 1989) — see (McDermott, 1988)). To compound the problem, there was no reliable way to select the right model-based tool for a particular task even if one did exist.

In response to these shortcomings, many researchers began to explore alternative ways to develop knowledge-based systems (for example, PROTEGE (Puerta et al, 1992), TAQL (Yost, 1993), and DIDS (Runkel & Birmingham, 1993)). The SBF research was one such path.

In 1988, we began to focus on indexing problem-solving methods by the domain or task characteristics for which they were appropriate (McDermott, 1988). This index was intended to be used to select an appropriate model-based tool for a given task based solely on task-level, non-computational information about the task. We soon realized that the index was extremely complicated even for small sets of problem-solving methods. We wrote a program that would use knowledge of the index to interview task developers and suggest appropriate knowledge acquisition tools for their task. This program was the first version of Spark, but there was not yet a Burn or Firefighter.

Building Spark proved to be very difficult — we were unable to come up with understandable questions with appropriate discriminating power (more on this in later sections). Moreover, within a few months, we realized that building a tool-selection program was ultimately futile — there were far too many tasks in the world to be covered by a manageable number of narrow, brittle, isolated knowledge acquisition tools. At the same time, we observed that existing model-based tools did not use single, atomic problem-solving methods. Instead, each tool used a problem-solving method that could be decomposed into components we called *mechanisms*. Our group set about extending Spark to be able to index into the component mechanisms and configure selected mechanisms into a complete problem-solving method for a given task. This extension of Spark became the first version of SBF.

3. SBF v1 (April 1989 - April 1990)[1]

SBF v1 was based on three hypotheses:

1. *Spark hypothesis:* Based only on characteristics of a task that are obvious to non-programmers, relevant pre-defined computational mechanisms can be identified and configured to form a method for performing the task.

2. *Burn hypothesis:* Given a set of configured mechanisms, predefined knowledge acquisition tools associated with those mechanisms can elicit expertise from a non-programmer and encode that expertise, thereby creating a program to perform the task.

3. *Firefighter hypothesis:* Given an indication from a non-programmer that an application program is inadequate, it is possible to determine whether the inadequacy is due to missing expertise or to an inappropriate method and then to remedy the inadequacy.

SBF v1's goal was to make it easier to evolve effective application programs, to a point where even non-programmers could develop applications. It consisted of three related systems — Spark, Burn, and Firefighter — corresponding to the three hypotheses.

Spark was much like the pre-SBF Spark. It had knowledge about how task features corresponded to suitable problem-solving mechanisms, and used this knowledge to interview the task developer (the domain expert). The interview was conducted in task-level terms, not mechanism-level terms. For example, after Spark determined that the expert used a historical database of cases for estimating resources for a new project, it would ask a question such as:

Spark: **If you have two different examples of specific cases and appropriate solutions, in what ways can you compare the solutions?**
1. **some or all of the characteristics of the solution can be compared arithmetically (for example, twice as big, or 10% larger)**
2. **some or all of the characteristics of the solution can be compared only non-numerically (for example, bigger or smaller)**

Spark used information gathered in the interview to index into a library of predefined mechanisms based on the mechanism's inputs and outputs and the expertise required to instantiate it. Its dialog was directed by a simple constraint-satisfaction algorithm where each question it asked differentiated among potential mechanisms based on the above criteria. When ambiguities were resolved and mechanism requirements met, Spark configured the selected mechanisms into a problem-solving method by matching inputs, outputs and expertise. Spark had to

---

[1]SBF v1 was never completely described in a paper. (Steels & McDermott, 1994) gives some glimpses into our early thoughts about SBF, but the view presented there is substantially different from the one presented here. In particular, the Burn mentioned in (Steels & McDermott, 1994) was a knowledge acquisition tool for case-based sizing systems, and should not be confused with the Burn in the SBF framework.

configure the mechanisms in a way such that the configuration (1) produced all of the outputs required by the task; and (2) required only inputs and expertise available in the task: this meant that all inputs required by any mechanism in the configuration were available either as task inputs or as outputs from prior mechanisms in the configuration. Sometimes, Spark had to add additional mechanisms to produce an acceptable configuration, or ask additional questions to select among multiple potential configurations.

Spark then passed a description of the configuration to Burn. Each mechanism in Spark's library had a corresponding mechanism-specific knowledge acquisition tool. For each mechanism in the configuration, Burn invoked the corresponding tool to acquire the knowledge required by that mechanism. Burn ensured that if more than one mechanism required the same information, the user was only asked for that information once. This turned out to be the most difficult part of building Burn and the knowledge acquisition tools because we required the SBF framework to be capable of configuring together mechanisms and knowledge acquisition tools built by different developers and not specifically intended to work together. For SBF v1, we created a common language for describing these disparate mechanisms, but extending and evaluating this language is one area of SBF that has not received further attention. Finally, Burn generated code linking the instantiated mechanisms into a single program.

After Burn, the application was ready to run. If it behaved incorrectly, the user could invoke Firefighter. Firefighter interviewed the user or developer to diagnose the problem. If the problem involved incorrect expertise, Firefighter would tell Burn to reinvoke the knowledge acquisition tool for the faulty mechanism. If the problem involved an incorrect mechanism configuration, it would reinvoke Spark, passing it information about the configuration and the problem with it.

Lessons

While Firefighter was able to diagnose and resolve some problems, it was never a robust component of SBF in any version. Like Spark, it had to interview the expert in domain terms, but the large number of possible failure modes made Firefighter's problem even more difficult than Spark's. While we have always believed that progress could be made on Firefighter, in practice we have devoted most of our efforts to Spark and Burn. Firefighter remains an open research problem and we will have little more to say about it in this paper. For more details on Firefighter and some examples of it in action, see (Marques et al., 1992).

As described at the end of Section 1, we initiated the SBF project to overcome problems with the earlier Spark system:

1. The earlier work assumed that a single method from a preexisting set of methods would be selected to automate a task. This implied that an unmanageable number of methods and KA tools had to be built by hand.

2. It was hard to come up with understandable necessary and sufficient questions to map task characteristics onto problem-solving methods.

There was progress on the first problem. Given a reasonable mechanism configuration, Burn worked fairly well. In building a few application prototypes using SBF v1, we did in fact reuse a variety of mechanisms and reconfigure them in different ways for different tasks. This experience was confirmed by a larger number of application-building efforts with SBF v2, which used essentially the same version of Burn as SBF v1 (see (Marques et al., 1991; Klinker et al., 1991)).

There was no progress on the second problem, however. The questions Spark asked were still of the same sort the pre-SBF Spark asked, which were both inadequate to select appropriate mechanisms and difficult for developers to understand and know how to answer.

4. SBF v2 (May 1990 - January 1991)[2]

SBF v1's main shortcoming was that it could not effectively produce a usable mechanism configuration. We found it very difficult to design questions that (1) a non-programming developer could understand and know how to answer and (2) could be used to index into appropriate computational mechanisms for the task. To address these problems, we designed SBF v2 to select and configure mechanisms in a very different way. In SBF v2, Spark did not ask the developer a series of questions to converge on an appropriate mechanism configuration. Instead, it presented the developer with a hierarchy of industry models and process models. These models represented the way a variety of tasks were performed in several types of businesses. The developer selected entries in the models that most closely matched their task. After each selection, Spark presented the developer with a more detailed model corresponding to that selection. The lowest level of the model contained detailed process models; the developer could edit these process models in limited ways to more closely match the processes involved in their task. Our hypothesis was that by leading the developer through progressively more detailed business models, they would be better able to understand the choices Spark asked them to make, since the choices would be presented in a hopefully-familiar business context. In SBF v1, the developer described their task in terms of its inputs, outputs, and the expertise available to perform it; in SBF v2 (and v3), the developer described their task in terms of the processes, activities, agents and information involved in performing it.

Each lowest-level process model in SBF v2 contained pre-built associations to appropriate mechanism configurations for that model. Spark only showed the developer the process models, not the associated mechanisms. But, by navigating through the process models and selecting/customizing appropriate models, the developer was in fact also selecting and configuring appropriate mechanisms for encoding their task. This is very different from the way mechanisms were configured in SBF v1. There, Spark used the answers to its questions to select a set of candidate mechanisms; it then used a variety of input/output matching heuristics

---

[2]SBF v2 is described more completely in (Marques et al., 1992; Marques et al., 1991; Klinker et al., 1991).

to configure the individual mechanisms into a complete problem-solving method. In SBF v2, Spark did not have to perform any mechanism configuration; by selecting and customizing process models, the developer was implicitly selecting and configuring the hidden mechanisms that were attached to those models. Some models had multiple mechanism configurations attached to them. In these cases, Spark still had to ask questions to select among those configurations. For example:

> *Spark:* **Will you be able to provide formulas for combining the user's facts to determine, for example, the megabytes of disk space?**
>
> 1. **yes**
> 2. **no**
> 3. **the above does not make sense.**

The term "megabytes of disk space" is one that the developer entered as a customization of the business process model.

An Example

Spark in SBF v2 presented a graphic process model of predefined activities that other developers in similar endeavors had automated. The activities were indexed by industry type and were grouped into broad categories. Because the industry type affected both the vocabulary to be used and the method for accomplishing tasks, Spark's first few screens determined the industry in which the developer worked. Figure 1 shows one of the industry screens. In this example, the developer is a salesperson who wants to create an application to help them estimate the size of computers to sell to their customers, for use in giving customers a rough idea of the amounts and kinds of computer support that would best suit their needs. (Marques et al., 1992) presents this example in much more detail; here we present only the aspects that distinguish SBF v2 from SBF v1.

After the developer selected the industry subcategories, Spark presented the appropriate top-level activity model and asked the developer to locate the activities that best described their task. After the developer chose "Solutions" in Figure 1, Spark displayed an activity model showing the interrelationships and information flow among a variety of activities related to the discrete manufacturing of computer solutions. The model included activities such as marketing, engineering, manufacturing, selling and servicing. In this example, the developer selected the "Selling" activity (since their task is a sales task), causing Spark to show a more detailed model of the activities involved in selling computer solutions. The sales model included activities such as needs assessment, account management, feasibility and qualifying, and pricing. The developer in this example wanted to build an application to help them give a customer a rough idea of their computing needs, for use in qualifying a sale. So they selected "Feasibility and qualifying".

Figure 2 shows the expansion of the "Feasibility and qualifying" activity. (To help developers who have different views of their work but do essentially the same thing, Spark had several different paths to the same detailed screen.) At this point, the developer selected the "Create a ballpark estimate" activity and indicated to

Spark that this was the activity they wanted to build an application for. Next, Spark asked the developer to customize the terminology in the ballpark-estimate model to use terminology relevant to their task. Spark then asked the developer a few questions in order to choose between two different mechanism configurations associated with the ballpark-estimation activity. Spark phrased these questions in domain terms, not mechanism terms, using the customized terminology that the developer entered. The Spark question near the beginning of this section is one of the questions Spark asked at this point. After selecting the appropriate mechanism configuration, Spark passed control to Burn. Burn invoked the knowledge acquisition tools associated with each mechanism to acquire the detailed knowledge of the task, and finally linked all of the information into an executable application.

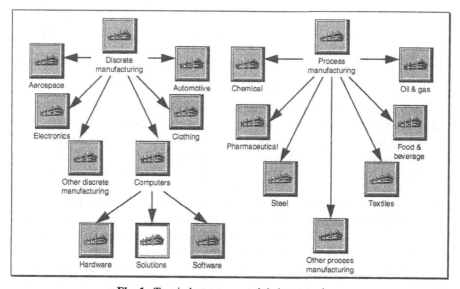

Fig. 1. Two industry types and their categories.

Lessons

How successful was SBF v2 in overcoming SBF v1's shortcomings? (Marques et al., 1991) and (Marques et al., 1992) describe our usability experiments in detail; here we describe some of the insights those experiments provided into SBF v2's strengths and weaknesses.

SBF v2 was intended to solve two problems with SBF v1: (1) it was difficult to index into mechanisms based on task features; and (2) it was difficult to present the indexing criteria to the developer in an understandable way.

SBF v2 made considerable progress on the first problem. Tying mechanism configurations directly to business process models eliminated nearly all of Spark's responsibilities for selecting and configuring mechanism; the domain expert implicitly selected an appropriate configuration by selecting and editing process models.

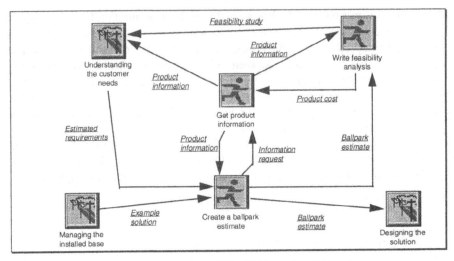

Fig. 2. The expansion of "Feasibility and qualifying."

SBF v2 made some progress on the second problem. Developers found SBF v1's questions hard to understand largely because they were expressed in thinly-veiled computational terms — we were usually unable to design non-computational questions that could discriminate among computational mechanisms. Changing the mechanism index to be in terms of business process models removed the computational flavor of the indexing criteria and created a communication context that developers could better relate to. However, it only partially solved the problem. We observed that different individuals and workplaces describe their processes differently, even if they actually use the same processes. There are a number of efforts now underway to describe generic business processes — for example (Malone et al., 1993) — but these process descriptions stop at a level of detail above that to which it is appropriate to add automated assistance. We found that when these models are taken to sufficient detail to attach mechanism configurations, then in many cases the differences between different workplaces doing the same basic business functions became greater than their similarities. Developers often had a hard time recognizing their processes in Spark's models because of differences in terminology, emphasis, or structuring. Presenting tasks in non-computational terms proved to be only a small step toward presenting understandable process descriptions; developers seemed to recognize and wish to describe their processes using their own idiosyncratic terms and viewpoints.

SBF v2 had two main additional problems:

1. Mechanisms were statically associated with process models and hidden from the user. Developers could not add new models or significantly change existing models, because Spark would be unable to suggest automation for the new or modified models. Therefore, SBF v2 was only useful for tasks that were very similar to tasks appearing in one of the prebuilt models. While this

was not ideal, it was a significant advance over earlier tools such as SALT that were useful for only a single kind of task.

2. The applications we developed using SBF v2 tended to have low user acceptance. Our analysis of the ways people were using our applications showed that this was mainly because the applications did not mesh well with the users' normal work patterns (Dallemagne et al., 1992). SBF v2 focused too narrowly on automating a single task, without explicitly taking into account the way the task fit into a particular workplace. This is related to the problem of developers not recognizing their task processes in SBF v2's models — while the models captured the context of a task, they did it in terms of a rather abstract model that could be very different from the actual workplace context. In retrospect this was surely a problem with SBF v1 as well, but we did not build enough applications with that version to clearly see the problem and its causes.

5. SBF v3 (February 1991 - present (March 1994))[3]

As outlined in the prior section, SBF v2 had three main problems: (1) developers had a hard time locating their task in the process models because the terms used in the models were often unfamiliar or ambiguous to them; (2) it was inflexible because the set of process models was static, as was their association with mechanism configurations; and (3) SBF-built applications had low user acceptance because they did not fit well with their users' accustomed work processes. All of these problems were rooted in SBF v2's use of static, prespecified process models. Our observations of people using SBF v2 indicated that it is difficult for people to understand somewhat generic, abstract models of their task unless they have participated in creating those models. People doing real tasks are buried in the details of the task; details that make their task unique. These details are exactly those by which a person would recognize their task, and yet these are the same details that an abstract model has removed. So, our approach in SBF v3 (the current version) is to allow the developer to enter a process model from scratch in their own terms, and help find similar models in a model library, together with any potentially-reusable mechanisms or mechanism configurations. For SBF v2, we had developed a graphical editor for entering process models. In SBF v3, this editor is part of Spark, and the developer uses it to enter their process model.

In many ways, this is very similar to SBF v2. We still assume that there is a library of process models, mechanisms, and mechanism configurations. The change is in how the developer indexes into those models. Instead of selecting progressively more detailed models from a static hierarchy (which developers found difficult to understand), SBF v3 bases its indexing on the developer's process model description. A tool called the Active Glossary (Klinker, Marques and McDermott, 1993) helps

---

[3]SBF v3 is described more completely in (Klinker et al., 1994; Klinker, Marques and McDermott, 1993; Dallemagne et al., 1992). The latter paper presents a very early and somewhat different view of SBF v3.

the developer find similar process models or model components in the model library; it also helps find potentially-reusable automation. Automation for the developer's task is based on these similar models and suggested mechanisms. If the models are quite similar, the existing model's mechanism configuration may be reusable in its entirety. Otherwise, a programmer may have to help the developer assemble and configure mechanisms. Once the mechanisms have been configured, Burn invokes knowledge acquisition tools to instantiate the mechanisms as in SBF versions 1 and 2. Finally, the developer's new process model and its associated automation can be added to the model library so that it may be reused in the future.

One of the problems with SBF v2 was that because it did not explicitly take into account how a task fit into the overall workplace processes, users resisted using the applications it built. There is evidence that this is a common problem with applications in general (see, for example, (Leonard-Barton, 1987)), and research on situated action gives insights into why this is so (Suchman, 1987; Wenger, 1990). Workers find it difficult to think of one task in isolation. We observed that in creating process models, developers were not just describing a monolithic task that was to be automated by an expert system. Instead, they were describing the cooperative workplace interactions required to perform their task. In effect, the process models specified the cooperative information flow among a set of agents (some human, some software).

Originally we had viewed the process model simply as a way to improve communication with the developer and index into a library of mechanisms and mechanism configurations. The model's role in SBF v3 is much more significant. It serves as an explicit representation not just of a set of agents and activities that are to be replaced by an expert system, but of all of the agents and activities that are involved in working together to perform a task. The key shift in viewpoint here is that a mechanism need not be simply a program component that interacts only with other program components. A mechanism can act as an agent in its own right (perhaps with quite limited capabilities), cooperating with other agents in a workplace, both human and software. Earlier versions of SBF focused on how to automate a given task; SBF v3 focuses on how to build a cooperative multi-agent human-computer system that effectively performs a task.

SBF had to change very substantially to accommodate this new focus, and the work is still incomplete. The primary change is in the way Burn links together mechanisms to form a complete system. Formerly, each mechanism was a piece of OPS5 code. Burn's job (after invoking knowledge acquisition tools to instantiate the mechanisms) was to generate the additional code required to link the individual mechanisms into a single executable program. In SBF v3, this is no longer adequate. Some activities in the system will be performed by software, but others may be performed by people. And we can no longer assume that we have complete control over the mechanisms, since they may include legacy applications that cannot be modified. Our solution is to change Burn to

1. Convert each mechanism into an independent agent program that can send and respond to mechanism-specific messages and translate data between the mechanism's required forms and a canonical inter-mechanism form.

2. Generate instructions for a workflow-control program that will manage the activities and agents (human and software) that are involved in the process model. A workflow controller is a computer system that takes a process model as input and sends pieces of work to the agents involved, in the sequence dictated by the model. It also keeps track of any data involved in the processes (such as documents or data variables) and supplies the agent responsible for an activity with the data required to perform that activity.

The first step yields mechanisms whose behavior is accessible through a standardized interface, regardless of how the mechanism is implemented. Therefore, the workflow controller only needs to know about the standardized interface. The agent interface is implemented as additional code wrapped around a mechanism that translates between the mechanism's native interface and the standardized interface. The standardized interface we use in our current SBF implementation permits messages to be sent and received either as structured electronic mail messages or as remote procedure calls via Digital's ObjectBroker product. Burn currently automatically generates object wrappers only for mechanisms implemented in OPS5. A programmer must supply the wrapper code for other mechanisms.

An Example

The section's example describes a workplace automation that we developed for *NewSoft, Inc.* (all names in this example are fictional). NewSoft has several specialized and geographically-distributed consulting organizations, called *Custom Product Providers (CPPs)*, that sell custom software solutions. In the CPPs, the process of developing a proposal for a customer, negotiating the terms and conditions, and finally obtaining a purchase order typically takes several weeks. Not all bids submitted to a customer result in a delivery contract. The CPPs refer to the collection and compilation of data about the state of the bids, proposals, and negotiations as "Revenue & Recovery Forecasting." The example here describes the support we developed for the Knowledge-Based Systems CPP.

The first step in creating a solution using SBF v3 is to create a model of the processes, agents, and information involved in the workplace for which automated support is to be provided. A business analyst creates this model using some business analysis technique and enters the information gathered into Spark. ((Dallemagne et al., 1992) and (Linster et al., 1994) describe two business analysis techniques we have used that map quite naturally to Spark models.) Figure 3 shows a Spark representation of the original, manual "Revenue Recovery" process as it was performed by the CPP's administrator, Kay Fields. External events triggered the process and led Kay to contact all of the managers responsible for business domains within the CPP (Activity: *Collect revenue recovery forecast data*). Kay compiled this data (*Rollup revenue recovery forecast data*) into a consistent picture and went back to the managers to review the compiled report with them to eliminate misunderstandings and typing errors. Finally, the report was distributed and handed out at management meetings. This process was repeated weekly.

After entering the initial process model in Figure 3, the developer uses the Active Glossary to look for similar processes in Spark's library having automation that could be reused in the current context. First, the developer describes the Spark model of the process in Figure 3 in less application-specific terms by linking the elements of the model to existing terms in the Glossary (Figure 4). The same glossary has been used to describe other models in Spark's library, so its terms can now be used to relate the Revenue&Recovery-Forecast model to other models.

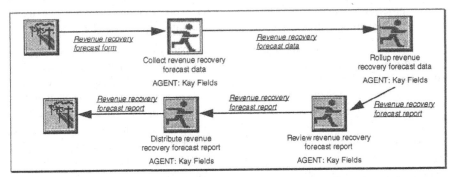

Fig. 3. Revenue Recovery in the Knowledge-Based Solutions CPP.

The Active Glossary suggests the "Collect hours" process as most similar to "Collect revenue recovery forecast data". Figure 5 shows the hours-collection process model. "Collect hours" describes how information about time spent in customer engagements is collected in the CPP. In addition to describing the manual process, "Collect hours" also describes the automation elements that were introduced to make this process more effective. Since the processes of collecting hours and of collecting revenue/recovery data appeared to be similar enough, we used Burn to specialize the hours collector to become a revenue/recovery collector.

However, once we started testing the system with our users, we found that the data collector for revenue and recovery forecasting needed to be able to calculate weighted forecasts of revenue. These capabilities were beyond the scope of the existing form-based data-collection mechanism in Spark's library (the one that was used in the hours-collection task). Thus, a programmer had to be called in to design and implement new mechanisms appropriate for this new situation. This should not be seen as a failure of the SBF framework, but rather as a part of it. It is unrealistic to expect that a library of reusable components will already contain the components required for every task. SBF's response to this situation is to have a programmer implement new mechanisms that are then added to Spark's library so that they can be reused in the future. To extend the library, one only needs to associate the new mechanisms with glossary terms describing their inputs, outputs, functions, and the process models that the mechanisms were originally designed to assist with. The developer uses the Active Glossary to create these associations.

In the current example, we (in the role of mechanism programmers) decided to reengineer the forecasting process and to develop customized mechanisms. Instead of supporting the process shown in Figure 3 with a linear collector simulating Kay Fields' behavior, we used distributed spreadsheets. This solution accommodates the need for calculated fields and local data management, ownership and storage.

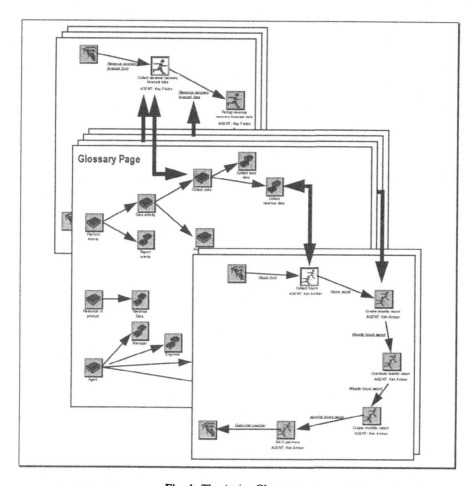

Fig. 4. The Active Glossary.

Each manager uses a dedicated Microsoft Excel spreadsheet to keep track of his/her data. The administrator (Kay Fields) has a rollup spreadsheet that uses Excel's dynamic links to access data on other spreadsheets across the LAN. This allows the individual managers to maintain their own data locally and to use it for other purposes, which was an important requirement. Additionally, spreadsheets allow the necessary computations of calculated fields.

Figure 6 shows the new "Revenue & Recovery Forecast" process. Kay Fields initiates the process (*Start collection and compilation*) and issues a request that every manager (in Figure 6: *Henri Nord, Tom Sud,* and *Ed Ouest*) update his spreadsheet (for example, *Work management revenue recovery forecast data*) and publish that information on a certain date. Kay then compiles the overall report using a rollup spreadsheet that collects the data from the managers' reports.

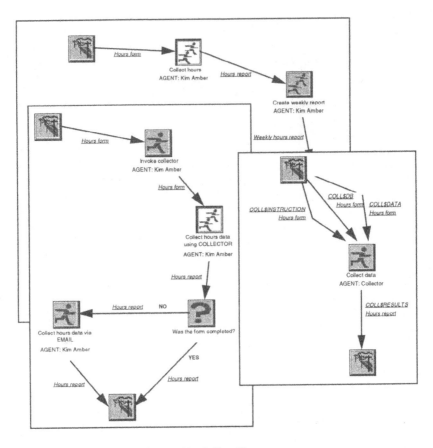

Fig. 5. The Collect Hours process.

The data collection mechanism used at each activity in this process is written in Excel, a standalone Microsoft Windows spreadsheet development platform. This is very different from the mechanisms we had used previously in SBF (all of which were written in OPS5, and were not standalone applications). Therefore, Burn was not able to automatically generate an object wrapper for Excel. We had to design and implement a new kind of wrapper by hand, one that could invoke a Windows application. Just as it is unrealistic to expect that Spark's mechanism library will always contain the required mechanisms, it is unrealistic to expect Burn to be able to generate wrappers for all possible kinds of mechanisms. However, whereas SBF v3 provides a fairly easy way to add new mechanisms to the library, it does not provide a way for developers to add new kinds of mechanism wrappers to Burn. This shortcoming needs to be addressed.

After we wrote the Windows-application wrapper (which simply responds to messages containing an application name and a data file name by invoking the application on the file), Burn generates instructions for our workflow controller that will cause it to invoke the mechanisms in accordance with the flow indicated in the new process model. The workflow controller runs the process shown in Figure 6 weekly. It sends messages to users, informing them about tasks that need to be done. If the user chooses to perform the task, the workflow controller brings up the application (here, Excel) with the appropriate document (here, the right spreadsheet). Thus, besides reminding users of tasks to be done, the workflow controller supplies the task's data and forwards the task's results to the next activities that use them as input.

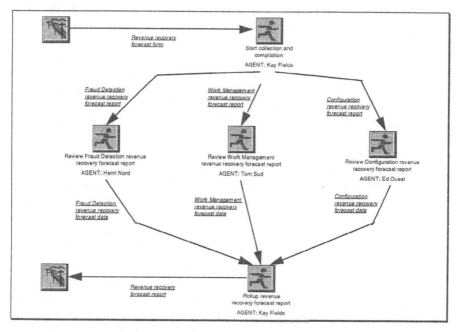

Fig. 6. The new Revenue & Recovery Forecasting process.

Lessons

SBF v3 addresses SBF v2's three main problems as follows:

1. *Problem: Developers were unable to locate their task in SBF v2's process models.* While the terms in the SBF v2 models were often familiar to a developer, the developer was also aware that those terms were often used in different ways by different people, and so was unsure how to interpret them. SBF v3's Active Glossary lets the developer map their preferred terminology and task structuring to existing terms and structures in Spark's model library. To help developers understand the context-specific meaning of model terms, the Active Glossary maintains links from glossary terms to the contexts in which they are used.

2. *Problem: The static process models and static indexing hierarchy made SBF v2 inflexible.* In SBF v2, it was implausible that people other than the SBF creators could extend the library of process models. Each new model had to

be carefully situated in the static process hierarchy that was used to index into the models, and the framework provided no guidelines or assistance for doing this. SBF v3, however, uses a data-driven matching scheme (via the Active Glossary) to index into the model library. Therefore, when a developer enters a new process model, or a programmer attaches a new mechanism or mechanism configuration to a process model, it is feasible for them to add the new process model and associated automation to the library. The tools developers use to integrate new models into the library are the same ones they use to specify their initial process models (Spark's graphical model editor and the Active Glossary).

3. *Problem: Applications built using SBF v2 had low user acceptance because they did not fit well with their users' accustomed work processes.* SBF v2 presented developers with a fixed set of process models from which they selected one most closely matching their situation. These models were somewhat abstract, and certainly did not model the detailed individualities of a specific workplace. Consequently, SBF v2 could provide no explicit support for ensuring that the applications it built would fit into the workplaces they were deployed in. In SBF v3, developers create their own models using a graphical model editor, and so can model all of the detailed aspects that make their situation unique. Also, SBF v3 does not build a single application as earlier SBF versions did. It builds a set of loosely-coupled applications and uses a workflow controller to manage their interactions with each other and with workers in the workplace. Through the workflow controller, SBF v3 provides explicit support for cooperative human-computer activities.

We have used SBF v3 to build workplace-support systems for four tasks: administering university research grants (Dallemagne et al., 1992); assigning offices to personnel in a research lab (Klinker et al., 1994); managing hours collection and reporting for a consulting organization; and managing revenue/recovery data collection, reporting and forecasting for a consulting organization (the example used in this section). The office assignment task is an artificial task created as part of *Sisyphus*, an ongoing research effort to evaluate a wide variety of knowledge acquisition tools. The other three tasks were created for and deployed in real workplaces.

The original revenue/recovery system described in this section has evolved substantially to incorporate new capabilities and use new technologies for its components. We delivered the updated system to 42 *NewSoft* CPPs in the US. While all of the CPPs needed to manage their revenue/recovery data, the details of what they needed to collect and how they needed to collect it varied substantially. For example, some CPPs were located in a single building and their desired reporting processes used the closer interaction that that enabled. Other CPPs were geographically distributed and so used different reporting processes. The CPPs' information requirements also varied. Some CPPs, including the one for which we originally developed our solution, needed the data to be collected and reported in terms of business segments, where each segment was the responsibility of a single manager. Others needed the data to be collected in terms of line-of-business activities where each line of business intersected several managers' areas of responsibility. Such variations in details made this task a particularly good testbed for seeing how well SBF v3 enabled reconfiguring loosely-coupled applications to best match a particular organization's accustomed work processes and information requirements. To configure our solution for a new CPP, we first informally developed models of the individualized reporting structure and data requirements of that CPP, and then used those models to customize the solution components and their interactions. Our first version of the revenue/recovery solution was deployed in a single CPP, and the workflow controller managed task interactions as described in this section's example. Unfortunately, our workflow controller is not yet robust enough to be widely deployed, so the rest of the CPPs had to be trained to manage the interactions of the various solution components themselves. Interestingly, about two-thirds of our training time was spent explaining how to do things that the workflow controller would automate if it was robust enough to be deployed.

Our solution was specified, developed, and implemented across the US operations of *NewSoft* in seven weeks by a two-person team, and immediately provided more than twice as much business data bi-weekly as the CPPs had been able to collect previously. The seven weeks includes development of training materials and delivery of training at four sites. The very short solution-delivery time span can be attributed to SBF's capability of configuring a complex information system from simple building blocks. The ability to easily customize the overall reporting system based on individual CPPs' business processes was critical to both our ability to rapidly deploy the solution and to its user acceptance. We believe that a monolithic reporting application would not only have been harder to build initially, but would not have been accepted by users because it did not accommodate their existing, familiar business practices and individualized information requirements. Our loosely-coupled, configurable solution should also be easier to change as the CPPs change their practices and new technologies become available for its components. (Linster et al., 1994) gives a detailed description of our experiences with this task.

Our experiences to date lead us to believe that SBF v3 is substantially more effective than earlier versions. Evaluating it is also substantially harder. Earlier versions of SBF assumed a single developer implementing a single task that they knew how to perform. Building a solution with SBF v3 requires active participation from all of the people in a workplace that cooperate to perform a task. Moreover, SBF v3 solutions span workplaces, which means that they are multi-seat systems that incorporate sets of communicating applications — SBF v1 and V2 solutions were confined to an individual workstation. This makes experimental setups and studies very expensive. As a result, we have so far only gathered evidence about some aspects of SBF v3. The revenue/recovery task, for example, suggests that building systems out of components that can be reconfigured to match individualized workplace models leads to increased user acceptance. Other aspects of SBF v3 remain untested. For example, we do not yet have data that lets us evaluate the Active Glossary's effectiveness.

6. Discussion and Conclusions

Section 1 discussed the prominent role our explorations of task context would have in SBF's evolution. This section presents what we believe are some of the most important implications of our use of workplace models as the context in which knowledge is acquired and computer-based support is developed.

Prior to 1992, the SBF project's primary goal was to make application development easier. The assumption — a common one in the knowledge acquisition and expert system fields — was that there was a predetermined task that was to be automated, and that the problem was to acquire the detailed knowledge and to operationalize it in a computer system. Our new primary goal is to discover how to build automated support that fits into a workplace, specifically complementing work done by human workers.

The shift in focus did not happen all at once. It began with Spark's failure to configure mechanisms in SBF v1, due primarily to the lack of a shared context in which to communicate with developers. It continued in 1991 when our SBF v2 user studies showed that developers could not make contact with the terminologies and structures imposed by the static, predefined workplace models we used at the time. That shortcoming led us to use workplace process models that would be custom-designed for each task that was to be implemented. The intent was that an automated mechanism would be associated with each activity in the model, and that the communication links between model activities would define how the individual mechanisms should be configured into a computer system automating the complete task. As we began to accumulate models of real workplaces, however, several things became apparent:

1. Some activities are time-consuming or error-prone, and others are unproblematic. Many activities involved using computer applications that either were adequate for their task or imposed by organizational policies; other activities involved coordination with individuals or organizations that were necessarily outside the scope of any automation effort.

2. Our models broke tasks down into fairly modular activities. At the lowest level of the model, nearly all activities were done by a single person who needed only a specified set of resources to perform the task, and who produced a specified set of results.

The first observation implies that fully automating a task may be unnecessary or undesirable. A more desirable approach would be to automate only the problematic activities, and to provide some way of propagating resources from producing activities to consuming activities. The second observation made a person performing an activity look a lot like a mechanism: the inputs, outputs, and expertise required could be specified reasonably well. Together, these observations made it seem desirable and feasible to change SBF so that it produced not single applications, but integrated, loosely-coupled human-computer systems in the context of complete workplaces. Based on our experiences with earlier versions of SBF, we believe that building applications without first explicitly modeling the workplace context in which they will reside is a hit-or-miss proposition: no task exists in isolation, and so useful applications cannot be designed in isolation.

A further benefit of building loosely-coupled systems of people and applications is that solutions can be delivered incrementally. Some assistance can be provided as soon as the business process models have been created: the workflow controller can manage those processes, informing workers of work that needs to be done and keeping track of what work has been done. This gives early insight into the adequacy of the process models, so that they can be refined even before workplace-specific application support is developed. Later, problematic activities can be identified, and custom application support integrated into the workflow for those activities. We call this approach to software development *incremental deployment*. Incremental deployment combines advantages of rapid prototyping and classical software development. Rapid prototyping delivers limited functionality quickly, but it is intended to be throwaway code. Classical software development carefully analyzes requirements and designs and implements a complete solution; the solution may be high-quality, but the customer does not get the solution until the developers believe it is nearly complete. Our incremental deployment approach allows us to deliver some non-throwaway support early on (the workflow controller and process models), and gradually deliver new applications as appropriate. The feature that enables this is that our systems are built of loosely-coupled applications that are coordinated through workflow control. Thus plugging in new applications and reconfiguring the ways they coordinate is relatively easy.

As mentioned at the end of Section 5, SBF has become large enough (and our group small enough!) that we can no longer properly attend to it as a whole, and it has become quite difficult for us to evaluate SBF's effectiveness as a complete framework. For the foreseeable future, we will work not on the framework *per se* but on what we believe are the most significant outcomes of our five-year mission. For instance, we will suspend work on Burn and Firefighter and

1. Continue the Spark work on exploring what constitutes a useful workplace model and what business analysis methods can be used to construct such models.

2. Continue the Active Glossary work on exploring how we can help people navigate through libraries of process models and automation, and understand and reuse what they find there.

3. Continue to explore the implications of solutions built as loosely-coupled systems of people and applications coordinated by a workflow controller. We are beginning an effort to understand how work from a workflow controller can best be presented to workers. Current workflow interfaces are not well-integrated with any non-workflow-controlled work a person might have to do, and we are developing an interface that unifies these two kinds of work.

While these research directions might seem well outside the realm of knowledge acquisition when taken in isolation, we hope this paper has shown why we believe they should be taken very seriously by knowledge acquisition researchers.

Acknowledgments

These people are or were part of the SBF team: Carlos Bhola, Renata Bushko, Michael Calvin, Glee Cameron, Rabih Chacar, Fred Conrad, Geoffroy Dallemagne, Patrice Gautier, Andy Latto, Cindy Maddern, Therese Mersereau, Henrik Nordin, Charlie Reed, Linda Stinson, Yuri Tijerino, David Tung, Jacquie Watkins and Tina Whitney.

References

Barker, V.E., O'Connor, D.E., Bachant, J., and Soloway, E. (1989). Expert systems for configuration at Digital: XCON and beyond. *Communications of the ACM, 32*(3), 298-317.

Birmingham, W.P. and Siewiorek, D. (1989). Automated knowledge acquisition for a computer hardware synthesis system. *Knowledge Acquisition, 1*(4), 321-340.

Chandrasekaran, B. (1986). Generic tasks in knowledge-based reasoning: High-level building blocks for expert system design. *IEEE Expert, 1*, 23-30.

Chandrasekaran, B. and Johnson, T.R. (1993). Generic tasks and task structures: History, critique and new directions. In David, J.M., Krivine, J.P. and Simmons, R. (Eds.), *Second Generation Expert Systems*. Berlin: Springer-Verlag.

Dallemagne, G., Klinker, G., Marques, D., McDermott, J., and Tung, D. (1992). Making application programming more worthwhile. In Schmalhofer, F. and Strube, G. (Eds.), *Knowledge Engineering and Cognition*. Berlin: Springer-Verlag.

Eshelman, L., Ehret, D., McDermott, J., and Tan, M. (1988). MOLE: A tenacious knowledge-acquisition tool. In Boose, J. and Gaines, B. (Eds.), *Knowledge Acquisition Tools for Expert Systems*. San Diego, CA: Academic Press.

Klinker, G. (1988). KNACK: Sample-driven knowledge acquisition for reporting systems. In Marcus, S. (Ed.), *Automating Knowledge Acquisition for Expert Systems*. Boston, MA: Kluwer Academic Publishers.

Klinker, G., Boyd, C., Dong, D., Maiman, J., McDermott, J. and Schnelbach, R. (1989). Building expert systems with KNACK. *Knowledge Acquisition, 1*, 299-320.

Klinker, G., Bhola, C., Dallemagne, G., Marques, D., and McDermott, J. (1991). Usable and reusable programming constructs. *Knowledge Acquisition, 3*, 117-135.

Klinker, G., Linster, M., Marques, D., McDermott, J. and Yost, G. (1994). Exploiting problem descriptions to provide assistance with the Sisyphus task. *International Journal of Human-Computer Systems, 40*(2).

Klinker, G., Marques, D., and McDermott, J. (1993). The Active Glossary: Taking integration seriously. *Knowledge Acquisition, 5*, 173-197.

Leonard-Barton, D. (Fall 1987). The case for integrative innovation: An expert system at Digital. Sloan Management Review.

Linster, M., Klinker, G., McDermott, J. and Yost, G. (1994). Business-process modeling and information-system configuration in the SBF approach. *Proceedings of the First European Conference on Cognitive Science in Industry*. To appear.

Malone, T.W., Crowston, K., Lee, J., and Pentland, B. (1993). *Tools for inventing organizations: Toward a handbook of organizational processes*. (Tech. Rep. CCS WP

#141, Sloan School WP #3562-93). Center for Coordination Science, Sloan School of Management, MIT.

Marcus, S. (1988). Taking backtracking with a grain of SALT. In Boose, J. and Gaines, B. (Eds.), *Knowledge Acquisition Tools for Expert Systems*. San Diego, CA: Academic Press.

Marcus, S., McDermott, J. and Wang, T. (1985). Knowledge acquisition for constructive systems. *Proceedings of the Ninth International Joint Conference on Artificial Intelligence*.

Marques, D., Klinker, G., Dallemagne, G., Gautier, P., McDermott, J., and Tung, D. (1991). More data on usable and reusable programming constructs. *Proceedings of the 6th Banff Knowledge Acquisition for Knowledge-Based Systems Workshop*. Banff, Alberta, Canada.

Marques, D., Dallemagne, G., Klinker, G., McDermott, J., and Tung, D. (1992). Easy programming: Empowering people to build their own applications. *IEEE Expert, 7*(3), 16-29.

McDermott, J. (1988). Preliminary steps toward a taxonomy of problem-solving methods. In Marcus, S. (Ed.), *Automating Knowledge Acquisition for Expert Systems*. Boston, MA: Kluwer Academic Publishers.

Musen, M.A., Fagan, L.M., Combs, D.M. and Shortliffe, E.H. (1988). Use of a domain model to drive an interactive knowledge-editing tool. In Boose, J. and Gaines, B. (Eds.), *Knowledge Acquisition Tools for Expert Systems*. San Diego, CA: Academic Press.

Musen, M.A. and van der Lei, J. (1988). Of brittleness and bottlenecks: Challenges in the construction of expert-system and pattern-recognition models. In Gelsema, E.S. and Kanal, L. (Eds.), *Pattern Recognition and Artificial Intelligence: Towards an Integration*. New York: Elsevier.

Newell, A. (1982). The knowledge level. *Artificial Intelligence, 18*(1), 87-127.

Puerta, A.R., Egar, J.W., Tu, S.W., and Musen, M.A. (1992). A multiple-method knowledge acquisition shell for the automatic generation of knowledge-acquisition tools. *Knowledge Acquisition, 4*, 171-196.

Runkel, J.T. and Birmingham, W.P. (1993). Knowledge acquisition in the small: Building knowledge-acquisition tools from pieces. *Knowledge Acquisition, 5*(2), 221-243.

Steels, L., and McDermott, J. (1994). *The Knowledge Level in Expert Systems: Conversations and Commentary*. San Diego: Academic Press.

Suchman, L. (1987). *Plans and Situated Actions*. Cambridge University Press.

Wenger, E. (1990). *Toward a theory of cultural transparency*. Doctoral dissertation, Department of Information and Computer Science, University of California, Irvine.

Yost, G.R. (1993). Acquiring knowledge in Soar. *IEEE Expert, 8*(3), 26-34.

Applying the REKAP Methodology to Situation Assessment

Nigel Major, James Cupit and Nigel Shadbolt *

Artificial Intelligence Group
Department of Psychology
University of Nottingham
Nottingham NG7 2RD
England
Email: nigel,jc,nrs@psyc.nott.ac.uk

Abstract. This paper outlines a principled methodology, based on KADS, for generating runnable expert system knowledge-bases from the output of high-level knowledge acquisition tools. This methodology is based upon a synthesis of earlier work arising from the UK CONSENSUS, ESPRIT P2576 ACKNOWLEDGE and P5365 VITAL projects. REKAP integrates knowledge elicitation techniques, real-time structured analysis and a model of the the desired run-time architecture within a common framework based upon extensions to the original KADS four-layer model of expertise. The methodology has been realised as a compiler between ProtoKEW, a knowledge acquisition toolkit, structured task-analysis tools and MUSE, a real-time expert system shell. The paper focuses on a particular example of the use of the methodology, in the domain of situation assessment.

1 Introduction

Our central goal when developing the REKAP methodology was to facilitate the development of knowledge-based systems in MUSE, a commercially available AI toolkit. Within the context of our application areas, the KBSs developed are highly situated within their environment and must operate in real-time. The target applications must also model complex patterns of reasoning that are performed by multiple experts working in conjunction. The systems developed can thus be thought of as distributed at a conceptual as well as implementational level. As experts are performing different, though interacting, problem solving tasks to realise an overall goal, one must model the interaction between experts as well as their individual, component expertise. An example of such a domain is that of co-ordinating a military operation. This task involves many sub-tasks such as data gathering, situation assessment and planning.

At present, no methodology encompasses the complete life cycle of developing such systems. Whilst the VITAL project (Shadbolt *et al*, 1993) is concerned with general issues of the complete life cycle of KBS development, its methodology is not tailored to meet the real-time and distributed nature of our target applications. The requirements of the KBS software able to handle these applications meant that we had to reconsider the ways in which a knowledge acquisition workbench ought to be used for KBS construction. The REKAP methodology is the result of this process.

The REKAP methodology envisages three `key stages of progression: the construction of a conceptual requirements model specifying the knowledge possessed by existing expertise; the construction of a technical design model specifying the structure of the system and the processes it will perform; and finally the construction of an implementation model, consisting of executable code. These three stages do not include any explicit treatment of project costs, risks or general project management.

* A previous version of this paper was presented at the 4th KADS User Meeting held at Sankt Augustin, Bonn, 1994. This work was sponsored by the Flight Systems Division of the Defence Research Agency, Farnborough, as part of contract no. FRN1c/348, and was carried out jointly with Cambridge Consultants Limited.

REKAP seeks to facilitate these processes by integrating two existing methodologies for conceptual and functional modelling and by automating the process of implementation. To fully explain how this is achieved, we will outline the existing methodologies and how, when employed in conjunction, they complement each other. A description of how these methodologies are unified within a framework which supports automated code production is then presented, giving details of each stage in the process. We then give a worked example, showing how REKAP was employed to develop a KBS for situation assessment, a single process within an overall application to do with a military co-ordination task. After a pragmatic consideration of the strengths and weaknesses of the methodology, we draw some concluding remarks.

2 Elements of modelling in REKAP

A key phase in developing any intelligent system is the acquisition of knowledge. Within REKAP, the knowledge acquisition process is based around extensions to the KADS acquisition methodology (Wielinga *et al*, 1992) and work arising from the ACKNOWLEDGE (Anjewierden *et al*, 1992) and VITAL (Shadbolt *et al*, 1993) projects.

2.1 The KADS methodology and the GDM approach

Within KADS, the central concern of knowledge acquisition is the construction of a conceptual model of expertise. A KADS conceptual model is a description of the knowledge constructed from a variety of sources, as opposed to the technical design model that provides a description of the desired KBS. Conceptual models are thus formulated at the knowledge level (Newell, 1982), free from any implementational concerns. Knowledge within a KADS model is thought of as residing within 4 layers within the knowledge level. These layers are outlined below.

- The domain layer. Knowledge within the domain layer is specific to the problem domain, such as a knowledge of teleologically relevant concepts and relations between such concepts.
- The inference layer. Contains knowledge of the basic inferences involved in problem solving. Such inferences take "meta-classes" of domain knowledge (also known as roles) as input and output and are independent of the specific domain.
- The task layer. Contains knowledge of the relationship between inferences and tasks. The task layer may be thought of as providing a default control flow for inferences.
- The strategic layer. Contains meta-control knowledge of how problem solving should be sequenced according to different environmental circumstances.

During acquisition, KADS promotes the idea of a library of interpretation models (Breuker *et al*, 1987). These are abstract pre-defined models of the inferences involved in certain types of problem-solving, such as diagnosis or design. An interpretation model should be thought of as the summation of inference and task-layer knowledge; that is, the basic inferences and meta-classes of domain knowledge required for problem solving together with a default flow of control. Interpretation models possess utility as they act as abstracted templates for expertise (O'Hara, 1993). The knowledge engineer can select a template to complete as opposed to constructing a new model for every application. The character of the directive model is used to suggest appropriate knowledge acquisition activity. Knowledge acquisition thus becomes "knowledge based". Identifying the type of knowledge a model contains allows the selection of appropriate acquisition strategies and tools.

Thus the task layer says how and why the inference model should be traversed, and the strategic layer decides which task knowledge about inference control should be used. It is worth noting that more recently the KADS-II project has tended to merge the knowledge in the task and strategic layer. We think this may ultimately be counter-productive. In our applications we have needed to continue with the strategic layer. This is because in our real-time domains there are a number of possible signals which cause priorities to be reassigned and consequently reconfigure the task structure. Typically one agent will interrupt another with such a signal. So we were unable to discard the fourth layer of KADS.

A problem in employing interpretation models to guide knowledge acquisition is that of initial model selection. No one-to-one correspondence between a generic problem solving task (Chandrasekaran, 1988) and a specific interpretation model appears to exist. It is rather the case that the mapping is, in fact, many to many. More than one interpretation model may be applicable to a given generic task (O'Hara and Shadbolt, 1993a) and, after redescription, generic tasks may become equivalent (O'Hara and Shadbolt, 1993b). The knowledge engineer may thus be faced with a wide range of choices when selecting an interpretation model. This means that a crucial stage in the model-based knowledge acquisition process, the stage of choosing the model, is done without the aid of a model at all. That is, knowledge acquisition to choose a model is clearly important, yet we run the risk of not being able to offer help to the initial engineer in how to perform it.

To overcome this dilemma, research within the ACKNOWLEDGE and VITAL projects introduced the notion of a generalised directive model (GDM) (Terpstra et al, 1993; Van Heijst et al, 1992) which is progressively refined. A GDM is a KA model in which the inference steps are decomposed into more and more detailed sub-models, until no further refinement is possible. This decomposition is done according to a grammar, which provides rewrite rules for the inference steps. The knowledge engineer is aided in choosing between rewrites by means of a series of interview questions, eliciting critical aspects of the problem solving mechanism. As acquisition progresses, the GDM provides an increasingly fine-grained account of reasoning within the domain and, correspondingly, an increasing amount of guidance for further elicitation.

2.2 ProtoKEW, an automated acquisition toolkit

Within our specific instantiation of the REKAP methodology, conceptual model construction is performed within ProtoKEW, an automated knowledge acquisition toolkit (Reichgelt and Shadbolt, 1992; Shadbolt, 1992). ProtoKEW provides support for five main acquisition activities; interpretation model construction; hierarchical laddering (Major and Reichgelt, 1990); card sorting (Major, 1992); repertory grid construction and analysis (e.g. Shaw and Gaines, 1987) and rule induction (Major and Shadbolt, 1992).

Conceptual models are represented with partitions that correspond to the meta-classes of domain knowledge specified within the interpretation model being employed. Knowledge within these is represented within first-order logic; this provides clear proof-theoretic semantics and allows redundancy and consistency checking when augmenting or merging partitions. Translation tools are provided to convert between acquisition tool-specific representations and the central logical representations. The process of translating between the central logical representation and the acquisition tools has been found to be an elicitation activity in its own right, eradicating any ambiguities that may exist within a tool-specific representation. The tools provided within ProtoKEW are designed to be applied at each of the four levels of knowledge specified within KADS.

When for example the card sort tool is being used (see section 5), the sorts performed by the expert in this case must be constrained to meet the requirements of the MUSE toolkit. To handle real-time problems the conceptual vocabulary at the domain and inference layers needs to be well-defined. We shall return to this point again in section 4.

2.3 The MUSE AI toolkit

MUSE is an AI toolkit for the development of real-time expert systems. It offers a blackboard architecture on an object-oriented base (MUSE, 1987). A number of knowledge sources place entries on different blackboard partitions. The knowledge sources use separate forward and backward chaining rule sets to perform inferences over blackboard entries. These entries are instances of various object class definitions termed schema.

Within an extension to MUSE (D-MUSE), knowledge sources may be grouped into "agents" which may be implemented on different platforms, affording parallel processing across the system. Our initial work linked ProtoKEW to the undistributed version of MUSE but we have now extended this to combine with the distributed version.

AI toolkits in general suffer from the problem that only experienced knowledge engineers can use them. Although they offer a highly structured environment, it is nonetheless a programming environment. A domain expert could not be expected to sit alongside a knowledge engineer and help construct a KBS. Knowledge engineering workbenches, such as ProtoKEW, have always had the goal of being part of a process which delivers an expert system, but as yet, no really successful KA workbenches have been linked to standard AI toolkits. Consequently the REKAP methodology has made a significant step forward in these real-time application domains.

3 Real-time structured analysis in KADS and CONSENSUS

3.1 Outline

The REKAP methodology also draws upon the CONSENSUS methodology (Bokma *et al*, 1993) for acquiring knowledge concerning the requirements of a KBS. This adopts the view that a system specification consists of two models: a requirements model and an architecture model. The requirements model specifies basic requirements for the final system. The architecture model describes how the system is to be structured to achieve those requirements and details the means of implementation. A CONSENSUS requirements model has some features in common with a KADS conceptual model.

CONSENSUS requirement models are constructed by employing structured analysis and real-time (SA/RT) techniques. These provide guidance in the construction of large conventional software systems (Hatley and Pirbhai, 1988) and are supported by a number of CASE tools. These allow the user to produce hierarchies of data diagrams and process specifications which are supplemented by control flow diagrams, control specifications and timing specifications. Figure 1 shows an example of a data flow diagram produced within the toolkit using TurboCASE; it shows a single processing level within the situation assessment domain.

The processes formulated within a requirements model are, in effect co-ordinated by the interactions between their states; the media of the interactions are events and actions. These relations are described in control specifications using such devices as decision tables and finite state machine tables.

CONSENSUS architecture models make use of the CASSANDRA architecture (Craig, 1989). The basis of the CASSANDRA architecture is a distributed blackboard system. Instead of all knowledge sources having access to a global blackboard, the blackboard is split into distinct panels corresponding to "levels of abstraction" in the problem-solving. Distinct groups of knowledge sources concerned with a particular panel are coupled with that panel to form a separate Level Manager; and communication paths between Level Managers are defined. The full architecture model consists of a set of inter-connected Level Managers (or Knowledge-Based Agents, as they are termed in the CONSENSUS adaptation).

The CONSENSUS approach encourages a modular design, consisting of several independent communicating units. This allows an analysis of control interactions between processes, necessary for assessing the potential for task concurrency, interruptability and rescheduling. Such a design strategy is of obvious benefit when constructing real-time and distributed systems. CONSENSUS also improves the discipline of determining clear and consistent data flow through a model of the knowledge resources.

3.2 The benefits of integrating KADS and CONSENSUS methodologies

We have seen that both KADS and CONSENSUS methodologies are employed to construct an initial conceptual requirements model. When integrated, their interaction overcomes difficulties

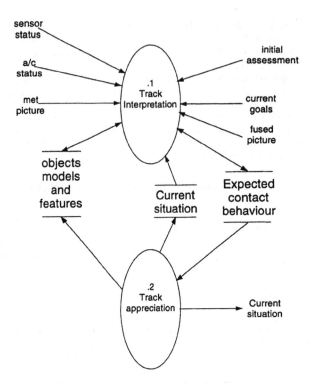

Fig. 1. A situation assessment data flow diagram

associated with their individual usage.

Whilst the CONSENSUS methodology and tools provide for support detailing and storing functional models, little help is provided for acquiring the structure and content of such models. ProtoKEW and the KADS methodology are being used to overcome this limitation. The KADS methodology directs the knowledge engineer to relevant knowledge types whilst ProtoKEW acquisition tools are employed to acquire a detailed domain-specific account.

The employment of generalised directive models and their progressive refinement not only overcomes the problem of interpretation model selection but also provides a solution to the complexity of task decomposition within real-time structured analysis. Within CONSENSUS, no principled methodology for managing the process of task decomposition is suggested. KADS interpretation models possess a structure which is known in advance and GDM refinement proceeds in a rule governed fashion towards such models. The GDM refinement methodology is thus employed to govern the decomposition process. Figure 2 shows a GDM interview tool performing this decompositional elicitation.

The benefits of integration are, we hope, bi-directional. In structured analysis terms the KADS task layer only allows one level of decomposition and there is a control sequence implied in the textual ordering of primitive processes. REKAP extends the KADS task layer to be more concerned with the composition and decomposition of complex tasks (as in CONSENSUS), where the acquisition of control knowledge may be deferred and modelled separately within the strategic layer.

The need for integration is also dominated by real-time concerns. The extended structured

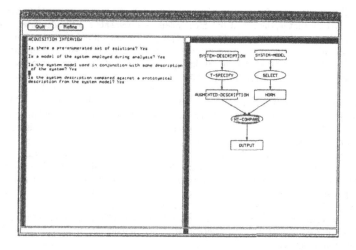

Fig. 2. The GDM interview tool

analysis techniques provide a rich language for modelling real-time aspects of systems. Conceptual modelling in the KADS framework is too easily dominated by the idea of a stand-alone, single-expert, non-real-time, system. This leads to a weak notion of control knowledge that is easily describable within the textual ordering of inferences within the task layer.

Indeed, it is likely that this rather simple task layer has been the reason for which the four layer model is currently being reduced to a three layer one. We suggest that in certain classes of application domain, this may be reasonable, but that in real-time domains the separation between task layer and strategic layer is necessary. In REKAP, the KADS domain layer is extended to include events and actions (involving domain objects). This extension signals the introduction of real-time concerns and reflects the fact that additional ontological elements are required to describe changes in both the control and process of reasoning through time. The REAKT Consortium (Fjellheim *et al*, 1992) has similar concerns. Relations between events and actions are described on the inference layer. The concerns of the KADS strategic layer are extended to include descriptions of the control interactions between tasks, necessary when constructing distributed systems.

3.3   Automatic run-time code generation within REKAP

The REKAP methodology not only attempts to provide a systematic means of constructing conceptual requirement models for real-time distributed systems but also attempts to automatically generate run-time implementation code. Whilst a conceptual model could be implemented in MUSE or any other software platform by hand, as is normally the case, the process of automatically generating MUSE code requires additional expertise. This expertise is required for two reasons.

Firstly, we might say that say that conceptual modelling belongs to a different discipline from functional and technical modelling. The difference of discipline may be reflected in a difference in the language used. Without a common framework relating these languages the process relating a conceptual model to functional and technical models may be fraught with ambiguity. Overcoming this ambiguity involves employing knowledge acquired in developing previous systems, where the process was done by hand, that relates elements of the conceptual requirements model to suitable implementational structures and techniques. If the ambiguity between the languages is too great, no realisation may be possible at all.

Secondly, a statement of system requirements is useful when assessing the risk involved in developing a system; that is, the extent to which system requirements can be adequately met. Whilst KA methodologies seek to avoid the fast prototyping of systems in order to encourage structured design and implementation, many contractors express dissatisfaction with the end product (Boy, 1993). This dissatisfaction does not appear due to the presence of structure within the end product but the misinterpretation of system requirements and goals! Expertise is involved in determining the correct requirements and whether the conceptual model is sufficiently complete to realise them.

Automatically generating run-time implementational code can be seen to be of benefit as it ameliorates many of these problems. If one can establish an appropriate mapping between the language of conceptual requirements and implementational structures then one is guaranteed an efficient and effective realisation. Automated code generation is also of benefit as it allows fast prototyping to occur in a principled fashion. The recursive procedure of conceptual model refinement and code generation helps make explicit the goals and requirements of the system during knowledge acquisition and also aids the assessment of KBS completeness. The risk involved in developing a system is reduced. Finally, the process of automating even part of the detailed and laborious implementation is likely to result in significant man-power savings.

Automatic code generation and the integration KADS and CONSENSUS methodologies within REKAP is achieved by extending the conceptual modelling language to provide a mapping to the implementation language.

4 Extensions needed to link knowledge types within REKAP

REKAP uses KADS and CONSENSUS ideas to implement its knowledge acquisition, so it is these two languages that must be mapped onto MUSE constructs to provide effective run-time code generation. The expressions translated into the MUSE target language have to form the source code for a viable application. The mapping is achieved by means of a common framework relating knowledge layers, knowledge types and languages. This allows all those involved in in KBS development (from domain expert to implementation programmer) to communicate more effectively. The common framework mapping KADS, structured analysis and MUSE constructs to the REKAP framework, together with the heuristic mapping between constructs and acquisition tools is shown in figure 3. The structured analysis/real-time component comes from the CONSENSUS work.

Level	ProtoKEW / CASE tools	REKAP	MUSE construct
domain	laddering, card sort rep-grid, induction	concept, attribute, value relation	schema, instance relation
inference	card sort, rep grid induction, data flows	inference complex state, event, action inference step meta-class	rule, rule-set function notice-board
task	laddering, data-flows	task task composition	knowledge source agent notice-board
strategic	card sort, rep-grid control flow editor	task priority task interactions task interruptions	priorities interrupts agent control

Fig. 3. The REKAP common framework

The common framework extends the conceptual vocabulary employed at a domain and inference level to meet real-time concerns. For every concept defined at the domain layer, a number of additional items are generated at the same level. These relate to the primitive types of states, events and actions that form what is termed an inference complex residing within the domain layer. This extension provides an interface between the domain, inference and strategic layers. These primitive types are shown in figure 4.

State	Event	Action
presence of an <object> absence of an <object>	appearance of an <object> disappearance of an <object> change in an <object>	construction of an <object> removal of an <object> modification of an <object>

Fig. 4. Extensions to the inference layer

The REKAP common framework is implemented within the translator designed to compile the conceptual models into implementation code. Translating the output of the knowledge acquisition tools into the implementation language is viewed as a compilation process. Files produced by the KA tools are compiled into "object modules" and entered in a token dictionary, organised according to the common framework. Code generation from the dictionary produces executables for the MUSE architecture.

5 REKAP in use - Situation Assessment

The problem scenario involves conducting a search of a target area for potentially hostile forces. This search procedure is complicated by the fact that there is not enough time to conduct a full, exhaustive search of the target area and that there is likely to be a high number of neutral or friendly civilian vessels within the area. The search procedure must therefore be directed towards assessing contacts that may pose a high threat as soon as possible. The overall aim of the situation assessment is to measure the threat level presented from the overall picture acquired during the search operation.

Preliminary knowledge elicitation sessions validated the following model (a composite of two KADS-1 library models) as applicable within the domain. Figure 2 has already shown the GDM tool in use and the final interpretation model for the situation assessment task is shown in figure 5.

It should be noted that the above model can be seen as highly suited to the domain of situation assessment as relevant domain-level knowledge is represented in a declarative form within the system model. In many cases, the model may thus be adapted to different problem scenarios by modifying the content of the system model without fundamentally altering the inference rules employed.

An interesting point to note with this model is that it is re-applied in different contexts during the assessment task. It emerged that in each of the major subtasks the same model was being reused.

5.1 Task description

The overall picture employed during situation assessment can be considered to consist of a table of "tracks" containing "fused" information from all available sensors together with additional

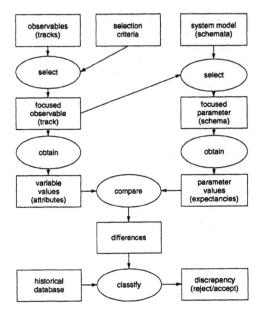

Fig. 5. The GDM for situation assessment

information concerning the position of the approaching task force, conditions within the area and status of vehicle performing the assessment.

Applied at the task level, ProtoKEW's laddering tool is employed to acquire knowledge of task-subtask decompositions. When translated, this is realised as MUSE agents, knowledge sources, rule sets and rule names. Attributes may be attached to the objects represented within the tool specifying the task's interest in a particular class of domain item. This knowledge is utilised within translation so as to partition the main noticeboard, to specify the linkages between rule sets and partitions and to create knowledge source specific notices where required. Figure 6 shows this decomposition.

These sessions showed the following three main subtasks:

- Track analysis. This stage involves classifying the behavioural characteristics of a potential target's track as instances of particular classes of behaviour. Tracks are also classified as instances of a particular class of vessel and as a possible member of a particular group.
- Track behaviour extrapolation. Having assigned an identity to a track, its expected behaviour is generated by computing "waypoints" which specify its expected location and behaviour.
- Track monitoring. Tracks are monitored to see if they deviate from expected behaviours. Assigned threat levels are adjusted in accordance with these deviations.

Whilst elicitation revealed that these subtasks roughly correspond to chronological phases, it was decided that this time sequence should not be rigidly enforced within the model but should emerge from the model in action. This decision arose from the recognition that tasks are dynamically prioritised upon the basis of incoming information and the extent of the current assessment. This arises due to the real-time nature of the application.

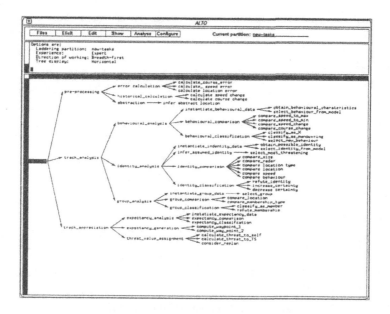

Fig. 6. Laddering at the task level

5.2 Populating the knowledge bases

When translating items from the common framework into MUSE implementation structures, there is an established, though heuristic, mapping. This is not, however, the case when translating the output of knowledge acquisition tools into the common framework. Given a file containing a set of expressions in the KA language, the translator cannot determine what items in the common framework the expressions denote. To do this, the intention of the knowledge engineer needs to be known.

Since REKAP involves re-applying a set of KA tools at each of the four KADS knowledge layers, to know the intended interpretation of the expressions one needs to know which layer they are describing. The translator is therefore provided with the "elicitation level" of the knowledge being translated; it then deduces how to compile and store the file according to the common framework.

In order to realise conceptual requirement models as MUSE implementation structures one must also employ the tools in a principled fashion within a single level. It is in this area that the REKAP methodology suggests novel usages for knowledge acquisition tools.

The hierarchical laddering tool within ProtoKEW, when used at a domain level, is used to acquire definitions of the objects within the domain. Figure 7 shows laddering in the domain layer.

These object definitions are, after translation, realised as MUSE schemas. The translated output of figure 7 is shown in figure 8.

The card sorting tool within ProtoKEW may be used at the domain level in a prototypical fashion to acquire object attribute values. Re-applied at the inference-level, the tool is employed to elicit the structure of individual "inference complexes" defined in terms of domain states, events and actions.

These items may be imported into the card sort tool and assigned a role within a particular inference. This is achieved by sorting the cards into piles representing the states, events and actions

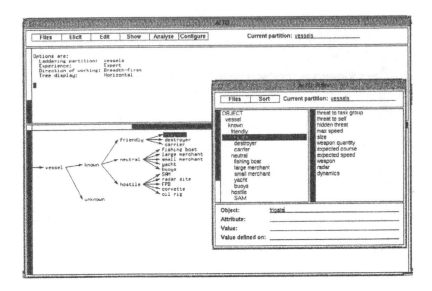

Fig. 7. Laddering for situation assessment

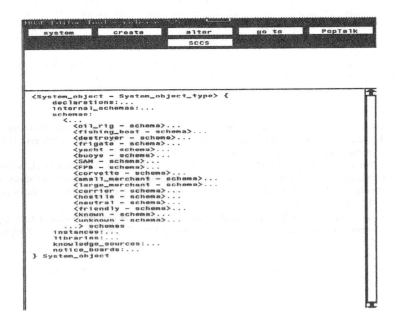

Fig. 8. Automatically produced MUSE schema

of a particular complex. Each sort at the inference level corresponds to a single inference complex. Figure 9 shows a sort in progress.

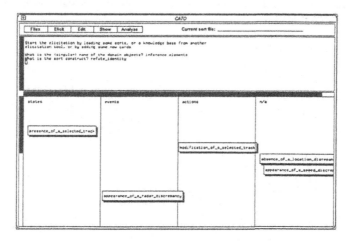

Fig. 9. Card sorting at the inference level

After translation, an inference complex is realised as a MUSE production rule and the translation of the inference complex defined in figure 9 can be seen in figure 10. At present, there is no translational difference between a state and an event within MUSE. The distinction is made within the conceptual modelling process however, as it is suggested in acquisition.

Fig. 10. Automatically produced MUSE rule

It was clear that the domain was viewed in terms of states which were affected by events and thus cause actions to happen. The definition of inference complexes has also led to the development of a new knowledge elicitation tool designed specifically for the REKAP methodology. A matrix tool has been designed to map the dependencies between the attributes of states, events and actions. The tool is shown in figure 11.

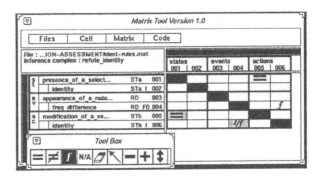

Fig. 11. Matrix tool mapping dependencies between states, events and actions

The mapping is achieved within a knowledge acquisition spreadsheet where functional dependency tokens may be placed to relate different inference element attributes. In figure 11, we can see that there is some functional dependency between the frequency discrepancy of the radar and the modification of an identity. Thus a particular frequency may suggest a particular class of ship for example. After translation, these mappings are realised as the variable bindings within a production rule, and functions will be implemented within Muse.

6 Goals and concerns

Given a complete conceptual model the translator tool is capable of generating a complete MUSE application. This, however, represents the ideal REKAP progression of removing implementational design skill from the KBS process. At present we envisage the process of KBS development more pragmatically for reasons outlined below.

Firstly, conceptual models are likely to undergo a number of revisions for reasons other than completeness and accuracy. Given the heuristic, not definitional, mappings established between the conceptual requirements model and the MUSE architecture, the code produced by the Translator may be inferior to those produced "by hand". Implementational skill may thus be required to optimise the automatically generated structures. The translator tool also processes a number of options that affect the translation process; this blurs the distinction between relying on automatic design and relying on design skills. Design skill, involving the usage of an explicit architectural model of MUSE and a model of the translator tool itself, is thus still required in operation.

Secondly, it is not always the case that conceptual requirement models are equivalent to technical design models. Constraints of time and budget may mean that only a part of the conceptual model is submitted to the translator. A role might be envisaged for the system for which some of the conceptual model is inappropriate. For example, if the system is to act as an advisor on a limited set of problems within the domain. A selection from the conceptual model will then need to made; making such a selection involved what can be seen as technical design expertise. The demands placed on the system may also exceed the knowledge encapsulated within the conceptual requirements models. It may be the case, for example, that the system requires a particular style of user interface or has to automatically process data received from external sensors. Realising such goals relies upon technical design skill outside of the KA modelling process.

Given these pragmatic concerns we do not realistically envisage the automated creation of KBSs, rather the automatic generation of code templates that dramatically reduces the time involved in KBS implementation but does not eradicate the need for implementational design skill *per se*.

7 Conclusions

This paper has attempted to outline the theoretical rationale behind the REKAP methodology whilst providing a picture of the methodology being applied within a specific domain. Whilst the application of this methodology was achieved through the usage of implementation specific tools, we believe the REKAP methodology is generic in nature and amounts to more than the specific toolset.

The REKAP methodology specifies the need to

- perform knowledge-level conceptual modelling within the context of the entire life-cycle of system development.
- employ principled methods to acquire the structure and content of knowledge residing at each of the four KADS levels.
- place a renewed emphasis upon strategic and task-level knowledge when modelling distributed expertise for real-time systems.
- to extend our conceptual vocabulary to meet these concerns.
- to formulate a framework relating conceptual structures to implementational structures to aid development.
- to automate the generation of implementation code where possible.

We would like to stress that the toolset designed to implement the REKAP progression has been applied to developing systems of an appreciable size. This process informally validates the REKAP methodology and shows that the toolset is robust when applied to problems of real-world complexity and real-time concerns.

Knowledge engineers familiar with developing MUSE applications by hand confirmed that they were could considerably reduce the time required to produce useful knowledge bases. Further, the amount of contact time with experts was relatively short due to the efficient nature of the contrived knowledge elicitation techniques used.

The development of the REKAP methodology also raises a number of research issues that have not been addressed. There would appear to be an absence of tools and techniques to automate the process of acquiring the strategic level control knowledge. The idea of employing GDM refinement methodology to manage the process of task decomposition is also dependent upon a suitable grammar for the refinement rules employed. Whilst the current grammar can be considered syntactically adequate for managing the refinement process, it is not yet clear whether the semantics employed relate clearly to identifiable tasks and subtasks within a multiple-level task hierarchy. Little support is also provided for assisting the acquisition and implementation of knowledge not strictly included within a conceptual model of expertise. Nevertheless this type of approach is likely to form the basis of our next generation of support tools for the construction of KBS systems.

References

Anjewierden, A., Wielinga, B. and Shadbolt, N. (1992) Supporting Knowledge Acquisition: The ACKnowledge Project. In Steels, L. and Lepape, B. (Eds.) ESPRIT-92 Knowledge Engineering, CEC, Brussels.

Bokma, A.F., Slade, A.J., Bateman, M.R., Kellaway, M. and Martin, S. (1993) The CONSENSUS Method, Final Report D17. IEATP Project 1365, British Aerospace.

Boy, G. (1993) Knowledge Acquisition in Dynamic Systems: How Can Logicism and Situatedness Go Together? In Aussenac, N., Boy, G., Gaines, B., Linster, M., Ganascia, J-G. and Kodratoff, Y. (Eds.) *Knowledge Acquisition for Knowledge-Based Systems - EKAW 93.* Springer-Verlag.

Breuker, J., Wielinga, B., Van Someren, M., De Hoog, R., Schreiber, G., De Greef, P., Bredeweg, B., Wielemaker, L., Billault, J-P., Davoodi, M. and Hayward, S. (1987) Model Driven Knowledge Acquisition: interpretation models. ESPRIT Project P1098 Deliverable D1. University of Amsterdam and STL Ltd.

Chandrasekaran, B. (1988) Generic tasks as building blocks for knowledge-based systems: the diagnosis and routine design examples. *The Knowledge Engineering Review*, 3(3), 183-210.

Craig, I.J. (1989) The Cassandra Architecture - Distributed Control in a Blackboard System. Ellis Horwood, UK.

Fjellheim, R.A., Pettersen, T.B. and Christoffersen, B. (1992) REAKT Application Methodology Overview, The REAKT Consortium.

Hatley, D.J. and Pirbhai, I.A. (1987) Strategies For Real-Time System Specification. Dorset House Publishing, New York.

Major, N.P. (1991) CATO - An Automated Card Sort Tool. In Linster, M. and Gaines, B. (Eds.) *Proceedings of EKAW 91.* GMD-Studien Nr. 211, September 1992.

Major, N.P. and Reichgelt, H. (1990) ALTO - An Automated Laddering Tool. In Wielinga B et al. (Eds.) Current Trends in Knowledge Acquisition. IOS Press, Amsterdam.

Major, N.P. and Shadbolt, N.R. (1992) CNN - Integrating Knowledge Elicitation with a Machine Learning Technique. In Mizoguchi, R., Motoda, H., Boose, J., Gaines, B. and Quinlan, R. (Eds.) *Proceedings of JKAW-92*, Osaka University.

MUSE Technical Description, Cambridge Consultants, 1987.

Newell, A. (1982) The Knowledge Level. *Artificial Intelligence*, 18, 87-127.

O'Hara, K. (1993) A Representation of KADS-I Interpretation Models Using A Decompositional Approach. In Löckenhoff, C. Fensel, D. and Studer, R. (Eds.) *Proceedings of the 3rd KADS Meeting*, pp 147-169. Siemens AG, Munich.

O'Hara, K. and Shadbolt, N. (1993a) AI Models as a variety of psychological explanation. In the *Proceedings of IJCAI-93*, pp 188-193.

O'Hara, K. and Shadbolt, N. (1993b) Locating Generic Tasks. *Knowledge Acquisition*, 5(4).

Reichgelt, H. and Shadbolt, N. (1992) ProtoKEW: A knowledge-based system for knowledge acquisition. In Sleeman, D. and Bernsen, N. (Eds.) *Research Advances in Cognitive Science, Volume 5.* Artificial Intelligence, Lawrence Erlbaum.

Shadbolt, N. (1992) Facts, fantasies and frameworks: the design of a knowledge acquisition workbench. In Schmalhofer, F., Strube, G. and Wetter, T. (Eds.) Contemporary Knowledge Engineering and Cognition. Springer Verlag, Heidelberg.

Shadbolt, N., Motta, E. and Rouge, A. (1993) Constructing Knowledge-Based Systems. *IEEE Software, November 1993, pp 34-39.*

Shaw, M. and Gaines, B. (1987) An Interactive Knowledge Elicitation Technique using Personal Construct Technology. In Kidd, A. (Ed.) *Knowledge Acquisition for Expert Systems: A Practical Handbook.* New York: Plenum Press.

Terpstra, P., Van Heijst, G., Shadbolt, N. and Wielinga, B. (1993) Knowledge Acquisition Process Support Through Generalised Directive Models. In David, J-M., Krivine, J-P. and Simmons, R. (Eds.) *Second Generation Expert Systems*, pp 428-454. Springer-Verlag.

Van Heijst, G., Terpstra, P., Wielinga, B. and Shadbolt, N. (1992) Using Generalised Directive Models in Knowledge Acquisition. In Wetter, T., Althoff, K-D., Boose, J., Gaines, B., Linster, M. and Schmalhofer, F. (Eds.) *Current Developments in Knowledge Acquisition - EKAW 92*, pp 112-132. Springer-Verlag.

Integration of learning into a knowledge modelling framework

Josep Lluís Arcos   Enric Plaza

Artificial Intelligence Research Institute, IIIA.
Spanish Council for Scientific Research, CSIC.
Camí de Santa Bàrbara, 17300 Blanes, Catalunya, Spain.
{arcos | plaza}@ceab.es

Abstract. In this paper we will report our current research on the NOOS language, an attempt to provide a uniform representation framework for inference and learning components supporting flexible and multiple combination of these components. Rather than a specific combination of learning methods, we are interested in an architecture adaptable to different domains where multiple learning strategies (combinations of learning methods) can be programmed. Our approach derives from the knowledge modelling frameworks developed for the design and construction of KBSs based on the task/method decomposition principle and the analysis of knowledge requirements for methods. Our thesis is that learning methods are methods with introspection capabilities that can be also analyzed in the same task/method decomposition. In order to infer new decisions from the results and behavior of other inference processes, those results and behavior have to be represented and stored in the memory for the learning method to be able to work with them.

1 Introduction

One of the key issues in the current development of knowledge-based systems (KBS) is the degree to which different components can be combined in a seamless way. Specifically, the integration of learning components, both for knowledge acquisition and for learning from experience, is viewed as an essential topic for future KBS building and design.

We have developed NOOS, a representation language for integrating inference and learning components in an uniform representation. Our approach derives from the knowledge-level analysis of expert systems and the knowledge modelling frameworks developed for the design and construction of KBS. These knowledge modelling frameworks like KADS [20] or components of expertise [15] are based on the task/method decomposition principle and the analysis of knowledge requirements for methods. Our thesis is that learning methods are methods with introspection capabilities that can be also analyzed in the same task/method decomposition. Thus, learning methods can be uniformly integrated into our framework and represented as methods in the NOOS language.

Although this will be explained in the paper, the main idea is that any time some knowledge is required by a problem solving method, and that knowledge is not *directly available* there is an opportunity for learning. We call those opportunities *impasses*, following Soar terminology [8], and the integration of learning methods is realized by methods that solve these impasses. A innovation required for integrating learning components into knowledge modelling frameworks is the definition of two levels: domain level and inference level. Domain level is where domain knowledge is modelled usually in knowledge modelling frameworks and is used to solve domain problems. Inference level is a level where domain knowledge shortcomings (impasses) are detected and learning components to overcome them can be defined. The inference level is thus a meta-level that deals with problems arising from the base-level problem-solving process. As we will see in section 3, different approaches to overcome an impasse are possible to be programmed into our system and integrated seamlessly. The second innovation to integrate learning into knowledge modelling frameworks is the notion of memory: memory of successes and failures of methods into solving tasks is necessary, as shown in section 2. This allows us to integrate case-based (analogical) reasoning and inductive learning methods in our framework, since the results of past problem solving cases are stored in the system's memory.

Next section describes the elements of our knowledge modelling framework and their implementation in the NOOS language. Section 3 shows an example where multiple learning components are applied to achieve the knowledge requirements of a (simplified) diagnosis task. Related work is compared in section 4 and, finally, section 5 discusses our approach and our future work.

2 The knowledge modelling framework

The elements that build up our framework are tasks, methods, theories and case models. This framework is close to the components of expertise [15], however our implementation of it, the NOOS language, departed from the original definition, so we do not claim we are using that componential framework. Our framework augments the ideas of the components of expertise with the notion of episodic memory: the memorization of problem-solving episodes allows learning methods to be integrated since they require to access the past experience to improve the system performance.

Let us shortly describe the elements of our knowledge modelling framework. Tasks are goals to be achieved by the system in a problem setting. Problem solving methods are specifications of ways to achieve tasks. Usually, tasks are decomposed into subtasks by means of a problem-solving method, e.g. the generate-and-test method applied to a task decomposes it into the generate and test subtasks. This recursive decomposition of task into subtasks by means of a method is called the task/method decomposition. This recursive task/method decomposition finishes when a task uses an elementary method (like union and intersection of sets) provided by NOOS language. Case models and theories embody the domain knowledge modelled for a given problem. A case model contains all factual knowledge of a topic and consists of the set of tasks that make sense for it. For instance, the case model of John are those tasks we have solved about John (like his fever being 39) and those tasks to be solved (like finding his diagnosis). Thus solving a problem consists on completing the case model of the problem (e. g. finding the diagnosis of John) by means of a method (e.g. generate-and-test). As the case model is characterized by its tasks, a theory is defined by the methods declared usable to solve the tasks of a case model. In particular, for every task in the case model the theory holds an object called metafunction containing (a) a set of methods declared usable for that task and (b) a set of preferences to choose among them (see Fig. 1). For instance, for task diagnosis of John we may declare usable the generate-and-test and the heuristic-classification methods plus a preference to try the first before trying the second.

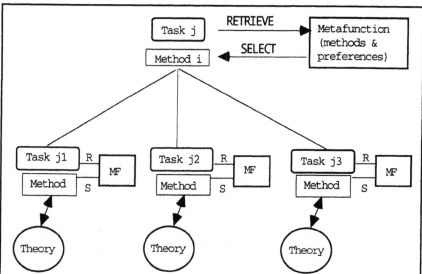

Figure 1. Schema of task-decomposition generated by a method M$_i$. Method M$_i$. has been retrieved from the set of applicable methods declared in the metafunction (MF). M$_i$. has subtasks for which methods can be retrieved and they will use knowledge from specific theories to solve the subtasks. These methods can recursively decompose the subtask into lower-level subtasks. A different method, say M$_j$, would generate different subtasks and use other kinds of knowledge from different theories.

How can we integrate case-based reasoning (CBR) and learning into this framework? The first step involves the memorization of successful methods mentioned above and the fact that all solved case models are also memorized as cases to be used by case-based or learning methods. The second step involves a metalevel above the *domain level* of methods and theories that will hold case-based and learning methods. This metalevel is called *inference level* and consists of inference methods and inference theories. An inference method is method that (1) examines selected parts of the domain level past problem solving behavior (these selected parts are to be considered "examples" or "cases"), and (2) construct some new piece of knowledge needed by the domain level to solve a problem. An example of inference method is the case-based method shown in figure 2. A CBR method for solving a task is decomposed on tasks retrieve, select, and reflect. An inference method (e.g. the CBR-method) is invoked when for a given task a domain method is missing (called No-Method impasse) and the result is retrieving and selecting a method from a case in memory able to solve the task at hand. This method is then instantiated (reflected down into the domain level) into the current task and executed there (like in derivational replay [3]). In fact, several methods can be retrieved from different cases in memory and tried out to see whether one of solve the current task (the select task selects among them using preferences). Different CBR methods can be described uniformly in this retrieve/select/reflect decomposition by using different methods in the retrieve and select subtasks. Inference theories hold several inference methods plus some preferences to choose among them (they are like metafunctions one level up). Examples of this are shown in section 3.

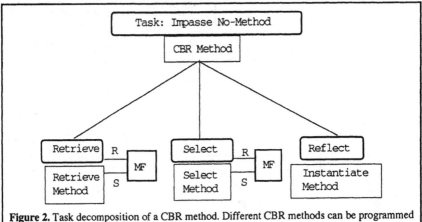

Figure 2. Task decomposition of a CBR method. Different CBR methods can be programmed by declaring different methods for the Rerieve/Select/Reflect task decomposition.

Thus, domain methods are grouped into domain theories and infer new factual knowledge by extending the case models. Similarly, one level up, inference methods are grouped into inference theories and infer domain knowledge by extending theories. We can design also other kinds of inference methods like inheritance methods that retrieve domain methods from supertype theories (e.g. John may inherit domain knowledge from theory person and theory mammal).

The last step to introduce learning regards the notion of *impasse*: whenever a the problem solving process requires some knowledge that is absent an impasse arises. An impasse then can be solved by some appropriate learning or knowledge acquisition method able to acquire the needed knowledge. This impasse-driven nature is the basis of learning integration, as we will see in the next section.

2.1 The framework implementation: The NOOS language

The knowledge modelling framework is supported by the implementation of the object-oriented frame-based language NOOS. In NOOS every concept of our framework is represented as an object: tasks, theories, methods, inference theories, and inference methods are NOOS objects. The dynamics of NOOS is impasse-driven: every time a lack of knowledge to do something is detected, an opportunity for learning arises and an impasse is generated. As in SOAR [8], there are two kind of impasses: either the next step is unknown (e.g. there is no known method to solve a task) or there are several ways to proceed (e.g. there are several possible methods that may be applicable to a task). Every time an impasse is generated the NOOS language generates a reflective task whose goal is to solve that impasse. Table 1 shows the typology of impasses and the reflective tasks generated. NOOS has a way (method) for dealing with every impasse that consists on subtasks Retrieve a Metaobject, Evaluate it, and Reflect down the result. For instance, if there is no method to solve a task, a No-Method impasse is generated, the task's metafunction is retrieved and its evaluation consists in take the methods declared there as applicable are try them out until one succeeds in solving the task. If no methods are known for a task the No-Metafunction impasse is generated and the task's inference method is evaluated to find domain knowledge (in the form of metafunctions) in other theories. For instance, a case-based method can be used to retrieve a metafunction from a precedent case and reuse it in the present task.

Table 1. Typology of impasses, tasks engaged from impasses and the constitutive methods for dealing with them. [key: MF = metafunction, IM = inference method, IT = inference theory.

IMPASSE	TASK	METHOD = Retrieve/Eval/Reflect (metaobject)
No-Referent	Infer(Referent)	Retrieve(Method)/Eval(Method)/Reflect(Referent)
No-Method	Infer(Method)	Retrieve(mf)/Eval(mf)/Reflect(Method)
No-Metafunction	Infer(mf)	Retrieve(im)/Eval(im)/Reflect(mf)
No-Inf-Method	Infer(I-Method)	Retrieve(it)/Eval(it)/Reflect(i-method)
No-Inf-Theory	Infer(I-Theory)	FAIL

The results of solving an impasse in a task are stored into that task for future usage: the successful method and the failed methods that were tried on a task are stored there so that future decisions may be based on this precedent (they are cases that record method utility). This is called the self-model of NOOS and can be used by NOOS learning methods to reason about its own performance and method usage. In a uniform way, inference methods that succeed an fail are also recorded at the inference level task so the system may learn from their usage.

An example of inference method is inheritance. Inheritance is not built-in but reified in NOOS objects, namely inference methods, and can be explicitly programmed in NOOS. Inheritance methods follows a task decomposition Retrieve/Select/ Reflect like the case-based methods, the difference being that the Retrieve method is a retrieve-along-link method [9]. In this way, retrieving along the type link NOOS achieves usual inheritance, but more specialized methods can be programmed. For instance, the family-name of a person can be computed by inheriting along the father relation. This is shown in the following figure, where this special inference method is ascribed only to the task family-name of the theory of person that inherits aling the father link starting from the case-model of the person we are interested in.

```
(define (theory (theory reify of person    ))
   (define (single-inheritance-method family-name)
      (link 'father)               ; the name of a relation-link
      (origin (>> referent)))      ; the case-model of the person considered
```

where the syntax can be summarized:

```
(define (type new-object)
   (task-name   value-specification)
   (define (method task-name   )
        <method-body> ))
```

where *type* may be a case model, a theory, an inference theory, a method, or an inference method. A value-specification is either an object or a *path* to an object of the form

```
(>> task-name-1 task-name-2 ... task-name-n of object).
```
If the object is the same we are defining it will be ommited, as in

```
(>> task-name-1 task-name-2 ... task-name-n).
```

Inference methods are characterized by the `Retrieve/Select/Reflect` task decomposition. The `Retrieve` tasks are achieved by several built-in retrieval methods that search the episodic memory of NOOS (the set of solved case models). In the example of section 3 several retrieval methods are shown and they allow to implement not only case-based methods but also induction methods. The `Reflect` task has also a built-in method; this method reinstantiates the retrieved knowledge into the case model of the current problem. If we compare it to usual object-oriented languages, this task is the binding of a method to a new object realized by inheritance; in NOOS inheritance is just a kind of inference method just like case-based methods.

Finally we mention two aspects of NOOS implementation: automatic backtracking and consistency maintenance. As we have seen, it is possible to declare in a metafunction several methods applicable to a specific task. NOOS assures that a method will be tried out to see if it solves the task (selected according to the declared preferences), backtracking to other declared methods if it fails. When all methods for a task fail, and this task is a subtask generated by a method of a super ordinate task, that method fails and a higher-level backtracking to new possible methods is performed. Thus, backtracking in NOOS assures that all methods declared in all tasks will be explored until a solution to the overall task is achieved, and that methods will be selected according to the preferences expressed in metafunctions. Moreover, NOOS has a consistency maintenance mechanism that supports incremental knowledge modelling. Every time some NOOS object (theory, method, task, etc.) is changed the consistency maintenance mechanism invalidates all objects that depend on that change.

3 Integration of Multiple Learning Methods

In this section we want to show, by means of a short example, how different strategies of learning can be developed and integrated into the NOOS language. We will illustrate these ideas with a simple example in the domain of diagnosis of car complaints. We will have examples that are cars with complaints and an explanation of the malfunction causing them. The task will be of diagnosing the malfunction that produces a complaint on a new car.

3.1 Learning Analogical Explanations

A first strategy for solving new problems is learning analogical explanations from past similar cases. With this strategy, a general method for solving car diagnosis will be used: a case-based method called `basic-analogy-method`. The knowledge required by these method is a set of cases, where each case contains a simple causal-explanation between its complaint and the diagnosis known for that case. The `basic-analogy-method` will use these causal-explanations for solving a new case. A causal explanation is simply a conditional method that when `cause` is true returns its `effect` as solution. We will use two examples of car diagnosis as illustration.

```
(define Peters-car
   (starts false)
   (complaint   does-not-start)
   (battery-voltage low-voltage)
   (gas-gauge-reading     full)
   (define (causal-explanation diagnosis)
      (cause (>> low-voltage?))
      (effect low-battery-malfunction))
   (define (identity low-voltage?)
      (item1 low-voltage)
      (item2  (>> battery-voltage))))

(define Carols-car
   (starts false)
   (complaint   does-not-start)
   (battery-voltage high-voltage)
   (gas-gauge-reading     empty)
   (define (causal-explanation diagnosis)
      (cause (>> empty-level?))
      (effect no-gas-malfunction))
   (define (identity empty-level?)
      (item1 empty)
      (item2  (>> gas-gauge-reading))))
```

Since causal explanations of the cases are in form of domain methods for task diagnosis, an analogical method can retrieve that domain method and apply it to the new problem to check whether that causal explanation also holds in that new problem. Since causal explanation is simply a NOOS method, we may define analogy as a kind of inference method that retrieves a method from a past case that has solved the task (here diagnosis). This is achieved, as shown below, by the retrieval method retrieve-by-task that recalls cases with successful methods for the current task and stores them into the contents slot.. The retrieved method is bounded to the new problem automatically (by the inference method semantics).

```
(define (im::basic basic-analogy-method)
    (define (retrieve-by-task contents )))
```

Car-diagnosis-analogy-method will apply the explanations to the new problem, ordering them by malfunction frequency in the retrieved cases, until one explanation succeeds. The successful explanation will be stored in the case model of the new problem as the method used to solve the task diagnosis.

```
(define (basic-analogy-method car-diagnosis-analogy-method     )
    (preferences (define (more-frequent-preference))))
```

For instance, diagnosing Karls-car can be achieved including car-diagnosis-analogy-method in the inference theory of Karls-car:

```
(define  karls-car
  (starts false)
  (complaint does-not-start)
  (battery-voltage low-voltage))

(define (inference-theory (meta reify of karls-car    ))
  (contents car-diagnosis-analogy-method))
```

Car-diagnosis-analogy-method retrieves from memory the cases Carols-car and

Peters-car. Then decides to select first Carols-car (since its malfunction no-gas-malfunction is more frequent). However the method retrieved from Carols-car fails since that causal explanation does not hold in Karls-car and thus Peters-car will then be selected. The domain method now retrieved will be successfully applied to Karls-car (since the causal explanation holds) yielding the no-battery-malfunction result for diagnosis task.

Car-diagnosis-analogy-method is a method that retrieves all the past cases that have solved the current task and tries to apply their task methods to the current problem. In this sense, Car-diagnosis-analogy-method is a general domain-independent method, because knowledge about car diagnosis is not necessary, the only knowledge used is the fact that the same task has been solved in those cases. If we have some knowledge of the domain we should be able add it and focus the analogical reasoning. This is what we can achieve in NOOS: adding this knowledge we can define a more specialized, domain specific, analogy method. For instance, in the car diagnosis domain, if we know that the complaint *determines* the set of possible malfunctions[1], we can build a new more specific analogy method based on determinations that profits from this knowledge:

```
(define (basic-analogy-method analogy-by-strict-determination)
   (determined-by   )
   (define (equal-solution-retrieve contents)
     (task-name   (>> determined-by))
   (preferences (define (more-frequent-preference)))))
```

where equal-solution-retrieve is a retrieval method that recalls past examples from the episodic memory with the same solution value for a given task (task-name) that the solution value of this task in the current problem. In our case, the determination is having the same complaint, so analogy-by-complaint-method is simply:

```
(define (analogy-by-strict-determination analogy-by-complaint)
   (determined-by   'complaint))
```

This method can then be used as inference method for the diagnosis task:

```
(define (theory (theory reify of karls-car))
   (define (analogy-by-complaint diagnosis )))
```

In our example, both Carols-car and Peters-car would be retrieved, since their complaint is equal to Karls-car, namely does-not-start, but no other cases with different complaints are retrieved. However, if our domain knowledge is weaker, for instance if we know that cases with the same complaint are more likely to give us a correct explanation but the other cases may be useful nonetheless, we may use a non-strict form of determination:

---

[1] The classical example of an analogy justified by a determination [12] is the following: the usual language spoken by a person is determined by the person's nationality. We know a case, Janos, that is Hungarian and speaks Magyar. The task language of another person can be solved by an analogy-by-determination method. If this method finds that a person is Hungarian then it concludes that he speaks Magyar because of the determination *and* the Janos precedent.

```
(define (basic-analogy-method analogy-by-determination)
  (determined-by   )
  (preferences (define (equal-solution-preference)
                  (task-name  (>> determined-by)))
```

where instead of only retrieving cases with the same complaints we retrieve all solved cases as before, and just *prefer* the causal explanations of the cases with the same complaint, i.e. we try them first but other, less preferred, cases can be tried out eventually.

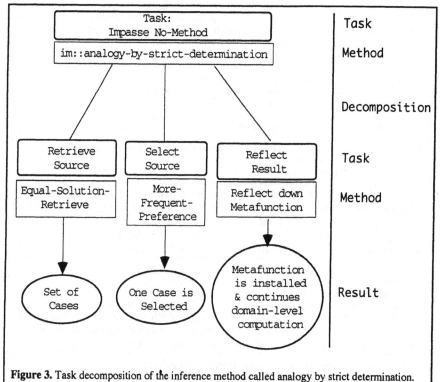

Figure 3. Task decomposition of the inference method called analogy by strict determination.

3.2 Analogical Generate-and-Test

Another learning strategy is to use a specific domain method for solving the diagnosis task and use an analogy method to infer the knowledge required for this domain method. A widely used method is *generate and test*. Generate and test methods, in general, require (1) the knowledge to generate hypotheses about the solution of a problem, and (2) knowledge to test whether a hypothesis is correct. We would like to learn the knowledge required for (1) and (2) from examples (cases). In this section we will acquire that knowledge in a case-based, analogical way, and in the next section we will show the use of an inductive method to acquire it.

In analogical generate and test we will learn type (1) and (2) knowledge from examples in a case-based way. Generation of hypotheses will be performed by looking at the malfunctions diagnosed in past examples. Testing of a hypothesis will be performed also by looking for causal explanations of that hypothesis in past examples. We will define g&t-by-analogy method consisting of two tasks (see Fig. 4). The first task is to generate a hypothetical solution for diagnosis, this will use the generate-hypothesis-by-analogy method (see below).

The second task is to check that hypothesis with the causal explanations of the malfunction-cases (those cases whose diagnosis is the malfunction we hold as current hypothesis). This second task is achieved in two parts: First, the method retrieve-explanations-by-analogy retrieves all cases in memory with the same solution value for diagnosis task as our current hypothesis. Second, the method of the recovered example (here a causal explanation) is then reflected down to the current case and applied (tested to see if it explains the hypothetical solution). If it fails the system automatically backtracks to other retrieved cases looking for new explanations. If all of them fail, the system backtracks to a new hypothesis.

```
(define (basic-analogy-method G&T-BY-ANALOGY  )
    (define (generate-hypothesis-by-analogy hypothesis))
    (define (retrieve-explanations-by-analogy malfunction-cases   )
        (hypothesis (>> hypothesis))
    (contents   (>> malfunction-cases)))

(define (solution-value-retrieve retrieve-explanations-by-analogy)
    (task-name  'diagnosis)
    (value (>> hypothesis))))
```

The hypothesis task is achieved by the generate-hypothesis-by-analogy method. This method prefers one hypothesis from a set of plausible hypotheses using a frequency criteria: more frequent hypotheses will be preferred to the others. If the most preferred hypothesis fails the testing phase, then the select-cliche will backtrack and select a less preferred (less frequent) hypothesis.

```
(define (select-cliche GENERATE-HYPOTHESIS-BY-ANALOGY)
    (define (generate-hypotheses-by-analogy contents ))
    (preferences (define (more-frequent-preference))))
```

Finally, generate-hypotheses-by-analogy method generates as the set of plausible hypotheses those malfunctions that are solutions to the task diagnosis in the past cases with the same complaint as the current problem.

```
(define (access-method GENERATE-HYPOTHESES-BY-ANALOGY)
    (task-name   'diagnosis)
    (domain (>> complaint-cases))
    (define (equal-solution-retrieve complaint-cases)
        (task-name   'complaint)))
```

The access-method is a method that obtains the solution value of a specific task (task-name) from all elements of a set (domain). In our example, access-method obtains malfunctions (the solution value for the task diagnosis) from the complaint-cases. The equal-solution-retrieve method retrieves those complaint-cases (precedent cases that have the same complaint as the current problem).

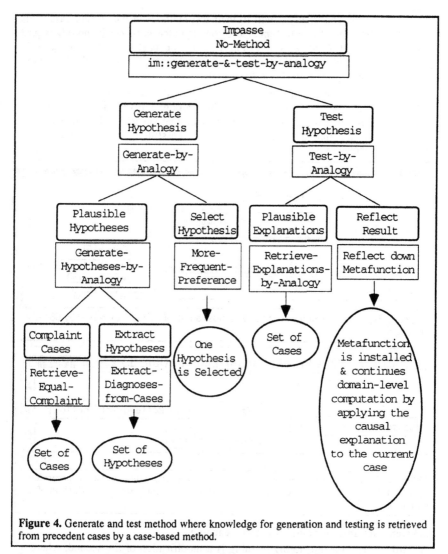

Figure 4. Generate and test method where knowledge for generation and testing is retrieved from precedent cases by a case-based method.

In order to use g&t-by-analogy as an inference method for diagnosis task of Johns-car we can define the following:

```
(define Johns-car
  (starts false)
  (complaint does-not-start)
  (battery-voltage low-voltage))

(define (G&T-by-analogy (diagnosis theory reify of Johns-car)))
```

In the Johns-car example G&T-by-analogy will obtain the set of plausible hypotheses (low-battery-malfunction and no-gas-malfunction). Then, for each hypothesis it will retrieve the past cases with this hypothesis as solution to diagnosis task, and finally it will trytheir test-methods in the current case. This method assures that if one test-method of one hypothesis succeeds, no others past cases will be retrieved. In our example, only the past cases with diagnostic hypothesis low-battery-malfunction will be retrieved if this hypothesis is more frequent than no-gas-malfunction hypothesis.

The browsing of objects in Figures 5 and 6 show that all elements of inference involved in the task are explicit and accessible through introspection. For instance, we can observe that the generated hypothesis that succeeded is low-battery-malfunction, and that the domain method successfully reused is the causal explanation shown in Fig. 6.

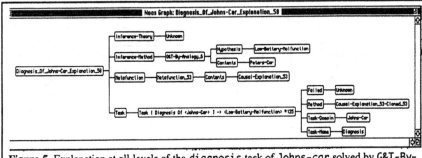

Figure 5. Explanation at all levels of the diagnosis task of Johns-car solved by G&T-By-Analogy.

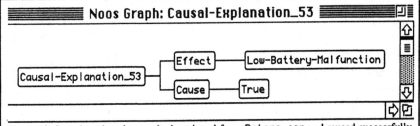

Figure 6. Causal explanation method retrieved from Peters-car and reused successfully upon Johns-car. In order to see why the Cause is true we should examine the Method of the Cause task

3.3 Generate-and-Test and Inductive Learning

A third strategy for integrating learning is a modification of the second, where a learning method is used to infer the knowledge required by a problem solving method. A problem solving method like generate and test requires, as we saw, (1) knowledge to generate plausible hypotheses from complaints, and (2) knowledge to propose tests that check that a given hypothesis holds. We can use a learning method to construct this knowledge once for all, e.g. using an inductive learning method.

Let us start analyzing the sort of knowledge needed by generate and test. Knowledge to generate hypotheses is a mapping from complaints to a set of hypothetical malfunctions:

$$plausible\text{-}hypotheses(complaint)=\{malfunction\} \qquad (1)$$

while knowledge to propose tests is mapping from malfunctions to its possible

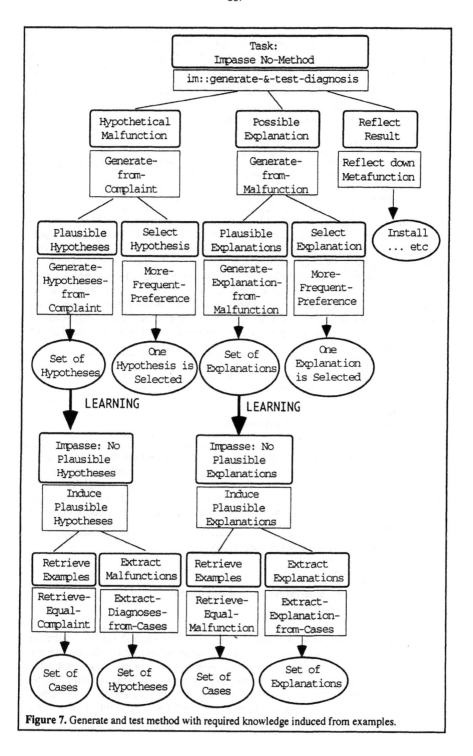

Figure 7. Generate and test method with required knowledge induced from examples.

explanations:

$$\text{possible-explanations(malfunction)=\{explanation\}} \qquad (2)$$

Therefore, the generate and test method using knowledge (1) and (2) will have a method for hypotheses generation using plausible-hypotheses and a method for proposing tests using possible-explanations, as in the following.

```
(define (theory G&T-DIAGNOSIS-THEORY)
   (define(im::G&T-Diagnosis diagnosis )))

(define (im::basic im::G&T-DIAGNOSIS)
   (define (select-cliche hypothetical-malfunction)
     (contents (>> plausible-hypotheses complaint referent task-domain task))
     (preferences (define (more-frequent-preference))))
   (contents (>> possible-explanations hypothetical-malfunction))
   (preferences (define (more-frequent-preference)))))
```

From this requirements, the task of learning is that of providing to G&T-Diagnosis the missing knowledge. We have to define learning methods that learn from past examples (1) the plausible malfunctions given a complaint and, (2) the possible causal explanations for every malfunction (see Fig. 7). In the following expression we only need to define an inductive method for plausible-hypotheses of complaints and another inductive method for possible-explanations of malfunctions. We define this for all complaints and all malfunctions by specifying that there is an inductive method to compute the plausible-hypotheses of complaint and another inductive method to compute the possible-explanations of malfunction.

```
(define COMPLAINT
   (define (hypotheses-induction plausible-hypotheses)
     (for-complaint    (>>))))       ; the current conplaint

(define MALFUNCTION
   (define (tests-induction possible-explanations)
     (for-malfunction (>>))))     ; the current malfunction
```

The inductive methods retrieve all the known examples and use them for inducing the required mappings. For inducing hypothesis generation, the method Hypotheses-Induction retrieves examples with the same complaint as the complaint of our current case (complaint-cases). Then it stores (as plausible hypotheses) the malfunctions that have been found in complaint-cases to be the solutions of their diagnosis tasks.

```
(define (access-method HYPOTHESES-INDUCTION)
   (access-name 'diagnosis)
   (domain (>> complaint-cases))
   (for-complaint   )
   (define (solution-value-retrieve complaint-cases)
     (task-name   'complaint)
     (value (>> for-complaint)))))
```

For inducing possible explanations of a malfunction, the method Tests-Induction retrieves all past examples in memory with the same malfunction as the one we are dealing with and then stores all the *different* methods used in diagnosis tasks that lead to that malfunction (i.e. all alternative explanations of that malfunction). In the following, to define the inductive methods we will need only the retrieval method solution-value-retrieve that recalls examples with the same solution value for a given task (task-name):

```
(define (solution-value-retrieve TESTS-INDUCTION)
    (for-malfunction )
    (task-name    'diagnosis)
    (value (>> for-malfunction)))
```

In order to use the G&T-Diagnosis☐method for the diagnosis task in new examples, like Janets-car, we declare it to be the inference method corresponding to the diagnosis task, while all other tasks about Janets-car can be solved by the basic analogy as before:

```
(define Janets-car
    (complaint    no-lights)
    (starts true)
    (battery-level    high-voltage))

(define (im::G&T-Diagnosis (diagnosis theory reify of Janets-car)))
(define (it::basic-analogy (meta  reify of Janets-car)))
```

3.4 Issues in integrating learning

We have used this simplified example to show different ways of integrating learning methods into a knowledge modelling framework. First, it has to be stressed that the learning methods themselves are analyzed and represented uniformly in the knowledge modelling framework (see Fig. 3, 4, and 7). Secondly, the learning methods can be seamlessly implemented and integrated using the NOOS representation language. Some methods like case-based analogical methods integrate learning and problem solving implicitly: case-based problem solving will improve as more cases are learned and stored in memory. When using a specific domain method, like the generate and test method, we can explicitly analyze the knowledge required for this method to work. Then we can design the learning methods that will fulfil these requirements exploiting the solved cases stored in the system's memory to provide the needed knowledge. We have seen that this can be done in two ways: (1) dynamically, when an analogical method generates hypotheses and tests from cases in memory to solve a specific new problem, or (2) statically, inducing from the set of all known cases the knowledge needed to generate hypotheses and tests. In a given application we can experiment with and evaluate the different options, and choose the most appropriate among them. Our goal in this paper has been to argue of the feasibility of this experimenting and choosing in general, rather than on experimenting and choosing in a specific domain (but see [2] for a discussion on the integration of case-based and inductive methods applied to a knowledge based system for the purification of proteins developed in NOOS).

It is clear that case-based methods can be integrated in our framework because of the notion of memory: the specific problem solving episodes are stored in memory and can be recalled using the retrieval methods. The implementation of this memory notion requires NOOS to be a reflective language: part of its problem-solving behavior has to be represented in the language itself, mainly the successful and failed methods for every task should be stored and moreover, NOOS has to be capable of recalling and reusing them for new problems. We can summarize the rôle of learning methods in our framework as follows: a learning method is like a problem solving method with introspective capabilities. As we have seen, a learning method (1) examines selected parts of the domain level past problem solving behavior (these selected parts are then considered "examples" or "cases" for learning), and (2) construct some new piece of knowledge needed by the domain level to solve a problem. For instance, as we have seen, a case-based analogical method retrieves and selects from a memory of precedent cases a method and reuses this method to solve a new task; on the other hand, an inductive method selects a set of past problem solving episodes as "examples" and generates the knowledge needed by a domain method (e.g. generate and test).

The second important issue in integrating learning methods is the notion of *impasse*. Whenever there is a lack of knowledge directly usable by a method, an impasse arises. For instance, generate and test method requires some knowledge to generate plausible hypotheses from problem descriptions: if this knowledge is lacking in the needed form, an impasse arises. In fact, the NOOS language then generates a metalevel task, the task of solving that impasse [10]. Learning methods are then integrated as methods to solve the tasks generated by impasses. In this way, using the knowledge modelling framework, we can analyze the knowledge requirements of a domain method and, if this knowledge is not directly available, include some learning methods that may derive the knowledge the domain method requires. Thus, the goal of a learning method is to generate knowledge in a form directly usable by a domain method.

4 Related work

Related work on knowledge-level modelling of AI systems includes the components of expertise framework [15], the KADS methodology [20], and the PROTEGE-II system [11]. Our approach is closer to the components of expertise [15] in that the ontology of models, tasks and methods proposed by it is related to NOOS's ontology of theories, methods and tasks. However, components of expertise lacks the two layers of NOOS: domain theories and methods and inference theories and methods, having only the domain layer. This is reasonable, since the components of expertise is intended as *a prescriptive framework* for expert systems where all options searched for in NOOS are dictated by the expert's knowledge through the process of knowledge engineering. Although this may involve lack of flexibility in general, it has evident advantages regarding efficiency in most expert system applications.

The KADS methodology is much more different but in [1] a reflective framework has been used to describe the KADS four-layer architecture. Their reflective framework, called "knowledge-level reflection" uses the KADS model to specify the system self-model of structure and process, very much like our inference-level model of theories, tasks, and methods allows NOOS to have a self-model. However, neither components of expertise nor KADS have been used to perform learning tasks, and in fact NOOS is the first attempt to apply knowledge level analysis to learning tasks and to develop a computational architecture that embodies that approach.

The PROTEGE-II system [11] is also related to our work. There is a difference in implementation of the support system: mechanisms, the basic building blocks in PROTEGE-II, are implemented in Lisp and thus new mechanisms require new programs in Lisp. The philosophy of NOOS is different: methods can be decomposed in a finer grain into elementary subtasks that use a set of elementary methods (e.g. conditionals, set intersection, etc.) provided by NOOS. There is a difference between our goals and the goals of components of expertise, KADS,

PROTEGE-II, etc., but they are complementary. The knowledge modelling community is interested in acquiring a wide library of components, while we are interested in integrating learning methods with those libraries of components. Related work on the use of knowledge level models to describe learning methods are [18], describing EBL methods, and [13], describing decision tree induction methods and implementing them in KREST (the workbench of the components of expertise framework).

Our work on NOOS is related to cognitive architectures like Soar [8], and specially with the frame-based THEO representation language [6]. However, THEO does not provide a knowledge modelling framework and does not incorporate analogical reasoning. Related work on reflection is [6], [4], and [14], and specially related viewpoints of inference-level reflection are projects like REFLECT [16]and KADS-II [21]. The NOOS language is to be considered a descendant of languages RLL-1 [5] and KRS [17].

5 Conclusion and future work

In this paper, we have presented a knowledge modelling framework for KBS modelling and its implementation into the NOOS language. Our main goal has been how learning could be integrated into this framework, for instance in the classical setting of a generate and test method for diagnosis. Integration of learning methods is possible due to the introduction in the modelling framework of two new notions: memory and a new level (so called inference level) that work upon domain knowledge. Memory is required so as to have old decisions and failures to guide future decision-making. The uniform nature of NOOS assures that at every decision point it can be guided if need be in a case-based manner by past experience. Inference methods are methods that deal with failures of domain methods on domain tasks and explicitly search for new knowledge and new methods that may overcome the impasses produced by failures. The nature of the relationship between learning and this two notions is further discussed in [10].

As a framework for KBS including learning, we are currently developing a case-based knowledge-intensive expert system for purification of proteins from animal tissues. Currently, we are exploring the usage of case-based and inductive learning, as shown in this paper, for different subtasks involved in the proteins purification process[2]. In [2] we show how an induction method can generate general plans for protein purification and be integrated with a case-based method that also generates protein purification plans. Also a classification-based system for sponge identification is being developed for a family of sponge species using a form of top-down classification called recognize-prototype-and-refine. This is a test for comparing our approach to a classical rule-based expert system on the same domain developed at our Institute and may help understand us the differences and the utility of our knowledge modelling framework for KBS design and the utility of learning methods for different subtasks. Research on planning as a general form of problem solving is currently under way. We focus on case-based planning, non-linear search-based planning, and interleaving case-based/search-based planning. Comparing it to other systems, like derivational analogy [19] NOOS supports its two main capabilities: non-linear planning and interleaving planning and learning. Comparison of planning domains in KBS knowledge modelling frameworks will be pursued, specifically using the workbench project Sisyphus on floor planning, used as a standard for comparison by the KBS knowledge acquisition community.

Acknowledgements

The research reported on this paper has been developed at the IIIA inside the ANALOG Project funded by CICYT grant 122/93 and a CSIC fellowship.

References

1. Akkermans, H., van Harmelen, F., Schreiber, G., Wielinga, B.: A formalisation of knowledge-level model for knowledge acquisition. Int Journal of Intelligent Systems , **8** (1993) 169-208.

2. Armengol, E., Plaza, E.: Integrating induction in a case-based reasoner. Proc. 2nd European Workshop on Case-based Reasoning, (to appear).

3. Carbonell, J. G.: Derivational analogy and its role in problem solving. Proc. AAAI-83 (1983) 45-48.

4. Giunchilia, F., and Traverso, P.: Plan formation and execution in an architecture of declarative metatheories . Proc of META-90: 2nd Workshop of Metaprogramming in Logic Programming.. MIT Press (1990).

5. Greiner, R., Lenat, D.: RLL-1: A Representation Language Language, HPP-80-9 Comp. Science Dept., Stanford University (1980). Expanded version of the same paper in Proc. First AAAI Conference.

6. Kiczales G., Des Rivières J., Bobrow D. G.: The Art of the Metaobject Protocol, The MIT Press: Cambridge (1991).

7. Mitchell, T.M., Allen, J., Chalasani, P., Cheng, J., Etzioni, O. Ringuette, M., Schlimmer, J. C.: Theo: a fra-mework for self-improving systems. In K Van Lenhn (Ed.) Architectures for Intelligence. Laurence Erlbaum, (1991).

8. Newell, A.: Unified Theories of Cognition. Cambridge MA: Harvard University Press (1990).

9. Plaza, E.: Reflection for analogy: Inference-level reflection in an architecture for analogical reasoning. Proc. IMSA'92 Workshop on Reflection and Metalevel Architectures, Tokyo, November (1992) 166-171.

10. Plaza, E., Arcos J. L.: Reflection and Analogy in Memory-based Learning, Proc. Multistrategy Learning Workshop (1993) 42-49.

11. Puerta, A., Egar, J., Tu, S., Musen, M. A.: A multiple-method knowledge acquisition shell for the automatic generation of knowledge acquisition tools. In Procs. of the AAAI Knowledge Acquisition Workshop (1991).

12. Russell, S.: The Use of Knowledge in Analogy and Induction. Morgan Kaufmann (1990).

13. Slodzian, A.: Configuring decision tree learning algorithms with KresT, Knowledge level models of machine learning Workshop preprints. Catania, Italy (1994).

14. Smith, B. C.: Reflection and semantics in a procedural language, In Brachman, R. J., and Levesque, H. J. (Eds.) Readings in Knowledge Representation. Morgan Kauffman, California, (1985) 31-40.

15. Steels, L.: The Components of Expertise, AI Magazine, **11** (1990) 30-49.

16. van Harmelen, F., Balder, J. R.: $(ML)^2$: A formal language for KADS models of expertise. Knowledge Acquisition, **4** (1992).

17. van Marcke, K.: KRS: An object-oriented representation language, Revue d'Intelligence Artificielle, **1** (1987) 43-68.

18. Van de Velde, W.: Towards Knowledge Level Models of Learning Systems, Knowledge level models of machine learning Workshop preprints. Catania, Italy, April (1994).

19. Veloso, M.: Learning by analogical reasoning in general problem solving. Ph.D. thesis, Carnegie Mellon University, Pittsburgh, PA (1992).

20. Wielinga, B., Schreiber, A., Breuker, J.: KADS: A modelling approach to knowledge engineering. Knowledge Acquisition **4** (1992).

21. Wielinga, B., Van de Velde, W., Schreiber, G., Akkermans, H.: Towards a unification of knowledge modelling approaches. In J. M. David, J. P. Krivine, and R. Simmons (eds.) Second Generation Expert Systems, Springer Verlag: Berlin, (1993) 299-335.

Knowledge level model of a configurable Learning System

Céline Rouveirol[1], Patrick Albert[2]

[1] Laboratoire de Recherche en Informatique, URA 410 du CNRS, Équipe Inférence et Apprentissage, Université Paris Sud, bât 490 F-91405 Orsay, France. Email: celine@lri.fr.
[2] ILOG, 2, avenue Galliéni, BP 85, 94253 Gentilly Cedex, France. Email: albert@ilog.fr

Abstract. This paper presents the knowledge level model of a configurable learning system that follows a Generate and Test strategy. The knowledge level model makes explicit the elementary functionalities of the learning tool (referred to as *learning operations*), the control of the learning primitives (referred to as *bias*), and the different implementations of the learning primitives. The proposed model is based upon the inference structure formalism of KADS and will be used as an interface when interacting with the user. This explicit representation of learning operations and related bias will make the experimentation of different configurations of the proposed learning tool easier for a knowledge engineer developing a Knowledge Based application.

1 Introduction

The growing complexity of the knowledge based applications makes it necessary to use some kind of (semi-)automated techniques during the knowledge acquisition phase. Furthermore, knowledge engineering may require the use of various Machine Learning systems (ML) of different types, accepting different concept description languages, using different learning techniques, or managing different natures and complexities of the example set.

The knowledge engineer may thus need to quickly experiment different variants of the learning algorithms. In this context, she/he is faced to the following loop:

1. select a ML tool suited to her/his task,
2. set the parameters that control the behavior of the tool,
3. run the tool, analyze the results, stop or goto step 2 (or 1.).

In many cases, running the previous loop may be a difficult and tedious process. Selecting the appropriate tool may take time, and finding the setting of parameters that fits well to the problems characteristics may also be long and difficult.

Systems that provide a family of learning algorithms in a unified environment, rather than a single one, seem to provide an effective solution to shorten the complexity and duration of the above loop.

A first solution has been proposed within the Machine Learning Toolbox Esprit Project [9]. This project has led to the implementation of a ToolBox gathering a set of Machine Learning within a unifying global framework. The framework defines a common language for inputs and outputs, and a "consultant", implemented as an expert system, that helps the user in selecting the algorithms suited to her/his specific needs.

Though this system has proved to be a valuable step, the level of integration of the different algorithms is weak . Its building blocks are very large (full fledged learning systems), and the support of the user is quite low, but the variety of learning systems is quite large, ranging from numerical techniques to knowledge intensive symbolic learning systems. This systems implements one view of the approach, that may be well suited to experimented users, knowing the properties of the different tools and willing to experiment a variety of techniques.

We are working on a slightly different approach that proposes more support to the user, while restricting the range of available learning techniques. Our work aims at implementing a machine learning tool providing access to a family of learning algorithms (Generate and Test) and allowing the user to configure graphically different variations of algorithms and control parameters.

The support of the interaction with the user relies upon a knowledge level model of the Generate and Test systems. The knowledge level model provides both the set of modeling formalisms useful for representing the family of algorithms and the set of graphical notations that may be used to interact with the user.

The range of accessible learning tools is smaller than the MLT but we expect to provide a better support and smaller grained adaptation capability because we address only one class of machine learning system. We also expect to provide a simpler and more efficient interaction with the user, because of the use of a knowledge level model of the systems. Choosing a specific learning model, will be made by selecting high-level learning operations, and setting appropriate control parameters.

Within this overall objective, the paper presents the first results of this work : the definition of a set of knowledge level formalisms used to the represent the possible configurations, and the knowledge level model of Generate and Test learning methods. We emphasize specifically the role of *bias*, that represent in the ML terminology the parameters used to control the behavior of the different methods.

The rest of the paper is organized as follows. We first present our approach, and the research results in machine learning and in knowledge acquisition that we use. We follow by an in depth description of a generic knowledge level model of a class of learning systems, insisting on the nature and role of certains parameters (called bias) for describing and controlling their behavior.

2   A configurable ML tool

Our objective is to provide a configurable ML tool supporting a class of ML algorithms and that a user could configure graphically.

The interest of such a tool is described below:

- adaptable: depending upon her/his goals, upon the nature and complexity of the examples, and upon the type of domain theory available, the user will be able to assemble a set of learning procedures suited to the problem's characteristics and to instantiate the definition of the control parameters. This will greatly simplify the experimentation of different learning algorithms.
- simple and homogeneous: the configuration of a given learning system will be made by assembling a set of predefined learning operations, and by instantiating bias related to the chosen components. The unified graphical notation representing the possible decompositions of each steps of the learning algorithm will make it possible to specify graphically a given configuration in an intuitive way.

Such an objective is ambitious, but will make possible a wider use of ML techniques. By selecting a family of learning systems (G-&-T) and embedding them into a unified framework based upon an explicit knowledge level representation of the learning models underlying the algorithms, we will provide an easier access and understanding of the machine learning techniques.

As the objects that we represent are learning tasks, we need to represent their decompositions and the way they may be assembled. We use a knowledge level representation of the learning models based upon an extension [2] of the CommonKADS notations [39].

Mainly two formalisms are used:

A *Task decomposition tree* graphically represents the possible decompositions of the learning procedures into subtasks, while a specific notation makes explicit the possible alternatives while decomposing a task.

The *Inference Structure* notation provides a simple mean for expressing the data-flow within the decomposition of a task. It also provides a notation for specifying the configuration parameters that have to be set during the configuration process.

2.1 What is to be represented?

The objects to be represented are the learning operations, their parameters and their connections.

These entities are the data used by the configurer. The output of the configurer represents the resulting learning system: a set of connected learning operations with values for the associated control parameters.

We need to make explicit the set of possible configurations that represent all the possible decompositions of the top-level goal. The entities are the following:

learning operations: these are the operations to be realized by the learning algorithms. These operations may be primitives, corresponding to a piece of code, or abstracts, decomposed into less abstract operations.

possible decompositions of a learning operation: these are the different methods for implementing an abstract operation.

data-flow between learning operations: this represents the connection between operations within a decomposition.

control parameters: these parameters, control the behavior of the learning operations.

constraints controlling the decompositions: these entities, represent the conditions that attached to a given decomposition.

Except the latter, all these entities and their relations are represented graphically.

The controlling of a decomposition may be done at different levels of complexity: either by selecting one specific assembly of tasks, or by setting the value of parameters that control the behavior of a given assembly. The elicitation of such control parameters, named *bias*, is an important issue in the machine learning community (see section 3.1 for a precise description).

This work is tightly connected to different trends in machine learning and in knowledge acquisition. We describe below how it is related to research about the influence of bias and about adaptive machine learning on the one hand, and to research about knowledge level modeling on the other hand.

3 Inputs from Machine Learning and Knowledge Acquisition

3.1 Inputs from Machine Learning

The work presented here stems from the research in the ML community about elicitation of bias. The first paper in ML that referred to *bias* was [22]. In this paper, bias represents any kind of information (except examples of the target concept) that allows to prefer a target concept definition over a set of candidate ones. Bias is thus some additional information, not always explicitly stated within the learning system, expressing what a "good" target definition should be. This definition of bias is very general and since then, many authors in ML developed their own view of bias (see among others, [47], [16], and more recently [12], [15]).

We adopt here a more restricted and operational definition of bias. Given a set of learning algorithms that share the same overall structure (behavior), bias is control knowledge that allows to define a learning strategy within that structure. They represent a set of parameters that, besides the learning algorithms, define some of the characteristics of the learning tool and task. We have focussed here on three categories of bias. The so-called *Language bias*, that defines the target concept language, has been recognized for long as a major factor that influences learning. Another well identified bias, that will be referred in the rest of the paper as *Validation bias* states the properties on the target concept to be learned. Another kind of bias, which was less studied up to now, the *Search bias*, defines the dynamics of the learning system, such as for example, the type of search used to cross the search space [35].

More generally, biases represent the hypotheses underlying machine learning tools. Though their importance is well acknowledged, they are often hard-wired in the coding of the tools and thus are most often static. The user of the tool usually does not have access to their definition.

Recent works have focussed on elicitation of the biases used in different ML systems and on the definition of generic algorithms allowing to describe in a unified framework ML algorithms that have close behaviours. The generic algorithm presented here elaborates on GENCOL [11] that was the first generic algorithm for empirical concept learning proposed in ILP. The *ontology of bias* we propose is a synthesis (oriented by the purpose of building a ML system configurer) of previous works on declarative bias. Another line of research In ML that will benefit to our work studies the effects of bias (mostly language bias up to now) on learning results and performances. More positive results in this field will allow us to define a set of "safe" configuration rules.

3.2 Inputs from Knowledge Acquisition

The knowledge acquisition field has gained increased interest since the last ten years. It aims at proposing formalisms to represent knowledge based applications and methods to help the knowledge acquisition. This field is tightly connected to machine learning because of the similarity of the objectives, even if the methods differ.

Research in knowledge acquisition has produced a set of so-called Knowledge Acquisition Methods that provide both a set of graphical knowledge representation formalisms, and a set of directives used by the knowledge engineer to map the knowledge used by a human to solve a problem into a computer usable representation.

We can distinguish two main streams of results : the *problem specific methods* and the *problem independent methods*. The problem specific methods — as for example [18] [19] — are dedicated to a class of problems (diagnosis , configuration, etc.). They usually propose a knowledge representation dedicated to the problem, and a set of tools that operationalize the knowledge. Though very useful these methods lack of generality to satisfy our needs.

The "generic" approach, examplified by KADS [39], [50] Commet [42] or VITAL [30] aims at proposing general formalisms suited to describe knowledge level representations of problem solving methods representing how a problem, or a class of problems, may be represented and solved. These methodologies all come with the notion of library or of reusable components[6], [43]. We analyze below the adequacy of the two main generic knowledge acquisition methods to our needs.

Commet The Component of Expertise method (Commet) is mainly oriented toward the reuse of components. This method provides graphical formalisms for representing *task decomposition* and *control flow*. A task may be decomposed into subtask and the data-flow is graphically represented, allowing to specify the connection between subtasks and the domain entities onto which the tasks are applied.

Predefined problem solving methods may be used to precisely specify the type of decomposition used. Specific editors are used to define the data types of the parameters and a propagation engine ensures the coherency of the overall design.

An important characteristic of Commet is the dividing of the domain specific knowledge into two types of knowledge represented into two different models: the *domain model* that holds all of the domain dependent knowledge that does not change from one session to another, and the *case model* that holds all task specific knowledge what will be built and used during the use of the application.

This distinction is important regarding reusability, because the domain model may be more reusable than the case-model which is much more closely related to the problem solved by the specific application.

KREST [43], the tool associated to the methodology, puts the emphasis on reusability. It provides a service of library management used to store and retrieve predefined or user defined components. An important aspect of KREST is its ability to produce an executable program from the graphic specification.

CommonKADS CommonKADS shares some of the objectives of Commet but puts the emphasis at a different level. The main concern of CommonKADS is the reusability of knowledge level representations of classes of problems.

CommonKADS distinguishes three levels of modeling. The *domain level* that represents the domain dependent knowledge, the *inference level* that represents the problem dependent knowledge at an abstract level, using a extended data-flow formalism, and the *task level*, that represent the precise algorithmic of the task to be performed.

We are especially interested by the inference-level formalisms, the "Inference Structures", that allow to specify both the problem solving components and their mapping onto the domain knowledge.

4 Selected formalism

Both approaches, KADS and KREST, provide elements, but none yet provides the solution, though recent advances in KREST may provide support for reasoning about tasks [48].

Among others, the two main functionalities that we need are not provided in the same framework:

- Commet provides a solution for representing the resulting configured system, and for generating the operational program from its specification ;
- KADS provides the formalisms to represent the set of components and their possible decompositions.

For the first step of our work, we have thus selected — and extended — the CommonKADS notations , for representing the knowledge level model of G-&-T systems. The models has been designed using KADS-TOOL [2] a case tool that supports the CommonKADS method, extended for supporting the decomposition of inference steps.

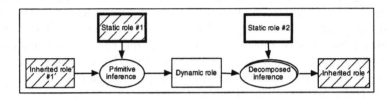

Fig. 1. Examples of graphical notations.

The inference structure shown in figure 1 contains the set of notations we rely upon. These notations, based upon CommonKADS, allow to represent both the possible configurations, and the resulting system. An *inference structure* shows the organization of a set of operations, the *inference steps*, represented by ellipsis. A simple ellipsis represents a primitive inference step, directly associated to an algorithm. A greyed ellipsis represents an intermediate inference step, that may be decomposed. Such an inference step may be decomposed through many inference structures. A simple box represents a *dynamic role*. It specifies the data flow between two or more inference steps. A bold box represents a *static role*, that is, a role that is used but not modified during the reasoning process.

The mapping between our entities and the CommonKADS concepts is as follows:

learning operations: these operations are represented by *inference steps*.

possible decompositions of a learning operation: these are the different *inference structures* that represent the decompositions of a composite inference step.

data-flow between learning operations: this is represented by the *dynamic roles* that link together the inference steps within an inference structure.

bias: the bias are represented by the *static roles* associated to the inference steps.

constraints controlling the decomposition: these entities, are not represented graphically.

5 Modeling Generate and Test Learning systems

5.1 Knowledge Level Model of Learning Systems

Let us first situate ourselves w.r.t. the idea of Knowledge Level Modeling of learning systems, especially with the work of Dietterich [13]. Our goal here is not to model a ML system integrated in a KA loop[3] or Knowledge Base system that improves its performance thanks to its learning component, as in [13]. Our focus here is modeling of ML systems *in the aim of building a configurable learning tool.* We are thus aiming at modeling learning systems in isolation of any performance system that may use their results. Moreover, recent research in ML (specially about bias in learning) seem to attenuate the conjecture of [13] about bias, or at least give a more respectable status to bias within learning systems, which may allow us to believe that it is possible to build conceptual models of ML system.

More practically, our claim is that complex learning systems, just like any complex apparatus or complex computer program should provide to their users some manual about the way they perform and consequently, some way to customize them to meet their actual needs. The adequacy of the Knowledge Level for this purpose, as well as for comparison of learning methods and elicitation of implicit (control) knowledge has already been discussed in [49].

This goal is very ambitious, we therefore address here a limited class of learning systems, and we do not provide for a complete guide of biases for such learning systems. The proposed model is fine-grained, sometimes as fine grained as one may object it does not belong to a Knowledge Level description anymore. We partly alleviate this objection by stating that for most biases that are considered to belong to the symbol level, a knowledge level characterization can be provided to/by the user as a first approximation, instantiations of such biases being delayed to the operationalisation phase, if any.

5.2 Generate-and-Test ML systems

The ML systems that are the scope of this paper are empirical learners. Unformally, one can state that they learn the definition of a target concept (denoted TC) from examples of TC (dynamic role *Environment* in the top level Inference Structure in fig. 2) and some background knowledge (dynamic role *Domain Theory*) which represents the domain model of the application domain. The most commonly used formalization in the Inductive Logic Programming community is : given a set of positive examples of TC, denoted E^+, a set of negative examples of TC, denoted E^- and some background knowledge, denoted BK, the learning goal is to find a hypothesis H such that $BK, H \models E^+$ and $B, H, E^- \not\models \square$), where $\models$ denotes logical entailment and $\square$ denotes the empty clause whihc means contradiction[4]).

---

[3] This is indeed another viewpoint when considering possible interactions between Knowledge Acquisition and Machine Learning, but out of the scope of this work.

[4] For a survey of different logical formalizations of empirical learning, see [26]

We focus here on empirical ML systems that use a *Generate and Test* strategy (denoted `G-&-T` in the rest of the paper) according to Mitchell's definition [21], as opposed to *Example Driven* learners.

Example driven learners modify their hypothesis space to dynamically adapt to newly incoming examples. More precisely, the learning process of example driven learners reduces HS by rejecting hypotheses of HS that do meet a validity criterion w.r.t. to a set of examples of TC. When the learning process is incremental, it is thus implicitly controlled by the order in which examples are provided or handled by the learning system. On the opposite, `G-&-T` learning systems, given a current hypothesis, first compute some relevant alterations of this hypothesis w.r.t. some strategic knowledge which is stated independently from the examples. The so generated hypotheses are then tested against some examples that validate or invalidate the proposed alterations. T

The `Generate-&-Test`[5] family of ML systems includes for example "historic" systems such as ID3 [32], CN2 [20], more recent ones such as MARVIN [37], INBF [41], ML-SMART [3], and Inductive Logic Programming systems (among all, FOIL [33], CLINT [10]). Note that these includes incremental systems that have a special policy w.r.t. the order of the examples as well as "batch" learning systems that handle a whole base of preclassified examples.

5.3 The KL model

In order to describe `G-&-T` systems at the knowledge level, we adopt a problem solving view of ML, that was first introduced in [21]: learning can be seen as a search for an appropriate definition of TC into a set of candidate definitions for TC. In the rest of the paper, a (partial) candidate definition for TC is called *hypothesis*, and the search space for a learning algorithm is denoted HS.

The learning task is decomposed into two tasks : the *computation of an initial representation* for HS and the *search* into HS.

The computation of the initial HS is mainly controlled by the so called *language bias* (section 6.2) which defines the language of the target concept definition, and a *search bias* that defines the direction of the search through HS.

The Search process in HS is controlled in the proposed model by two biases : a *search bias* (section 6.3), setting search strategies within HS and a *validation bias* (section 6.4) that specifies a validity criterion for hypotheses of HS. The learning process loops on those two tasks until the stopping criterion for learning, which is the validation of the final definition for TC (section 6.4), is fulfilled or until learning fails.

Those two tasks and their associated biases are interdependent. The chosen representation for HS will determine the type of search that will be performed and therefore the search bias. Another issue is about the relative importance of those two tasks w.r.t. to the overall learning process. On the one hand, when much information about the form of the target concept to be learned is available, it is computationnally interesting to put much attention to the task of computing

---

[5] See [29] for details about the ML aspects of the model presented here

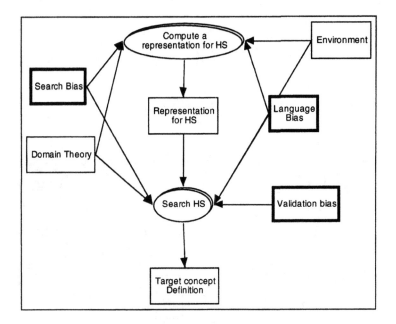

Fig. 2. The Problem Solving view of empirical learning

a representation of HS that "precompiles" the search process [4]. In this case, defining an adequate language bias alleviates most of the search problems. On the other hand, when few information is known beforehand about the target concept, the task of computing a representation for HS may be trivial. Therefore, most of the learning effort is left to the search process that, by combining an efficient search strategy and a clever access to the information stored in the examples of the target concept will allow to reach the expected TC definition.

6 Decomposition of bias

We now introduce a decomposition of biases for G-&-T algorithms (fig. 3). All of those biases, except for the search bias are applicable to other learning systems, including Example Driven ML systems. The role of each bias is illustrated by commenting the inference structures associated to each learning step. For all biases, a list of typical instantiations in G-&-T systems is given as well as some unformal rules about how they can be tuned to meet user's goals.

6.1 Representation of *HS*

We will assume in the remainder of the paper that HS is represented by a set of hypotheses that are a bound of HS : either the set of most specific or the set

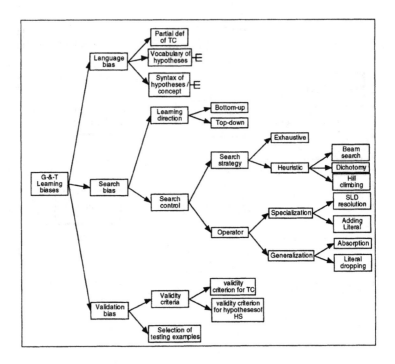

Fig. 3. Composition of bias for G-&-T systems

of most general hypotheses of HS that satisfy the validity criterion. This bound will be denoted CBD (for Current Best Definition). This representation requires that a generality relationship (a partial order) is explicitly given on the formulas of the target concept description language.

6.2 Language bias

The language bias defines restrictions on the language in which the target concept is expressed[6]. We give in the following a list of language biases commonly used in Inductive Logic Programming systems that learn target concept definitions in subsets of first order logic (see [45] and [4] for a more exhaustive survey).

Syntax and vocabulary of hypotheses of HS

- any constraint on the type/number of connectors, on the type/number of variables allowed in a hypothesis (namely, existentially and/or universally quantified variables) [10]. Sophisticated constraints on possible instantiations

---

[6] We do not consider as an explicit bias the language in which the examples and the background knowledge are expressed, although they have an influence on the target concept language.

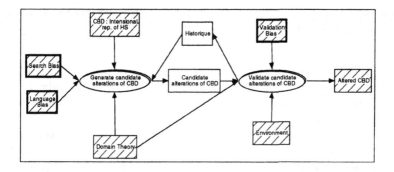

Fig. 4. Computation of alterations for the *Current Best Definition*

of such variables (determination, input/output modes, [38], ij-determination [27]) are also used.

- Higher order schemata [24], [45].
- For top-down systems such as [38], refinement graph that explicitly defines HS.

Syntax of the target concept The target concept language may be conjunctive; in this case, the final TC definition has to contain a single hypothesis, but still CBD contain several hypotheses that represent alternative choices for TC that should be resolved when learning stops. If the target concept language is disjunctive, the final TC definition is a set of hypotheses, such that each hypothesis is a partial definition of the target concept.

Influence of language bias The language bias acts *statically* when defining the initial representation for HS and also *dynamically* in the search process (see fig. 4). During search, it may be used to check that the alterations of CBD generated by the learning operators indeed belong to HS. Its influence on the learning results is crucial: the definition for TC must belong to the target concept language so that learning has any chance to succeed. With respect to the performance of the learning system, the size of HS and the complexity of the search through HS increases while the language bias weakens.

The exact influence of the syntax of hypotheses of HS on the performance of a ML system is still an open research issue in the ML community. Moreover, acquiring on even tuning such a bias may be quite difficult a "naive" ML system user. The two above objections raise the question of having such a bias as part of a knowledge level model of ML systems. Operationally, most of them are indeed justified by the necessity of bounding the complexity of the search process or by implementation choices that are not accessible at the level of detail of the inference structure. But, one may hope that syntactic criteria have some interpretation at the knowledge level: for example, finding a syntactically simple definition for the target concept (which translates into various syntactic criteria depending on the language bias) is something which, according to us, belongs to a Knowledge Level Model.

Configuration strategies Working in a conjunctive target concept language is the more constrained choice : learning will succeed if and only if at least one hypothesis of HS satisfies the stopping criterion. The vocabulary of the target concept language has therefore to be very carefully chosen. Working in a disjunctive concept language allows to express more complex concepts. Therefore, the choice of the vocabulary of TC has less influence on the success of learning but it also makes the search process in HS much more expensive. (see section 6.3). Therefore, the usual way to proceed is to start with a very strong syntactic bias on the hypothesis and/or concept language and to gradually shift to a more complex language when learning fails (see [1] or [10] for example).

6.3   Search bias

The search process, when the learning system handles a representation of HS with one of its bounds CBD, amounts to building a candidate alterations of CBD by applying a learning operator to it (fig. 5), and then checking the validity of the generated alterations against a set of examples for the target concept (fig. 6).

As an explicit generality relation is available to such learning systems, the search process has an interesting side effect on HS. For example, when the learning direction is bottom up and when a given CBD is not validated against examples of TC, all hypotheses more general than CBD are incorrect and must not be considered during the learning process (this is one reason why the dynamic role *Historic* appears in fig. 6). Note that we only consider in this paper search processes that monotonically reduces HS, therefore the alteration of CBD will be always from specific to general or from general to specific.

Learning direction CBD is modified by the application of a learning operator, one of a list of generalization or specialization operator. The user, depending on its learning goal will choose either to search HS from specific hypotheses to more general ones, CBD will therefore be a lower bound for HS, or to search HS from general to more specific hypotheses, in the latter case, CBD will be the upper bound of HS.

The choice of the learning direction is influenced by the validity criterion (see section 6.4) for the final TC definition. A top down learning algorithm is preferred when learning (maximally) discriminant concept definitions, that is, when the ML system user privileges learning complete concept definitions over learning correct concept definition. symmetrically, using a bottom up learning algorithm provides as a result more specific concept definitions that a top down algorithm does. Bottom up learning is more conservative and better suited when the correctness criterion is considered more important than the completeness one

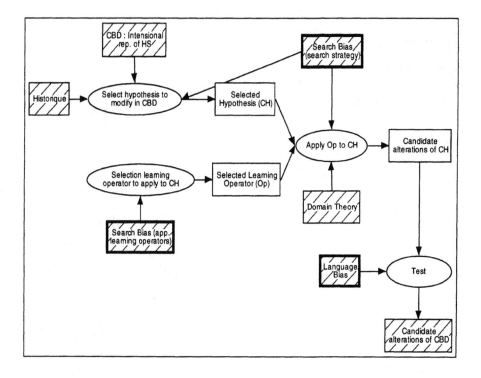

Fig. 5. Generation of candidate alterations of CBD

(that is, when it is not necessary to cover all positive examples but it is crucial that no negative example is covered by the learned concept definition).

The other search biases in **G-&-T** learning systems that operate on a representation of HS by a bound define dynamic constraints on possible alterations of CBD. They can be decomposed into:

Applicable learning operators Several learning operators have been described in ML. We have extracted from the Inductive Logic Programming literature the following (non exhaustive) list:

1. the dropping literal generalization operator that drops a literal in the body of a clause ([10], [34]), and its dual operator for specialization that adds literals to the body of a clause [3], the well known *least general generalization* operator ([31], [27]).
2. for operators that dynamically make use of the domain theory: the inverse resolution operator [25] and its dual operator for specialization, resolution [3].

Each learning operator generates its own search space denoted H_{Op}, which may not coincide exactly with HS. An operator may not be complete with

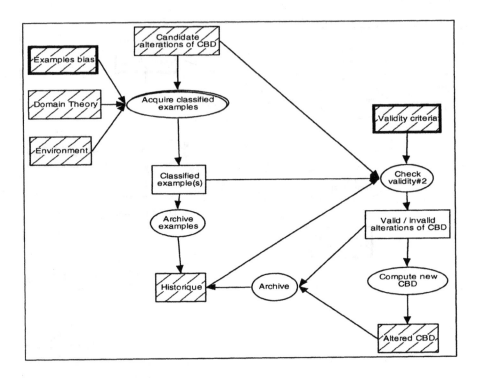

Fig. 6. Validity checking of candidate alterations of CBD

respect to the language bias, i.e., they may not be able to reach all hypotheses of HS. Thus, chosing an operator which is incomplete w.r.t. the language bias is a way to prune hypotheses of HS that will never be considered through learning (the search bias is then restrictive, in the terminology introduced by [36]).

Search strategy In case the target concept language is disjunctive (CBD may therefore contain more than one hypothesis), the search strategy defines an order on hypotheses of CBD that are to be altered by the learning operator. The set of possible strategies here are the usual ones in Problem Solving : depth first, breadth first, iterative deepening for uniformed strategies, best first, hill climbing, stochastic [23], etc. If the target concept is conjunctive, no choice is to be done at that step.

Any strategy can be defined to search H_{Op}. One may choose to exhaustively search through H_{Op} (smallest step [28], [10]) which is a careful strategy, considering that each generated alteration has to be validated. This strategy is applied, when the user does not want to degrade theoretical properties for the learning algorithm (see for example, [10], [14], [8]) are defined with the hypothesis of exhaustive search), or when the domain theory is incorrect or incomplete. The largest possible step w.r.t. to given operator allows (as in [41]) to minimize memory storage. Dichotomy search (as described in [17]) minimizes the number of examples needed for learning.

Each of these strategies is adapted to specific learning situations (expressed in terms, for example of distributions of the positive and negative examples of TC in the instance space, the space of all possible example descriptions) and learning goals (such as minimizing the number of intermediate CBD to build before learning, bounding the estimation of the error rate of the target concept definition learned, minimizing memory storage, etc.)

6.4 Validation bias

The biases of validation include :

Validity criterion that assess the validity of an intermediate CBD. Note that this criterion may be different than the stopping criterion that assesses the final target concept definition to be learned. For example, when the target concept language is disjunctive a partial definition is validated when it is correct but not necessarily complete, whereas the final TC definition has to be correct **and** complete. The most used validity criteria are the *completeness* criterion : a hypothesis of HS has to cover all positive examples of TC and the *correctness* criterion : a hypothesis of HS must not cover any negative example of TC. These are absolute validity criteria, usually applied in incremental learning systems. When a pre-classified database of examples for the target concept is available, a heuristic measure evaluating some gain in discrimination or some expected error rate of the learned target concept can be applied (for example, [32], [33], [3]).

Selection of testing examples. A candidate alteration of CBD which is acceptable w.r.t. the language bias has to be checked against the above validity criteria against a set of examples. The subset of examples of TC that are pertinent for validating the alteration of a given CBD into a new bound $NCBD$ (denoted S_{pex}) is defined as : for a bottom up strategy, the set of examples of TC covered by $NCBD$ and not by CBD ($NCBD$ is more general than CBD) and and symmetrically for a top down strategy the set of examples of TC covered by CBD and not by $NCBD$ ($NCBD$ is then more specific than CBD). Still, this set of examples may be large, and when the validation mode is a set of queries to the user, enumerating all such examples may be tedious. Diverse heuristics can then be applied to reduce this set, sometimes up to a singleton (see for example [5]), increasing the risk to miss an example that would contradict the alteration.

7 Related work

Our work takes place at the border between machine learning and knowledge acquisition. One promising and related approach, illustrated by [46], is to use

KADS domain level of a given application to control machine learning. In this work, the model driven analysis promoted by KADS defines *what* has to be learned, and its role within the overall knowledge based application.

Some works in the Inductive Logic Programming are also close to ours : GENCOL [11] (as quoted in section 3.1, MILES [44] which also has some strong links with our work, but up to now, has put much more stress on the study of language bias. Our originality w.r.t. those two works is our representation in a Common KADS formalism of our model on the one hand, and our explicit concern of building a configurer that will use our knowledge level model for interaction with the user on the other hand.

Within the knowledge acquisition community, [49] argues on some possible roles of Machine Learning within a Common Kads Methodology. We agree on the fact ([49], p13) that the Knowledge Level is a good level of description for analyzing, comparing and here configuring learning systems. Some very recent work, presented by [40], provides a configurable library of a family of ID3 like learning algorithms within KREST, is exactly in the same philosophy than ours.

Finally, let us quote a work [7] about the status and representation of control in a knowledge in KA methodologies that is quite related to our concern of building a knowledge level model of G-&-T systems parameterisable in terms of bias.

8   Conclusion - Perspectives

We have presented first results for building a configurable machine learning kit. The basis of the configurer is a knowledge level description of a family of empirical learners represented as a set of decomposed inference structures. This formalism provides a knowledge level representation of learning models and supports the explicit representation of some bias. The ML system is assembled by choosing decompositions of learning operations and by setting the associated biases.

As a first step, we have used these formalisms to represent the G-&-T family of learning algorithms. This work, though still incomplete, seems to validate the approach. As a useful side-effect, the knowledge level modeling puts the emphasis on bias and their role in the learning process. The models have been designed with KADS-TOOL and a first mockup has been implemented in Prolog.

The next step is now to complete the model, to formalize the configurer (and especially answering the questions related to the dynamic configuration process), and to set up a first prototype allowing some experiments.

Acknowledgements

This work is partially supported by ESPRIT III BRA 6020 (Inductive Logic Programming) and by the French MRT through PRC-IA. The authors thank Claire Nédellec for her involvement in the definition of the generic model which is the basis of this paper and Karine Causse for most helpful comments on the

KA aspects of this paper. This work has also benefited from discussions with members of the ILP project, specially those participating in the Declarative Bias Task. We would like to finally thank the anonymous referees of this paper for very useful suggestions.

References

1. H. Ade, L. De Raedt, and Bruynooghe M. Declarative bias for specific-to-general ilp systems. *Machine Learning*, 1994. Special Issue on Declarative Bias, submitted.
2. P. Albert, E. Brunet, J. Gonzague, and I. Bousquet. Kads-tool, a case tool for the *commonk*ads methodology. In *Conference of International Association of Knowledge Engineers*, 1992.
3. F. Bergadano and A. Giordana. A knowledge intensive approach to concept induction. In *Proceedings of the 5th International conference on Machine Learning*. Morgan Kaufmann, 1988.
4. F. Bergadano and D. Gunetti. Learning clauses by tracing derivations. Technical report, University of Torino, 1993.
5. R.C. Berwick. Learning from positive-only examples : The subset principles and three cases studies. In R.S Michalski, J.G. Carbonell, and T.M. Mitchell, editors, *Machine Learning II : An Artificial Intelligence Approach*, pages 625–646. Morgan Kaufmann, 1986.
6. Breuker, Bredeweg, Valente, and Van de Velde. Reusable problem solving components: the *commonk*ads library. In 3rd *KADS User Meeting, Munich.*, 1993.
7. K. Causse. A model for control knowledge. In *Proceedings of the 8th Knowledge Acquisition for Knowledge-Based Systems Workshop (Banff'94)*, Banff, Alberta, Canada, 1994.
8. W. Cohen. Learnability of restricted logic programs. In *Proceedings of the Inductive Logic Programming Workshop*, pages 41–71, 1993. Bled, Slovenia.
9. MLT CONSORTIUM. Final public report. Technical report, 1993. Esprit II Project 2154.
10. L. De Raedt. *Interactive Theory Revision: an inductive logic programming approach*. Academic Press, 1992.
11. L. De Raedt and M. Bruynooghe. A unifying framework for concept-learning algorithms. *The Knowledge Engineering Review*, 7(3):251–269, 1992.
12. M. Desjardins. *Proceedings of the AAAI 92 workshop on Declarative Biases*. 1992.
13. T.G. Dietterich. Learning at the knowledge level. *Machine Learning*, 1:287–316, 1986.
14. S. Džeroski, S. Muggleton, and S. Russel. Pac learnability of logic programs. In ACM, editor, *Proceedings of the 1992 Workshop on Computational Learning Theory*, pages 128– 135, 1992.
15. D. Gordon. *Proceedings of the ML92 workshop on Biases in Inductive Learning*. 1992. Aberdeen.
16. B. Grosof and S. Russell. Shift of bias as non-monotonic reasoning. In P.B. Brazdil and K. Konolige, editors, *Machine Learning, Meta-Reasoning and Logics*. Kluwer Academic Publishers, 1990.
17. D. Haussler. Applying valiant's learning framework to ai concept-learning problems. In Y. Kodratoff and R.S. Michalski, editors, *Machine Learning : an artificial intelligence approach*, volume 3. Morgan Kaufmann, 1990.

18. S. Marcus. Salt: a knowledge acquisition tool for propose and revise systems. In Marcus, editor, *Automating Knowledge Acquisition for Expert Systems*. Kluwer Academic, 1988.

19. S. Marcus and J. McDermott. Salt: A knowledge acquisition language for propose and revise systems. *Artificial Intelligence*, 39(1):1–38, 1989.

20. R.S. Michalski. A theory and methodology of inductive learning. In R.S Michalski, J.G. Carbonell, and T.M. Mitchell, editors, *Machine Learning : an artificial intelligence approach*, volume 1. Morgan Kaufmann, 1983.

21. T.M. Mitchell. Generalization as search. *Artificial Intelligence*, 18:203–226, 1982.

22. T.M. Mitchell. The need for biases in learning generalizations. In *Readings in Machine Learning*. Morgan Kaufmann, 1991.

23. D. Mladenic. Combinatorial optimization in inductive concept learning. In *Proceedings of Int. Conf. on Machine Learning*. Morgan Kaufmann, 1993.

24. K. Morik, S. Wrobel, J.-U. Kietz, and W. Emde. *Knowledge Acquisition and Machine Learning - Theory, Methods, and Applications*. Academic Press, 1993.

25. S. Muggleton and W. Buntine. Machine invention of first order predicates by inverting resolution. In *Proceedings of the 5th Int. Conf. on Machine Learning*, pages 339–351. Morgan Kaufmann, 1988.

26. S. Muggleton and L. De Raedt. Inductive logic programming: Theory and methods. *Journal of Logic Programming*. to appear.

27. S. Muggleton and C. Feng. Efficient induction of logic programs. In *Proceedings of the 1st conference on algorithmic learning theory*. Ohmsha, Tokyo, Japan, 1990.

28. C. Nédellec. How to specialize by theory refinement. In *Proceedings of ECAI-92*, 1992.

29. C. Nédellec and C. Rouveirol. Hypothesis selection biases for incremental learning. In *Proceedings of the AAAI Spring Symposium Series workshop on Issues for Incremental Learning*, 1993.

30. L. O'Hara. Knowledge acquisition in vital. Technical Report D2.1.2, Esprit Project 5365, 1992.

31. G. Plotkin. A note on inductive generalization. In *Machine Intelligence*, volume 5. Edinburgh University Press, 1970.

32. J.R. Quinlan. Induction of decision trees. *Machine Learning*, 1:81–106, 1983.

33. J.R. Quinlan. Learning logical definition from relations. *Machine Learning*, 5:239–266, 1990.

34. C. Rouveirol. Extensions of inversion of resolution applied to theory completion. In S. Muggleton, editor, *Inductive Logic Programming*, pages 63–93. Academic Press, 1992.

35. C. Rouveirol. *Working Notes of the Declarative Bias MLNet workshop*. 1994. Catania.

36. S. Russell and B. Grosof. A sketch of autonomous learning using declarative bias. In P.B. Brazdil and K. Konolige, editors, *Machine Learning, Meta-Reasoning and Logics*, pages 19–54. Kluwer Academic Publishers, 1990.

37. C. Sammut and R. Banerji. Learning concepts by asking questions. In R.S. Michalski, J.G. Carbonell, and T.M. Mitchell, editors, *Machine Learning : an artificial intelligence approach*, volume 2, pages 167–192. Morgan Kaufmann, 1986.

38. Ehud Y. Shapiro. *Algorithmic Program Debugging*. The MIT press, 1983.

39. G. Shreiber, B. Wielinga, and J. Breuker. *KADS: a Principled Approach to Knowledge-Based System Developpement*. Academic Press, 1992.

40. A. Slodzian. Configuring decision tree learning algorithms with krest. Technical report, VUB, 1994.

41. B.D. Smith and P.S. Rosembloom. Incremental non-backtracking focusing: A polynomially bounded generalization algorithm for version space. In *AAAI-90 : proceedings of the ninth conference*, pages 848–853. Morgan Kaufmann, 1990.

42. L. Steels. Reusability and configuration of applications by non programmers. Technical Report AI-memo 92-4, AI Lab. Free University of Bruxelles, 1992.

43. L. Steels. The componential framework and its role in reusability. In David J-M., Krivine J-P., and Simmons R., editors, *Second Generation Expert Systems*. Springer-Verlag, 1993.

44. B. Tausend. Biases and their effects in inductive logic programming. In Springer Verlag, editor, *Machine Learning: European Conference on Machine Learning-94*, pages 431–434, 1994.

45. B. Tausend. Representing biases for inductive logic programming. In Springer Verlag, editor, *Machine Learning: European Conference on Machine Learning-94*, pages 427–430, 1994.

46. J. Thomas, J.G. Ganascia, and P. Laublet. Model-driven knowledge acquisition and knowledge-biased machine learning. In G. Tecuci, S. Kedar, and Y. Kodratoff, editors, *Proceedings of the IJCAI-93 Workshop on Machine Learning and Knowledge Acquisition*, pages 220–235, 1993.

47. P.E. Utgoff. Shift of bias for inductive concept-learning. In R.S Michalski, J.G. Carbonell, and T.M. Mitchell, editors, *Machine Learning : an artificial intelligence approach*. Morgan Kaufmann, 1986.

48. W. Van de Velde. Invited talk: Toward a toolkit for knowledge engineering. *Journées Acquisition des Connaissances*, 1994.

49. W. Van de Velde and A. Aamodt. Machine learning issues in commonkads, 1992.

50. B. Wielinga, W. Van de Velde, G. Shreiber, and D. Akkermans. The commonkads framework for knowledge modelling. In *AAAI Knowledge Acquisition Workshop 1992, Banff, Canada*, 1992.

Reflective, Self-Adaptive Problem Solvers

Eleni Stroulia and Ashok K. Goel *

College of Computing
Georgia Institute of Technology
Atlanta, GA 30332-0280

Abstract. Problem-solving systems, situated in the real world are faced with a great challenge, that is, the dynamic nature of their environment. In any realistic environment the state of the world changes, and therefore, the system's knowledge about the world often becomes incomplete and incorrect. Furthermore, the constraints and the requirements imposed on the system's behavior may also evolve, and as a result, the system's functional architecture may become insufficient to meet the requirements of the evolving task environment. In principle, we would like our systems to be able to adjust themselves in their environments and to sustain quality performance across such environmental changes. To enable a system with the capability of self-adaptation, we have developed a framework for endowing it with the competence of reflection. In this framework, the system's problem-solving behavior is modeled in terms of a SBF model. This model captures a deep comprehension of the system's task structure, world knowledge and their inter-dependencies. The knowledge captured in the SBF model of a system enables it, when it fails, to identify the need to update its world knowledge and also appropriately redesign its functional architecture.

1 Introduction

Problem-solving systems, situated in the real world are faced with a great challenge, i.e., the dynamic nature of their environment. In any realistic environment the state of the world changes not only as a result of the system's actions, but also due to the actions of other agents acting in this environment. Therefore, the system's knowledge about the world is often incomplete and incorrect. Furthermore, the constraints and the requirements imposed on the system's behavior may also evolve. For example, the system may be presented with novel types of problems which are not part of its original design specification but which are quite similar to the types of problems it is able to solve. Alternatively, the system may be required to produce solutions of a quality slightly different than the types of solutions which it was originally designed to produce. In such situations, the

* This work has been supported by the National Science Foundation (research grant IRI-92-10925), the Office of Naval Research (research contract N00014-92-J-1234), and the Advanced Projects Research Agency. In addition, Stroulia's work has been supported by an IBM graduate fellowship.

system's original functional architecture may become insufficient to meet these novel requirements. In principle, we would like our systems to be able to adjust themselves in their environments and to sustain quality performance across such environmental changes.

To develop problem-solving systems, which can be effectively used in the real world over a long period of time, we have to provide them with the ability of self-adaptation so that they can keep up with the changes in their environment, they can meet evolving constraints and requirements, and they can take advantage of potentially new opportunities. To exhibit such self-adaptive behavior, a system would have first, to recognize its needs for new knowledge, second, to acquire and integrate this new knowledge within the body of its existing knowledge, and potentially, to reuse its existing knowledge for new purposes.

One way of enabling this kind of competence in a system is by a-priori identifying the possible changes that might occur in the system's environment, identifying the adjustments that would be necessary for the system to cope with these changes, and provide a method for each one of these adjustments. Clearly, this is a prohibitively costly and often impossible way of addressing the problem. An alternative way is by enabling the system to reflect on its own problem-solving process. More specifically, if the system has a comprehension of its own problem-solving process, it can reason about it, identify its shortcomings and redesign itself when necessary. The reflection approach to adaptability raises two questions that we, as AI designers, have to address: first, we have to provide a language in which to analyze and describe problem solving in a manner that makes explicit the interactions between the knowledge of the system and the way it is used; second, we have to develop a specific method for reflection which will use the model of the system's behavior as a basis for identifying its shortcomings and for proposing appropriate modifications to it.

In our work, to address the first question, we have adopted Chandrasekaran's [3] framework of task structures. In this framework, problem solving is analyzed in terms of the tasks a problem solver accomplishes, the methods available to it, and the knowledge used by these methods. Further, to describe how a problem solver works, we have adapted the language of structure-behavior-function (SBF) models for describing how physical devices work [8]. To address the second question, we have developed a failure-driven method for reflection. In that method, the system monitors its own reasoning on each specific problem, and when it fails, it uses the model of its own reasoning and the record of the failed problem-solving episode to assign blame for the failure to some element of its task structure and to redesign it appropriately.

In this paper, we focus mainly on the blame-assignment subtask of the reflection process. The blame-assignment subtask takes as input the record of the failed problem-solving episode, and the feedback from the world. It has the goal of producing as output a (set of) suggestion(s) on modifications to the system's task structure which, if implemented, could potentially enable the system not to fail again for a similar reason. [2] The range of modifications, which the blame-assignment subtask can suggest, define the extent to which the system can adapt itself. We have developed a method which can suggest (i) modifications to the system's world knowledge, (ii) reorganization of the world knowledge, (iii) use of the available world knowledge in new ways, (iv) redefinition of the role that a subtask plays in the overall system's reasoning process, and (v) more effective use of the system's alternative reasoning strategies. The AUTOGNOSTIC system implements and evaluates our reflection process in multiple task domains.

2   The Modeling Framework

Task Structures We adopt the task-structures framework [3] as an initial step for capturing the types of problem-solving meta-knowledge required for reflection: first, knowledge of the different types of world knowledge available to the system, and, second, knowledge of the expected behavior of each type of reasoning step the system can perform. A task consumes some type(s) of information as input and produces some other type(s) of information as output. A task can be recognized as an instance of a generic task [2], and it can be accomplished by one or more methods, each of which decomposes it into a set of simpler subtasks. A method is characterized by the kinds of knowledge it uses, the subtasks it sets up, and the control it exercises over the processing of these subtasks. These subtasks can, in turn, be accomplished by other methods, or, they may be solved directly by some non-inspectable operator. The task structure of a problem solver thus provides a recursive decomposition of its overall task in terms of methods and subtasks. [3]

SBF Model of Problem Solving To describe the task structure of a system, we have adapted the language of structure-behavior-function (SBF) models for describing how physical devices work [7, 8, 24]. A problem-solving task, in this SBF language, is specified as a transformation from an input information state to an output information state, annotated by a set of semantic relations between the input and output information. The specification of a task in the SBF language also includes a pointer to the prototypical task of which it is an instance,

---

[2] This is a slightly different formulation for the task of blame assignment. In its original definition, [18, 15], it produces a (set of) fault(s) which caused the failure. We prefer the notion of corrective modifications instead of faults as output of the blame-assignment task because our notion of failure is also slightly different: in the context of self-adaptive systems failure may be a mismatch between the system's behavior and the ever-evolving external requirements, instead of simply a mismatch of the system's behavior and its design specifications. We'll discuss our notion of failure in greater detail later.

[3] Tasks can be thought of as roughly equivalent to goals, and "leaf" tasks (that is, tasks not further decomposable by methods) are similar to operational goals, i.e., elementary goals which the system knows how to accomplish. Methods can be thought of as general plans for how the solutions to different subgoals combine to accomplish higher-level goals.

and pointers to the methods than can potentially accomplish it, or to the operator which directly solves it. The task's semantic relations constitute a partial description of the expected, correct behavior of the task, and specify its role in the context of the overall system behavior. If the task is accomplished by a method which decomposes it into a set of subtasks, then the semantic relations of the subtasks and the ordering relations that the method imposes over them constitute a partial description of a correct reasoning strategy for this task.

In an extension of the task-structure framework, the SBF model of a system in our work also includes a description of its world knowledge in terms of the types of objects in the world and the relations applicable to them. The types of information that the problem solver consumes and produces are related to the types of world objects, and the semantic relations of the tasks in its task structure are related to the relations between the world objects. Figures 1, 2, 3, 4, 5 describe the language of SBF models of problem solving. We will discuss the types of knowledge that the SBF model of the system contains in more detail as we explain their role in assigning blame.

$Tsk(task) :=$

$\quad (info\_state_{input}, info\_state_{output}, \{instance\_of\}, by\_methods\|op, under\_conditions,$
$semantic\_rels)$

where

$info\_state_{input} := \{Info\_Type\}^{*}$, a set of types of information that the task consumes as input.

$info\_state_{output} := \{Info\_Type\}^{*}$, a set of types of information that the task produces as output.

$instance\_of := Tsk$, a (generic) task that accomplishes a transformation equivalent to or more general than the transformation of the current task.

$by\_methods := \{M\}^{+}$, a list of methods potentially applicable to the task.

op the name of the operator which accomplishes the task i.e., whose functional abstraction the task is. Only tasks which are not further decomposed by methods are associated with operators; we call these tasks "leaf tasks".

$under\_conditions := \{p(info\_state_{input})\}^{*}$, a set of predicates on the input information of the task, under which it is meaningful to accomplish the task.

$semantic\_rels := \{p(info\_state_{input}, info\_state_{output})\}^{*}$, a set of predicates that hold true between the input and the output of the task, i.e., rules that define the transformation that the task imposes on its inputs to produce its outputs.

Fig. 1. The language of SBF models: Task

The Case Study AUTOGNOSTIC is an operational system that uses the SBF model of a given system for monitoring its reasoning (subtasks performed, the information produced, and alternative methods considered but not chosen), assigning blame when it fails and redesigning it appropriately. In this paper, we describe AUTOGNOSTIC's blame-assignment method on top of a multistrategy navigational planner called ROUTER [10, 11].

$M(method) :=$

  $(applied\_to, under\_conditions, subtasks, control)$

where

$applied\_to := Tsk$, the task to which the method is applicable.

$under\_conditions := \{p(Info\_Type)\}^*$ a set of predicates that need to be true in order for the method to be applicable to the task. The types of information on which these predicates are applied, are all information types the values of which have been produced before the method selection.

$subtasks := \{Tsk\}^+$ a set of subtasks into which the method decomposes the task it is applied to.

$control := \{ctrl\_op(subtasks(M))\}^*$ a set of control operators applied to the subtasks of the method. Control operators define a partial order among these subtasks. They define precedence among tasks, potential parallelism, and repetitions of tasks until a condition is met.

Fig. 2. The language of SBF models: Method

$WO(worldobject) :=$

  $(domain, attrs, id\_test)$

where

$domain :=$ the data structure with the possible values for the object that the system knows; only enumerated types of objects have domains, and these are objects that directly refer to instances in the world, as opposed to conceptual objects.

$attrs := \{(name, definition\_function, type)\}^*$, the set of attributes characteristic of the objects of this type. Each one of them is specified in terms of a name, a definition of a function evaluating its value given an instance of this type, and the type of this value which can be either another world object or a number.

$id\_test :=$ the definition of a function to evaluate identity between instances of this type.

Fig. 3. The language of SBF models: World Object

$DR(domainrelation) :=$

$(input\_args, output\_args, \{truth\_table\}, \{predicate\}, \{inv\_predicate\}, organizational)$

where

$input\_args :=$ the set of types of world objects that constitute the key of this relation.

$output\_args :=$ the set of types of world objects that constitute the dependent element of this relation.

$truth\_table :=$ the data structure containing the tuples belonging in the relation.

$predicate :=$ a predicate which, given a key, produces the dependent element under this relation.

$inv\_predicate :=$ a predicate which, given a dependent element, produces the key under this relation; this is applicable only to inversible relations.

$organizational := F/T$ depending on whether this relation takes its truth value from the state of the world or simply through design conventions.

Fig. 4. The language of SBF models: Domain Relation

$Info\_Type :=$

$(is\_a, input\_to, produced\_by)$

$is\_a := WO$ a world object, of which this type of information is an instance.

$input\_to := \{Tsk : Info\_Type \in info\_state_{input}(Tsk)\}^*$ a set of tasks consuming this type of information.

$produced\_by := \{Tsk : Info\_Type \in info\_state_{output}(Tsk)\}^*$ a set of tasks that can potentially produce this type of information as output.

Fig. 5. The language of SBF models: Information Type

ROUTER's task is to find a path from an initial location to a goal location in a physical space. ROUTER has a topographic model of its world, which contains knowledge about specific world objects (i.e., streets, intersections) and the relations between them (i.e., connectivity). It also has an episodic memory of past problem-solving cases. ROUTER knows two methods for accomplishing the path-planning task: a model-based method, and a case-based method. When presented with a problem, ROUTER chooses one of them based on a set of heuristic rules which evaluate the applicability and utility of the two methods for the given problem.

AUTOGNOSTIC understands ROUTER's problem solving in terms of a SBF model. The SBF model explicitly specifies the two methods that ROUTER can use to plan paths, and the way they decompose the overall problem-solving task in different trees of subtasks, using different types of knowledge. The subtasks resulting from the use of the first method refer to model relations while the subtasks resulting from the use of the second method refer to case-memory relations. Finally, the SBF model contains a meta-level description of the system's world knowledge (i.e., general descriptions of the different types of objects, such as streets, intersections, and paths, and relations, such as connectivity) and their respective organizations (i.e., general descriptions of the different types of organizational relations, such as organization of the world model in a neighborhood hierarchy, and associations between paths and their initial and final intersections).

3 The Method for Blame Assignment

Our method for blame-assignment consists of three major subtasks. The first subtask, *feedback assimilation*, investigates the possibility that the feedback was not produced because it includes references to objects in the world that are unknown to the system or are in conflict with the system's world knowledge. The second subtask, *blame assignment within the problem-solving strategy used*, investigates whether the strategy (i.e., the sequence of subtasks accomplished) used in the failed problem-solving episode, could have produced the feedback under different world-knowledge conditions, or with slight modifications to the way these subtasks were performed. The third subtask, *exploration of alternative strategies*, investigates whether an alternative strategy should have been more appropriate to solve the problem at hand.

Assimilate(*info value*)

1. IF there is a domain, *d*, for the type of object, *wo*, of which *info* is an instance,
2. THEN
   (a) IF *value* $\notin$ *d*
   (b) THEN
       include-value-in-domain to improve the system's knowledge and inform it
       of the existence of *value*
3. FOR-ALL attributes *attr* of *info*,
   (a) calculate the value, *v*, of attribute *attr* of the instance *value*
   (b) assimilate(type(*info attr*) v)
   (c) i. IF impossible to calculate the value of *attr*
           or there is a mismatch between the form of *v* and the type(*info attr*)
        ii. THEN
           modify-object-representation to allow the instance *value* to meet the
           representational commitments of the object

Fig. 6. Feedback Assimilation Algorithm.

3.1 Assimilation of Feedback Information

The feedback assimilation process uses the meta-model of the system's world knowledge to "parse" the desired solution, *value*, for the information type, *info*, in order to elicit all the information it contains about the world. If some of this information is not part of, or is in conflict with the system's world knowledge, then this is evidence that the feedback does not belong in the domain of solutions that the problem solver can produce. The assimilation process suggests appropriate modifications to the world knowledge.

As shown in Figure 3, the SBF model includes a general description of each type of world object that the system knows about. For each attribute of an object type, the SBF model specifies the type of object this attribute is, and also a function which, given an instance of this object type, returns the value of this attribute for the given instance. The assimilation process examines whether the system knows the instance presented as feedback to it, i.e., whether the instance belongs in the corresponding world-object domain. If not it suggests the inclusion of this instance to the domain, *include-value-in-domain*, and infers its attributes to further examine whether they agree with their corresponding expected types and whether their values are known to the system.

If at any point, the assimilation process faces an inconsistency between the feedback and the types of attributes it expects, (i.e., the value of some attribute of the feedback instance is incompatible with its expected type, or some attributes cannot be inferred for the feedback instance) this is evidence that a change in the representation framework of the system's world knowledge may be necessary, *modify-object-representation*, in order for the assimilation to become possible. When the assimilation process suggests a representation modification, it also suggests that modifications may be necessary to any subtasks of the system whose semantic relations refer to this attribute. Figure 6 shows in detail the algorithm for the feedback assimilation process.

	PATH		**INTERSECTION**
id_test	path-equivalence		intersection-equivalence
domain	–		intersection-domain
attrs	nodes	length	streets
	(lambda(x) x)	(lambda(x) (length x))	(lambda(x) x)
	(list-of intersection)	number	(list-of 2 street)
rels	begins-in-zone		connected-to
	ends-in-zone		belongs-in-zone

Fig. 7. AUTOGNOSTIC's meta-level comprehension of ROUTER's world knowledge.

Examples Let us consider the problem [4] of going from *(8th-1 mcmillan)* to *(north cherry-3)*. For this problem ROUTER produces the path *(8th-1 mcmillan) (mcmillan test-3) (test-3 hemphill) (hemphill ferst-2) (ferst-2 ferst-3) (ferst-3 cherry-3) (cherry-3 north)* which is correct but suboptimal to the path *(8th-1 mcmillan) (mcmillan 6th-1) (6th-1 ferst-2) (ferst-2 ferst-3) (ferst-3 cherry-3) (cherry-3 north)*.

In this example, the assimilation process uses its general description of paths to "understand" the feedback. This description (see Figure 7) specifies that a path is a sequence of "nodes" each of which is an intersection. Therefore, the assimilation process uses its general description of intersections to assimilate the specific intersections that constitute the path at hand. Intersections are elementary objects in ROUTER's world knowledge, (see Figure 7), i.e., all the intersections that ROUTER knows about are listed in a data structure. By investigating the contents of the intersection domain, the assimilation process finds that the intersections *(mcmillan 6th-1)* and *(6th-1 ferst-2)* do not belong in the intersection domain. Moreover, in its effort to assimilate *(mcmillan 6th-1)* and *(6th-1 ferst-2)*, the assimilation process finds that *6th-1* does not belong in the street domain. Therefore, the assimilation process suggests as modifications that could potentially enable ROUTER to produce the desired path, the incorporation of *6th-1* in the street domain, and the incorporation of *(mcmillan 6th-1)* and *(6th-1 ferst-2)* in the intersection domain.

Let us now consider how the feedback path *(8th-1 mcmillan) (mcmillan 6th-1) (6th-1 ferst-2) (ferst-2 ferst-3 ponders) (ferst-3 cherry-3) (cherry-3 north)* would have been assimilated. While assimilating *(ferst-2 ferst-3 ponders)* as an intersection, the process faces an inconsistency between the type of the attribute *streets* and its value in the specific intersection. That is, while the *streets(intX?)* is a list of two elements, each of which is a street, *(ferst-2 ferst-3 ponders)* is a list of three elements. At this point, the assimilation suggests a modification to the representation of the attribute *streets* of intersections in ROUTER's world knowledge.

---

[4] A problem specification in ROUTER consists of a pair of street intersections to be connected. A solution is a path, i.e., a sequence of adjacent intersections, between them.

3.2 Within the Strategy used for Problem Solving

If the assimilation process proceeds without errors, i.e., all the information conveyed by the desired solution is already known to the system, the blame-assignment process starts to investigate the strategy which was using during problem solving, in order to identify modifications which can potentially enable this same strategy to produce the desired solution. It is possible that, although the desired solution is within the class of solutions that this problem-solving strategy can produce, it was not actually produced because (a) some piece of world knowledge is missing (the successful assimilation of the feedback only means that the constituent elements of the solution are known to the system; still, there may be types of information used by intermediate problem-solving steps, for which the system's world knowledge is incomplete), or (b) some type of world knowledge is incorrectly organized, so that although all the necessary information is available to the system, it cannot access it appropriately, or (c) the problem-solving strategy allows the production of several solutions to the same problem, one of which is more desirable than the others.

The blame-assignment process first identifies the highest task in the task structure whose output is the information for which the problem solver produced an undesirable value. The process then investigates whether the desired feedback value meets the criteria for the expected correct behavior of the task, i.e., it evaluates the semantic relations of the task under inspection with the feedback value. If the feedback value and the input of this task are verified by the semantic relations, the blame-assignment process infers that the feedback value is within the class of values produced by the task under inspection, and thus it could have been produced by this task. Thus, the reason why this value was not actually produced must lie within the internal mechanism of the task, that is, it must be due to some of the subtasks which were performed to accomplish the task under inspection. From the record of the failed problem-solving episode, the blame-assignment process infers which method was actually used to solve this task, and, as above focuses the assignment of the blame to the subtask which produced the undesired value. If the task under inspection is an instance of a known prototypical task, then the blame-assignment process shifts to the performance of the prototypical task.

If at some point, the semantic relations of a task do not hold true between the input of this task and the desired value, then the blame-assignment process attempts to infer alternative input values [5] which would satisfy the failing semantic relations. If there is some intermediate type of information, for which an alternative value, (i.e., a value different from the value actually used in the problem-solving process), can be inferred, the focus of the blame-assignment process shifts to identifying why this value was not produced.

---

[5] When the task's input information is not part of the overall problem specification, that is, the types of information for which alternatives are sought are not part of the givens of the problem.

	CROSSINGS	CONNECTED-TO	BELONGS-IN
input_args	street	intersection	intersection
output_args	(list-of intersection)	(list-of intersection)	neighborhood
truth_table	crossings-table	–	zones-of-ints-table
predicate	–	adjacent-ints	–
inv_predicate	–	adjacent-ints	–

Fig. 8. The description of a domain relation (crossings), an organization relation (belongs-in) and a predicated relation (connected-to) in AUTOGNOSTIC's meta-model of ROUTER's world knowledge.

AB-in-TS-used-for-PS(*task info value*)

1. IF the *value* belongs in the class of values produced by *task* for *info*
2. THEN
   (a) IF *task* is accomplished by an operator
   THEN
   insert-selection-task to reason about the possible .values of *info*
   make-semantic-relation-false for the value of *info* actually produced by the *task*.
   (b) IF *task* is accomplished by a method M
   THEN AB-in-TS-used-for-PS(*task-i info value*)
   where $task\text{-}i \in$ subtasks(*task M*) and $info \in$ output(*task-i*)
   (c) IF *task* is accomplished by the instantiation of *task-i* where $task\text{-}i =$ prototype(*task*)
   THEN AB-in-TS-used-for-PS(*task-i info value*)
3. ELSE
   (a) IF there is alternative value, v, for information i, where $i \in$ input(*task*) for which *task* could have produced *value* for *info*
   (b) THEN AB-in-TS-used-for-PS(*task-i i v*)
   where $i \in$ output(*task-i*) and $\not\exists$ *task-j*: $i \in$ output(*task-j*) and $task\text{-}i \in$ subtasks(*task-j*)
   (c) ELSE
   redefine-task-semantics to extend the competence of the *task*
   make-semantic-relation-true for *value* of *info*

Fig. 9. The Algorithm for Blame Assignment within the strategy used for problem solving.

A short discussion on the different types of semantic relations is required here. Semantic relations are usually domain relations, and as such they can be either defined in terms of a truth table or in terms of a predicate. From the ones that are analytically defined, i.e., in terms of a truth table, some are relations whose truth value depends on the state of the world, and some are organizational relations which are designed to improve the system's efficiency. For example, in ROUTER's domain, the relation *connected-to* is one of the former kind, and the relation *belongs-in* is one of the latter. Relations defined in terms of a truth table can be modified by simple operations to their truth table; however the modification of a domain relation may require the approval of a domain expert, where the modification of an organizational relation does not. Predicated relations are non-modifiable. The meta-level descriptions of some of ROUTER's relations in the SBF model of ROUTER's problem solving are shown in figure 8.

The way that the blame-assignment process infers alternative values for the input of the under-inspection task depends on the type of the failing semantic relation. If it is evaluated by a predicate, the inverse predicate may also be known to the system. If the failing semantic relation is a relation exhaustively described in an truth table, then the inverse mappings can be inferred from this table. Finally, if the input information is a type of world object the instances of which belong in some exhaustively described domain, the blame-assignment process can search the domain to find these values which would satisfy the semantic relations of the task.

If there are no possible alternative values for the the input of the task under inspection that can satisfy its semantic relations, then the blame-assignment process suggests as possible modifications the following: (a) if the semantic relations refer to domain relations exhaustively described by truth tables, the updating of the corresponding truth tables to include the mapping of the task's input to its desired output, *make-semantic-relation-true*, or else (b) the redefinition of the task's semantic relations, so that they don't get violated by the mapping of the task's input to its desired output, *redefine-task-semantics*. In the first case, if the relation is an organizational relation, the modification can be performed directly by the system, and it results in the reorganization of the system's domain knowledge. Otherwise, it results to a modification to the system's world knowledge, and a domain expert may have to approve it. The second modification results to an extension of the competence of the task at hand, so that it performs a different class of information transformations which includes the currently violating feedback value. This modification is possible when the system can find a new relation to characterize the new extended behavior of the task at hand.

The blame-assignment process may thus reach a task which can produce two alternative values, both of them consistent with its semantic relations, one of which leads to the desired problem solution and the other to the unacceptable one. This is an indication that the task structure is not sufficiently tailored to producing the right kind of solutions. In this case, the blame-assignment process suggests as possible modifications the following: (a) if the semantic relations refer to domain relations exhaustively described by truth tables, the updating of the corresponding truth tables to exclude the mapping of the task's input to its old output, *make-semantic-relation-false*, or (b) the introduction of some new task in the task structure which, using some type of world knowledge, will distinguish between the possible alternatives and will "steer" the problem-solving process towards the correct solution, *insert-selection-task*. Again, in the first case, if the relation is an organizational relation, the modification can be performed directly by the system, and it results in the reorganization of the system's domain knowledge. Otherwise, it results to a modification to the system's world knowledge, and a domain expert may have to approve it. The second modification results to a refinement of the competence of the task at hand, so that it performs an information transformation tailored to the "kind of solutions" preferred by the environment, as exemplified by the feedback value. This modification is possible when the system can find a new relation which can differentiate between the actual and the desired feedback value of the task's output. Figure 9 shows in detail the algorithm for blame assignment within the strategy used for problem solving.

Examples Let us consider for example, the problem of going from *(10th center)* to *(ferst-1 dalney)*, for which ROUTER produces the path *(center 10th) (10th atlantic) (atlantic ferst-1) (ferst-1 dalney)* which is suboptimal to the path presented as feedback to AUTOGNOSTIC *(center 10th) (10th dalney) (dalney ferst-1)*.

In this example, the blame-assignment process first focuses on the *route-planning* task, as the highest task producing the *path*, and consequently on the *increase-of-path* task, as the subtask of *intrazonal-method*, the method used for *route-planning* when both intersections belong in the same neighborhood. The semantic relation of *increase-of-path*, *FORALL n in nodes(path) belongs-in(n initial-zone)*, fails for the desired *path* value and the actual *initial-zone* value. The relation *belongs-in* is an organizational relation, and from its truth table, the alternative *initial-zone* value is inferred, *za*. Thus, the blame-assignment process focuses on identifying why *za* was not produced as the value for *initial-zone*. The task producing the *initial-zone* is the task *elaborate*. Its semantic relations verify both *za* and *z1* as *initial-zone* values. Therefore the blame-assignment process suggests as possible modifications the reorganization of the relation *belongs-in* so that *((10th center) z1)* $\notin$ domain(belongs-in), and the insertion of a new task which will reason about the potential values of *initial-zone* and select the most appropriate one in the context of the given problem.

3.3 Exploring Alternative Strategies

Often, the desired solution cannot be produced by the strategy used in the failed problem-solving episode. Different methods produce solutions of different qualities, and often the desired solution exhibits qualities characteristic of a method other than the one originally used for problem solving. The blame-assignment process described above recognizes this "incompatibility" between the desired solution and the method used for problem solving as a suggestion for a redefine–task-semantic-relations modification. The suggestion for a modification of this type is an indication that the feedback is in conflict with the very definition of some subtask involved in the actual problem-solving. Before revising the very definition of this subtask (from now on, we will refer to it as the problem-task, *task-p*) to resolve the conflict, it is worthwhile investigating whether it is possible to pursue another course of reasoning which will avoid it.

The blame-assignment process identifies the last task in the task structure, before the problem-task, for which there exist multiple methods, and which, dur-

ExploreAlternatives(*task-p info value*)

1. IF there is *M-alt* applicable to *task-c* but not chosen such that *task-p* ∉ subtree(*M-alt*)
2. THEN
   (a) invoke *M-alt*
   (b) IF *value* produced for *info*
       THEN **revise-method-selection-criterion**
       to prefer *M-alt* over the method used
3. ELSE
   (a) IF there is *M-alt* not chosen such that *task-p* ∉ subtree(*M-alt*)
   (b) THEN
       i. Evaluate with *value* semantic relations of subtree(*M-alt*) which relate *info* to other information available at the selection point.
       ii. IF there is a relation, *rel*, which is true
           THEN
           A. invoke *M-alt*
           B. IF *value* produced for *info*
              THEN
              make-method-selection-criterion-true to allow *M-alt* to be used
              revise-method-selection-criterion to allow *M-alt* to be used
   (c) ELSE **acquire-new-method** capable of producing the type
       of values for *info* exemplified by *value*.

Fig. 10. The Algorithm for Blame Assignment within strategies alternative to the one used for problem solving.

ing problem solving, was accomplished by a method that resulted in the problem-task. We will call this task choice-task, *task-c*. If at the time of method selection, during problem solving, there was another applicable method, this is an indication that this method should have been chosen. Therefore, the blame-assignment process suggests as possible modification the refinement of the method-selection criteria, *revise-method-selection-criterion*, so that under similar circumstances the alternative method is chosen over the one actually used.

If none of the alternative methods were applicable at the time of method selection, then this is an indication that the system may need to acquire another method, *acquire-new-method*. It is possible, however, that a particular alternative method could have produced the desired solution, although it was not applicable. To collect evidence for this possibility, the blame-assignment process evaluates the semantic relations of the tasks arising from the decomposition of the choice-task by each alternative method. If, for some method, there are semantic relations, which relate the solution with types of information available at the time of method selection, that validate the feedback value for the solution, then this is evidence that indeed the feedback value fits the "quality" of solutions that this method produces. Therefore, although the method was not applicable at the time, it maybe should have been. Therefore, the blame-assignment process may suggest that the problem solver should try to this alternative method. If its applicability criteria refer to domain or organizational relations, modifications to these relations is necessary before actually testing the method, *make-method-selection-criterion-true*. If it produces the desired solution, the domain/organizational modifications become permanent. If the applicability criterion was a predicate, the blame-assignment process suggests the redefinition of the selection criteria, *revise-method-selection-criterion*, so that the successful method is applicable under similar circumstances in the future. Figure 10 shows in detail the algorithm for blame assignment within strategies alternative to the one actually used for problem solving.

Examples Let us for example, consider the problem of going from *(fowler 3rd)* to *(fowler 4th)*. Although spatially close, these locations belong in different neighborhoods, and thus ROUTER uses the *interzonal-model-based* (ROUTER's model based method has really two versions, the intrazonal, i.e., search within a single common neighborhood, and the interzonal one) method to solve the problem which results in the path *(fowler 3rd) (3rd techwood) (techwood 5th) (5th fowler) (fowler 4th)*. The desired path should have been *(fowler 3rd) (fowler 4th)*

The blame assignment within the used strategy identifies that the feedback path is in conflict with the semantic relation of the *plan-synthesis* subtask of the *interzonal-model-based* method. This subtask synthesizes the overall path from smaller paths, produced as solutions to the subproblems into which the original problem is decomposed. It takes as input three paths and concatenates them; as a result, the length of the paths it produces is greater than six nodes, which is not true for the feedback path. The blame-assignment process exploring alternative strategies identifies that the semantic relations of *increase-of-path* subtask of the *intrazonal-model-based* method specify that the paths it produces are shorter than six nodes. This is an indication that *intrazonal-model-based* could have produced the path, had it been applicable. Its applicability condition refers to an organizational relation, *belongs-in(final-point initial-zone)*, therefore the blame-assignment process reorganizes the world model to so that *belongs-in((fowler 4th) zd)*. Afterwards, it solves the problem once again. Indeed, the *intrazonal-model-based* is applied and the desired solution is produced. Had it not been the case, it would have undone the modification.

4 Discussion

The effectiveness of the blame-assignment method relies, to a great extent, on the quality of the SBF model of the problem solver. There are three important aspects to the quality of such a model:

1. the quality of the task-structure analysis of the problem-solving process, i.e., the level of detail and the level of precision in which the problem-solver's reasoning process is described,
2. the quality of the meta-model of the problem-solver's domain knowledge, i.e., the level of detail in which the domain knowledge that the problem solver has available to it is described, and

3. the degree to which the level of these descriptions match, i.e., the degree to what the semantic relations of the problem-solver's subtasks can be expressed in terms of domain relations it knows about.

If the SBF model is not precise, i.e., if the expected correct behavior of the problem-solver's tasks is poorly described, (i.e., sparse semantics or no semantics at all), then the blame-assignment method has no basis of evaluating whether or not the feedback solution is within the class of solutions the task structure is able to produce, and cannot suggest modifications to the task structure. Furthermore, it cannot suggest changes to the domain knowledge either, since changes to some part of the domain knowledge are suggested after there is evidence that a task which uses this domain knowledge has failed.

If the SBF model does not explain in enough detail the problem-solver's subtasks, i.e., if it only analyses its process in terms of big, complex subtasks, then the blame-assignment method may not able to localize enough the potential cause of the failure. Too big tasks are bound to be complex and may play multiple roles in the context of the overall problem-solving task. Thus, it becomes difficult to suggest precise operational modifications, because they may have many, undetectable consequences and thus lead to inconsistent problem-solving task structure.

If the meta-model of the problem-solver's domain knowledge is described in little detail, then the blame-assignment method may not be able to trace failures of the subtasks to errors in the domain knowledge. Also if the meta-model is poor, then the reflective system may not be able to recognize new uses for this domain knowledge, and consequently, it may not be able to introduce new tasks in the task structure or modify the semantics of its existing tasks.

From this discussion, it must also be evident that a good match between the level of description of the task structure and the level of description of the domain meta-model is critical to the effectiveness of the reflection process. If the meta-model of the problem-solver's domain knowledge is described in terms different than the semantics of its tasks, then the blame-assignment method may not be able to trace failures of subtasks to errors in the domain knowledge, or to postulate new uses of its existing domain knowledge in the task structure.

5 Related Research

Previous work on modifying knowledge-based systems has focused mainly on the revision of the set of rules included in the system's knowledge base. Teiresias [5, 6] is an interactive knowledge-base validation system. In Teiresias the system guides the domain expert to identify erroneous and missing rules. The rules added and modified by the expert may result in modifications to the strategy used in problem solving or to the domain knowledge of the system; however, in Teiresias there is no explicit separation between strategic rules and simple domain-knowledge rules, and therefore the contribution of each modification is not made explicit. AUTOGNOSTIC on the other hand, explicitly postulates strategic and domain knowledge needs through its blame-assignment process.

Quawds [25] is an autonomous knowledge-base validation system. It uses an explicit model of the expert-system's diagnostic method to identify the error. The model used in Quawds is based in the task-structure framework also. However, unlike AUTOGNOSTIC it does not allow for multiple problem-solving strategies, and, it includes expected faulty behaviors of these subtasks, which requires from the designer an a-priori analysis of these faults. Recently, Marques, Dallemagne, Klinker, McDermott and Tung [13] have developed a set of tools, Spark, Burn and Firefighter which are meant to guide domain experts to develop a system beginning from a rough idea of the task to a working program. Spark helps the expert map its task to a fairly generic predefined task model and customize it to meet its task specification. Burn builds tools for acquiring the knowledge necessary for this task model. Finally, Firefighter interacts with the expert to further modify and customize the program. AUTOGNOSTIC's task is similar to Firefighter's task.

The blame-assignment method in Hacker, [20], identifies as possible causes of failure the problematic interactions between the plan's steps; therefore, it only suggests reorganization of these steps. The blame-assignment methods developed for Lex [17] and for Prodigy [16], assume a relatively static task environment and identify as only shortcomings of the system its suboptimal efficiency. The blame-assignment method in Gordius, [19], triggered by the failure of the system to explain a given datum, searches for possible causes for the failure its assumptions regarding the state of the world; therefore it only suggests modifications to the system's world knowledge.

Functional models similar to the SBF models of problem solving have been used to model abstract devices such as programs for software verification [1], and students in the context of a tutoring system [12]. The framework of task structures shares many features with other task and method oriented theories of problem solving, e.g., [4, 14, 21, 26].

6 Evaluation

AUTOGNOSTIC is a fully operational system. It presently operates in two widely different task domains: on top of ROUTER, in the domain of navigational planning, and on top of KRITIK2 [9, 22], in the domain of engineering design. Both ROUTER and KRITIK2 are autonomous multistrategy systems developed independently of AUTOGNOSTIC but within the task-structures framework.

We have tested AUTOGNOSTIC quite extensively in the context of ROUTER. In particular, we have tested AUTOGNOSTIC–on– ROUTER for some three dozen problems in each of which ROUTER produced a suboptimal navigation plan, AUTOGNOSTIC–on– ROUTER received the desired plan as feedback, and then AUTOGNOSTIC assigned blamed and suggested modifications. Together the test set of problems covered a number of different kinds of modifications to ROUTER: (i) modifications to ROUTER's world knowledge, for example, the acquisition of the knowledge of streets and intersections, (ii) reorganization of ROUTER's knowledge, for example, modifying the region of space covered by a neighborhood in the system's spatial model of the navigation world, (iii) redesign of ROUTER's task structure, for example, by the insertion of new tasks in its task structure, and (iv) the use of the ROUTER's knowledge in new ways, for example, by using the old knowledge for the newly inserted task. The modified ROUTER had a wider coverage of its domain, it had imposed a hierarchical organization on its domain knowledge (note, in the beginning of this experiment ROUTER had a flat world model), and it had changed its concept of intersection to include three-street intersections. These are all modifications to its domain knowledge, however ROUTER's task structure was also improved: it had changed its concept of useful past experiences so that it was able to use its case-memory more often and thus become more efficient, it had learned to choose the "right" neighborhood in which to search for a path, it had learned to choose the "right" common intersections to connect neighborhoods, and it had learned to produce paths "legal" for driving, i.e., paths conforming with the traffic rules of the domain. The affects of domain-knowledge modifications and task-structure modifications to ROUTER's performance were evaluated separately, and both types of modifications were found to have significant positive affects to the class of problems ROUTER was able to solve and the (time and space) efficiency of its process. The quality of its paths, as far length–of–path is concerned, deteriorated slightly, due to the hierarchical organization of its domain knowledge, however the paths of the modified ROUTER were appropriate for drivers as well as pedestrians more often.

Our evaluation of AUTOGNOSTIC in the context of KRITIK2, has so far focused on a different type of modification. In KRITIK2's case, AUTOGNOSTIC performs blame assignment based purely on its monitoring of KRITIK2's reasoning (without requiring any specific type of feedback). AUTOGNOSTIC–on–KRITIK2 identifies errors in the selection and use of problem-solving strategies (design-modification plans) and suggests the migration of a subtask from one point in the task structure to another for improving strategy selection and application.

Since ROUTER and KRITIK2 solve widely different tasks in widely different domains, the success of AUTOGNOSTIC's blame assignment suggests that its SBF models of problem solving and model-based methods of blame assignment are quite general.

Of course assigning blame is pointless unless it results in the repair of the error and improved problem solving. In this sense, the repair task constitutes one part of the evaluation of any process of blame-assignment. AUTOGNOSTIC is able to redesign the failing system according to some of the types of modifications it can suggest, and evaluates it on the old problem. If the problem solver is successful in producing the desired solution, then AUTOGNOSTIC assumes that the whole process of blame assignment and repair was successful. AUTOGNOSTIC knows how to perform most of the modifications it can recognize as potentially useful to the system. For example, it knows how to change the content of a domain relation and how to ensure that the consequences of such modifications are propagated through the known domain constraints. Moreover, it knows how to discover a differentiating or unifying relation in its domain theory and how to integrate it in its problem-solving task structure as semantics for a new selection task or as semantics for a task that needs to be redefined and extended. At this point, AUTOGNOSTIC does not have a learning method for the *modify-object-representation* task, and sometimes, although it knows how to perform a certain type of modification, AUTOGNOSTIC may not have sufficient knowledge to actually perform it. For example, it may not be able to identify the semantics for a new selection task, and when the modification involves changes to the domain knowledge, *include-value-in-domain, make-semantic-relation-true/false,* AUTOGNOSTIC may also request the advice of a domain expert on whether to actually proceed with it or not. In that sense, the blame-assignment subtask of AUTOGNOSTIC's reflection, focuses the interaction between the system and the expert, and makes explicit the role of the knowledge that the expert is asked to provide to the system.

7 Conclusions

A general criticism for AI systems has been that they are brittle. They perform at a high level of expertise for a narrow set of problems, but when presented with a slightly different one, they fail. Systems working in realistic environments are bound to face novel problems, that is, problems which were not considered at the time of the original design of the system. The reason is twofold: (a) realistic environments are dynamic, and (b) often, the constraints and the requirements on the system's behavior may change depending on the context in which it is used. The possible states of the system's environment and the different contexts in which it will be used cannot be predicted a priori. Thus, as system designers we must enable our systems with the capability of self-adaptation. To address the issue of self-adaptation, we have developed a framework for endowing a system with the competence of reflection. In this framework, the system's problem-solving behavior is modeled in terms of a SBF model. This model captures a deep comprehension of the system's task structure, world knowledge and their inter-dependencies. More specifically, the SBF model of a system's reasoning makes explicit

1. the representational and organizational assumptions on which the system's world knowledge is based. Thus discrepancies between feedback information and representation assumptions can indicate errors to the world-knowledge representation scheme.
2. the role that the system's world knowledge plays in the accomplishment of its tasks and the selection of its reasoning methods. Thus, failures of tasks or misuse of reasoning methods can be related to errors in the world knowledge.
3. the interactions between subtasks in terms of information and control flow, and the role of each subtask to the accomplishment of the overall task of the system in terms of the information it consumes and produces. Thus, unde-sirable properties of the overall problem-solving behavior can be accounted for by undesirable behaviors of elementary subtasks, and failures of some subtask can be accounted for by failures of earlier subtasks to provide it with appropriate information.

4. the expectations regarding the information-processing role of each subtask. Thus, differences between environmental requirements and the prespecified role of a subtask can be accounted for by the incorrect specification of the role that this subtask should play in the context of the overall problem solving.

Using the SBF model of its own problem-solving, a system can identify the need to modify

1. the representation scheme of its world knowledge, (modify representation to accommodate discrepancies between feedback and object type)
2. the organization of its world knowledge, (make-relation-true/make-relation-false to organizational relations)
3. the content of its world knowledge, (make-relation-true/make-relation-false to domain relations, include new instances to domains)
4. the assumptions on the applicability and utility of the different problems-solving methods it has available to it, (revision to method selection criteria)
5. the role of a subtask in the overall reasoning process (insertion of selection tasks, redefinition of a task's semantic relations)

When performed, these types of modifications enable the improvement of the system's knowledge about the domain, the tailoring of the system's expertise towards producing certain types of solutions whose quality is desired by the environment, and the extension of the system's expertise to address an extended class of problems.

References

1. D. Allemang: Understanding Programs as Devices, PhD Thesis, The Ohio State University (1990)
2. B. Chandrasekaran: Towards a functional architecture for intelligence based on generic information processing tasks. In Proceedings of Tenth International Joint Conference on Artificial Intelligence, 1183-1192, Milan (1987)
3. B. Chandrasekaran: Task Structures, Knowledge Acquisition and Machine Learning. Machine Learning 4: 341-347 (1989)
4. W.J. Clancey: Heuristic Classification, Artificial Intelligence 27: 289: 350 (1985)
5. R. Davis: Interactive transfer of expertise: Acquisition of new inference rules, Artificial Intelligence 12: 121-157 (1977)
6. R. Davis: Meta-Rules: Reasoning about Control. Artificial Intelligence 15: 179-222 (1980)
7. J.S. Gero, H.S. Lee and K.W. Tham: Behaviour: A Link between Function and Structure in Design, In Proceedings IFIP WG5.2 Working Conference on Intelligent CAD, pp. 201-230. (1991)
8. A. Goel: Integration of Case-Based Reasoning and Model-Based Reasoning for Adaptive Design Problem Solving, PhD Thesis, The Ohio State University (1989)
9. A. Goel: A Model-Based Approach to Case Adaptation. In Proceedings of the Thirteenth Annual Conference of the Cognitive Science Society, Chicago, August 7-10, pp. 143-148 (1991)

10. A. Goel, T. Callantine, M. Shankar, B. Chandrasekaran: Representation, Organization, and Use of Topographic Models of Physical Spaces for Route Planning. In Proceedings of the Seventh IEEE Conference on AI Applications. 308-314, IEEE Computer Society Press (1991)

11. A. Goel, T. Callantine: An Experience-Based Approach to Navigational Route Planning. In Proceedings of the IEEE/RSJ International Conference on Intelligent Robotics and Systems (1992)

12. K. Johnson: Exploiting a Functional Model of Problem Solving for Error Detection in Tutoring, PhD Thesis, The Ohio State University (1993)

13. D. Marcques, G. Dallemagne, G. Klinker, J. McDermott, D. Tung: Easy Programming: Empowering people to build their own applications. IEEE Expert, June 1992, 16-29.

14. J. McDermott: Preliminary steps toward a taxonomy of problem-solving methods, In Sandra Marcus (ed.): Automating Knowledge Acquisition for Expert Systems, Kluwer Academic Publishers (1988)

15. M. Minsky: Steps Towards Artificial Intelligence. In Feigenbaum and Feldman (eds): Computers and Thought, McGraw-Hill, New York. (1963)

16. S. Minton: Qualitative results concerning the utility of explanation-based learning. Artificial Intelligence 42: 363-392 (1990)

17. T.M. Mitchell, P.E. Utgoff, B. Nudel, R.B. Banerji Learning problem-solving heuristics through practice. In Proceedings of the Seventh International Joint Conference on AI 127-134 (1981)

18. A. Samuel: Some studies in machine learning using the game of checkers. IBM Journal of RD. (1959) Reprinted in Feigenbaum and Feldman (eds.): Computers and Thought (1963)

19. R.G. Simmons: Combining Associational Causal Reasoning to Solve Interpretation and Planning Problems, MIT Report 1048.(1988)

20. J.G. Sussman: A Computational Model of Skill Acquisition, American Elsevier, New York, (1975)

21. L. Steels: Components of Expertise. AI Magazine 11: 30-49 (1990).

22. E. Stroulia and A. Goel: Generic Teleological Mechanisms and their Use in Case Adaptation. In the Proceedings of the Fourteenth Annual Conference of the Cognitive Science Society, pp. 319-324. (1992)

23. E. Stroulia, A. Goel: Functional Representation and Reasoning for Reflective Systems. Applied Artificial Intelligence: An International Journal (to appear). (1993)

24. Y. Umeda, H. Takeda, T. Tomiyama, H. Yoshikawa: Function, Behaviour, and Structure. In Gero (ed.): Applications of Artificial Intelligence in Engineering, vol 1, Design, Proceedings of the Fifth International Conference, Springer-Verlag, Berlin, pp. 177-193. (1990)

25. M. Weintraub: An Explanation-Based Approach to Assigning Credit, PhD Thesis, The Ohio State University (1991)

26. B.J. Wielinga, A.Th. Schreiber, J.A. Breuker: KADS: A modelling approach to knowledge engineering. In Knowledge Acquisition 4(1). Special issue "The KADS approach to knowledge engineering" (1992)

27. R. Wilensky: Planning and Understanding, A Computational Approach to Human Reasoning. Addison Wesley. (1983)

Springer-Verlag
and the Environment

We at Springer-Verlag firmly believe that an international science publisher has a special obligation to the environment, and our corporate policies consistently reflect this conviction.

We also expect our business partners – paper mills, printers, packaging manufacturers, etc. – to commit themselves to using environmentally friendly materials and production processes.

The paper in this book is made from low- or no-chlorine pulp and is acid free, in conformance with international standards for paper permanency.

Lecture Notes in Artificial Intelligence (LNAI)

Lecture Notes in Computer Science